MW01641166

Functional Programming and Parallel Graph Rewriting

INTERNATIONAL COMPUTER SCIENCE SERIES

Consulting Editor **A D McGettrick** University of Strathclyde

SELECTED TITLES IN THE SERIES

Distributed Systems: Concepts and Designs *G Coulouris and J Dollimore*
Software Prototyping, Formal Methods and VDM *S Hekmatpour and D Ince*
High-Level Languages and Their Compilers *D Watson*
Interactive Computer Graphics: Functional, Procedural and Device-Level Methods *P Burger and D Gillies*
Real Time Systems and Their Programming Languages *A Burns and A Wellings*
Fortran 77 Programming (2nd Edn) *T M R Ellis*
Prolog Programming for Artificial Intelligence (2nd Edn) *I Bratko*
Introduction to Expert Systems (2nd Edn) *P Jackson*
Logic for Computer Science *S Reeves and M Clarke*
Computer Architecture *M De Blasi*
The Programming Process: An Introduction using VDM and Pascal *J T Latham, V J Bush and D Cottam*
Analysis of Algorithms and Data Structures *L Banachowski, A Kreczmar and W Rytter*
Elements of Functional Programming *C Reade*
Handbook of Algorithms and Data Structures in Pascal and C (2nd Edn) *G Gonnet and R Baeza-Yates*
Algorithms and Data Structures *J H Kingston*
Principles of Expert Systems *P Lucas and L van der Gaag*
Discrete Mathematics for Computer Scientists *J K Truss*
Programming in Ada plus Language Reference Manual (3rd Edn) *J G P Barnes*
Software Engineering (4th Edn) *I Sommerville*
Distributed Database Systems *D Bell and J Grimson*
Software Development with Z *J B Wordsworth*
Program Verification *N Francez*
Concurrent Programming *A Burns and G L Davies*
Concurrent Systems: An Integrated Approach to Operating Systems, Database and Distributed Systems *J Bacon*
Comparative Programming Languages (2nd Edn) *L B Wilson and R G Clark*

Functional Programming and Parallel Graph Rewriting

Rinus Plasmeijer
Marko van Eekelen

University of Nijmegen, The Netherlands

Wokingham, England · Reading, Massachusetts · Menlo Park, California · New York
Don Mills, Ontario · Amsterdam · Bonn · Sydney · Singapore
Tokyo · Madrid · San Juan · Milan · Paris · Mexico City · Seoul · Taipei

Cover designed by Chris Eley
and printed by The Riverside Printing Co. (Reading) Ltd.
Typeset using Microsoft Word on an Apple Macintosh by the authors.
Printed and bound in Great Britain by T.J. Press, Padstow Cornwall.

First printed 1993.

ISBN 0–201–41663–8

British Library Cataloguing-in-Publication Data
A catalogue record for this book is available from the British Library.

Library of Congress Cataloging-in-Publication Data is available.

Preface

Functional languages

In a **declarative programming language** a computation is expressed in a static fashion, as a list of declarations. A program in such a language is regarded as a specification that happens to be executable as well. In this textbook we focus on a subclass of the declarative languages, the **functional programming languages**, sometimes called **applicative languages**. In these languages a program consists of a list of function definitions. The execution of a program consists of the evaluation of a function application given the functions that have been defined.

In this book we want to show that functional programming languages can be used to write compact, reliable and readable programs. As example languages we shall use the functional languages Miranda and Concurrent Clean. We shall explain the advantages and disadvantages of functional languages, show how efficient implementations can be obtained on sequential and parallel architectures, and discuss the important underlying theoretical frameworks. The expressive power of functional languages is shown not only by some small examples. The descriptions, transformation and compilation schemes, as well as the definitions of the abstract machine architectures given in this textbook are *all* presented in a functional style illustrating the suitability of functional languages as specification tools.

Graph rewriting systems

The concept of a function is a fundamental notion in mathematics. One of the very strong points of functional languages is the property that their semantics is based very directly on well-defined mathematical models of computation. In fact, functional languages can be regarded as sugared versions of these models. These models are very important because they abstract from unimportant language details. In this way they help to get a better understanding of the essential underlying concepts of a language. This knowledge can then be used to improve the language itself, but it can also be used to make better implementations.

The traditional model of computation used for functional languages is the **λ-calculus**. Field and Harrison (1988) give a very good, thorough survey of several functional languages and their implementations using the λ-calculus as the basic model of computation. They use HOPE as a functional language instead of Miranda and they restrict themselves mainly to sequential implementations.

This book differs from other textbooks in that it focuses on an alternative model of computation: **graph rewriting systems**. Like the λ-calculus this model has the advantage that it is simple and that it can model functions. Unlike the λ-calculus it additionally contains the important notions of patterns and graphs. Graphs (and the related notion of sharing) play a key role in any efficient (parallel) implementation. To reason about the computational complexity of a program it is essential to know whether computations are shared or not. Furthermore, the notion of uniqueness in graphs gives an efficient solution for modelling interaction and side-effects within a pure functional framework.

Implementation on sequential architectures

The implementation of functional languages is quite complex when efficient code has to be generated. In this book we shall explain how such an implementation can be achieved on traditional sequential architectures. The implementation of functional languages is explained in a number of steps. Starting from Miranda, we go down in level of abstraction until we reach the concrete machine level. In this compilation process the functional language Concurrent Clean (based upon graph rewriting systems) is used as intermediate language.

Concurrent programming and parallel evaluation

Another advantage of functional languages is that they are, in principle, suited for concurrent (parallel or interleaved) evaluation. However, an implementation on parallel hardware is much more difficult than on sequential hardware, mainly because parallel machines are hard to program anyway. Concurrent functional programming is being investigated at several research institutes but is still in its infancy. We shall demonstrate its potential power and discuss the implementation on loosely coupled parallel architectures.

About this book

This book is intended as a textbook for a one or two semester (term) course: an *introductory course* on functional programming, models of computation and the implementation of functional programming languages on traditional sequential machine architectures (Parts 1, 2 and 4), optionally followed by an *advanced course* focused on analysis methods (strictness analysis and type theory), concurrent functional programming and implementation on parallel architectures (Parts 3 and 5).

The prerequisite for this book is an introductory course in computer science including knowledge of programming in a high-level language as well as some basic understanding about (parallel) computer architectures and compiler construction.

This textbook is suited for advanced undergraduate students, for postgraduate students of computer science and for researchers interested in the area of functional programming and the implementation techniques on sequential and parallel architectures.

The subject of this textbook is a hot and very interesting research topic. It is not an easy topic because many aspects of computer science play a role in it. Although much progress has been made during the last decade, also many problems are still to be solved and are expected to remain unsolved for quite a while. Instead of covering all existing and proposed lines of research we have chosen to base this book mainly on the work performed by our research team at the University of Nijmegen. This has the advantage that one complete line of approach, involving theory, specification and implementation, can be described in detail based upon actual experience. For example, all translation schemes presented in this book are abstracts from the prototype specifications written in a functional formalism that have been used as blueprint for the actual implementations. The approaches explained in this book have produced good results. Furthermore, they have many things in common with other approaches, so one will still get a very good overall insight on the actual problems and how they can be handled.

About the Concurrent Clean software

The Concurrent Clean system, the software system developed at the University of Nijmegen using the approaches described in this textbook, can be ordered separately via the authors (from the address at the end of the Preface). This software can be used to obtain practical experience in (concurrent) functional programming. With this system one can develop real applications.

The Concurrent Clean system contains a programming environment (including text editor and project manager), an interpreter and a code generator for the lazy functional language Concurrent Clean (Brus *et al.*, 1987; Nöcker *et al.*, 1991b). The system is especially designed for the Apple Macintosh (Plasmeijer *et al.*, 1991) and generates efficient code for any Mac. An I/O-library is available offering a very high-level specification of modern I/O-handling (windows, dialogues and the like). Furthermore, it is possible to generate parallel code for Macs connected in a local area network (AppleTalk/Ethernet).

Concurrent Clean and the Concurrent Clean system are also available on other platforms. The Macintosh version runs on an Atari ST (using a Mac emulator). There is a version for Sun3 (Motorola) and Sun4 (SPARC) under UNIX using an X Window System with Open Look or OSF-Motif for the low-level I/O-handling. Clean programs can run on any of these platforms without the need to modify source code. A cross-compiler is available for ParSyTec's Supercluster (transputer). A version for the IBM-PC (look-alikes) is under development.

The Clean research team is working on the improvement of Concurrent Clean and the Concurrent Clean system. Please contact the authors for the latest information.

Outline of this book

This book is divided into five parts. In the first two parts we focus on *functional programming* and suitable underlying *models of computation*. Then, in Part 3 these models are used to show how properties of functional programs can be *analysed*. Part 4 uses a particular model to show in detail how functional programs can be *implemented* efficiently on traditional architectures. The final part (Part 5) covers the same kind of subjects as Parts 1, 2 and 4 respectively, but focuses on parallelism. Since the research in this area is less stabilized, this final part is of a more introductory and reflective nature. Exercises are given at the end of each chapter (difficult or large exercises are marked *).

Part 1: Functional programming

In this first chapter we give a description of the *basic language concepts* that most functional languages have in common (Chapter 1). Hereafter we show in more detail the descriptive power and syntactic sugar of the *advanced language concepts* as offered by one particular functional programming language: Miranda (Chapter 2).

Part 2: Models of computation

In this part we concentrate on three models of computation: *λ-calculus* (Chapter 3) as the best known computational model and *term rewriting systems* (Chapter 4) and *graph rewriting systems* (Chapter 5) as alternative models of computation. The latter is used throughout this book as a basis for implementations and for reasoning about efficiency aspects.

Part 3: Analysis of functional programs

The models of computation introduced in Part 2 are used in Part 3 to show how additional information can be obtained by static analysis. In particular, type assignment systems (Chapter 6) and strictness analysis (Chapter 7) are discussed. Type and strictness information is needed to obtain efficient implementations. This theoretical part might be skipped by readers with a greater interest in more practical subjects.

Part 4: Implementation on sequential architectures

This part of the book covers the implementation of functional languages on traditional machine architectures. The implementation is discussed in a number of steps. In each step we go down in level of abstraction until the concrete machine level is reached (Figure 0.1).

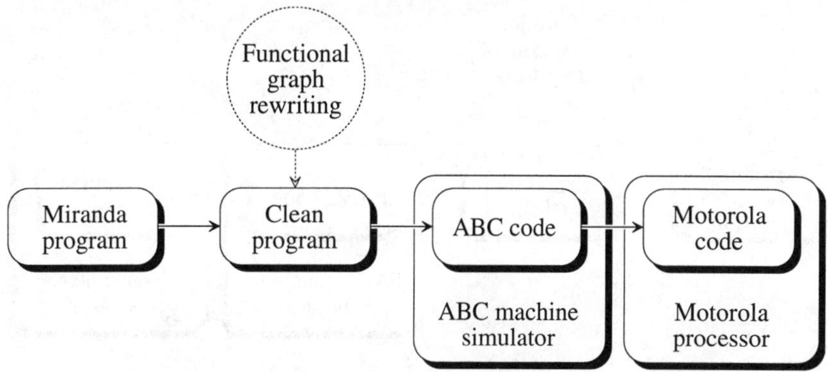

Figure 0.1 Sequential implementation of functional programming languages in four levels of abstraction.

The language *Clean* is introduced in Chapter 8. This language is based on *functional* graph rewriting systems. It is shown how a Miranda program can be translated into an equivalent Clean program (Chapter 9). Hereafter an abstract machine, the *ABC machine*, is introduced modelling traditional stack-based machine architectures (Chapter 10). The use of an abstract machine prevents us from getting lost in the details of concrete architectures. Step by step we shall deduce compilation schemes from Clean to the instruction set of the ABC machine (Chapter 11). Finally, the remaining problems of an actual implementation on concrete target machines are discussed (Chapter 12). As a representative target architecture the Motorola processor is used.

Part 5: Concurrency issues

There are several ways in which concurrency can be exploited in a functional program. Because loosely coupled parallel architectures are becoming widely available we concentrate on the implementation on this type of architecture. To get an optimal performance on these machines the parallelism should be *explicitly* specified by the programmer.

None of the existing well-known functional languages have language facilities to control parallelism. Therefore we introduce a possible extension to express concurrency in functional languages (Chapter 13). How the underlying model of computation can be extended to capture the notion of processes and process communication is the subject of Chapter 14.

Finally, the implementation of functional languages on loosely coupled parallel machine architectures is discussed. As in Part 4 the implementation is explained through a series of abstraction steps down to the concrete machine level (Figure 0.2).

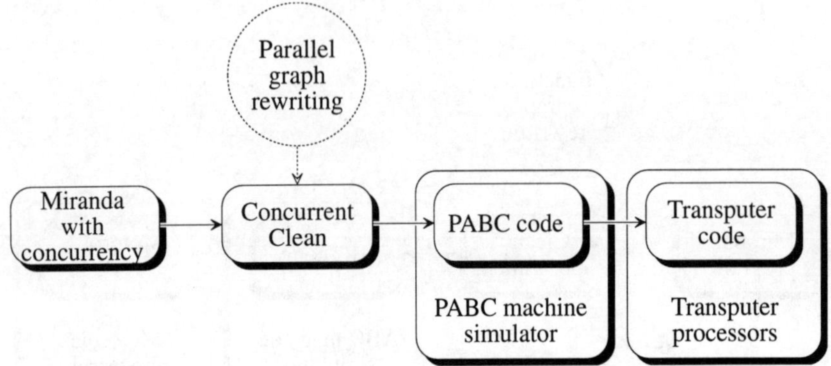

Figure 0.2 Parallel implementation of functional programming languages in four levels of abstraction.

First, we introduce the extension of *Clean* to *Concurrent Clean* and show how a concurrent functional program can be translated into an equivalent *Concurrent Clean* program (Chapter 15). Then, we extend the ABC machine (Chapter 10) to a *parallel ABC machine* modelling loosely coupled machine architectures and show how Clean's concurrency primitives are translated to abstract machine instructions (Chapter 16). Finally, we discuss the remaining problems of an actual implementation (Chapter 17) on a concrete parallel target machine. As a representative target architecture the transputer processor is used.

Acknowledgements

The following members of the Nijmegen research team have made important contributions to specific aspects of this book: Peter Achten (Clean's event I/O), Steffen van Bakel (type assignment systems), John van Groningen (code generators and machine wizarding), Halbe Huitema (I/O library, testing), Marco Kesseler (transputer code generator), Pieter Koopman (transformation schemes, (P)ABC machine), Eric Nöcker (transformation schemes, strictness analysis, PABC machine), Sjaak Smetsers (transformation schemes, Concurrent Clean, PFGRSs, (P)ABC machine) and Ronny Wichers Schreur (Concurrent Clean environment).

We would like to thank the following people who each in their own way made an important contribution to the realization of this book and to the design and the construction of the Concurrent Clean system: Christ Aarts, Erik Barendsen, Henk Barendregt, Tom Brus, Cor de Cloe, Guido van Dam, Wil Dekkers, Maurice Klein Gebbink, John Glauert, Johan Goos, Harco de Hilster, Martin van Hintum, Jeroen ter Hofstede, Richard Kennaway, Mathieu Knops, Hans Koetsier, Frank van Latum, Maarten van Leer, Mieke Massink, Paul de Mast, Angelo Melis, Betsy Pepels, Leon Pillich, Ab Reitsma, Richard van Schelven, Ronan Sleep, Daniël Tuynman, Marten Wensink, Koen Wouters and Mariëlle van der Zandt.

We appreciate very much the work of the referees who have helped us with several very good suggestions for improvement of this textbook.

We are very grateful for the financial injection of the *'Dienst Wetenschapbeleid'* of the Dutch *Department of Science and Education* which initiated the research that forms the basis for this textbook. Furthermore, we would like to thank the *ESPRIT* projects *Tropics* and *Semagraph* for supporting the more advanced parts of that research.

Rinus Plasmeijer and Marko van Eekelen

April 1993

Computer Science Department
University of Nijmegen
Toernooiveld 1
6525 ED Nijmegen
The Netherlands

email: rinus@cs.kun.nl
marko@cs.kun.nl

To Trees and Lianne

Contents

Part 1
Functional programming

This part serves as an introduction to functional programming.

Since there are many different functional programming languages, the first chapter focuses on the basic concepts most functional languages have in common. By first focusing on these concepts it will be relatively easy to master the basics of any functional language with its own syntactical sugar. The concrete examples in Chapter 1 are given in a subset of Miranda.

In Chapter 2 the more sophisticated features of Miranda are shown to demonstrate the expressive power and notational elegance of a specific state-of-the-art functional programming language. More elaborate program examples are given with modest suggestions for a functional programming methodology.

For readers who want to study the art of functional programming in more detail good introductory books are available (e.g. Bird and Wadler, 1988).

Chapter 1
Basic concepts

This chapter first explains the advantages and drawbacks of a functional programming style compared with the commonly used classical imperative style of programming (Section 1.1). The difference in objectives between a mathematical specification of a function and a function specification in a functional programming language is explained in Section 1.2.

This is followed by an overview of the basic concepts of most functional programming languages (Sections 1.3–1.7). These concepts are explained using a concrete functional programming language: Miranda (Turner, 1985). Functions can be defined by a single equation (Section 1.3) as well as by more than one equation using guards and patterns to discriminate between the alternative equations (Section 1.5). Other topics that are covered are: higher order functions and currying (Section 1.7), lists as basic data structures (Section 1.6) and (lazy as well as eager) function evaluation (Section 1.4).

Traditional proof techniques like symbolic substitution and mathematical induction can be used to prove correctness of functional programs (Section 1.8). Finally, some small example programs are presented in Section 1.9.

1.1 Why functional programming?

Imagine the availability of perfect computer systems: software and hardware systems that are user-friendly, cheap, reliable and fast. Imagine that programs can be specified in such a way that they are not only very understandable but that their correctness can easily be proven as well. Moreover, the underlying hardware ideally supports these software systems and superconduction in highly parallel architectures makes it possible to get an answer to our problems at dazzling speed.

Well, in reality people always have problems with their computer systems. Actually, one does not often find a bug-free piece of software or hardware. We have learned to live with the *software crisis*, and have to accept that most software products are *unreliable*, *unmanageable* and *unprovable*. We spend money on a new release of a piece of software in which old bugs are removed and new ones are introduced. Hardware systems are generally much more reliable than software systems, but most hardware systems appear to be designed in a hurry and even well-established processors contain errors.

Software and hardware systems clearly have become very complex. A good, orthogonal design needs many person years of research and development, while at the same time pressure increases to put the product on the market. So it is understandable that these systems contain bugs. The good news is that hardware becomes cheaper and cheaper (thanks to very large scale integration) and speed can be bought for prices one never imagined. But the increase of processing power automatically leads to an increase of the use of that power with an increasing complexity of the software as a result. So computers are never fast enough, while the complexity of the systems is growing enormously.

The two key problems that the computer science community has to solve are:

- How can we, at low cost, make large software systems that remain reliable and user-friendly?
- How can we increase processing power at low cost?

Researchers are looking for solutions to these problems: by investigating *software engineering techniques*, to deal with problems related to the management of software projects and the construction and maintenance of software; by designing new *proof techniques* to tackle the problems in proving the correctness of systems; by developing *program transformation techniques*, to transform the specification of a problem into a program that solves it; and by designing new (parallel) *computer architectures* using many processors (thousands or more). In the mean time the quest for revolutionary new *technologies* (e.g. optical chips, superconduction) is always going on.

Another approach is based on the idea that the problems mentioned above are *fundamental* problems that cannot be solved unless a totally different approach is used and hardware and software are designed with a completely *different model of computation* in mind.

1.1.1 An imperative programming style

Most computer programs are written in an **imperative programming language** in which algorithms are expressed by a sequence of commands. These languages, such as FORTRAN, C, Algol, COBOL, PL/1 and Pascal, are originally deduced from (and form an abstraction of) the computer architectures they are running on (see Figure 1.1). These computer architectures, although different in detail, are all based on the same architecture: the **Von Neumann computer architecture** (Burks *et al.*, 1946). The Von Neumann computer architecture is based on a mathematical model of computation proposed by Turing in 1937: the **Turing machine**.

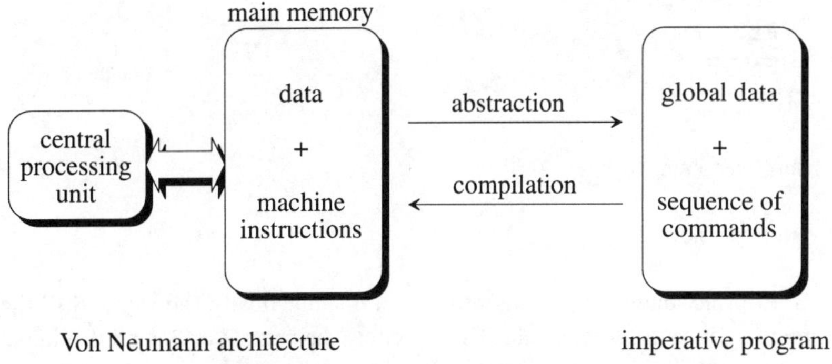

Figure 1.1 Imperative programming and the Von Neumann computer architecture.

The great advantage of this model and the corresponding architecture is that they are extremely simple. The Von Neumann architecture consists of a piece of memory that contains information that can be read and changed by a central processing unit (the **CPU**). Conceptually there are two kinds of information: program **instructions** in the form of machine code, information that is interpreted by the CPU and that controls the computation in the computer; and **data**, information that is manipulated by the program. This simple concept has made it possible to make efficient realizations in hardware at a relatively low cost.

In the beginning of the computer era, the 'high-level' imperative programming languages were designed to provide a notation to express computations in a machine-independent way. Later on, one recognized the importance of expressing computations such that programs are understandable for the human being and their correctness can be proven. It became clear that, in order to make it possible to reason about programs, not every machine instruction should have a direct equivalent in the high-level programming language. For instance, it is common knowledge that with the use of GOTO statements, which are the direct abstraction of the branch and jump instructions that are available on any computer, programs can be written in such a way that reasoning about them is almost impossible (Dijkstra, 1968). We strongly believe that a similar kind of problem is caused by the assignment statement.

Consider the following example written in an imperative programming style:

```
BOOLEAN even := TRUE;
...
PROCEDURE calculate (INTEGER value) : INTEGER;
BEGIN
   even := NOT even;
   IF even
   THEN value + 1
   ELSE value + 2
   ENDIF
END;
...
print(calculate (6));
...
print(calculate (6));
```

Both print statements in this program are syntactically the same. Still they may produce different results. Clearly either the value 7 or 8 is printed in both cases, but the exact value printed depends on the number of times the procedure calculate is called. The result returned by the procedure not only depends on the actual value of its argument, but also on the value the global boolean has at that particular moment. This value is 'secretly' changed in each procedure call. Such side-effects cause the result of a procedure call to be context dependent. Results become very hard to predict when, in a large program, global variables are changed all over the place.

One of the most important drawbacks of an imperative programming style is that an imperative program consists of a sequence of commands of which the dynamic behaviour must be known to understand how such a program works. The assignment causes problems because it changes the value (and often even the meaning) of a variable. Owing to side-effects it can happen that evaluating the same expression in succession produces different answers. Reasoning about the correctness of an imperative program is therefore very difficult.

Furthermore, because of the command sequence, algorithms are more sequential than is necessary. Therefore it is hard to detect which parts of the algorithm can or cannot be executed concurrently. This is a pity, since concurrent evaluation seems to be a natural way to increase execution speed.

A conjecture adopted by many researchers nowadays is that the software crisis and the speed problem are inherent to the nature of imperative programming languages and the underlying model of computation. Therefore, other styles of programming, such as *object oriented*, *logical* and *functional* styles of programming are investigated.

1.1.2 A functional programming style

John Backus (1978) pointed out that the solution for the software problems has to be found in using a new discipline of programming: a functional programming style instead of an imperative one.

In a **functional program** the result of a function call is uniquely determined by the actual values of the function arguments. No assignments are used, so no side-effects are possible. As a consequence, it makes no difference where and under what conditions a function is called. The result of a function will, under all conditions, be determined solely by the value of its arguments. For instance, in the program below the value printed will be 42 in both cases.

```
FUNCTION increment (INTEGER value) : INTEGER;
BEGIN
  value + 1
END;
...
print(increment (41));
...
print(increment (41));
```

It is much easier to reason about the result produced by a function that has no side-effects than about the result of an imperative procedure call with side-effects (see also Section 1.8).

Advantages of functional programming languages

So perhaps a functional programming style is important and side-effects, and hence the assignment statement, should be abandoned. But why should we use a functional programming language? Is it not possible to use the familiar languages? The common imperative languages also have functions, so why not restrict ourselves and only use the functional subset of for instance C, Algol or Modula2?

Well, one can use the functional subset of imperative languages (i.e. only using functions and leaving out the assignment), but then one is deprived of the expressive power of the new generation of functional languages that treat functions as 'first class citizens'. In most imperative languages functions can only be used restrictively. An *arbitrary* function cannot be passed as an argument to a function nor yielded as result.

For instance, the function twice takes a function and an argument, applies the function 'twice' to the argument and yields the result that again might be a function. The function twice can be used in various ways, e.g. by applying the result again as a function to respectively one or two arguments, etc.

```
FUNCTION
twice (f : FUNCTION from ANYTYPE to ANYTYPE, x: ANYTYPE ) :
  result ANYTYPE;
BEGIN
     f ( f (x) )
END;
...
print( twice (increment, 0) );
print( ( twice (twice, increment) ) (0) );
print( ( twice (twice, twice) ) (increment, 0) );
print( ( ( twice (twice, twice) ) (twice, increment) ) (0) );
...
```

Functions like twice are hard to express in a classical imperative language.

Functional programming languages have the advantage that they offer *a general use of functions* which is not available in classical imperative languages. This is a fact of life, not a fundamental problem. The restricted treatment of functions in imperative languages is due to the fact that when these languages were designed people simply did not know how to implement the general use of functions efficiently. It is also not easy to change the imperative languages afterwards. For instance, the type systems of these languages are not designed to handle these kinds of function. Also the compilers have to be changed dramatically.

In a traditional imperative language one would probably have severe problems expressing the type of twice. In a functional language such a function definition and its application can be expressed and typed in the following way:

```
twice:: (* -> *) -> * -> *          || type definition
twice f x    =  f (f x)             || function definition

?twice increment 0                  || function application, yields a number
```

```
?twice twice increment 0           || function application, yields a number
?twice twice twice increment 0     || function application, yields a number
...
```

Another advantage is that in most modern functional programming language(s) (FPLs) *the functional programming style is guaranteed*: the assignment statement is simply not available (like GOTOs are not available in decent modern imperative languages). FPLs in which there are no side-effects or imperative features of any kind are called **pure** functional languages. Examples of pure functional languages are Miranda, LML (Augustsson, 1984), HOPE (Burstall *et al.*, 1980), Haskell (Hudak *et al.*, 1992) and Concurrent Clean (Nöcker *et al.*, 1991b). LISP (McCarthy, 1960) and ML (Harper *et al.*, 1986) are examples of well-known functional languages which are impure. From now on only *pure* aspects of FPLs are considered.

In pure FPLs the programmer can only define functions that compute values uniquely determined by the values of their arguments. The assignment statement is not available, and nor is the heavily used programming notion of a variable as something that holds a value that is changed from time to time by an assignment. Rather, the **variables** that exist in purely functional languages are used in mathematics to name and refer to a yet *unknown constant value*. This value can never be altered. In a functional style a desired computation is expressed in a static fashion instead of a dynamic one. Due to the absence of side-effects, program correctness proofs are easier than for imperative languages (see Section 1.8). Functions can be evaluated in any order, which makes FPLs suitable for parallel evaluation (see Section 1.4). Furthermore, the guaranteed absence of side-effects enables certain kinds of analysis of a program, for example strictness analysis (see Chapter 7) and uniqueness analysis (see Chapter 8).

Besides the full availability of functions, the new generation functional languages also offer an elegant, user-friendly notation. Patterns and guards provide the user with simple access to complex data structures; basically one does not have to worry about memory management any more. Incorrect access of data structures is impossible. Functional programs are in general much shorter than their conventional counterparts and thus in principle easier to enhance and maintain.

The question arises, is it possible to express any possible computation by using pure functions only? Fortunately, this question has already been answered years ago. The concept of a function is one of the fundamental notions in mathematics. One of the greatest advantages of functional languages is that they are based on a sound and well-understood mathematical model, the **λ-calculus** (Church, 1932; 1933). One could say that functional languages are sugared versions of this calculus. The λ-calculus was introduced at approximately the same time as the Turing model (Turing, 1937). *Church's thesis* (Church, 1936) states that the class of **effectively computable functions**, i.e. the functions that intuitively can be computed, is the same as the class of functions that can be defined in the λ-calculus. Turing formalized machine computability and showed that the resulting notion of *Turing computability* is equivalent to *λ-definability*. So the power of both models is the same. Hence *any* computation can be expressed using a functional style only. For more information on λ-calculus we refer to Barendregt (1984).

Disadvantages of functional programming languages

The advantages mentioned above are very important. But although functional languages are being used more frequently, in particular as a language for rapid prototyping and as a language in which students learn how to program, functional languages are not yet commonly used for general purpose programming. The two main drawbacks lie in the fields of

- *efficiency* and
- *suitability* for applications with a strongly *imperative nature*.

Firstly, until recently programs written in a functional language ran very, very slowly in comparison with their imperative counterparts. The main problem is that the traditional machine architectures on which these programs have to be executed are not designed to support functional languages. On these architectures function calls are relatively expensive, in particular when the lazy evaluation scheme (see Section 1.4) is used. Our computers are ideally suited for destructive updates as present in imperative languages (assignments), but these are conceptually absent in functional languages. It is therefore not easy to find an efficient compilation scheme. Another big problem is caused by the fact that for some algorithms, due to the absence of destructive updates, the time and space complexity can be much worse for a functional program than for its imperative equivalent. In such a case, to retain the efficiency, program transformations are necessary.

As will be shown in this textbook, by using several new (and old) compilation techniques, the efficiency of (lazy) functional programs can nowadays be made acceptable in many (but certainly not all) cases. New compilation techniques have been developed at several research institutes. These techniques are quite complex. Commercial compilers are therefore not widely available yet. This will soon change. Anyhow, in our opinion, the advantages of functional languages are so important that some loss of efficiency is quite acceptable. One has to keep in mind that decades ago we accepted a loss of efficiency when we started to use high-level imperative languages instead of machine assembly languages.

Secondly, a very important drawback of functional languages was that some algorithms could not be expressed elegantly in a functional programming style. In particular, this seemed to hold for applications that strongly interact with the environment (interactive programs, databases, operating systems, process control). But, the problem is largely caused by the fact that the art of functional programming is still in development. We had and still have to learn how to express the different kinds of applications elegantly in a functional style. We now know that strongly interactive applications can be expressed very elegantly in a functional programming style. One example is the way interactive programs that use windows, dialogs, menus and the like can be specified in Clean (see Chapter 8). Another example is the definition of the abstract imperative machine given in Chapter 10.

The advantages of a functional programming style are very important for the development of reliable software. The disadvantages can be reduced to an acceptable level. Therefore we strongly believe that one day functional languages will be used worldwide as general purpose programming languages.

1.2 Functions in mathematics

Before discussing the basic concepts of most functional languages, we want to recall the mathematical concept of a function. In mathematics a **function** is a mapping from objects of a set called the **domain** to objects of a set called **co-domain** or **range** (see Figure 1.2).

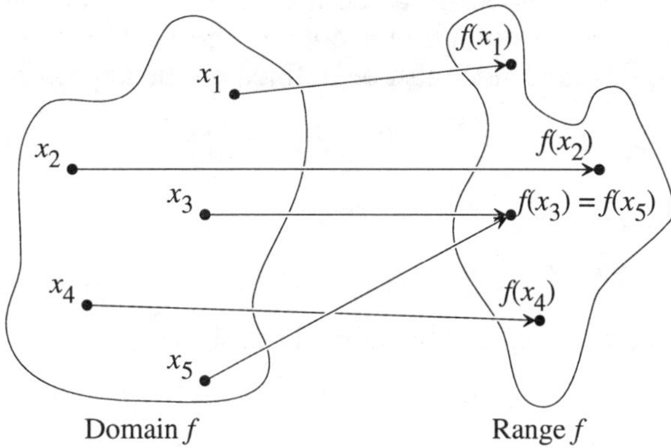

Figure 1.2 A function f maps objects x from the domain set to objects $f(x)$ in the range set.

This mapping need not be defined for all objects in the domain. If the mapping is defined for an object, this object is mapped to exactly one object in the range. This object in the range is called the **image** of the corresponding object in the domain. If all objects in the domain have an image, the function is called a **total function**, otherwise it is called a **partial function**. If x is an object in domain A and f is a function defined on domain A, the image of x is called $f(x)$.

The **type of a function** is defined as follows. If x is an object in the domain A, x is said to be of *type A*. If y is an object in range B, y is said to be of *type B*. If a function f maps objects from the domain A to the range B, f is said to be of *type* $A \to B$, which is pronounced as 'from A to B'. The type of f is generally specified as:

$$f\colon A \to B$$

In mathematics, there are several ways to define a function. The type of a function can be specified separately from the function definition.

One way to define a function is by explicit *enumeration* of all objects in the domain on which the function is defined with their corresponding images. An example of this is the following partial function (domain names Z and N are used for the domains of integers and natural numbers).

$$\begin{aligned} &abs\colon Z \to N \\ &abs(-1) = 1 \\ &abs(\ 0) = 0 \\ &abs(\ 1) = 1 \end{aligned}$$

Another way to define functions is by using definitions that consist of one or more (recursive) *equations*. For example, with this method the *abs*-function above can easily be defined as a total function, applicable for all objects in the domain. Of course, the functions and operators used on the right-hand side must be defined on the appropriate domains.

$$\begin{aligned} &abs\colon Z \to N \\ &abs(n) = n, \quad n > 0 \\ & = 0, \quad n = 0 \\ & = -n, \quad n < 0 \end{aligned}$$

A function like factorial can be defined as follows:

$$\begin{aligned} &fac\colon N \to N \\ &fac(n) = 1, \quad n = 0 \\ & = n * fac\ (n-1), \quad n > 0 \end{aligned}$$

or an alternative definition method is:

$$\begin{aligned} &fac\colon N \to N \\ &fac(0) = 1 \\ &fac(n) = n * fac\ (n-1), \quad n > 0 \end{aligned}$$

A mathematician would consider the definitions above as very common, ordinary function definitions. But these examples are also perfect examples of function definitions in a functional programming language. Notationally a function definition in a functional language has many similarities with a function definition in mathematics. However, there is an important difference in objective. The objective in a functional language is not only to define a function, but also to define a *computation* that automatically computes the image (result) of a function when it is applied to a specific object in its domain (the actual argument of the function).

Some function definitions, well-defined from a mathematical point of view, cannot be defined similarly in a functional language, because the images of some functions are very difficult to compute or even cannot be computed at all.

Consider, for example, the following function definition:

halting: All_Programs $\rightarrow$ *N*
halting(p) = *1*, *if the execution of p will stop*
0, *otherwise*

The *halting* function as indicated above is a problem that is not computable, and therefore an attempt to express it will not produce the desired computation. Suppose that a function in an FPL would try to calculate the image of the *halting* function for an arbitrary program. The only way of doing this is more or less running the program. But then the function would simply not terminate if the argument program does not terminate, in which case the result 0 would never be produced. For another example, consider:

$$f: R \rightarrow R,\ g: R \rightarrow R$$
$$f'' - 6g' = 6 \sin x$$
$$6g'' + a^2 f' = 6 \cos x$$
$$f(0) = 0,\ f'(0) = 0,\ g(0) = 1,\ g'(0) = 1$$

The equations for f, g and their derivatives f', f'', g' and g'' are solvable, but it is not easy to compute such functions.

Some special purpose programming languages are able to calculate functions by applying special purpose calculation techniques (symbolic computation using computer algebra techniques or formula transformations). But a general purpose functional programming language uses a very simple model of computation, based on substitution. So when functions are defined in an FPL a computation through substitutions is defined implicitly (see Section 1.4).

1.3 A functional program

A program written in a functional language consists of a collection of *function definitions* written in the form of *recursive equations* and an *initial expression* that has to be evaluated. From now on a Miranda-based syntax (see Appendix A) will be used.

1.3.1 Function definitions

A **function definition** consists of one or more equations. An **equation** consists of a left-hand side, an equals symbol (=) and a right-hand side.

The left-hand side defines the **function name** and its **formal arguments** (also called **formal parameters**). The right-hand side specifies the **function result**. It is also called the **function body**. This function body consists of an expression. Such an **expression** can be a denotation of some *value*, or it can be a *formal argument*, or a *function application*.

In a **function application** a function is applied to an expression, the **actual argument**. The application of a function f to an expression a is denoted as $f\ a$. So function application is denoted by simple juxtaposition of the function and its argument. An important syntactical convention is that in every expression function application has always the *highest* priority (on both sides of the equations). A function definition can be preceded by its *type definition* (indicated by post-fixing the function name with a '::' followed by its type).

Below are some examples of function definitions (now in Miranda-based notation). In Section 1.6 more complex definitions can be found with more than one alternative per function and guards or patterns to indicate which alternative has to be chosen. The || indicates that the rest of the line is a comment.

```
ident:: num -> num                      || ident is a function from num to num,
ident x  =  x                           || the identity function on numbers

alwaysseven:: num -> num                || a function from num to num,
alwaysseven x   =  7                    || that yields 7, independent of arg. x

inc:: num -> num                        || a function from num to num,
inc x =  x + 1                          || that returns the value of its arg. + 1

square:: num -> num                     || square function
square x   =  x * x

squareinc:: num -> num                  || square increment of argument
squareinc x   =  square (inc x)

fac:: num -> num                        || the factorial function
fac x =  cond (x = 0) 1 (x * fac (x – 1))
```

In the last example cond is a predefined operator with three arguments: a boolean, a then part and an else part. Its semantics corresponds to a conditional choice in imperative languages.

A formal argument, such as x in the example above, is also called a **variable**. The word variable is used here in the mathematical sense of the word that is not to be confused with the use of the word variable in an imperative language. This variable does not vary. Its scope is limited to the equation in which it occurs (whereas the defined function names have the whole program as scope).

Functions defined as above are called **user-defined functions**. One can also denote and manipulate objects of certain *predefined types* with given *predefined operators*. These predefined basic operators can be regarded as **predefined functions**. For mathematical–historical reasons, and therefore also for user convenience, such primitive functions are often defined as *infix* functions or operators. This is in contrast to the user-defined functions that are generally defined as *prefix* functions.

Examples of predefined types (numbers, booleans, characters), corresponding to predefined operators (functions), denotation of values (concrete objects) of these types, and the 'real-life' domain with which they can be compared.

Types	Operators	Denotation of values	Comparable with
num	+, –, *, …	0, 1, 34.7, –1.2E15, …	real numbers
bool	and, or, …	True, False	truth values
char	=, <, …	'a', 'c', …	characters

1.3.2 The initial expression

The **initial expression** is the expression whose value has to be calculated.

For example, in the case that the value of 2 + 3 has to be calculated, the initial expression 2 + 3 is written. But one can also calculate any application of user-defined functions: squareinc 7.

1.4 The evaluation of a functional program

The execution of a functional program consists of the evaluation of the initial expression in the context of the function definitions in the program called the **environment**.

A functional program: a set of function definitions and an initial expression.

```
ident:: num -> num
ident x  =  x
```

```
inc:: num -> num
inc x = x + 1

square:: num -> num
square x    = x * x

squareinc:: num -> num
squareinc x    = square (inc x)

squareinc 7
```

The evaluation consists of repeatedly performing *reduction* or *rewriting steps.* In each **reduction step** (indicated by a '→') a function application in the expression is replaced (*reduced, rewritten*) by the corresponding function body (the right-hand side of the equation), substituting the formal arguments by the corresponding actual arguments. A (sub)expression that can be rewritten according to some function definition is called a **redex** (**red**ucible **ex**pression). The basic idea is that the reduction process stops when none of the function definitions can be applied any more (there are no redexes left) and the initial expression is in its most simple form, the **normal form.** This is the result of the functional program that is then printed out.

For instance, given the function definitions above (the environment), the initial expressions below can be evaluated (reduced) as follows. In the examples the redex that will be reduced has been underlined.

```
ident 42          →    42

squareinc 7       →    square (inc 7)    →    square (7 + 1)
→    square 8     →    8 * 8             →    64

square (1 + 2)    →    (1 + 2) * (1 + 2) →    3 * (1 + 2)  →    3 * 3 →    9
```

However, the initial expression may *not* have a normal form at all. As a consequence, the evaluation of such an initial expression will not terminate. Infinite computations may produce partial results that will be printed as soon as they are known (see Section 1.6.3).

Example of a non-terminating reduction. Take the following definition:

```
inf    = inf
```

then the evaluation of the following initial expression will not terminate:

```
inf    →    inf    →    inf    →    ...
```

1.4.1 The order of evaluation

Because there are in general many redexes in the expression, one can perform rewrite steps in several orders. The actual order of evaluation is determined by the **reduction strategy** which is dependent on the kind of language being used. There are a couple of important things to know about the ordering of reduction steps.

Due to the absence of side-effects, the result of a computation does *not* depend on the chosen order of reduction (see also Chapter 3). If all redexes are vanished and the initial expression is in normal form, the result of the computation (if it terminates) will always be the same: the normal form is *unique*.

For instance, one can compute one of the previous expressions in a different order, but the result is identical:

```
square (1 + 2)  →  square 3         →  3 * 3  →  9
```

It is sometimes even possible to rewrite several redexes at the same time. This forms the basis for *parallel* evaluation.

Reducing several redexes at the same time:

```
square (1 + 2)  →  (1 + 2) * (1 + 2)  →  3 * 3  →  9
```

However, the order is not completely irrelevant. Some reduction orders may not lead to the normal form at all. So a computation may not terminate in one particular order while it would terminate when the right order was chosen (see again Chapter 3).

Example of a non-terminating reduction order. Assume that the following (recursive) functions are defined:

```
inf            = inf

alwaysseven x  = 7
```

Now it is possible to repeatedly choose the 'wrong' redex which causes an infinite calculation:

```
alwaysseven inf  →  alwaysseven inf  →  alwaysseven inf  →  ...
```

In this case another choice would lead to termination and to the unique normal form:

```
alwaysseven inf  →  7
```

The reduction strategy followed depends on the kind of FPL. In some languages, e.g. LISP, ML and HOPE, the arguments of a function are always reduced before the function application itself is considered as a redex. These languages are called **eager** or **strict** languages. In most recent FPLs, e.g. Miranda and Haskell, the rewriting is done lazily. In **lazy functional languages** the value of a subexpression (redex) is calculated if and only if this value must be known to find the normal form. The lazy evaluation order will find the normal form if it exists.

Illustrating lazy rewriting:

```
alwaysseven inf    →    7
```

A more complex example to illustrate lazy evaluation is shown below. The predefined conditional function demands the evaluation of its first argument to make a choice between the then and else parts possible. The equality function forces evaluation in order to yield the appropriate Boolean value. Multiplication and subtraction are only possible on numbers; again evaluation is forced.

```
fac 2
→    cond (2 = 0) 1 (2 * fac (2 – 1))
→    cond FALSE 1 (2 * fac (2 – 1))
→    2 * fac (2 – 1)
→    2 * cond (2 – 1 = 0)1 ((2 – 1) * fac ((2 – 1) – 1))
→    2 * cond (1 = 0) 1 ((2 – 1) * fac ((2 – 1) – 1))
→    2 * cond FALSE 1 ((2 – 1) * fac ((2 – 1) – 1))
→    2 * (2 – 1) * fac ((2 – 1) – 1)
→    2 * 1 * fac ((2 – 1) – 1)
→    2 * fac ((2 – 1) – 1 )
→    2 * cond ((2 – 1) – 1 = 0) 1 (((2 – 1) – 1) * fac (((2 – 1) – 1) – 1))
→    ...    →    2 * 1 * 1    →    2 * 1 →    2
```

1.5 Functions with guarded equations and patterns

In the previous section ordinary recursive equations were used to define a function. But often one needs a function description that depends on the actual values of the objects in the domain, or one wants to make a separate description for each subclass of the domain that has to be distinguished. Of course, a (predefined) function can be used, like cond in the factorial example in Section 1.3. However, it is much more convenient to use *guarded equations* or *patterns* for such a case analysis.

1.5.1 Guarded equations

The right-hand side of a definition can be a guarded equation. A function definition using **guarded equations** consists of a sequence of *al-*

ternative equations, each having a **guard**: an expression yielding a Boolean result, the textual first alternative for which the corresponding guard is True being selected. Guards can be preceded by the keyword if. The guard of the last alternative can be just the keyword otherwise and the corresponding alternative is chosen if and only if all other guards evaluate to False. Although it is allowed, it is good programming style not to use overlapping guards.

Function definitions with guarded equations:

```
fac:: num -> num
fac n    = 1,                if n = 0
         = n * fac (n – 1),  if n > 0

abs:: num -> num
abs n    = n,    if n >= 0
         = –n,   otherwise
```

It is quite possible to define partial functions using guards. When a function is called with actual parameters that do not satisfy any of the guards, it is considered to be a fatal programming error.

For example, the Fibonacci function below will cause a fatal error when it is called with an argument less than one (the V-operator denotes the logical OR).

```
fib:: num -> num
fib n  =  1,                          if (n = 1) V (n = 2)
       =  fib (n – 1) + fib (n – 2),  if n > 2
```

The programmer should of course avoid this situation. One way to avoid it is to specify the domain (type) of a function accurately, in such a way that a total function is defined on that domain. The type system of the language should therefore allow the specification of new types or of subtypes (see Chapter 2). However, an arbitrary accurate specification of the domain is generally not possible because it leads to undecidable type systems. Total functions can be accomplished in another way by adjusting the definition of the partial function. The guards should then always cover the whole domain the function is defined on. To make this possible in an easy way most languages are equipped with an error routine that fits in any type.

The Fibonacci function above is now changed into a total function. It will still yield a run-time error when it is called with an argument less than one. But now this situation is handled by the programmer and an appropriate error message can be given.

```
fib:: num -> num
fib n  =  1,                                                    if (n = 1) V (n = 2)
       =  fib (n – 1) + fib (n – 2),                            if n > 2
       =  error "Fibonacci called with argument less than one", otherwise
```

1.5.2 Patterns

It is also possible to discriminate between alternative equations by using *patterns* on the left-hand side. These **patterns** are *values* (e.g. 0) including *data constructors* (see the next section) or *variables*. The meaning of a pattern is that the equation in question is only applicable if the actual arguments of the function match the pattern. An actual argument **matches** a corresponding *pattern value* if it has the *same* value. A *pattern variable* is matched by any actual argument. An equation is only applicable if all the actual arguments match the corresponding patterns. Patterns are tried from left to right, equations are tried in textual order: from top to bottom. When an actual argument is matched against a non-variable pattern, the argument is evaluated first after which the resulting value is compared with the specified pattern.

A function definition with patterns:

```
fac:: num -> num
fac 0    =  1
fac n    =  n * fac (n – 1)
```

0 and n are the patterns of the first two rules (a variable as formal parameter indicates that it does not matter what the value is). Calling fac (7 – 1) will result in a call to the pattern-matching facility, which decides that (after the evaluation of the actual argument) only the second rule is applicable (6 ~= 0).

Patterns can also be used in combination with guarded equations.

```
fac:: num -> num
fac 0    =  1
fac n    =  n * fac (n – 1),                                    if n > 0
         =  error "factorial called with argument less than zero",  otherwise
```

1.5.3 The difference between patterns and guards

Patterns have a limited power: they can only be used to test whether actual arguments are of a certain value or form. Using guards any function yielding a Boolean result can be applied to the actual arguments. So guards are more powerful than patterns, but, on the other hand, patterns are easier to read and sufficient for most definitions. Using patterns in combination with guards often leads to clearer and more concise definitions and is highly recommended.

1.6 Data structures

In imperative languages one can define global data structures that are globally accessible for reading and writing during execution. Since this is not possible in functional languages it will be clear that the use of data structures in these languages is quite different. After creation of a data structure, the only possible access is read access. Data structures cannot be overwritten. Furthermore, data structures are not globally available but they must always be passed as arguments to the functions that need them.

Modern functional languages allow the definition of structured data objects like the records in Pascal. How user-defined data structures can be defined is explained in the next chapter. In this chapter only lists are treated.

Lists are the most important basic data structure in any FPL. **Lists** in FPLs are actually linked lists, each element in the list has the *same*[1] type *T* (see Figure 1.3). The *last* element in the list is indicated by a special element, generally called Nil.

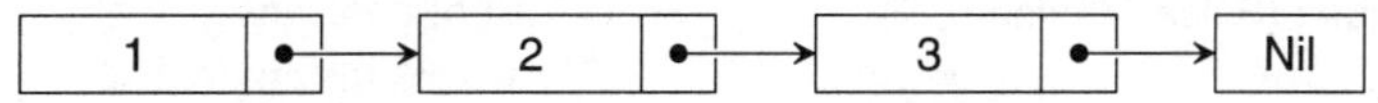

Figure 1.3 An example of a list.

Because lists are so important, they are generally predefined. A list is conceptually not different from any other user-defined data structure (see Chapter 2).

Lists, like any data structure in an FPL, are built using *data constructors*. A **data constructor** is a special constant value that is used as a tag that *uniquely* identifies (and is part of) an object of a certain type. So one can recognize the type of a data structure just by looking at the data constructor it contains. Several different data constructors can be used to identify the different objects of the same type.

Lists are constructed using two data constructors (see Figures 1.4 and 1.5). A list element is tagged with a constructor that is usually named 'Cons' (prefix notation) or ':' (infix notation, as used in Miranda). The end of a list is an empty list that just contains a tag, the constructor 'Nil' or '[ ]'. A non-empty list element contains, besides the constructor 'Cons' (or ':'), a value of a certain type *T* and (a reference

[1] Note that in most languages all elements of a list have to be of the same type. In some other languages (e.g. LISP) the types of the list elements may differ from each other. In Miranda tuples are used for this purpose (see Chapter 2).

to) the rest of the list of that same type *T*. A *list of elements of type* T is denoted as [T].

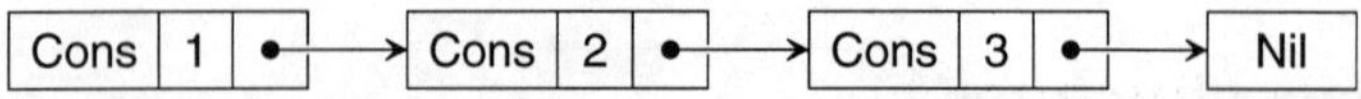

Figure 1.4 A list prefix tagged with the constructors Cons and Nil.

Hence, in Miranda, a non-empty list element contains the infix constructor ':', while the end of the list only contains a '[ ]'.

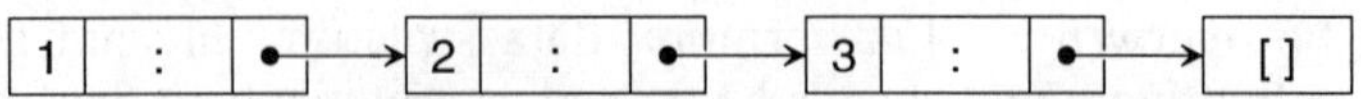

Figure 1.5 Miranda lists are infix tagged with the constructors : and [ ].

1.6.1 Denotation of lists

In Miranda, lists are denoted as follows.

Denotation of lists:

```
1 : (2 : (3 : (4 : (5 : [ ]))))       || list of numbers from 1 up to 5
True : (False : (False : [ ]))        || list of booleans
[ ]                                   || denotes the empty list
1 : 2 : 3 : 4 : 5 : [ ]               || list of numbers from 1 up to 5
```

Note that the list constructor ':' is right associative. For the convenience of the programmer Miranda allows a special notation for lists, with square brackets:

Lists, shorthand notation:

```
[1, 2, 3, 4, 5]                       || same as 1 : 2 : 3 : 4 : 5 : [ ]
[True, False, False]                  || same as True : False : False : [ ]
0 : [1, 2, 3]                         || same as [0, 1, 2, 3]
```

1.6.2 Predefined functions on lists

The data constructors ':' and '[ ]' are special constant values. The elements of a list can therefore easily be selected by using the pattern match mechanism in which these data constructors appear.

The (usually predefined) projection functions on lists are head (hd) and tail (tl). Projection functions like these are of general use and can be defined on lists of any type (see Chapter 2). The functions given below are restrictively defined on list of numbers.

```
hd:: [num] -> num              || hd is a function from list-of-num to num
hd (first : rest)   = first    || yields the first element of a non-empty list

tl:: [num] -> [num]            || a function from list-of-num to list-of-num
tl (first : rest)   = rest     || returns the tail of the list
```

Note that the parentheses on the left-hand side are not part of the list denotation. They are added to disambiguate the patterns concerning the application.

This way of handling lists is very user-friendly. One does not need to worry about 'memory management' nor about 'updating pointers'.

Below some other predefined operations on lists are given. These are: *length of a list* (denoted by #), *subscription,* followed by a number indicating the subscript (counting from zero), and *concatenation* (++).

List operations:

```
# [2, 3, 4, 5]         || length of list, yields 4
[2, 3, 4, 5] ! 2       || subscription, yields 4
[0, 1] ++ [2, 3]       || concatenation, yields [0, 1, 2, 3]
```

1.6.3 Infinite lists

One of the powerful features of lazy FPLs is the possibility of declaring infinite data structures by recursive definitions.

Definition of a function yielding an infinite list of numbers n, equal to [n, n, n, n, ...]:

```
infnums:: num -> [num]
infnums n  =  n : infnums n
```

The following program, the sieve of Eratosthenes, yields an infinite list of prime numbers. First an infinite list of all numbers [n, n+1, n+2, ...] is defined using the function gen.

```
gen:: num -> [num]
gen n    =  n : gen (inc n)
```

filter has two arguments: a number and a (possibly infinite) list. The filter removes all multiples of the given number pr from the list. Note the type of this function. It is explained in the next section.

```
filter:: num -> [num] -> [num]
filter pr (x : xs)   =  x : filter pr xs,  if  x mod pr ~= 0
                     =  filter pr xs,      otherwise
```

sieve yields an infinite list of primes. It is assumed that the first element in the infinite list is a prime. This value is delivered as result in the head of a list. The function recursively calls itself, filtering all multiples of the found prime from the input list.

```
sieve:: [num] -> [num]
sieve (pr : rest)   =  pr : sieve (filter pr rest)
```

The initial expression that will yield the infinite list of all prime numbers [2, 3, 5, 7, 11, ...] is the following:

```
sieve (gen 2)
```

Programs having infinite data structures as results do not terminate, of course. When an infinite list is yielded, the lazy evaluation scheme will force the evaluation of the list elements from 'left to right'. It would not be wise to postpone printing this list until the last element has been calculated. Therefore, one after another the values of the elements of the list are printed as soon as they have been evaluated.

Infinite data structures are of more practical importance than one may conclude from the examples above. One has to remember that, if functions are evaluated with the lazy evaluation scheme, the computation of a value is only started when its value is needed to produce the result. For instance, if one needs a certain element of an infinite list, the computation will not force the evaluation of the whole list, but only of the part that is needed for the evaluation of the required element. Therefore, such a computation can be performed in finite time, even if an infinite list is being used. Of course, if an attempt to find the last element of an infinite list is made, the computation will not terminate.

So in *lazy* languages *infinite* data structures can be defined; moreover, they make elegant programs possible. For example, if a function has to be defined that yields the first thousand prime numbers, one can simply take the first thousand elements of the list of all primes.

The following initial expression will yield the second prime number of an infinite list of all primes. The evaluation will terminate even if an infinite list is being used.

```
hd (tl (sieve (gen 2)))
→    hd (tl (sieve (2 : gen (inc 2))))
→    hd (tl (2 : sieve (filter 2 (gen (inc 2)))))
→    hd (sieve (filter 2 (gen (inc 2))))
→    hd (sieve (filter 2 (inc 2 : gen (inc (inc 2)))))
→    hd (sieve (filter 2 (3 : gen (inc (inc 2)))))
→    hd (sieve (3 : filter 2 (gen (inc (inc 2)))))
```

```
→    hd (3 : sieve (filter 3 (filter 2 (gen (inc (inc 2))))))
→    3
```

Infinite data structures cannot be handled in *eager* languages, because they evaluate arguments regardless of whether they are needed or not, which leads to infinite computations.

The evaluation of the initial expression in the previous example in eager FPLs will not terminate.

```
hd (tl (sieve (gen 2)))
→    hd (tl (sieve (2 : gen (inc 2))))
→    hd (tl (sieve (2 : gen 3)))
→    hd (tl (sieve (2 : 3 : gen (inc 3))))
→    hd (tl (sieve (2 : 3 : ...)
```

In a lazy functional programming language most functions that are defined on lists can also be used to handle infinite lists. For instance, the hd function (defined above) can take the head of all lists, regardless of whether the list is finite or infinite.

1.7 Higher order functions and currying

Compared with the traditional imperative languages, which normally allow also the declaration of functions, functional programming languages such as Miranda have a more general view of the concept of functions: they are treated as 'first-class citizens', i.e. functions are treated just like other objects in the language. As a consequence, functions can have *functions* as arguments and as results.

1.7.1 Higher order functions

Functions that have functions as actual arguments or yield a function as result are called **higher order functions**, in contrast to **first-order functions,** which have only non-function values as argument or as result.

Example of a higher order function that takes a function as argument (note how this is reflected in the type):

```
atzero:: (num -> num) -> num
atzero f  =  f 0
```

Now consider the following initial expressions (inc, square and ident are taken to be defined as in Section 1.3):

```
atzero inc      →  inc 0     →  0 + 1  →  1
atzero square   →  square 0  →  0 * 0  →  0
atzero ident    →  ident 0   →  0
```

Example of a higher order function that yields a function as result (note the type):

```
funcresult:: num -> (num -> num)
funcresult 0   =  inc
funcresult 1   =  square
funcresult n   =  ident
```

And consider the following initial expressions:

```
funcresult 0 6  →  inc 6     →  6 + 1  →  7
funcresult 1 6  →  square 6  →  6 * 6  →  36
funcresult 2 6  →  ident 6   →  6
funcresult 3 6  →  ident 6   →  6
```

At first sight the substitutions in the example above may seem a bit strange. But, remember that the application of a function *f* to an expression *a* is denoted as *f a*. So if a function is applied to more than one argument, say n, this can be denoted as:

$(\dots ((f\ a_1)\ a_2) \dots a_n)$

Function application is left associative. So this can be denoted in an equivalent, more readable way:

$f\ a_1\ a_2 \dots a_n$

Hence, the expression funcresult 0 6 is equivalent to (funcresult 0) 6, which immediately explains why the substitution above is allowed. Higher order functions are very natural and provide a powerful programming tool, as is shown below.

1.7.2 Currying

The possibility of yielding a function as result makes it unnecessary to have functions with more than one argument. A function with *n* arguments can be simulated by a higher order function with *one* argument that returns a new function. Now this new function can be applied to the *next* argument, and so on, until finally *all n* arguments are handled.

The idea of handling functions with *n* arguments by using a sequence of applications of higher order functions with one argument is called **currying** (Schönfinkel, 1924; Curry and Feys, 1958), see also

Chapter 3. The final result of such a sequence of applications of higher order functions with one argument is the same as the result yielded by the equivalent function with *n* arguments.

Consider a function definition, in Miranda, of a function with more than one argument, say n. Assume that these arguments are, respectively, of type A_1, A_2, ..., A_n and that the result of the function is of type B. In general such a function definition has the following form:

```
function-name arg1 arg2 ... argn  =  expression
```

In Miranda, all functions are used in a curried manner. Functions with more than one argument are simulated by a sequence of applications using currying. Therefore the definition above should be read as:

```
( ... ((function-name arg1) arg2) ... argn)   =  expression
```

The type of this function is not

```
function-name:: A1 x A2 x ... x An -> B
```

which is the mathematical type with as domain the Cartesian product of the n argument types, but

```
function-name:: A1 -> (A2 -> ... -> (An -> B) ... )
```

The arrow -> is defined to be right associative, so the type can also be specified as

```
function-name:: A1 -> A2 -> ... -> An -> B
```

1.7.3 The use of currying

The question arises: why should one use this currying scheme and make things more complicated? Well, notationally it is almost equivalent to having functions with more than one argument: function application is left associative, so the parentheses can be left out. Currying enables the use of a familiar notation; only the types of the functions are different. But a great advantage of currying is that it increases the expressive power of a functional language.

Parametrizing functions

The currying scheme makes it possible to apply a function defined on *n* arguments to any number of arguments from 1 up to *n*, resulting in a *parametrized* function. A function defined with *n* arguments can, without currying, only be applied when all these *n* arguments are available.

In the curried variant some of the arguments can be 'fed' to the function; the result (a **parametrized function**) can be passed to another function that can fill in the remaining arguments.

Consider the following definition:

```
plus:: num -> num -> num
plus x y = x + y
```

This definition is equivalent to:

```
plus:: num -> (num -> num)
(plus x) y   =  x + y
```

Now take the following initial expression:

```
plus 1
```

Clearly, we need another argument to be able to actually perform the addition specified in the function body. The result of this initial expression is a function of type num -> num. It is a function of one argument; the function has no name.

Assuming plus to be defined as above, the function incr can be defined in two ways: as a function with an explicit formal argument:

```
incr:: num -> num
incr x    =  plus 1 x
```

or as a parametrized version of plus:

```
incr:: num -> num
incr   =  plus 1
```

The only difference between the two incr functions is that the second definition is more concise.

It is very useful to be able to create new functions by adding parameters to more general functions. So currying enables a new way of programming by elegantly specifying general purpose functions.

Another example of parametrized functions. The function map takes a function of type num -> num, a (possibly infinite) list of numbers and applies the given function to all numbers in the list. incr and plus are assumed to be defined as above.

```
map:: (num -> num) -> [num] -> [num]
map f [ ]       =  [ ]
map f (x : xs)  =  f x : map f xs
```

A function that increments the elements of a list can now simply be constructed as follows:

```
mapincr:: [num] -> [num]
mapincr     =  map incr
```

or as

```
mapincr:: [num] -> [num]
mapincr     =  map (plus 1)
```

In Miranda it is, in general, not the intention to yield a function as the final result of a program. Functions cannot be printed. The intention is to yield some non-function value, probably a string of characters, as the final result. Therefore, in ordinary programs curried functions will in the end receive all arguments needed to do the computation.

The following example of an expression with mapincr as defined above (the second definition) shows how evaluation might actually proceed when currying is used.

```
mapincr [1,2,3]
→    map (plus 1) [1,2,3]
=    map (plus 1) (1 : 2 : 3 : [ ])
→    plus 1 1 : map (plus 1) (2 : 3 : [ ])
→    2 : map (plus 1) (2 : 3 : [ ])
→    2 : (plus 1) 2 : map (plus 1) (3 : [ ])
→    ...    →    2 : 3 : 4 : [ ] = [2,3,4]
```

1.8 Correctness proof of functional programs

A functional programming style has advantages that are common in any mathematical notation:

- There is consistency in the use of names: variables do not vary, they stand for a, perhaps not yet known, constant value throughout their scope.
- Thanks to the absence of side-effects, in FPLs the same expression *always* denotes the same value. This property is called **referential transparency.**

A definition like x = x + 1 would mean in an imperative language that x is incremented. In a functional language however this definition means that *any* occurrence of x can always be substituted by x + 1. Clearly the initial expression x does not have a normal form: substitution will continue forever (some systems recognize such situations in certain simple cases and report an error message).

$$\underline{x} \rightarrow \underline{x} + 1 \rightarrow (\underline{x} + 1) + 1 \rightarrow \ldots$$

Due to the referential transparency[1] one is allowed to replace in *any* expression *any* occurrence of *any* left-hand side of a definition by its corresponding right-hand side and vice versa.

Referential transparency makes it possible to use common mathematical techniques such as *symbolic substitution* and *induction*. With the help of these techniques a program can be transformed into a more efficient one or certain properties of a program, such as its correctness, can be proven. Take again the factorial example:

```
fac:: num -> num
fac 0   = 1                                                    || (1)
fac n   = n * fac (n – 1),                         if n > 0 || (2)
        = error "factorial called with argument less than zero", otherwise
```

The Miranda definition of this function has a great similarity to the mathematical definition of factorial. In order to prove that this function indeed calculates the mathematical factorial written as n! for n >= 0, mathematical induction is used: first it has to be proven that the function calculates factorial for a start value n = 0 (step 1). Then, under the assumption that the function calculates factorial for a certain value n (the induction hypothesis), it has to be proven that the function also calculates factorial for the value n + 1 (step 2). The proof is trivial:

step 1: fac 0 = 1 , by applying rule (1)
1 = 0! , by the definition of factorial

step 2: Assume that fac n = n!, n >= 0 (induction hypothesis)
fac (n + 1) = (n + 1) * fac n , by applying rule (2): n+1>0
(n + 1) * n! , by the induction hypothesis
(n + 1)! , by the definition of factorial

---

[1] Sometimes the notion 'functional programming language' is used for languages which support higher order functions and the notion 'applicative programming language' for languages which support referential transparency. Outside the functional programming community the notion 'functional' is widely used as a synonym for 'useful'.

Note that the proof assumes, as is common in mathematics, that the function is only applied to arguments on which it is defined: the mathematical definition does not concern itself with 'incorrect input' ($n < 0$). In general, a proof must cover the complete domain of the function.

There is a strong correspondence between a recursive definition and an induction proof. Recursive functions generally have the form of a sequence of definitions: first the special cases (corresponding to the start values in an induction proof), textually followed by the general cases that are recursively expressed (corresponding to the induction step).

1.9 Program examples

This section illustrates the expressive power of the functional programming languages in two small examples.

1.9.1 Sorting a list

The function (quick) sort needs a list of numbers as argument and delivers the sorted list as result.

```
sort:: [num] -> [num]
sort [ ]  = [ ]
sort (x : xs)    = sort (smalleq x xs) ++ [x] ++ sort (greater x xs)
```

The functions smalleq and greater take two arguments, namely an element and a list. This element must be of the same type as the type of the elements of the list. It is assumed that the elements are of type num; the operators <= and > are therefore well defined.

```
smalleq:: num -> [num] -> [num]
smalleq a [ ]          = [ ]
smalleq a (x : xs)     = x : smalleq a xs,  if x <= a
                       = smalleq a xs,      otherwise

greater:: num -> [num] -> [num]
greater a [ ]          = [ ]
greater a (x : xs)     = x : greater a xs,  if x > a
                       = greater a xs,      otherwise
```

1.9.2 Roman numbers

Outline of the problem
Roman numbers consist of the characters (roman ciphers) M, D, C, L, X, V and I. Each of these characters has its own value. The values of roman ciphers are: M := 1000, D := 500, C := 100, L := 50, X := 10, V := 5, I := 1.

These characters always occur in sorted order, characters with a higher value before characters with a lower value. Exceptions to this rule are a number of 'abbreviations', given below. The value of a roman number can be found by adding the values of the characters that occur in the roman number (MCCLVI = 1000 + 100 + 100 + 50 + 5 + 1 = 1256). The following abbreviations are commonly used: DCCCC := CM, CCCC := CD, LXXXX := XC, XXXX := XL, VIIII := IX, IIII := IV. These abbreviations make it less simple to calculate the value of a roman number because now the value of the character depends on its position in the string. Negative numbers and the number zero cannot be expressed in roman numbers.

Task

- Develop an algorithm that calculates the integer value of a roman number, represented as a string, assuming that the string is a proper roman number.
- Develop an algorithm that converts an integer value into a roman number without abbreviations, assuming that the integer value is positive.

Solution

First the value of a roman cipher is defined:

```
value:: char -> num
value 'M'   =  1000
value 'D'   =   500
value 'C'   =   100
value 'L'   =    50
value 'X'   =    10
value 'V'   =     5
value 'I'   =     1
```

The function romtonum converts a roman number to a decimal number. It assumes that the supplied argument is a proper roman number.

```
romtonum:: [char] -> num
romtonum ('C' : 'M' : rs)   = value 'M' – value 'C' + romtonum rs
romtonum ('C' : 'D' : rs)   = value 'D' – value 'C' + romtonum rs
romtonum ('X' : 'C' : rs)   = value 'C' – value 'X' + romtonum rs
romtonum ('X' : 'L' : rs)   = value 'L' – value 'X' + romtonum rs
romtonum ('I' : 'X' : rs)   = value 'X' – value 'I' + romtonum rs
romtonum ('I' : 'V' : rs)   = value 'V' – value 'I' + romtonum rs
romtonum ( r : rs)          = value r + romtonum rs
romtonum [ ]                = 0
```

The function numtorom converts a decimal number to a roman number by repeated subtraction of 1000, 500, 100, 50, 10, 5 and 1, in this order. It assumes that the argument is a number greater than zero.

```
numtorom:: num -> [char]
numtorom n  =  countdown n ['M','D','C','L','X','V','I']

countdown:: num -> [char] -> [char]
countdown 0 rs        =  [ ]
countdown n (r : rs)  =  [r] ++ countdown (n – value r) (r : rs), if  n >= value r
                      =  countdown n rs,                        otherwise
```

The style in which these algorithms were presented (bottom-up) is not the way in which they were deduced. In Chapter 2 styles of functional programming are discussed.

Summary

- A *functional program* consists of a collection of (predefined) *function definitions* and an *initial expression* that has to be evaluated according to these definitions.
- A *function definition* consists of a sequence of one or more alternative *equations*. The choice between these alternatives is determined by *patterns* and/or *guards*.
- The evaluation of a functional program is called *reduction* or *rewriting*.
- A function application that can be rewritten according to a function definition is called a *redex*.
- In each *reduction step* a redex is replaced by the corresponding function body, *substituting* formal arguments by actual arguments.
- The evaluation of a functional program stops if there are no more redexes left in the resulting expression. Then the expression is in *normal form*.
- Redexes can be chosen in *arbitrary* order; in principle it is even possible that they are reduced in parallel.
- A *reduction strategy* determines the order in which redexes are reduced.
- In a *lazy* FPL redexes are only chosen if their result is needed to achieve the normal form.
- In an *eager* FPL the arguments of a function are reduced to normal form before the function application itself is reduced.

- *Data structures* in FPLs are not globally available but constructed in expressions, passed as arguments, decomposed and used as components for the construction of new structures.
- Data structures in FPLs are composed using *data constructors*. With pattern matching data structures can be decomposed.
- The most important basic data structure in FPLs is a *list*.
- Lazy FPLs can handle *infinite* data structures, eager FPLs cannot.
- A function with *n* arguments can be simulated using higher order functions with at most *one* argument (*currying*).
- FPLs have a high expressive power due to the availability of higher order functions, pattern matching and guarded equations.
- Due to *referential transparency* traditional mathematical proof techniques, such as *induction* and *substitution*, can be used for the correctness proof of functional programs.

EXERCISES

1.1 Write in your favourite imperative language a program that finds the maximum element in a list of numbers. Rewrite the program so that only the functional subset of the imperative language is used.

1.2 Consider the following function definition:

```
maxi:: num -> num -> num
maxi x y   = x,  if x >= y
           = y,  if x < y
```

Check whether the following initial expressions are legal, and if so, give the result yielded:

- maxi 5 6
- maxi (5)
- maxi 5
- maxi (5,6)
- maxi maxi 5 6 4
- maxi [5,6]
- maxi (maxi 5 6) 4
- maxi 'a' 4

1.3 Write a function maxilist that uses the function maxi of Exercise 1.2 to calculate the *greatest* element of a list of numbers. How does maxilist react on the empty list? Are there lists for which your program does not terminate? Does it make any difference if you change the order of the guards or patterns in your program?

1.4 Suppose you now want to find the *smallest* element of a list with minimal rewriting of the programs written in Exercise 1.3. To solve this problem first write a higher order function find in Miranda that gets a list of numbers and a function f of type num -> num

-> num as arguments and produces a num as its result such that find [a_1,a_2,...,a_n] f = f a_1 (f a_2 (... (f a_{n-1} a_n))).

Then, write down the stepwise lazy evaluation of the function application find [1,2,3] s with s:: num -> num -> num and s a b = a + b. What does find list s calculate?

Finally, write a function to find the smallest element of a list.

1.5 Define functions that print a list of characters on the screen in different ways: vertically below each other; each character in the same place; with two spaces between the characters; diagonally.

1.6 Define a function which yields the last two elements in a list.

1.7 Define a function which yields the average of a list of numbers.

1.8 Define a function search that takes two arguments of type [char] yielding a bool indicating whether the first argument is part of the second.

1.9 Examine the definition of the function map in this chapter. Define a function mapfun that applies a list of functions to a number and returns a list of the results of the function applications. So the following must hold: mapfun [f,g,h] x = [f x, g x, h x].

1.10 Define a function that yields all factorial numbers.

Chapter 2
Advanced concepts: Miranda

In this chapter the more sophisticated language features as found in modern lazy functional languages are discussed. Again Miranda (Turner, 1985) is taken as example language. The intention of this chapter is to show the programming power and notational elegance provided by such a state-of-the-art-language.

Many of the advanced concepts treated in this chapter can also be found in other languages. Those who are already familiar with similar languages like ML (Harper *et al.*, 1986), LML (Augustsson, 1984), HOPE (Burstall *et al.*, 1980), Haskell (Hudak *et al.*, 1992) or others will recognize most concepts.

Examples of simple function definitions using patterns and guarded equations have been shown in the previous chapter. In addition Miranda allows function definitions with a local scope to support a more modular programming style (see Section 2.1). Besides lists, tuples are also available as predefined data structures. Furthermore, a powerful and elegant notation based on mathematics is provided to generate all kinds of lists (Section 2.2). Miranda's type system has many features useful for programming. Functions can be of polymorphic type (Section 2.3). User-defined data structures (Section 2.4) can be declared using algebraic type declarations or abstract type declarations. The use of (higher order) functions as basic building blocks (Section 2.5) is a useful and reliable method for producing more complex functions. Due to lazy evaluation it is possible to write fairly general interactive programs in a functional language (Section 2.6). Finally, in Section 2.7 some guidelines are given on how to perform a top-down design of a functional program.

2.1 Defining functions

The basic ideas of Miranda are taken from earlier functional languages such as SASL (Turner, 1979b). The word 'Miranda' is Latin and it means 'she who is to be admired'.

Miranda is a *lazy* functional programming language featuring the basic concepts discussed in the previous chapter. Miranda is equipped with many additional features such as a rich type system that helps the user to develop meaningful, elegant and compact programs.

A Miranda program consists of two parts: a collection of declarations, called the **script**, and an **initial expression** to be evaluated. The declarations in the script can be function definitions or type declarations. In general, a function definition has the following form:

f_name $pattern_1$ $pattern_2$ ... $pattern_n$ = expression

Some examples of valid Miranda expressions:

```
x                 || an identifier
127               || a value of type num(eral)
True              || a value of type bool(ean)
'a'               || a value of type char(acter)
"hello world"     || a value of type [char]
y * x – 17        || an expression of type num using predefined operators
[1,5,7,9]         || a list of nums
[+, –, *, /]      || a list of operators of type num -> num -> num
fac 3             || a function application
(any_expression)  || an expression
```

There are a variety of predefined infix and prefix operators, of various binding powers (see below).

List of prefix and infix operators, in order of increasing binding power. The table reveals that Miranda allows functions of polymorphic type (see Section 2.3). Comparison operators can be continued, e.g. 0 <= x < 5.

Left associative operators:	+ , – , * , / , div , mod , !
Right associative operators:	++ , – – , : , ^
Associative operators:	., V , &
Prefix operators:	~ , # , –
Continuable operators:	> , >= , = , ~= , <= , <

Operator	**Type**	**Meaning**
:	* -> [*] -> [*]	prefix an element to a list
++, – –	[*] -> [*] -> [*]	list concatenation, list subtraction
V, &	bool -> bool -> bool	logical OR, AND

~	bool -> bool	logical negation
>, >=, =, ~=, <=, <	* -> * -> bool	greater, greater than, equal, not equal, less than, less
+, –	num -> num -> num	plus, minus
–	num -> num	unary minus
*, /, div, mod	num -> num -> num	times, divide, integer divide, remainder
^	num -> num -> num	to the power of
.	(** -> ***) -> (* -> **) -> * -> ***	function composition
#	[*] -> num	length of list
!	[*] -> num -> *	list subscription

The evaluation strategy in Miranda is lazy. Function alternatives are tried in textual order and the patterns in an alternative are tried from left to right. This strategy is intuitively easy to understand. However, it is not *truly lazy*, i.e. it does not always find a normal form if it exists.

Miranda's evaluation strategy is not truly lazy. Take the following definitions:

```
f 1 [ ]       = 0
f x (a : b)   = a

inf   = inf
```

With the initial expression f inf [1..2] the evaluation in Miranda will not terminate since the first argument will be evaluated first. So the strategy will not find the normal form 1. However, one would expect that a truly lazy strategy would evaluate the second argument of f first, but the strategy of Miranda first tries to match the patterns of the topmost rule from left to right and therefore it first evaluates the first argument of f.

Furthermore some specific aspects of Miranda are:

- Named constants in patterns are not possible: you can define a function linewidth = 80 for usage as a named constant throughout your program, but it is not possible to use this constant as a pattern on the left-hand side of a function definition: syntactically it would be a pattern variable.
- A string actually is a list of characters; hence "It is fun" is shorthand for 'I' : 't' : ' ' : 'i' : 's' : ' ' : 'f' : 'u' : 'n' : [ ]. This implies that one can use the pattern match mechanism for lists to decompose strings.

2.1.1 Local function definitions

Ordinary functions defined in Miranda have a **global** scope. This means that such a function can be applied in any expression anywhere in the program script. It is also possible to define functions with a **local** scope using a *where clause*. Such a **local** function is only defined in the smallest surrounding *block*. Outside a block such a function is not visible. In most programming languages the beginning and the end of a block structure are indicated by special keywords such as 'begin' or 'end', or in other languages a block is surrounded by parentheses. In Miranda a block is indicated by the *layout* of a program: a **block** consists of all expressions and definitions within one function definition or where clause that is either directly below or to the right of the first token after the equal sign of the function definition. A token that is outside the block of a definition is said to be **offside** (Landin, 1966).

The boxes indicate the blocks of, respectively, the function definition and the where clause:

```
glob_func a1 ... an = | expr1
glob_func b1 ... bn = | expr2
                      | where
                      | local_func1 c1 c2 ... cm  = | expr3
                      | local_func2 d1 d2 ... ds  = | expr4
```

A **where clause** can contain any number of definitions. The where clause must be indented, to show that it is part of the right-hand side.

```
primes:: [num]
primes =   | sieve (from 2)
           | where
           | sieve (p : x)     =  | p : sieve (filter p x)
           | from n            =  | n : from (n + 1)
           | filter p (a : x)  =  | filter p x,     if a mod p = 0
           |                   =  | a : filter p x, otherwise
```

A disadvantage of the offside rule is that it can lead to errors when names are changed globally in the script.

A not-offside program:

```
f a    = g
         where g = 3
```

An offside program:

```
a_meaningful_long_name_for_this_function a = g
         where g = 3
```

Actually (for purists), it is a consequence of the offside rule that a Miranda program is no longer referentially transparent: a uniform substitution can introduce an error and hence change the meaning of a program. One can overcome this problem by using a layout that is *safe* with respect to global name changes.

An example of such a safe layout is given below:

```
f a
= g
  where g = 3
```

2.2 Predefined data structures

In Miranda two kinds of data structure are predefined: *lists* and *tuples*. In the first part of this section tuples are discussed and compared with lists which were already introduced in the previous chapter.

Modern languages like Miranda and Haskell furthermore offer compact alternative notations to define lists: *list comprehensions*. These list comprehensions offer the possibility of defining lists in a style commonly used in mathematics. In the second part of this section these notations are discussed.

2.2.1 Tuples

The most important difference between lists and tuples is that the elements of a tuple can have *different* types while all the elements of a list must be of the *same* type. Furthermore a list is a linked list, possibly of *infinite* length. A tuple is just a record with some *finite* number of fields (Figure 2.1). There must be at least two fields in the tuple. Each field contains an object of a certain type.In Miranda, the notation for lists and tuples is quite similar: brackets are used to denote lists, parentheses are used to denote tuples. Parentheses are also used for disambiguating the structure of expressions. There is no concept of a 1-tuple, so the use of parentheses for disambiguating never conflicts with their use for tupling.

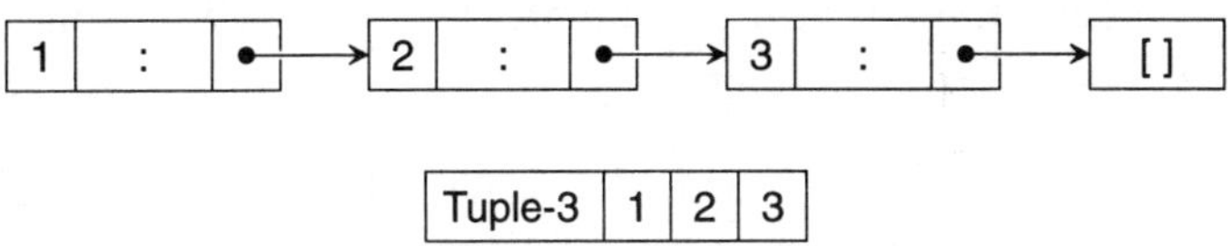

Figure 2.1 General difference between a list and a tuple.

The correspondence between the Miranda notation for lists and tuples:

```
[1, 2, 3]          || the list 1 : 2 : 3 : [ ]
(1, 2, 3)          || a tuple containing the elements 1, 2 and 3
```

In a tuple the elements can have *different* types. If the elements of a tuple are of type T_1, T_2 … T_n, the type of that tuple is indicated by (T_1, T_2, … , T_n) (see also Section 2.3).

Example of tuples and their types:

```
(3, 0, 'a')        || 3-tuple of type (num, num, char)
([0,1,2], +)       || 2-tuple of type ([num], num -> num -> num)
```

As with any other data structure, pattern matching can be used to access elements. In this way projection functions can be constructed that select a certain element from a tuple.

Using pattern matching to select an element of a tuple with three elements:

```
first (x, y, z)    = x
second (x, y, z)   = y
last (x, y, z)     = z
```

Here follows a summary of the differences between the two predefined data structures lists and tuples:

- the length of lists can vary and can even be infinite, the length of tuples will always be fixed and finite;
- all the elements in a list must be of the same type, the elements in a tuple need not;
- lists are enclosed in square brackets, tuples are enclosed in round parentheses;
- in a pattern match and in a denotation all the elements in a tuple must be enumerated, whereas for lists this is not necessary;
- subscription as in lists is not defined in tuples; however there is the possibility of extracting elements of a tuple by using pattern matching.

As will be shown in Section 2.4, both lists and tuples could have been defined as ordinary user-defined algebraic data types. The reason that they have been predefined is that they are used so frequently that both data structures deserve a compact notation as well as special attention in an implementation.

2.2.2 List comprehensions

Miranda offers three alternative notations to define lists in a style commonly used in mathematics: by means of *dotdot expressions*, *ZF-expressions* and *recurrent generators*. These notations do not offer any additional expressive power, but are just syntactic sugar. The advantage of the notations is that they may be used to express certain algorithms concisely and elegantly (although the concept of recurrent generators is a bit overdone in our opinion). A disadvantage of the notations is that it may be less clear how the list will be computed. As a result programmers may sometimes find their programs to be unexpectedly slow or even non-terminating.

Dotdot expressions

The following abbreviations are provided for defining lists whose members form a finite or infinite arithmetic series.

Dotdot notations (let a, b, c stand for arbitrary numeric expressions):

[a..b]	finite list of numbers from a with interval 1, last member not exceeding b
[a..]	infinite list from a with interval 1
[a,b..c]	finite list from a with interval (b–a), last member not exceeding c
[a,b..]	infinite list from a with interval (b–a)

The following examples show the use of these abbreviations together with an equivalent definition showing that it is all just syntactical sugar.

Two auxiliary functions that are used in the expansion of the abbreviations:

```
inbetween:: num -> num -> num -> [num]
inbetween start limit interval
= start : inbetween (start + interval) limit interval,
            if (interval >= 0 & start <= limit) \/ (interval <= 0 & start >= limit)
= [ ],      otherwise

from:: num -> num -> [num]
from start interval  =  start : from (start + interval) interval
```

Examples of the use of dotdot expressions with (on the right) an equivalent ordinary definition.

The ciphers from 0 up to 9:

```
ciphers:: [num]                  |  ciphers:: [num]
ciphers  =  [0..9]               |  ciphers  =  inbetween 0 9 1
```

The natural numbers:

```
nats:: [num]                          nats:: [num]
nats  =  [1..]                        nats  =  from 1 1
```

Even ciphers:

```
evenciphers:: [num]                   evenciphers:: [num]
evenciphers  =  [0, 2..9]             evenciphers  =  inbetween 0 9 (2–0)
```

Even natural numbers:

```
evens:: [num]                         evens:: [num]
evens  =  [2, 4..]                    evens  =  from 2 (4–2)
```

ZF-expressions

ZF-expressions give a concise syntax for a general class of iterations over lists. The notation is adapted from the Zermelo–Fraenkel set theory (Fraenkel, 1922; Zermelo, 1908). Note that Miranda is dealing with lists and not with sets. A *ZF*-expression has two possible forms:

```
[ exp | qualifiers ]    or    [ exp // qualifiers ]
```

The above must be read as 'list of all exp such that qualifiers'. The expression yields a list with elements of the form dictated by exp. The elements are produced by qualifiers. When multiple qualifiers are specified, they are separated by semicolons. There are two kinds of **qualifiers**: *generators* and *filters*. A qualifier can be a **generator**, of the form:

$\text{pattern}_1, \text{pattern}_2, \ldots, \text{pattern}_n$ <- exp

which is a shorthand for the following multiple generators:

pattern_1 <- exp; pattern_2 <- exp; ... ; pattern_n <- exp

The '<-' sign denotes that the patterns, of which the variables are locally introduced on its left, range over all the elements of the list on its right.

The function squares yields an infinite list containing (in order) the squares of all natural numbers. The *ZF*-expression is read aloud as 'list of all n*n such that n is drawn from the list [1..]'. The pattern n is just a local variable.

```
squares:: [num]
squares    =  [ n*n | n <- [1..] ]
```

The function sqlist employs a more complex pattern to yield a list of tuples. With the pattern (x, y) these tuples are generated from that list and used to yield the list of cubes, i.e. the list of all numbers to the power 3.

```
cubes:: [num]
cubes   = [ x*y | (x, y) <- sqlist ]

sqlist:: [(num,num)]
sqlist   = [ (n, n*n) | n <- [1..] ]
```

If there is more than one generator specified as qualifier, the rightmost will vary first, as if the generators were specified as nested for loops.

Example of the use of multiple generators:

```
list:: [(num, num)]
list   = [ (x, y) | x, y <- [1..2] ]
```

is an abbreviation for

```
list   = [ (x, y) | x <- [1..2]; y <- [1..2] ]
```

The rightmost generator varies first, so list yields the following list of tuples: [(1,1), (1,2), (2,1), (2,2)].

A qualifier can also be a **filter**, i.e. a Boolean expression used to impose restrictions on the objects generated by the generators.

The function factors gives the list of all factors of a given number n using a filter qualifier.

```
factors:: num -> [num]
factors n   = [ r | r <- [1..n div 2]; n mod r = 0 ]
```

A nice demonstration of the elegance of *ZF*-expressions is given by the following definition of the quicksort algorithm:

```
quick_sort:: [num] -> [num]
quick_sort [ ]        = [ ]
quick_sort (a : x)    = quick_sort [b | b <- x ; b <= a] ++
                        [a] ++
                        quick_sort [b | b <- x ; b > a]
```

Since in the case of multiple generators the rightmost generator will vary first, other generators cannot produce new solutions if the rightmost generator yields an infinite sequence. Hence, one has to be aware of the possibility that a specification looks fine at first sight, but is not producing any result due to the way the computation is performed.

The Pythagorean numbers with multiple generators varying over infinite lists:

```
pyths:: [(num, num, num)]
pyths    = [ (a, b, c) | a, b, c <- [1..]; a^2 + b^2 = c^2]
```

This 'solution' will not yield anything because of the order in which the generators vary: [(1, 1, 1), (1, 1, 2), (1, 1, 3), ...]

The problem can be solved by **diagonalizing** generators such that all generators have equal priority, i.e. these generators are evaluated breadth-first from left to right instead of depth-first. This different type of generator is specified by using '//' instead of the '|'.

Example: the Pythagorean numbers with diagonalized generators:

```
pyths:: [(num, num, num)]
pyths    = [ (a, b, c) // a, b, c <- [1..]; a^2 + b^2 = c^2]
```

Now the generators yield a list of tuples in the following way: [(1, 1, 1), (1, 1, 2), (2, 1, 1), (1, 2, 1), (2, 1, 2), (3, 1, 1), (1, 1, 3), (2, 2, 1), ...].

Recurrent generators

Recurrent generators allow the construction of lists from arbitrary recurrence relations using the dotdot notation:

$\text{pattern} <- \text{exp}_1, \text{exp}_2 ..$

The meaning of a recurrent generator is expressed by expanding it to a normal generator in the following way:

$\text{pattern} <- \text{iterate f exp}_1$
$\quad\quad\quad\quad \text{where f pattern} = \text{exp}_2$

```
iterate:: (* -> *) -> * -> [*]
iterate f x   =  x : iterate f (f x)
```

The result of iterate is the infinite list [x, f x, f (f x), f (f (f x)), ...]. The meaning of the type specification of iterate will be explained in the next section.

The recurrent generator combines the pattern and the second expression into a recurrent relation f. This f is iterated with start expression exp_1 yielding a list.

With a recurrent generator the Fibonacci series can be defined as:

```
fibs:: [num]
fibs  =  [ a | (a,b) <- (1,1), (b,a+b).. ]
```

This can be expanded to:

```
fibs  =  [ a | (a,b) <-   iterate f (1,1) ]
         where
         f (a,b)   =  (b, a+b)
```

The generator yields [(1,1), (1,2), (2,3), (3,5), (5,8),...]

Recurrent generators are special syntactical constructs for a special kind of recursive definition, generating a list.

2.3 The type system

Miranda is a **strongly typed** language, i.e. every expression and every subexpression has a type. The type system of Miranda is based upon the type assignment systems of Milner–Mycroft (Milner, 1978; Mycroft, 1984). Explicit type declarations are not required. If the types are not specified, they are inferred by the compiler by analysing the function definitions. Any inconsistency in the deduced types or any conflict with the specified types results in a compile-time error message. However, the explicit specification of types is highly recommended. It gives a lot of information about the specified functions. By choosing meaningful names for user-defined types (and for all other identifiers used in the program) the readability can be improved dramatically.

The advantages of adding a type system to a language are twofold. Firstly, it stimulates the programmer to write correct programs: only correctly typed programs are accepted by the compiler. Hence, for example, if the type of a function application is inconsistent with the type of the corresponding function definition, a compile-time error is generated. In this way the type system is of help in writing programs that make (more) sense.

Given the type of the infix + to be num -> num -> num, the expression

```
1 + 'a'
```

will be detected by the compiler as a type error.

A second advantage of having a typed language is that the type information can be used to generate efficient code. This is explained in Part 4.

There are also some disadvantages in having a typed language. To obtain the advantages claimed above, it is necessary to determine the consistency of types at compile-time. It can be proven that it is in general impossible to determine a proper type for *all* sensible expressions (see also Chapter 6). Fortunately, powerful type systems such as the Milner–Mycroft scheme used in Miranda can deduce and check the types of *most* expressions. As shown in this chapter later on, some expressions cannot be typed in this system and a compile-time error is generated even if the expression made sense. A peculiarity of the combination of the Milner type system (type *deduction* of a function that has not been typed) and the way the Mycroft system is used (*checking* a type specified by a programmer) is that in some cases expressions are accepted when they are explicitly typed by the programmer, but rejected otherwise (see also Section 2.3.6).

Hence, a type system always limits the number of legal programs. In most cases this limitation is of great help for the programmer, because an illegal program generally contains a program error. But in some more rare cases an illegal program does not contain a programming error at all. It simply could not be handled by the type system. In such cases the programmer is obliged to change the program to make it acceptable for the type system.

2.3.1 Basic types

In Miranda three basic types are predefined: num(bers), bool(eans) and char(acters). There is no type distinction between integer and floating-point numbers: they are both of type num. At run-time integer numbers are taken where possible. They are automatically converted into floating-point numbers when needed. It is important to note that due to the nature of floating-point numbers (rounding errors) this automatic conversion can create a conflict with referential transparency.

2.3.2 Type constructors

Complex types can be constructed by using *type constructors*. **Type constructors** make it possible to construct new types by combining existing types. The available type constructors are '[' and ']' (for constructing lists), '(' and ')' (for constructing tuples) and '->' (for constructing functions).

For these type constructors the following holds:

- If T is a type, then [T] denotes the type *list of* T.
- If T1,...,Tn are types, then (T1,...,Tn) denotes the type *tuple of* T1,...,Tn.
- If T1,T2 are types, then (T1 -> T2) denotes the type *function from* T1 *to* T2.

The best way to understand complex types built with the type constructors is to read them aloud, as in the following example.

Using type constructors to build complex types:

```
[ [num] ]                   || list of list of num
([char],[num] -> bool)      || tuple with list of char and
                            || function from list of num to bool
num -> num -> num           || function from num to
                            || function from num to num
```

2.3.3 Polymorphic types

A useful type system should not restrict the programmer too much. The example below illustrates this.

Function reverse:

```
reverse [ ]       = [ ]
reverse (a : as)  = reverse as ++ [a]
```

If the function reverse is applied to a list of characters, it will yield a list in which all characters are in reversed order. On the other hand, if applied to a list of numbers, it will yield this list in reversed order too. Hence it would be nice if the type system would allow the use of such a function for *any* sort of list. The Miranda system allows such a type specification. The type of reverse is denoted by

```
reverse:: [*] -> [*]
```

which indicates that reverse takes a list with elements of an *arbitrary* type as an argument and yields a list with elements of the *same* type.

To indicate arbitrary types there is an alphabet of **generic type variables** denoted by the symbols *, **, ***, and so on. A variable name can occur more than once in a type definition. In such a case each occurrence of the *same* name denotes the *same* type. Unequal names only indicate that the corresponding types can differ from each other (they could be the same). If a type variable occurs in the type definition of a function, the type of the function is said to be **polymorphic (or generic)** in the sense of Milner (1978).

Some examples of polymorphic functions:

```
ident:: * -> *
ident x  =  x
```

```
hd:: [*] -> *
hd (x : xs)  =  x

second:: (*, **, ***) -> **
second (x, y, z)  =  y
```

2.3.4 Type deduction

Generally a programmer will know the type of the function that he or she is defining. It is not always clear what the type of a concrete function is. For example, consider the function twice and try to deduce (infer) its type.

```
twice f x     =  f (f x)
```

In order to solve this problem the programmer actually has to perform the same kind of analysis that is performed by the type system incorporated in the Miranda compiler. This is only possible in all cases if the type system and the *type inference* mechanism are fully understood by the programmer. For the moment we shall only present a basic inference scheme that helps to derive the type of a function in most cases. Type systems and type inference mechanisms are explained in detail in Chapter 6.

The general idea of the inference scheme is the following: first the *left-hand side* of a function definition is analysed, making assumptions for the type of the function, its arguments and its result. The next step is to analyse this *right-hand side* using all assumptions already made. The type of the result must be compatible with the type of the right-hand side. Furthermore, function and arguments must be used consistently in the right-hand side. This analysis leads to *equations* that have to be solved to infer the type of the function.

Below the basic inference scheme is explained in more detail. For reasons of readability Greek characters are used for type variables instead of the *s that are used in Miranda.

1. Left-hand side analysis

For the general case f x_1 x_2 ... x_n = right-hand side for each argument and for the result a new type variable is introduced leading to the following assumptions:

$$x_1{::}\ \alpha_1,\ x_2{::}\ \alpha_2,\ \ldots,\ x_n{::}\ \alpha_n,\ \text{result}{::}\ \alpha_{n+1}$$
$$f{::}\ \alpha_1 \text{ -> } \alpha_2 \text{ ->} \ldots \text{ -> } \alpha_n \text{ -> } \alpha_{n+1}$$

If a pattern is specified, the corresponding type information is incorporated directly in the assumptions.

Incorporating pattern information in assumptions for left-hand side type analysis:

```
hd (x : y)   = x
```

The constructor ':' is a constructor of the type list, so the following types are assumed:

(x : y):: [α_1], x:: α_1, y:: [α_1], result:: α_2, hd:: [α_1] -> α_2.

2. *Right-hand side analysis*

The right-hand side is analysed using the assumptions made so far, leading to one or more equations. First of all, the assumed result type must be compatible with the type of the right-hand side as a whole. Furthermore, every application must be type-consistent. So for every occurrence of an application (function argument) on the right-hand side the required equation for the type of the function, the argument and the result of the application itself is:

function type = argument type -> result type.

Remember that all functions are considered to be curried. So for a function with multiple arguments several applications must be considered.

Already known types of functions are used in such a way that for each application of a polymorphic function in the assumed type fresh variables are taken. When no assumption is available new assumptions are made introducing fresh variables. Equations are constructed that specify the conditions that have to be fulfilled to make every application type consistent.

Right-hand side type analysis of previous example: hd (x : y) = x. Left-hand side assumptions were: (x : y):: [α_1], x:: α_1, y:: [α_1], result:: α_2, hd:: [α_1] -> α_2. Inspecting the right-hand side shows that the result type must equal the type of x (the right-hand side):

$\alpha_2 = \alpha_1$

This equation is solved in the next step.

3. *Solving equations*

The equations are solved by substituting for the type variables other type variables or actual types. In general there are many solutions for the equations. The solution we want is of course the most general solution. The process of finding such a solution is called **unification**, and the requested solution is called the **most general unifier.** In Chapter 6 a method will be given that performs the unification by solving the equations during the analysis.

Solving equations for the running example: hd (x : y) = x. Assumptions: (x : y):: [α_1], x:: α_1, y:: [α_1], result:: α_2, hd:: [α_1] -> α_2. Equations: $\alpha_2 = \alpha_1$.

Solution: substitute α_2 by α_1, leading to the following derived types:

(x : y):: [α_1], x:: α_1, y:: [α_1], result:: α_1, hd:: [α_1] -> α_1

We could also substitute α_1 by α_2 yielding the same solution, since the names of the type variables can be chosen freely. The compiler would have deduced the type hd:: [*] -> *. A different solution of the equation would have been found by substituting both α_2 and α_1 by num, leading to hd:: [num] -> num. Obviously, this is not the most general solution.

These three steps complete the basic type inference scheme. In this scheme not all syntactic constructs of Miranda, such as local definitions, type synonyms, algebraic data types, *ZF*-expressions etc., are taken into account. It is left to the reader to extend the scheme where necessary. To illustrate the basic type inference scheme it is applied to the following examples:

```
doublehd x    =  hd (hd x)
```

Left-hand side analysis: x:: α_1, result:: α_2, doublehd:: α_1 -> α_2

Right-hand side analysis: generally, it is easier to do the innermost application first.
Analysis of application: hd x leads to: type of hd = (type of x)->(type of (hd x))
Take fresh variables for the type of hd:: [α_4] -> α_4. The type of x is already assumed to be α_1. For hd x no assumption is available, so assume hd x:: α_3.
The resulting equation: [α_4] -> α_4 = α_1 -> α_3
The application hd (hd x) leads in the same way to the following equation:
[α_5] -> α_5 = α_3 -> α_2

Solving the equations: both sides of -> have to be equal:
[α_4] = α_1, $\alpha_4 = \alpha_3$, [α_5] = α_3, $\alpha_5 = \alpha_2$.
Leading to the following substitutions: α_1 = [[α_5]], $\alpha_2 = \alpha_5$.
So doublehd:: [[α_5]] -> α_5.
The compiler would have deduced the type of doublehd as [[*]] -> *.

Another example: twice f x = f (f x)

Left-hand side analysis: f:: α_1, x:: α_2, result:: α_3, twice:: α_1 -> α_2 -> α_3.

Right-hand side analysis:
Analysis of application: f x leads to: type of f = (type of x) -> (type of (f x))
For f x no assumption is available, so assume f x:: α_4.
The resulting equation: $\alpha_1 = \alpha_2 \text{ -> } \alpha_4$
Analysis of application: f (f x) leads to: (type of f) = (type of (f x)) -> (type of (f (f x)))
f (f x) is the right-hand side, so its type is assumed to be the result type: α_3.
The resulting equation: $\alpha_1 = \alpha_4 \text{ -> } \alpha_3$

Solving the equations leads to $\alpha_2 = \alpha_4 = \alpha_3$ and $\alpha_1 = \alpha_2 \text{ -> } \alpha_2$.
So the derived type is twice:: (α_2 -> α_2) -> α_2 -> α_2.
The compiler would have deduced the type of twice as (* -> *) -> * -> *.

2.3.5 Untypable function definitions

Not all functions can be typed in Milner's type system (see also Chapter 6). Two different kinds of untypable functions are given below:

A Milner untypable function:

```
selfapplication f = f f
```

This function cannot be typed in Milner's system because f cannot have both * and * -> * as type since the equation $\alpha_1 = \alpha_1 \text{ -> } \alpha_1$ has no solution.

The function definition in the example above cannot be typed. In this case one can argue that such functions should not be written. However, although the Milner type system is very powerful compared with the type systems generally available in more traditional languages, some very reasonable functions also cannot be expressed.

A Milner untypable function:

```
length:: [*] -> num
length [ ]          =  0
length (a : b)   =  1 + length b

fun:: ([*] -> num) -> [*] -> [*] -> num
fun f list1 list2     =  f list1 + f list2

missionimpossible   =  fun length [1,2,3] "abc"
```

The actual argument f is not allowed to have two different types within the body of the function fun. In this case f has to have type [num] -> num when applied to list1 but type [char] -> num when applied to list2.

Milner's type inference scheme inherently does not allow **internal polymorphism**, where the same object is used with different types within one function definition. Although the deduction scheme used can be improved for some cases, a satisfactory algorithm for general cases is not possible.

The problem mentioned above can be solved by making the polymorphism external:

```
fun2:: ([*] -> num) -> ([**] -> num) -> [*] -> [**] -> num
fun2 f1 f2 list1 list2  =  f1 list1 + f2 list2

missionpossible:: num
missionpossible  =  fun2 length length [1,2,3] "abc"
```

2.3.6 Differences between type deduction and checking

Explicit declaration of types makes it possible to declare the type of twice more restrictively as (num -> num) -> num -> num. In this way a type declaration can also be used to impose additional restrictions on a function (the declared type is more restrictive than the general derived type). Another difference between type deduction and type checking is due to the fact that the *type checking* algorithm uses an algorithm of Mycroft that differs from the *type deduction* algorithm of Milner (this is discussed in more detail in Chapter 6).

Difference between type inferencing and type checking:

```
g x = 1 : g (g 'c')
```

The type *deduction* algorithm of Milner cannot deduce the type of g. Hence an error message will be produced. In this case g is used polymorphically in the right-hand side of its own definition, with type instances: char -> [num] and [num] -> [num]. However, when the user *explicitly* specifies the type of g as g:: * -> [num] the type *checker* has no problems handling this case: the specified type is accepted and no error message is produced.

Maybe it would be better to insist always on explicit specification of types and to have a type inference tool assisting with this specification.

Another example with a difference between type checking and type deduction:

```
g x = g 1
```

Type deduction yields g:: num -> * while type checking will accept g:: ** -> *.

2.3.7 Type synonym declaration

In Miranda it is possible to define a new name for a given type by means of a type synonym declaration.

Examples of type synonym declarations:

```
string   ==  [char]
matrix   ==  [ [num] ]
```

For obvious reasons (what should be substituted for what), recursive type synonyms are not permitted. Type synonyms are entirely transparent to the type system, and it is best to think of them as macros.

Using generic type variables, it is also possible to introduce a new name for a family of types.

Type synonym for a family of types:

```
array *  ==  [*]
```

In the examples above the predefined type [[num]] is renamed. It can be called matrix, but also array (array num). In both cases, an object of the newly defined type will be checked by the type system against the type [[num]], illustrating that indeed the type synonyms are entirely transparent (which is the only way to handle synonym types in the case that the type system must be able to deduce the type of the objects on its own).

Example of a type synonym declaration:

```
invert * **   ==   (* -> **) -> (** -> *)
string        ==   [char]
```

invert num string is then shorthand for (num -> [char]) -> ([char] -> num).

2.4 User-defined data structures and their types

Data structures are defined by defining new types. For this purpose it is possible to define (polymorphic) types using *algebraic type definitions* and *abstract type definitions*. Such a type specifies all legal occurrences of the user-defined data structure. With an *algebraic data type* a new data structure (like a record) can recursively be defined that is composed of existing data structures. Each record contains a discriminating *data constructor* (see also the section on lists in the previous chapter) and zero or more other objects called the **arguments of the data constructor**. The data constructor is an identifier (tag) that uniquely identifies an object to be of a specific type. *Abstract data types* make it possible to create data structures of which the actual implementations are hidden from the user. On such a data structure only the functions specified in the *abstract signature* can be applied. The concrete definition of these functions can be defined elsewhere.

2.4.1 Algebraic data types

A (recursive) **algebraic data type** definition enumerates the new data constructors with their arguments. Every alternative of an algebraic type definition begins with a unique discriminating data constructor.

Examples of algebraic type definitions:

```
day       ::=  Mon | Tue | Wed | Thu | Fri | Sat | Sun
numlist   ::=  Nillist | Numlist num numlist
numtree   ::=  Niltree | Node num numtree numtree
```

In these definitions there are predefined types (num), user-defined algebraic types (day, numlist, numtree) and user-defined data constructors (Mon, Tue, … , Sun, Nillist, Numlist, Niltree, Node). In Miranda, data constructors have to start with a capital letter.

The data constructors defined in an algebraic type can be used in function definitions. They appear in expressions to construct new objects of the specified algebraic type. They appear in patterns, for instance to discriminate between objects of the same algebraic type or to make projection functions for accessing the arguments of the data constructor. The influence of pattern matching on soundness criteria for type systems is discussed in Chapter 6. There it is shown that the use of algebraic data constructors as proposed here is indeed sound with respect to the type inference mechanism.

Constructing objects of an algebraic type:

```
payment_day:: day
payment_day    = Fri

tree1:: numtree
tree1    = Node 1 (Node 3 Niltree Niltree) Niltree
```

Using data constructors as patterns, the following function yields the mirror image of a numtree.

```
mirror:: numtree -> numtree
mirror Niltree         = Niltree
mirror (Node n l r)    = Node n (mirror r) (mirror l)
```

In a definition of an algebraic data type a new discriminating constructor is needed for every new type and for every new alternative. Consequently, it is impossible to define a general Nil. Every new type must have its own special constructor to denote an empty object of that type.

2.4.2 Polymorphic algebraic types

Algebraic types can also be **polymorphic**. One or more generic type variables can be used as parameters in the type definition.

Polymorphic algebraic type definition:

```
tree *    ::=   Niltree | Node * (tree *) (tree *)
```

This definition can be used for instance as follows:

```
numtree    ==   tree num
```

In this way a family of tree types can be defined (including tree num, tree bool, tree char, tree (num -> num), and so on). It is important to know that, in principle, all predefined types of Miranda can be defined using polymorphic algebraic type definitions. So in theory no built-in predefined types are needed. In practice, however, representing all predefined types algebraically would be rather inconvenient and inefficient.

Algebraic type definition for predefined types:

```
bool      ::=   True | False
char      ::=   'A' | 'B' | 'C' | ...
[*]       ==    list *          ::=   Nil | Cons * (list *)
(*, **)   ==    tuple2 * **     ::=   Tuple2 * **
```

2.4.3 Abstract data types

An **abstract data type** is a *hidden* (algebraic or synonym) type for which functions are defined. These functions are the only way to create and access objects of that specific abstract type. The concrete definition of the abstract type and the concrete definitions of the functions, the **concrete signature**, are not visible to the outside world. Only the abstract type itself and the type of its functions, called the **abstract signature**, are visible.

Example: the well-known abstract data type stack with its signature.

```
abstype stack *                   || the abstract data type
with  empty      ::  stack *      || and its abstract signature
```

```
isempty     :: stack * -> bool
push        :: * -> stack * -> stack *
pop         :: stack * -> stack *
top         :: stack * -> *
```

The concrete definition of the abstract type and the functions defined on it are specified separately. The outside world cannot make use of the particular implementation chosen.

For example: the abstract data type stack can be implemented as a list. The outside world cannot make use of this fact: [ ] and empty are incomparable objects of two different and unrelated types, [*] and stack * respectively.

```
stack *      == [*]          || the concrete data type
empty        = [ ]           || its implementation equations
isempty [ ]  = True
isempty s    = False
push e s     = e : s
pop (e : s)  = s
top (e : s)  = e
```

The implementation equations do not have to appear immediately after the corresponding abstype declaration. They can occur anywhere in the script, but it is probably best to keep them nearby.

2.5 The use of functions as basic building blocks

In this section some important functions are given that, due to their general nature, are often used as basic building blocks in functional programs. The availability of higher order functions in combination with polymorphic types makes it possible to write very powerful functions that cannot be defined in most imperative languages that often use a more rigid type system. These powerful higher order functions can be used as basic building blocks for the creation of more sophisticated functions. Bird and Wadler extensively show the use of higher order functions as basic building blocks in the construction of functional programs and their correctness proofs (Bird and Wadler, 1988).

Function composition

There is a special operator to compose two functions. This associative operator is denoted as a single dot '.' and can be used in infix notation like the other operators in Miranda. The composition of two functions, say f and g, is a *function* comp f g, such that

```
comp f g x = f (g x)
```

or, using the infix operator:

```
(f . g) x  =  f (g x)
```

The operator '.' takes two functions as arguments and yields a new function: the composition of the two argument functions. The type of the composition operator is therefore (** -> ***) -> (* -> **) -> (* -> ***). The rightmost parentheses are not necessary, but they make it more clear that the composition of two functions yields a function as result. This type can be deduced as follows. Look at the function body in the definition of the composition operator: f (g x). Assume that x is of type *. Then g must be a function of type (* -> **). Hence f must be of type (** -> ***). The composition of f and g therefore yields a function of type (* -> ***).

Example of function composition. The function code is a predefined function in Miranda that returns the ASCII code of a character. The function decode is also predefined and returns the corresponding ASCII character when it is applied to a number between 0 and 256. The function nextchar is constructed by using function composition and yields the next character in the ASCII table when it is applied to a character with ASCII code less than 255.

```
code:: char -> num
decode:: num -> char

nextchar:: char -> char
nextchar    =  decode . (+ 1) . code
```

The predefined operator + is used in a special curried way here. The following expressions are all equivalent in Miranda: a + b, (+) a b, (a +) b, (+ b) a. The same holds for other predefined infix operators.

Evaluation of the function nextchar:

```
nextchar 'b'
→    ((decode . (+ 1)) . code) 'b'
→    (decode . (+ 1))(code 'b')          || according to the definition of '.'
→    decode ((+ 1) (code 'b'))           || according to the definition of '.'
→    decode ((+ 1) 98)
→    decode 99
→    'c'
```

Three alternative definitions of nextchar that are equivalent to the one above:

```
nextchar1 x   =  (decode . (+ 1) . code) x
nextchar2 x   =  decode ((+ 1) (code x))
nextchar3 x   =  decode (code x + 1)
```

The example above also illustrates that a sequence of functions can be combined as one new function using function composition. One can regard a composition of the form (f_n . f_{n-1} . ... . f_1) x as a pipeline of functions applied to x, as illustrated in Figure 2.2.

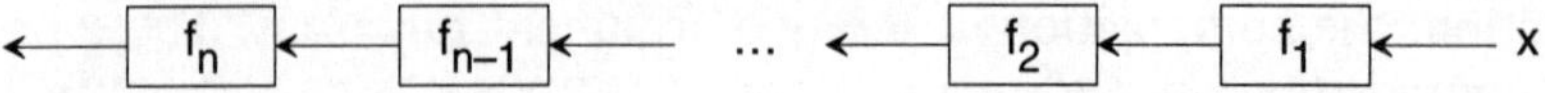

Figure 2.2 A 'pipeline' of functions created with function composition.

Functions to manipulate lists

There are several handy functions that are frequently used to manipulate lists. In this section an overview is given of these functions and their use is illustrated with some examples.

The polymorphic function map is very powerful: it applies any function of appropriate type to all the elements of a list.

```
map:: (* -> **) -> [*] -> [**]
map f [ ]        =  [ ]
map f (x : xs)   =  f x : map f xs
```

For example, if

```
max:: num -> num -> num
max a b     =  a,  if a > b
            =  b,  otherwise
```

then

```
map (max 0) [–2, 3, –5]   →    ...    →    [0, 3, 0]
```

The function filter has as arguments a predicate and a list. The result list will contain only those elements from the argument list that satisfy the predicate.

```
filter:: (* -> bool) -> [*] -> [*]
filter pred [ ]         =  [ ]
filter pred (x : xs)    =  x : filter pred xs,   if pred x
                        =  filter pred xs,       otherwise
```

```
filter (> 0) [2, –3, 5, 1, –2, –100]   →    ...    →    [2, 5, 1]
```

The function take has as arguments a number, say n, and a list and yields the first n elements of that list.

```
take:: num -> [*] -> [*]
take n [ ]          = [ ]
take n (x : xs)     = x : take (n – 1) xs,  if n > 0
                    = [ ],                  otherwise

take 2 [1, 2, 3, 4]   →   ...   →   [1, 2]
take 3 "abcd"         →   ...   →   "abc"
```

The function drop when applied to a number, say n, and a list of elements returns that list without the first n elements.

```
drop:: num -> [*] -> [*]
drop n [ ]          = [ ]
drop n (x : xs)     = drop (n – 1) xs,  if n > 0
                    = x : xs,           otherwise

drop 2 ['a','b','c']    →   ...     ['c']
```

The function takewhile has a predicate and a list as arguments. It takes elements from the front of the input list as long as they satisfy the predicate, and returns these elements in a list.

```
takewhile:: (* -> bool) -> [*] -> [*]
takewhile pred [ ]        = [ ]
takewhile pred (x : xs)   = x : takewhile pred xs,  if pred x
                          = [ ],                    otherwise

takewhile (~= "stop") ["hello","world","stop","nice"]
→   ...   →   ["hello","world"]
```

The function dropwhile is analogous to takewhile, but now the elements that satisfy the predicate are dropped. The rest of the list is the result of this function.

```
dropwhile:: (*->bool)-> [*] -> [*]
dropwhile pred [ ]        = [ ]
dropwhile pred (x : xs)   = dropwhile pred xs,  if pred x
                          = x : xs,             otherwise

dropwhile (~= "stop") ["hello","world","stop","nice"]
→   ...   →   ["stop","nice"]
```

The function zip2 has two lists as arguments and yields a list of pairs. The *n*th pair of the result list consists of the *n*th element of the first list together with the *n*th element of the second list. Analogous functions that 'zip' three, four, five or six lists together are also useful. The resulting list of tuples is as long as the shortest of the argument lists.

```
zip2:: [*] -> [**] -> [(*,**)]
zip2 (x : xs)   (y : ys)  =  (x,y) : zip2 xs ys
zip2 xs         ys        =  [ ]

zip2 [1..] "index" →   ...   →   [(1,'i'),(2,'n'),(3,'d'),(4,'e'),(5,'x')]
```

The function last yields the last element of a given list. This is the dual function of the function hd, which yields the head of a list.

```
last:: [*] -> *
last (x : xs)    = x,         if xs = [ ]
                 = last xs,   otherwise
last [ ]         = error "last of [ ]"

last [1,2,3]       ...   →   3
```

The function init is the dual function of the tail-function tl. It takes a list and yields a list of all elements of the input list without the last one.

```
init:: [*] -> [*]
init (x : xs)  =  [ ],           if xs = [ ]
               =  x : init xs,   otherwise
init [ ]       =  error "init of [ ]"

init ['g','r','a','v','e', 'l']   →   ...   →   ['g','r','a','v','e']
```

A frequently used function is the function foldr. foldr is used to apply a function, say f, recursively in an accumulating way on all elements, say a_1, a_2, ... a_n, of a list as follows:

$$f\ a_1\ (f\ a_2\ (\ \ldots\ (f\ a_n\ i)\ \ldots\ ))$$

The initial value i indicates the value to be substituted for the empty list.

```
foldr:: (* -> ** -> **) -> ** -> [*] -> **
foldr f i [ ]        = i
foldr f i (x : xs)   = f x (foldr f i xs)
```

Using foldr it is easy to give examples defining functions that calculate the product of all elements of a list, or their sum etc.

```
product = foldr (*) 1
sum     = foldr (+) 0
```

```
and     = foldr (&) True
or      = foldr (\/) False
```

In these examples predefined operators are passed as arguments to the function foldr. To disambiguate this use of a predefined operator with its ordinary use the additional parentheses are needed.

```
product [1, 2, 3, 4]
→   foldr (*) 1 [1, 2, 3, 4]
→   (*) 1 (foldr (*) 1 [2, 3, 4])
→   (*) 1 ((*) 2 (foldr (*) 1 [3, 4]))
→   (*) 1 ((*) 2 ((*) 3 (foldr (*) 1 [4])))
→   (*) 1 ((*) 2 ((*) 3 ((*) 4 (foldr (*) 1 [ ]))))
→   (*) 1 ((*) 2 ((*) 3 ((*) 4 1)))
→   ...   →   24
```

On finite lists foldr is often used instead of recursion.

Example of the use of foldr

This example shows how to design an algorithm for computing the powerset of a given set of elements with the help of the function foldr.

Example of the function :

```
powerset [1,2,3] = [ [ ],[1],[2],[3],[1,2],[1,3],[2,3],[1,2,3] ]
```

The result list represents a set of elements, so it is not allowed to have more than one occurrence of an element. powerset [1,2,3] can be made out of powerset [2,3] by adding 1 to every element of the powerset [2,3] and concatenating it with powerset [2,3]:

```
powerset [2,3]   = [ [ ],[2],[3],[2,3] ]
powerset [1,2,3] = [1 : [ ],1 : [2],1 : [3],1 : [2,3] ] ++ powerset [2,3]
```

Recursive definition of the function powerset:

```
powerset:: [*] -> [ [*] ]
powerset [ ]        = [ [ ] ]
powerset (x : xs)   = map (x :) (powerset xs) ++ powerset xs
```

The above example contains a halting criterion: powerset [ ] = [[ ]]. The definition also clearly reflects the above described method for making the powerset of a list (x : xs) out of the powerset of the list xs.

The definition of foldr has three formal arguments. These arguments are in the following way related to aspects of a recursive definition. The halting criterion, in the definition of foldr called i (derived from init), can be defined as [[ ]], like the halting criterion in the recursive definition. The relation between the powerset of list (x : xs) and the list xs can be represented by the function f from the parameter list of foldr. Define f as:

```
f:: * -> [ [*] ] -> [ [*] ]
f x powersofar    =  map (x :) powersofar ++ powersofar
```

powersofar stands for the result of the powerset of the list without the new element x.

The new definition of the function powerset using the function foldr:

```
powerset:: [*] -> [ [*] ]
powerset xs   =  foldr f [ [ ] ] xs
```

So combining the halting criterion with a constructive inductive recursion step leads to a short definition with foldr.

2.6 Interactive programs

Requiring that a functional program is interactive at first sight seems to be in contrast with referential transparency. An interactive system does not always react in the same way on the same input value. Take for example a program that repeatedly gets a value as input and outputs the sum of *all* the values so far. Such a program reacts differently when it gets the same value two times in a row. However, it always reacts in the same way on the whole input so far. This observation leads to the conclusion that interactive programs can be written in a functional language by considering the input as an argument that is a conceptually infinite list of values (called a **stream**). The output is also a stream: the result of the program. Owing to lazy evaluation such infinite lists can be handled. On the input side this means that not all the input has to be given at once. On the output side it means that those parts of the result that are already available can be printed. Together this allows interactive programs to be written.

Combining both input and output it is possible to write a program that gives a prompt (part of the result is already evaluated), reads a value (the head of an infinite input list is needed for the evaluation), responds and prompts again. One has to take care that the rest of the input list is passed as a parameter to functions that require input and furthermore one has to take care that no cyclic dependencies are required.

One way to create an interactive functional program in a lazy language:

```
function:: * -> [char] -> [char]
function state input = response ++ function newstate restinput
                       where
                       response  = ...
                       newstate  = ...
                       restinput = ...
```

Generally some kind of state is adapted due to the input. Furthermore, one has to be able to indicate that a certain argument is actually the input of the program. In Miranda the input of the program can be indicated in the initial expression by specifying $– as an argument. So a typical call of the function above would be:

```
function initialstate $–
```

in which initialstate is a function that produces the initial state.

A program that repeatedly checks an input line for palindromicity (a word or sentence is a **palindrome** if it is the same as its reverse, e.g. 'able was I ere I saw elba' is a palindrome). The basic function is rather simple using the previously defined function reverse.

```
palindrome:: [char] -> bool
palindrome    chars   =     chars = reverse chars
```

Extending the program for interactive use requires some extra definitions in which the interaction with the user is defined. The program will prompt for an input line, respond and stop when an empty line is given as input:

```
pal_io:: [char] -> [char]
pal_io input   = prompt ++ pal_react input

prompt:: [char]
prompt  = "Type in a line, please?\n"

pal_react:: [char] -> [char]
pal_react input  = "Have a good day.\n",           if thisline = ""
                 = response ++ pal_io restlines,   otherwise
                   where
                   response   = "Is a palindrome!\n", if palindrome thisline
                              = "Is not a palindrome.\n", otherwise
                   (thisline, restlines)  = splitline input
```

```
splitline:: [char] -> ([char], [char])
splitline chars    = (line, restlines)
                     where
                     line        = takewhile (~= '\n') chars
                     restlines   = tl (dropwhile (~= '\n') chars)
```

The function splitline is defined using the basic functions tl, takewhile and dropwhile defined previously. Note that this is not a very efficient program: it would have been more efficient to define a new function that combined the definitions of takewhile and dropwhile producing both results together. The program is called with the following initial expression:

```
pal_io $–
```

In Koopman (1987) it is shown how using this method one can write strongly interactive programs like an editor. The basic structure of, for example, such an editor is given below:

```
commandinterpreter:: [char] -> [char] -> [char]
commandinterpreter text commands
   = response ++ prompt ++ commandinterpreter newtext nextcommands
     where
     (commandline, rest)    = splitline commands
     editoperation          = parse commandline
     (response, newtext, nextcommands) = editoperation text rest
     prompt        = ...
     splitline x   = ...
     parse x       = ...
```

This command interpreter parses a command line and produces directly a function (not some encoding for a function) that performs the required operation.

A disadvantage of the given method for writing interactive functional programs is that every part of the output has to be part of the result of the whole program on the top level. As a consequence it is not a trivial task to change a program in such a way that for a specific function that is used somewhere in an expression the value of its arguments is printed every time the function is called. A change like that, which can be of interest for tracing or debugging, requires a change of the structure of the whole program.

Furthermore, it does not seem to be very practical to program file handling and menu and mouse-driven applications with the facilities that are provided by Miranda. In the language Concurrent Clean a different method for writing interactive programs is given that offers the required practical facilities for such applications (see Chapter 8).

2.7 Top-down functional programming

There is already much knowledge about programming in imperative programming languages. The two most important programming styles used are the *top-down* method and the *bottom-up* method.

Generally, when a large program is developed, several layers of abstraction are created. Each layer of abstraction is based on layers on a lower level of abstraction. Each layer has its own locally defined data structures with operations on them and performs its own task.

In a **bottom-up** style one starts with the lowest layer upwards to the next layer and finally one defines the top layer. In this style one designs data structures and the corresponding operations on them that are made available for the next layer. In a **top-down** style it is exactly the other way around. The problems left in each layer are solved in the next layer. In this way one refines the problems step-wise down to the basic level. Generally both methods are mixed when large programs are developed. One could say that with the bottom-up approach one designs the programming tools needed on a certain level of abstraction, whereas with the top-down approach one decides how these tools are being used.

These programming styles, commonly used to develop imperative programs, can also be used for the development of functional programs. For a bottom-up style of programming one can use, for instance, abstract data types. An example of their use was given in Section 2.4.3. The kind of data structures and operations will strongly depend on the kind of problem one has to solve. Top-down programming is based on **step-wise refinement**, which means that a problem is divided into subproblems if there is no simple way to write down the solution directly with the help of basic language constructs. In functional programming languages there is an excellent way to glue those partial solutions together, for solutions will consist of function definitions, and functions can be composed using function composition or function application. And of course, there is no danger of side-effects. Furthermore the strong typing provides an extra test of whether the functions are composed correctly.

2.7.1 A check-list for a top-down design

The check-list in Table 2.1 may be useful for designing functional programs. The check-list consists of seven parts that reflect the common phases of a top-down program design. Each phase consists of issues to think about when designing a program. It is not strictly necessary to work out all the issues nor to do them in the given order: experienced programmers can merge some of these steps or do them unconsciously or implicitly.

Table 2.1 A check-list for a top-down design.

1 Analysis

1.1 Work out some examples to get an understanding of the problem.
1.2 Write down the essential aspects of the given problem.
1.3 Give the relation between these aspects and the desired result.
1.4 Work out concrete examples.
1.5 Try to find general constraints and exceptions.
1.6 Find out whether there are special constraints for the solution.

2 Specification

2.1 Give the type of the arguments of the function(s).
2.2 Give the type of the result of the function(s).
2.3 Give the type of the function(s).
2.4 Look for inconsistencies and missing specifications in the problem.
2.5 Formulate the specification with the help of mathematics or a graphical representation.

3 Design

3.1 Make the data structure that will be used explicit.
3.2 Formulate a global algorithm that will solve the problem.
3.3 Decide whether the solution can be given directly with the help of language elements and if not
3.4 Divide the problem into subproblems.
3.5 Apply the method of this check-list to each of the subproblems.
3.6 Make alternative designs and choose the best one to implement.

4 Implementation

4.1 Work out the designed algorithm (including the data structures and the operations on them) into a Miranda script with comments, significant names and a structured layout.
4.2 Type the script into the computer.

5 Test and debug

5.1 Design critical test values to test all designed functions.
5.2 Test functions that solve subproblems before testing the total solution.
5.3 Debug functions if necessary.

6 Documentation

6.1 Check comments and names on consistency with (revised) functions.

7 Reflection

7.1 Note why decisions were made, and check whether this is documented.
7.2 Summarize what you have learned about designing an algorithm for the given problem.

In addition to this check-list it is useful to pay attention to the following points:

- use significant names everywhere;
- include meaningful comments where needed;
- always write down the type of a function explicitly;
- do not combine too many function compositions as this may make a program unreadable;
- use pattern matching where possible.

Example of a top-down design

Take again the roman number problem from the previous chapter. A closer look shows that the designed function romtonum is not very robust. It assumes that its argument will always be a correct roman number. With the help of the check-list below a function will be designed that decides whether a list of characters represents a correct roman number. Not all the points of the check-list are worked out because most of the points are trivial for experienced programmers (in an imperative language) and they do not differ much from the way one could handle them in the design of an imperative language. Names of subproblems that are not solved yet are printed in italic.

1 Analysis

1.1 Work out some examples to get an understanding of the problem.

```
MDCCCLXXXVIII  = 1888
MCDXCII        = 1492
```

1.2 Write down the essential aspects of the given problem.

It is important to know what exactly a roman number is. From the description of the problem one can find that:

- Roman ciphers consist of the following characters: M, D, C, L, X, V and I.
- These characters have values, respectively: 1000, 500, 100, 50, 10, 5 and 1.
- The characters in the roman numbers are always sorted from the highest value to the lowest from left to right, with the exception that some combinations of characters are abbreviated:

```
DCCCC  = CM      LXXXX = XC      VIIII = IX
CCCC   = CD      XXXX  = XL      IIII  = IV
```

1.3 Give the relation between these aspects and the desired result.

Given: Description of roman numbers.

Desired result: A function that decides whether a list of characters is a roman number.

1.4 Work out concrete examples.

```
MCDXCII    = MCCCCLXXXXII
```

1.5 Try to find general constraints and exceptions.
It is not possible to denote negative numbers or zero.

2 Specification

2.3 Give the type of the function(s).

Let us call the desired function `isroman`; it will be of type `[char] -> bool`.

2.4 Look for inconsistencies and missing specifications in the problem.

According to the description of the problem, `IVI` is a correct roman number (5). However, this is not true. An extra constraint on Roman numbers has to be added, namely that roman numbers are always written in the shortest possible way.

2.5 Formulate the specification with the help of mathematics or a graphical representation.

isroman romnumber → true <=>

romnumber is a non-empty character sequence that obeys the syntax of roman numbers. The syntax of roman numbers is as follows (a BNF-like notation (Backus–Naur form) is used; literals are put between quotes):

```
Roman-number  = Thousands;
Thousands     = {'M'} Fivehundreds;
Fivehundreds  = 'CM' Fifties   | 'D'   Hundreds
              | 'CD' Fifties   | Hundreds;
Hundreds      = ['C'] ['C'] ['C']  Fifties;
Fifties       = 'XC' Fives     | 'L'   Tens
              | 'XL' Fives     | Tens;
Tens          = ['X'] ['X'] ['X']  Fives;
Fives         = 'IX'           | 'V'   Ones
              | 'IV'           | Ones;
Ones          = ['I'] ['I'] ['I'];
```

3 Design

3.1 Make the data structure that will be used explicit.

```
rom_num  ==  [char]
```

3.2 Formulate a global algorithm that will solve the problem.

Apart from a global test for non-emptiness for each syntax rule there is a function that handles that rule.

3.4 Divide the problem into subproblems.

3.5 Apply the method of this check-list to each of the subproblems.

```
rom_num == [char]

isroman:: rom_num -> bool
isroman    [ ]        = False
isroman    roms       = syntax_check roms

syntax_check:: rom_num -> bool
syntax_check roms     = thousands roms

thousands:: rom_num -> bool
thousands ('M' : rest) = thousands rest
thousands roms         = fivehundreds roms

fivehundreds:: rom_num -> bool
fivehundreds ('C' : 'M' : rest)   = fifties rest
fivehundreds ('D' : rest)         = hundreds rest
fivehundreds ('C' : 'D' : rest)   = fifties rest
fivehundreds roms                 = hundreds roms

hundreds:: rom_num -> bool
hundreds  ('C' : 'C' : 'C' : rest)  = fifties rest
hundreds  ('C' : 'C' : rest)        = fifties rest
hundreds  ('C' : rest)              = fifties rest
hundreds  roms                      = fifties roms

fifties:: rom_num -> bool
fifties    ('X' : 'C' : rest)    = fives rest
fifties    ('L' : rest)          = tens rest
fifties    ('X' : 'L' : rest)    = fives rest
fifties    roms                  = tens roms

tens:: rom_num -> bool
tens  ('X' : 'X' : 'X' : rest)  = fives rest
tens  ('X' : 'X' : rest)        = fives rest
tens  ('X' : rest)              = fives rest
tens  roms                      = fives roms
```

```
fives:: rom_num -> bool
fives ['I', 'X']     = True
fives ('V' : rest)   = ones rest
fives ['I', 'V']     = True
fives roms           = ones roms

ones:: rom_num -> bool
ones    ['I', 'I', 'I']   = True
ones    ['I', 'I']        = True
ones    ['I']             = True
ones    [ ]               = True     || all possibilities have been checked:
ones    roms              = False    || if anything is left, it must be incorrect
```

3.6 Make alternative designs and choose the best one to implement.

It is much more efficient to combine the functions for checking and for calculating the value described in this chapter and in the previous chapter into one function that runs through the character sequence only once. So the design (and in fact even the task definition) is changed accordingly.

4 Implementation

4.1 Implement the designed algorithm (including the data structures and their operations) into a Miranda script with comments, significant names and a structured layout.

```
|| An efficient algorithm that computes the value of a proper roman number.
|| Error messages will be given for incorrect arguments.
|| Roman numbers are represented as character sequences
|| rom_num = = [char]
|| The main function is    rom_to_num:: rom_num -> num

rom_num   = =   [char]

rom_to_num:: rom_num -> num
rom_to_num  [ ]        = error "an empty sequence is not a roman number"
rom_to_num  roms       = compute_and_check roms

compute_and_check:: rom_num -> num
compute_and_check roms   = thousands roms

thousands:: rom_num -> num
thousands ('M' : rest)  = value 'M' + thousands rest
thousands roms          = fivehundreds roms
```

```
fivehundreds:: rom_num -> num
fivehundreds ('C' : 'M' : rest)  = value 'M' – value 'C' + fifties rest
fivehundreds ('D' : rest)        = value 'D' + hundreds rest
fivehundreds ('C' : 'D' : rest)  = value 'D' – value 'C' + fifties rest
fivehundreds roms                = hundreds roms

hundreds:: rom_num -> num
hundreds ('C' : 'C' : 'C' : rest) = 3 * value 'C' + fifties rest
hundreds ('C' : 'C' : rest)       = 2 * value 'C' + fifties rest
hundreds ('C' : rest)             = value 'C' + fifties rest
hundreds roms                     = fifties roms

fifties:: rom_num -> num
fifties  ('X' : 'C' : rest)  = value 'C' – value 'X' + fives rest
fifties  ('L' : rest)        = value 'L' + tens rest
fifties  ('X' : 'L' : rest)  = value 'L' – value 'X' + fives rest
fifties  roms                = tens roms

tens:: rom_num -> num
tens ('X' : 'X' : 'X' : rest) = 3 * value 'X' + fives rest
tens ('X' : 'X' : rest)       = 2 * value 'X' + fives rest
tens ('X' : rest)             = value 'X' + fives rest
tens roms                     = fives roms

fives:: rom_num -> num
fives ['I', 'X']     = value 'X' – value 'I'
fives ('V' : rest)   = value 'V' + ones rest
fives ['I', 'V']     = value 'V' – value 'I'
fives roms           = ones roms

ones:: rom_num -> num
ones   ['I', 'I', 'I']  = 3 * value 'I'
ones   ['I', 'I']       = 2 * value 'I'
ones   ['I']            = value 'I'
ones   [ ]              = 0
ones   roms             = error ( "not a proper roman number: " ++
                                    roms ++ " is the incorrect part" )

value:: char -> num
value 'M'   =   1000
value 'D'   =    500
value 'C'   =    100
value 'L'   =     50
value 'X'   =     10
value 'V'   =      5
value 'I'   =      1
```

5 Test and debug

5.1 Design critical test values to test all designed functions.

Check types, design critical test function. For example, test the function rom_to_num with arguments IVI, –I, IIIII, IVXLCDM, CMI, I.

6 Documentation

6.1 Check comments and names on consistency with (revised) functions.

Check the significance of names, check the comments to see if they are consistent with the latest version of the program.

7 Reflection

7.2 Summarize what you have learned about designing an algorithm for the given problem.

To avoid running through a list structure more times than necessary it is in many cases more efficient to combine function definitions that manipulate a list structure into new function definitions that produce multiple results, e.g. in a tuple. Accordingly, the algorithm was changed (for further reflection see Exercise 2.9).

Summary

- The functional programming language Miranda extends the basic concepts with *syntactical sugar* incorporating most of the advanced concepts found in modern functional languages.
- The language has a *nice*, purely functional *notation* fully based on *function application*.
- *Pattern matching* can be used in combination with *guarded equations*.
- *Local function definitions* can be defined in a nested way inside the scope of a global function definition.
- Data structuring facilities are given by the presence of *lists*, *tuples*, *list comprehensions*, *algebraic data types* and *abstract data types*.
- Milner's *type inference* algorithm provides *strong polymorphic typing*. However, for some cases Mycroft's *type checking* algorithm is used allowing more functions to be correctly typed.
- With these sophisticated features one can write *compact* and *elegant* (even *interactive*) functional programs.
- The elegant mathematical style of programming common in the functional programming community still requires, of course, a programmer to pay attention to a good *programming methodology*.

EXERCISES

2.1 Define a function takesum that takes two functions f:: num -> num, g:: num -> num and a number n to calculate

$$\sum_{i=0}^{n} f(g^i(0)) = f(0) + f(g(0)) + f(g(g(0))) + \ldots$$

For instance, if $f(x) = x^2$, $g(x) = x + 1$ and $n = 2$ than the result must be: $0^2 + g(0)^2 + g(g(0))^2 = 0^2 + 1^2 + 2^2 = 5$

Show how this function can be used to approximate $e = \sum_{i=0}^{\infty} \frac{1}{i!}$

2.2 Write functions that compute the following lists using *list comprehensions* where possible:

(a) All 5-tuples of integers such that their sum is less than 7 and greater than –7.

(b) All perfect natural numbers (natural numbers that are equal to the sum of their dividers; e.g. 6 = 1 + 2 + 3)

2.3 The function numchar yields the number of times a given character is appearing in a finite list of characters. Define numchar (a) with recursion, (b) with foldr and (c) with list comprehension.

2.4 Define the function map (a) with foldr and (b) with a *ZF*-expression.

2.5 Write a function eightqueens that yields all solutions of the eight queens problem: the queens should be put down on a 8 * 8 chessboard such that they cannot take each other.

2.6* A binary search tree *T* is an AVL-tree if for every node *v* in *T*: *–1 <= depth (right (v)) – depth (left (v)) <= 1* with *depth*, *right* and *left* defined as usual. The *balance factor* of a node *v* is: *depth (right (v)) – depth (left (v))*. So in an AVL-tree the balance factor of every node is –1, 0 or +1. Inserting or deleting a node cannot be done in the way it is done in ordinary binary search trees. The AVL-tree may not be balanced any more after a deletion or insertion. In such a case there is a node with balance factor +2 or –2. Define an abstract data type avl_tree * with, as operations:

empty	delivers an empty AVL-tree.
key	delivers the value of the root.
left, right	gives the left or right subtree of an AVL-tree.
is_empty	tests if an AVL-tree is empty.
depth	gives the depth of an AVL-tree.

retrieve	delivers the *i*th value in the AVL-tree.
find	decides if a certain value is contained in the tree.
insert	inserts a given value in the AVL-tree.
delete	deletes a value in the AVL-tree.

2.7* Write a small editor. An editor operates on a set of lines, called the buffer. Implement the buffer as an abstract data type with appropriate operations (get_line, remove_ line). An editor should be able to show lines, insert lines, delete lines and change lines (replace a substring).

2.8* Write an interactive program that can play the Mastermind game. The program has to guess a secret code of 4 numbers (0–9). For each guess given by the program a player returns how many numbers appear in the code and how many of these numbers are on a correct position.

2.9 In the final program in Section 2.7 an error is given if the argument is incorrect. So the function cannot be used in a context in which the programmer wants to specify what has to be done for incorrect arguments. Write a function that produces a tuple with a boolean indicating the correctness and a number indicating the value if the argument was correct.

Part 2
Models of computation

This part contains an overview of three important models of computation: λ-calculus, term rewriting systems and graph rewriting systems. In three consecutive chapters these models are compared with respect to their ability to serve as the basic model for functional languages and their implementation.

The best-known model is the **λ-calculus** introduced by Church (1932; 1933). This calculus is a model of computation based on consistent substitution of variables in nameless functions. Evaluation is done by two rules only: α-conversion and β-reduction. Many semantic properties that are deduced for the λ-calculus immediately carry over to functional languages. Therefore, the λ-calculus is studied intensively and used as *the* basic model of computation. But, although the model is very suitable as a model to study the basic semantics of functional languages, it is in our opinion not very suitable to study implementation aspects of functional languages.

Term rewriting systems (Huet and Oppen, 1980; Klop, 1992) form a model of computation based on pattern matching on terms that do not contain variables. In term rewriting systems evaluation is not done using a fixed set of reduction rules but in every term rewriting system a set of rules is specified that define how terms can be rewritten. Semantically, a functional program can be seen as a specific term rewriting system in a special class of term rewriting systems. Implementations of functional languages are usually more close to term rewriting systems than to the λ-calculus.

Graph rewriting systems (Barendregt *et al.*, 1987a; 1987b) extend term rewriting systems with the notion of sharing such that a model of computation is obtained based on pattern matching on graphs not containing variables. Every *efficient* implementation of functional languages avoids duplication of work by *sharing* subexpressions. Therefore, graph rewriting systems are considered to be best suited to serve as the basic model for functional languages and their implementation.

Chapter 3
The λ-calculus

The theory of the *λ-calculus* has been introduced by Church (Church, 1932; 1933) to describe the properties of mathematical functions using a textual substitution model, and has since been investigated further. All functions that are effectively computable can be expressed in the calculus (see also Section 1.1.2). Another important property of the calculus is the *Church–Rosser property*, which states that alternative evaluation orders cannot yield different results. Many of the theoretical properties of functional programming can be deduced from the (known) theoretical properties of the λ-calculus. The semantics of a high-level functional language can be explained by giving the translation schemes to the calculus. The close relation between the (relatively old) calculus and (relatively new) functional languages makes it clear why anyone interested in the underlying basic concepts of functional languages should study the λ-calculus.

In Sections 3.1–3.6 a short overview is given of the theory of the λ-calculus. Readers interested in a detailed overview of the λ-calculus (including proofs of the theorems discussed in this chapter) are referred to the book of Barendregt (1984).

One can regard the λ-calculus also as a very simple low-level functional programming language that is as equally powerful as a high-level functional language such as Miranda. One often regards these high-level functional programming languages as sugared versions of the λ-calculus. It is possible to translate programs written in an arbitrary functional programming language into an equivalent expression in the λ-calculus. In Section 3.7 it is shown how, in principle, Miranda functions can be translated into equivalent λ-expressions.

Since the λ-calculus can be considered as a basic functional language, a λ-calculus machine should be suited to executing all functional programs. However, as discussed in Section 3.8 an efficient realization of a λ-calculus machine is not so easy to achieve. The computational models that are introduced in Chapters 4 and 5 are more closely related to functional languages and the way they are generally implemented.

3.1 λ-expressions

In the λ-calculus one can write down expressions (**λ-terms** or **λ-expressions**) in which anonymous functions can be defined together with the expressions on which these functions have to be applied. Furthermore there are a couple of evaluation rules called **reduction rules** (or **rewrite rules**) defined in the calculus that specify how a λ-expression can be transformed into an equivalent λ-expression, i.e. an expression denoting the same value. In this section the λ-expressions are introduced, in the next section reduction rules are discussed.

Syntax definition

Syntax of λ-expressions in BNF-like notation (literals between quotes):

```
Lambda-expression    = Lambda-abstraction   | Application
                     | Variable             | Constant ;
Lambda-abstraction   = '(' 'λ' Variable '.' Lambda-expression ')' ;
Application          = '(' Lambda-expression Lambda-expression ')' ;
```

Further syntactical aspects are the following: variables will always start with a lower case character and constants with an upper case character or some special character (a digit, an asterisk, etc.); in general, the outermost parentheses are left out; as in Miranda, application (juxtaposition) is left associative; λ-abstraction (.) is right associative; application has a stronger binding than abstraction; and parentheses can be omitted when they are redundant (see Section 3.1.2).

3.1.1 λ-abstraction

With λ-abstraction **anonymous functions** are specified, i.e. functions that have no name. A **λ-abstraction** is a λ-expression with which one can define an anonymous function of a certain variable. This variable can be considered as the **formal argument** of the function. The variable is called the **bound variable** of the abstraction. The general form of a λ-abstraction is:

λ-abstraction:

```
λ            v               .     expression
↑            ↑               ↑     ↑
a function   of variable v   that  returns this value
```

The expression behind the dot is again a λ-expression that expresses the **body** of the function. In general, the value denoted by the expression will depend on the bound variable.

Examples of λ-abstraction. It is assumed that Inc and * are externally defined functions (see the end of this section on constants):

```
λ                 x  .     Inc x
↑                 ↑  ↑     ↑
the function of   x  that  increments x

λ                 x  .     * x 2
↑                 ↑  ↑     ↑
the function of   x  that  multiplies x by 2
```

In the λ-calculus only functions with one argument can be specified. Functions with more than one argument are simulated by using a cascade of (higher order) functions each with exactly one argument (see also Section 1.7.2). A higher order function yielding a function can be defined by specifying another λ-abstraction as function body.

Defining higher order functions:

```
λ                 x  .     (λ                y  .     + x y)
↑                 ↑  ↑     ↑                 ↑  ↑     ↑
the function of   x  that  yields
                           the function of   y  that  adds x and y
```

This is equivalent to the Miranda definition:

```
f x y  =  x + y
```

In Miranda most functions have a name, whereas in the λ-calculus all functions are anonymous; in the λ-calculus all functions are specified in prefix notation.

3.1.2 Function application

As in functional programming languages, application is fundamental in the λ-calculus and it is denoted simply by juxtaposition.

Function application:

```
f                        a
↑                        ↑
f  has to be applied to  a
```

If f is a function (λ-abstraction), the expression to which the function is applied is called the **actual argument** of the function.

Example of function application:

```
(λ x.Inc x)                                              5
↑                                                        ↑
this function of x   has to be applied   to the constant  5

((λx.(λy.+ x y))                          4)                 5
↑                                         ↑                  ↑
this function of x     has to be applied to 4
and the result which is a function of y       has to be applied to  5
```

Notational conventions

Parentheses can be left out when they are redundant. The main cases are given below with other ways to abbreviate λ-expressions. The symbol '≡' means: 'is an abbreviation for'.

$$\lambda x.exp_1\ exp_2 \equiv \lambda x.(exp_1\ exp_2)$$
$$exp_1\ exp_2\ exp_3 \equiv (exp_1\ exp_2)\ exp_3$$
$$\lambda x.\lambda y.exp \equiv \lambda x.(\lambda y.exp)$$
$$\lambda xy.exp \equiv \lambda x.\lambda y.exp$$

Although functions have no name in the λ-calculus it is sometimes convenient to use an *abbreviation* as a synonym for a complex λ-expression. Such an abbreviation is generally an identifier in upper case characters. Do not confuse this notation with a (possibly recursive) function call in Miranda. The identifier is just an abbreviation for the corresponding λ-expression and nothing else.

A common abbreviation for a specific λ-expression:

TWICE ≡ (λf.λx.f (f x))

3.1.3 Constants

In the original λ-calculus model, **pure** λ-calculus, constants were not included. Nevertheless, any computable function can be expressed in pure λ-calculus. For notational convenience however, we do include **constants** in the model to represent constant values (such as numbers) or externally defined functions (such as arithmetical functions). Such a function is called a **δ-rule** or a **δ-function** (see Section 3.2.3).

Some λ-expressions containing constant values (2, 3 and 5) and externally defined functions (+, *, –):

```
5
+ 2 3
λx.* (+ 2 x) (– y x)
```

3.1.4 Representing λ-expressions as trees

Sometimes a λ-expression is also represented as a tree, which clarifies the structure of an expression.

Figure 3.1 A tree representation of, respectively, λ-abstraction (λv.E) and application (F A).

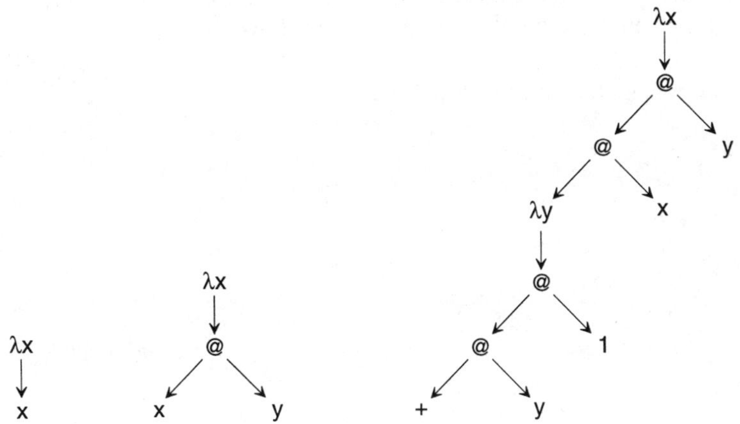

Figure 3.2 Tree representations of λx.x, λx.x y and λx.(λy.+ y 1) x y.

As shown in Figures 3.1 and 3.2, a λ-abstraction λv.E is represented in such a tree by a vertical line with on the top the λv and on the bottom the tree representing E, the function body of the anonymous function of v. An application of an expression F applied to an expression A is represented by a binary tree with @ (indicating an application) as root, a left subtree representing F and a right subtree representing A.

3.1.5 Bound and free variables

A λ-expression can contain variables. Traditionally, a one-character identifier (x, y, z, v, w, a, b, c, …) is used to denote a variable. There are *free* variables and *bound* variables. Informally it can be stated that a variable occurs *bound* in a λ-expression if and only if there is an enclosing λ-abstraction that *binds* it, i.e. the variable is the formal argument of an enclosing λ-abstraction. Otherwise, the variable occurs *free* in this λ-expression. The notion of free and bound variables plays an important role in the reduction rules (see Section 3.2).

The precise definition of bound and free variables can easily be given using the tree representation of a λ-expression:

- An occurrence of a variable, say x, is **bound** if on the path starting from the occurrence of the variable (this will always be a leaf in the tree) going up to the root of the tree a λ is encountered with a variable with the same name you started with, i.e. λx. The first occurrence of λx in the path from the leaf up to the root is said to **bind** the occurrence of x.
- An occurrence of a variable is **free** if it is not bound.

Follow this algorithm for the variables in the trees given in Figure 3.2 and compare the results with the examples below.

Illustrating free and bound variables:

```
x                          |  λx.  x       y
↑                          |       ↑       ↑
free variable              |       bound   free
                           |
λx.  x                     |  λx.(λy. + y  1)   x       y
     ↑                     |           ↑        ↑       ↑
     bound variable        |           bound    bound   free
```

Note that a variable can occur bound as well as free in one and the same expression.

3.1.6 α-conversion

In the λ-calculus the term λx.x is considered to be equivalent to λz.z. A λ-expression can be converted into another equivalent one by renaming *bound* variables. It can be compared to a function definition in Miranda in which the names of the formal arguments can be chosen freely (without changing the semantics) as long as they do not conflict with other names. Expressions that can be made textually equivalent by renaming bound variables are called **α-convertible** or **alphabetically equivalent**. The renaming process is called **α-conversion**.

If names are changed, a new name which is chosen must not be in *conflict* with one of the old names. Therefore α-conversion only allows us to change the name of a bound variable under the following conditions:

Definition of α-conversion

$$\lambda x.E =_\alpha (\lambda y.E\ [x{:=}\ y])$$

where E [x := A] means E in which all free occurrences of x (which means occurrences of x not bound by other λs inside E) are replaced by y. The variable y has to be a **fresh variable**, i.e. y does not occur free in E *and* y does not get bound in E by the substitution.

Here are some examples of valid and invalid α-conversions on λ-expressions (the α-converted variables are underlined):

Examples of valid α-conversions:

$\underline{\lambda x}$.Succ x	$=_\alpha$	λy.Succ y
$\underline{\lambda x}$.(λy.y) x	$=_\alpha$	λy.(λy.y) y
(λx.$\underline{\lambda y}$.* x y) y	$=_\alpha$	(λx.λz.* x z) y

Examples of invalid α-conversions:

$\underline{\lambda x}$.Succ x y	$\neq_\alpha$	λy.Succ y y, because y occurs free in Succ x y
$\underline{\lambda x}$.(λy.y x)	$\neq_\alpha$	λy.(λy.y y), because y will get bound in λy. y x
λy.y $\underline{x}$	$\neq_\alpha$	λy.y z, because x is not bound

One has to be careful because the same name does not always stand for the same variable. Whether or not the same name stands for the same variable is determined by the context: when the variables are bound by the same λ or when they are both free then they also stand for the same variable. From now on, two λ-expressions are considered to be **equal** if they are α-convertible to each other.

3.2 Reduction rules for λ-expressions

There are a number of *reduction rules* or *rewrite rules* that define how λ-terms can be converted to other, equivalent, λ-terms. Two transformation rules are treated in this section: *β-reduction* and *δ-reduction.*

3.2.1 β-reduction

β-reduction is a reduction rule that describes how to evaluate an application of a function (a λ-abstraction) to its actual argument. In the λ-calculus, β-reduction states that any function applied to an argument forms a **β-redex**, a **red**ucible (sub)**ex**pression according to the β-reduction rule. The result of β-reduction is the body of the λ-abstraction in which all occurrences of the formal argument are *textually substituted* (replaced, reduced, rewritten) by the actual argument on which the function is applied. Hence, all occurrences of the variable that are bound by the corresponding λ are replaced by the actual argument. The replacement is also called a **β-reduction step** or a **rewrite step**.

Definition of β-reduction

$$(\lambda x.E)\ A \quad \rightarrow_\beta \quad E\,[x := A]$$

where E [x := A] means E in which all free occurrences of x are replaced by expression A. Furthermore, as explained below, it is not allowed that one of the free variables in A becomes bound when substituted in E.

As an example some λ-terms are given together with some β-reduction steps. As usual, the chosen redexes are underlined.

β-reduction on a simple λ-term:

$$\underline{(\lambda x.x)\ 0} \quad \rightarrow_\beta \quad 0$$

Using currying to simulate functions with more than one argument:

$$\underline{(\lambda x.(\lambda y.x)\ )\ 0}\ 1 \quad \rightarrow_\beta \quad \underline{(\lambda y.0)\ 1} \quad \rightarrow_\beta \quad 0$$

In the example above an anonymous function is returned after application of the function to the first argument. When λ-calculus is used to model currying, a new anonymous function is explicitly created each time a curried function is applied to another one of its arguments.

A function with another function as its argument:

$$\underline{(\lambda f.f\ 0)\ (\lambda x.x)} \quad \rightarrow_\beta \quad \underline{(\lambda x.x)\ 0} \quad \rightarrow_\beta \quad 0$$

A β-redex can easily be recognized in a tree representation. It is a function application with as left subtree a λ-abstraction (see Figure 3.3).

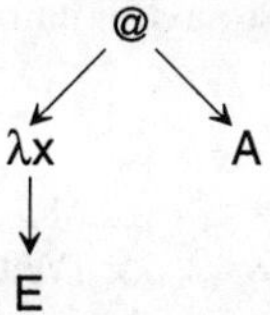

Figure 3.3 A β-redex, the application (@) of a λ-abstraction ($\lambda x.E$) to an expression (A).

3.2.2 α-conversion and β-reduction

According to the definition, β-reduction is only valid if the free variables that are present in the actual argument remain free after substitution.

Example of an illegal β-reduction: after substitution, the free variable y has become a bound variable. The name of the free variable 'conflicts' with the name of the bound variable.

$$(\lambda x.\lambda y.x\ \underset{\substack{\uparrow\\ \text{bound}}}{y})\ \underset{\substack{\uparrow\\ \text{free}}}{y} \not\to_\beta \lambda y.\ \underset{\substack{\uparrow\ \uparrow\\ \text{both bound}}}{y\ y}$$

The name conflict can be avoided by performing α-conversion first, replacing the function of y by an equivalent function of, say z.

$$(\lambda x.\lambda \underline{y}.x\ y)\ y =_\alpha \underline{(\lambda x.\lambda z.x\ z)\ y} \to_\beta \lambda z.y\ z$$

Note that the illegal substitution above would have changed the meaning of the expression: $\lambda y.y\ y \neq_\alpha \lambda z.y\ z$. For the same reason it is not allowed to avoid the name conflict by renaming the free variable y.

The examples show why β-reduction is only allowed when the substitution is 'safe', i.e. when no names of free variables get bound through the substitution. From now on it will be assumed that α-conversion will always be performed where needed to make β-reduction possible.

α-conversion needed during β-reduction

At first sight it may seem possible to avoid name conflicts by choosing different names for the different variables in the initial λ-expression. However, name conflicts can arise during β-reduction even if in the initial expression all different variables had different names.

Consider the following λ-expression: TWICE ≡ (λf.λx.f (f x)). α-conversion is necessary during β-reduction to avoid name conflicts:

$$\begin{array}{lll}
\underline{(\lambda y.y\ y)\ \text{TWICE}} & & \\
\rightarrow_\beta\ \ \text{TWICE TWICE} & \equiv & \underline{(\lambda f.\lambda x.f\ (f\ x))\ \text{TWICE}} \\
\rightarrow_\beta\ \ \lambda x.\text{TWICE}\ (\text{TWICE}\ x) & \equiv & \lambda x.\text{TWICE}\ (\underline{(\lambda f.\lambda x.f(f\ x))\ x})
\end{array}$$

In this term the underlined subterm is not allowed to be β-reduced since otherwise the free variable x would get bound. So first the names have to be changed: α-conversion is applied, renaming all occurrences of x that are bound by the innermost λx:

$$\begin{array}{lll}
\lambda x.\text{TWICE}\ ((\lambda f.\underline{\lambda x}.f(f\ x))\ x) & =_\alpha & \lambda x.\text{TWICE}\ (\underline{(\lambda f.\lambda y.f(f\ y))\ x}) \\
\rightarrow_\beta\ \ \lambda x.\text{TWICE}\ (\lambda y.x(x\ y)) & &
\end{array}$$

The example shows that changing of names can in general be necessary after any β-reduction because as a consequence of (self-)application new conflicts can come up. Note that α-conversion is not considered to be an explicit step in the reduction process: it is a renaming process that does not change the structure of an expression and it is assumed to be performed implicitly where needed.

Practical ways to deal with α-conversion are explained in Section 3.8. Furthermore, in that section it will be shown that there are certain conditions under which α-conversion is not needed at all.

3.2.3 δ-reduction

As explained in Section 3.1, the impure λ-calculus can contain externally defined functions which are called **δ-rules** or **δ-functions**. Such δ-functions can be defined on predefined constants, such as, for instance, constants that represent numbers. Although it is possible to define most of these functions and constants directly in the pure λ-calculus (see Section 3.7), it is sometimes more convenient for readability and illustration purposes to assume the availability of these external functions. δ-rules are sometimes also introduced to increase efficiency: with one δ-*reduction* one can obtain the same result that otherwise would have cost many β-*reductions* in the pure λ-calculus.

If a δ-function is applied to the number of arguments it needs and these arguments are of the correct type, the corresponding subexpression is called a **δ-redex**. If the external function is applied it is called a **δ-reduction step**.

For example, assume that an external δ-rule + is defined which requires that its arguments are constants of a specific type, e.g. constant numbers. An application of the function + is not a δ-redex until this restriction is satisfied. This implies that one first has to reduce the arguments of + to obtain the required constant numbers, before this δ-rule can be applied.

Example of a δ-reduction step, assuming that +, 2, 3 and 5 are externally defined δ-rules:

$\underline{+\ 2\ 3} \quad \rightarrow_{\delta+} \ 5$

The function + cannot be applied until its arguments are constant numbers:

$+\ (\underline{*\ 1\ 2})\ 3 \quad \rightarrow_{\delta*} \ \underline{+\ 2\ 3} \quad \rightarrow_{\delta+} \ 5$

In principle, it is allowed that external functions investigate the internal structure of their arguments. This means that, for instance, it is possible to have δ-rules that can determine whether two arbitrary λ-expressions are syntactically equal. Such a function cannot be defined in the pure λ-calculus. Hence with δ-rules one can introduce arbitrary computational power in the λ-calculus (see also Section 3.7).

3.3 Reduction sequences and normal forms

A **reduction sequence** of a λ-expression consists of zero or more reduction steps (rewrite steps) performed on that expression. If expression E_1 can be reduced to expression E_2 by a reduction sequence, E_2 is called a **reduct** of E_1. This is denoted as: $E1 \rightarrow_* E2$. So $\rightarrow_*$ is the reflexive transitive closure of $\rightarrow$.

A λ-expression that does not contain a redex is in **normal form**. A λ-expression *has* a normal form if there exists some sequence of reduction steps starting with this expression that results in an expression in normal form. Not all expressions have a normal form. In that case there exists an infinite reduction sequence (see the example below).

A reduction sequence (of length 1), where the reduct is in normal form:

$\lambda x.\underline{(\lambda y.y)\ (\lambda x.x)} \quad \rightarrow_{\beta} \quad \lambda x.(\lambda x.x)$

Example of an expression that has no normal form :

$\underline{(\lambda x.x\ x)\ (\lambda x.x\ x)} \quad \rightarrow_{\beta} \quad \underline{(\lambda x.x\ x)\ (\lambda x.x\ x)} \quad \rightarrow_{\beta} \quad \ldots$

Note the difference between being in normal form and having a normal form:

x	is in normal form, because it does not contain a redex.
(λx.x)(λx.x)	is not in normal form, but it has a normal form: λx.x.
(λx.x x)(λx.x x)	is not in normal form, and it has no normal form.

3.4 Properties of the λ-calculus

3.4.1 Church–Rosser property

A λ-expression can contain several redexes:

Example: the following expression:

$(\lambda x.(\lambda y.y)\ (\lambda z.z))\ (\lambda u.u)$

contains two redexes, namely: $(\lambda x.\underline{(\lambda y.y)\ (\lambda z.z)})\ (\lambda u.u)$
and $\underline{(\lambda x.(\lambda y.y)\ (\lambda z.z))\ (\lambda u.u)}$

If more than one redex occurs in an expression, different reduction sequences are possible. Hence, the available redexes can be reduced in different **reduction orders**. An interesting question is: is it possible that an expression has more than one normal form depending on the chosen order of reduction?

Two alternative reduction orders leading to the same result. First method:

$$(\lambda x.\underline{(\lambda y.y)\ (\lambda z.z)})\ (\lambda u.u) \quad \to_\beta \quad \underline{(\lambda x.\lambda z.z)\ (\lambda u.u)} \quad \to_\beta \quad \lambda z.z$$

or, with an alternative reduction order

$$\underline{(\lambda x.(\lambda y.y)\ (\lambda z.z))\ (\lambda u.u)} \quad \to_\beta \quad \underline{(\lambda y.y)\ (\lambda z.z)} \quad \to_\beta \quad \lambda z.z$$

Two different reduction sequences: one leads to a normal form, the other is an infinite reduction sequence:

$$\underline{(\lambda y.\lambda z.z)((\lambda x.x\ x)(\lambda x.x\ x))} \to_\beta \quad \lambda z.z$$

$$(\lambda y.\lambda z.z)(\underline{(\lambda x.x\ x)(\lambda x.x\ x)}) \to_\beta \quad (\lambda y.\lambda z.z)(\underline{(\lambda x.x\ x)(\lambda x.x\ x)}) \quad \to_\beta \quad \ldots$$

The examples show that not all reduction orders lead to a normal form, not even if the initial expression has a normal form.

A reduction system (such as the λ-calculus) has the **Church–Rosser property** (Church and Rosser, 1936) or is **confluent** if and only if for every two 'divergent' reduction sequences $E \to_* E_1$ and $E \to_* E_2$ there are two 'convergent' reduction sequences $E_1 \to_* E_3$ and $E_2 \to_* E_3$. The Church–Rosser property is also called the **diamond property** (Figure 3.4).

Theorem: The λ-calculus satisfies the Church–Rosser property.

The Church–Rosser theorem has a very important consequence: in a reduction system, in which the Church–Rosser property holds, every expression has at most one normal form: *the normal form is unique*. Assume that an expression has two normal forms. The Church–Rosser property implies that there must be a common reduct to which both these normal forms can be reduced. Since both expressions are already in normal form, they must have been the same.

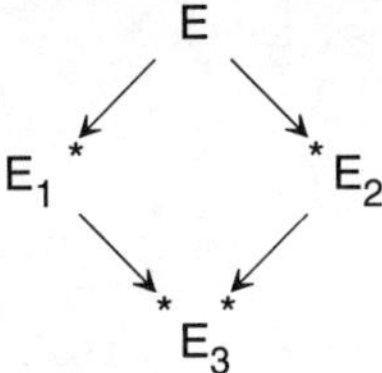

Figure 3.4 The Church–Rosser property.

If a λ-term can be reduced by several reduction sequences and several of these sequences lead to a normal form, the result is always the same, independent of the reduction order chosen. λ-expressions that have a common reduct are **β-convertible** ($=_\beta$). Due to the Church–Rosser property the following holds: if $E_1 \rightarrow_* E_3$ and $E_2 \rightarrow_* E_3$ then $E_1 =_\beta E_2 =_\beta E_3$ and if $E_1 =_\beta E_2$ then there is an E_3 such that $E_1 \rightarrow_* E_3$ and $E_2 \rightarrow_* E_3$.

3.4.2 Computability

Conjecture (Church's thesis)**:** The class of effectively computable functions, i.e. functions that intuitively can be computed, is the same as the class of functions that can be defined in λ-calculus (Church, 1936).

Theorem: The class of Turing computable functions is the same as the class of λ-definable functions (Turing, 1937).

So the power of Turing machines is the same as the power of the λ-calculus. Both models capture the intuitive idea of computation.

3.5 Reduction strategies

A **reduction strategy** in the λ-calculus is a mathematical function that prescribes which redex in a given, arbitrary λ-expression has to be rewritten. When it is repeatedly applied to a λ-expression and its reducts, a strategy defines the **order** in which redexes are reduced. In this way a (possibly infinite) reduction sequence can be defined. A **normalizing reduction strategy** is a reduction strategy that results, after repetitive application, in the normal form, if this normal form exists.

3.5.1 Normal order reduction

In the **normal order** reduction strategy the leftmost-outermost redex in a given expression is rewritten and therefore it is also known as the **leftmost-outermost** reduction strategy, or as the **leftmost** strategy. The **leftmost-outermost redex** of a λ-expression is the redex that is not surrounded by any other redex (outermost) and is to the left of all the other outermost redexes in that expression (leftmost).

The notion leftmost-outermost redex:

$$(\underline{(\lambda x.x\ x)\ (\lambda y.y)})\ (\underline{(\lambda x.x\ x)\ (\lambda x.x\ x)})$$
$$\uparrow r_1 \qquad\qquad \uparrow r_2$$

r_1 is the leftmost redex, because this redex is to the left of all other redexes in that expression. Furthermore this redex is also an outermost redex, because there is no other redex in this expression that surrounds r_1. Note that r_2 is also an outermost redex, but not the leftmost one.

$\underline{(\lambda z.(\lambda x\ x)\ z)\ (\lambda z.z)}$ $\uparrow r_1$	$(\lambda z.\underline{(\lambda x\ x)\ z})\ (\lambda z.z)$ $\uparrow r_2$

r_1 is the leftmost-outermost redex. r_2 is not an outermost redex.

Theorem: In the λ-calculus the normal order strategy is a normalizing strategy (Curry and Feys, 1958).
So reducing normal order will always yield the normal form if it exists.

3.5.2 Applicative order reduction

The **applicative order** reduction strategy prescribes rewriting the leftmost-innermost redex in a given expression and therefore it is also known as the **leftmost-innermost** reduction strategy, or the **innermost** strategy. The **leftmost-innermost redex** of a λ-expression is the redex that does not contain any other redex (innermost) and is to the left of all the other innermost redexes in that expression (leftmost). Hence, the innermost reduction strategy will always rewrite the argument of a function first, before a β-reduction is performed on that function and its argument.

Innermost reduction: The third example shows that the innermost reduction strategy is not normalizing (the expression does have a normal form: 0).

$$(\lambda x.x)\ (\underline{(\lambda z.z\ z)\ y}) \quad \rightarrow_\beta \quad \underline{(\lambda x.x)\ (y\ y)} \quad \rightarrow_\beta \quad y\ y$$

$$(\lambda x.x)\ (\underline{(\lambda x.x)\ (\lambda x.x)}) \quad \rightarrow_\beta \quad \underline{(\lambda x.x)\ (\lambda x.x)} \quad \rightarrow_\beta \quad \lambda x.x$$

$$(\lambda x.0)\ (\underline{(\lambda x.x\ x)\ (\lambda x.x\ x)}) \ \rightarrow_\beta\ (\lambda x.0)\ (\underline{(\lambda x.x\ x)\ (\lambda x.x\ x)}) \ \rightarrow_\beta\ \ldots$$

Analogous to leftmost-outermost and leftmost-innermost one can define the notions *rightmost-outermost* and *rightmost-innermost*. To find leftmost, rightmost, innermost or outermost redexes, again the tree representation is very helpful (Figure 3.5).

λ-term as tree: (λx.λy.x y) ((λz.z) ((λx.x) z)) ((λx.x) ((λx.x) ((λx.x) z)))

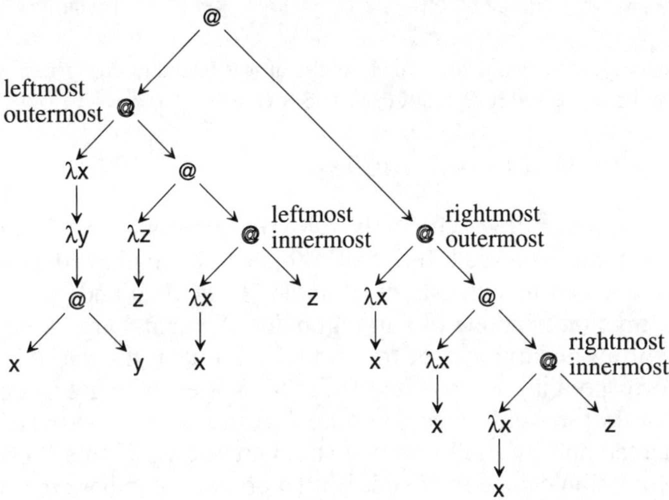

Figure 3.5 Tree showing leftmost, rightmost, innermost and outermost redexes (marked with @).

3.6 Properties of subclasses of the λ-calculus

3.6.1 Combinatory logic

A **combinator** is a λ-expression (a λ-abstraction) without free variables. The theory of such λ-terms is the **combinatory logic** (Curry, 1930).

The combinators S and K:

S ≡ λx.λy.λz.x z (y z)
K ≡ λx.λy.x

Combinators can be regarded as function constants, e.g. S and K are functions with the following property:

S x y z = x z (y z) (distributor)
K x y = x (cancellator)

With these combinators **applicative expressions** can be constructed, i.e. expressions in which only applications (of combinators) occur. It turns out that with only the two combinators, S and K, one can construct a system that has the same power as the pure λ-calculus: one can construct all effectively computable functions with it:

With an applicative expression of the combinators S and K one can build for example the identity combinator (often referred to as I), with the property

I x = x (identity)

Generally, for convenience, the I-combinator is added to the system, although it can be expressed in S and K (e.g. as S K S or S K K).

$$\mathsf{I\ e} \equiv \underline{\mathsf{S\ K\ S\ e}} =_{\mathsf{S}} \underline{\mathsf{K\ e\ (S\ e)}} =_{\mathsf{K}} \mathsf{e}$$

It is amazing that with only two combinators, any computable function can be expressed. Intuitively this can be explained as follows. The pure λ-calculus consists of variables, functions and applications. When a function is applied to an argument, the actual argument is substituted for all occurrences of the formal argument, the variable bound by the corresponding λ. So actually all that matters is to get a copy of an expression in the right place. With an S combinator an expression can be duplicated and inserted into two subexpressions. With a K combinator an expression can be removed. With a proper combination of the two one can copy any expression into another until it is in the right place. If a copy arrives at a place where it is not needed, it is simply removed by a K.

Transforming λ-expressions to combinators

An algorithm for translating λ-expressions into an applicative expression of SKI-combinators is presented below.

All translation rules used in this textbook are presented in a functional style. These functions define how a (part of a) language can be translated into another language. The objects of the translation are syntactic objects. To make a translation description in a functional formalism as short and as readable as possible a notational convenience is added that allows specification of arbitrary syntactic objects. To emphasize that these objects are special they are placed between double square brackets (⟦ and ⟧). If one would like to specify these transformations directly in Miranda, one would actually need a data structure (an abstract syntax tree) that is able to represent any sentence in the language one wants to translate. The algorithm for translating λ-expressions into combinators, known as **bracket-abstraction** (probably due to the use of the double square brackets), is defined below.

Algorithm for bracket-abstraction: x and y are variables, c is any constant, E, E_1 and E_2 are λ-expressions. The rules have to be tried in textual order.

```
LamToSKI ⟦ λx.x ⟧        = I
LamToSKI ⟦ λx.y ⟧        = K y
LamToSKI ⟦ λx.c ⟧        = K c
LamToSKI ⟦ λx.E1 E2 ⟧    = S (LamToSKI ⟦ λx.E1 ⟧) (LamToSKI ⟦ λx.E2 ⟧)
LamToSKI ⟦ λx.E ⟧        = LamToSKI ⟦ λx.LamToSKI ⟦ E ⟧ ⟧
LamToSKI ⟦ E1 E2 ⟧       = (LamToSKI ⟦ E1 ⟧) (LamToSKI ⟦ E2 ⟧)
LamToSKI ⟦ E ⟧           = E
```

For example, consider the following λ-expression:

```
INV  ≡  λx.λf.f x
```

The bracket-abstraction algorithm applied to this λ-expression:

```
LamToSKI ⟦ INV ⟧  ≡   LamToSKI ⟦ λx.λf.f x ⟧
→     LamToSKI ⟦ λx.LamToSKI ⟦ λf.f x ⟧ ⟧
→     LamToSKI ⟦ λx.S (LamToSKI ⟦ λf.f ⟧)) (LamToSKI ⟦ λf.x ⟧) ⟧
→*    LamToSKI ⟦ λx.S I (K x) ⟧
→     S (LamToSKI ⟦ λx.S I ⟧) (LamToSKI ⟦ λx.K x ⟧)
→     S (S (LamToSKI ⟦ λx.S ⟧) (LamToSKI ⟦ λx.I ⟧))(LamToSKI ⟦ λx.K x ⟧)
→*    S (S (K S)(K I)) (S (LamToSKI ⟦ λx.K ⟧) (LamToSKI ⟦ λx.x ⟧))
→*    S (S (K S)(K I)) (S (K K) I)
```

This complicated expression will, when it is applied to two arguments (say X and F), yield the same result as the original λ-expression:

```
S (S (K S)(K I)) (S (K K) I) X F          =S    (S (K S)(K I) X) (S (K K) I X) F
=S      (K S X) (K I X) (S (K K) I X) F   =K,K  S I (S (K K) I X) F
=S      I F (S (K K) I X F)               =I,S  F ((K K X) (I X) F)
=K      F (K (I X) F)                     =K    F (I X)
=I      F X
```

The example above shows that there is a slight disadvantage when only these few combinators are used: the resulting expression is of exponential length with respect to the original expression. This can be improved by the following optimization rules (Curry and Feys, 1958):

```
S (K E1) (K E2)  =  K (E1 E2)
S (K E) I        =  E
```

These equalities can be proven as follows:

```
S (K E1) (K E2) anything  =S   (K E1 anything) (K E2 anything)   =K,K  E1 E2
```

K (E1 E2) anything =K E1 E2

Since the combinators yield the same result for any argument, they are equal. Likewise

S (K E) I anything =S (K E anything) (I anything) =K,I E anything

So the following rules can be added to the translation scheme that *Tr*ansforms an SKI-expression inside out into a more optimal one:

```
Tr ⟦ E1 E2 ⟧   = OptiSKI ⟦ (Tr ⟦ E1 ⟧) (Tr ⟦ E2 ⟧) ⟧
Tr ⟦ c ⟧       = c

OptiSKI ⟦ S (K E1) (K E2) ⟧  = K (OptiSKI ⟦ E1 E2 ⟧)
OptiSKI ⟦ S (K E) I ⟧        = E
OptiSKI ⟦ E ⟧                = E
```

These optimizations can be applied to our example expression

```
Tr ⟦ S (S (K S)(K I)) (S (K K) I) ⟧
→  OptiSKI ⟦ (Tr ⟦ S (S (K S)(K I)) ⟧) (Tr ⟦ S (K K) I ⟧) ⟧
→  OptiSKI ⟦ (Tr ⟦ S (S (K S)(K I)) ⟧) (OptiSKI ⟦ (Tr ⟦ S (K K) ⟧)(Tr ⟦ I ⟧) ⟧) ⟧
→  OptiSKI ⟦ (Tr ⟦ S (S (K S)(K I)) ⟧) (OptiSKI ⟦ (Tr ⟦ S (K K) ⟧) I ⟧) ⟧
→* OptiSKI ⟦ (Tr ⟦ S (S (K S)(K I)) ⟧) (OptiSKI ⟦ S (K K) I ⟧) ⟧
→  OptiSKI ⟦ (Tr ⟦ S (S (K S)(K I)) ⟧) K ⟧
→* S (K (S I)) K
```

and indeed:

```
S (K (S I)) K X F      =S    (K (S I) X) (K X) F     =K    S I (K X) F
=S   (I F) (K X F)     =I,K  F X
```

Further optimizations involve the introduction of new combinators, e.g.:

```
B ≡ λf.λg.λx.f (g x)
C ≡ λf.λx.λy.f y x
```

with corresponding new optimization rules (note that only two new rules are added):

```
OptiSKI ⟦ S (K E1) (K E2) ⟧  = K (OptiSKI ⟦ E1 E2 ⟧)
OptiSKI ⟦ S (K E) I ⟧        = E
OptiSKI ⟦ S (K E1) E2 ⟧      = B E1 E2
OptiSKI ⟦ S E1 (K E2) ⟧      = C E1 E2
OptiSKI ⟦ E ⟧                = E
```

These optimizations are easily proven to be correct. With the help of these new combinators and optimization rules the complexity can be improved to $O(n^2)$, where n is the length of the original expression.

In this way INV can be expressed as B (S I) K. But on the other hand there is nothing wrong with introducing INV itself as an extra combinator. Many other combinators can be defined. It is an interesting line of research to find out which set is the best in a certain sense.

3.7 λ-calculus as a basis for functional languages

As stated before, the λ-calculus can be seen as a desugared functional language to which all existing functional languages can be translated. The same is possible for the other models of computation treated in this part of the book. An exhaustive transformation scheme from Miranda to a graph rewriting system is given in Chapter 9. The intention of this section is to illustrate how, in principle, the basic concepts of functional languages (see Chapter 1) can be expressed in the *pure* λ-calculus. This will give the reader an intuitive idea how it can be proven that in the pure λ-calculus all recursive functions can be expressed. The transformation of the more advanced language concepts can be found, for example, in Peyton Jones (1987).

3.7.1 Functions and applications

A simple Miranda function definition without patterns and guards is easy to translate to the λ-calculus since application is a basic operation in both languages. Furthermore, all Miranda functions are considered to be curried so they are actually functions with one argument.

$$\text{MirToLam} [\![\text{f } a_1\ a_2 \ldots a_n = \text{expression}]\!] = \lambda a_1.\lambda a_2 \ldots \lambda a_n.\ (\text{MirToLam} [\![\text{expression}]\!])$$

$$\text{MirToLam} [\![\text{f a}]\!] = (\text{MirToLam} [\![\text{f}]\!])\ (\text{MirToLam} [\![\text{a}]\!])$$

The notation means: a function definition in a Miranda program is translated into a λ-expression with a λ for each argument of the function definition. The body of the λ-expression is the translation of the body of the function. The resulting λ-expression is replaced for every application of f, possibly abbreviated by a symbolic name. Furthermore, any application of operands is translated directly to an application of the translated operands.

For instance,

```
twice f x   =  f (f x)
```

will be translated into

```
TWICE ≡ λf.λx.f (f x)
```

Since all functions are anonymous, an application of the function twice in Miranda results in a textual substitution of the λ-expression TWICE in the corresponding λ-expression.

3.7.2 Booleans and the conditional

Boolean values can be translated as follows:

```
MirToLam ⟦ True ⟧    = λx.λy.x
MirToLam ⟦ False ⟧   = λx.λy.y
```

The translation of True and False is not a value, but a function that is able to select the first or second argument to which it is applied. This function corresponds to the conditional in Miranda. So the conditional itself disappears in the translation. Hence a conditional expression can be translated as follows:

```
MirToLam ⟦ cond boolexpr thenpart elsepart ⟧
= MirToLam ⟦ boolexpr ⟧ (MirToLam ⟦ thenpart ⟧) (MirToLam ⟦ elsepart ⟧)
```

because

```
TRUE THENPART ELSEPART            ≡     (λx.λy.x) THENPART ELSEPART
→β  (λy.THENPART) ELSEPART        →β    THENPART
```

and

```
FALSE THENPART ELSEPART           ≡     (λx.λy.y) THENPART ELSEPART
→β  (λy.y) ELSEPART               →β    ELSEPART
```

The names in upper case characters are again abbreviations that represent λ-expressions that are the translation of corresponding Miranda expressions, e.g. TRUE ≡ λx.λy.x, FALSE ≡ λx.λy.y

3.7.3 Recursion

In the λ-calculus functions have no name. So recursion cannot be achieved by using recursive function calls, as in Miranda.

The factorial function in Miranda:

```
fac n    = cond (n = 0) 1 (n * fac (n – 1))
```

cannot be translated into

```
FAC ≡ λn. (EQUAL n 0) 1 (TIMES n (FAC (MINUS n 1)))
```

In the recursive abbreviation above an infinite λ-expression is actually expressed. However, the λ-calculus deals with finite terms only. There is a trick to solve this problem. There exist special λ-expressions, called **fixed point combinators**, having the following property (Y is a fixed point combinator, f is any λ-expression):

$$Y\ f \quad =_\beta \quad f\ (Y\ f)$$

Recursive functions now will get an additional parameter in which such a special duplicate of their own code is filled in, but this time this will happen only when the function is applied. Hence there is a kind of lazy duplication of code. In the following Y stands for any fixed point combinator.

A correct translation of the factorial function:

```
FAC ≡ Y F
F   ≡ λf.λn.(EQUAL n 0) 1 (TIMES n (f (MINUS n 1)))
```

Now,

```
FAC 3  ≡   Y F 3
=    F (Y F) 3  ≡ (λf.λn.(EQUAL n 0) 1 (TIMES n (f (MINUS n 1)))) (Y F) 3
≡    (λf.λn.(EQUAL n 0) 1 (TIMES n (f (MINUS n 1)))) FAC 3
→β   λn.(EQUAL n 0) 1 (TIMES n (FAC (MINUS n 1))) 3
→β   (EQUAL 3 0) 1 (TIMES 3 (FAC (MINUS 3 1)))
→*   FALSE 1 (TIMES 3 (FAC (MINUS 3 1)))
≡    (λx.λy.y) 1 (TIMES 3 (FAC (MINUS 3 1))
→*   TIMES 3 (FAC (MINUS 3 1))
≡    TIMES 3 (Y F (MINUS 3 1)), ...
```

Each time Y F is applied, F is returned, and the original expression Y F is duplicated which guarantees that this kind of lazy code duplication can be repeated in the sequel. The property of fixed point combinators may seem very magical at first sight. Therefore an example of the definition of such a fixed point combinator is given below.

```
θ ≡ A A
A ≡ λx.λy.y (x x y)
```

The following reduction steps show that $\theta\ f \rightarrow_* f\ (\theta\ f)$, which implies that θ indeed has the fixed point property:

$$\theta\, f \equiv A\, A\, f \equiv (\lambda x.\lambda y.y\,(x\,x\,y))\, A\, f$$
$$\rightarrow_\beta (\lambda y.y\,(A\,A\,y))\, f \rightarrow_\beta f\,(A\,A\,f) \equiv f\,(\theta\, f)$$

3.7.4 Representation of natural numbers

In the λ-calculus one can represent natural numbers and arithmetical functions. In this section every numeral n is represented by the nth Church numeral. The **Church numerals** c_0, c_1, c_2, ... are defined by ($f^0(x)$ stands for x, $f^{n+1}(x)$ stands for $f(f^n(x))$):

$$c_n \equiv \lambda f.\lambda x.f^n(x)$$

Hence,

$$0 \equiv c_0 \equiv \lambda f.\lambda x.x$$
$$1 \equiv c_1 \equiv \lambda f.\lambda x.f(x)$$
$$2 \equiv c_2 \equiv \lambda f.\lambda x.f(f(x))$$

Now it is possible to represent the arithmetical functions +, * and exp in the λ-calculus. Rosser defines the following λ-expressions:

$$A_+ \equiv \lambda x.\lambda y.\lambda p.\lambda q.\ x\, p\, (y\, p\, q)$$
$$A_* \equiv \lambda x.\lambda y.\lambda p.\ x\, (y\, p)$$
$$A_{exp} \equiv \lambda x.\lambda y.\ y\, x$$

Now for all $n,m \in N$

(i) $A_+\, c_n\, c_m \rightarrow_* c_{n+m}$
(ii) $A_*\, c_n\, c_m \rightarrow_* c_{n*m}$
(iii) $A_{exp}\, c_n\, c_m \rightarrow_* c_{(n^m)}$, except for m=0

Below it is shown that A_+ yields the Church numeral representing the arithmetical sum of the two Church numerals it is applied to:

$$A_+\, c_n\, c_m \equiv (\lambda x.\lambda y.\lambda p.\lambda q.\ x\, p\, (y\, p\, q))\, c_n\, c_m$$
$$\rightarrow_\beta (\lambda y.\lambda p.\lambda q.\ c_n\, p\, (y\, p\, q))\, c_m$$
$$\rightarrow_\beta (\lambda p.\lambda q.\ c_n\, p\, (c_m\, p\, q)) \equiv (\lambda p.\lambda q.(\lambda f.\lambda x.f^n(x))\, p\, (c_m\, p\, q))$$
$$\rightarrow_\beta (\lambda p.\lambda q.(\lambda x.p^n(x))\, (c_m\, p\, q))$$
$$\rightarrow_\beta (\lambda p.\lambda q.p^n(c_m\, p\, q) \equiv (\lambda p.\lambda q.p^n((\lambda f.\lambda x.f^m(x))\, p\, q)$$
$$\rightarrow_\beta (\lambda p.\lambda q.p^n((\lambda x.p^m(x))\, q)$$
$$\rightarrow_\beta (\lambda p.\lambda q.p^n(p^m(q)) =_\alpha (\lambda f.\lambda x.f^n(f^m(x)) \equiv c_{n+m}$$

So the arithmetic operations +, * and exp on the numerals can be represented respectively by the λ-terms A_+, A_* and A_{exp} operating on the Church numerals. It will be clear that it is much more efficient to actually use the machine representation of numerals.

3.7.5 Lists

The translation of lists is not as intuitively simple as the translation of simple function definitions. The trick is to translate every constructor with its arguments to a λ-term representing a function that given a projection as an argument produces the desired component. So the constructors are translated as follows (implicitly defining CONS and NIL):

```
MirToLam [[ x:xs ]]   =  λz.z (MirToLam [[ x ]]) (MirToLam [[ xs ]])
MirToLam [[ [ ] ]]    =  λx.TRUE
```

Functions like head and tail are translated into λ-terms that given a list as an argument apply the list to the appropriate projection (implicitly defining HD and TL):

```
MirToLam [[ hd ]]   =  λx.x TRUE
MirToLam [[ tl ]]   =  λx.x FALSE
```

such that hd (x:xs) is translated into HD (CONS X XS) ≡ (λx.x TRUE) (λz.z X XS). In an analogous way, tl (x:xs) is translated into: TL (CONS X XS) ≡ (λx.x FALSE) (λz.z X XS). Below it is shown that the translations are correct:

```
HD (CONS X XS)
≡    (λx.x TRUE) (λz.z X XS)
→β   (λz.z X XS) TRUE
→β   TRUE X XS
≡    (λx.λy.x) X XS
→*   X
```

```
TL (CONS X XS)
≡    (λx.x FALSE) (λz.z X XS)
→β   (λz.z X XS) FALSE
→β   FALSE X XS
≡    (λx.λy.y) X XS
→*   XS
```

3.7.6 Patterns

One can simulate pattern matching by using conditionals in combination with a test for equality.

Modelling pattern matching by conditionals:

```
fac 0   =  1
fac n   =  * n (fac (– n 1))
```

can be written as (in which the conditional is created in λ-calculus as above):

```
fac n   =  cond (= n 0) 1 (* n (fac (– n 1)))
```

A test for syntactic equality is however not easy to achieve in pure λ-calculus. It can be realized in two ways.

The first way is choose a suitable representation (λ-term) such that each constant one would like to compare can be examined via an application of a specially designed test function. The comparison is done by applying the test function to the object and reducing the application to normal form. If the normal form is the λ-term that corresponds to TRUE, then they are equal; if it is the λ-term that corresponds to FALSE they are not. The disadvantage of this method is that it is sometimes hard to come up with an appropriate representation.

For instance, define

ZERO ≡ CONS TRUE NIL
ONE ≡ CONS FALSE ZERO
TWO ≡ CONS FALSE ONE

Now a test on the equality on ZERO can be performed by taking the head of the representation of the numeral. A test on ONE can be performed by taking the head of the tail, and so on.

The second way is to add additional power to the model by the introduction of a special δ-rule (Church's δ) that is defined on normal forms. This δ-rule returns TRUE or FALSE depending on the syntactic equality of its arguments. The strategy has to ensure that the arguments are reduced to normal form before the δ-rule is applied.

3.8 λ-calculus as a basis for implementations

A **reducer** is a piece of hardware and/or software that evaluates an expression by performing reductions. Although the λ-calculus appears to be simple, an implementation of a λ-reducer is not straightforward, particularly if efficiency is important. This section discusses some of the problems that have to be solved.

First of all, for efficiency reasons δ-rules will have to be used for pattern matching and for dealing with basic values.

Then, since our prime interest is a reducer that tries to reduce to normal form, one of the problems is caused by the α-conversion. Implementation of α-conversion has a considerable impact on efficiency. Below the relevant issues related with α-conversion will be discussed.

But there are more implementation problems. During the reduction process the reducer has to look up the actual argument to substitute for a particular variable. For this substitution process a rather complicated administration is needed. Only via the proper λ that binds the variable can the corresponding argument be found. The consequence is that in the actual implementation either all arguments accessible in a function body are passed to a function or a pointer structure has to be set up that makes it possible to switch back to the appropriate environment in which an argument can be evaluated.

3.8.1 α-conversion

It is clear that performing α-conversions after every reduction will never yield an efficient implementation. De Bruijn (1972) and Berkling and Fehr (1982) have developed solutions to the problem of name conflicts. Both their solutions are described here. They are basically equivalent to each other. The general idea is that in every variable name it is encoded via a counter to which λ the variable is bound.

Berkling and Fehr introduce the *λ-bar operator*: '#'. The number of **λ-bar operators** in front of a variable indicates the number of surrounding λs, which bind variables with the same name, to skip. A λ **surrounds** a variable in a λ-term if the λ is above the variable in the tree representation of that λ-term. In that case the variable is in the body of the function corresponding to that λ. The following example illustrates the function of this operator.

```
λ-bar operator:

λx.x                  || x is bound.

λx.#x                 || the # indicates to skip the first λ-occurrence
                      || that binds x. So x is free in this expression.

λx.λx.#x              || x is bound by the indicated λ, because #
↑                     || indicates to ignore the first surrounding λ.

λx.λx.λx.##x          || x is bound by the indicated λ.
↑

λx.λy.λx.#x           || x is bound by the indicated λ.
↑

λx. λx. #x (λx. ##x)  || both xs are bound by the same indicated λ.
↑

λx.(λx. #x) (λx. #x)  || both xs are bound by the same indicated λ.
↑                     || note that the second λ does not surround the second #x.
```

The following problem arises: doing a β-reduction implies that the number of λ-bar operators in the expression has to be adjusted in the body of the function as well as in the argument.

Examples of the adjustment of the number of λ-bar operators:

```
(λx.(λy.x y))  y  →β  λy.#y y
               ↑
```

It is not λy.y y, because the indicated y is a free variable of the expression and β-reduction should not change the meaning of variables.

λy.($\underline{(\lambda\text{y.\#y y) z}}$) $\rightarrow_\beta$ λy.y z

Not λy.#y z, because in λy.#y z, #y is a free variable whereas #y was bound in the expression before the β-reduction took place.

The solution of De Bruijn uses *nameless dummies*: instead of named variables. A **nameless dummy** is a number that replaces a named variable. The nameless dummy indicates by which λ the replaced variable is bound. The λs are counted starting from the nameless dummy going to the top of the tree representation of the term. For free occurrences of variables nameless dummies are replaced as if extra λs binding them were added in front of the term. In this way effectively also the names of the free variables are modelled by the nameless dummies. Note that De Bruijn's $\underline{\text{n}}$ means that the *n*th surrounding λ binds, while Berkling and Fehr's $\#^{\text{n}}$x means to skip *n* surrounding λs that bind x.

Nameless dummies:

$\lambda.\ \underline{1}$ || $\underline{1}$ is a dummy for a variable bound by the indicated λ.
↑

$\lambda.\ \underline{2}$ || $\underline{2}$ is a dummy for a variable that is free.

$\lambda.\ \lambda.\ \underline{2}\ (\lambda.\ \underline{3})$ || $\underline{2}$ and $\underline{3}$ indicate the same variable, bound by indicated λ.
↑

$\lambda.\ (\lambda.\ \underline{2})\ (\lambda.\ \underline{2})$ || $\underline{2}$ and $\underline{2}$ indicate the same variable, bound by indicated λ.
↑

As with the # operator, the numbers of the nameless dummies have to be adjusted when doing a β-reduction.

Adjusting the numbers of De Bruijn:

$(\lambda.\ (\lambda.\ \underline{2}\ \underline{1})\ )\ \underline{1}$ $\rightarrow_\beta$ $\lambda.\ \underline{2}\ \underline{1}$ || not $\lambda.\ \underline{1}\ \underline{1}$
$\lambda.((\lambda.\ \underline{2}\ \underline{1})\ \underline{2})$ $\rightarrow_\beta$ $\lambda.\ \underline{1}\ \underline{2}$ || not $\lambda.\ \underline{2}\ \underline{2}$

3.8.2 Avoiding α-conversion

It has been shown that, in general, α-conversion cannot be avoided during β-reduction. However, if redexes are reduced in a special order and the final result does not have to be in normal form, α-conversion can be avoided. This can be used in a reducer that reduces a λ-expression which is the result of a translation of a Miranda program.

Suppose, when reducing in normal order, the leftmost-outermost redex is rewritten. Starting from Miranda the initial expression is a closed term, i.e. it does not contain free variables. So if the corresponding argument is substituted in the function body it is not possible that free variables in the argument get bound. Name conflicts cannot arise if the leftmost-outermost redex is repeatedly reduced in this way and the reduction process is stopped as soon as the result is a function. As long as reduction inside the body of a function (under an abstraction) does not occur, no α-conversion is needed.

> Example: if the underlined redex inside the function body is reduced, name conflicts arise:
>
> $(\lambda y.\underline{(\lambda x.\lambda y.x\ y)\ y})\ (\lambda x.\lambda y.x\ y)$
>
> However, reducing in normal order will not give any problems:
>
> $\underline{(\lambda y.(\lambda x.\lambda y.x\ y)\ y)\ (\lambda x.\lambda y.x\ y)} \rightarrow_\beta \underline{(\lambda x.\lambda y.x\ y)\ (\lambda x.\lambda y.x\ y)} \rightarrow_\beta \lambda y.(\lambda x.\lambda y.x\ y)\ y$
>
> Now conversion problems would arise if reduction would continue inside the body of the function.

So the evaluation has to be stopped as soon as the result is known to be a function. Starting from Miranda this is all right. In general, Miranda programs do not yield a function but a value of a basic type, e.g. a string. In the case that a function is yielded, the message <function> is printed and no further reduction to normal form takes place. So it is possible to proceed with reduction in the way that is described above. Below the formal foundation for this approach will be given.

An expression E in the pure λ-calculus is in **head normal form** if it is of the form $\lambda x_1.\lambda x_2. \ldots \lambda x_n.x\ E_1\ E_2 \ldots E_m$ with $x_1, x_2, \ldots x_n, x$ (not necessarily different) variables and $n, m \geq 0$. In that case x is the **head variable** of the expression E. If E is of the form $\lambda x_1.\lambda x_2. \ldots \lambda x_n. (\lambda x.E_0)\ E_1\ E_2 \ldots E_m$ with $n \geq 0$, $m \geq 1$, then $(\lambda x.E_0)\ E_1$ is called the **head redex** of E. An expression E in the pure λ-calculus is in **weak head normal form** if it is an expression of either the form $\lambda x.E$ or the form $x\ E_1\ E_2 \ldots E_m$ with $m \geq 0$. A head normal form is always a weak head normal form.

A head normal form does not contain a head redex. A λ-abstraction in weak head normal form may still contain a head redex in its body. So a (weak) head normal form does not have to be a normal form.

The notion of reduction in which reduction never takes place under an abstraction is called **weak reduction** (conversely, reduction under an abstraction is sometimes called **strong reduction**). When only weak reduction is performed, no α-conversion is needed if initially the free variables are chosen to be distinct from the bound variables. Since weak reduction cannot reduce under a λ-abstraction it generally cannot yield a head normal form but only a weak head normal form.

Abramsky's work on lazy λ-calculus formalizes the notion of lazy (leftmost) reduction to weak head normal form (Abramsky, 1990; Ong, 1988). Lazy reduction is a form of weak reduction, so in lazy λ-calculus no α-conversion is necessary.

3.8.3 Sharing of expressions to avoid duplication of work

Consider the following expression:

```
(λx.+ x x) heavy-computation
```

Assume that the evaluation of the argument involves many reductions. The following reduction steps are performed if the expression is evaluated in normal order:

```
(λx.+ x x) heavy-computation
→β  + heavy-computation heavy-computation
→*  + easy-number heavy-computation
→*  + easy-number easy-number
→δ+ twice-the-easy-number
```

The argument is substituted for each occurrence of the variable in the function body. But if such an argument is a complicated expression requiring many reductions then each additional substitution implies duplication of work. This is of course a terrible waste because the result of the computation will be the same for each occurrence. In the example above this problem can be solved by reducing the expression in applicative order.

```
(λx.+ x x) heavy-computation
→*  (λx.+ x x) easy-number
→β  + easy-number easy-number
→δ+ twice-the-easy-number
```

In general, it is much more efficient to reduce in applicative order instead of in normal order. But unfortunately, when reduction is performed in applicative order, termination is no longer guaranteed (see Section 3.3).

There are several solutions to retain the efficiency. One solution is to analyse the arguments of a function to determine whether or not they can be reduced in applicative order instead of in normal order. This is allowed if the termination behaviour compared with normal order reduction is not changed (see Chapter 7). If such arguments can be found a mixture of normal order and applicative order evaluation is obtained. The analysis to determine whether or not arguments can be evaluated in applicative order is known as *strictness analysis* (see Chapter 7).

The problem of the duplication of work can be partly solved by choosing a different representation for a λ-expression. A computer scientist would use pointers, i.e. use a *graph* representation instead of using *strings* or *trees*. However, this changes the reduction behaviour since several redexes are now contracted at once. So it is not sufficient just to use a different representation. The pure λ-calculus has to be extended with some notion of sharing of terms. The first proposal for using λ-calculus **graph reduction** instead of the ordinary **string reduction** is due to Wadsworth (1971). Graphically this sharing can be expressed as in Figure 3.6.

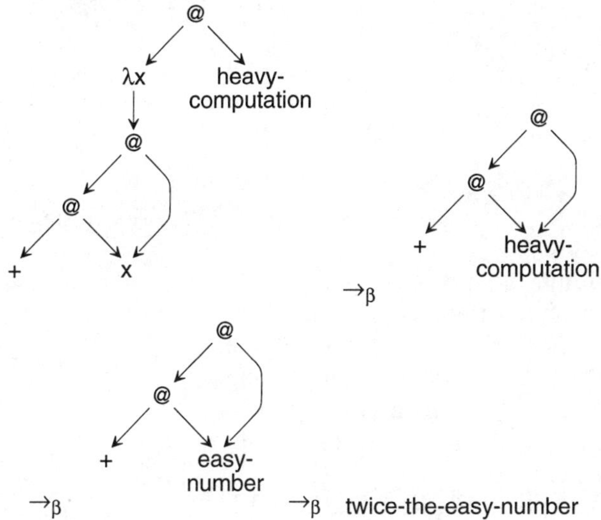

Figure 3.6 Sharing of λ-expressions to avoid duplication of work.

The following linear notation is chosen to indicate shared λ-expressions:

$\underline{(\lambda x.+ x\ x)\ S}$, where S ≡ heavy-computation
$\rightarrow_\beta$ + S S, where S ≡ $\underline{\text{heavy-computation}}$
$\rightarrow_*$ $\underline{+ S\ S}$, where S ≡ easy-number
$\rightarrow_{\delta+}$ twice-the-easy-number

Unfortunately, the sharing has to be broken if the shared expression is a function that is applied to different arguments (Figure 3.7).

For instance, consider the following expression:

S 3 (S 4), where S ≡ λx.+ x (Fac 1000)

If the argument 3 were to be substituted in the function S, this shared function would be corrupted. Consequently, the shared expression S has to be partially **deshared** (i.e. a copy is made of the shared structure) as shown in Figure 3.7.

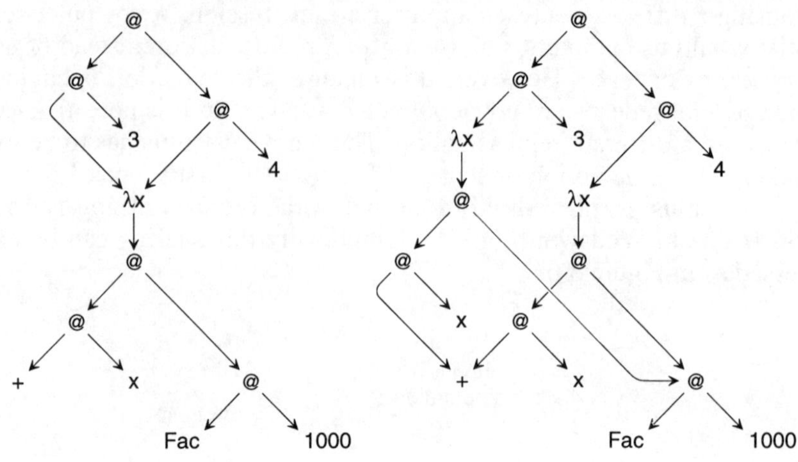

Figure 3.7 Desharing needed when the shared expression is a function.

To keep things sound, that part of the shared function has to be copied that is affected by a possible substitution of the variable. This process of partly desharing is also called **peeling off a copy** (Wadsworth, 1971). It increases the complexity of an implementation.

The example of Figure 3.8, due to J.J. Lévy, shows that, because of the forced copy action, duplication of work is sometimes hard to avoid. When the leftmost redex is reduced, there seems to be no way to deshare (parts of) the λf expression without introducing a copy of a λx-redex. This is due to the fact that when a copy is peeled off, a copy has to be made of all applications above the variable to be substituted up to the λ that binds it. So the application f 1 has to be copied but also the two applications above it including the λx redex.

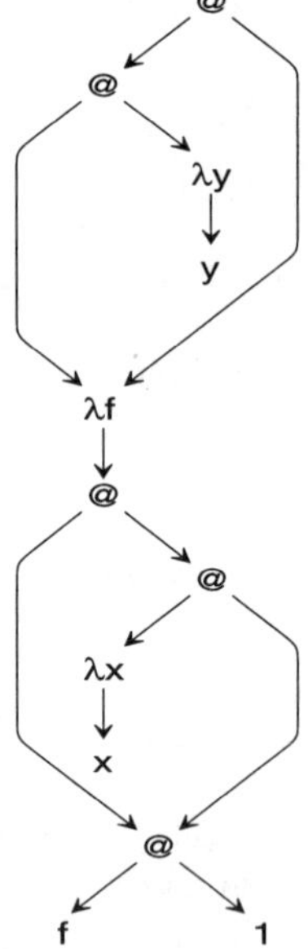

Figure 3.8 J.J. Lévy example.

The problem of avoiding duplication of work is called the optimality problem (Lévy, 1980). Recently, in Lamping (1990) an algorithm is given that solves the optimality problem. However, the algorithm is very complex. A lot of administration is needed to always avoid duplication of work. In practice, for most cases it may be more efficient to duplicate the work instead.

3.8.4 Implementations based on combinatory logic

The use of combinators has been studied very extensively in the context of implementing functional languages. Combinators do not suffer from the problems with copying shared subexpressions that are treated in the previous section. Expressions of these combinators do not contain variables. So if combinators are implemented as basic primitives, no administration for variables is needed at all.

David Turner was the first to introduce an implementation of a functional language using combinators as an intermediate language (Turner, 1979a). He used about 15 combinators including S, K, I, B and C named above and of course some δ-rules. This paper led to a lot of research on the question of which set of combinators was best for implementation purposes (e.g. super-combinators (Hughes, 1982) and categorical combinators (Curien, 1986)) and even to research on machine architectures based on such sets of combinators.

Striving for ultimate efficiency recent implementations tend to employ sharing not with a fixed set of combinators but with a dedicated set of combinator-like definitions (rewrite rules) that are deduced from the program. The next chapters cover the concepts of (graph) rewrite rules of which combinators are treated as a special case.

3.8.5 Translating evaluation orders

In the translation schemes given in Section 3.7 the evaluation order was not taken into account. Actually, when λ-terms were reduced in the examples, normal order evaluation was used. This is not remarkable since Miranda is a lazy language. *Lazy evaluation* corresponds with *normal order reduction* in the λ-calculus, whereas *eager evaluation* corresponds to *applicative order reduction*. Lazy languages can handle infinite lists as long as the evaluation of the last element is not being asked for. This corresponds with normal order reduction that will find the normal form if it exists.

Languages can also be characterized by the way parameters are passed, the **calling mechanisms**. *Call-by-value* implies *applicative order reduction*, *call-by-name* corresponds with *normal order reduction*; and *call-by-need* corresponds to *normal order reduction* in a context in which the arguments are *shared* such that they are evaluated only once.

Summary

- The *λ-calculus* can be considered to be the computational basis of all functional languages.

- In the λ-calculus *anonymous functions* are defined.
- *Reduction rules* translate λ-expressions into equivalent ones.
- The most important reduction rule is *β-reduction* that defines how a function applied to an argument is evaluated by applying *textual substitution.*
- With *α-conversion* bound variables can be renamed.
- In general α-conversion is needed when doing β-reduction.
- α-conversion can be avoided when only *weak reduction* is done.
- *Lazy evaluation* in functional languages corresponds to *normal order reduction* in the λ-calculus.
- *Eager evaluation* in functional languages corresponds to *applicative order reduction* in the λ-calculus.
- Theoretical and practical properties of functional languages can be derived directly from the λ-calculus:
  - all effectively computable functions can be defined;
  - normal forms are unique;
  - not every expression has a normal form;
  - lazy evaluation is normalizing;
  - with lazy evaluation work can be duplicated while eager evaluation avoids duplication of work;
  - eager evaluation is not normalizing.
- The λ-calculus is not very well suited as a basis for efficient implementation for the following reasons:
  - full sharing of expressions is difficult to maintain;
  - testing on syntactic equality is not possible in the pure λ-calculus. The extension of the calculus with Church's δ-rule is rather artificial. For reasoning about implementations of functional languages it seems to be a better approach to start with a computational model in which syntactical tests (pattern matching) are inherently present (see the next chapter).

EXERCISES

3.1 Make tree-representations of the following λ-expressions:

(a) (λx.λy. x+y) ((λx. y) 1) ((λy.λz. x z) ((λx. 2*x) z) 5)
(b) FAC y

where FAC is the abbreviation of the λ-expression for the factorial function given in Section 3.7.3.

Mark the free variables and the leftmost-outermost, leftmost-innermost, rightmost-outermost and rightmost-innermost redexes.

3.2 Consider the λ-expression λx.x ((λx.λy.x y) y) x. Give its tree representation. Reduce the expression normal order to weak head normal form and to normal form.

3.3 Reduce the following expressions in normal order, once using the λ-bar operator and once using the numbers of De Bruin.

(a) λx.((λx.λy.y z x) y x)
(b)* (λf.λx. f(f x)) x) ((λf.λx. f(f x)) x)

3.4 Show that $A_{exp}\ c_n\ c_m$ ->* $c_{(n^m)}$, except for m = 0, where c_n and c_m are the Church numerals and A_{exp} = λx.λy.y x.

3.5 Define λ-expressions AND, OR and NOT with standard semantics.

3.6 Represent the following expression by a graph, and so build a tree but share (sub)expressions where possible.

(+) (F (F 3)) (F 300)   where F = λx. * (Fib 10) x

Fib represents the Fibonacci function. Show with the help of the graph what happens when the following redexes will be β-reduced:

(a) (+) (F (F 3)) (F 300)
(b) (+) (F (G)) (F 300) where G stands for result of previous reduction
(c) (+) (H) (F 300) where H stands for result of previous reduction

3.7* Write a reducer for λ-expressions in Miranda. This function should reduce a λ-expression to normal form using normal order reduction. The program should accept a list of characters as input and deliver the reduced λ-expression again as a list of characters. Take as internal data structures to represent λ-expressions:

```
lcalc   ::=  AP lcalc lcalc | ABS var lcalc | VAR var | CONST const
var     ==   [ char ]
const   ==   [ char ]
```

Furthermore, define a *parser* function to parse the input string to this data structure lcalc, a *reducer* (of type reduce:: lcalc -> lcalc) and a *display function* that converts the data structure back to a list of chars. Make sure that your reducer does α-conversion when necessary (this is probably the most difficult part of this exercise).

Chapter 4
Term rewriting systems

Term rewriting systems (TRSs) form an important computational paradigm for which applications are found in several fields, including formal software specification, analysis of algebraic specifications, design and implementation of functional languages, computing by means of equations and mechanizing deduction systems. Surveys of theory of TRSs are given in Huet and Oppen (1980) and Klop (1992).

A TRS consists of a collection of rewrite rules. Rewrite rules have many similarities with function definitions in a functional language but it is only possible to define rules on one global level. The rules in a TRS are used to rewrite a given term in the same way as function definitions in a functional language are used to evaluate a given initial expression. In TRSs tests on syntactic equality (using pattern matching) form a key concept in the semantics of reduction. The left-hand side of a rewrite rule consists of a pattern that determines whether or not the rule can be applied to rewrite a (sub)term.

One can regard TRSs as the extension of combinatory logic with pattern matching. TRSs are also related to the λ-calculus. The descriptive power of TRSs is greater than of these systems, e.g. non-determinism can be expressed in a TRS but not in λ-calculus nor in combinatory logic. TRSs are a subset of *Graph rewriting systems* (GRSs) which will be explained in the next chapter. A good understanding of TRSs is a prerequisite for a good understanding of GRSs.

An important difference between TRSs and functional languages is that in the basic semantics of TRSs there is no ordering in the rewrite rules (all rules have equal priority) and furthermore no strategy is predefined that prescribes in which order redexes in the term are rewritten. So in a certain sense one can say that TRSs are 'more declarative' than functional languages. They just contain a collection of rules that can be applied to a given term. No reduction order is specified explicitly that determines how a given term has to be evaluated.

The bad news is that in contrast with the λ-calculus, there does not exist a decidable normalizing strategy for a general TRS (see Section 4.5). Since the basic semantics of TRSs is quite simple (Sections 4.1, 4.2 and 4.3), the emphasis of this chapter lies in a quest for an efficiently implementable, intuitively clear, reduction strategy that is normalizing for a large class of TRSs. One of the problems encountered in this quest is caused by the possibility of defining ambiguous rules (partly due to the fact that all rewrite rules have equal priority in the basic semantics). On one hand this has the advantage that TRSs allow the expression of non-deterministic computations. But on the other hand this has the disadvantage that (of course) the uniqueness of normal forms is no longer guaranteed (Section 4.4). With certain restrictions imposed on TRSs (*orthogonal* TRSs, see Sections 4.4 and 4.6), uniqueness of normal forms can be guaranteed. Also, there exists a normalizing strategy (*parallel outermost*) for such orthogonal systems. Unfortunately, this normalizing strategy is certainly not efficiently implementable. Efficiently implementable normalizing strategies are possible, but they will only work for certain subclasses of orthogonal TRSs. Furthermore, it is not always intuitively clear how these strategies proceed nor for which subclass they can or cannot be applied (see Section 4.6).

It appeals to the intuition to take priority of rules into account. The basic problems encountered in a TRS with standard semantics also appear in TRSs extended with a functional language-like priority in their rules (Section 4.7). Forcing evaluation of arguments to tell whether or not they match a corresponding pattern in a rule definition now seems to be the only sensible thing to do. The disadvantage of forcing evaluation is that infinite computations can occur, even if a normal form exists according to the priority semantics. As a special case of this general approach of forcing evaluation the *functional strategy* is presented. When reduced with the functional strategy *priority rewrite systems* (PRSs) capture priority of rules similar to a functional language.

A functional language is easily translated to various subclasses of TRSs (Section 4.8). Implementations of functional languages are usually more close to term rewriting systems than to the λ-calculus. An implementation based on TRSs causes fewer problems than an implementation based on the λ-calculus. Efficient implementations of functional language-like PRSs can be obtained (Section 4.9). If graphs are used instead of terms even state-of-the-art efficiency is possible (see Part 4).

4.1 TRSs

Term rewriting systems consist of a collection of *rewrite rules*. These rewrite rules specify how a given *term* can be translated (*reduced*, *rewritten*) to another term.

4.1.1 Terms

A collection of **terms** over a set of *constant symbols* and a set of *variables* is defined by the following syntactic definition (the curly braces specify *zero or more* occurrences of the enclosed objects):

```
Term    = Variable    |  Constant   |   '(' Constant {Term} ')' ;
```

Variables always begin with a lower case character; constant symbols with an upper case character or some special character (a digit, an asterisk etc.). The outermost brackets of a term are usually omitted. The (zero or more) terms following a constant are called the **arguments** of the constant. The fixed **arity** of an occurrence of a particular constant is equal to its number of arguments. A term that does not contain any variables is called a **closed term**, otherwise it is an **open term.**

Examples of terms:

x	Reverse (Cons 2 Nil)
1000	Select 3 (Array 1 2 3 4 5 6)
Fac x	Sqrt (– (* b b) (* 4 (* a c)))
Fac 1000	Ap (Ap x z) (Ap y z)

A non-example:

```
x z (y z)
```

A term τ' is a **subterm** of a term τ iff (i.e. if and only if) τ' is contained in τ and τ' is a term in the syntactic construction of τ. A subterm τ' of τ is a **proper subterm** if τ' and τ are not the same. Subterms do differ from subexpressions in Miranda and in the λ-calculus. This is due to the absence of implicit application. Implicit application would allow any two expressions to be put together by juxtaposition to form a new expression. With explicit application one has to specify a function that defines application (see Section 4.1.4).

Subterms of the term Ap (Ap x K) K are (see Figure 4.1):

Ap (Ap x K) K	x
Ap x K	K (occurs twice)

The following are *not* subterms of the term Ap (Ap x K) K:

Ap	x K
Ap (Ap x K)	(Ap x K) K
Ap x	

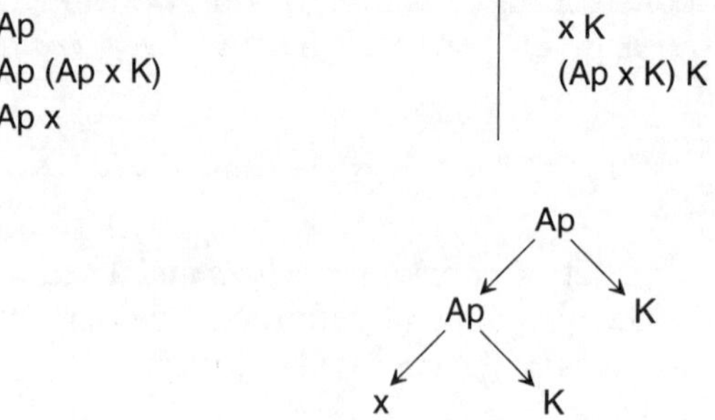

Figure 4.1 Tree representation (see Section 4.1.2) of Ap (Ap x K) K.

4.1.2 Representing terms as trees

A term can be represented as a tree (Figure 4.2).

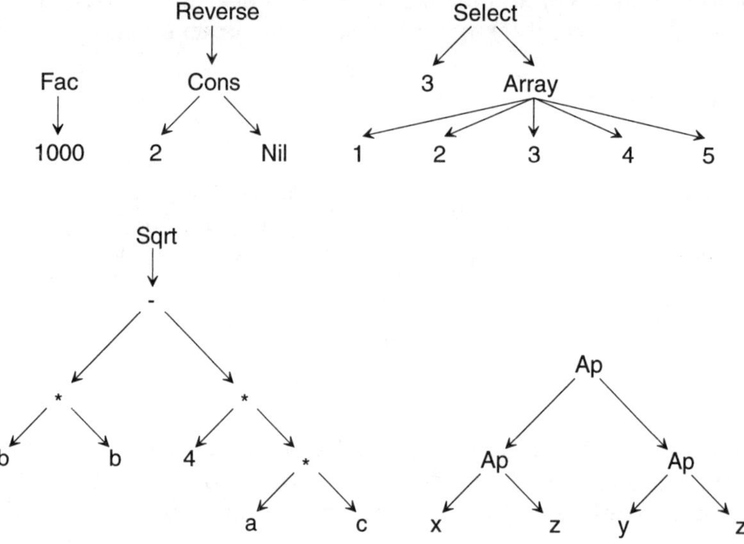

Figure 4.2 Tree representation of the term Fac 1000, Reverse (Cons 2 Nil), Select 3 (Array 1 2 3 4 5 6), Sqrt (– (* b b) (* 4 (* a c))), Ap (Ap x z) (Ap y z).

This tree representation makes the structure of a term clearer in most cases. A constant symbol is represented by a node labelled with that constant. A directed arc is drawn to each argument of a constant. Hence, the arity of a constant determines the number of outgoing arcs from the corresponding node. A subtree of a tree consists of a node with all nodes that are reachable (following the arcs) from that node. Any subtree represents a subterm.

4.1.3 Term rewriting systems

A **term rewriting system** (TRS) is a collection of **rewrite rules** $\alpha_i \rightarrow \beta_i$ over sets of constants and variables, where α_i, β_i are terms, such that all variables in β_i also occur in α_i and none of the α_i is a term consisting of a single variable.

Example of a TRS:

```
Fac 0           →   1
Fac n           →   * n (Fac (– n 1))

Cond True x y   →   x
Cond False x y  →   y
```

Non examples:

```
x           →   1

Illegal x   →   y
```

Syntax of TRSs

```
TRS               =  {TRS-Rule} ;
TRS-Rule          =  Left-Hand-Side '→' Right-Hand-Side ;
Left-Hand-Side    =  Constant {Term} ;
Right-Hand-Side   =  Term ;
```

The constants used in a TRS are divided in two classes. All constant symbols in a TRS that appear as the leftmost constant on the left-hand side of a rule are called **(recursive) functions**. The corresponding rule is then called **a rule for** the function and the corresponding occurrence of the symbol is called a **defining occurrence** of the symbol. All other constants are called **constructors**. The term on the left-hand side is called a **pattern**. A subterm of a left-hand side is called a **(sub)pattern**.

4.1.4 Notation used in this book

The notation for TRSs used in this textbook is a variant of the *functional style*. We use an alternative bracketing, resulting in a LISP-like notation. In the literature this notation is very unusual. Either an *applicative style* (like in Miranda, with implicit application functions) or a *functional style* is used. In a **functional style** application is written down *ex-*

plicitly as a function (say the function Ap which, of course, stands for Application). However, traditionally, in a functional style the arguments of functions and constructors are placed between brackets and separated by commas.

Example of the notation used in this book (the combinatory logic example; see also Section 3.6.1):

```
Ap (Ap (Ap S x) y) z   →   Ap (Ap x z) (Ap y z)
Ap (Ap K x) y          →   x
```

The SK example in the traditional functional notation (compare this with our notation in the example above):

```
Ap (Ap (Ap (S, x), y), z)   →   Ap (Ap (x, z), Ap (y, z))
Ap (Ap (K, x), y)           →   x
```

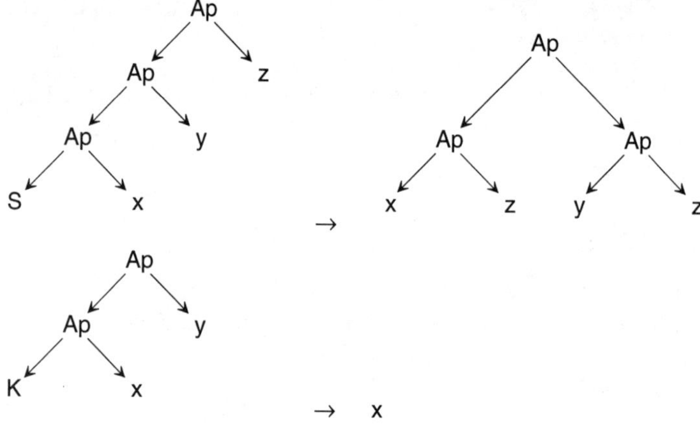

Figure 4.3 Tree representation of SK rules in (alternative) functional style.

When the rewrite rules of a TRS are represented graphically (see Figure 4.3) using the tree notation for terms, it is immediately clear that the difference in both notations is a matter of syntax only.

In a TRS using an **applicative style** function applications are *implicit*. The applicative style is commonly used when application is the only actual function that is being used and all other symbols have arity zero (Figure 4.4). When application is the only function, it can be left out in the notation and juxtaposition can stand for application.

In this textbook we generally want to consider also other functions than apply (Ap) but we do not like to write down too many brackets. Therefore we have chosen a functional style with a LISP-like bracketing. We will use this notation throughout this textbook.

The SK example in the applicative notation:

```
S x y z    →    x z (y z)
K x y      →    x
```

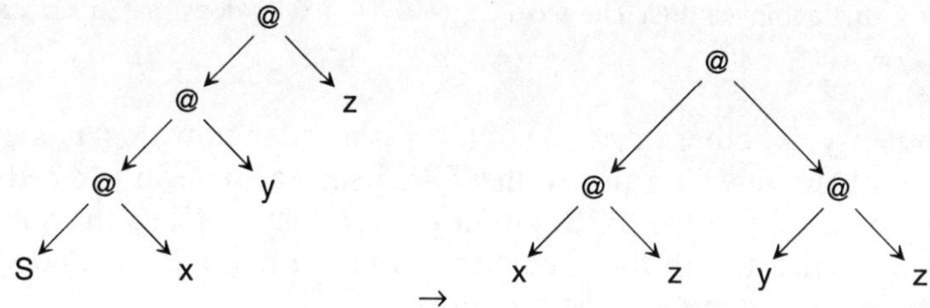

Figure 4.4 Tree representation of a TRS with implicit application functions (indicated by @ labels).

4.2 Rewriting with a TRS

A TRS can be used to rewrite a given *closed* term τ, which consists of constants only. This closed term can be compared with the initial expression to be evaluated in Miranda.

4.2.1 Redexes

A (sub)term is a redex iff there is a left-hand side of a rule (a pattern) that matches this term. A left-hand side matches a (sub)term if this term is syntactically equal with respect to all constants in the pattern.

More formally: a **redex** of a closed term τ is a subterm τ' that is syntactically equal to an *instance* of a left-hand side α_i of a rule of the TRS. An **instance** of a term α_i is a term $\sigma(\alpha_i)$ where σ is a substitution of closed terms for all variables in α_i. One also says: τ' **matches** α_i. By σ every variable of a left-hand side is bound to a subterm of the redex.

Example of pattern matching; consider again:

```
Ap (Ap (Ap S x) y) z    →    Ap (Ap x z) (Ap y z)
Ap (Ap K x) y           →    x
```

and the term

```
Ap (Ap K K) (Ap S K)
```

This term matches the pattern Ap (Ap K x) y. The corresponding substitution is σ(x) = K, σ(y) = Ap S K, yielding σ(Ap (Ap K x) y) = Ap (Ap K K) (Ap S K).

Consider the following TRS:

Eq x x → True

The term Eq (+ 0 1) 1 does *not* match Eq x x. There is simply no substitution for x that achieves this. The term Eq (+ 0 1) (+ 0 1) does match Eq x x with σ(x) = + 0 1.

Consequently, whether or not a subterm is a redex now depends on the *structure* of the rewrite rules in the TRS itself: a subterm is a redex iff there exists a rule in the TRS with a pattern that matches the subterm. This is in contrast with the λ-calculus where a redex is created whenever a function is applied to an argument.

4.2.2 Rewriting a term

A **rewrite** (or **reduction**) of a term τ is the replacement of a redex of τ, say τ', by the right-hand side of the rule using the substitution function of the corresponding match: σ. The redex τ', which is equal to $\sigma(\alpha_i)$, is replaced by $\sigma(\beta_i)$: the right-hand side in which the substitution function is applied on the variables (by σ every variable is bound to a subterm of the redex).

Consider the TRS

Hd (Cons a b) → a

The term Hd (Hd (Cons (Cons 0 Nil) Nil)) can be rewritten as follows using the only rewrite rule in the TRS:

Hd (<u>Hd (Cons (Cons 0 Nil) Nil)</u>)	‖ σ(a) = Cons 0 Nil,	σ(b) = Nil
$\rightarrow_{Hd}$ <u>Hd (Cons 0 Nil)</u>	‖ σ(a) = 0,	σ(b) = Nil
$\rightarrow_{Hd}$ 0		

where the subscript Hd on the arrow indicates that the rule for Hd is used.

This rewriting of terms is the TRS equivalent of β-reduction in the λ-calculus. The main difference is that a λ-expression like (λx.M) N is always a redex and that it binds exactly one variable. For TRSs it depends on the set of rules in a concrete TRS whether a (sub)term is a redex or not. Furthermore, in TRSs functions can be specified with more than one argument. These rules can only be applied if *all* the arguments are present and match the pattern. Therefore, no currying is needed to simulate functions with more than one argument.

Example of functions with more than one argument:

```
G x y    →   x
H x y z  →   G z x
```

The term G 2 3 $\rightarrow_G$ 2, but the term G 2 will not be reduced: it is not a redex because it has only one argument and not two.

Name conflicts, as they occurred in the λ-calculus, cannot arise in TRSs. The initial term is a closed term and free variables cannot be introduced in the rewrite rules. So the term that is rewritten will never contain variables, therefore no name conflicts occur.

4.2.3 δ-rules

As in the λ-calculus there can exist externally defined functions and constants. Such an externally defined function is called a **δ-rule** or a **δ-function**. If a δ-function is applied to the number of arguments it needs, the corresponding subexpression is called a **δ-redex**. If the external function is applied it is called a **δ-reduction step.** Although it is possible to define rewrite rules with the same behaviour directly in TRSs, it is sometimes more convenient for readability and illustration purposes to assume the availability of these external functions.

Example of a δ-reduction step, assuming that + is an externally defined δ-rule and 2 and 3 are externally defined constants:

$\underline{+\ 2\ 3}$ $\rightarrow_{\delta+}$ 5

An external function like + requires that its arguments are indeed constants of a specific type, in this case the arguments should be constant numbers. If this is not the case, the corresponding subexpression is not a δ-redex until this restriction is satisfied. This implies that one first has to reduce the arguments of + before this δ-rule can be applied.

4.3 Reduction sequences and normal forms

One reduction is often called a **reduction step** (or **rewrite step**). A **reduction sequence** (or **rewrite sequence**) of a term is a sequence of zero or more reduction steps (or rewrites) performed on that term. If term τ_1 can be reduced by a sequence of reductions to expression τ_2, τ_2 is called a **reduct** of τ_1. This is denoted as $\tau_1 \rightarrow^* \tau_2$. So $\rightarrow^*$ is the reflexive transitive closure of $\rightarrow$.

Given a TRS, a term is in **normal form** if no rule in the TRS matches the term or one of its subterms. Note that whether or not a term is in normal form depends on the concrete TRS. Given a TRS, a term has a normal form if there exists some sequence of reduction steps that results in a term in normal form.

A term is in **head normal form** if the term as a whole is not a redex and the term as a whole will never become a redex. Such a term need not be in normal form since it may contain subterms that are redexes. Whether or not a term as a whole will ever become a redex is in general undecidable, so it is also undecidable whether a term is in head normal form. In many cases, however, the head normal form property is decidable, e.g. when the term begins with a constructor it is trivially in head normal form.

Examples of head normal forms; take the following rules:

```
H (Cons a b) 0   →   a
H Nil 1          →   Nil
```

Cons (H Nil 1) 1 is clearly in head normal form because the head of the term is a constructor

H (H Nil 1) 0 is in head normal form although the head is a function and the second argument matches. However, the first argument is a redex that reduces to Nil

H (H Nil 1) 1 is not in head normal form

Since the head normal form property is in general undecidable, the following notion is used to define a decidable approximation. A **rule partially matches** a term if its pattern partially matches the term. A **pattern α_i partially matches** a term τ if firstly the first constant of α_i equals the first constant of τ and secondly for each argument τ' of the first constant of τ corresponding to a non-variable argument α_i' of the first constant of α_i, α_i' also partially matches τ' or there exists a rule with a pattern partially matching τ'. Intuitively, a rule partially matches a term if by just looking at the left-hand sides the rule might after some reductions match the term. In Klop (1992), a term for which there exists a partially matching rule is called a **soft term**.

Illustrating the definition of a partial match:

```
H (Cons a b) 0   →   a
H Nil 1          →   Nil
```

H Nil 0 there is no rule with a pattern partially matching this term

H (H Nil 1) 0 partial match for the first rule of H; H Nil 1 is a redex

H (H (H Nil 1) 0) 0 partial match for the first rule of H; H (H Nil 1) 0 itself partially matches the first rule of H

A term is in **strong head normal form** if none of the rules partially matches this term. It is decidable whether or not a term is in strong head normal form. A term in strong head normal form does not partially match any rule so it is also in head normal form. A term in head normal form need not be in strong head normal form (see the examples above).

It is important to note that because of the rewrite semantics of TRSs there is a difference between TRSs and functional languages with respect to normal forms for the case of partial functions:

Difference between functional languages and rewriting system for a partial function:

```
F 1  →  2
F 2  →  3
```

Suppose the term to be reduced is F 3: in a functional language this would result in an error because it does not match any of the rules; in a rewriting system it is just not rewritten because it does not match, and the normal form is then simply F 3.

A function that is applied with a number of arguments that does not correspond to the number of arguments specified on a left-hand side, will never be a redex. This is why one can consider occurrences of constants with different numbers of arguments as different constants. This has no influence on the semantics.

4.4 Properties of TRSs

In this section some properties of TRSs are considered that are independent of the specific term one wants to rewrite and independent of the specific reduction strategy (see Section 4.5) that is used.

4.4.1 Ambiguity

The patterns specified in a TRS determine whether or not a (sub)term is a redex. However, it is possible that a term matches several left-hand sides of the rewrite rules of the TRS. In that case there are several alternative rewrite rules by which the term can be rewritten. A TRS is **ambiguous** iff it contains rules of one of the following types:

- **non-deterministic** rules, i.e. their left-hand sides are totally overlapping;
- **partially ambiguous** rules, i.e. their left-hand sides are partially overlapping.

Two left-hand sides of two *different* rules are **totally overlapping** if a term exists that is an instance of both left-hand sides. Two left-hand sides α_1 and α_2 of two (not necessarily different) rules are **partially overlapping** if a term exists that is an instance of α_1 and that is also an instance of a non-variable, *proper* subterm of α_2. Two such (partially) overlapping left-hand sides are also called a **critical pair**. Depending on the right-hand sides the existence of a critical pair can invalidate uniqueness of normal forms.

Example of non-deterministic rules:

```
Choose x y   →   x
Choose x y   →   y
```

Given this TRS, the term Choose 1 2 can be reduced to either 1 or to 2: there is no unique normal form.

The following very familiar looking set of definitions forms a TRS that is non-deterministic. The term Fac 0 matches both left-hand sides. Unlike function definitions in Miranda, in ordinary TRSs all rules have equal priority. Choosing the wrong rule will lead to unexpected and unwanted results.

```
Fac 0   →   1
Fac n   →   * n (Fac (– n 1))
```

Example of partial ambiguity:

```
G ( K n 1 ) →   1
K x y       →   x
```

Given this TRS, the term K 0 1 is a redex and an instance of the subterm K n 1 in G (K n 1). The term G (K 0 1) can be reduced to either 1 or to G 0.

A more subtle example of a partial ambiguous TRS:

```
F ( F x )   →   A
```

This TRS is ambiguous with itself. The term F (F 1) is a redex and an instance of the subterm F x in F (F x). Given this TRS the following term can be reduced as follows:

F (<u>F (F 1)</u>) $\to_F$ F A | <u>F (F (F 1))</u> $\to_F$ A

So the term F (F (F 1)) has two different normal forms in this TRS.

4.4.2 Comparing

A TRS is **comparing** iff one or more left-hand sides of the rules of the TRS is **comparing**, i.e. it contains a multiple occurrence of the same variable, such as

```
Eq x x  →   True
```

A comparing rule is also called **non-left-linear** because of the correspondence with multiple occurrences of variables in multiplicative terms of polynomial expressions.

Restricting a TRS to be non-comparing is natural. A rewrite rule using a left-hand side that contains a multiple occurrence of the same variable induces a test on *syntactic* equality of the corresponding arguments of the term. However, it is possible that the arguments are *semantically* equal but syntactically not. In general, it is undecidable whether two terms are semantically equal. Comparing is therefore only sound if the two terms are in normal form, i.e. they do not contain any redexes (this is similar to Church's δ, see Section 3.7.6). In that case terms that are semantically the same are also syntactically equal, because the only semantics is the rewriting semantics.

In the term below the arguments are not always syntactically equal. If they are in normal form, then syntactic equality implies semantic equality.

Eq (+ 1 1) (+ 1 1) $\rightarrow_{\delta+}$ Eq 2 (+ 1 1) $\rightarrow_{\delta+}$ Eq 2 2 $\rightarrow_{Eq}$ True

4.4.3 Confluency

A TRS is **confluent** (or has the **Church–Rosser property**) iff for every two (divergent) reduction sequences $\tau \rightarrow_* \tau_1$ and $\tau \rightarrow_* \tau_2$ there is a τ_3 such that there are two (convergent) reduction sequences $\tau_1 \rightarrow_* \tau_3$ and $\tau_2 \rightarrow_* \tau_3$ (see also Section 3.4). The Church–Rosser property implies the *unique normal form property*. As in the λ-calculus, this does not imply that every term has a normal form. It states only that *if* there is a normal form, it is a unique one.

Not every term has a normal form in a confluent TRS:

```
F x  →   G x
G x  →   F x
H 0  →   1
```

This TRS is confluent. H 0 has as normal form 1, However, the term F 1 does not have a normal form.

But, in contrast with the λ-calculus, a TRS is in general *not* confluent.

The examples in the previous section show that ambiguity can interfere with confluency. However, ambiguity does not necessarily lead to non-confluency in all cases. Furthermore, comparing can also be a source of non-confluency. The following examples clarify this.

Ambiguity versus confluency:

- a non-ambiguous and confluent TRS:

```
K x y   →   x
```

- 'parallel OR', an ambiguous but confluent TRS:

```
Or   True    x       →   True
Or   x       True    →   True
Or   False   False   →   False
```

- an ambiguous and non-confluent TRS:

```
F 0   →   0
F x   →   1
```

The following marvellous example is due to J.W. Klop. It shows that comparing is also a source of non-confluency. This is caused by the fact that the terms that are compared need not be in normal form.

- a non-ambiguous and non-confluent TRS (Klop's example):

```
D x x   →   E
C x     →   D x (C x)
A       →   C A
```

Explanation: the term C A can be reduced in the following ways:

C A	C A
$\rightarrow_C$ D A (C A)	$\rightarrow_A$ C (C A)
$\rightarrow_A$ D (C A) (C A)	$\rightarrow_C$ C (D A (C A))
$\rightarrow_D$ E	$\rightarrow_A$ C (D (C A) (C A))
	$\rightarrow_D$ C E
	$\rightarrow_C$ D E (C E)

The term D E (C E) cannot be reduced to E any more. Note that just before the D-reductions are done the terms can still be reduced to a common reduct. Further note that the arguments of D are not in normal form when the D-rule is applied.

Orthogonal TRSs

A TRS is **orthogonal** iff it is non-ambiguous and non-comparing.

Theorem (Klop, 1992): Every orthogonal TRS is confluent.

Hence, in an orthogonal TRS a unique normal form is guaranteed. As in the λ-calculus it depends on the chosen reduction order whether or not the reduction process will find the normal form (if it exists). In Section 4.6 a normalizing strategy for orthogonal TRSs is presented.

4.5 Reduction strategies

A **reduction strategy** is a function that, given a TRS and a term, prescribes which redexes in the term have to be rewritten next. It also prescribes for each redex, if there is more than one matching rule, which one of these rules has to be applied. It is possible that the strategy function prescribes more than one redex to be reduced next in arbitrary order. Such a strategy is called a **parallel reduction strategy**. It is also possible that the strategy function returns more than one redex or rule to choose from. In that case the strategy function is called **non-deterministic**. Note that for the λ-calculus we only considered non-parallel and deterministic strategies. In TRSs parallel and non-deterministic strategies play a more important role than in the λ-calculus.

Without knowing the reduction strategy it is in general impossible to reason about the actual evaluation of terms in a TRS: a TRS with a term specifies many possible computations. When the reduction strategy is known, a term with a TRS fully specifies the computation and then it is possible to reason about properties of this computation.

A **reducer** is a process that consecutively reduces the redexes that are indicated by some strategy. The result of a reducer is reached as soon as the reduction strategy does not indicate any more redexes. A reduction strategy is **normalizing** iff for any term, having a normal form, the reducer applying the strategy will terminate at a normal form. **Parallel reducers** are assumed to reduce the redexes indicated by a parallel reduction strategy in parallel, i.e. in arbitrary order. **Non-deterministic reducers** should choose non-deterministically one of the redexes offered by a non-deterministic strategy.

If the intention of non-deterministic rules is indeed to make a non-deterministic choice between the overlapping rules, a non-deterministic reduction strategy must be used. Such a strategy will yield both rules as candidate to rewrite a matching redex. A non-deterministic reducer will arbitrarily choose one of these rules.

The reduct depends on the chosen rewrite rule (the first or the second rule for Choose):

```
Choose x y   →   x
Choose x y   →   y
```

Choose 1 2 $\rightarrow_{\text{Choose}_1}$ 1 | Choose 1 2 $\rightarrow_{\text{Choose}_2}$ 2

Of course it is possible to define an algorithm that finds the normal form for all TRSs: just produce breadth-first the reduction tree of a term with all possible reductions. If a normal form exists it will certainly be found and then the algorithm can stop. This is not a very efficient algorithm. The algorithm is not a strategy since the algorithm does not just indicate which redexes are to be reduced next possibly in parallel, but indicates which possible reducts have to be investigated and remembered. In the following we shall only investigate proper strategies.

A redex in a term is **needed** iff for all possible reduction sequences of this term ending at a normal form this redex (or if it is copied by a rule, one of these copies) must have been reduced. In confluent TRSs a reduction strategy is trivially normalizing if it chooses needed redexes only.

Needed redex: consider the following (part of a) TRS:

```
If True x y    →   x
If False x y   →   y
```

Consider the term If (= 0 0) (+ 1 1) (+ 2 2) (assume that the TRS has rules for + and =). Then it contains three redexes, namely (= 0 0), (+ 1 1) and (+ 2 2). Enumerating all possible reduction sequences shows that (= 0 0) and (+ 1 1) are needed redexes and (+ 2 2) is not.

Whether or not a redex is needed is in general undecidable. It is even undecidable for orthogonal TRSs. So always choosing the needed redexes is not a practical strategy for orthogonal TRSs or indeed for confluent TRSs in general. However, for (subclasses of) orthogonal TRSs it is possible to define decidable strategies that are normalizing for that class. Sometimes it is even possible to define for a certain subclass a decidable normalizing strategy that only reduces needed redexes.

4.6 Orthogonal TRSs

Orthogonal TRSs are confluent (see Section 4.4.3). In this section various *rule-based* and *non-rule-based* reduction strategies are investigated. There is a normalizing strategy for orthogonal TRSs (parallel outermost), but this strategy is not efficient: generally too many redexes are indicated. There are other more efficient strategies, but they are only normalizing for certain subclasses of orthogonal TRSs.

4.6.1 Classes with non-rule-based normalizing strategies

In a **non-rule-based strategy** the decision of which redex to reduce depends only on the position of the redex in the term.

Given the following rule:

F x y → 1

and the following term (Figure 4.5): Triple (F 0 (F 1 2)) (F (F 3 4) 5) (F 6 7)

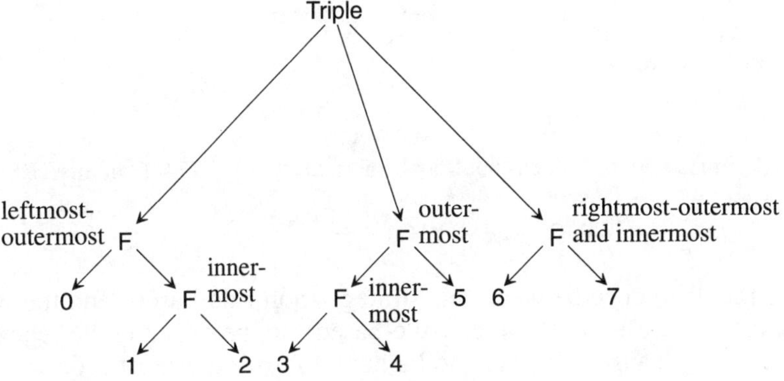

Figure 4.5 Leftmost, rightmost, outermost and innermost redexes in the tree of the term Triple (F 0 (F 1 2)) (F (F 3 4) 5) (F 6 7).

Definitions of *leftmost*, *rightmost*, *innermost*, *outermost redexes* and *strategies* are similar to the definitions for the λ-calculus (see Chapter 3). For TRSs *parallel* versions of innermost and outermost strategies are also considered.

Innermost strategy

Innermost strategies are not normalizing for arbitrary orthogonal TRSs.

An orthogonal TRS for which innermost strategies are not normalizing:

K x → 0
W → W

Using an innermost strategy the reduction process starting with the term K W will not terminate. On the other hand, using the leftmost-outermost strategy the reduction process starting with K W will terminate with the normal form 0.

Innermost strategies are normalizing for those confluent TRSs for which infinite reduction sequences do not exist, called **strongly normalizing TRSs**. Innermost strategies correspond with eager evaluation in functional languages. So innermost strategies rule out concepts similar to lazy evaluation.

Leftmost-outermost strategy

The leftmost-outermost strategy chooses the leftmost of the outermost redexes. In the λ-calculus the leftmost-outermost reduction strategy is normalizing, but even for orthogonal TRSs this is not true.

An orthogonal TRS for which a leftmost-outermost reducer is not normalizing:

```
F x 0   →   1
G       →   0
W       →   W
```

Leftmost-outermost does not find the normal form 1 of F W G in this TRS:

F $\underline{\text{W}}$ G $\rightarrow_{\text{W}}$ F $\underline{\text{W}}$ G $\rightarrow_{\text{W}}$ F $\underline{\text{W}}$ G $\rightarrow_{\text{W}}$ ...

Note the difference between this strategy (non-rule-based) and the way redexes are chosen in Miranda (rule-based). In the example the redex W is reduced because it happens to be the leftmost-outermost redex in the term to be reduced. But from the pattern of the rewrite rule for F it can be deduced that the evaluation of this argument was not needed.

Left-normal TRSs

An orthogonal TRS is called **left-normal** if in no left-hand side a variable occurs before a constant.

Example of a left-normal system:

```
Hd (Cons a b) →   a
```

Not a left-normal system:

```
F (Cons a b) (Cons c d) →   0
```

The variable a on the left occurs before the second Cons.

In left-normal systems the leftmost-outermost redex is always needed. So leftmost-outermost is normalizing for left-normal systems.

The restriction that in a pattern no variable occurs before a constant is a serious restriction. It implies that many patterns are not allowed. Still, the expressive power of such systems is very high. For instance, every combinatorial system (see below) is left-normal.

Combinatorial TRSs

A subclass of left-normal systems is the class of **combinatorial systems** (see also Section 3.6.1). Rules in combinatorial systems all have the following form:

Combinatorial systems, general form:

Ap (Ap... (Ap C x_1)... x_{n-1}) x_n → *A term with only Aps and variables*

Such a rule defines the *combinator* C. These combinators are equivalent to those defined in the λ-calculus in the previous chapter:

Equivalent definition to the one above:

C ≡ $\lambda x_1. \dots \lambda x_{n-1}.\lambda x_n$.*term with juxtaposition instead of Aps*

Consider the following λ-calculus combinators:

```
S  ≡  λx.λy.λz. x z (y z)
K  ≡  λx.λy.x
I  ≡  λx.x
```

The same combinators defined in a TRS:

```
Ap (Ap (Ap S x) y) z   →   Ap (Ap x z) (Ap y z)
Ap (Ap K x) y          →   x
Ap I x                 →   x
```

The only function that is present in these combinatorial TRSs is the dyadic function Ap(ply). The combinators are *discriminating* constructors: they determine which of the alternative rules for the apply function is applicable.

An example of reduction in a combinatorial system:

Ap (Ap (Ap S K) K) X $\to_S$ Ap (K̇ X) (K X) $\to_K$ X

Every combinatorial system is left-normal. Therefore, leftmost-outermost is normalizing for the class of combinatorial systems.

Parallel-outermost strategy

Leftmost-outermost is not normalizing for arbitrary orthogonal TRSs. It is even impossible to define a decidable normalizing strategy that indicates separately for each rule which argument has to be reduced first. The normal form can only be found using a parallel reduction strategy.

The example given by G. Berry shows that TRSs can be constructed for which it is undecidable to indicate an argument that has to be reduced first:

```
B 0 1 x  →   1
B 1 x 0  →   2
B x 0 1  →   3
```

Berry's TRS is orthogonal, so it guarantees a unique normal form. Suppose the term B R_1 R_2 R_3 has to be reduced, given that the reduction process performed on one of the arguments may not terminate. The strategy still has to choose one of the arguments, but unfortunately it does not know beforehand which one will not terminate. So enforcing argument evaluation at one of the arguments for which a pattern is specified may start a non-terminating computation. The only safe way to reach the normal form is to reduce each argument of B a finite number of steps to see if the term as a whole has become a redex. The parallel-outermost strategy satisfies this idea of reducing each argument of B one step at a time.

The **parallel-outermost** reduction strategy indicates all outermost redexes. It is assumed that all these redexes are reduced in parallel (i.e. in arbitrary order) in one reduction step of the reducer. The parallel-outermost reduction strategy is not normalizing for a general TRS.

Consider the following (ambiguous) TRS:

```
F G 0  →   W
F A 0  →   B
G      →   A
W      →   W
```

A parallel-outermost reducer would reduce the next term as follows:

P G (F A 0) $\rightarrow_{G,F_2}$ P A B

Parallel-outermost does not find the normal form B of F G 0 in this TRS:

$\underline{\text{F G 0}} \rightarrow_F \underline{\text{W}} \rightarrow_W \underline{\text{W}} \rightarrow_W \ldots$

Theorem (O'Donnell, 1985): Parallel outermost is normalizing for orthogonal TRSs.

By reducing all outermost redexes by one step a breadth-first reduction order is chosen. Clearly, at least one of the outermost redexes is needed for the reduction to normal form, but it is unknown which ones are needed and which are not. So it is apparent that the parallel-outermost strategy is not always the most efficient one. It indicates all outermost redexes, but not all of them might be needed.

Parallel-outermost finds the normal form of the following orthogonal TRS that includes Berry's example. However, too many redexes are reduced: the W-steps performed with the parallel-outermost reduction are not needed.

$$
\begin{array}{lll}
\mathsf{B}\ 0\ 1\ \mathsf{x} & \rightarrow & 1 \\
\mathsf{B}\ 1\ \mathsf{x}\ 0 & \rightarrow & 2 \\
\mathsf{B}\ \mathsf{x}\ 0\ 1 & \rightarrow & 3 \\
\mathsf{W} & \rightarrow & \mathsf{W} \\
\mathsf{A} & \rightarrow & 1 \\
\mathsf{C} & \rightarrow & \mathsf{A}
\end{array}
$$

$$
\mathsf{B}\ \underline{\mathsf{W}}\ 0\ \underline{\mathsf{C}} \rightarrow_{\mathsf{W,C}} \mathsf{B}\ \underline{\mathsf{W}}\ 0\ \underline{\mathsf{A}} \rightarrow_{\mathsf{W,A}} \underline{\mathsf{B}\ \mathsf{W}\ 0\ 1} \rightarrow_{\mathsf{B_3}} 3
$$

4.6.2 Classes with rule-based normalizing strategies

In a **rule-based strategy** the decision which redex to choose depends on the kind of rules in the TRS. Since analysis of the rules that takes the right-hand side into account is bound to be undecidable, only left-hand side analysis is treated. Even by looking only at the left-hand side it is in general undecidable for orthogonal TRSs to indicate needed redexes, as is illustrated by Berry's example. So, in this section, for orthogonal TRSs restrictions are imposed on the left-hand side that allow a decision tree to be defined that is used by the reduction strategy to point out the next needed redex.

Discriminating positions strategy

Next we will present a strategy that uses the patterns of the rewrite rules to produce a decision tree. In contrast with the term-based strategies the decision tree does not always indicate a redex if there is one in the term to be reduced. So the strategy will be normalizing only for certain classes of orthogonal TRSs.

The discriminating position strategy: consider the set of all **partially matching rules**, i.e. all rules that partially match the given *term*;

- if this set of rules is empty no redex is indicated: the term is in strong head normal form;
- if the term is a redex for one of the rules in the set, then this redex is indicated;

- otherwise:

  - if there is a proper subterm of the given term for which in every rule in the set in the corresponding position in the pattern a non-matching subpattern appears then this subterm is in a **discriminating position**;

  - if there are subterms on discriminating positions, first the strategy is recursively applied on the leftmost-outermost of such subterms, and afterwards the strategy is recursively applied again on the given term;

  - otherwise, no redex is indicated.

If a normal form is required the strategy must recursively be applied to all subterms of obtained head normal forms.

Illustrating discriminating positions:

```
G (Pair a 1) 0   →   a
G (Pair a 0) 1   →   Nil
A                →   Pair A B
B                →   0
```

For G A B both the first and the second arguments are in a discriminating position. A will be indicated since it is the leftmost-outermost redex. For G (Pair A B) B the second subargument of the pair will be indicated.

An orthogonal TRS without discriminating positions:

```
B 0 1 x  →   1
B 1 x 0  →   2
B x 0 1  →   3
```

In Berry's example given above there is a variable on each argument position so no redex on these positions is indicated by the strategy. Clearly, for this TRS the discriminating position strategy is not normalizing.

The example above shows that when discriminating positions do not exist the strategy is not normalizing. The examples below show that the discriminating position strategy is not always normalizing even if discriminating positions do exist. The reason for this is that the strategy when it is recursively applied on a discriminating position does not examine the term as a whole but only tries to match subterms locally against the discriminating patterns.

An orthogonal TRS for which the discriminating position strategy is normalizing:

```
F  (Cons a b)  (Cons 1 c) →    a
F  (Cons a b)  (Cons 2 c) →    b
F  Nil               c    →    c
```

The discriminating position strategy will first choose the first argument a_1 of a term F a_1 a_2 for evaluation. The second argument of F is only chosen if the term after evaluation partially matches the first two rule alternatives.

Another orthogonal TRS for which the discriminating position strategy is normalizing:

```
F (D x A) B   →   1
F (D A x) C   →   2
```

In the term F a_1 a_2 the subterms a_1 and a_2 are in a discriminating position. First a_1 will be chosen, then a_2.

An orthogonal TRS for which the discriminating position strategy is not normalizing:

```
F (G x A) B   →   1
F (G A x) C   →   2
G D D         →   3
```

In the term F (G a_1 a_2) a_3 the subterm (G a_1 a_2) is in a discriminating position. The strategy is recursively applied on G a_1 a_2. Now it finds that both a_1 a_2 are in discriminating positions in the rule for G. They are chosen next. A more clever strategy would reduce a_3 in F (G a_1 a_2) a_3 next. Compare this with the example above, where this order was taken by absence of the G rule.

For left-normal systems the discriminating position strategy coincides with the leftmost-outermost strategy. Therefore the discriminating position strategy is trivially normalizing for left-normal systems. The class of orthogonal TRSs for which the discriminating position strategy is normalizing is called **locally discriminating** TRSs since each recursive call of the strategy considers only locally the given subterm. For this class of TRSs the strategy always indicates a needed redex. The class is characterized by a decidable syntactical test that guarantees that a discriminating position is indeed needed.

Huet–Lévy strategy

Huet and Lévy (1979) have defined a class of orthogonal TRSs and a corresponding strategy (the **Huet–Lévy** strategy) in which they always take as much of the term as a whole into account as necessary. In their **strongly sequential** or **globally discriminating** systems needed redexes are identified by looking at the left-hand sides of the rules. Strongly sequential systems are a *decidable* subclass of *sequential systems*. In sequential systems the right-hand sides are also taken into account to identify a needed redex. Berry's TRS is clearly not strongly sequential. Below we give examples of TRSs that are globally discriminating but not locally discriminating. Furthermore another example of an orthogonal not strongly sequential TRS is given.

A strongly sequential TRS that is not locally discriminating:

```
F (G x A) B   →   1
F (G A x) C   →   1
G D D         →   2
```

For this TRS it turns out to be possible to identify in every term a needed redex if it exists. For instance, in F (G a_1 a_2) a_3 the subterm a_3 is needed.

Another strongly sequential TRS that is not locally discriminating:

```
F (F x A) B   →   ...
F C (F D x)   →   ...
```

For this TRS it turns out to be possible to identify in every term a needed redex if it exists. For instance, in F (F x_1 x_2) (F x_3 x_4) both x_2 and x_3 are needed. The TRS is not locally discriminating because x_1 would have been indicated wrongly by the discriminating position strategy.

An orthogonal TRS that is not strongly sequential:

```
F (G A x) (F B y)   →   ...
F (G x A) (F C y)   →   ...
G D D               →   ...
```

In the term F (G x_1 x_2) (F (G x_3 x_4) x_5) one cannot identify a needed redex (supposing the xs are complicated expressions with undecidable reducts). If the second rule for F is applicable x_2 has to be reduced and if the first rule for F is applicable x_1 has to be reduced. Which rule for F is applicable is determined by the second argument of F. It is important to note that this argument by itself can also be a redex for one of the rules for F and that, in order to determine for which rule this is the case, the reduction of x_5 is needed. This means that on the one hand it depends on the reduction of G x_3 x_4 (and consequently on the reduction of x_3 and x_4) whether the rule as a whole might be a redex for the first or the second rule for F. On the other hand it depends on the reduction of x_5 whether F (G x_3 x_4) x_5 might become a redex as a whole for one of the rules for F. So it is impossible to indicate a needed redex, i.e. to make a choice between the xs.

Unfortunately there does not exist an efficient test to determine whether a system is strongly sequential or not. Furthermore it is hard to see whether or not a specific TRS is strongly sequential and how evaluation will proceed. The Huet–Lévy strategy will not be fully treated here. It would require extending the notions of partial match and strong head normal form to definitions that recursively take more of the whole term into account.

4.7 Priority rewrite systems

There are several other interesting related systems for term rewriting that are not treated in this textbook, such as **conditional rewriting systems** (Meinke and Tucker, 1992), in which rewriting can only proceed if a guard is fulfilled (like in Miranda) and **narrowing rewriting systems** (De Groot and Lindstrom, 1986), in which the term that is rewritten may have free variables. **Narrowing** means that the variable in the term is instantiated with (is narrowed to) the value that is specified in a pattern. There are various ways of using this mechanism. Narrowing rewriting systems are investigated in the context of logical programming languages.

This section treats term rewriting systems with priorities (Baeten *et al.*, 1987), also called ***priority rewrite systems*** (PRSs), that try to capture the theoretical basis of the order dependency in the rules. The difference with an ordinary TRS is that in a PRS, whenever a rule matches a given redex, it can only be chosen if none of the rules with higher priority can *ever* match the (internally rewritten) term. A reduction step is called **internal** if it proceeds entirely within the arguments of the leftmost symbol of the term.

In a PRS the factorial function can be defined as follows:

```
  Fac 0  →   1
> Fac n  →   * n (Fac (– n 1))
```

The greater than sign indicates that the top rule has priority over the bottom rule. If the argument of Fac is 0 then the first rule is applicable. However, if it is somehow known that the argument can never be reduced to 0, then the priority of the rules makes it possible to choose the second rule without actually reducing the argument. So the second rule can be applied on Fac (+ 1 1) but not on Fac (– 1 1).

Of course it is in general undecidable whether or not a term can ever be made to match a pattern via internal rewrites. So a practical approximation is simply to force the evaluation of the term. **Forcing evaluation** means reduction to strong head normal form via some strategy. **Uniformly forcing evaluation** means that the choice for a rule with lower priority is only made if the subterms on ambiguous positions are reduced to strong head normal form. In this way, no choice for a rule with lower priority is ever made wrongly.

Forcing evaluation solves the problems in examples like Fac above. Fac (+ 1 1) and Fac (– 1 1) are first reduced to, respectively, Fac 2 and Fac 0, and then the choice between the prioritized rules is made. However, due to forcing evaluation non-termination may occur, although semantically this was avoidable.

Non-termination caused by forcing evaluation:

```
  G 0  →   1
> G n  →   2
  F    →   G F
```

A very clever strategy could know that F can only reduce to G (G (…(G F)...)) so never to G 0, so the second rule of G can be applied. The normal form of F is 2. Forcing evaluation of the argument of G leads to non-termination. The argument of G is not in strong head normal form since a partial match occurs.

Furthermore, in partially ambiguous cases a normal form may not be reached, just as was the case without priorities.

Normal forms in partially ambiguous cases not reached by forcing evaluation:

```
  F G  →   1
> F A  →   F G
  G    →   A
```

The normal form of F G is 1. However, forcing evaluation of the argument of F would lead to non-termination.

A strategy still must indicate which of the arguments must be forced for evaluation. This is essentially the same problem as with ordinary TRSs. For orthogonal TRSs the priorities do not make a difference. It is possible to investigate again various non-rule-based and rule-based strategies for PRSs. However, we only investigate one specific strategy: the functional strategy.

4.7.1 The functional strategy

The **functional strategy** combines the discriminating position strategy with uniformly forcing evaluation in priority rewrite systems such that the reduction proceeds in a similar way to most functional languages; subtle uses of priority for only certain sets of rules are not used, but textual order is assumed always to correspond to increasing priority; if a normal form is required the strategy is recursively applied to all subterms of obtained head normal forms. Effectively, this means that the discriminating position strategy is applied for one rule alternative at a time, with as a consequence that each non-variable subpattern under consideration induces a discriminating position. This leads to an efficient reduction strategy that is relatively easy to understand. Priority rewrite systems with an additional restriction that the functional strategy is being used are called **functional term rewriting systems** (FTRSs).

In other words, the functional strategy chooses redexes as follows: if there are several rewrite rules for a particular function, the rules are tried in textual order; patterns are tested from left to right; and evaluation of an actual argument is always forced when this argument must match a non-variable in the corresponding pattern (even in overlapping cases). This forcing of the evaluation of an argument reduces the argument to strong head normal form. If in the resulting term the argument matches the corresponding part of the pattern, the next (sub)argument is tried until the whole pattern matches and the rule can be applied. If in the resulting term the argument does not match the corresponding part of the pattern, the left-hand side of the next rule is tried to match the resulting term, proceeding in the same way, enforcing evaluation of subterms. If in the end none of the rules matches, the whole term is in strong head normal form. If a normal form is required the strategy is recursively applied to all subterms of obtained head normal forms.

A natural way to define the factorial function is:

```
Fac 0   →   1
Fac n   →   * n (Fac (– n 1))
```

This example has the intended semantics if the functional strategy is chosen. Fac (– 1 1) will be reduced to Fac 0 and the priority of the rules guarantees that Fac 0 matches the first rule and not the second.

If the functional strategy yields a normal form, it is a correct one with respect to the priority semantics. Of course, the functional strategy is not normalizing for a general PRS.

A (non-ambiguous) PRS for which the functional strategy is not normalizing:

```
F 0 0  →  1
F x 1  →  2
W      →  W
```

F W 1 $\rightarrow_W$ F W 1 $\rightarrow_W$ ...

Owing to the forced evaluation the normal form 2 of F W 1 is not reached in this PRS: owing to the priority of the rules the functional strategy does not first reduce the second argument of F, but first forces evaluation to establish whether or not the first argument reduces to 0.

So the functional strategy is actually a practical compromise: it is efficiently implementable and it makes it possible to express computations in a user-friendly manner. It has the following advantages:

- it is easy to explain;
- it is easy to use: the priority in the rules makes alternative rules similar to an if-then-else control structure;
- it is easy to understand, such that a programmer will not often specify unintended infinite computations;
- it can be implemented very efficiently.

The class of TRSs without priority for which the functional strategy is normalizing is characterized in Toyama *et al.* (1993).

4.8 TRSs as a basis for functional languages

TRSs have much in common with functional languages. Since TRSs have even greater expressive power than the λ-calculus, it will certainly be possible to translate functional programs into equivalent rewrite rules. An initial expression will be translated into a term that has to be rewritten.

However, there are several translation schemes possible depending on the kind of TRS one would like to obtain, such as an orthogonal, left-normal, combinatorial or priority system. This choice will influence:

- the complexity of the compilation scheme;
- the complexity of the obtained code (the number and size of the rewrite rules);
- the reduction strategy to be used;

- the number of reduction steps needed to reach the normal form (assuming that the compilation is correct and the normal form will be found if it exists);
- the efficiency of the reducer.

For instance, one can choose to compile to an orthogonal TRS and use the parallel-outermost strategy. This means that one has to make sure that patterns do not overlap, as is possible in functional languages.

Here we illustrate how the basic concepts of functional languages can be translated to an FTRS. It should not come as a surprise that such a compilation is a very straightforward one. Most of the details of an actual translation can be found in Chapter 9, where the translation from Miranda to GRSs is given. In most cases these translation schemes are also applicable to the translation to TRSs.

Booleans and the conditional

Booleans can be expressed as constants: True, False. Now a conditional expression can be created by

```
Cond True x y   →   x
Cond False x y  →   y
```

Recursion

Recursion can be expressed directly, e.g.

```
Fac 0   →   1
Fac n   →   * n (Fac (– n 1)
```

Representation of natural numbers

In TRSs one can represent natural numbers and arithmetical functions.

Define

```
0 ≡ Zero
1 ≡ Succ Zero
2 ≡ Succ (Succ Zero)
```

etc. Now a function for addition can be defined as follows:

```
Add x Zero       →   x
Add x (Succ y)   →   Add (Succ x) y
```

It will be clear that the use of the machine representation of numerals and δ-rules yields a much more efficient implementation.

Lists

Lists and other data structures can be defined easily using constructors.

```
x : y     ≡ Cons x y
[ ]       ≡ Nil
```

Now functions on these lists can be defined via pattern matching on the constructors:

```
Hd (Cons x y)   →   x
Tl (Cons x y)   →   y
```

Patterns

Patterns are part of TRSs as well as of FPLs.

Currying

In Miranda, all functions are curried and have at most one argument. Curried applications of functions can be realized in TRSs by introducing additional rewrite rules for those functions that are actually used in a curried way. These additional rules explicitly transfer curried applications of these functions into uncurried ones. Hence, currying is only performed when it is needed.

For instance, consider the well-known function Map:

```
Map  f  Nil          →    Nil
Map  f  (Cons a b) →    Cons (AP f a) (Map f b)
```

Assume that all elements of an integer list have to be multiplied with the number 2, using this function Map. Assume that * is a predefined δ-rule for integer multiplication that is defined with arity 2. Now its curried application can be realized as follows by defining the following additional rule:

```
AP (AP * a) b →     * a b
```

This AP-rule transforms the curried application of the multiplication into an uncurried application as shown in the following rewrite sequence:

```
Map (AP * 2) (Cons 3 (Cons 4 Nil))
→Map2   Cons (AP (AP * 2) 3) (Map (AP * 2) Cons 4 Nil)
→AP     Cons (* 2 3) (Map (AP * 2) Cons 4 Nil)
```

```
→*      Cons 6 (Map (AP * 2) Cons 4 Nil)
→Map2   Cons 6 (Cons (AP (AP * 2) 4) (Map (AP * 2) Nil))
→Ap     Cons 6 (Cons (* 2 4) (Map (AP * 2) Nil))
→*      Cons 6 (Cons 8 (Map (AP * 2) Nil))
→Map1   Cons 6 (Cons 8 Nil)
```

In general, an extra AP-rule has to be defined for every function that is actually used in a curried way.

4.9 TRSs as a basis for implementations

In contrast with implementations based on the λ-calculus, name conflicts cannot occur in an implementation based on TRSs. Still, an implementation of general TRSs is not straightforward, in particular when efficiency is important. Only some subclasses and strategies can be implemented efficiently. Orthogonal systems require parallel-outermost as strategy, which is inherently inefficient. Left-normal systems can be implemented efficiently by means of the leftmost-outermost reduction strategy. Locally and globally discriminating systems can be efficiently implemented, but their characterization is difficult to comprehend. Efficient implementations of FTRSs which use the functional strategy can be obtained via the introduction of sharing (see the next chapter).

4.9.1 Combinators

As explained in the previous chapter, combinators (and hence also combinatorial systems) can be implemented efficiently. However, an advantage of the use of more general TRSs is that pattern information is explicitly present in the model allowing special kinds of analysis (for example the strictness analysis using abstract reduction in Chapter 7).

4.9.2 Sharing

To avoid unnecessary computations one can share terms in the actual implementation. In such a case, graphs are rewritten instead of terms. Because local definitions do not exist in TRSs, the problem that parts of the graph sometimes have to be copied does not occur. However, using graphs instead of terms will change the semantics in certain cases. This is discussed in the next chapter.

4.9.3 The functional strategy

The functional strategy chooses redexes in a similar way as in Miranda. So, as shown in Chapter 9, a functional program can be compiled to a PRS using a functional strategy in such a way that:

- the compilation scheme is straightforward;
- the length of the obtained code is linear with respect to the length of the original program.

If graphs are being used instead of terms, even state-of-the-art efficiency is possible (see Part 4). The language Clean (introduced in Chapter 8) which uses the functional strategy, is based on this extension to graph rewriting. In Chapters 10, 11 and 12 it is explained how an efficient implementation of Clean can be achieved.

Summary

- In TRSs tests on syntactic equality (*pattern matching*) are used to rewrite *terms* according to the specified *rewrite rules.*
- Most notions like *normal forms*, *strategies* and *rewriting* are similar to the corresponding notions in the λ-calculus. But for a general TRS:
  - *normal forms* are *not* unique;
  - the *head normal form* property is *undecidable*;
  - the *strong head normal form* property is *decidable*;
  - there is *no normalizing strategy.*
- *Ambiguity* and *comparing* are the sources of non-confluency, so *orthogonal systems* are confluent.
- The *parallel-outermost strategy* is normalizing for *orthogonal systems*; it is an inefficient strategy because it can indicate redexes that are not needed.
- The *leftmost-outermost strategy* is normalizing for *left-normal systems* among which are *combinatorial systems*; left-normal systems allow only a very restricted use of patterns.
- The *discriminating position strategy* as well as the *Huet–Lévy strategy* are normalizing for, respectively, *locally* and *globally discriminating systems*. The strategies are efficient but their classes of TRSs are difficult to characterize and it is difficult to understand how evaluation will proceed.
- The *functional strategy* combines the discriminating position strategy with uniformly forcing evaluation to *strong head normal form* in systems with priority in the rules. It is similar to the way evaluation proceeds in most lazy functional programming languages. The functional strategy is efficiently implementable and intuitively clear.
- Conceptually there are fewer problems in making an implementation based on a TRS than on the λ-calculus:

- there is no need for α-conversion, as name conflicts cannot arise;
- sharing of terms is easy to use as an optimization in the implementation (see the next chapter).

EXERCISES

4.1 Give all subterms of the expression

```
Ap (Ap x z) (Ap y z)
```

Is Ap a subterm in the expression above? If so, say why; if not can you tell whether there is a term in which Ap is a subterm? Give an example.

4.2 Indicate for each of the following TRSs whether it is partially ambiguous, non-deterministic, comparing, confluent or left-normal.

```
(a) F F       →  1
    F F       →  2
(b) F x (G x) →  1
    F x (H y) →  2
    G x       →  1
    H x       →  2
(c) F x       →  H x
    F x       →  G
    H x       →  F (F x)
```

4.3 For each of the following TRSs, give a reduction sequence of the given term using respectively the leftmost-outermost reduction strategy, the parallel-outermost reduction strategy, the discriminating position strategy and the functional strategy.

```
(a) F x 0     →  0          Term:  F G G
    F 0 x     →  1
    F 0 0     →  2
    G         →  0
(b) F x (G x) →  F (G x) x  Term:  F G G
    F G x     →  F x (G x)
    G         →  G
(c) F x y 1   →  1          Term:  F (F 1 1 2) (F 1 1 2) (F 1 1 2)
    F x 1 2   →  2
    F 1 2 2   →  3
```

4.4 Try to translate Berry's example into the λ-calculus and show that for every possible translation the resulting λ-expression can be normalized with the leftmost-outermost reduction strategy.

Chapter 5
Graph rewriting systems

Graph rewriting systems (GRSs) (introduced in Barendregt *et al.* (1987a, b) are an extension of term rewriting systems where the terms are replaced by directed graphs. The main goal is to obtain a sound extension of the TRS model in which duplication of work is avoided via sharing of subgraphs (see Section 5.1). More information on this approach and on related approaches can be found in Ehrig *et al.* (1973), Raoult (1984), Staples (1980) and Kennaway (1990).

A computation in a GRS is specified by a set of graph rewrite rules that are used to rewrite a given initial graph to its final result. The rules contain graph patterns that can match some part of the graph. If the graph matches a rule it can be rewritten according to the specification in that rule. This specification makes it possible to construct an additional graph structure which is linked to the existing graph by redirecting all arcs from the root of the redex to the root of the result (Sections 5.2 and 5.3).

Many notions in GRSs are similar to the notions in TRSs and also many properties of subclasses carry over from TRSs to GRSs (Sections 5.4, 5.6 and 5.7). For instance, GRSs are also in general not confluent. However, similar to the TRS world it is possible to define confluent subclasses with normalizing strategies. As with term rewriting, priority can be added to graph rewrite rules. The functional strategy can be used to rewrite graphs in a GRS with priorities (Section 5.8).

A TRS can be converted (lifted) to a GRS (Section 5.8). This conversion has been made very easy by a special shorthand notation that is defined for GRSs (Section 5.5). In most cases a GRS obtained via lifting is syntactically equivalent to the original TRS. The GRS semantics is then applied instead of the TRS semantics. Rewriting graphs instead of terms has the advantage that duplication of work is avoided. Generally, fewer rewrite steps are needed to reach a normal form. The resulting graph in normal form can be converted back to a term again (unravelled). Under certain conditions the same reduct is obtained via this *term graph rewriting* as would have been the case when the original term was reduced in the term world. In particular, sharing can be used safely in lifted FTRSs.

Graph rewriting can be generalized to allow multiple redirections (Section 5.9). Such a generalized graph rewriting model allows much more complex changes of a graph structure than is necessary for lifted TRSs. Generalized graph rewriting can model basic concepts of other languages than pure functional languages, such as those found in logic languages and even in imperative languages. Generalized GRSs are used for instance to investigate the possibility of combining different kinds of language concepts into one framework.

GRSs are referentially transparent, since in a rewrite step all arcs to the root of the subgraph matching a pattern are redirected to the result. GRSs with priority and the functional strategy very much resemble a functional language and therefore can serve very well as a basis for functional languages (Section 5.10). Transformation schemes that specify the conversion of a functional program into an equivalent GRS are discussed in detail in Part 4. An efficient implementation of a generalized GRS is very hard to obtain. However, efficient implementations of functional language-like GRSs are very possible (Section 5.11). In Part 4, efficient implementations of functional languages based on GRSs are treated in detail.

5.1 Extending TRSs to GRSs

In this section the differences and correspondences between *term* and *graph* rewriting are briefly explained in order to give the reader a first intuition on the subject.

TRS terms can be regarded as trees (see Chapter 4). The basic motivation behind the extension of TRSs to GRSs is to include the notion of *sharing of computation*. For this purpose the objects of rewriting become directed acyclic graphs instead of trees. The GRS model is even more general: it also allows cyclic structures to be manipulated. In TRSs rewriting of terms consists of replacing a subterm by another subterm. In graph rewriting the natural extension of sub*term* replacement is sub*graph* replacement. This subgraph replacement is achieved via a change of the graph structure retaining as much sharing as possible.

5.1.1 Terms versus graphs

There are many similarities between the tree representation of terms and the graphs as used in GRSs. However, in order to be able to express sharing and cycles a unique *label* (like an address) is added to every node, called the **node identifier** or **node-id** (Figure 5.1). A node is then referred to by its node-id. A subgraph can be identified via the node-id of the root of that subgraph.

Tree representation of a closed term: A closed graph:

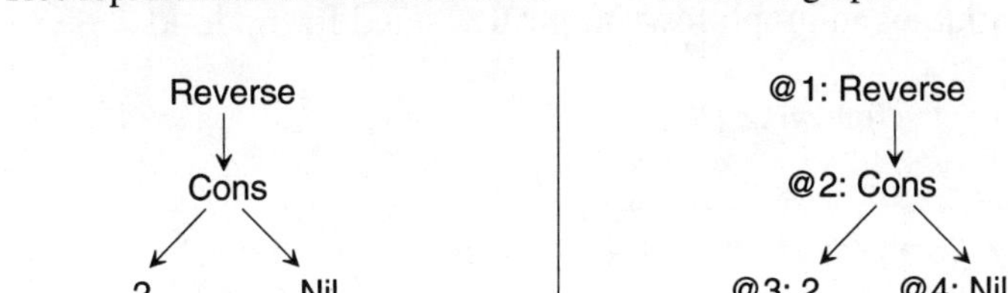

Figure 5.1 Closed terms in TRSs versus closed graphs in GRSs.

5.1.2 Term rewrite rules versus graph rewrite rules

In a *graph rewrite rule* graphs are specified instead of terms.

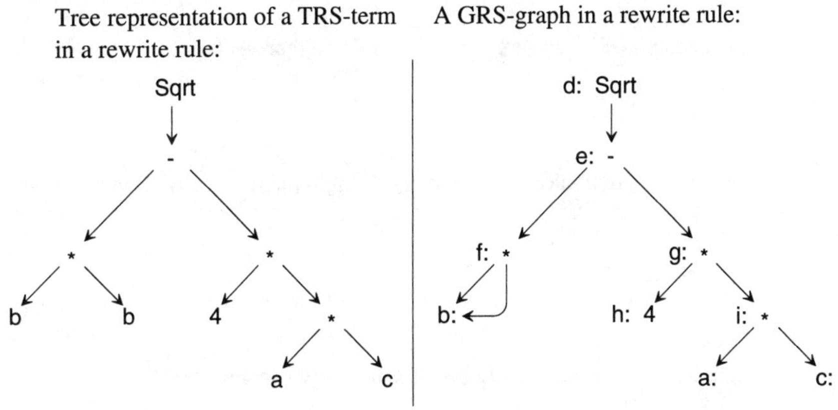

Tree representation of a TRS-term in a rewrite rule:

Sqrt
-
* *
b b 4 *
a c

A GRS-graph in a rewrite rule:

d: Sqrt
e: -
f: * g: *
b: h: 4 i: *
a: c:

Figure 5.2 Terms versus graphs in rewrite rules.

The graphs that are specified in the rewrite rules of a GRS are **open graphs**, i.e. these graphs are labelled with node-id *variables*. The graph that is rewritten is a **closed graph**, i.e. the nodes of the graph are labelled with node-id *constants*. There is a difference between variables in TRSs and variables in GRSs. Variables that appear in the rewrite rules of a TRS are bound to a whole subterm (or subtree) of the term to be rewritten. Since a subgraph of a graph to be rewritten can be identified by the node-id of the root node of that subgraph, a node-id variable in a GRS-rule is bound to just a simple node-id constant.

5.1.3 Term rewriting versus graph rewriting

An important difference between term rewriting and graph rewriting is that with term rewriting subterms are duplicated if a corresponding variable appears more than once on the right-hand side whereas with graph rewriting the subterms will be shared. This is caused by the fact that the variables in graph rewriting rules stand for node-ids.

Consider the following TRS:

```
Double x               →    + x x
Heavy_Computation      →    Easy_Number
```

The term Double Heavy_Computation will be reduced in this TRS as follows (using a lazy strategy):

```
Double Heavy_Computation
→Double               + Heavy_Computation Heavy_Computation
→Heavy_Computation    + Easy_Number Heavy_Computation
→Heavy_Computation    + Easy_Number Easy_Number
```

which is displayed in Figure 5.3. using the tree representation of TRS terms.

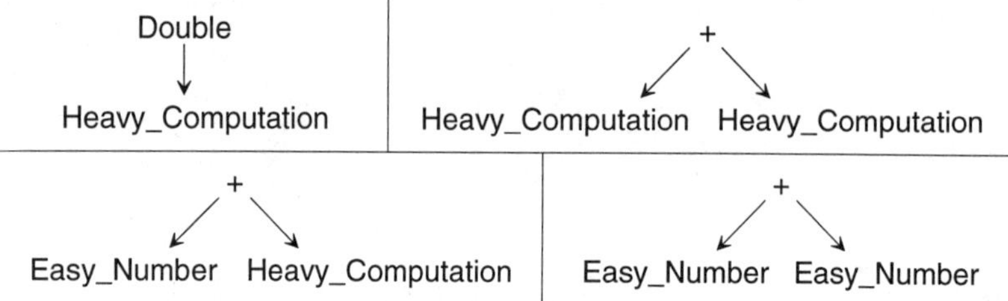

Figure 5.3 Four snapshots of the term rewriting process.

The example above shows that in term rewriting work may be duplicated by subtree replacement. In GRSs duplication of work is avoided. The graph structure makes it possible to share a subgraph representing a computation that has to be performed (see also Section 5.8). If such a subgraph is replaced by the subgraph representing the result of the computation all arcs pointing to the computation automatically become arcs pointing to that result. Subgraph replacement in GRSs is accomplished via redirection of arcs in the graph.

Avoiding duplication of work by sharing computations.

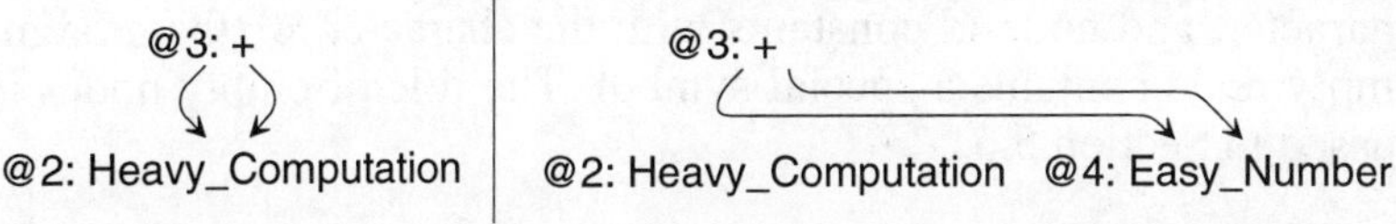

Figure 5.4 Two snapshots of the graph rewriting process.

In Figure 5.4 the same rules as above are used with graph rewriting semantics instead of term rewriting semantics. The snapshots in Figure 5.4 show that the right-hand side of the Double rule induced the sharing of the expression representing the heavy computation. The reduction of the heavy computation to the easy number is only done once after which all arcs to the root of the heavy computation subgraph are redirected to the root of the result (2nd snapshot).

5.2 GRSs

A GRS consists of a collection of rewrite rules. These rewrite rules specify how a given *graph* can be *rewritten* (*reduced*) to another graph.

In a GRS there are two syntactic ways of specifying graphs and rules: the shorthand form and the canonical form. In the *shorthand form* the graph structure need not be fully specified if it can be deduced from the notation. The shorthand notation is designed in such a way that those GRSs that very much resemble TRSs can also be written in a syntactic form that is very much like a TRS. In the *canonical form* everything is specified explicitly. Generally, the shorthand form is used for specifying computations whereas the canonical form is mainly used to analyse the semantics of GRSs. Keep in mind that both forms denote exactly the same rules and objects, so they can be interchanged freely.

In this section the canonical form will be treated. This form will also be used in explaining the semantics in Section 5.3. In Section 5.5 the more readable TRS-like shorthand form will be explained.

5.2.1 Graphs

A collection of **graphs** over a set of *constant symbols* and a set of *node identifiers* (or *node-ids*) is defined by the following syntactic definition:

```
Graph       = NodeDef {',' NodeDef} ;
NodeDef     = Nodeid ':' Node ;
Node        = Symbol {Arg}      |  EmptyNode ;
Symbol      = Constant ;
Arg         = Nodeid ;
Nodeid      = NodeidVariable  |  NodeidConstant ;
EmptyNode   = '⊥' ;
```

Constants always begin with an upper case character or some special character (a digit, an asterisk etc.), node-id variables with a lower case character, and node-id constants with the character @ (the *at* sign). An empty node contains a special symbol. The role of empty nodes is discussed in Section 5.6.

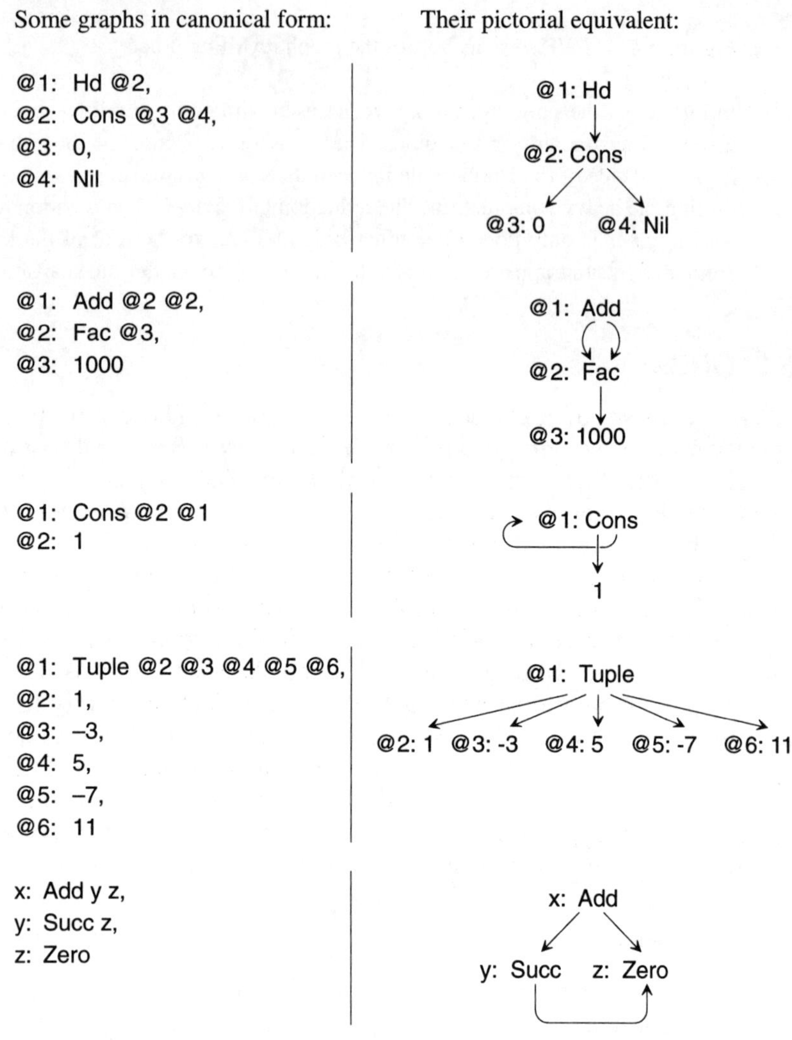

Figure 5.5 Some graphs.

A **graph** consists of a set of **node definitions**. Each node in the graph has a unique **node-identifier** or **node-id** associated with it (Figure 5.5). Occurrences of node-ids before a colon are **defining occurrences**. Each **node** consists of a **constant symbol** with a (possibly empty) sequence of **arguments**: node-ids defining *arcs* pointing to (other) nodes in the graph. There are **node-id constants** and **node-id variables.** A graph that contains no node-id variables is called a **closed graph**, otherwise it is called an **open graph.** A **subgraph** of a graph is a set of node definitions contained in the given graph. A graph can be cyclic. Symbols have fixed arities.

There is a distinguished node in every graph that is the *root* of that graph. When the set of node-id definitions is textually enumerated, the topmost node-id definition is always the definition of the **root** of the graph. A **path** in a graph is a sequence of node-ids of the graph such that each node-id is an argument of the node associated with its predecessor in the sequence; the path is said to be a **path from** A **to** B where A and B are the nodes associated with respectively the first and the last node-id of the path. A node A is **reachable** from a node B if there exists a path from B to A. When all nodes in the graph are reachable from the root of the graph, the graph is said to be a **connected graph**. In GRSs all graphs (also in the rules) are connected. **The subgraph of a node-id** n in a graph g is defined as the connected subgraph of g which is rooted at n and contains the node definitions of all nodes in g that are reachable from n.

Two closed graphs are considered to be **equivalent** when the graphs are identical up to the node-id constants. This means that the graphs have the same graph structure and that corresponding nodes contain the same symbol with the same arity. So between two equivalent graphs there exists a rooted isomorphism. From now on graphs will be considered to be indistinguishable with respect to this equivalency.

From a standard graph theory point of view, a GRS graph is a *connected directed graph* in which each node is labelled with a symbol whose set of out-arcs is given an ordering. In standard graph theory, cycles in directed graphs are usually referred to as *circuits*.

5.2.2 Graph rewriting systems

A **graph rewriting system** (GRS) is a collection of *rewrite rules* $\alpha_i \rightarrow \beta_i, \varphi_i$ over sets of constant symbols and node-id variables obeying the syntactical restrictions described below. The object that is manipulated in a GRS is a connected closed graph called the **data graph.** When there is no confusion, the data graph is simply called the **graph**.

Syntax of GRSs (canonical form)

In the notation below the square brackets specify an optional occurrence of the enclosed objects:

```
CanonicalGRS    = {Rule} ;
Rule            = RedexPattern '→' [ContractumPattern ','] Redirection ;
RedexPattern    = Graph ;
```

```
ContractumPattern = Graph ;
Redirection       = Nodeid ':=' Nodeid ;
```

The left-hand side α_i of a rewrite rule consists of a connected open graph that is called the **redex pattern.** The right-hand side β_i consists of a connected open graph called the **contractum pattern** (optional) and a **redirection** φ_i.

The patterns are *open* graphs not containing node-id constants (only node-id *variables*). Every node-id variable must have at most one defining occurrence within a rule. A node-id variable that appears on the right-hand side of a rule, must either have a defining occurrence on this right-hand side or it must appear on the corresponding left-hand side. Note that node-id variables are allowed only in rewrite rules whereas node-id constants are allowed only in the data graph.

The left node-id of the redirection is always the root of the redex pattern. The right node-id of the redirection must either be the root of the contractum pattern or a node-id that occurs in the redex pattern. The redirection specifies to which node arcs to the root of the redex pattern are redirected.

The first symbol in a redex pattern is called the **function symbol**. Function symbols can also occur at positions that are not the head of the pattern. A symbol that does not occur at the head of any pattern in the GRS is called a **constructor symbol**.

Example of a GRS (compare this with the example in Section 5.5 that uses the much more readable shorthand notation):

```
r: Hd x,
x: Cons a b   →   r := a

r: Fac x,
x: 0          →   r': 1,     r := r'

r: Fac n      →   r': * n u,
                  u:  Fac v,
                  v:  – n w,
                  w:  1,     r := r'

r: Start      →   r': Fac a,
                  a:  Hd b,
                  b:  Cons c d,
                  c:  1000,
                  d:  Nil,    r: = r'
```

5.3 Rewriting with a GRS

In this section the full operational semantics for GRSs is given. As said before, a GRS is used to rewrite a given closed data graph γ. The data graph that is to be rewritten can be compared with the initial expression to be evaluated as present in TRSs and in Miranda.

5.3.1 The initial graph

One can specify on which data graph the set of rules has to be applied. However, since change of graph structure is obtained via redirecting existing arcs, it is more convenient for the specification of the semantics to assume a fixed initial graph to be present. This initial graph consists of the root node that always remains the root of the data graph, even after rewriting. The purpose of the root node is always to have an arc pointing to the actual graph to be rewritten. Initially the root node contains an arc to the start node. A GRS should contain a rule matching the start node to initiate the computation.

The initial graph in linear notation:	In pictorial notation:
@DataRoot: Graph @StartNode, @StartNode: Start	@DataRoot: Graph ↓ @StartNode: Start

Requiring an initial graph does not impose a serious restriction because on the right-hand side of a start rule one can always specify the desired graph one would actually like to rewrite. When such a start rule is applied, the arc pointing from the root node to the start node will be redirected to this desired graph. This graph then becomes the object of rewriting. For reasons of simplicity sometimes the start rule is omitted in examples and a desired graph is specified directly.

5.3.2 Redexes

As explained above, a redex pattern consists of constant symbols and node-id variables. An **instance** of a redex pattern is a subgraph of the data graph, such that there is a mapping from the pattern to this subgraph. Such a mapping must be the identity on symbols and it has to preserve the node structure. The corresponding subgraph is called a **redex** (*red*ucible *ex*pression). The redex pattern (and the corresponding rewrite rule) is said to **match** the redex. As in TRSs, it depends on the rules present in the GRS whether or not a subgraph is a redex or not.

In order to define a match more formally, some terminology has to be introduced. Let F be a set of symbols and N be a set of node-ids. Further, let C be a function (the *contents function*) from N to $F \times N^*$.

Then C specifies a GRS graph over F and N. Furthermore, for each GRS graph γ there is a unique contents function: C_γ. The canonical form can be regarded as a tabulation of the contents function. Let γ be a GRS graph, and ρ the set of rewrite rules. Then μ is a mapping from the node-id variables in a redex pattern π of ρ to node-id constants of the graph γ such that for every node with node-id x in π with contents, say $C_\pi(\mathsf{x}) = \mathsf{S}\ \mathsf{x}_1\ \mathsf{x}_2 \ldots \mathsf{x}_n$ it holds that $C_\gamma(\mu(\mathsf{x})) = \mathsf{S}\ \mu(\mathsf{x}_1)\ \mu(\mathsf{x}_2) \ldots \mu(\mathsf{x}_n)$. That is, μ preserves the node structure.

Consider the following GRS:

```
r:  Hd x,
x:  Cons a b        →            r := a
```

and the following data graph:

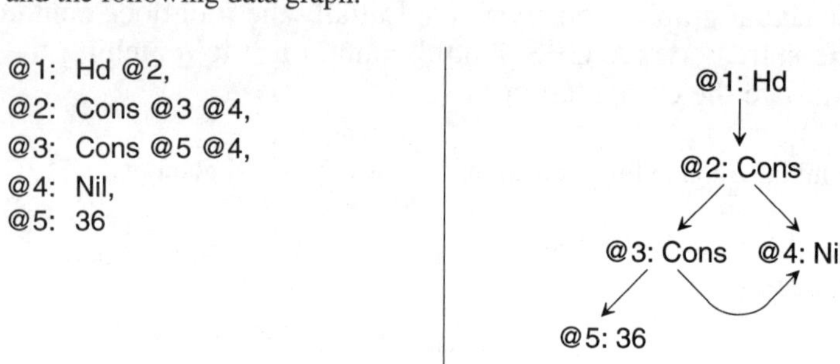

The mapping μ is defined by: μ(r) = @1, μ(x) = @2, μ(a) = @3, μ(b) = @4.

5.3.3 Rewriting a graph

The semantics of a GRS is explained using the canonical form. The operational semantics (Barendregt *et al.*, 1987b) is similar to Staples' model of graph rewriting (Staples, 1980). A categorical semantics of graph rewriting is given in Kennaway (1990).

A **rewrite** (or **reduction**) of a graph γ and the set of rewrite rules ρ is performed in a number of steps. Consider a rewrite rule and a redex that matches the rule with a corresponding concrete mapping μ. The basic idea is to construct a new data graph out of the old data graph and out of a graph called the **contractum** via redirection of arcs. The contractum is only constructed if a contractum pattern is specified on the right-hand side of the chosen rule. More precisely, the operational semantics of graph rewriting is defined by the following steps:

(1) Choose a redex together with a matching rule and a mapping μ.
(2) When a contractum pattern is specified in the matching rule the contractum is constructed in the following way:

- invent new constant node-ids (not present in γ) for each node-id variable on a defining occurrence in the contractum pattern. This mapping is called μ'. These new node-ids correspond to the identifiers of new nodes to be introduced during rewriting.
- apply μ'', the combination of μ and μ', to the node-ids in the contractum pattern of the rule yielding the contractum graph γ'.

If no contractum pattern is specified, then γ' is empty.

(3) A graph γ'' is constructed by taking the union of γ and γ'.

(4) The redirection in a rule takes the form r := n where r is the root node of the redex pattern. Now all arcs pointing to the root node of the redex are redirected to the specified node-id. By applying μ'', node-id constants @R and @N are determined from the node-id variables that occur in the redirection. In terms of the syntactic representation, redirection is performed by substituting @N for every occurrence of @R *as an argument* in every node of the graph γ''. This results in the new graph γ'''. Note that the node *definition* of @R still remains.

(5) The graph γ''' thus constructed may be a graph that is disconnected. In order to make the resulting new data graph connected again only those nodes are considered to be part of the new data graph that are reachable from @DataRoot, the root of the initial graph. All nodes that are not reachable from the root of the graph are removed from the graph. This is known as **garbage collection**.

Since the node that is the root of the redex plays such an important role in the rewrite, one sometimes by abuse of language speaks of **rewriting** or **reducing a node** when one means rewriting the *graph* of which the node is the root.

5.3.4 A small example

When the rewriting process starts, the data graph γ always consists of the following initial graph:

```
@DataRoot : Graph @StartNode,
@StartNode: Start
```

```
@DataRoot: Graph
      |
      v
@StartNode: Start
```

In the following example the data graph will be rewritten until it contains no redexes (to *normal form*) given the following graph rewrite rules.

```
x: Add y z,
y: Zero      →   x := z                                   (1)

x: Add y z,
y: Succ a    →   m:   Succ n,
                 n:   Add a z,
                 x := m                                   (2)

x: Start     →   m:   Add n o,
                 n:   Succ o,
                 o:   Zero,
                 x := m                                   (3)
```

The following semantic actions are performed:

(1) The start node is the only redex matching rule (3). The mapping is trivial: μ(x) = @StartNode.

(2) Invent new node-ids for the node-id variables defined in the contractum pattern: μ'(m) = @A, μ'(n) = @B, μ'(o) = @C. Applying μ'' (the combination of μ and μ') to the node-ids in the contractum pattern will leave this unchanged as x does not appear in it. Now the contractum γ' can be constructed:

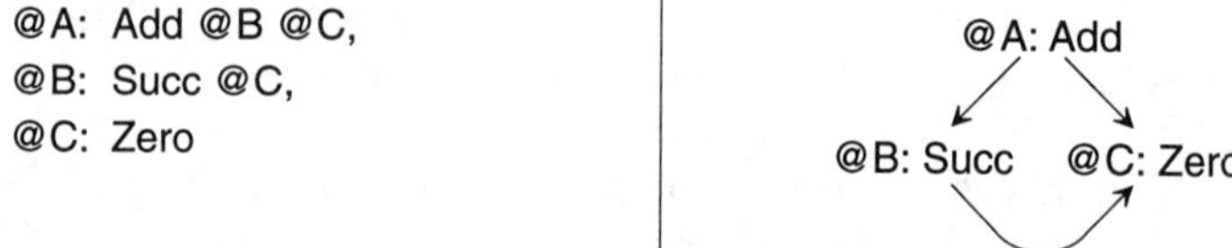

(3) The union of contractum γ' and graph γ is the new graph γ'':

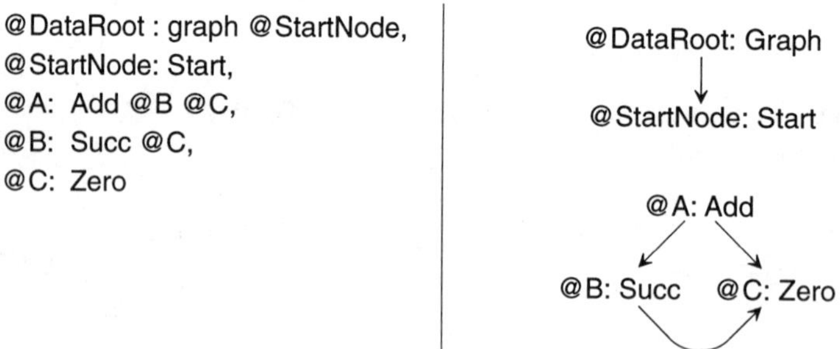

(4) μ''(x) = @StartNode has to be redirected to μ''(m) = @A. All occurrences of @StartNode as an argument will be replaced by occurrences of @A. The graph γ''' resulting after rewriting is now:

```
@DataRoot : Graph @A,
@StartNode: Start,
@A: Add @B @C,
@B: Succ @C,
@C: Zero
```

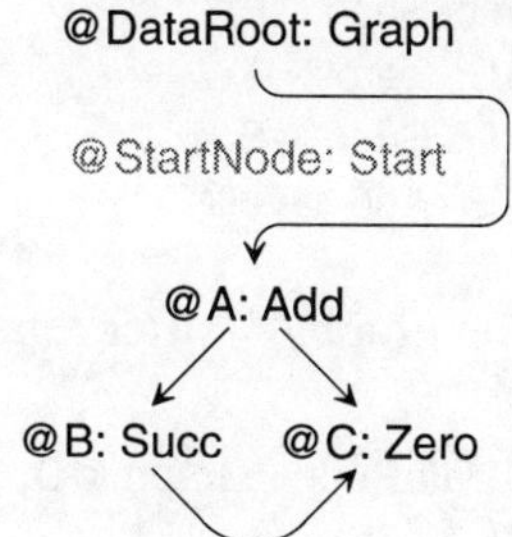

(5) The start node is no longer reachable from the data root node: it is garbage. Hence it is removed:

```
@DataRoot: Graph @A,
@A: Add @B @C,
@B: Succ @C,
@C: Zero
```

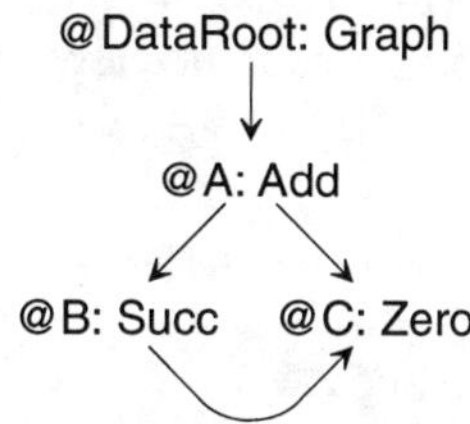

This completes one rewrite. The graph still contains a redex. So reduction can go on:

(1) There is only one redex to choose.
It matches rule 2: $\mu(x)$ = @A, $\mu(y)$ = @B, $\mu(z)$ = @C, $\mu(a)$ = @C.

(2) Invent new node-ids and map the variables as follows: $\mu'(m)$ = @D, $\mu'(n)$ = @E. The contractum can now be constructed:

```
@D: Succ @E,
@E: Add @C @C
```

(3) The union of γ' and γ is γ'':

```
@DataRoot: Graph @A,
@A: Add @B @C,
@B: Succ @C,
@C: Zero,
@D: Succ @E,
@E: Add @C @C
```

(4) $\mu''(x)$ = @A is redirected to $\mu''(m)$ = @D:

```
@DataRoot: Graph @D,
@A: Add @B @C,
```

```
@B: Succ @C,
@C: Zero,
@D: Succ @E,
@E: Add @C @C
```

(5) The graph γ''' after removing garbage is:

```
@DataRoot: Graph @D,
@C: Zero,
@D: Succ @E,
@E: Add @C @C
```

It is now clear how this process may continue: @E is a redex and it matches rule 1: μ(x) = @E, μ(y) = @C, μ(z) = @C. The strategy chooses this redex; there is no new contractum graph but just a single redirection that takes μ''(x) = @E to μ''(z) = @C, yielding the expected normal form:

```
@DataRoot: Graph @D,
@C: Zero,
@D: Succ @C
```

5.3.5 δ-rules

δ-rules are used in the same way as in TRSs and λ-calculus.

5.4 Reduction sequences and normal forms

The notions defined in this section are all very similar to the corresponding notions in TRSs with the exception that computation is initiated by the start rule.

One reduction is often called a **reduction step** (or **rewrite step**). A **reduction sequence** (or **rewrite sequence**) of a graph is a sequence of zero or more reduction steps (or rewrites) performed on that graph. If graph γ_1 can be reduced by a sequence of reductions to graph γ_2, γ_2 is called a **reduct** of γ_1. This is denoted as: $\gamma_1 \rightarrow_* \gamma_2$. So $\rightarrow_*$ is the reflexive transitive closure of $\rightarrow$.

Given a GRS, a graph is in **normal form** if no rule in the GRS matches the graph or one of its subgraphs.

The root normal form property in GRSs is the natural generalization of the head normal form property in TRSs: a graph is in **root normal form** if the graph as a whole is not a redex and the graph as a whole will never become a redex. In general it is undecidable whether a graph is in root normal form.

A pattern **partially matches** a graph if firstly the symbol of the root of the pattern equals the symbol of the root of the graph and secondly in positions where symbols in the pattern are not syntactically equal to symbols in the graph, the corresponding subgraph is a redex or the subgraph itself is partially matching a rule. A graph is in **strong root normal form** if the graph does not partially match any rule. It is decidable whether or not a graph is in strong root normal form. A graph in strong root normal form does not partially match any rule, so it is also in root normal form. A graph in root normal form need not be in strong root normal form (see also the previous chapter). In the graph world the notions partial match and strong root normal form are only partially defined. The cases where these notions are not defined are cases of cycle-in-spine errors (see also Section 5.8).

Consider the following GRS:

```
A 0     →    1
```

For the term `@N: A @N` the notion partial match is undefined.

5.5 Shorthand form

Before some important properties and aspects of GRSs are discussed, first the shorthand notation is introduced. In the canonical form every node has a definition and definitions are not nested. Redirection is explicitly specified. In the **shorthand form** it is not necessary to specify all the node-ids. Furthermore redirection need not be specified explicitly. This notation makes it possible to use a more readable TRS-like notation for GRSs. The shorthand notation will be used throughout the rest of this chapter.

Syntax of GRS graphs and GRSs (shorthand form)

```
GRS                = {Rule} ;
Rule               = RedexPattern '→' ContractumPattern [',' Redirection]
                   | RedexPattern '→' Redirection ;
RedexPattern       = Graph ;
ContractumPattern  = Graph ;
Graph              = [Nodeid ':'] Node {',' NodeDef} ;
Nodeid             = NodeIdVariable       | NodeIdConstant ;
Node               = Symbol {Arg}         | EmptyNode ;
Symbol             = Constant ;
Arg                = Nodeid               | [Nodeid ':'] Symbol
                   | [Nodeid ':'] '(' Node ')' ;
EmptyNode          = ⊥ ;
NodeDef            = Nodeid ':' Node ;
Redirection        = Nodeid ':=' Nodeid  |  Nodeid ;
```

Some graphs in shorthand form (compare this with the equivalent examples of Section 5.2 that use the canonical form):

```
Hd (Cons a b)   →   a

Fac 0   →   1
Fac n   →   * n (Fac (– n 1))

Ones    →   n: Cons 1 n

Start   →   Fac (Hd (Cons 1000 Nil))
```

The shorthand notation is more readable and hence generally this form is used for specifying computations. Both forms denote the same rules and objects so there is no semantic difference between them. The shorthand form is not only used in the rules, but also to denote graphs that are being reduced:

Consider the following example in shorthand form:

```
Add Zero z          →   z
Add (Succ a) z      →   Succ (Add a z)
```

and the following data graph:

```
Add (Succ @1) @1, @1: Zero
```

The data graph can be rewritten in the following way:

<u>Add (Succ @1) @1</u>, @1: Zero
$\rightarrow_{\text{Add}_2}$ Succ (<u>Add @1 @1</u>), @1: Zero
$\rightarrow_{\text{Add}_1}$ Succ Zero

The reduction of this graph is also given in canonical form in Section 5.3.

Translating shorthand form to canonical form

The shorthand form can be translated into canonical form via two steps:

(1) *Add explicit node-ids and flatten*

In the canonical form all nodes have explicit node-ids and there are no nested node definitions. In each rule for every argument that does not consist of a single node-id, a new node is defined with the same contents as that argument. The new node is labelled with a new unique node-id. The original argument is replaced by this new node-id. With this replacement brackets disappear. Adding explicit node definitions and replacing corresponding arguments is repeated until there is no nesting and all node-ids are explicit.

The rules that were used before in the small example to illustrate the semantics of GRSs, denoted in the shorthand form:

```
Add Zero z       →   z                          (1)
Add (Succ a) z   →   Succ (Add a z)             (2)

Start            →   Add (Succ o) o,
                     o: Zero                    (3)
```

Note the sharing on the right-hand side of the Start rule. The first transformation step towards canonical form replaces the rules by:

```
x: Add y z,
y: Zero          →   z                          (1')

x: Add y z,
y: Succ a        →   m: Succ n,
                     n: Add a z                 (2')

x: Start         →   m: Add n o,
                     n: Succ o,
                     o: Zero                    (3')
```

(2) *Make redirection explicit*

The root of the redex pattern is redirected to the root of the contractum pattern or if the right-hand side consists of a single node-id variable, it is redirected to that node-id variable.

The same example with explicit redirections in the canonical form:

```
x: Add y z,
y: Zero          →   x := z                     (1")

x: Add y z,
y: Succ a        →   m: Succ n,
                     n: Add a z,
                     x := m                     (2")

x: Start         →   m: Add n o,
                     n: Succ o,
                     o: Zero,
                     x := m                     (3")
```

5.6 Properties of GRSs

Although there are many notions in GRSs that are similar to the notions in TRSs and also many properties of subclasses carry over from TRSs to GRSs (Smetsers, 1993), there are also subtle differences between these two worlds. These similarities and differences are discussed briefly in this section.

5.6.1 Sources of non-confluency

A GRS is **confluent** (or has the **Church–Rosser property**) iff for every two 'divergent' reduction sequences $\gamma \rightarrow_* \gamma_1$ and $\gamma \rightarrow_* \gamma_2$ there are two 'convergent' reduction sequences $\gamma_1 \rightarrow_* \gamma_3$ and $\gamma_2 \rightarrow_* \gamma_3$ (similar to the definition in TRS and the λ-calculus). The Church–Rosser property implies the *unique normal form property*.

Ambiguity

Just like in a TRS (partial) overlapping patterns in a GRS give rise to ambiguity and they can be a source of non-confluency. However, cyclic structures make it also possible that a subgraph can be matched in several ways on the same partially overlapping rule.

Example of several ways of matching with a cyclic structure:

```
r: F x,
x: F a  →    r := a
```

Take the following graph:

```
@1: F @2,
@2: F @1
```

This graph matches the rule in two ways. There are two possible mappings: μ(r) = @1, μ(x) = @2, μ(a) = @1 but also μ(r) = @2, μ(x) = @1, μ(a) = @2.

Comparing is not a source of non-confluency

In a TRS multiple occurrences of a variable in the left-hand side mean that the arguments are tested on their syntactic equality. In a GRS however, this means that a test is done on the equality of the node-ids of the arguments. If the node-ids are the same, the arguments are also syntactically equal. But subgraphs with the same contents need not have the same node-id of course. We conjecture that because of the different semantics, in a GRS comparing is *not* a source of non-confluency.

Consider the following example as a GRS (see also Section 4.4.3):

```
D x x   →   E
C x     →   D x (C x)
A       →   C A
```

In the rule for C on the right-hand side for the second argument of D a new node-id is invented for the node C x. This new node-id cannot be the same as the node-id corresponding with x. Since there is no rule C x → x these node-ids will remain different such that the rule for D can never be applied.

Self-embedding redexes

In GRSs a very special source of non-confluency exists, called *self-embedding redexes*. A redex is **self-embedding** iff there is a mapping μ for a rule ρ with redirection φ such that the corresponding μ'' applied to the redirection maps both left- and right-hand sides of the redirection to one and the same node-id constant in the graph. In other words: the root of the redex has to be redirected to itself. So such a self-embedding redex reduces to itself.

Consider the following GRS:

```
I x →  x
```

The graph @1: I @1 is a self-embedding redex. It will be reduced to itself as follows with the semantics as described up to now:

@1: I @1 $\rightarrow_I$ @1: I @1 $\rightarrow_I$ ...

The example below shows that with self-embedding redexes a non-confluent situation can occur.

Self-embedding redexes can give rise to a non-confluent situation:

```
A x →  x
B x →  x
```

The graph

```
@1: G @2 @3,
@2: A @3,
@3: B @2
```

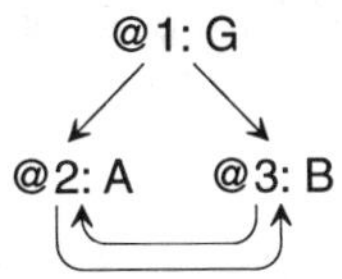

@1: G
@2: A @3: B

contains two redexes.

Depending on the order of evaluation two different self-embedding redexes are created:

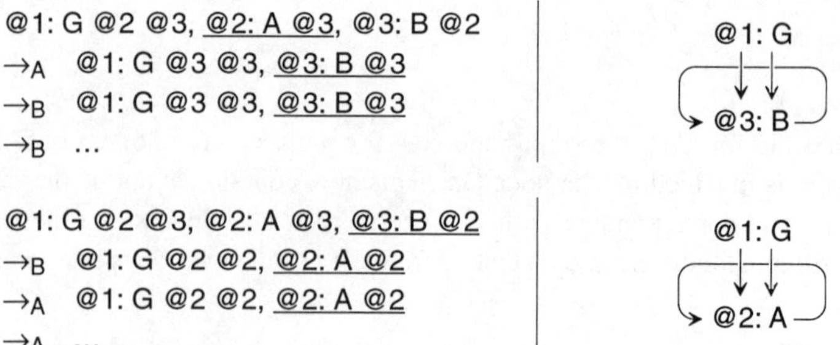

In the two resulting graphs there are no other redexes than the self-embedding redexes reducing to themselves, so the two graphs have no common reduct.

The only case in which this kind of non-confluency occurs is the case where self-embedding redexes do not have a common reduct (Kennaway *et al.*, 1993a). This source of non-confluency can only be taken away by changing the *semantics* of graph rewriting by adding a special **empty node** with the property that a self-embedding redex is reduced to this empty node instead of to itself. Besides removing the source of non-confluency, this solution has the advantage that it allows a categorical description of the semantics with only one push-out instead of two (Kennaway, 1990).

In the operational semantics it means a slight adaptation of step 4 (Section 5.3.3): a special case is inserted for a redirection of a self-embedding redex; in such a case instead of the standard redirection a redirection to an empty node is performed.

In the sequel it will always be assumed that the semantics is changed in this way. This has as a consequence that self-embedding redexes are not a source of non-confluency any more.

The graph @1: G @2 @3, @2: A @3, @3: B @2 reduced with the new semantics and the same rules described above. Both self-embedding redexes are reduced to an empty node.

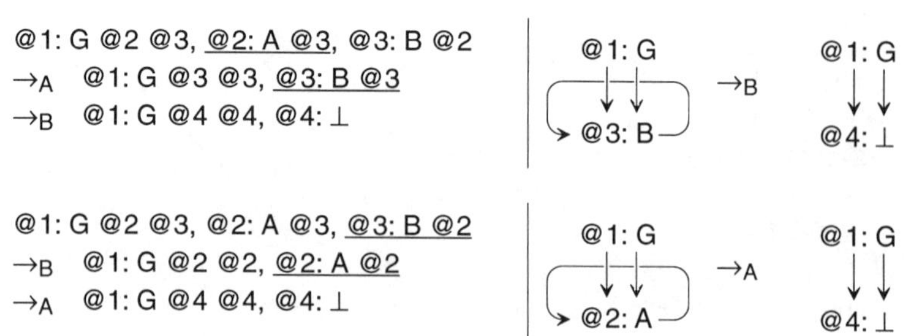

5.6.2 Sharing and computational complexity

Sharing can be used on the right-hand side of rewrite rules to avoid duplication of work by creating shared subgraphs or even cyclic graphs. Node-ids can be used on the left-hand side to address subgraphs in various ways.

In the following example cyclic objects are reduced to other cyclic objects. It is a solution for a Hamming problem: it computes an ordered list of all numbers of the form 2^n3^m, with $n, m \geq 0$. An efficient solution to this problem can be obtained by means of creating cyclic sharing in the contractum making heavy use of computations already done.

```
Ham →    x: Cons 1 (Merge (Map (* 2) x) (Map (* 3) x))
```

The map and merge functions (mapping a function on a list and merging two sorted lists into one sorted list with no multiple elements) can be defined as follows (IF, <, = and * are assumed to be defined elsewhere, Cons and Nil are just constructors with no special (predefined) meaning):

```
Merge   Nil             Nil             →   Nil
Merge   f: (Cons a b)   Nil             →   f
Merge   Nil             s: (Cons c d)   →   s
Merge   f: (Cons a b)   s: (Cons c d)   →   IF    (< a c)
                                                (Cons a (Merge b s))
                                                (IF    (= a c)
                                                       (Merge f d)
                                                       (Cons c (Merge f d)))

Map  f  Nil            →    Nil
Map  f  (Cons a b)     →    Cons (Ap f a) (Map f b)

Ap (* a) b  →    * a b
```

Note the use of Ap for the rewriting of a curried application of * (used as a constructor with one argument) to an application of * as a δ-rule (a function with two arguments). Further note that because f is specified in the redex pattern of Merge, both the components a and b as well as the subgraph f as a whole are available on the right-hand side.

The cyclic solution presented above has a polynomial complexity. The behaviour of this solution is much better than a solution in which recursion was used instead of this cyclic structure. The recursive solution specified below has an exponential complexity because previous computations performed by a call of Ham have to be recomputed.

```
Ham →    Cons 1 (Merge (Map (* 2) Ham) (Map (* 3) Ham))
```

5.6.3 Copying

GRSs are designed to exploit sharing wherever possible. As GRSs are an extension of TRSs, in GRSs one would expect a possibility of creating copies of subgraphs similar to the creation of duplicates of subterms in TRSs. However, in an ordinary GRS it is not possible to copy an arbitrary unknown data structure since in the contractum pattern multiple references to node-ids always imply sharing. In Chapter 14 an extension of GRSs is discussed that provides copying of arbitrary graph structures.

5.7 Reduction strategies

A **reduction strategy** is a function that, given a GRS and a graph, prescribes which redexes in the graph have to be rewritten next. It is possible that the strategy function prescribes more than one redex to be reduced next in arbitrary order. Such a strategy is called a **parallel reduction strategy**. It is also possible that the strategy function returns more than one redex or rule to choose from. In that case the strategy function is called **non-deterministic**. A **reducer** is a process that repeatedly reduces the redexes that are indicated by some strategy. The result of a reducer is reached as soon as the reduction strategy does not indicate redexes any more. A reduction strategy is **normalizing** iff, for any graph, having a normal form, the reducer applying the strategy will terminate at a normal form.

Another property a strategy can have is being *hypernormalizing*. A reduction strategy is **hypernormalizing** iff the strategy is normalizing even if it is diluted with a finite number of arbitrary reduction steps. The notion of hypernormalizing strategies can in the same way be defined in the TRS world and in the λ-calculus. However, the notion is particularly important in the context of *term graph rewriting* (see Section 5.8). It is also an important property when GRSs are used as the basis for a programming language. It makes it possible to deviate from the standard strategy to allow a more efficient evaluation order (see Part 4).

Parallel reducers are assumed to reduce the redexes indicated by a parallel reduction strategy in parallel, i.e. in arbitrary order. **Non-deterministic reducers** should choose non-deterministically one of the redexes offered by a non-deterministic strategy.

As is the case with TRSs, there exists no normalizing strategy for an arbitrary GRS. Instead of starting another independent quest for subclasses and normalizing strategies for GRSs, it seems to be more natural to investigate GRSs as extensions of TRSs.

5.8 Term graph rewriting

Although it is possible to search for confluent subclasses of GRSs with corresponding normalizing strategies we shall only investigate properties of TRSs that are converted into the GRS world to see whether it is possible to use sharing of subterms in general. Special attention is paid to the conversion of the most important TRS subclass for functional languages: priority rewrite systems with the functional strategy.

Term graph rewriting means that first a TRS and the term to be rewritten is converted (*lifted*) to a GRS; then in the GRS world reduction takes place and a normal form which is a graph is converted again (*unravelled*) to a term in the TRS world (Figure 5.6). Term graph rewriting (Barendregt *et al.*, 1987a) formally connects TRSs with GRSs.

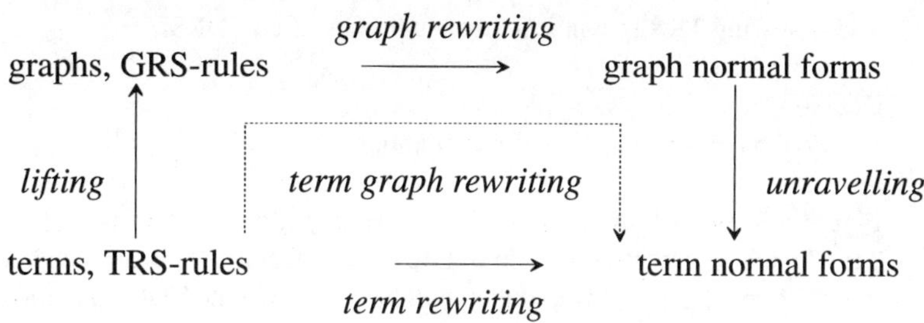

Figure 5.6 Diagram of term graph rewriting.

The conversion of a TRS to a GRS is called the **lifting** of a TRS to a GRS. One can easily convert a TRS to a GRS almost without any syntactic change in the rules, because the TRS notation is also a valid GRS (shorthand) notation. Although the rules of that GRS are syntactically the same as the TRS rules, semantically they get a different meaning. Note that TRSs and GRSs work on different objects and the comparing of terms in TRSs is not at all the same thing as the comparing of node-ids in GRSs. However, many properties of TRSs are inherited if TRSs are lifted. In many cases the only difference between TRSs and GRSs will be that, through sharing, fewer steps are needed to reach a normal form.

The conversion of a graph to a term is called the **unravelling** of the graph. A graph is unravelled by recursively duplicating all shared subgraphs starting from the root of the graph. This yields a tree representation of the term that is the result of the unravelling. When the graph to be unravelled is cyclic, recursive duplication goes on forever resulting in an infinite term.

There are various ways of lifting TRSs and they have led to the investigation of special classes of GRSs. Since the semantics of a comparing rule that is lifted would change too dramatically, these classes have in common that no rule is comparing. This restriction implies that it is impossible to pattern match on equivalency of node-ids (sharing). So a left-hand side in these classes is always a graph without sharing (like a term). Because of this restriction the classes are called **term … rewriting systems** where **…** indicates what kind of right-hand sides are allowed. The most simple subclass is **term tree rewriting systems** (TTRSs) in which right-hand sides must be trees. In order to express this properly a special semantic action for duplication of arguments on the right-hand side is necessary (see Section 5.6.3). TTRSs are equivalent to TRSs.

The most natural subclass of TGRSs is **term dag rewriting systems** (TDRSs) in which right-hand sides must be **dags** (*d*irected *a*cyclic *g*raphs). When a TRS is lifted to a TDRS all rules remain syntactically the same.

The following TRS is syntactically equal to its lifted TDRS:

```
Double x             →   + x x
Heavy_Computation    →   Easy_Number
```

Figure 5.3 shows how the term Double Heavy_Computation is reduced in a TRS (using a lazy strategy). In a TRS four reduction steps are needed. The graph Double Heavy_Computation will be reduced in the TDRS as follows:

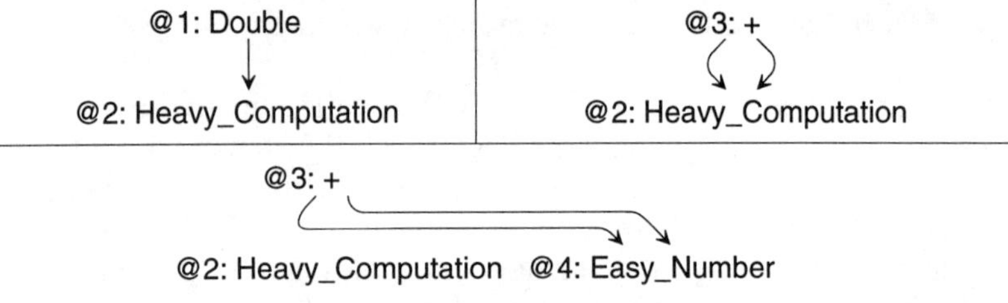

Figure 5.7 Sharing of computations in graph rewriting.

Figure 5.7 shows that in a GRS only three reduction steps are needed to perform the corresponding computation. Due to sharing the Heavy_Computation is only reduced once. The results of both computations, modulo unravelling, are the same.

In Barendregt *et al.* (1987a) it is proven that lifted *orthogonal* TRSs are also confluent as TDRSs. It is shown that if strategies are hypernormalizing for an orthogonal TRS, these strategies are normalizing when they are used in the corresponding TDRS. This can be explained as follows: if a shared subgraph is chosen by a strategy, not only is the GRS counterpart of the original term reduced, but as a side-effect (due to the sharing) also the counterpart of other equivalent terms. If the original strategy is hypernormalizing, the additional rewriting steps that are performed cannot influence the outcome of the computation.

Lifting is not always safe for a *general* TRS. There are some subtle differences between TRSs and corresponding TDRSs. It is possible that the corresponding TDRS has less normal forms than its original TRS.

The normal form properties can change when an *ambiguous* TRS is lifted to a TDRS :

```
A x    →  B x x
C      →  D
D      →  C
B C D  →  E
```

The normal form of A C in the TRS world is E according to A C $\to_A$ B C C $\to_C$ B C D $\to_B$ E (Figure 5.8).

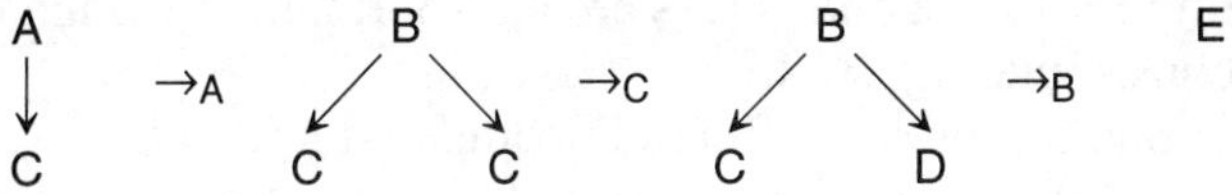

Figure 5.8 Reduction to normal form in the original TRS.

In the graph world the TDRS with the same rules will reduce the graph A C to

```
    @1: A @2,     @2: C
→A  @3: B @2 @2,  @2: C
→C  @3: B @4 @4,  @4: D
→D  @3: B @5 @5,  @5: C  →*  ...
```

There is no normal form. The double occurrence of x on the right-hand side of the A-rule creates sharing that (in this example) will exist forever (Figure 5.9).

```
@1: A        @3: B        @3: B        @3: B
  |    →A    (   )   →C   (   )   →D   (   )   →C  ...
@2: C        @2: C        @4: D        @5: C
```

Figure 5.9 Fewer normal forms in the lifted TRS than in the original TRS.

Via term graph rewriting in TDRSs it is proven that, independent of the chosen strategy, sharing terms is *sound* (i.e. an unravelled normal form of the TDRS is also a normal form for the TRS) for all TRSs and *complete* (i.e. for any normal form in the TRS, the TDRS will have a normal form that can be unravelled to it) for orthogonal TRSs.

Well-known strategies that are hypernormalizing for certain subclasses are, for example, parallel-outermost, leftmost-outermost, the discriminating position strategy and the Huet–Lévy strategy. So a TRS with one of these hypernormalizing strategies can be lifted to a TDRS safely. The result (modulo unravelling) will be the same. In general, due to the sharing of subterms, fewer reduction steps will be needed in the TDRS to reach the normal form.

The most general subclass is the one in which no further restrictions are given: **term graph rewriting systems** (TGRSs). In a TGRS right-hand sides are GRS graphs that may contain cycles. For certain simple recursive rewrite rules in a TRS (see, for example, the solution for the Hamming problem in Section 5.6) rules with cycles on the right-hand side are created in the corresponding TGRS. In this way infinite data structures can be implemented efficiently with cyclic graphs.

Lifted orthogonal TRSs are also confluent as TGRSs (due to the changed semantics introduced in Section 5.6.1). Strategies that are hypernormalizing for orthogonal TRSs are also normalizing when they are used in the corresponding TGRS.

There is one important difference compared with TDRSs. The reduction in the TGRS may yield a normal form that is a cyclic graph, while the corresponding reduction in the TRS does not terminate.

Consider the following TRS:	Lifting this to a TGRS yields:
F x → A x	F x → A x
G → F G	G → x: F x
Start → G	Start → G

The normal form of the TGRS is @N: A @N. In the TRS the computation does not terminate. The term reduces to terms of the following form: A(A(A(...))).

The unravelling of a cyclic graph in normal form results in an infinite term. Note that it is impossible to specify infinite terms in TRSs. However, an infinite term can be seen as a limit of a non-terminating computation. In a TGRS an infinite term can be specified in a cyclic graph. But, if such a cyclic graph normal form is unravelled to a term, the unravelling process does not terminate either. If in an implementation the result of the unravelled graph would be printed it is indistinguishable from the printing of the head normal form parts of the non-terminating computation obtained via term reduction. Both prints produce equal output and do not terminate.

The unravelling of an empty node results in a **bottom** symbol, ⊥, i.e. a special symbol in the TRS world that represents a non-terminating computation producing no result. Again the results are indistinguishable since in both cases *no* resulting output is produced.

So in that sense also lifting a TRS to a TGRS is *sound* (i.e. an unravelled normal form of the TGRS is also a normal form for the TRS if the unravelled normal form is a finite non-bottom term while the results are indistinguishable otherwise) for all TRSs and *complete* (i.e. for any normal form in the TRS, the TGRS will have a normal form that can be unravelled to it) for orthogonal TRSs (Kennaway *et al.*, 1993b).

Empty nodes in the context of functional languages:

f = h f h x = x f?	F → x: H x H x → x Start → F

In a functional language a computation corresponding to an empty node is assumed to be not intended. The Miranda program on the left halts with a black hole error. The GRS reduces the initial graph to an empty node. In the functional graph rewriting language Clean (see Chapter 8) a cycle_in_spine error would be given.

So a TRS with a hypernormalizing strategy can also be lifted to a TGRS safely. Due to the presence of cycles even fewer reduction steps may be needed in the TGRS world than in the TDRS world.

5.8.1 Functional graph rewriting systems

FTRSs can also be lifted to a GRS class called **functional graph rewriting systems** (FGRSs): TGRSs with priorities added using the functional strategy. Lifting is accomplished in the same way as explained above. FGRSs will be heavily used in this textbook. In Parts 4 and 5 it is shown that efficient state-of-the-art implementations on sequential and parallel hardware can be obtained by compiling functional languages to Clean, a language that is based on FGRSs.

Adding priorities in GRSs has similar semantics as in TRSs, i.e. a matching rule can only be chosen if no rule with higher priority can ever match on the (internally rewritten) graph. As in TRSs this has the following properties:

- it is undecidable whether a term can ever match a pattern via internal rewrites;
- forcing evaluation leads to a decidable approximation of the priority semantics in which reduction is always correct with respect to the priority semantics; however, in some cases forcing evaluation leads to non-termination, although semantically it was avoidable;
- textual order is defined to correspond to increasing priority;
- the functional strategy effectively applies the discriminating position strategy to one rule alternative at a time.

Factorial as an FGRS (syntactically unchanged by the lifting process):

```
Fac 0   →   1
Fac n   →   * n (Fac (– n 1))
```

Note that n is shared on the right-hand side of the second alternative.

The definition of the functional strategy has to be slightly adapted for FGRSs. Evaluation is not uniformly forced to strong head normal form but to its analogue in GRSs: strong root normal form. The functional strategy is efficiently implementable, intuitively clear and normalizing for a large class of FGRSs (see the previous chapter). The functional strategy is even hypernormalizing for this class. Of course, only diluted reductions are allowed that are not in conflict with the priority in the rules.

So also lifting a TRS with priorities and the functional strategy to a FGRS is *sound* (i.e. an unravelled normal form of the FGRS is also a normal form for the TRS if the unravelled normal form is a finite non-bottom term while the results are indistinguishable otherwise) for all TRSs and *complete* (i.e. for any normal form in the TRS, the FGRS will have a normal form that can be unravelled to it).

Due to the use of the functional strategy FGRSs can be regarded as a very simple functional language with a more explicit notion of controlling the sharing of terms.

The functional strategy is a partial function for FGRSs

There is a subtle difference between the functional strategy in TRSs and its analogue in FGRSs: owing to the presence of cycles the functional strategy is a partial function for FGRSs. The explanation for this is that it can happen that the functional strategy itself does not terminate when it recursively searches for a redex on a cycle.

Consider the following TRS:	The FGRS resulting from lifting this TRS:
F (F a) → 1	F (F a) → 1
G → F (F G)	G → x: F (F x)
initial term: G	Start → G

In the TRS the functional strategy tries to force the evaluation of the argument of F (after reduction of G). Since the argument of F contains an F again, also this argument is forced. This leads to reduction of G resulting in further applications of F. The reduction process will not terminate.

Also in the FGRS the functional strategy tries to force the evaluation of the argument of F (after reduction of Start and G). Since on the cycle every node consists of F with an argument, the process of selecting a candidate for evaluation will go on for ever. Reduction will never take place.

Note that in both systems termination would have been possible if evaluation was not forced.

Non-termination of the strategy in the FGRS corresponds to non-termination of the computation with the functional strategy in the TRS.

A special aspect of the non-termination of the functional strategy in FGRSs is that non-termination can be detected as an erroneous situation: whenever it occurs, the strategy is running on a cycle.

One could be tempted to change the semantics of the functional strategy such that when the strategy runs on a cycle, evaluation is not forced. Instead, a test could be performed to see whether the pattern matches the graph and a redex is indicated accordingly. Then, the strategy becomes a total function. But an important property of the functional strategy would be lost: the strategy would not be hypernormalizing any more. The problem is caused by an interference between partial ambiguity in the rule system and a cyclic graph structure that matches in various ways.

The functional strategy would not be hypernormalizing if it would not always force evaluation:

```
F (F a)  →   1

G 1 x    →   1
G x y    →   G x y
```

Take the following graph:

```
@1: G @2 @3,
@2: F @3,
@3: F @2
```

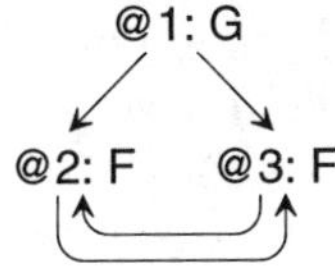

Then, the normal form would be 1 since it would be detected that the strategy runs on a cycle: forcing evaluation is stopped, the cycle matches the redex pattern of the F rule and reduction to normal form takes place.

$@1{:}\ G\ @2\ @3,\ \underline{@2{:}\ F\ @3},\ \underline{@3{:}\ F\ @2}$

$\rightarrow_F\ \ \underline{@1{:}\ G\ @4\ @3},\ \underline{@4{:}\ 1,\ @3{:}\ F\ @4}$

$\rightarrow_{G_1}\ @4{:}\ 1$

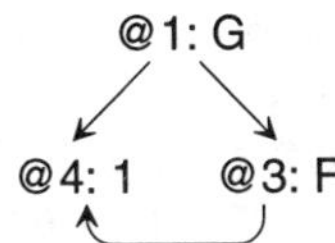

If such a reduction is diluted with reduction of the second argument of G, then afterwards the functional strategy will not reach the normal form any more:

```
@1: G @2 @3, @2: F @3, @3: F @2
→F   @1: G @2 @4, @2: F @4, @4: 1
→G2  @1: G @2 @4, @2: F @4, @4: 1
→*   ...
```

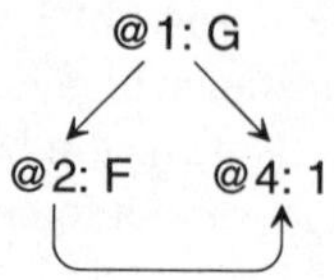

The functional strategy being a partial function for FGRSs is just a new aspect of the fact that forcing evaluation is a decidable approximation of the priority semantics: for graphs that correspond to infinite computations in the term rewrite world, the non-termination may not only concern the reduction process but also the strategy itself.

5.8.2 GRSs versus TRSs

We have shown that many interesting TRSs can be lifted safely to GRSs. For these systems the outcome of a computation in the TRS world is equal to the unravelled outcome of the corresponding computation in the GRS world. It has been shown that this is not a general property as one might have expected.

Different behaviours between TRSs and GRSs are generally possible when graphs with cyclic structures are being used. Also comparing in TRSs has quite a different meaning than comparing in GRSs and is therefore forbidden when TRSs are lifted to GRSs. But fortunately the lifting process is sound and complete for important (sub)classes of orthogonal TRSs and TRSs with priorities.

As a consequence one can say that the most important difference between these kinds of TRSs and GRSs is that in the latter duplication of work is avoided. This is an efficiency aspect: fewer rewrite steps are needed in the GRS than in the original TRS. Although GRSs can be regarded as an extension of TRSs one should realize that in general it is impossible in a standard GRS to duplicate work explicitly since it is impossible to copy arbitrary graph structures in these systems. An extension of GRSs in which copying as well as sharing can be expressed is given in Chapter 14.

5.9 Generalized graph rewriting systems

A very high expressive power is realized in **generalized graph rewriting systems** (Barendregt *et al.*, 1987b) because the transformations that can be performed are extended. This induces a trade-off: adding restrictions decreases expressiveness but it may yield important properties for reasoning or implementation (e.g. referential transparency or efficient fine-grain parallelism). In a generalized GRS the right-hand side of a rewrite rule may contain several redirections. Any node can be redirected to another one. All redirections specified in the rule are done in parallel in one reduction step.

This extension makes it possible to express much more complex changes of a graph structure than simple subgraph replacement. A generalized GRS can be regarded as a very powerful graph assembler. In such a system confluency is by no means guaranteed. Assignment can be modelled very well. Unification can be expressed. Any concrete machine language can be modelled in such a generalized system. As a consequence, referential transparency is no longer guaranteed.

So generalized graph rewriting can model other languages than pure functional languages, such as logical languages and even imperative languages (Glauert *et al.*, 1987). Although generalized graph rewriting systems are not of direct importance in the context of this textbook they are explained here briefly to illustrate their conceptual power.

5.9.1 Multiple redirections

With multiple redirections side-effects can be expressed. All redirections specified in a rule are done in parallel in one reduction step. As a consequence, parallel redirections act like parallel assignments with which it is possible to interchange values of variables. With parallel redirections it is possible to effectively interchange node-ids.

Illustration of parallel evaluation of multiple redirections:

```
r: F x y z        →     r := x, y := z
```

Take the following graph @1: F @2 @2 @1. This graph matches the rule and the redirections that have to be performed are @1 := @2, @2 := @1. Because of the parallel evaluation (like in a parallel assignment) the effect will be that the applied occurrences of @1 and @2 are exchanged. So the result will be @1: F @1 @1 @2.

Now suppose that with the same rule the graph is @1: F @2 @1 @3. Also this graph matches the rule and now the redirections that have to be performed are @1 := @2, @1 := @3. Because of the parallel evaluation of the substitutions either all applied occurrences of @1 will be replaced by @2 or all applied occurrences of @1 will be replaced by @3. The choice between these two possibilities is made non-deterministically. Note that the semantics does not allow some of the applied occurrences of @1 to be replaced by @2 and others to be replaced by @3. In this sense a redirection is indivisible.

It is intuitively clear that side-effects can be created with multiple redirections. This will be further illustrated by an example designed by E. Meijer: a GRS that implements a simple unification algorithm, using multiple redirections. It operates on representations of two types, returning 'cannot unify' in case of failure. The types are constructed from three basic types I(nteger), B(oolean) and V(ariable) and a composition constructor Com(position). Different type variables are represented by distinct nodes. References to the same shared node are taken to be references to the same type variable. The unification rule has as arguments the two types that have to be unified. During the unification process the graph representing the unification is constructed and delivered as the result. However, it may also turn out that unification is not possible. Then, the graph constructed so far has to be replaced by 'cannot unify' in cases of failure. To make this possible the root of this graph is passed as a third argument such that it can be redirected when unification is not possible.

```
   Unify  x           x            r  →  x
o: Unify  t1:(Com x y) t2:(Com p q) r  →  n: Com (Unify x p r) (Unify y q r),
                                          o := n, t1 := n, t2 := n
o: Unify  t1:V        t2           r  →  o := t2, t1 := t2
o: Unify  t1          t2:V         r  →  o := t1, t2 := t1
   Unify  (Com x y)   I            r  →  n: "cannot unify",  r := n
   Unify  (Com x y)   B            r  →  n: "cannot unify",  r := n
   Unify  I           (Com x y)    r  →  n: "cannot unify",  r := n
   Unify  B           (Com x y)    r  →  n: "cannot unify",  r := n
   Unify  I           B            r  →  n: "cannot unify",  r := n
   Unify  B           I            r  →  n: "cannot unify",  r := n
```

For instance, find the unification of a cycle y: Com I y and the same cycle unravelled once z: Com I (Com I z). The result will be u: Com I u. Hence, assume that the start rule is

```
Start →   x: Unify y z x,
          y: Com I y,
          z: Com I (Com I z)
```

After reduction of the start rule there is the following graph:

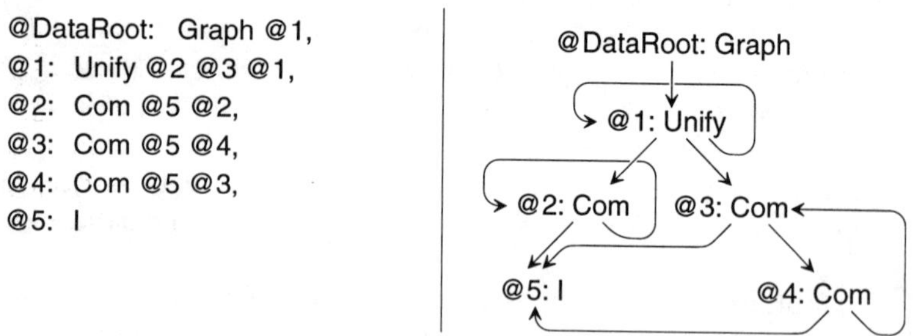

It can be rewritten as follows by applying the second rule for Unify:

μ(o) = @1, μ(t1) = @2, μ(t2) = @3, μ(x) = @5, μ(y) = @2, μ(p) = @5, μ(q) = @4, μ(r) = @1

The contractum is:

```
@6: Com @7 @8,   @7: Unify @5 @5 @1,   @8: Unify @2 @4 @1
```

After redirection and garbage collection this yields

```
@DataRoot:  Graph @6,
@6:  Com @7 @8,
@7:  Unify @5 @5 @6,
@5:  I,
@8:  Unify @6 @4 @6,
@4:  Com @5 @6
```

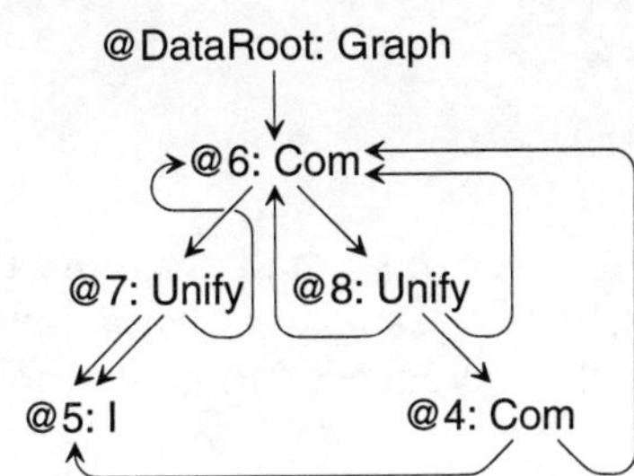

Rewriting this graph by applying the first rule for Unify to @7 yields:

```
@DataRoot:  Graph @6,
@6:  Com @5 @8,
@5:  I,
@8:  Unify @6 @4 @6,
@4:  Com @5 @6
```

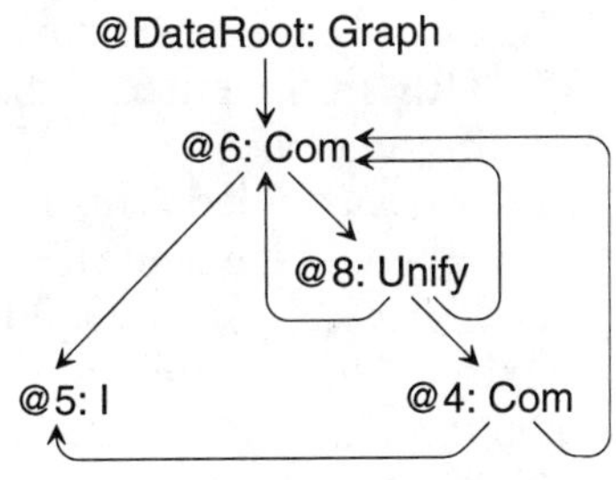

This can be rewritten by applying the second rule for Unify to @8:

μ(o) = @8, μ(t1) = @6, μ(t2) = @4, μ(x) = @5, μ(y) = @8, μ(p) = @5, μ(q) = @6, μ(r) = @6

The contractum is

```
@9: Com @10 @11,   @10: Unify @5 @5 @6,   @11: Unify @8 @6 @6
```

After redirection and garbage collection this yields

```
@DataRoot:  Graph @9,
@9:     Com @10 @11,
@10:    Unify @5 @5 @9,
@5:     I,
@11:    Unify @9 @9 @9
```

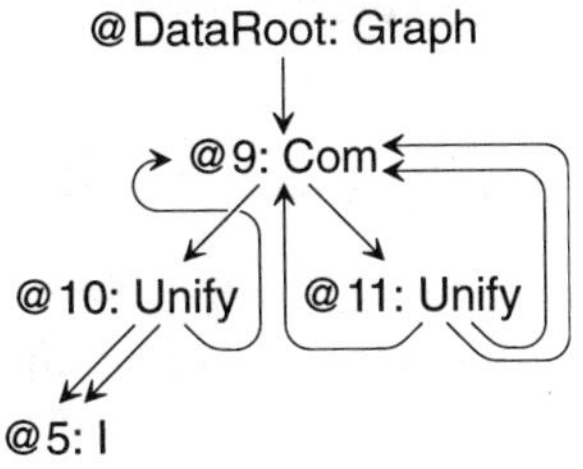

Finally, on this graph the first rule for Unify on @10 and on @11 can be applied, yielding the wanted unifier:

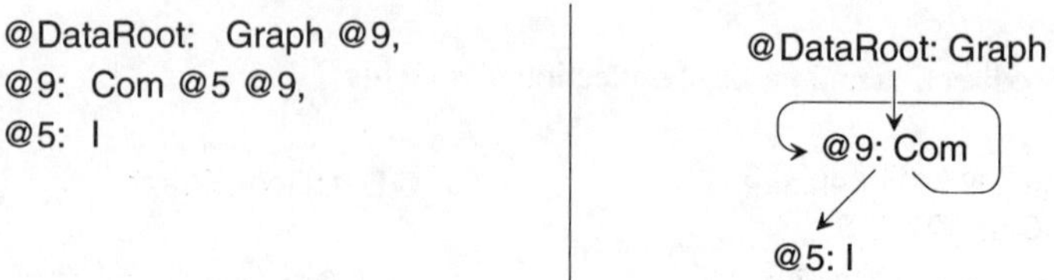

Of course, this small example does not model unification in general. But, it gives an idea of the power of redirection and how it might be used to solve these kinds of problems.

5.10 GRSs as a basis for functional languages

In the previous chapter we have seen that there are several kinds of TRSs that can be used as a basis for functional languages. Most properties of a TRS are inherited if the TRS is lifted to a GRS. The most important difference between TRSs and GRSs is that in the latter duplication of work is avoided. This makes GRSs more suited to serve as a basis for functional languages if efficiency is of interest.

As with TRSs, if a functional program is translated to a GRS the complexity of the compilation scheme, the complexity of the obtained code and the efficiency of the reducer are heavily influenced by the kind of GRS chosen. For a lazy functional language without explicit graph rewriting semantics one has to assume that sharing is created and that for certain recursive definitions a cyclic structure is created (which in fact means that assumptions are made about some *unknown* graph rewriting semantics). These assumptions may be essential not only for reasoning about the efficiency of the program but in certain cases even for reasoning about the computational complexity of the program (see Section 5.6.2).

The most obvious choice is to use FGRSs as a basis. Owing to the use of the functional strategy FGRSs can be regarded as a very simple functional language with a more explicit notion of controlling the sharing of terms. Part 4 treats the translation from Miranda to the FGRS based language Clean.

5.11 GRSs as a basis for implementations

In practice almost all implementations of functional languages use sharing in one way or another. Many implementations (e.g. of HOPE, Haskell, LML and Miranda) can therefore be regarded as implementations of GRSs. For instance, the implementation of Sasl, described in Turner (1979a), is based on the following combinatorial GRS:

```
Ap (Ap (Ap S x) y) z   →   Ap (Ap x z) (Ap y z)
Ap (Ap K x) y          →   x
Ap I x                 →   x
```

Note that in the S-rule sharing of the distributed argument z is maintained. Leftmost-outermost is hypernormalizing for a combinatorial TRS and therefore this strategy can be used as normalizing strategy for a combinatorial GRS also. Of course, when an implementation is made for a GRS, special attention is paid to make such an implementation as fast as possible. This may lead to exploiting stacks, registers, δ-rules, avoiding building of graphs whenever possible, implementation of redirection via overwriting of nodes or via creation of indirection nodes, etc. In Parts 4 and 5 of this book we show in detail how efficient state-of-the-art implementations of the FGRS-based language Clean is achieved.

Summary

- In GRSs *graphs* are being rewritten instead of *terms*. This makes it possible to *share* computations during rewriting such that duplication of work can be avoided.
- There are many similarities between TRSs and GRSs; many notions like *normal forms*, *strategies* and *rewriting* in GRSs are similar to these notions in TRSs; many properties of GRSs are similar to properties of TRSs:
  - *normal forms* are not *unique*;
  - the *root normal form property* is *undecidable*;
  - the *strong root normal form property* is *decidable*;
  - there is *no normalizing strategy*.
- There are some important differences between TRSs and GRSs:
  - in GRSs connected, possibly cyclic *graphs* are being rewritten instead of *trees* (*terms*);
  - *comparing* in GRSs implies a test that checks whether two subgraphs are shared or not; two syntactically equivalent subgraphs are considered to be unequal in GRSs if they are not shared; in TRSs two syntactically equivalent subterms are always considered to be equal.
- Ambiguity is a source of non-confluency in GRSs. *Comparing* is conjectured to be not a source of non-confluency. The introduction of *empty nodes* removes *self-embedding redexes* as a source of non-confluency.

- A TRS can be *lifted* to a GRS; this transformation can be performed almost without any change in syntax.
  - Owing to the difference in semantics comparing is not allowed in TRSs that are lifted.
  - If lifting is sound and complete, reduction can be performed in the GRS world instead of the TRS world; if the resulting graph is converted back to a term the result is equivalent with the result that would have been obtained in the TRS world; owing to the sharing the number of reduction steps that is needed to reach the normal form is generally decreased.
- A TRS can be lifted to a GRS without cycles (resulting in a *term dag rewriting system*) or to a GRS with cycles (resulting in a *term graph rewriting system*).
  - Strategies that are *hypernormalizing* for an orthogonal TRS are *normalizing* when they are used in the corresponding TDRS/TGRS: parallel-outermost, leftmost-outermost, the discriminating position strategy and the Huet–Lévy strategy are hypernormalizing and hence normalizing in a lifted context.
  - When a TRS is lifted to a TDRS/TGRS, sharing of terms is *sound* for all TRSs and *complete* for orthogonal TRSs; these properties are independent of the reduction strategy.
  - Lifting a FTRS to a FGRS is *sound* and *complete*.
- Graph rewriting can be *generalized* in such a way that *non-functional concepts* as found in logic languages and imperative languages can also be modelled.
- Graph rewriting semantics is required to make it possible to *reason* about the actual *computational complexity* of a lazy functional program.
- The class of FGRSs seems best suited to be used as a computational model for functional languages; important concepts in FGRSs also play an important role in functional languages:
  - *pattern matching* is available;
  - *sharing* is used as an optimization in the implementation;
  - reduction proceeds with the *functional strategy*.

EXERCISES

5.1 Write the GRS-rules in their canonical form.

(a) `F (F 5)  →  G 5 5`
(b) `F x y    →  G x (F x y)`
(c) `F x:5 x  →  G x (H 5)`

5.2 Write the GRS-rules in shorthand form, as short as possible.

(a)
```
r: F x,
x: Cons x y,
y: F r          →   a: G r b,
                    b: F a
```
(b)
```
r: F x x,
x: Cons x r     →   a: Cons b c,
                    b: Cons c b,
                    c: Cons b r
```
(c)
```
r: F x,
x: Cons y z,
z: Nil          →   y
```

5.3 The following GRS and initial graph is given:

```
Eq x x     → True
Eq x y     → False
F (G x y)  → G (F x y) y
```
initial graph: @0:F @1:(G @2:(Eq @3:5 @4:5) @1)

Show all redexes in the graph. Give, for each redex, the mapping from the corresponding rule to the graph. Rewrite, step by step, the redex corresponding to the rule for F (the third rule).

5.4* Write a GRS-rule generating a list of pairs, each pair containing a natural number (in ascending order) and a reference to the pair in the list containing half of that number (rounded downwards). So

```
Cons a:(Pair 0 a) (Cons b:(Pair 1 a) (Cons c:(Pair 2 b) (Cons d:(Pair 3 b) ...
```
is the initial segment of this list.

5.5 Write a GRS-rule that traverses a tree from left to right, yielding a list of all nodes in this tree in the order in which they are visited. The tree is built with the constructor Tree, taking two arguments, and the constructor Leaf, which has no arguments (e.g. Tree Leaf (Tree Leaf (Tree Leaf Leaf)) is a tree).

5.6 Give the possible results of the following systems both when you consider them as TRSs and when you consider them as GRSs.

(a)
```
F x          →   G x x
G (+ 0 1) 1  →   0
```
initial expression: F (+ 0 1)

(b)
```
F g (Cons a b)  →   Cons (g a) (F g b)
F g Nil         →   Nil
```
initial expression: F (+ 1) (Cons 1 (Cons 0 Nil))

Part 3
Analysis of functional programs

This part treats two important kinds of static analysis of functional programs: *type assignment systems* and *strictness analysis.*

The purpose of static analysis is to deduce certain properties of a particular program at compile-time. The properties that are of interest can vary from properties that are important for the *correctness* of the program, such as type checking, to properties that are important for an *efficient execution,* such as complexity analysis, termination analysis, reference count analysis and strictness analysis.

Properties are generally studied on the level of the model of computation. Most interesting properties turn out to be undecidable. Therefore, with a static analysis usually only a decidable approximation of the desired property can be derived. This results in a methodology for the analysis that can be applied on the level of the model and also in practice directly on some internal data structure of a compiler. Every static analysis tries to deduce at compile-time as much information as possible from the program.

Type systems are traditionally studied in the λ-calculus via formal schemes to infer types of λ-terms. We also study a type system for TRSs that can easily be transferred to FGRSs.

Strictness analysis is usually also studied in the λ-calculus via a technique called *abstract interpretation.* We also describe a methodology for the analysis that is performed in rewriting systems via a technique called *abstract reduction.*

Chapter 6
Type assignment systems

Adding type information to a program is important for several reasons. Type information makes a program more *readable* because it gives a human being additional information about the structure of a program. Furthermore, type information plays an essential role in the implementation: the information is needed to obtain an *efficient implementation* and it also makes *separate compilation* of program modules possible (see Part 4). However, one of the most important aspects of type systems is that they warn the programmer at an early stage (at compile-time) if a program contains *severe errors.* If a program is type-error free, it is assumed to be safe to run: *'Typed programs cannot go wrong'* (Milner, 1978). So a compile-time analysis of a program rejects programs in which errors may occur at run-time. However, some errors depend on the values computed at run-time (e.g. divide by zero or stack overflow). They cannot be detected at compile-time. So only some *special classes of run-time errors* can be found at compile-time.

Typing concerns the analysis of the domain and the range on which functions are defined and a check that these functions are indeed applied consistently. The exact domain and range of a function can depend on its run-time behaviour and is therefore undecidable at compile-time. A decidable compile-time approximation can be found by looking at the syntactic structure of the program only. This chapter deals with such type assignment systems for functional languages.

Although, as shown in Part 2, graph rewriting systems are best suited as a basis to reason about functional languages and their implementation, a type system that exploits the special properties of GRSs (e.g. by using cyclic types) has not yet been developed. Therefore, type systems for functional languages are still based upon type systems for the λ-calculus. In this chapter, type systems are treated in their historical context: the λ-calculus, followed by a context that is more close to functional languages: term rewriting systems. These type systems for the λ-calculus and TRSs can be transferred easily to FGRSs.

The basis of every type system for the λ-calculus (Section 6.1) has been defined by H.B. Curry (Curry and Feys, 1958). Type assignment in this system is decidable and most type assignment algorithms used in functional programming languages are based upon it. Unfortunately, the type system can only type terms that are **strongly normalizing**, i.e. terms that reduce to normal form in all possible reduction orders. Furthermore, the type system can only type a subclass of these strongly normalizing terms. This subclass does not contain terms in which self-application occurs. Examples of terms with self-application are fixed point combinators which play an essential role in dealing with recursion.

The λ-calculus, and a type assignment system for it, can be extended in a natural way to incorporate recursion. In this chapter it will be done by presenting an intermediate language Λ^+ (Section 6.2) in which λ-terms can be named such that recursion can be expressed. Both Milner's as well as Mycroft's type assignment systems are presented. Their properties are analysed and compared.

Finally, also type assignment on TRSs is discussed (Section 6.3) as a generalization of the Mycroft type assignment system for Λ^+. It turns out that some general properties of Mycroft's system (like subject reduction) are only valid for TRSs under certain restrictions.

6.1 Type assignment for the λ-calculus

H.B. Curry was the first to study typing for the pure λ-calculus. He designed a straightforward system that is completely syntax-directed: like the definition of the set of λ-terms, the Curry type system also expresses *abstraction* (function definition) and (function) *application*.

First, the basic concepts of this system are explained using the concept of *typed trees*. A tree representation of a λ-term can be labelled with types according to *type assignment rules*. The resulting typed tree corresponds with a formal logic deduction in standard type theory. Such a deduction is constructed with inference rules that correspond directly to the type assignment rules that label the tree.

Then, it is shown how intuitively a type can be derived in this system. A formal specification of several related type assignment algorithms is given in a functional style.

Finally, some general properties of the Curry system are discussed.

6.1.1 Basic concepts of the Curry type system

Intuitively, the Curry type system restricts all occurrences of the *same bound variable* to have the *same type* and furthermore in every application the *argument* is of the desired *domain type* and the *result* of the function applied to that argument has to be of the desired *range type*. This means that a function *definition* is of type $\sigma \rightarrow \tau$ if the function body is of type τ (the range) and in the body the argument is used consistently with type σ (the domain). For a function *application* this means that the application is of type τ when a function of type $\sigma \rightarrow \tau$ is applied to an argument of type σ.

Curry types

The set of Curry types contains all types that can be built from type variables and the type constructor $\rightarrow$ (arrow). Its inductive definition is:

(1) all type variables φ_0, φ_1, ... are Curry types.

(2) if σ and τ are Curry types, then $(\sigma \rightarrow \tau)$ is a Curry type.

In this chapter, σ, τ, ρ_0, ρ_1, ... are used to name arbitrary Curry types. M and N are used to name arbitrary λ-terms. Not all brackets are used in the notation of a type. The arrow constructor is *right associative* and *outermost brackets* are omitted.

Typed trees

Assigning a type to a λ-term consists of first constructing a tree representation of that term (see Chapter 3), extended with an edge to the root node. Then, the nodes and edges of this tree are labelled by adding labels of the form '::', followed by a type. This results in a *typed tree* (Figure 6.1).

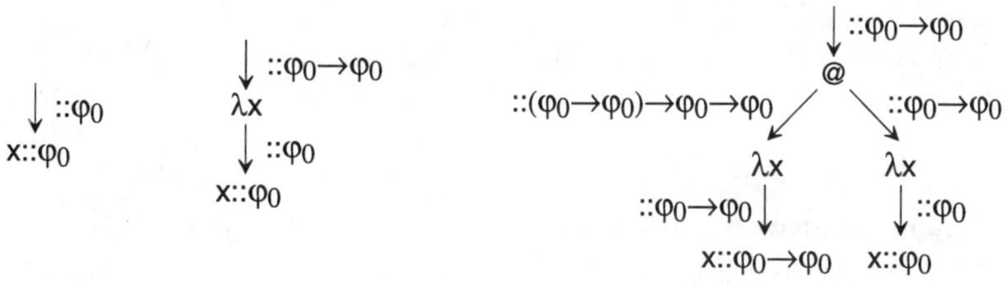

$::\varphi_0$
$x::\varphi_0$

$::\varphi_0 \rightarrow \varphi_0$
λx
$::\varphi_0$
$x::\varphi_0$

$::\varphi_0 \rightarrow \varphi_0$
@
$::(\varphi_0 \rightarrow \varphi_0) \rightarrow \varphi_0 \rightarrow \varphi_0$ $\quad$ $::\varphi_0 \rightarrow \varphi_0$
λx $\quad$ λx
$::\varphi_0 \rightarrow \varphi_0$ $\quad$ $::\varphi_0$
$x::\varphi_0 \rightarrow \varphi_0$ $\quad$ $x::\varphi_0$

Figure 6.1 A typed tree for respectively, x, λx.x and (λx.x)(λx.x). Note that in the rightmost tree $x::\varphi_0 \rightarrow \varphi_0$ was assumed in the left subtree while $x::\varphi_0$ was assumed in the right subtree.

A **typed tree** is a tree representation of a λ-expression labelled with type information in such a way that the types of variables, application nodes and abstraction nodes are *consistent* with respect to the Curry type restrictions mentioned above. Then, the type at the top edge of a typed tree is a correct Curry type for the λ-term involved. The leaves of the tree (containing term variables) are called **assumptions**, and the set of all assumptions for a term is called the **basis**. The combination of type σ at the top edge and basis is called a **pair** for the term N. The notation N::σ is called a **statement** and expresses the fact that σ is a suitable type for N; the combination of this type and λ-term is called the **conclusion** of the typed tree.

Type assignment constraints

Type assignment constraints are a translation of the Curry type restrictions to consistency requirements for typed trees: assigning types to a λ-term is **consistent** if it satisfies the type assignment constraints defined below. There are only two type assignment constraints in Curry's system (Figure 6.2), the **application constraint** (@), and **abstraction constraint** (λ). In the literature these constraints are defined by giving type assignment rules respectively **arrow elimination** (→E) and **arrow introduction** (→I). Here, starting with typed subtrees a constraint states how these subtrees can be combined into other typed trees. Furthermore, the type assignment constraints play an important role in the type assignment algorithm that constructs a typed tree.

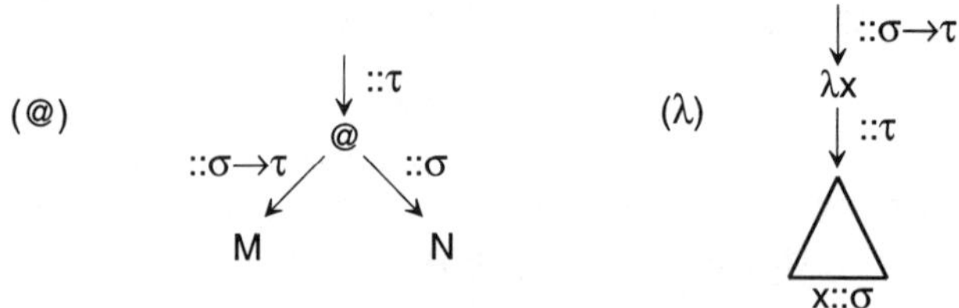

Figure 6.2 The two constraints of the Curry type system.

The type assignment constraint (@) assumes a type σ→τ was found for M and σ for N. Put together this gives type τ for the application M N.

In both subtrees the assumption x::φ_0 is made giving rise to a conflict in the root of the tree. No conclusion is possible since the types do not obey the application-constraint (@).

::?
@
::φ_0→φ_0 ::φ_0→φ_0
λx λx
::φ_0 ::φ_0
x::φ_0 x::φ_0

Figure 6.3 *Impossible* typed tree for (λx.x)(λx.x): inconsistent types.

The type assignment constraint (λ) is used to construct a type to a λ-abstraction term λx.M. It assumes that constructing the typed tree for M was successful and the type found for M was τ. If the assumption x::σ is the only assumption for x needed to reach the conclusion $M::\tau$ (so no other assumption like $x::\rho$ is used where ρ is different from σ) the (λ)-step can be performed. The result will be that finding a type for the λ-term λx.M was successful and the type found is $\sigma\to\tau$.

There is no separate constraint for term variables. The constraints (λ) and (@) only limit the possible combinations of typed (sub)trees (see Figure 6.3). These constraints do not express *how* a type is found for a specific λ-term: they only formalize *what* a consistent typed tree should look like.

6.1.2 Finding a type for a term

Type assignment is decidable in Curry's system. There is an algorithm that, given a λ-term M, will say 'NO' if there is no possible typed tree for M and will yield a type for M if there is a possible typed tree for M. In this algorithm, *unification* (described below) plays a crucial role.

The basic idea of the type deduction algorithm is the following. It starts at the variables in the leaves of the tree. It assumes that a variable is of the most general type and assigns a *fresh* (i.e. new, not yet used) type variable to it. Then the tree is traversed upwards. For each visited node the consistency of the subtree with that node as root is checked against the type assignment constraints. If there is an inconsistency an attempt is made to make the tree consistent by deriving more accurate types. This is done by unification. If the unification succeeds the algorithm continues, otherwise no typed tree can be created at all.

Unification

Types consist of arrows and type variables. Types can be obtained from other types by replacing, in a consistent way, type variables by types. An operation that uniformly replaces type variables by types (i.e. each occurrence of the same variable is replaced by the same type) is called a **substitution**. Substitution is a **sound** operation on typed trees, i.e. if in a typed tree all types are replaced by a substitution with other types, then the resulting typed tree is consistent. A type that is produced by substitution is called an **instance** of the original type.

Two types that are not equal can have a common instance:

$((\varphi_6\to\varphi_6)\to\varphi_5)\to\varphi_6\to\varphi_6$ can be obtained from the type $\varphi_2\to\varphi_3\to\varphi_3$ by uniformly replacing φ_2 by $(\varphi_6\to\varphi_6)\to\varphi_5$ and φ_3 by φ_6.
$((\varphi_6\to\varphi_6)\to\varphi_5)\to\varphi_6\to\varphi_6$ is also an instance of the type $(\varphi_0\to\varphi_1)\to\varphi_0$.

Two types are **equivalent** if there exists both a substitution of type variables to type variables such that the substitution applied to the first type gives the second type as well as a similar substitution from the second type to the first type. In the following, types are considered modulo this equivalency. So equivalent types are considered to be **equal**.

A type that is an instance of two different types is called a **unifier** of these types. If two types have a unifier, they also have a **most general unifier**, i.e. all unifiers of the two types are instances of their most general unifier. Trying to find the most general unifier for two types is called **unification**. Two types are **unifiable** if a (most general) unifier exists. For Curry types, unification is decidable.

Robinson's unification algorithm

In Robinson (1965) an algorithm unify is given that takes two types σ and τ and either fails, or succeeds yielding a substitution S such that:

- $S\,\sigma = S\,\tau$, so S unifies σ and τ;
- $S\,\sigma$ is the most general unifier of σ and τ;
- S is only defined on variables occurring in σ and τ.

For example, let

$$S = \text{unify}\ \varphi_2{\rightarrow}\varphi_3{\rightarrow}\varphi_3\ \ (\varphi_0{\rightarrow}\varphi_1){\rightarrow}\varphi_0$$

then S unifies $\varphi_2{\rightarrow}\varphi_3{\rightarrow}\varphi_3$ and $(\varphi_0{\rightarrow}\varphi_1){\rightarrow}\varphi_0$ and

$$\begin{aligned} S\,\varphi_0 &= \varphi_3{\rightarrow}\varphi_3 \\ S\,\varphi_1 &= \varphi_1 \\ S\,\varphi_2 &= (\varphi_3{\rightarrow}\varphi_3){\rightarrow}\varphi_1 \\ S\,\varphi_3 &= \varphi_3 \end{aligned}$$

and therefore

$$\begin{aligned} S\,\varphi_2{\rightarrow}\varphi_3{\rightarrow}\varphi_3 &= ((\varphi_3{\rightarrow}\varphi_3){\rightarrow}\varphi_1){\rightarrow}\varphi_3{\rightarrow}\varphi_3 \\ S\,(\varphi_0{\rightarrow}\varphi_1){\rightarrow}\varphi_0 &= ((\varphi_3{\rightarrow}\varphi_3){\rightarrow}\varphi_1){\rightarrow}\varphi_3{\rightarrow}\varphi_3 \end{aligned}$$

which gives that $((\varphi_3{\rightarrow}\varphi_3){\rightarrow}\varphi_1){\rightarrow}\varphi_3{\rightarrow}\varphi_3$ is the most general unifier of $\varphi_2{\rightarrow}\varphi_3{\rightarrow}\varphi_3$ and $(\varphi_0{\rightarrow}\varphi_1){\rightarrow}\varphi_0$. Another unifier of these two types is $((\varphi_4{\rightarrow}\varphi_4){\rightarrow}\varphi_4{\rightarrow}\varphi_4){\rightarrow}\varphi_4{\rightarrow}\varphi_4$. It is indeed an instance of the most general unifier by substituting φ_1 by $\varphi_4{\rightarrow}\varphi_4$ and φ_3 by φ_4.

Robinson's algorithm, written in a functional style:

```
type           ::=  Typevar typevar |  Arrow type type
substitution   ==   type -> type
typevar        ==   num
```

```
unify:: type -> type -> substitution
unify (Typevar φ0) (Typevar φ1)  =  sub φ0 (Typevar φ1)
unify (Typevar φ)  τ             =  sub φ τ,              if not_in τ φ
unify σ            (Typevar φ)   =  unify (Typevar φ) σ
unify (Arrow σ0 σ1) (Arrow τ0 τ1) = res1 . res0
                                    where  res0  = unify σ0 τ0
                                           res1  = unify (res0 σ1) (res0 τ1)

sub:: typevar -> type -> substitution
sub φ0 τ   = s
          where  s (Typevar φ1)  =  τ,              if φ0 = φ1
                                 =  Typevar φ1,     otherwise
                 s (Arrow σ ρ)   =  Arrow ((sub φ0 τ) σ) ((sub φ0 τ) ρ)

not_in:: type -> typevar -> bool
not_in (Typevar φ0) φ1    =  φ1 ~= φ0
not_in (Arrow σ τ) φ1     =  not_in σ φ1   & not_in τ φ1
```

In this algorithm sub φ σ returns the substitution that replaces the type variable φ by the type σ and does not affect other type variables. *R.T* (the function composition of *R* and *T*) is the substitution that first performs *T* and afterwards performs *R*.

The result of the function unify is built by function composition of the substitutions found while unifying subtypes. The substitution found while unifying the left-hand sides of two arrow types is first performed on the right-hand sides before unifying them.

Assigning types to trees

The general idea of the method to find the most general type for every λ-term in Curry's system is as follows. Start by building a tree in which all labels are empty. Then, traverse the tree to label the nodes containing variables and the edges with types, making use of the type assignment constraints. Sometimes, while trying to assign a type to a node, a unification is performed. In that case the resulting substitution is performed on the whole tree. Because substitution is a sound operation, such replacing of type variables by types in a correctly typed tree will always give a correctly typed tree. If unification fails, the whole term cannot be typed.

More precisely, the following algorithm is used: traverse the tree depth-first from left to right performing at each position one of the following three steps:

- If a leaf is encountered, the variable and the edge going into this node are labelled with the same fresh type variable.

- If an abstraction node is visited, the subtree below it is a tree that is already typed, say M. Now an abstraction step (λ) to a variable, say x, is performed, to type λx.M.

  The algorithm therefore checks the assumptions made on the corresponding x (all labelled) to see whether they are all typed with the same type. If they are the same, everything is fine. If no assumptions have been made, because the variable x did not occur in the term, a fresh type variable will be assumed. If the assumptions on x are not the same, the algorithm tries to unify the assumed types. If this succeeds, the substitution generated by this unification will be performed on the typed subtree, giving a typed subtree in which all assumptions on x are labelled with the found unifier.

  In either case the result will be a typed subtree with conclusion, say, M::τ in which all assumptions on x are labelled with the same type, say ::σ. The edge going into the abstraction node λx.M is then labelled with ::$\sigma \rightarrow \tau$.

- If an application node is visited, there are two typed subtrees with conclusions, say M::σ and N::τ. Now an application step (@) is performed. To perform this step, the types on both subtrees should match the requirements of (@).

  The algorithm employs a fresh type variable φ_0 and unifies the types σ and $\tau \rightarrow \varphi_0$. If this unification is successful, a substitution S is yielded such that $S(\sigma) = S(\tau \rightarrow \varphi_0) = \rho_0 \rightarrow \rho_1$, so $S(\sigma) = \rho_0 \rightarrow \rho_1$ and $S(\tau) = \rho_0$. Applying this substitution to the two typed subtrees yields a left subtree with conclusion M::$\rho_0 \rightarrow \rho_1$, and a right subtree with conclusion N::ρ_0. Now the (@)-constraint can be taken into account labelling the edge into the application node with ::ρ_1.

The type assignment algorithm returns the unused fresh variables, the type found for the term, and the set of typed term variables that are free in the term. The algorithm is illustrated below with two examples.

Example 1: (λa.λb.a b)(λx.x). First, an untyped tree is constructed (Figure 6.4(a)). Then the algorithm visits the left subtree, assuming a::φ_1 and b::φ_2. An (@)-step should be performed, so a new type variable φ_3 is picked and the algorithm unifies φ_1 and $\varphi_2 \rightarrow \varphi_3$. This yields that φ_1 will be replaced by $\varphi_2 \rightarrow \varphi_3$. The edge going into the application node will be labelled by φ_3. The two abstraction nodes give no difficulties (this results in Figure 6.4(b)). Then, the algorithm visits the right subtree. It assumes a type variable for the assumption x::φ_4. Again the abstraction node gives no difficulties. This yields Figure 6.4(c). Lastly, the algorithm visits the top node. It is an application node so the subtree should satisfy the @-constraint. The types involved are $(\varphi_2 \rightarrow \varphi_3) \rightarrow \varphi_2 \rightarrow \varphi_3$ and $\varphi_4 \rightarrow \varphi_4$; a fresh type variable φ_5 is taken and $(\varphi_2 \rightarrow \varphi_3) \rightarrow \varphi_2 \rightarrow \varphi_3$ and $(\varphi_4 \rightarrow \varphi_4) \rightarrow \varphi_5$ are unified. This yields the substitution that replaces both φ_2 and φ_3 by φ_4, and φ_5 by $\varphi_4 \rightarrow \varphi_4$ (Figure 6.4(d)).

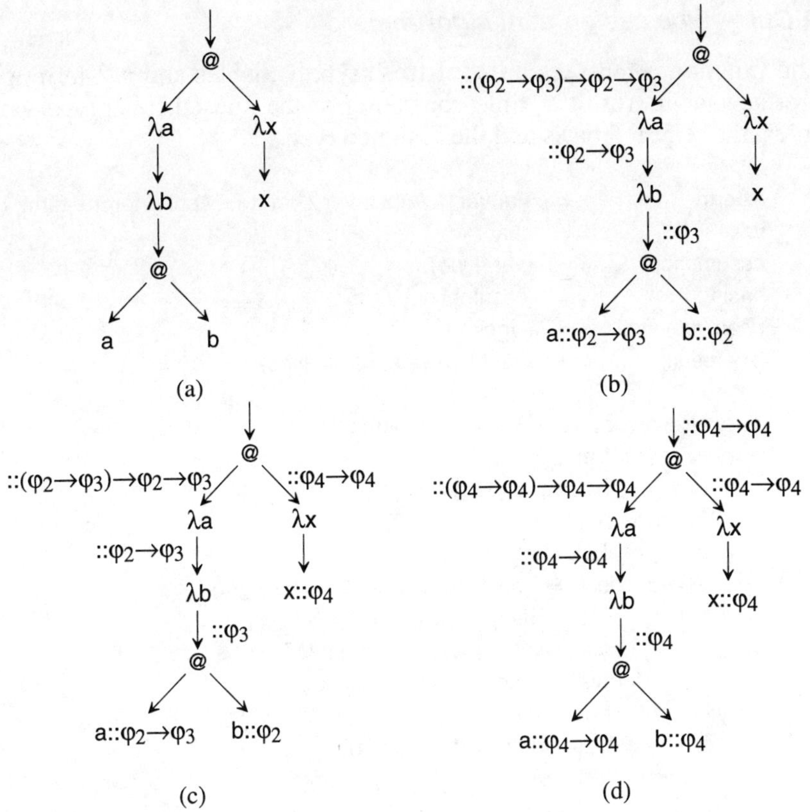

@
λa λx
λb x
@
a b

(a)

@
$::(\varphi_2 \to \varphi_3) \to \varphi_2 \to \varphi_3$
λa λx
$::\varphi_2 \to \varphi_3$
λb x
$::\varphi_3$
@
$a::\varphi_2 \to \varphi_3$ $b::\varphi_2$

(b)

@
$::(\varphi_2 \to \varphi_3) \to \varphi_2 \to \varphi_3$ $::\varphi_4 \to \varphi_4$
λa λx
$::\varphi_2 \to \varphi_3$
λb $x::\varphi_4$
$::\varphi_3$
@
$a::\varphi_2 \to \varphi_3$ $b::\varphi_2$

(c)

$::\varphi_4 \to \varphi_4$
@
$::(\varphi_4 \to \varphi_4) \to \varphi_4 \to \varphi_4$ $::\varphi_4 \to \varphi_4$
λa λx
$::\varphi_4 \to \varphi_4$
λb $x::\varphi_4$
$::\varphi_4$
@
$a::\varphi_4 \to \varphi_4$ $b::\varphi_4$

(d)

Figure 6.4 (a) Initial tree, (b) typed left subtree, (c) right subtree, (d) conclusion.

Example 2: λa.λb.a. In the initial tree (Figure 6.5(a)) it is assumed that a has type φ_0. For the first abstraction node, there is no assumption made on b yet. This means that any type can be taken for b, because the typed tree puts no limits on the type for b. The result is shown in Figure 6.5(b).

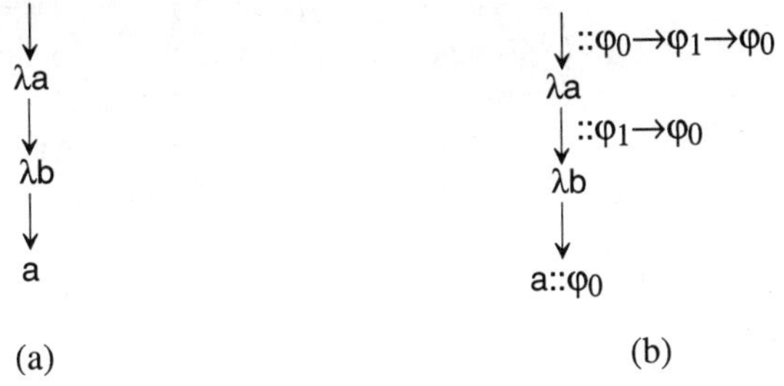

Figure 6.5 (a) Initial tree, (b) final typed tree.

A Curry-type assignment algorithm

The function curry takes a list of fresh type variables and a λ-term and produces as its result a triple consisting of the unused fresh type variables, the required basis and the assigned type.

```
λ-term          ::=  Var var  |  Abstr var λ-term  |  Appl λ-term λ-term
var             ==   char
assumption      ==   (var, type)
basis           ==   [assumption]
freshtypevars   ==   [typevar]
typeresults     ==   (freshtypevars, basis, type)

curry:: freshtypevars -> λ-term -> typeresults
curry (φ : ftvs) (Var x)
   = (ftvs, [(x, Typevar φ)], Typevar φ)
curry (φ : ftvs) (Appl f g)
   = (ftvs", basis, s (Typevar φ))
     where basis = substitute s (basleft ++ basright)
           s     = unify ρ (Arrow σ (Typevar φ))
           (ftvs', basleft, ρ)     = curry ftvs f
           (ftvs", basright, σ)    = curry ftvs' g
curry (φ : ftvs) (Abstr x g)
   = (ftvs', basis, s (Arrow (Typevar φ) τ))
     where (basis, s)       = check_assmptn (x, Typevar φ) bas
           (ftvs', bas, τ)  = curry ftvs g

substitute:: substitution -> basis -> basis
substitute s [ ]               = [ ]
substitute s ((x, σ) : rest )  = (x, s σ) : substitute s rest

check_assmptn:: assumption -> basis -> (basis, substitution)
check_assmptn ass    [ ] =  ([ ], identsub)
check_assmptn (x, σ)  ((y, τ) : rest)
              = (substitute (s2 . s1) bas1, s2 . s1),  if y = x
              = (substitute s ((y, τ) : bas), s),       otherwise
                where s1           = unify σ τ
                      (bas1, s2)   = check_assmptn (x, s1 σ) rest
                      (bas, s)     = check_assmptn (x, σ) rest

identsub:: substitution
identsub   σ    = σ
```

The function check_assmptn goes through the basis and unifies the type it has already found (initially φ) with the types for the term variable. It returns a basis that equals the original one from which all statements for the term variable are removed, together with the substitution that unifies all types in the statements for the term variable.

6.1.3 Properties of the Curry system

Curry's type assignment system satisfies the **subject reduction property**: if σ is a suitable type for M, and M can be reduced to N, then σ is also a suitable type for N. So a type found for a λ-term will also be a type for any of its reducts (such as the normal form). In a way, this property formalizes the notion that typed programs cannot go wrong.

Curry's system also has the **principal type property** (Hindley, 1969): for every closed λ-term M that is typeable, a type σ_M can be found such that all other types that can be found for M in Curry's system are instances of σ_M and can therefore be obtained by substitution. This type σ_M is called the **principal type** of M.

For open terms there exists a **principal pair**, consisting of the *principal basis* and the *principal type*. All other pairs for this open term can be obtained from this principal pair by substitution. The algorithm presented above returns the principal pair for each typeable λ-term: the last part of its result is the principal type.

The principal type of λx.x is $\varphi_0 \to \varphi_0$. All other possible types are instances of this principal type. For example: $(\varphi_2 \to \varphi_1) \to \varphi_2 \to \varphi_1$ is such a type.

The principal type of a term M can be used as a scheme for the construction of the actual type of M when it occurs as a subterm in a specific context: the actual type must be an instance of the principal type. This property forms the basis for polymorphic type systems, as described in the next section.

Principal types are not preserved under reduction: if σ is the principal type for M, and M can be reduced to N, σ does not need to be the principal type for N; it can be that N has a principal type τ that is different from σ. Of course, σ and τ are in such cases related: because of subject reduction, σ is a correct type for the reduct N, and because τ is its principal type, σ is then an instance of τ. The intuition behind this is the following: an application generally contains more information than its reduct. So the type of an application will in general be more specific than the type of its reduct.

The principal type of (λx.λy.λz.x z (y z)) (λa.λb.a) is $(\varphi_0 \to \varphi_1) \to \varphi_0 \to \varphi_0$, that of λy.λz.z is $\varphi_2 \to \varphi_3 \to \varphi_3$. (λx.λy.λz.x z (y z)) (λa.λb.a) reduces in three steps to λy.λz.z, and $(\varphi_0 \to \varphi_1) \to \varphi_0 \to \varphi_0$ is an instance of the type $\varphi_2 \to \varphi_3 \to \varphi_3$. The function in the original application requires its second argument y to be applicable on the third argument z. The reduct does not require this any more.

Drawbacks

Curry's type assignment system is decidable but an important class of terms is not typeable within this system.

The typed subtree $x::\varphi_0$ uses two different assumptions for x that cannot be unified. This is easily checked by computing the result of unify $\varphi_1 \to \varphi_0\ \varphi_1$.

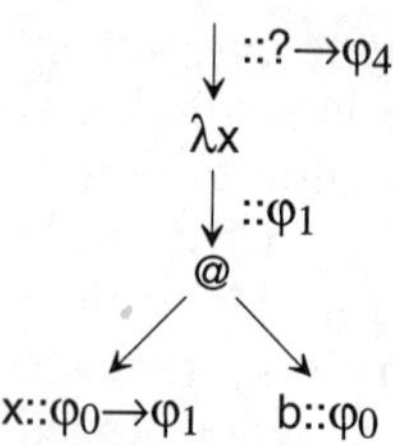

Figure 6.6 λx.x x is not typeable in Curry's type system.

Curry's type assignment system can only type a subclass of the strongly normalizing terms. This subclass does not contain terms in which self-application occurs (Figure 6.6). Hence, recursion cannot be modelled since all fixed combinators contain self-application.

6.2 Polymorphism and recursion

The language Λ^+ presented in this section is an extension of the λ-calculus that enables us to focus on polymorphism and recursion by introducing names for closed λ-terms. Several solutions for finding a type for recursive definitions are discussed.

6.2.1 Syntax of Λ^+

```
Program      = {Definition} Term ;
Definition   = Name '=' Term ;
Term         = Var | Name | Abstraction | Application ;
Abstraction  = '(' 'λ' Var '.' Term ')' ;
Application  = '(' Term Term ')' ;
```

Variables are characters, names are strings starting with a capital. This syntax allows recursive definitions. Redundant brackets will be omitted.

Example of a program written in Λ^+:

```
S = λx.λy.λz.x z (y z)
K = λx.λy.x
I = λx.x

S K I
```

Programs written in Λ^+ can easily be translated into λ-terms. For non-recursive programs the translation consists of replacing, starting with the final term, all names by their bodies. In the case of a recursive definition, the translation to the λ-calculus has to use a fixed point combinator.

6.2.2 Finding a type in Λ^+

Type assignment in Λ^+ is an extension of Curry's type assignment for the λ-calculus. Basically, principal Curry types are assigned to named λ-terms. Furthermore, there is a special way to deal with recursion, as described below.

When trying to find a type for the final term in a program, each definition is typed separately. Its right-hand side is treated as a closed λ-term. So in principle the typed tree representing the principal type of the term is derived as usual.

For every definition, a pair, consisting of the principal type (found for the right-hand side) and the name of the defined function, is put in a list, the **environment**. The environment is represented as a function from names to types. This representation of an environment is possible assuming that all names are (made) different. The environment is used to find types for terms that contain names: each occurrence of a name Name in the program can be regarded as an abbreviation of the right-hand side in its definition, and, therefore, the type associated with the occurrence should be an instance of the principal type of Name in the environment. The different occurrences of Name can have different types, the only relation between their types is that they are all instances of the principal type of Name. The type used for an occurrence of Name does not affect the type of Name in the environment: the type of Name is called **generic**, and the function defined by Name is called a **polymorphic function**.

Every time Name is encountered in a right-hand side, the algorithm looks in the environment to see what its type is. It takes a **fresh instance** of this type, i.e. an instance which is produced by substituting all type variables consistently with fresh type variables. This fresh instance is used to find a type for the right-hand side. In this way, the types actually used for Name in the final typed tree will always be instances of the principal type that is associated with Name in the environment.

For reasons of simplicity, it is assumed that names are defined before they are used. A problem arises when Name does not occur in the environment. This can be the case when the program is recursive. Recursion is dealt with later on.

Consider I = λy.y and the application I I

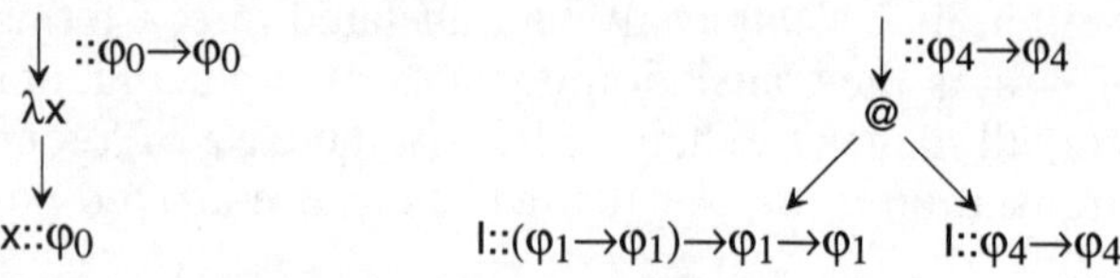

Figure 6.7 Typed trees for I and I I.

The term I I in the program above is typeable by $\varphi_1 \to \varphi_1$. In finding this type the polymorphism of I is used. The first I in I I is typed by $(\varphi_1 \to \varphi_1) \to \varphi_1 \to \varphi_1$, whereas the second one is typed by $\varphi_1 \to \varphi_1$. Both types are substitution instances of the principal type found for I, $\varphi_0 \to \varphi_0$ (see also Figure 6.7).

Solving recursion with a fixed point construction

Also for occurrences of recursively defined names in a right-hand side the types actually used for the occurrences of a name G have to be at least instances of the type found for that name. However, a problem arises when dealing with the occurrences of G in its own body, because when finding the type for G, no type is associated with G in the environment. So in the case of recursive definitions, this condition is difficult to meet. In general, a fixed point construction is necessary to solve the repeated unifications that are involved.

For *mutually recursive* definitions one needs a special kind of fixed point construction that treats all mutually dependent definitions together. For reasons of clarity that kind of recursive definition is *not* considered here. In the rest of this chapter only directly recursive definitions are considered.

A fixed point construction is a general method to find solutions of recursive equations (see also Section 7.3). Starting from an initial approximation of the solution the equations are solved and the solution is taken as a new approximation. If in this approximating process a solution is found that equals the previous approximation, the *fixed point* is reached: the solution of the original equation.

Take for example the following program with a recursive definition:

```
I = λx.x
K = λa.λb.a
G = λv.K (G I) (G K)
```

To find the type for G, a fixed point construction is needed: the first approximation assumes a type variable φ_0 for G. When building the type for the body of G, this type variable will be instantiated to, respectively, $(\varphi_1 \to \varphi_1) \to \varphi_2$ and $(\varphi_3 \to \varphi_4 \to \varphi_3) \to \varphi_5$. The type found for the body of G is $\varphi_6 \to \varphi_2$. The original assumption for G, φ_0, is not an instance of the type found. Apparently this assumed type was too general. It should be replaced by a type that is at least an instance of $\varphi_6 \rightarrow \varphi_2$. So in the fixed point construction a next approximation is made to find the type for G, using as a new assumption the type $\varphi_6 \rightarrow \varphi_2$ found for G in the first try. In this case, this second attempt will give exactly the same typed tree for the body of G (Figure 6.8). So the fixed point is reached.

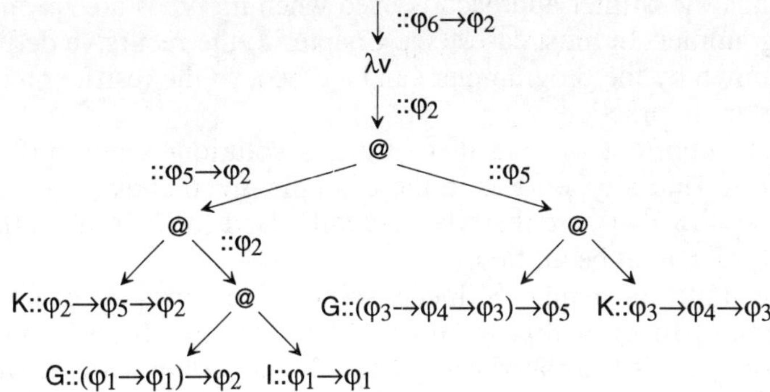

Figure 6.8 Typed tree for G in the example above.

This fixed point construction *always* finds a correct type *if one exists*. Unfortunately, type assignment with the fixed point construction is undecidable due to the possibility of non-termination, as is shown in the next example.

Example of non-termination of the fixed point construction:

F = λx.F

The fixed point construction for F starts with assuming that F is of type φ_0. Then it performs the (λ)-step and finds $\varphi_1 \rightarrow \varphi_0$ for λx.F. Obviously, the type φ_0 is not an instance of $\varphi_1 \rightarrow \varphi_0$. So a second approximation has to be made assuming $\varphi_1 \rightarrow \varphi_0$ for F. The type found is then $\varphi_2 \rightarrow \varphi_1 \rightarrow \varphi_0$ and another approximation has to be made. This will go on and on.

Two different solutions for the problem of recursive definitions are commonly used, both avoiding the fixed point calculation such that both systems become decidable. In fact, they each perform only the first step of the fixed point calculation, each in a different way.

Milner's solution

The first solution is part of Milner's type assignment algorithm defined for the functional programming language ML (Milner, 1978) in which naming of terms is possible via special constructs: the let-construct for non-recursive definitions and the fix-construct for recursive ones.

Instead of calculating the fixed point, Milner's solution simply requires that all types used for a recursively defined name in its definition are one and the same. This seems to be a severe restriction, but with Milner's solution surprisingly many programs can be adequately typed. In Miranda the Milner approach is used when no types are specified by the programmer. In most cases (see Chapter 2) the recursive definitions written down by the programmer can be typed, so the restriction is not a big problem in practice.

It is important to note that Milner's solution is not sufficiently powerful to find a type for G in the example given above. $(\varphi_1 \to \varphi_1) \to \varphi_2$ and $(\varphi_3 \to \varphi_4 \to \varphi_3) \to \varphi_5$ are the types actually used for G in its definition. These types cannot be unified.

The intuition behind Milner's solution becomes apparent in the translation of functional programs in Λ^+ to λ-terms. In this translation the fix-construct is translated using a fixed point combinator Y, which is assumed to be typeable by the type $(\varphi_0 \to \varphi_0) \to \varphi_0$. Note that in the translation the λ-term λf.(λx.f (x x))(λx.f (x x)) is not used, because it cannot be typed. The algorithm below will assume that occurrences of a recursively defined name in its own definition are represented as Defrecname name.

The Milner algorithm

```
program        ==   ([definition], term)
definition     ==   (name, term)
name           ==   [char]
term           ::=  Var var  | Defrecname name     | Name name
                             | Abstr var term      | Appl term term
environment    ==   name -> type

find_type:: freshtypevars -> environment -> program -> type
find_type ftvs env ([ ], t)
= σ
   where   ((ftvs', bas, σ), s)     = milner ftvs env t
find_type (φ:ftvs) env (((n, body) : defs), t)
= find_type ftvs' (addto env n (s1 σ1)) (defs, t),      if occurs_in n body
= find_type ftvs'' (addto env n σ2) (defs, t),          otherwise
   where   ((ftvs', bas1, σ1), s2)    = milner ftvs
                                             (addto env n (Typevar φ)) body
           s1                         = unify (s2 (Typevar φ)) σ1
           ((ftvs'', bas2, σ2), s3)   = milner (φ:ftvs) env body

milner:: freshtypevars -> environment -> term -> (typeresults, substitution)
milner (φ:ftvs) env (Var x)
```

```
    = ((ftvs, [(x, Typevar φ)], Typevar φ), identsub)
  milner ftvs env (Defrecname n)
    = ((ftvs, [ ], env n), identsub)
  milner ftvs env (Name n)
    = ((ftvs', [ ], typeinstance), identsub)
      where  (ftvs', typeinstance)     = fresh_instance ftvs (env n)
  milner (φ:ftvs) env (Appl f g)
    = ((ftvs'', bas, s (Typevar φ)), s2 . s1)
      where  bas   = substitute s (basl ++ basr)
             s     = unify ρ (Arrow τ (Typevar φ))
             ((ftvs', basl, ρ), s1)  = milner ftvs env f
             ((ftvs'', basr, τ), s2) = milner ftvs' (s1 . env) g
  milner (φ:ftvs) env (Abstr x g)
    = ((ftvs', resultbas, s2 (Arrow (Typevar φ) τ)), s2 . s1)
      where  (resultbas, s2)       = check_assmptn (x, Typevar φ) bas
             ((ftvs', bas, τ), s1)  = milner ftvs env g

  addto:: environment -> name -> type -> environment
  addto env x σ      = newenv
                       where  newenv z  = σ,       if x = z
                                        = env z,   otherwise
```

The function find_type takes three operands, a list of fresh variables, the environment and the program. An infinite list of fresh variables is assumed to be passed initially as an argument.

As its result find_type produces the type for the final term. When find_type encounters a definition, it checks whether it is a recursive definition (with the function occurs_in, which is left undefined here). If so, it assumes the name is typed by a type variable and it tries to find a type for its body, by calling the function milner. The type variable assumed will very probably be changed by the resulting substitution s_2. The final type should be the same as the type used for the name and therefore the resulting type σ_1 is unified with $s_2\ \varphi$, yielding s_1. If this unification is successful, $s_1\ \sigma_1$ is the type found for the name.

The algorithm milner takes three operands: the fresh variables list, the environment and the term to be typed, and returns the type results found for the term and a substitution. The algorithm milner is almost the same as the algorithm curry. It differs in the way it is capable of dealing with recursive definitions. For recursive definitions, all occurrences of the defined name in the recursive definition (Defrecnames) must have the same type. If a non-recursive name is encountered in a term, the type that is associated with that name in the environment can be instantiated: the function fresh_instance (not defined here) returns a fresh instance of its argument and the remaining part of the list of fresh variables.

If an identifier occurs in its own body, the type in the environment is taken itself instead of being instantiated. This type can be changed in the process of finding a type for the recursive definition: the substitution that is found can also affect the environment. Therefore this substitution is passed as a result of the function milner, and the substitution that is returned by the first recursive call when dealing with an application is also performed on the environment when performing the second recursive call. So all types used for a name in its body will be the same. The substitution is passed as an argument for this purpose only.

Mycroft's solution

The second solution is based on a type assignment system defined by A. Mycroft (Mycroft, 1984). This solution deals with the problem in a way frequently used for many hard problems in computer science: the programmer has to specify the solution; it insists on the type for a recursively defined name being given by the programmer. Instead of calculating the fixed point, this solution simply requires that all types used for a recursively defined name in its definition are instances of the given type. This always terminates, since in looking for a type for the body, the given type is instantiated and no new assumptions are made. Of course, the given type also has to correspond with the type derived for the body. It is even sufficient to require that the given type is an instance of the type derived. This makes it possible that the programmer specifies a type that is more restrictive than the type derived.

Mycroft's solution solves the example:

```
I:: φ1→φ1
I  = λx.x

K:: φ1→φ2→φ1
K  = λa.λb.a

G:: φ1→φ2
G  = λv.K (G I) (G K)
```

Again the types actually used for G are $(\varphi_1 \to \varphi_1) \to \varphi_2$ and $(\varphi_3 \to \varphi_4 \to \varphi_3) \to \varphi_5$. These are both instances of the type given, which is the same as the type found. Therefore Mycroft's solution succeeds.

For any σ and τ, Mycroft's solution rejects the following typed definition:

```
F:: σ→τ
F  = λx.F
```

The Mycroft algorithm

```
mycroft:: freshtypevars -> environment -> term -> typeresults
mycroft (φ:ftvs) env (Var x)
            = (ftvs, [(x, Typevar φ)], Typevar φ)
mycroft ftvs env (Name n)
            = (ftvs', [ ], typeinstance)
              where  (ftvs', typeinstance)   = fresh_instance ftvs (env n)
mycroft (φ:ftvs) env (Appl f g)
            = (ftvs'', bas, s (Typevar φ))
              where  bas   = substitute s (basl ++ basr)
                     s     = unify ρ (Arrow σ (Typevar φ))
                     (ftvs', basl, ρ)   = mycroft ftvs env f
                     (ftvs'', basr, σ)  = mycroft ftvs' env g
mycroft (φ:ftvs) env (Abstr x g)
            = (ftvs', resultbas, s (Arrow (Typevar φ) τ))
              where  (resultbas, s) = check_assmptn (x, Typevar φ) bas
                     (ftvs', bas, τ) = mycroft ftvs env g

check_type:: freshtypevars -> environment -> program -> type
check_type ftvs env ([ ], g)
            = σ
              where  (ftvs', bas, σ)    = mycroft ftvs env g
check_type ftvs env ((n, body):defs, g)
            = check_type ftvs' env (defs, g), if equal_types σ τ
              where  σ                  = env n
                     (ftvs', bas, τ)    = mycroft ftvs env body
```

The algorithm mycroft differs from the algorithm milner in some points. mycroft does not distinguish between different kinds of occurrences of names. All names are dealt with in the same manner (so Defrecname is assumed never to be used). Furthermore, the algorithm assumes that in the environment a type is returned for every name that appears in the program. So if mycroft encounters a name, it takes an instance of the type that is already in the environment. Hence, this algorithm does not affect types in the environment, and the resulting substitution need not be performed on the environment as in milner. Consequently, this substitution is not returned as a part of the result.

The function equal_types (not defined here) checks whether two types are equal.

A mixed approach solution

The functional programming language Miranda uses a combination of Milner's and Mycroft's solutions. If the programmer has defined a type for a recursive definition, the algorithm tries to find it using Mycroft's solution, otherwise it uses Milner's. In Miranda therefore there is a major difference between **type checking**, taking types supplied for definitions by the programmer and checking whether these types are correct, and **type inferencing**, analysing the definitions in a program and trying to find the principal types for them (see also Chapter 2).

The mixed approach algorithm

```
mixed_type:: freshtypevars -> environment -> program -> type
mixed_type ftvs env ([ ], t)
        = σ     where  ((ftvs', bas, σ), s)   =  milner ftvs env t
mixed_type ftvs env (((n, body):b), t)
        = find_type ftvs env (((n, body):b), t),        if env n = Undefined
        = check_type ftvs env (((n, body):b), t),      otherwise
```

In order to be able to test whether in the environment a type is already defined for a name, the definition of type is assumed to be extended with Undefined. As a consequence, functions that are applied on objects of type type have to be extended accordingly.

6.2.3 Properties of type assignment in Λ^+

Both type assignment systems for Λ^+ cover important features of functional programming languages: polymorphism and recursion. They also have the principal type property and satisfy subject reduction.

However, some terms still cannot be typed in the proposed systems. For example, self-applications like λx.x x cannot be typed. Moreover, the type systems cannot deal with definitions that have **internal polymorphism**: i.e. different occurrences of a defined object have different types *inside the definition.*

Take for example the following program:

```
I  =  λy.y
E  =  λc.λd.c d
K  =  λa.λb.a
F  =  λf.λg.λc.λi.f (g c)(g i)

F K I K E
```

While reducing the term F K I K E, I will be applied to two different terms K and E, whose principal types are not unifiable. One might think that, because I is polymorphic and can be used several times with different, maybe even non-unifiable types, the final term will be typeable. This is not true.

The problem is the λ-term that is at the basis of the Milner untypeable function given in Chapter 2. In the tree for the principal type of λf.λg.λc.λi.f (g c) (g i) (and therefore in all possible types for that term) the types for c and i should be the same. This is best illustrated by giving the principal typed tree for the λ-term λc.λi.f (g c) (g i) (Figure 6.9) and performing the (λ)-step to g. Until this step two different assumptions for g, g::$\varphi_0 \rightarrow \varphi_1$ and g::$\varphi_5 \rightarrow \varphi_3$ are used. The (λ)-step to g unifies these types, giving a substitution that replaces φ_0 by φ_5 and φ_1 by φ_3. Therefore it is concluded that the types used for c and i are to be the same (see Figure 6.10). This conclusion is too restrictive. Since the types for c and i are the same, when trying to find a type for the final term F K I K E instances of the types for K and E are unified. This will fail.

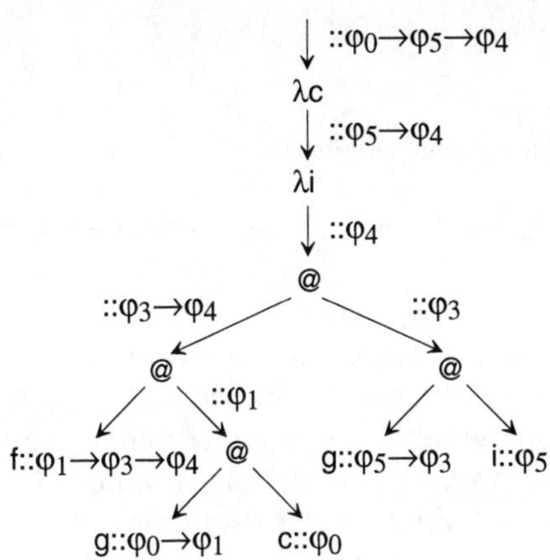

Figure 6.9 Typed tree for λc.λi.f (g c) (g i).

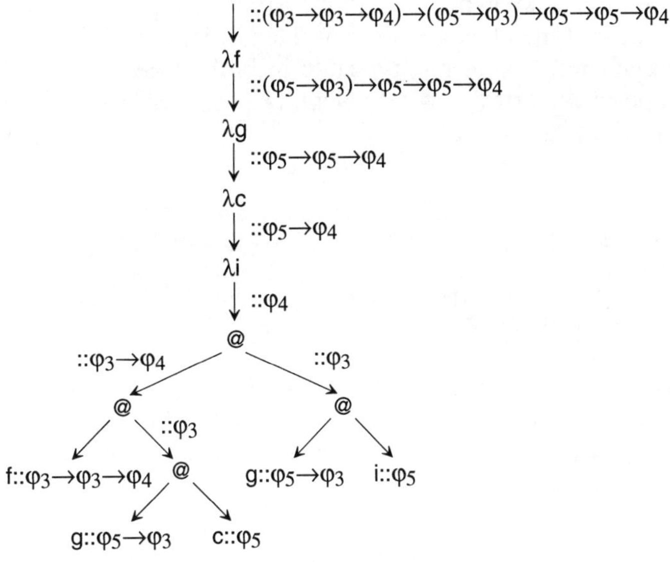

Figure 6.10 Typed tree for λf.λg.λc.λi.f (g c) (g i).

Furthermore, it can happen that applications of functions in which at run-time some arguments are not used, are typed too restrictively since at compile-time their possible use is taken into account.

Consider the following well-known definitions:

```
S:: (φ0→φ1→φ2)→(φ0→φ1)→φ0→φ2
S = λx.λy.λz.x z (y z)

K:: φ1→φ2→φ1
K = λa.λb.a

S K S:: (φ3→φ4→φ5)→φ3→φ4→φ5
```

Although S K S reduces to I, neither the Milner nor the Mycroft algorithm finds the type $\varphi_0 \to \varphi_0$, due to the imposed restrictions.

There is one final remark to make on the type assignment systems that use Milner's and Mycroft's approaches. In both systems all occurrences for a function symbol are assigned types that are substitution instances of the type provided by the environment for this symbol. One could easily think that since all substitutions are allowed on types, one could replace the type in the environment by any arbitrary substitution instance. For the system that uses Milner's approach, in which of course also types could be provided for definitions, this holds: substitution is a sound operation for terms as well as for definitions.

However, as shown above, in the Mycroft approach recursive definitions can be typed that are not typeable in Milner's. It is not very well known that there are terms, typeable in both systems for which Mycroft's approach allows a more general type than Milner's. Take for example the definitions

```
K:: φ1→φ2→φ1
K = λa. λb. a

R:: (φ1→φ2→φ1) → (φ1→φ2→φ1) → φ1→φ2→φ1
R = λx. λy. R (R y K) x
```

The types for the definitions (note in particular the type for R) are correct in both Milner's and Mycroft's systems. In Mycroft's system, however, it is possible to take a more general type for R; also the following is correctly typed:

```
K:: φ1→φ2→φ1
K = λa. λb. a
```

```
R:: φ1→φ2→φ3
R = λx. λy. R (R y K) x
```

This same program can be used to illustrate that in Mycroft's system substitution is no longer a sound operation on definitions. Although the type assignment algorithm is allowed to take any substitution instance of the type $\varphi_1 \to \varphi_2 \to \varphi_3$, not every substitution instance of this type can be put in the environment. For example, using the type $\varphi_1 \to \varphi_1 \to \varphi_1$, the definition for R cannot be typed. The underlying problem here is in fact the same as, for example, in the program:

```
K = λa. λb. a
I = λc. c

I K
```

This program is typeable with the types $\varphi_1 \to \varphi_2 \to \varphi_1$ for K, and $\varphi_3 \to \varphi_3$ for I, but *not* when the type for I is replaced by $(\varphi_4 \to \varphi_4) \to \varphi_4 \to \varphi_4$. The only thing that can be said about this 'problem' is that in Mycroft's system it becomes apparent *within* definitions.

Instead of the very common idea that supplying a type for a definition is equivalent to *asking* if the definition has this type, it is in fact *giving the algorithm the instruction* that all occurrences should have types that are instances of the supplied type. So systems that allow programmers to specify types should not be called type-check systems. The notion *partial type assignment system* is better.

6.3 Type assignment for term rewriting systems

6.3.1 Extending Λ^+ to a functional programming language

It is, from the type assignment point of view, no real problem to extend the language Λ^+ to a real functional programming language. This can be done by, for example, defining the set of types as follows:

(1) all type variables $\varphi_0, \varphi_1, \ldots$ are types;

(2) num, real and bool are types;

(3) if σ and τ are types, then $(\sigma \to \tau)$ and $[\sigma]$ are types, where $[\sigma]$ denotes a list of objects of type σ.

The unification algorithm for such types will be almost the same as unify, extended with conditions to solve the problems with the added types. Of course unification of, for example, num and real fails.

When instead of

```
F = λa.G
```

the notation

```
F a = G
```

is used, the operand a can be given a structure, making programs written in the functional programming language look like term rewriting systems. Then the type assignment algorithm would also have to cope with pattern matching by finding the types for the given operands. In this section it will be shown that, if arbitrary patterns are allowed, the subject reduction property is lost.

Another extension is the introduction of **constructors** and **algebraic type definitions**. Constructors are symbols that, when applied to the right arguments, construct an object of a certain type. They are defined by giving an algebraic type definition. It is also customary to introduce constructors that do not take operands. Take, for example:

```
List σ   ==  Nil  |  Cons σ (List σ)
num      ==  1 | 2 | 3 | ...
```

The first definition is one for the algebraic type List; this definition defines two constructors, Nil and Cons. The second defines the numerals that have type num. Then Cons 1 (Cons 2 Nil) is an object of type List num.

When assigning types to definitions that use (objects of) these algebraic types, before analysing the definitions the environment must contain types for all the constructors, like

```
Nil    :: List φ
Cons   :: φ → (List φ) → (List φ)
1      :: num
2      :: num
```

In functional programming languages rule alternatives are also introduced, forcing the algorithm to unify the resulting types of alternatives such that a function always yields the same type.

To get programming convenience, the type assignment algorithm also has to deal with definitions used before they are defined (and mutually recursive definitions). This is not difficult to implement.

6.3.2 Type assignment and term rewriting systems

In this section we focus on type assignment in TRSs (see Chapter 4), since in TRSs pattern matching is closer to functional programming languages than in the λ-calculus. Such a type system can easily be transferred to FGRSs (see Chapter 8). Since the proposed type system does not make use of graph information it is best studied in TRSs. The strategy used to assign types to the tree representation of terms will be similar to the previous defined type systems for the language Λ^+. There are, however, some differences, due to the differences between a λ-term and a TRS-term (see Sections 4.1.1 and 4.1.4).

- As for Λ^+, an environment is used to store the types for the constants. However, unlike in Λ^+, there can be more than one rule that defines a constant. In finding a type assignment for the second rule, all constants will already have a type. For convenience, the choice has been made to require that the environment initially provides a type for *every* constant that appears in the TRS.
- As with Mycroft's solution it is required that the type assigned to a defining occurrence of a symbol (see Section 4.1.3) equals its type provided by the environment, while to other occurrences an instance of this type can be assigned.
- In TRSs symbols have fixed arity. Standard Curry types seem to be more appropriate for a variable arity context. So Curry types are extended with a Cartesian product (denoted as x) which is used for the types of the arguments of a function. This means that the definitions of type, unify, sub and not_in of Section 6.1.2 have to be extended accordingly (this is left to the reader).
- For type assignment on rewrite rules the left- and right-hand sides are treated as terms. A rewrite rule Lhs → Rhs is correctly typed if Lhs and Rhs are typed with the same type, and all the types assigned to one term variable (that appears in the left- and right-hand sides' bases) are one and the same.
- For type assignment on TRS-terms there is only one constraint, the **constant constraint** (C). If F is a constant symbol, and $F\ A_1 \ldots A_n$ is a TRS-term, then there is a substitution *S*, and types $\sigma_1, \ldots, \sigma_n$ and σ, such that *S* applied to the type for F provided by the environment is $(\sigma_1 \times \ldots \times \sigma_n)\to\sigma$. In the tree representation, typing is performed accordingly (see Figure 6.11).

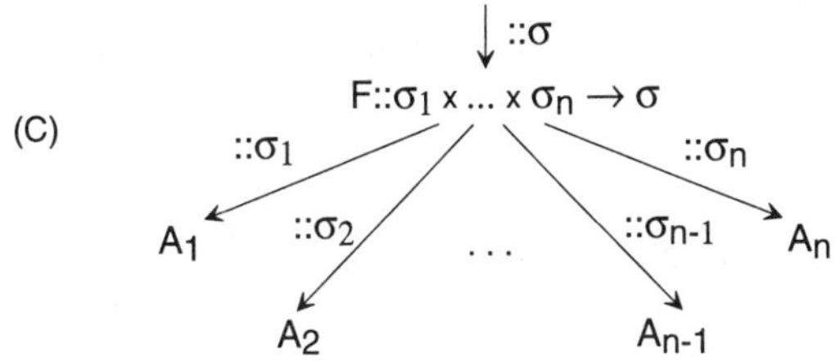

Figure 6.11 The constant constraint.

This notion of type assignment has the principal type property.

Example: stack handling. This example deals with stacks of natural numbers and contains, next to the standard stack functions Top and Pop, the function Alternate that combines two stacks. The types that are assigned are similar to the types that are assigned in the approach using sorts, as in Dershowitz and Jouannaud (1990). The main difference between the two typing approaches is that the approach presented here also allows higher order and polymorphic types. Stacks of natural numbers are represented as terms of the form

Push S_1 (Push S_2 . . .(Push S_n Empty). . .)),

where Empty is the empty stack, and the S_i denote representations of the natural numbers 0, Succ (0), Succ (Succ (0)), etc. according to the following algebraic type definitions:

```
Nat     ==  Zero    |  Succ (Nat)
Stack   ==  Empty   |  Push (Nat, Stack)
```

Push and Empty are stack constructors, and Zero and Succ are number constructors. The functions Top, Pop and Alternate are defined by:

```
Top:: Stack → Nat
Top (Push x y)   →   x

Pop:: Stack → Stack
Pop (Push x y)   →   y

Alternate:: (Stack x Stack) → Stack
Alternate Empty z        →   z
Alternate (Push x y) z   →   Push x (Alternate z y)
```

With these rules it can be shown, for example, that the term Alternate (Push (Top (Push Zero Empty)) Empty) (Pop (Push (Succ Zero) Empty)) rewrites to: Push Zero Empty.

In term rewriting systems function symbols are also allowed on other positions in left-hand sides of rules than just the left-most one (note that this is not allowed in Miranda, see also Section 8.2.3). So it is possible to define optimizations like:

```
Push x (Pop (Push z y))                    →   Push x y
Push (Top (Push x z)) y                    →   Push x y
Push (Top (Push x w)) (Pop (Push z y))     →   Push x y
```

With these rewrite rules for Push the TRS can still be typed correctly.

Currying

In term rewriting systems currying is modelled via an extra symbol for explicit curried application: Ap. Furthermore, for each symbol F a curried variant F_0 is used as an argument of such explicit applications. Finally, for each curried symbol a rewrite rule is added that transforms the curried application into an uncurried one. With respect to typing such (partly) curried systems some special actions have to be taken:

- For the symbol Ap in the environment the higher order type $((\varphi_1 \to \varphi_2) \times \varphi_1) \to \varphi_2$ has to be added. When typing occurrences of this symbol the standard constant-constraint is applicable.
- For each pair of related symbols F and F_0 the types in the environment have to be equivalent with respect to currying, as explained in Section 1.7.2.
- The added rules for transforming curried applications into uncurried applications need to be typed as defining rules for the curried symbols (and not as alternative defining rules for Ap).

Consequently, the following rules for combinator application are typeable, for example, with the given environment:

```
I   ::  φ1 → φ1
K   ::  (φ1 x φ2) → φ1
S   ::  ((φ1→φ2→φ3) x (φ1→φ2) x φ1 )→φ 3
Ap  ::  ((φ1→φ2) x φ1 )→ φ2
I0  ::  φ1→φ1
K0  ::  φ1→φ2→φ1
S0  ::  (φ1→φ2→φ3)→(φ1→φ2)→φ1→φ3

I x                      →   x
K x y                    →   x
S x y z                  →   Ap (Ap x z) (Ap y z)

Ap I0 x                  →   I x
Ap (Ap K0 x) y           →   K x y
Ap (Ap (Ap S0 x) y) z    →   S x y z
```

Subject reduction

In general, when assigning types to TRSs as defined above, the subject reduction property is lost.

Take the following rules that are well typed with the given environment:

```
I    :: φ1→φ1
K    :: (φ1 x φ2) → φ1
S    :: ((φ1→φ2→φ3) x (φ1→φ2) x φ1 )→φ 3
M    :: (((φ1→φ2)→φ3) x (φ1→φ2))→ φ2
Ap   :: ((φ1→φ2) x φ1 )→ φ2
I0   :: φ1→φ1
K0   :: φ1→φ2→φ1
S0   :: (φ1→φ2→φ3)→(φ1→φ2)→φ1→φ3
M0   :: ((φ1→φ2)→φ3)→(φ1→φ2)→φ2

I x                  →  x
K x y                →  x
S x y z              →  Ap (Ap x z) (Ap y z)
M (Ap (Ap S0 x) y)   →  Ap (Ap S0 I0) y

Ap I0 x                  →  I x
Ap (Ap K0 x) y           →  K x y
Ap (Ap (Ap S0 x) y) z    →  S x y z
Ap M0 x                  →  M x
```

Then, the term M (Ap (Ap S_0 K_0) I_0) is typeable with the type $(\varphi_4 \rightarrow \varphi_5) \rightarrow \varphi_5$. A rewrite rule matches this term, so it can be rewritten to Ap (Ap S_0 I_0) I_0. This last term, however, is not typeable with the type $(\varphi_4 \rightarrow \varphi_5) \rightarrow \varphi_5$. In fact, it is not typeable at all.

It is possible to filter out the rewrite rules that do not satisfy the subject reduction property. Rules are called **safe** if they satisfy the following condition which is needed and sufficient for the required property (see Bakel *et al.*, 1992):

- If (basis, σ) is the principal pair for the left-hand side term, then it is possible to type the right-hand side with σ such that all term variables are typed with the same type as in basis, so if (basis, σ) is the principal pair for the left-hand side term, then (basis, σ) is a pair for the right-hand side.

The Miranda type system satisfies this safety criterion due to the fact that in Miranda in left-hand sides functions can appear as left most symbols only, in combination with the way algebraic type definitions are specified.

6.3.3 The type check algorithm

The goal of the type check algorithm presented below is to determine whether a safe type assignment can be constructed such that all the conditions on type assignment of term rewrite systems are satisfied. The main function of the algorithm, type_rules, has a set of rules, as well as an environment, as parameters. It returns a boolean that indicates whether the construction of the type assignment to all rules was successful and safe. The algorithm type_term returns the principal pair for every term.

```
trs      ==   ([rule] , trsterm)
rule     ==   (trsterm, trsterm)
trsterm  ::=  Var var  |  Const const [trsterm]  |  DefSymb const [trsterm]
const    ==   name
```

The last alternative for trsterm (defining the constructor DefSymb) is used to indicate that the corresponding (sub)term starts with the defined symbol. So using DefSymb only makes sense when specifying the left-hand side of a rewrite rule. Of course, it would have been very possible to determine the defined symbol of a certain left-hand side of a rewrite rule without such a construct. This, however, would have made the algorithm somewhat more complicated and less clear.

The type of a constant is either an instance of the type for that constant given by the environment (in the case of a Const) or that type itself (in the case of a DefSymb). The distinction between the two is determined by the function type_term.

The defining node of a rewrite rule can only be typed with *one* type. So any substitution resulting from a unification is forbidden to change this type. This is solved by using as the unification algorithm not unify but unify_types, an extension of Robinson's unification algorithm which is not defined here; it is capable of deciding whether or not a type variable is special (so it appears in some environment type) and it refuses to substitute this variable by other types. This extension can be encoded easily by taking corresponding negative numbers as representation for such variables. The function unify_types must be used throughout instead of unify also where unify is applied in auxiliary functions such as check_assmptn.

```
type_trs:: freshtypevars -> environment -> trs -> typeresults
type_trs ftvs env (rules, term)
                = type_term ftvs env term,   if type_rules ftvs env rules

type_rules:: freshtypevars -> environment -> [rule] -> bool
type_rules ftvs env rules  =  foldr (&) True (map (type_rule ftvs env) rules)
```

```
type_rule:: freshtypevars -> environment -> rule -> bool
type_rule ftvs env (lhs, rhs)
= equal_bases (substitute (s2 . s1) basl) basl
  where  s2          = unify_basis (substitute s1 basl ++ substitute s1 basr)
         s1          = unify_types σ τ
         (ftvs', basl, σ)    = type_term ftvs env lhs
         (ftvs", basr, τ)    = type_term ftvs' env rhs

type_term:: freshtypevars -> environment -> trsterm -> typeresults
type_term (φ:ftvs) env (Var var)
          = (ftvs, [(var, Typevar φ)], Typevar φ)
type_term ftvs env (DefSymb const args)
          = type_func_app ftvs env (env const) args
type_term ftvs env (Const const args)
          = type_func_app ftvs' env typeinstance args
            where   (ftvs', typeinstance) =  fresh_instance ftvs (env const)

type_func_app:: freshtypevars-> environment-> type -> [trsterm]->typeresults
type_func_app ftvs env σ [ ]     = (ftvs, [ ], σ)
type_func_app (φ:ftvs) env σ terms
          = (ftvs', substitute s bas, s (Typevar φ))
            where   s                  = unify_types (Arrow τ (Typevar φ)) σ
                    (ftvs', bas, τ)    = type_args ftvs env terms

type_args:: freshtypevars -> environment -> [trsterm] -> typeresults
type_args ftvs env [ t ]     = type_term ftvs env t
type_args ftvs env (t : ts)  = (ftvs", bas ++ rbas, CartProd σ1 σ2)
                               where   (ftvs', bas, σ1)    = type_term ftvs env t
                                       (ftvs", rbas, σ2)   = type_args ftvs' env ts

unify_basis:: basis -> substitution
unify_basis [ ]                = identsub
unify_basis ((x, σ): rest)     = unify_basis bas . s
                                 where   (bas, s) =  check_assmptn (x, σ) rest
```

The algorithm type_rule returns TRUE only for rewrite systems that are safely typeable. For every term variable occurring in a rewrite rule, all the types assigned to this variable in the bases for both the left- and the right-hand sides should be the same. This is provided in type_rule by unifying all those types after a rule has been type checked. These unifications are performed by the function unify_basis. The function type_rule also takes care of checking the safety constraint, by checking, using equal_bases, if the unification of left- and right-hand sides of a rewrite rule has changed the left-hand side basis. This last function is not specified, because its definition is rather tedious while its intention is clear.

The function type_func_app looks for the type of a function application. It calls type_args, which is an auxiliary function that derives the types for all arguments of a node and constructs an arrow type out of these types. type_args assumes that the definition of type is extended with a binary constructor CartProd denoting a Cartesian product. Of course, such an extension also requires an adjustment of several other function definitions used in this chapter.

Summary

- Type assignment systems are used to perform a compile-time check on the type consistency of a program. Most type assignment algorithms for functional programming languages are based upon the *Curry system* for the λ-calculus.
- Type assignment in the Curry system takes place just by looking at the *syntactic structure* of a λ-term: there is one type assignment constraint for a *λ-application* (the arrow elimination) and one for a *λ-abstraction* (the arrow introduction). All instances of the same variable are assumed to have the same type.
- Type assignment in the Curry system is *decidable* and the principal type for a typeable term is found.
- *Self-application* cannot be typed with the consequence that the Curry system cannot be used to type recursive functions.
- By *naming* λ-terms *recursive* definitions can be introduced. Functions can be *polymorphic*.
- With a *fixed point construction* it is possible to find a type for *any (recursive) function definition*, if one exists. But whether there exists a type or not is *undecidable*.
- Milner's solution is a decidable algorithm that finds a type for *many* recursive definitions. It requires that all types used for a recursive definition can be *unified*. All instances of the *same variable* have the *same type*.
- Mycroft's solution checks on consistency of *given* types and is also decidable. It can approve more types than can be derived with the Milner algorithm.
- Neither Milner's nor Mycroft's solution can type *self-application* nor can they handle *internal polymorphism*.
- Type assignment in term rewriting systems is a *natural extension* of type assignment in the λ-calculus. But not all properties of type assignment for the λ-calculus are inherited by term rewriting systems. *Subject reduction* only holds for *safe* rewrite rules.

EXERCISES

6.1 Give a formal derivation for the type of:

(a) λab.a

(b) λxyz. x z (y z)

(c) (λxyz. x z (y z)) (λab.a)

(d) (λxy.x y) (λa.a) (λa.a)

6.2 Show that the term (λz.(λxy.x y) z z) (λa.a) cannot be typed.

6.3 Derive the types for the Push rules of the TRS in Section 6.3.2.

Chapter 7
Strictness analysis

Programs in lazy functional languages are evaluated lazily. The order of evaluation corresponds to normal order reduction of an equivalent λ-term in the λ-calculus. It also corresponds to evaluation according to the functional strategy for an equivalent FTRS or FGRS. Each of these evaluation orders is normalizing for its corresponding system.

However, in practice, lazy evaluation has as a disadvantage that this order of evaluation is not very efficient. In many cases, a lot of efficiency (both in space and time) can be gained when eager evaluation is chosen instead of lazy evaluation, both for sequential (see Part 4) as well as for parallel implementations (see Part 5). Eager evaluation corresponds in the λ-calculus to applicative order reduction, while in FTRSs and FGRSs it corresponds to innermost strategies.

As shown in the previous part of this book one cannot simply change the overall evaluation order from lazy to eager. The normal order reduction strategy as well as the functional strategy are both hypernormalizing (see Part 2). So if the corresponding evaluation orders are diluted with an arbitrary *finite* number of reduction steps, the result will always be the same. The problem is that by switching to eager evaluation the default strategy might be diluted with an *infinite* number of reduction steps. This can lead to a change in the termination behaviour of the program. So the evaluation order can only be changed at those places where it is certain that the termination behaviour of the program is not affected. The arguments in which a function is strict have this property.

A function is *strict* in a certain argument if the (eager) evaluation of that argument does not change the termination behaviour of the program. *Strictness analysis* is a compile-time analysis of a program that is used to tell whether or not a function is strict in its arguments. This *strictness information* is used to change the default reduction order at certain points in the program such that the performance of that program is improved. Whether or not a function is strict in a certain argument is, of course, in general undecidable. So strictness analysers use some kind of *approximation* method. Such an approximation method must be safe, i.e. the termination behaviour of a program has to remain unchanged.

There are various kinds and levels of approximations and therefore also various kinds of strictness analysers. Good strictness analysers are complex programs: for a good approximation it is not sufficient just to look at the syntactic structure of a program, as is the case with type assignment systems. For an accurate analysis some kind of approximation of the run-time behaviour of a program has to be performed at compile-time. This technique is known as *abstract interpretation.*

Strictness is explained in Section 7.1. A general introduction in abstract interpretation is given in Section 7.2. Some necessary basic formal knowledge about domain theory is presented in Section 7.3. Then, strictness analysis for lazy functional languages based on abstract interpretation is explained. This technique, introduced by Mycroft (1981), can only deal with first-order functions and flat domains (Section 7.4). In Section 7.5 we explain how one can deal with recursive functions and higher order functions (Burn *et al.*, 1985). The analysis for lists (Wadler, 1987) is treated in Section 7.6.

Sections 7.7 and 7.8 explore a related approximation method that can deal with arbitrary data structures. This method is known as *abstract reduction* (Nöcker, 1988; 1993). An analyser based on abstract reduction is incorporated in the Clean System (see Chapter 8).

7.1 Strictness

A function is **strict** in a certain argument if the (eager) evaluation of that argument does not change the termination behaviour of the program. Formally, this can be defined as follows: a function f of arity n is *strict* in its *i*th argument iff

$$f\ x_1 \dots x_{i-1} \perp x_{i+1} \dots x_n \quad = \perp$$

for all possible values x_j ($j \neq i$). In this definition $\perp$ (bottom) stands for any non-terminating expression.

A **strict argument** can arise in two situations. In the first place it can be the case that an argument is **needed** (see Chapter 4), i.e. it certainly has to be reduced in each possible application of the function. So when an argument is needed it can be evaluated in advance without changing the termination behaviour of the function. This property is very important for changing lazy evaluation into eager evaluation. In the second place an argument is strict when the function represents an infinite computation, even disregarding the argument.

Example of strictness due to neededness:

```
g x   = x + 1
```

The function g is strict in x because the value of x is needed for the addition. Hence, x can be evaluated safely before applying g. If the evaluation of x does not terminate, the lazy strategy would also end up in non-termination because x would be evaluated anyway. So indeed: g $\perp = \perp$.

Example of strictness due to non-termination:

```
g x   = g x
```

In spite of the fact that x is not needed in g, it is still safe to evaluate it before applying g. The termination properties remain the same: g $\perp = \perp$.

Strictness analysis is a compile-time analysis of the strictness properties of a program. Strictness is in general undecidable. So inherently strictness analysers use some kind of *approximation* method which is safe, i.e. the termination behaviour of a program has to remain unchanged. Two analysis methods are described in this chapter: *abstract interpretation* and *abstract reduction.*

7.2 Abstract interpretation

The technique of abstract interpretation is used to perform a compile-time analysis of certain properties of a complex computation. It is often used to perform strictness analysis, but the technique can also be used to analyse many other properties, such as the complexity of a program, or to predict whether a computation is shared or not. The basic idea of the method is that the *standard interpretation* at run-time (the ordinary, possibly non-terminating, evaluation of the program) is approximated by a terminating *abstract interpretation* at compile-time. To make this compile-time evaluation possible, only those evaluation aspects are regarded that are needed for the derivation of the desired property. So the kind of analysis is highly dependent upon the property of interest.

7.2.1 Rule of signs

As an example the well-known 'rule of signs' is presented. Assume that one is interested in the sign of the result of a multiplication of integer values. The sign of the result can be calculated in two ways: either by first calculating the result and then taking the sign or by first taking the sign of the arguments and then deducing the sign of the result.

Take the following computation:

```
–33 * 728 * –301    →    +7231224
```

The obvious way to find out the sign of the result is by simply calculating the result, +7231224, which obviously is positive. The other method only looks at the signs of the arguments:

```
(–) * (+) * (–)  →    (+)
```

The sign of the result follows by applying a special 'multiplication' on signs.

Formally, the first method starts with calculating the result in the domain Z of numbers as usual (with the standard interpretation). Then, an abstraction of the result from that domain to an abstract domain $Z^{\#}$ of representations of signs is made.

The first method calculates the sign after performing a standard multiplication.

```
abs +7231224    →    plus
```

where the abstraction function abs and the domains Z and $Z^{\#}$ are defined as:

```
Z     = { ..., –2, –1, 0, 1, 2, ... }
Z#    = {minus, zero, plus}

abs:: Z → Z#
abs x     = plus,     if x > 0
          = minus,    if x < 0
          = zero,     otherwise
```

The second method first abstracts numbers to signs with the abstraction function from Z to $Z^{\#}$. Then, instead of the standard multiplication in Z an abstract multiplication is performed in $Z^{\#}$.

Abstract multiplication is an abstract function from $Z^{\#}$ to $Z^{\#}$. Do not confuse such an abstract function with the abstraction function that is defined from Z to $Z^{\#}$.

The second method uses an abstract multiplication *#: an abstract version (in prefix form) of the standard multiplication, working on abstracted values.

```
*# (abs –33) (*# (abs 728) (abs –301))
→    *# minus (*# plus minus)  →    *# minus minus  →    plus
```

where the abstract multiplication *# is defined as:

```
*#:: Z# x Z# → Z#
*# plus    plus    = plus
*# plus    zero    = zero
*# zero    plus    = zero
*# plus    minus   = minus
*# minus   plus    = minus
*# minus   zero    = zero
*# zero    minus   = zero
*# zero    zero    = zero
*# minus   minus   = plus
```

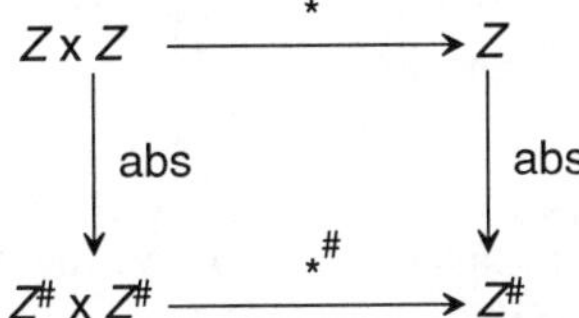

Figure 7.1 Two ways to calculate the sign of a multiplication.

So the sign of the result of a multiplication can be obtained in two ways (see Figure 7.1). The first way corresponds to the arrows going from $Z \times Z$ to Z (using the *standard interpretation*) and then from Z to $Z^{\#}$ (an abstraction from Z). The second way corresponds to the arrows going from $Z \times Z$ to $Z^{\#} \times Z^{\#}$ (an abstraction from $Z \times Z$) and then from $Z^{\#} \times Z^{\#}$ to $Z^{\#}$ (using an *abstract interpretation*). Both ways reach the same property, represented by an element of $Z^{\#}$. But, with abstract interpretation the result can be obtained more easily and faster.

In the running example the result of both calculation methods is the same:

```
abs (x * y)  =  *# (abs x) (abs y)
```

So the abstract interpretation can replace the standard interpretation.

We have shown that abstract interpretation can be used to derive signs of multiplicative expressions. However, not all properties can be derived via abstract interpretation.

Assume that we want to calculate the sign of the result of integer addition via abstract interpretation. Then, an abstract function +# has to be defined:

```
+#:: Z# x Z# → Z#
+# plus plus   = plus
```

```
+# plus zero  =  plus
+# plus minus =  ??
...
```

The third alternative is problematic. The sign of the addition of a positive and a negative value can only be computed by actually doing the computation. In the abstract domain the result is unknown. This can be expressed by adding a new element to $Z^{\#}$: unknown. The definition of $+^{\#}$ can now be completed. One also has to take care that the new value unknown can appear as an argument of $+^{\#}$ as well.

```
+# plus minus      = unknown
+# plus unknown    = unknown
+# zero zero       = zero
+# zero unknown    = unknown
...
```

When the outcome of the abstract addition yields the value unknown nothing can be said of the sign of the actual result in the standard interpretation.

In the abstract domain various approximations are possible. If a value y in the abstract domain represents many elements in the concrete domain, it is a coarser approximation than an abstract value x representing fewer of these concrete elements. The operator ≤ (less than or equal) expresses this ordering. If x ≤ y then x represents *fewer* concrete *elements* than y. So x contains *more information* than y. The inverse abstraction function abs^{-1} yields, given a value $v^{\#}$ in the abstract domain, the set of all corresponding values v in the concrete domain for which $abs^{-1}\ v^{\#} = v$. Formally, the **abstract ordering** is defined as x ≤ y iff $abs^{-1}\ x \leq abs^{-1}\ y$.

All integers in the concrete domain Z correspond to the value unknown, whereas, for instance, only the positive integers correspond to the abstract value plus. Hence the value unknown holds less information than plus.

```
plus     ≤  unknown
```

Not all elements in $Z^{\#}$ contain the same amount of information. So in some cases the abstract interpretation is less informative. Therefore only an approximation of the desired property can be found. Such an approximation should not yield wrong results, i.e. be in contradiction with the results obtained by using the standard interpretation. However, being an approximation it may contain less information. The main requirement for an abstract interpretation is that it is *safe* (correct), i.e.

```
abs . f  ≤  f# . abs
```

for all elements in the concrete domain ('.' stands for function composition). This important criterion is called the **safety criterion**.

For deriving the sign for multiplication there is no difference between the outcome with abstract interpretation or without abstract interpretation, since

```
abs . *  =  *# . abs
```

For deriving the sign for addition only an approximation can be achieved:

```
abs . +  ≤  +# . abs
```

So due to the loss of information, abstract interpretation will generally only give an approximation. This does not have to be a serious problem. A decidable analysis at compile-time that can predict an undecidable run-time property of a program can only be achieved by using an approximation method.

For a further understanding of strictness analysis via abstract interpretation, a short informal introduction to domain theory is needed.

7.3 Basic domain theory

The fundamental concept in domain theory is a **semantic domain**, a set of elements grouped together because they share some common property or use. In the literature many approaches, more or less equivalent, can be found (see, for example, Markovsky (1976), Stoy (1977)). All of them are based on the concept of a **c**omplete **p**artial **o**rdering (**cpo**). A set D with an ordering relation over that set $\leq_d$ (or $\leq$ for short) is a **complete partial ordering** $(D, \leq)$ if it has the following properties:

(1) It is a partially ordered set (a **poset**), i.e. $\leq$ is
- **reflexive**: $d \leq d$ for all $d \in D$;
- **transitive**: if $d \leq e$ and $e \leq f$ for $d,e,f \in D$ then $d \leq f$;
- and **anti-symmetric**: if $d \leq e$ for $d,e \in D$ and $d \neq e$, then not $e \leq d$.

(2) It is **complete**, i.e.
- D has a **least** element $\perp_d$ (or $\perp$) such that $\perp \leq d$ for all $d \in D$;
- and, for each **increasing sequence** $S = d_1 \leq d_2 \leq \ldots \leq d_n \leq \ldots$ in D, there exists a *least upper bound* $\cup S \in D$.

A **least upper bound** is defined as:
- it is an **upper bound**: $d_j \leq \cup S$ for all $d_j \in S$;
- and it is **least**: if $d_j \leq u$ for all $d_j \in S$ and some $u \in D$, then $\cup S \leq u$.

The **l**east **u**pper **b**ound (lub) is also used as an infix operator.

From now on all domains are assumed to be cpos.

A pictorial representation of a finite semantic domain is shown in Figure 7.2. All points represent elements of the domain. The arcs define the ordering. If x and y are connected and x is 'below' y in the picture, then $x \leq y$.

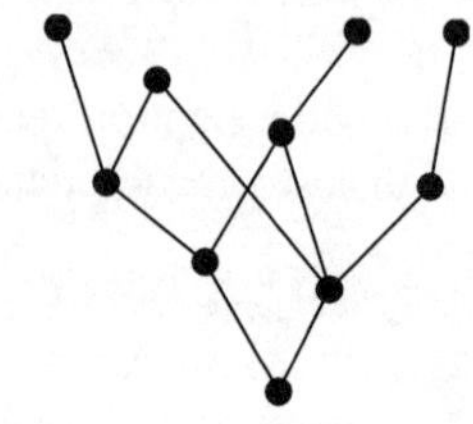

Figure 7.2 A finite cpo.

A domain $<D, \leq>$ is **flat** (Figure 7.3) iff:

- for all $a,b \in D$: if $a \leq b$ then $a = b$ or $a = \perp$.

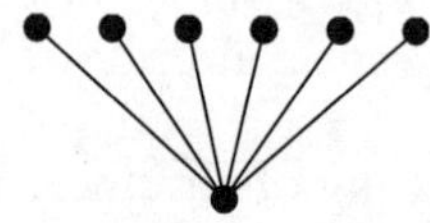

Figure 7.3 Pictorial representation of a flat domain.

Some examples of complete partial orderings:

$<\{0,1\}, \leq>$ with $0 \leq 1$. The least element is 0; for the sequence $0 \leq 1$ the least upper bound is 1. This is a flat domain.

$<N_\perp, \leq>$ with $\perp \leq$ n, n $\in N_\perp$ where $N_\perp$ is the set of natural numbers extended with a bottom element: $N \cup \{\perp\}$ (also called the **lifted domain** of N). Note that the $\leq$ has nothing to do with the ordinary less than or equal: elements of N are incomparable in this domain. Further note that this is a flat domain.

$<$P$(\{0, 1, 2\}), \leq>$ where P$(\{0, 1, 2\})$ is the powerset of the set $\{0, 1, 2\}$ containing all subsets of this set: $\{\{\}, \{0\}, \{1\}, \{2\}, \{0, 1\}, \{0, 2\}, \dots, \{0, 1, 2\}\}$ where $\leq$ is the standard subset relation defined on sets.

The functions over domains are in general *monotonic* and *continuous*:

- A function f:: $D \to E$ is **monotonic** iff for all $d,e \in D$, if $d \leq e$, then $f\ d \leq f\ e$.
- A monotonic function f:: $D \to E$ is **continuous** iff for every increasing sequence S in D, $f\,(\cup S) = \cup\ \{f\ d_i \mid d_i \in S\}$.

If a function is continuous, it is also monotonic. For finite domains the two are equivalent. The intuitive meaning of monotonicity is that all 'nice' properties and the structure of a domain are maintained. For example, an increasing sequence stays an increasing sequence after function application. Continuity ensures that there is no surprise at least upper bounds: the least upper bound of an increasing sequence stays a least upper bound after function application.

Starting with domains new domains can be constructed. Suppose D and E are domains. Then the **product domain** $D \times E$ is defined as: $D \times E = <\{(x,y) \mid x \in D, y \in E\}, \leq_x>$. The **ordering relation** $\leq_x$ **for the product domain** is defined as: $(x,y) \leq_x (x',y')$ iff $x \leq_d x'$ and $y \leq_e y'$.

The **function domain** $D \rightarrow E$ contains all continuous functions from D to E. It is defined as: $D \rightarrow E = <\{f \mid f$ is a continuous function from D to $E\}, \leq_{\rightarrow}>$. The **ordering relation for the function domain** is defined as: $f \leq_{\rightarrow} g$ iff $f\ d \leq_e g\ d$ for all $d \in D$.

Take for example the following domain with its product domain:

$$D = <\{0,1\}, \leq> \text{ with } 0 \leq 1$$
$$D \times D = <\{(0,0), (0,1), (1,0), (1,1)\}, \leq_X>$$

The domain D contains only two values, 0 and 1. Therefore only four functions from D to D can be constructed:

$f_{\perp}$ x = 0
f_{I} x = x
$f_{\sim I}$ x = ~x (~ is negation)
f_{T} x = 1

Only the function $f_{\sim I}$ is not continuous, so the function domain $D \rightarrow D$ is (Figure 7.4):

$$D \rightarrow D = <\{f_{\perp}, f_{I}, f_{T}\}, \leq_{\rightarrow}>$$

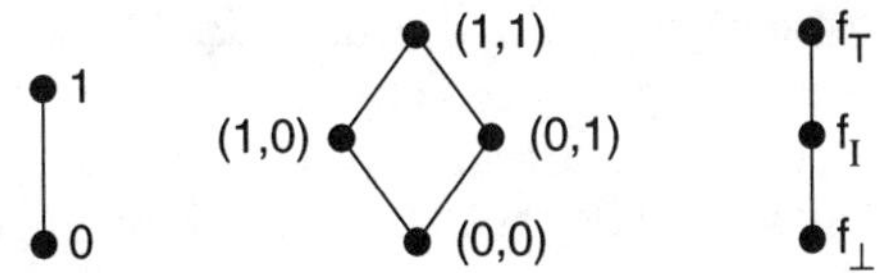

Figure 7.4 Pictorial representation of the domains D, D x D and D → D.

For continuous functions the **fixed point theorem** holds: if f:: $D \rightarrow D$ is continuous, then

- f has a **least fixed point** $d \in D$ with the following properties:
  - d is a fixed point: $f\ d = d$;
  - d is least: if $f\ e = e$, $e \in D$, then $d \leq e$.

This least fixed point d can be constructed as follows: $d = \cup \{f^n \perp \mid n \geq 0\}$. This set equals $\{\perp, f\perp, f(f\perp), \ldots\}$. So it follows that *if* the domain D is *finite*, the least fixed point can be found in finite time: just start computing the sequence $\perp, f\perp, f(f\perp), \ldots$ (which is increasing since f is continuous) until two consecutive values are the same.

7.4 Strictness analysis using abstract interpretation

In this section strictness analysis is discussed for a very restricted situation: only simple non-recursive functions are considered working on a flat domain D of integers, booleans and the like. Function bodies can only contain function applications (non-recursive, no higher order), constants (numbers, booleans etc.) and variables. So it is assumed that generally a function f is defined as:

$$f :: D^n \to D$$
$$f\ x_1 \ldots x_i \ldots x_n \quad = \ E$$

To make an abstract interpretation to determine strictness two things have to be done (Figure 7.5).

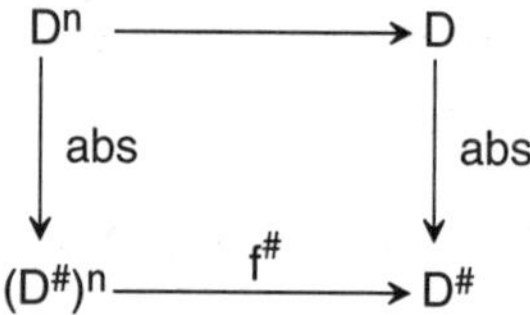

Figure 7.5 Abstract interpretation diagram for strictness analysis.

First an abstraction function abs and a domain $D^\#$ have to be found in which the strictness property can be expressed. Then, the interpretation function $f^\#$ has to be defined working on the abstract domain. For each possible function f such an abstract interpretation function $f^\#$ has to be found.

The strictness question contains entities like 'all possible values' and 'any non-terminating expression'. So it is natural to represent these notions as elements of $D^\#$.

Define:

1 the value representing all possible (terminating as well as non-terminating) expressions (generally also indicated as 'top');

0 the value representing all non-terminating ($\perp$) expressions (generally also indicated as 'bottom');

and define the abstraction function abs accordingly:

```
abs:: D → D#
abs x    = 0, if x does not terminate
         = 1, otherwise
```

where

```
D#   = {0, 1}
D    = {expressions}
```

$D^\#$ is a domain with $0 \leq 1$ (since the set of all non-terminating expressions is a subset of the set of all possible expressions); 0 is the least element; 1 is the least upper bound for the increasing sequence $0 \leq 1$.

The abstraction function abs is clearly undecidable. Fortunately, the abstraction does not actually have to be made. Suppose that for an abstract function $f^\#$ the equation

```
f# 1 ... 1 0 1 ... 1    = 0
```

can be solved. Then, the remaining problem is to find the proper abstract version $f^\#$ for each function f, and to prove that this abstraction is safe (abs . f $\leq$ $f^\#$. abs). It can be proven that it is possible to construct abstract functions in such a way that the abstraction is safe. Proofs like this go beyond the scope of this book. For a more formal treatment of strictness analysis and abstract interpretation the reader is referred to Mycroft (1981), Burn *et al.* (1985) or Renardel (1988).

Owing to the safety criterion the actual determination of the undecidable abs functions can be avoided, since, when it is known that

```
f# 1 ... 1   0 1 ... 1      = 0
```

it follows that

$$f\ x_1 \dots x_{i-1} \perp x_{i+1} \dots x_n = \perp$$

which can be shown as follows (using the safety criterion):

$$
\begin{aligned}
&(\text{abs} . f)\ x_1 \dots x_{i-1} \perp x_{i+1} \dots x_n \leq f^\#\ (\text{abs}\ x_1 \dots x_{i-1} \perp x_{i+1} \dots x_n) \\
\Rightarrow\quad &(\text{abs} . f)\ x_1 \dots x_{i-1} \perp x_{i+1} \dots x_n \leq f^\#\ 1 \dots 1\ 0\ 1 \dots 1 \\
\Rightarrow\quad &(\text{abs} . f)\ x_1 \dots x_{i-1} \perp x_{i+1} \dots x_n \leq 0 \\
\Rightarrow\quad &(\text{abs} . f)\ x_1 \dots x_{i-1} \perp x_{i+1} \dots x_n = 0 \\
\Rightarrow\quad &\text{abs}\ (f\ x_1 \dots x_{i-1} \perp x_{i+1} \dots x_n) = 0 \\
\Rightarrow\quad &f\ x_1 \dots x_{i-1} \perp x_{i+1} \dots x_n = \perp
\end{aligned}
$$

For the construction of an abstract function $f^\#$ a transformation function # can be defined that translates an arbitrary function f over D^n to its abstract counterpart $f^\#$. If f is defined by

$$f :: D^n \rightarrow D$$
$$f\ x_1 \ldots x_i \ldots x_n \quad = E$$

then $f^\#$ is defined using a transformation function #:

$$f^\# :: (D^\#)^n \rightarrow D^\#$$
$$f^\#\ x_1 \ldots x_i \ldots x_n \quad = \#[\![E]\!]$$

Next we show how this transformation function # has to be defined. The resulting functions will satisfy the safety criterion.

7.4.1 Constants, variables and function applications

First, assume that a right-hand side of a function body only consists of constants, variables and applications of other functions. Constant expressions always terminate, so $\#[\![\text{constant}]\!] = 1$. The translation function # then becomes:

$\#[\![c]\!]$	$= 1$	where c is a constant
$\#[\![x]\!]$	$= x$	where x is a variable
$\#[\![f\ E_1 \ldots E_n]\!]$	$= f^\#\ \#[\![E_1]\!] \ldots \#[\![E_n]\!]$	where f is a function

7.4.2 δ-rules

Now consider abstract versions of simple functions like δ-rules. Take, for example, the addition. To perform an addition both arguments are needed. So clearly, $\bot + E = \bot$ for all expressions E. In the abstract world this means that always $+^\#\ 0\ x = 0$. In this way $+^\#$ can be defined for all possible arguments. It follows that $+^\#$ equals the logical AND operator & (where 0 and 1 represent Boolean values):

```
& 0 x   = 0
& x 0   = 0
& 1 1   = 1
```

The same holds for multiplication and many other δ-rules. So the abstraction function # can now be refined:

$$\#[\![+\ E1\ E2]\!] = \&\ \#[\![E1]\!]\ \#[\![E2]\!]$$
$$\#[\![*\ E1\ E2]\!] = \&\ \#[\![E1]\!]\ \#[\![E2]\!]$$
...

A more difficult standard function is the conditional. The condition in a conditional expression is needed, so: $\text{if}\ \bot\ t\ e = \bot$. Hence, in the abstract world: $\text{if}^\#\ 0\ t\ e = 0$ for all t and e in $D^\#$. Furthermore, either the 'then' or the 'else' part is needed. Non-termination is possible if only one of these branches is non-termination. Non-termination is certain when both 'then' and 'else' parts are non-terminating. The abstract conditional is defined as

```
if# c t e  =  & c (| t e)
```

where | is the logical OR operator. So:

$$\#[\![\text{ if } E_c\ E_t\ E_e]\!] = \&\ \#[\![E_c]\!]\ (|\ \#[\![E_t]\!]\ \#[\![E_e]\!])$$

7.5 Analysing function definitions

The definitions above can be used for deriving abstract versions of simple functions. Clearly, it can be the case that in the resulting abstract functions information is lost.

Consider the following example:

```
f x y z   = if (x = 0) (y + z) (x – y)
```

then

```
f# x y z
= # [[ if (x = 0) (y + z) (x – y) ]]
= & # [[ (x = 0) ]] (| # [[ (y + z) ]] # [[ (x – y) ]] )
= & (& # [[ x ]] # [[ 0 ]] ) (| (& # [[ y ]] # [[ z ]] ) (& # [[ x ]] # [[ y ]] ))
= & (& x 1) (| (& y z) (& x y))
```

Now this abstract function can be used for deriving strictness information by evaluating f# 0 1 1, f# 1 0 1 etc.:

```
f# 0 1 1 →    & (& 0 1) (| (& 1 1) (& 0 1))  →   & 0 (| 1 0) →   0
f# 1 0 1 →    & (& 1 1) (| (& 0 1) (& 1 0))  →   0
f# 1 1 0 →    & (& 1 1) (| (& 1 0) (& 1 1))  →   1
```

From the first two derivations it can be concluded that f is strict in x and y. This is what would be expected: x will always be evaluated in the condition, y will always be evaluated because it appears in both the 'then' and 'else' branches of the conditional. Of course, it cannot be concluded from the derivations above that f is *not* strict in z. Consider a slightly different definition of f:

```
f x y z   = if (x = x) (y + z) (x – y)
```

Abstract interpretation will give that f# 1 1 0 = 1. However, f is strict in z, because the 'then' part will always be chosen (so always: f x y ⊥ = ⊥).

7.5.1 Recursive functions

When recursive functions are considered the analysis is more complex.

> Consider the following recursive definition:
>
> | | | | |
> |---|---|---|---|
> | f x y | = | if (x = 0) y (f (x – 1) y) | |
> | then, $f^\#$ x y | = | & (& x 1) (I y ($f^\#$ (& x 1) y)) | |
> | hence, $f^\#$ 0 1 | → | & (& 0 1) (I y ($f^\#$ (& 0 1) y)) | → 0 |
>
> So the method described above finds f to be strict in its first argument.

In general, however, (mutually) recursive functions can lead to a non-terminating reduction in the abstract world. It is in principle undecidable whether or not this situation occurs.

> For instance, when the strictness of the second argument of the example above is calculated, the abstract reduction sequence is non-terminating:
>
> $f^\#$ 1 0 → & (& 1 1) (I 0 ($f^\#$ (& 1 1) 0)) → & 1 ($f^\#$ (& 1 1) 0)) → $f^\#$ 1 0 → ...

Since 1 is the upper bound of $D^\#$, it is always true that $f^\# \ x_1 \dots x_n \leq 1$. This can be used to stop a (possibly infinite) computation at any moment to approximate the result with 1. In this way the interpretation stays safe, but too much information is lost.

With some help from domain theory the problem can be solved. Because $D^\#$ is a domain, the continuous functions over it also form a domain. Since $D^\#$ is finite, the domain $D^\# \times D^\# \to D^\#$ is also finite. Abstract functions that are constructed with continuous functions like &, I and if are continuous as well.

With abstract functions that are defined by a recursive equation, initially the only thing that is known of the function is the recursive equation and the fact that it is continuous. Since for finite domains this means that the function is also monotonic, the function can be approximated from below by a fixed point computation as follows: if $f^\#$ is a function of arity n, defined by the equation $f^\# \ x_1 \dots x_n = E$, then functions $f^{\#m}$, $m \geq 0$, are defined as follows:

$$f^{\#0} \ x_1 \dots x_n = 0$$
$$f^{\#m} \ x_1 \dots x_n = E [\![f^\# := f^{\#m-1}]\!]$$

where $[\![x := y]\!]$ means that all occurrences of x have to be replaced by y. This sequence of functions is increasing. Therefore it has a least upper bound $f^{\#u}$, for which $f^{\#u} = f^{\#u+1}$ and therefore $f^{\#u} = f^\#$.

In the function domain the function defined by

$$F \ f \ x_1 \dots x_n = E [\![f^\# := f]\!]$$

takes a function and returns the next approximation which is a continuous function as well. Hence, this function has a fixed point for which $F\ d = d$, i.e. E ⟦ f# := f ⟧ = f. This corresponds directly to the solution of the equation being found. Therefore, the computation via an approximating increasing sequence is a proper fixed point computation. In the case of mutually recursive functions a set of equations has to be solved simultaneously with a fixed point calculation. As a first approximation all functions are returning the bottom element for all their arguments. Each iteration calculates the next approximation for each function.

The fixed point calculation applied to the example above:

```
f# x y   = & (& x 1) (| y (f# (& x 1) y))
```

then (by definition):

```
f#0 x y  = 0
```

and (by repeated substitution):

```
f#1 x y  = & (& x 1) (| y (f#0 (& x 1) y))  = & (& x 1) (| y 0)   = & x y

f#2 x y  = & (& x 1) (| y (f#1 (& x 1) y))  = & (& x 1) (| y (f#1 x y))
         = & x (| y (& x y))                = & x y
```

The sequence for this function converges quickly. The first and second element are already the same: $f^{\#1} = f^{\#2}$. So the solution is $f^{\#} = f^{\#1}$ and therefore:

```
f# x y   = & x y
```

such that f# 1 0 → 0. Hence, f is also strict in its second argument.

A disadvantage of the method is that it requires that functions are tested for equality. Two functions are **equal** if they yield the same value for each possible combination of arguments. Because the complexity of comparing functions is exponential in the number of arguments, the derivation of the fixed point can be computationally expensive. In practice, the fixed point can often be found quickly. In the example above, one can see directly without computing any result that $f^{\#1}$ and $f^{\#2}$ are equal. However, a brute force comparison of $f^{\#1}$ and $f^{\#2}$ requires 2^2 comparisons.

7.5.2 Higher order functions

Until now only functions working from D^n to D were considered. Strictness analysis is more complex when higher order functions are allowed.

Consider the following higher order function:

```
hof g a b   =  (g a b) + (g b b)
```

The first element of hof is a function: an element of D x D → D assumed that hof delivers an element of D. For finding the abstract function $hof^{\#}$ the same technique as before can be used:

$$hof^{\#}\ g\ a\ b\ =\ \&\ (g\ a\ b)\ (g\ b\ b)$$

The test for strictness becomes difficult because $hof^{\#}$ 0 1 1 cannot be computed. The first argument of $hof^{\#}$ is of the wrong type. It should be a member of the domain $D^{\#} \times D^{\#} \rightarrow D^{\#}$, so the appropriate top and bottom elements from this domain should be chosen.

In order to deal with higher order functions new functions for the top element and bottom element have to be defined in the appropriate domain. So the bottom element is represented by a function that always yields 0, and the top element by a function that always yields 1.

For example, for the domain $D^{\#} \times D^{\#} \rightarrow D^{\#}$ define $f_{\perp}$ and f_{T}

$$f_{\perp} :: D^{\#} \times D^{\#} \rightarrow D^{\#}$$
$$f_{\perp}\ x\ y = 0$$

$$f_{T} :: D^{\#} \times D^{\#} \rightarrow D^{\#}$$
$$f_{T}\ x\ y = 1$$

With these elements the strictness properties of hof can be determined: hof is only strict in its first argument.

$$hof^{\#}\ f_{\perp}\ 1\ 1\ =\ 0$$
$$hof^{\#}\ f_{T}\ 0\ 1\ =\ 1$$
$$hof^{\#}\ f_{T}\ 1\ 0\ =\ 1$$

Functions over higher order functions can be recursive as well. The fixed point technique for recursive functions must now be applied in more complex domains. Finding such a fixed point can be expensive.

```
rechof g x y   =  if  (x = 0) (g x y) (rechof g (x – 1) (y + 1))
```

The function $rechof^{\#u}$ has to be found in the domain $(D^{\#} \times D^{\#} \rightarrow D^{\#}) \times D^{\#} \times D^{\#}$. For testing whether rechof is strict in argument x no fixed point computation has to be done. But for determining the strictness in y a least upper bound has to be determined.

Fortunately, many programs do not contain very complex higher order functions. So in practice, fixed points can often be found fairly easily.

7.6 Analysing non-flat domains

So far, only functions over flat domains such as integers and booleans are considered. No lists or other data types (constructors) were involved. Again, the analysis method described above can easily be extended by mapping all constructors to top:

$$\# [\![\text{Con } E_1 \ldots E_n]\!] = 1$$

where Con is a constructor of arity n. The disadvantage of such a rough approximation is that too much information is lost.

> Consider for example the function that sums all elements of a list:
>
> ```
> sum [ ]        = 0
> sum (a : x)    = a + sum x
> ```
>
> It can easily be seen that sum is strict in its argument: the list given to sum can be evaluated to head normal form before applying sum to it. Furthermore, all the elements of the list can be evaluated in advance also.

The sum example above shows that for data structures like lists another kind of strictness analysis is required. The kind of strictness cannot be found by the abstract interpretation used thus far. But what abstract interpretation is strong enough for finding this kind of information? The most natural way seems to maintain the constructors in the abstract domain:

$$\# [\![\text{Con } E_1 \ldots E_n]\!] = \text{Con}^{\#} \; \# [\![E_1]\!] \ldots \# [\![E_n]\!]$$

So the abstract domain (for lists) contains elements like $\text{Nil}^{\#}$, $\text{Cons}^{\#}\ 0\ \text{Nil}^{\#}$, $\text{Cons}^{\#}\ 0\ (\text{Cons}^{\#}\ 0\ \text{Nil}^{\#})$ etc. This (non-flat) domain has a disadvantage: the domain is in general *infinite*. As a consequence, fixed point computations are no longer possible. Also, the kind of evaluation needed for the sum example is very difficult to express in this domain. What is needed is a finite domain in which several kinds of termination property can be expressed.

7.6.1 The four-point domain on lists

The method of Wadler (1987) is based on the observation that only some special kinds of reduction on lists are useful:

- reduction to head normal form:

```
is_empty (h : t)  =  False
is_empty [ ]      =  True
```

  is_empty does not terminate when its argument has no head normal form.

- **spine reduction:** reduction of the 'spine' $[e_1, e_2, \ldots, e_m]$ of a list, but no reduction of the list elements $e_1, e_2, \ldots, e_m$ themselves:

```
length [ ]       =  0
length (h : t)   =  1 + length t
```

  length only terminates for finite lists. The elements of the list are not needed.

- **element reduction:** reduction of the spine of the list and reduction to head normal form of all the list elements:

```
sum [ ]      =  0
sum (h : t)  =  h + sum t
```

  sum only terminates for finite lists with no non-terminating elements.

All these kinds of reduction have to be represented in the abstract domain. Therefore abstract values av_i have to be introduced such that:

```
is_empty#  av1  =  0
length#    av2  =  0
sum#       av3  =  0
```

Let LD be the domain of lists over the simple values of D. The following abstract values in the abstract domain LD# are defined:

Bot — the bottom element, representing *all certainly non-terminating expressions*;

Inf — represents the same as Bot extended with *all infinite lists*;

BotMem — represents the same as Inf extended with *all lists with at least one non-terminating element* (member);

TopMem — represents *all possible lists.*

These values are sometimes also represented as the numbers 0, 1, 2 and 3. We shall use the above notation to prevent confusion with the elements of the domain D# (0 and 1). In this analysis an infinite list can be a real infinite list as well as a list of which the tail is a non-terminating reduction. As a consequence, the domain LD# has the following ordering:

Bot ≤ Inf ≤ BotMem ≤ TopMem. The meaning of these values is explained by considering the function f::LD → D. Suppose that in the abstract domain the result of applying f# to the four abstract values can be derived:

- *reduction to head normal form*: if f# Bot = 0, it is known that calling f with a non-terminating reduction will result in non-termination (hence f ⊥ = ⊥). The argument of f can be reduced safely to head normal form before applying f. If f# Bot = 1, this is not possible.

```
is_empty# Bot = 0
length#   Bot = 0
sum#      Bot = 0
```

- *spine reduction*: if f# Inf = 0, it is known that calling f with an infinite list will result in non-termination (hence f inflist = ⊥, where inflist is some infinite list). Note that then also f# Bot = 0 since f# is continuous. In this case the spine of the argument of f can safely be evaluated before applying the function. If f# Inf = 1, this is not possible.

```
is_empty# Inf = 1
length#   Inf = 0
sum#      Inf = 0
```

- *element reduction*: if f# BotMem = 0, it is known that calling f with a list containing a non-terminating element will result in non-termination (hence f botelemlist = ⊥, where botelemlist is such a list). Note that then also f# Inf = 0 and f# Bot = 0. In this case both the spine and the elements of the argument of f can safely be evaluated before applying the function. If f# BotMem = 1, this is not possible.

```
is_empty# BotMem = 1
length#   BotMem = 1
sum#      BotMem = 0
```

- if f# TopMem = 0, an application of f will never terminate (then also f# BotMem = 0, f# Inf = 0 and f# Bot = 0).

```
is_empty# TopMem = 1
length#   TopMem = 1
sum#      TopMem = 1
```

7.6.2 Constructing abstract functions in the four-point domain

For the construction of the abstract functions so far only a translation of the right-hand side was necessary. Now also pattern matching on the left-hand side is taken into account.

The translation is explained by considering a more or less general function definition (in which E and N are functions with respectively zero and two arguments representing the right-hand sides of the alternatives):

```
f []      = E
f (h : t) = N h t
```

The abstract function f# is now examined for the four possible arguments in the domain LD#.

The result of f# Bot corresponds to the result of a call to f with a non-terminating element: f ⊥. Because the pattern matching never will terminate, the result of this will be ⊥, corresponding to bottom in the result domain. So f ⊥ = ⊥. Hence, we deduce f# Bot = bottom.

The result of f# Inf corresponds to the result of a call to f with an infinite list. Hence, the second member of f will always match. What can be said of the head and tail of an infinite list? The head (variable h) can have any value (Top), and in the abstract domain all occurrences of variable h can be replaced by 1. The tail of an infinite list can either be a non-terminating reduction (⊥), or it can also be an infinite list. Therefore, in the abstract domain variable t can be replaced by Bot or Inf. The result in the abstract domain will be the least upper bound of both possibilities (the smallest safe value in the abstract domain). Since all abstract functions are monotonic it is sufficient to replace the variable t by Inf.

A similar construction can be made for determining f# BotMem. This corresponds to calling f with a list containing at least one element that does not terminate. This implies that in this case the second member of f will always match. Again two possibilities arise: either the head of the list does not terminate, in which case nothing more can be said about the tail, or the head of the list might terminate, in which case the tail of the list has to contain the non-terminating element. In the abstract world the first case corresponds to replacing variable h by 0 and variable t by TopMem. The second case corresponds to replacing variable h by 1 and variable t by BotMem.

Lastly, the same procedure has to be followed for TopMem. Function f is called with some list. One of the two members will match. If the second one does, nothing special can be said of the tail of the list. So the least upper bound has to be taken of the two right-hand sides. Hence

```
f# Bot     = bottom
f# Inf     = # ⟦ N ⟧ 1 Inf
```

```
f# BotMem  = (# ⟦ N ⟧ 0 TopMem) ∪ (# ⟦ N ⟧ 1 BotMem)
f# TopMem  = # ⟦ E ⟧ ∪ (# ⟦ N ⟧ 1 TopMem)
```

Extending the method to functions with more arguments and more complex types is straightforward.

Another part of the translation scheme is formed by the right-hand sides. With the list constructors special things have to be done. Nil (or [ ]) is clearly a terminating list, and its abstract representation is TopMem. Cons (or :) becomes a predefined function: Cons#.

```
# ⟦ [ ] ⟧         = TopMem
# ⟦ E1 : E2 ⟧    = Cons# # ⟦ E1 ⟧ # ⟦ E2 ⟧
```

The Cons of a non-terminating expression and some list is a list with a non-terminating element, or abstractly: Cons# 0 TopMem = BotMem. Similarly, Cons# x y is defined for other arguments (see the table below).

Cons# x y	x = 1	x = 0
y = TopMem	TopMem	BotMem
y = BotMem	BotMem	BotMem
y = Inf	Inf	Inf
y = Bot	Inf	Inf

Consider for example the function reverse: it reverses a list by using the standard function append:

```
reverse [ ]     = [ ]
reverse (h : t) = append (reverse t) (h : [ ])
```

Convert the right-hand sides:

```
# ⟦ [ ] ⟧  = TopMem
# ⟦append (reverse t) (h : [ ])⟧ = ... = append# (reverse# t) (Cons# h TopMem)
```

Convert pattern matching (with E = [ ] and N h t = append (reverse t) (h:[ ])) and apply the Cons# table defined above:

```
reverse# Bot  =  Bot              || bottom
reverse# Inf                      || # ⟦ N ⟧ 1 Inf
   =  append# (reverse# Inf) (Cons# 1 TopMem)
   =  append# (reverse# Inf) TopMem
reverse# BotMem                   || (# ⟦ N ⟧ 0 TopMem)∪(# ⟦ N ⟧ 1 BotMem)
   =  (append# (reverse# BotMem) (Cons# 1 TopMem))
      ∪ (append# (reverse# TopMem) (Cons# 0 TopMem))
```

```
    = (append# (reverse# BotMem) TopMem)
       ∪ (append# (reverse# TopMem) BotMem)
reverse# TopMem                      || # ⟦ E ⟧ ∪(# ⟦ N ⟧ 1 TopMem)
    = TopMem ∪ (append# (reverse# TopMem) (Cons# 1 TopMem))
    = TopMem
```

The resulting equations will still have to be solved to achieve proper abstract function definitions. Also the following defining equations of abstract functions can be derived in the same way:

```
is_empty# Bot        = 0
is_empty# Inf        = 1
is_empty# BotMem     = 1
is_empty# TopMem     = 1

length#   Bot        = 0
length#   Inf        = length# Inf
length#   BotMem     = length# TopMem = 1
length#   TopMem     = 1

sum#      Bot        = 0
sum#      Inf        = sum# Inf
sum#      BotMem     = sum# BotMem
sum#      TopMem     = 1
```

Some of the resulting equations are solved directly, e.g. for the function is_empty. For a function like sum, however, the abstract equation is recursive. As for functions over the domain D, a fixed point computation has to be performed to solve this recursive equation. For the functions sum and length this is easy since sum# Inf, sum# BotMem and length# Inf are all 0.

The fixed point computation for the function sum:

```
sum#   Bot       = 0
sum#   Inf       = sum# Inf
sum#   BotMem    = sum# BotMem
sum#   TopMem    = 1
```

then (by definition):

```
sum#0  x         = 0
```

and (by substitution):

```
sum#1  Bot       = 0
```

$sum^{\#1}$	Inf	= $sum^{\#0}$ Inf	= 0
$sum^{\#1}$	BotMem	= $sum^{\#0}$ BotMem	= 0
$sum^{\#1}$	TopMem	= 1	

$sum^{\#2}$	Bot	= 0	
$sum^{\#2}$	Inf	= $sum^{\#1}$ Inf	= 0
$sum^{\#2}$	BotMem	= $sum^{\#1}$ BotMem	= 0
$sum^{\#2}$	TopMem	= 1	

The first and second approximations are equal, so the fixed point is found.

For reverse the computation is more complex: first the values for the function append should be known, then a fixed point of reverse can be determined in the domain $LD^{\#} \rightarrow LD^{\#}$ (see Exercise 7.3).

For mutually recursive function definitions fixed points cannot be calculated separately. In such a case the fixed points have to be calculated together.

7.6.3 Lists with more complex elements

To derive more information for lists with more complex elements, another abstract domain has to be constructed. Suppose the list consists of elements of a domain S for which the abstract domain $S^{\#}$ contains n elements s_i ($i \leq n$). The abstract domain $LS^{\#}$ is constructed as follows. $LS^{\#}$ contains the elements Inf and Bot. Furthermore, for each element s_i of $S^{\#}$ an equivalent element s_iMem is added to $LS^{\#}$.

Consider for example the construction of $LLD^{\#}$:

$D^{\#}$	$LD^{\#}$	$LLD^{\#}$	...
1 (Top)	TopMem	TopMemMem	...
0 (Bot)	BotMem	BotMemMem	
	Inf	InfMem	
	Bot	BotMem	
		Inf	
		Bot	

Then, for example, BotMemMem corresponds to lists that have at least one element that is a list containing at least one element that is bottom. Of course the same can be done for lists of functions etc.

It will be clear that this kind of strictness analysis is difficult when more complicated data structures (e.g. trees) are taken into account. In that case the abstract domains that have to be constructed are complicated as well. As a result, the complexity of the analysis can explode.

7.7 Abstract reduction

Another strictness information deduction method is based on **abstract reduction**. With both abstract interpretation and abstract reduction a compile-time abstract computation is performed in an abstract domain. An important difference is that abstract reduction takes arbitrary data structures (data constructors) into account as well as pattern matching on these data constructors. Abstract reduction can be regarded as a special kind of symbolic graph rewriting and is therefore based on GRSs, whereas abstract interpretation is based on the λ-calculus.

A disadvantage of the possibility of handling arbitrary data structures is that the abstract domain in which the abstract reduction takes place can become *infinite*. Hence the computation of a fixed point can take an infinite amount of time. So, in principle, strictness analysis based on abstract reduction may not terminate. In practice, an approximating analyser can be defined that will terminate and that will find strictness in many cases in a relatively short time.

In this section proofs of properties are omitted. For further details the reader is referred to (Nöcker, 1988; 1993).

7.7.1 The abstract domain

Strictness analysis via abstract reduction proceeds as follows: via an undecidable abstraction function abs the concrete domain S is abstracted to the abstract *power domain* PS#. PS# is defined by first taking the **powerset** of S, i.e. the set PS of all subsets of S. Then, PS# is constructed by joining every element of PS with the set Bot of all non-terminating and undefined expressions of S. In this way Bot is the least element of the domain PS#. The greatest element of PS# is S, from now on referred to as Top. PS# is in general an infinite domain since S can be infinite (S contains all possible terms).

No distinction is made between a partial function that is undefined for a particular value of its arguments and a function that is non-terminating for a particular value of its arguments. Both kinds of function are united in the least element Bot.

An important advantage of the abstract domain PS# is that it contains all subsets of all kinds of expressions. This enables reasoning about all kinds of structures without the necessity to define special abstract domains for it. Another consequence is that a least upper bound *always* exists for any two elements in the abstract domain and that this lub can be found by taking the set union of these elements.

Rewriting in PS# implies that rewriting is now defined on *sets*. The constructors that are used in the rewrite rules denote elements of PS#.

Top	≡	S
Bot	≡	the set of all non-terminating expressions
Constructor# Top	≡	the set of all terms starting with Constructor ∪ Bot

$Nil^{\#}$	$\equiv$ {Nil} $\cup$ Bot
$Cons^{\#}$ Bot $Nil^{\#}$	$\equiv$ the set of all lists of length 1 with a non-terminating element $\cup$ Bot

Below, the method of abstract reduction will be explained. Compared with abstract interpretation the construction of abstract functions will turn out to be a trivial task. The important aspect of the analysis now lies in the definition of abstract rewriting.

7.7.2 Transforming functions to abstract functions

Functions defined on S are transformed into abstract functions defined on $PS^{\#}$ in the following way. Assume that a function f of arity n is defined with k rule alternatives:

```
f:: S^n → S
f p11 ... p1n   = rhs1
...
f pk1 ... pkn   = rhsk
```

For the construction of an abstract function $f^{\#}$ the following transformation function # can be defined that translates an arbitrary function f over D^n to its abstract counterpart $f^{\#}::(PS^{\#})^n \rightarrow PS^{\#}$.

```
# [[ f p11 ... p1n   = rhs1
     ...
     f pk1 ... pkn   = rhsk ]]   = # [[ f p11 ... p1n ]]   = # [[ rhs1 ]]
                                   ...
                                   # [[ f pk1 ... pkn ]]   = # [[ rhsk ]]
# [[ s x1 ... xn ]]              = s# # [[ x1 ]] ... # [[ xn ]]
# [[ x ]]                        = x
```

Here s stands for a function or constructor symbol; x stands for a variable.

So the transformation is trivial: every symbol s is converted to $s^{\#}$.

For the following function definitions the corresponding abstracted functions are constructed by applying the transformation #.

```
f x                  = g (Constructor (h x))
g (Constructor x)    = x
h 0                  = 0
h x                  = x

f# x                 = g# (Constructor# (h# x))
g# (Constructor# x)  = x
```

```
h# 0#                     = 0#
h# x                      = x
```

7.7.3 Rewriting

In principle, the functional strategy is used for reduction as usual. However, rewriting in the abstract domain is defined on *sets*. In order to define rewriting on sets some small changes are necessary. A variable on a left-hand side now stands for the set of all expressions (Top). Furthermore, four situations have to be distinguished during the pattern matching phase (for each situation an example is given):

(1) There is a **total match**: the *formal* argument is a superset of the *actual* argument, i.e. the actual argument is contained in the formal argument. When there is a total match, the matching can continue.

The term h# 0# totally matches h# 0#

(2) There is a **partial match**: the *actual* argument is a superset of the *formal* argument. When there is a partial match another rule alternative may be applicable as well. So although a match has been found and matching can continue with this rule alternative, the next rule alternatives also have to be considered with as actual argument the remaining non-matching part of the original argument. The remaining part is defined as follows: if A is the actual argument, B the formal argument and A ⊃ B, then the remaining part C is all elements of A that are not contained in B, united with Bot. This is denoted as C = A \ B.

The term g# Top partially matches g# (Constructor# x).
The remaining part is Top \ (Constructor# Top)

(3) There is an **infinite match**: the formal argument is a non-variable; the actual argument is Bot. This case corresponds to forcing evaluation of a non-terminating expression to match it against a non-variable pattern. This will lead to a non-terminating reduction in the concrete world. In the abstract world the rule alternative is applicable: the term reduces to Bot, independent of its right-hand side.

The term g# Bot infinitely matches g# (Constructor# x)

(4) There is **no match**: none of the previous cases arises: the rule alternative is not applicable. Matching proceeds with the next rule alternative.

The term $g^{\#}$ $Nil^{\#}$ does not match $g^{\#}$ ($Constructor^{\#}$ x)

After the matching phase rewriting is done accordingly with the special extension that when more than one rule alternative is applicable (due to a partial match) the *union* of all possible results is taken.

If none of the rule alternatives matches, the result of the rewriting is Bot, indicating that the partial function is undefined.

One-step rewriting of the terms in the examples of Section 7.7.2:

$$
\begin{array}{lcl}
h^{\#}\ 0^{\#} & \rightarrow & 0^{\#} \\
g^{\#}\ Top & = & g^{\#}\ ((Constructor^{\#}\ Top) \cup (Top \setminus (Constructor^{\#}\ Top))) \rightarrow Top \cup Bot \\
 & = & Top \\
g^{\#}\ Bot & \rightarrow & Bot \\
g^{\#}\ Nil^{\#} & \rightarrow & Bot
\end{array}
$$

In an implementation of abstract reduction, for reasons of efficiency and termination, further approximations can be made (see also Section 7.8.1). For example, one can approximate all numbers by Top. In the case of a partial match one can continue with the complete argument instead of with the remaining non-matching part. Another optimization concerns the use of graph structures in the analysis. Combined with sensible criteria for termination (see Section 7.8.1), an efficient implementation of abstract reduction can be obtained.

7.8 Strictness analysis using abstract reduction

The concrete reduction in the standard domain is approximated by reduction on sets in the abstract domain. Approximation takes place in two ways. Firstly, the objects of reduction are sets of which the elements cannot be distinguished any more. Secondly, the reduct can be a set that is larger than necessary, e.g. the reduct always contains Bot.

Just as with abstract interpretation the safety criterion has to hold. For abstract reduction the *safety criterion* ($abs\ .\ f \leq f^{\#}\ .\ abs$) means that for every function, when it is applied with concrete arguments, the abstraction of all its results has to be a subset of the set of the results of the corresponding abstract function applied on all corresponding abstract arguments.

In other words, the **safety criterion for abstract reduction** requires that for all $x_1 \ldots x_n \in S$ it holds that when $t, t' \in PS^{\#}$ are defined as $t = \cup\ x^{\#} \mid f\ x_1 \ldots x_n \rightarrow_* x$ and $t' = \cup\ x^{\#} \mid f^{\#}\ x_1{}^{\#} \ldots x_n{}^{\#} \rightarrow_* x^{\#}$ then, $t \leq t'$.

Matching and rewriting on sets are defined in such a way that this safety criterion holds. As a consequence, the strictness question for the ith argument of a function f of arity n:

$$f\ x_1 \ldots x_{i-1}\ \bot\ x_{i+1} \ldots x_n \quad = \ \bot$$

can be approximated via abstract reduction as follows:

$f^{\#}$ Top ... Top Bot Top ... Top $\rightarrow_*$ Bot

This question can be answered via abstract reduction to normal form.

Consider again an example of Section 7.5: f x y z = if (x = 0) (y + z) (x – y). With pattern matching this function can now be defined as:

```
f 0 y z   = y + z
f x y z   = x - y
```

The abstract reduction for the various strictness questions yields the same answers as in Section 7.5:

$f^{\#}$ Bot Top Top $\rightarrow$ Bot
$f^{\#}$ Top Bot Top $\rightarrow$ (Bot $+^{\#}$ Top)$\cup$(Top $-^{\#}$ Bot) $\rightarrow \ldots \rightarrow$ Bot$\cup$Bot = Bot
$f^{\#}$ Top Top Bot $\rightarrow$ (Top $+^{\#}$ Bot)$\cup$(Top $-^{\#}$ Top) $\rightarrow \ldots \rightarrow$ Bot$\cup$Top = Top

However, with respect to the strictness of $f^{\#}$ of the example in Section 7.7.2 abstract reduction yields better results than abstract interpretation:

$f^{\#}$ Bot $\rightarrow$ $g^{\#}$ (Constructor$^{\#}$ ($h^{\#}$ Bot)) $\rightarrow$ $h^{\#}$ Bot $\rightarrow$ Bot

So $f^{\#}$ is strict in its first argument. This fact would not have been found using abstract interpretation as explained in this chapter.

Strictness analysis using abstract reduction on sets can be performed relatively easily. The introduction of new constructors does not increase the complexity of the analysis. Owing to the possibility of performing *pattern matching on abstract constructors*, results can be obtained that are much harder to obtain with strictness analysis based on abstract interpretation. However, abstract reduction has the disadvantage that it is not guaranteed to terminate.

Non-terminating abstract reduction:

$f^{\#}$ x = $f^{\#}$ x

$f^{\#}$ Bot $\rightarrow$ $f^{\#}$ Bot $\rightarrow$ ...

Since the domain $PS^{\#}$ is infinite a fixed point analysis cannot be performed. So termination of the analysis must be realized in another way.

7.8.1 Termination of abstract reduction

Although in principle the analysis is non-terminating, it can always be stopped. When it is stopped the result is approximated. Fortunately, it is always safe to approximate a reduction with Top since this set contains all possible terms. Some limit must be placed upon the reduction sequence. For instance, we can use the depth of the recursion in the reduction, or the number of reductions that have been performed in the analysis, or the length of the term that is analysed. An implementation criterion can also be the depth of the recursion stack, or the time needed, or the memory required, or a combination of these.

In certain special cases an analysis of the reduction path (**path analysis**) can introduce an extra stop criterion when the analysis leads to the conclusion that a non-terminating reduction is going on. An example of such an path analysis is the following:

Suppose an analysis of the reduction path yields the following about a term t: $t \rightarrow_* E(t)$ in which E(t) is an expression, not in head normal form, in which t occurs. When the reduction of t is needed to reduce E(t), the term t in E(t) can be replaced by Bot. When it is not known whether the reduction of t is needed to reduce E(t), the term t in E(t) can be replaced by Top.

Path analysis avoids non-termination in the previous example:

$f^{\#}$ Bot → $f^{\#}$ Bot → Bot

Clearly, reduction of the term $f^{\#}$ Bot is needed in the expression $f^{\#}$ Bot.

Consider one of the examples of Section 7.5.1: f x y = if (x = 0) y (f (x – 1) y). With pattern matching this function can now be defined as:

```
f 0 y  =  y
f x y  =  f (x – 1) y
```

For this case path analysis yields the same answer as the fixed point analysis in Section 7.5.1:

$f^{\#}$ Top Bot = $(f^{\#}\ 0^{\#}\ \text{Bot}) \cup (f^{\#}\ (\text{Top} \backslash 0^{\#})\ \text{Bot})$
→ $\text{Bot} \cup f^{\#}\ ((\text{Top} \backslash 0^{\#}) -^{\#} 1^{\#})\ \text{Bot}$ = $f^{\#}\ ((\text{Top} \backslash 0^{\#}) -^{\#} 1^{\#})\ \text{Bot}$
→ $f^{\#}$ Top Bot
→ Bot

7.8.2 Abstract reduction on non-flat domains

Other questions than the standard strictness question fit nicely in the general framework of abstract reduction. Consider, for example, strictness analysis on non-flat domains, e.g. list structures. With abstract interpretation the most simple analysis is done via the introduction of the four-point domain for which appropriate abstract functions have to be constructed. With abstract reduction a similar analysis can be performed directly. The elements of the four-point domain correspond directly with sets that are elements of the domain $PS^{\#}$:

Bot	≡ the set of all non-terminating expressions: least element of $PS^{\#}$
Inf	≡ the set of all infinite lists ∪ Bot
BotMem	≡ the set of all lists with at least 1 non-terminating element ∪ Inf
TopMem	≡ the set of all possible lists

These sets are elements of the domain $PS^{\#}$ and as sets they obey the following relation: Bot ⊆ Inf ⊆ BotMem ⊆ TopMem which corresponds to the ordering in the four-point domain.

In order to perform abstract reduction, first abstract functions have to be constructed, and then strictness questions can be asked. The results of the abstract functions for each of the indicated sets can be computed in the standard way using abstract reduction. Note that the abstract functions are not just defined on the four special sets, but are defined on the complete domain $PS^{\#}$.

Take again an example of Section 7.6: sum. The abstract function is now:

```
sum# Nil#           =  0#
sum# (Cons# a x)    =  a +# sum# x
```

In order to be able to perform the pattern matching on the indicated sets, more about the structure of these sets has to be known. The following recursive set equations are sufficient to perform pattern matching.

```
Inf       =  Cons# Top Inf
BotMem    =  (Cons# Top BotMem) ∪ (Cons# Bot TopMem)
TopMem    =  Nil# ∪ (Cons# Top TopMem)
```

With these equations and path analysis abstract reduction is performed.

The sum example with abstract reduction:

```
sum# Bot       →   Bot
sum# Inf       =   sum# (Cons# Top Inf)
               →   Top +# (sum# Inf)
               →   Top +# Bot
               →   Bot
sum# BotMem    =   sum# ((Cons# Top BotMem) ∪ (Cons# Bot TopMem))
               →   (Top +# (sum# BotMem)) ∪ (Bot +# (sum# TopMem))
               →   (Top +# (sum# BotMem)) ∪ Bot
```

$$
\begin{array}{lcl}
 & \rightarrow & \text{Top} +^{\#} (\text{sum}^{\#}\ \text{BotMem}) \\
 & \rightarrow & \text{Top} +^{\#} \text{Bot} \\
 & \rightarrow & \text{Bot} \\
\text{sum}^{\#}\ \text{TopMem} & = & \text{sum}^{\#}\ (\text{Nil}^{\#} \cup (\text{Cons}^{\#}\ \text{Top TopMem})) \\
 & \rightarrow & 0^{\#} \cup (\text{sum}^{\#}\ (\text{Cons}^{\#}\ \text{Top TopMem})) \\
 & \rightarrow & 0^{\#} \cup (\text{Top} +^{\#} (\text{sum}^{\#}\ \text{TopMem}))) \\
 & \rightarrow & 0^{\#} \cup (\text{Top} +^{\#} \text{Top}) \\
 & \rightarrow & 0^{\#} \cup \text{Top} \\
 & = & \text{Top}
\end{array}
$$

Another important aspect of abstract reduction is the fact that *a priori* no restriction is imposed on the considered structures. The strictness of functions that manipulate user-defined data structures can be investigated in the same way as the strictness of lists. Furthermore, the complexity of the analysis does not explode if more complex structures are considered. There is no necessity to define more complicated domains (with more complex fixed point analysis) for such structures. An increasing complexity of the structures that are considered only leads to increasing complexity of the arguments of the abstract functions. The complexity of the path analysis and of the abstract reduction itself does not increase.

Summary

- A function is *strict* in a certain argument if evaluation of that argument does not change the termination behaviour of the program.
- Strictness analysis is a *compile-time* analysis to obtain *strictness information*. It can be used to change the reduction order in such a way that the time and space behaviour of the program is improved.
- Strictness is inherently *undecidable*. Therefore, practical strictness analysis always deals with *approximations* that must be *safe*, i.e. the termination behaviour of a program has to remain unchanged.
- Two general techniques of strictness analysis are discussed: *abstract interpretation* on *finite* abstract domains and *abstract reduction* on the powerset domain that can be *infinite*.
- Abstract interpretation approximates strictness via an analysis in a *finite domain* that is constructed with the purpose of answering a special kind of strictness question.
  - The use of continuous functions on the finite domain makes it possible to deal with recursion via a *fixed point analysis*.
  - With the *four-point domain* list structures are handled.
  - For more complex information more complex domains have to be defined; the complexity of the analysis *explodes*.

- Abstract reduction approximates strictness via a special way of reducing *sets* of expressions.
  - Pattern matching and reduction with sets is defined in a *safe* way such that the reduct of a set contains at least all reducts of all expressions in the original set.
  - In principle, abstract reduction is *non-terminating*. However, *path analysis* and practical *heuristics* make it possible to avoid this non-termination in practice at the price of making further approximations.
  - *Recursive set equations* are used to deal with pattern matching and reduction on all kinds of sets.
  - Within the general framework of abstract reduction, strictness of all kinds of structures is *relatively easily* examined since it is not necessary to construct new domains and abstract functions for every new kind of question. No explosion of complexity takes place.

EXERCISES

7.1 Give for each element a of the four-point domain (TopMem, BotMem, Inf, Bot) an element x of the concrete domain such that $x \in abs^{-1}$ a and for all a' < a it holds that $x \notin abs^{-1}$ a'.

7.2 The definition of the append function is:

```
append:: LD->LD->LD
append [ ]       list   = list
append (h : t)   list   = h : append t list
```

Give the defining equations of the abstract function append# in the four-point domain. Solve the equations using fixed point analysis.

7.3 Solve with the resulting definition of append# the defining equations of reverse# in Section 7.6.2. Derive the required strictness information from the resulting definition.

7.4 Derive both using abstract interpretation as well as using abstract reduction the strictness information for f, as defined below.

```
head:: LD->D
head (a : as)  =  a

f:: D->D
f  x  =  head (x : [ ])
```

Part 4
Implementation on sequential architectures

An efficient implementation of a functional language can be obtained in many ways. We shall not give a general overview of the several available methods (e.g. Landin, 1964; Turner, 1979a; Augustsson, 1984; Peyton Jones, 1987). Instead, we shall describe *one* implementation method in detail (Smetsers *et al.*, 1991). We think it is highly illustrative to study one particular implementation starting from the level of a particular full-featured programming language, leading through intermediate levels (see Figure P4.1) and finally ending with concrete machine code. Furthermore, the described implementation method is state-of-the-art and has many aspects in common with other methods.

So an implementation is described for a particular functional language (Miranda) based on the model that we consider to be the most suited for this purpose: FGRSs. First, the language is translated into an intermediate language (Clean) based on FGRSs. Since the level of Clean is still rather high compared with the level of a concrete machine, a Clean program is translated into code for an abstract stack-based machine (the ABC machine). The abstract machine forms an additional more concrete intermediate level enabling a relatively easy production of interpreters and code generators for various target machines.

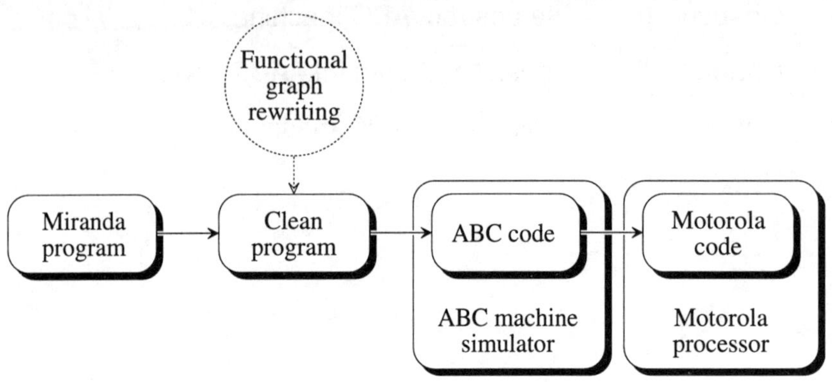

Figure P4.1 Two intermediate levels; three translations.

Owing to the intermediate levels, some of the information present in the original program might get lost, so some loss of efficiency might be introduced. This conceptual loss is generally well compensated since the compiler becomes more structured and easier to maintain.

Five chapters treat the two intermediate levels and the three corresponding translations. These transformations are also used in the Concurrent Clean system: the software package that goes with this book.

Chapter 8
Clean

Clean is an experimental lazy higher order functional programming language based on functional graph rewriting systems (FGRSs) (see Chapter 5). So Clean is a functional language in which computations are expressed in terms of graph rewriting. Clean is originally designed as an intermediate language to be used in the compilation path from (eager as well as lazy) functional languages to concrete machine architectures (Figure 8.1).

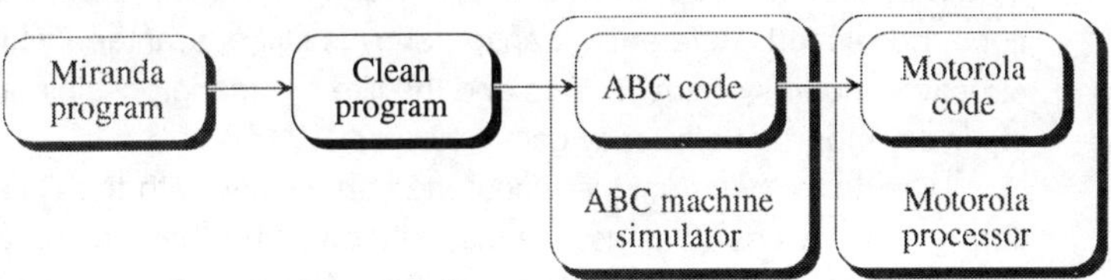

Figure 8.1 Clean as intermediate language.

In contrast with most other functional programming languages Clean supports only the most basic aspects of functional programming (see Chapter 1). Syntactical sugar (such as infix notation or *ZF*-expressions) is mainly excluded. Clean basically just realizes FGRSs syntactically extended with *macros* and *guards*. However, many additional semantic features have been added enabling an efficient and usable implementation, e.g. a *type system*, *annotations* to control evaluation order, a *modular structure* and *type attributes* enabling destructive updates of objects, as well as a library that enables a high-level specification of *input* and *output*.

Type information is important for programmers since it will help them to design programs which are correct and understandable. But, type information is also important because it can be used to generate efficient code. Furthermore, the type information can be used to create a modular environment. The type system of Clean is based on the type assignment system for TRSs as explained in Section 6.3. It includes polymorphic types, abstract types, algebraic types and synonym types, as well as basic types (see Section 8.2). Lists, tuples and function type constructors are predefined.

With *annotations* the evaluation order of a Clean program can be influenced by the programmer: the evaluation can be made (partially) *eager* instead of lazy. In this way a better space and time behaviour of functional programs can be obtained in a machine-independent manner (see Section 8.3). For efficient solutions of some problems the ability to share computations and to control the evaluation order is essential. In the extended language, Concurrent Clean (see Chapter 15), even parallel evaluation can be specified by the programmer.

Clean's *modular* structure (see Section 8.4) consists of separate implementation modules and definition modules, including a facility to import definitions from other modules implicitly and explicitly. There are predefined modules (libraries) for basic operations (δ-rules) on objects of basic types (integers, reals, characters, strings and booleans).

The interaction with the outside world has always been hard to incorporate in the functional framework. The Clean type system is extended with the *unique type attribute* that can be assigned to an object of any type (see Section 8.5). An object with the unique type attribute that is passed as an argument to a function can, under certain conditions, be reused. Referential transparency is still guaranteed while destructive updates of arrays, files and the like are made possible, resulting in an important efficiency gain.

Owing to these unique types one can specify with the Clean I/O library I/O devices (dialogs, menus, windows and the like) on a very high level of abstraction (see Section 8.6). As much as possible of the low-level I/O handling is done automatically by the library system. Predefined algebraic data types can be used to specify which devices should be activated and how these devices should be initialized. A programmer just specifies which (higher order) function is called when a certain part of an active device is triggered (e.g. a particular menu item has been chosen).

Using Clean as intermediate language has made it possible to concentrate on the implementation of the basic aspects only, instead of getting lost in the details of a specific full-featured functional language. Since Clean is an experimental language, it has been equipped with some special features that are not found (yet) in other functional languages. Major and minor changes and extensions can be expected in future versions of the language.

8.1 Clean, a language for functional graph rewriting

Clean (Brus *et al.*, 1987; Nöcker *et al.*, 1991b; Van Eekelen *et al.*, 1992) was designed at the University of Nijmegen and it stands for: **C**lean **Lean**[1]. Clean is based on functional graph rewriting systems (see Chapter 5).

8.1.1 Basic syntax of rewrite rules

Clean uses the shorthand notation of graph rewrite rules. Apart from some additions for typing and for programming convenience (see Appendix B for a full syntax description of the language) the only syntactic differences from FGRSs are:

- The rule alternatives of a function definition are grouped together.
- A ';' marks the end of each rule alternative.
- Redirections consist of a single node-id only.
- The keyword RULE indicates that a sequence of graph rewrite rule definitions follows (so that they can be distinguished from other kinds of declaration).
- '->' is used instead of an $\rightarrow$.
- Empty nodes cannot be denoted in Clean.
- Several functions on basic types are predefined (see Section 8.1.3).
- Guards are added for choosing between rule alternatives (see Section 8.1.4).
- Lists and tuples are predefined data structures (see Section 8.1.5).
- Currying is allowed. A curried application is transformed at compile-time to an application of an internal 'apply rule' (see Section 8.1.6).
- Macros are used for programming convenience (see Section 8.1.7).

8.1.2 Semantics

Clean's basic semantics are treated in Chapter 5 (semantics of FGRSs). There are, however, some differences between FGRSs and Clean:

- When at run-time an empty node is created, in Clean an error message is given (see Section 5.8).
- Clean rules are typed (see Sections 6.3 and 8.2).

---

[1] Lean (Barendregt *et al.*, 1988) stands for the **L**anguage of **E**ast **A**nglia and **N**ijmegen, jointly designed at both universities. Lean has been used to experiment with *generalized* graph rewriting systems (see Section 5.9).

- In Clean, the functional strategy can be influenced by using annotations that make the evaluation partially eager instead of lazy (see Section 8.3).
- Input/output is treated in a special way. In order to communicate with the outside world, the Start rule optionally can have a parameter of type UNQ WORLD, representing the environment in which the program is called (see Sections 8.5 and 8.6).

8.1.3 Predefined functions and basic types

For practical reasons it is convenient that rules for performing arithmetic on objects of basic types (integers, reals etc.) are predefined. Then they can be implemented efficiently with the concrete representation and corresponding instructions available on the concrete machine.

```
<<    The factorial function in Clean using predefined functions.
>>
RULE
:: Fac INT      ->    INT;                    ==    type definition
   Fac 0        ->    1;                      ==    the factorial function
   Fac n        ->    * n (Fac (-- n));

:: Start        ->    INT;                    ==    type definition
   Start        ->    Fac 20;                 ==    the initial expression
```

As in FGRSs prefix notation is used. Rules starting with '::' are type rules (see Section 8.2). Comments are placed between '<<' and '>>' or after a '=='.

Below, a list is given of several predefined functions (for a full list of the functions in the Clean library, see Appendix B).

Basic type	Examples of denotations	Examples of predefined functions
INT	1, 2, 2147483647	+, –, =, >=, AND%
REAL	1.5, 0.314E10	+R, –R, =R, >=R, SIN, EXP
CHAR	'a', 'b', 'c', '\n', '\007'	=C, >=C
BOOL	TRUE, FALSE	NOT, AND, XOR, =B
STRING	"This is a string \n"	+S, –S, =S, >=S, SLICE
FILE		StdIO, FOpen, FWriteC

8.1.4 Guarded expressions

In Clean, guards can be added to rewrite rules. A guard is a Boolean expression that can be seen as an extension of the pattern matching mechanism: a rule alternative is only chosen when its pattern matches a subgraph *and* its guard evaluates to TRUE. Pattern matching always takes place before the guard is evaluated. A guard is separated from the right-hand side of a rule by an optional comma and the keyword IF. In a guard the *infix* operators || (conditional OR) and && (conditional AND) can be used. The arguments of the operators are evaluated from left to right, and parentheses can be used to specify the priorities. Arguments of operators are not evaluated when their value is of no influence on the value of the result. For instance, when the first operand of || evaluates to TRUE, the second operand will not be evaluated: the result will be TRUE anyway.

Rule alternatives that have the same left-hand side (but different guards) can be grouped together separated by arrow symbols ('->'). When the last guarded expression has a guard that always evaluates to TRUE that guard can be omitted (the 'otherwise' or 'default' case).

Example of the use of guards in Clean:

```
:: Fib INT  ->   INT;
   Fib n    ->   1,                            IF  =n 1  ||  =n 2
            ->   + (Fib (– n 1)) (Fib (– n 2)),  IF  >n 2
            ->   ABORT "Fibonacci called with argument less than one";
```

8.1.5 Predefined data structures and type constructors

To provide some programming convenience, denotations for *lists* and *tuples* are predefined.

Lists

Lists are denoted as follows: Nil is denoted as [ ], Cons h t as [h | t] and the list with elements 1, 2, 3 and 4 is denoted as [1, 2, 3, 4]. Furthermore, [e_1, ... , e_n | r] denotes a list r prefixed with elements e_1 ... e_n. If T is a type, than [T] denotes the type *list of* T.

Merge merges two sorted lists of integers, removing double occurrences:

```
:: Merge [INT]       [INT]        ->   [INT];
   Merge [ ]         g            ->   g;
   Merge f           [ ]          ->   f;
   Merge f:[ a | b ] g:[ c | d ]  ->   [ a | Merge b g ],    IF  <a c
                                  ->   Merge f d,            IF  =a c
                                  ->   [ c | Merge f d ];
```

Tuples

Tuples and tuple type constructors are denoted as in Miranda. If T_1, ... , T_n are types, then (T_1, ..., T_n) denotes the type *tuple of* T_1, ..., T_n.

Example of Clean tuples and their types:

```
(3, 0, 'a')           ==   3-tuple of type (INT, INT, CHAR)
([0, 1, 2], +)        ==   2-tuple of type ([INT], => INT (=> INT INT))
```

In order to simplify the use of tuples a special syntactical construct is added that automatically generates projection functions. One can specify a definition of a number of node-ids simultaneously by placing a tuple of node-ids before a colon symbol in a node definition. The basic idea of this construct is illustrated by the example below:

Instead of

```
G ... ->    H a b,
            a: First g,
            b: Second g,
            g: F ...;

F ... ->    (x, y);

First    (a, b)   ->   a;
Second   (a, b)   ->   b;
```

one can define G more compactly (First and Second are no longer needed):

```
G ... ->    H a b,
            (a, b):   F ...;
```

The meaning of such a construct is that all these node-ids are bound at run-time to parts of the graph on the right-hand side of the colon symbol. This only makes sense if this graph denotes a function that delivers a tuple. The type checker (Section 8.2) verifies that this is true.

Example of the use of tuples before a colon symbol in a node definition.

```
RULE
==   FindElem traverses a list of lists of integers to search for the element el.
==   The list containing the element and its index in this list is returned.

:: FindElem [[INT]]    INT   ->   ([INT], INT);
   FindElem [ l | ls ] el    ->   (l, index),          IF found
                             ->   FindElem ls el,
                                  (found, index): Index l el 1;

:: Index [INT]    INT   INT   ->   (BOOL, INT);
   Index [ ]      el    n     ->   (FALSE, n);
```

```
Index [ f | r ]  el    n   ->  (TRUE, n),           IF = el f
                           ->  Index r el (++ n);

:: Start                   ->  ([INT], INT);
   Start                   ->  FindElem [ l1, l2, l3 ] 6,
                               l1: [ 2, 3, 5, 7, 11, 13, 17, 19 ],
                               l2: [ –9, –6, –3, 0, 3, 6, 9 ],
                               l3: [ 1, 4, 9, 16, 25, 36 ];
```

Besides the benefit of notational elegance, the list and tuple constructs have the advantage that they indicate special predefined cases that can be implemented more efficiently than the fully user-defined data structures. In the case of the tuples it might even lead to fewer reductions since it is not necessary any more to apply a selector function explicitly to access the elements of the tuple.

8.1.6 Currying

Clean conceptually uses the functional notation (see Section 4.1.4). As explained in Sections 4.8 and 6.3.2, curried applications of functions can be realized by introducing additional rewrite rules that transform curried applications into uncurried ones. This method has a disadvantage. Many of these additional 'AP-rule' alternatives are needed: one alternative for each function that is used in a curried manner. It is much more convenient if this curry conversion is performed automatically.

This automatic conversion has been realized in Clean in the following way: a generic internal rule _AP is predefined (internal here means that this _AP rule cannot be used by the programmer explicitly) with which curried applications of any symbol F are transformed into uncurried applications at compile-time.

The Twice function as defined in Clean is given below.

```
:: Twice (=> x x)   x  ->   x;
   Twice f          x  ->   f (f x);
```

The curried applications of f are internally transformed leading to

```
   Twice f          x  ->   _AP f (_AP f x);
```

The internal rewriting code for _AP provides that when a symbol is supplied with a sufficient number of arguments it will be rewritten according to the rule that corresponds to the curried symbol. This allows the programmer to use symbols with an arbitrary arity or to apply node-ids to arguments. If F is defined with arity n, say F a_1 a_2 ... a_n -> a_r, then _AP (... (_AP (_AP F a_1) a_2) ...) a_n reduces to F a_1 a_2 ... a_n. If there are too few arguments the expression is in root normal form (_AP is a partial function). Since the conversion of curried applications into uncurried ones will be done automatically there is no need at all for the programmer to be aware of the presence of this internal _AP rule.

This facility implies the need for a special predefined type constructor, the **curried function type**, denoted by =>. This predefined type can be compared with the function type constructor as predefined in Miranda, used in prefix notation. So the type => a b stands for a curried function (of arity one) that, when applied to an argument of type a, will produce a result of type b (pronounce => a b as: curried function from a to b). Consequently, the type axioms of the Clean type system include the equivalence of

```
:: F -> => t1 (=> t2 (=> ... (=> tn tr) ... )) ;   to   :: F t1 t2 ... tn -> tr ;
```

if F is defined with arity n. The internal function _AP is typed as:

```
:: _AP (=> a b) a -> b ;
```

The first argument of _AP (i.e. the function that has to be applied) always has to be evaluated in order to compute the result. So _AP is strict in its first argument.

With this syntactic sugar the Hamming example of Chapter 5 can be specified in Clean in the following way (with the IMPORT statement, general δ-rules for arithmetic are imported (see Section 8.4)):

```
MODULE Hamming;
IMPORT delta;
RULE
:: Ham ->    [INT];
   Ham ->    x: [ 1 | Merge (Map (* 2) x) (Map (* 3) x) ];

:: Map (=> x y) [x]      ->    [y];
   Map f        [ ]      ->    [ ];
   Map f        [ a | b ] ->   [ f a | Map f b ];
```

8.1.7 Macros

In Clean one can define **macros**: macros are special rewrite rules that are rewritten (*expanded*) at compile-time. Macros can be used to assign a meaningful name to a constant or to an expression (graph). They can reduce the number of function calls at run-time. Furthermore, macros can be used as a named constant in a redex pattern.

A MACRO block consists of a number of macro definitions of the form Left-hand-side-graph -> Right-hand-side-graph;. At compile-time the right-hand side of the macro definition will be substituted for every occurrence of the left-hand side. Macros may have parameters, but it is not allowed to specify a pattern on the left-hand side of a macro definition. Consequently, a macro rule always consists of a single alternative. It is clear that, at compile-time, the rewriting of the macros should always terminate. This is guaranteed by prohibiting macros that are mutually dependent or recursive.

Example of the use of macros in Clean.

```
MACRO
   Size               ->   6;
   UnsortedList       ->   [ 3, 1, 5, 2, 4 ];
   Singleton x        ->   [ x ];
   +SC string char    ->   +S string (CTOS char);
   *R4 r1 r2 r3 r4    ->   *R r1 (*R r2 (*R r3 r4));
```

8.2 The type system

Clean is a typed language conforming to the type system introduced in Section 6.3. So, in many cases, types in Clean are similar to but not exactly the same as those in Miranda. Note that in Clean each symbol is defined with a fixed arity. In Miranda functions are always curried and have at most one argument. As already explained in Section 8.1.4, the function type => (in prefix notation) is used for curried functions. Another difference is that identifiers are used for type variables instead of *s. Two major differences concern abstract types (in Clean abstract types are connected to the module structure; see Section 8.2.2) and typing patterns (see Section 8.2.3).

As in Miranda, types do not have to be specified explicitly by the programmer. For programmers in a hurry, types can be inferred by the Clean compiler if type information is left out. However, the programmer is strongly advised to give an explicit specification of the types.

As a special facility of the Clean system, type checking can be switched off. In that case specified types are not checked but *assumed* to be correct. When the type of a function is not specified at all, the most general type is assumed. This facility of Clean can be used to experiment with GRS rules that are not typeable in the usual system. It is also useful when Clean is used as intermediate language for an untyped functional language, such as SASL (Turner, 1979b). Of course, its use is very dangerous and it will generally lead to inefficient code.

8.2.1 Type definitions

The objects that are manipulated in Clean are graphs. With a type definition one specifies certain restrictions imposed on the graphs on which rewrite rules are defined. Syntactically, graph rewrite rules are used to define types. Semantically there is of course a great difference between type rules and rewrite rules. In fact, in Clean types specify restrictions on the underlying term structure, rather than on the specific graph structure. Therefore, all graphs in type definitions have to be *d*irected *a*cyclic *g*raphs (**dags**) without explicit node definitions.

Types are defined in a TYPE block, just like rewrite rules are defined in a RULE block. Blocks may be specified in any order. Each type rule must be preceded by a '::'. The function symbol of the type rule is called the **type symbol**. Each time the *same* **type variable** is used in a particular type rule, it stands for the *same* type.

8.2.2 Defining new types

As in Chapter 2 there are three kinds of type definition that introduce new types: *algebraic* type definitions, *synonym* type definitions and *abstract* type definitions.

Algebraic types

Algebraic types are specified by means of a type rule where each alternative has a right-hand side with a *fresh* root symbol: the **constructor**. All the arguments of the constructor are type instances. A **type instance** is either a type variable or a dag with a type symbol, as root of which all the arguments are type instances. The alternatives of an algebraic type definition can be separated either by an arrow symbol ('->') or by a vertical bar ('|').

Compare the following (polymorphic) algebraic type definitions with the corresponding definitions given in Chapter 2:

```
TYPE
:: Day      ->   Mon  | Tue | Wed | Thu | Fri | Sat | Sun;

:: Intlist  ->   NilList
            ->   IntList INT Intlist;

:: Tree x   ->   NilTree
            ->   NodeTree x (Tree x) (Tree x);
```

Synonym types

Synonym types permit the user to introduce a new name for an already existing type. Mutual dependencies of synonym type definitions are prohibited.

Example of a type synonym definition in Clean:

```
TYPE
:: Stack x ->     [x];
```

Abstract types

In Clean, *abstract type* definitions are only allowed in definition modules (see Section 8.4). Abstraction and hiding are considered to be two sides of a coin. So the module structure is used to hide the concrete signature of the abstract type to the outside world. An abstract type is actually a synonym type or an algebraic type of which the concrete definition is hidden in the corresponding implementation module. In the definition module only the left-hand side of the type definition is shown as well as the type of the functions defined on the abstract data structure (the abstract signature). To distinguish an abstract type definition from an ordinary type definition a special kind of type block is provided: an ABSTYPE block.

A well-known example of an abstract data type is given below:

```
DEFINITION MODULE Stack;
ABSTYPE
:: Stack x;

RULE
:: Empty                    ->    Stack x;
:: IsEmpty    (Stack x)     ->    BOOL;
:: Push     x (Stack x)     ->    Stack x;
:: Pop        (Stack x)     ->    Stack x;
:: Top        (Stack x)     ->    x;
```

The corresponding implementation module:

```
IMPLEMENTATION MODULE Stack;
IMPORT delta ;
TYPE
:: Stack x ->     [x] ;

RULE
:: Empty   ->     Stack x;
   Empty   ->     [ ];

:: IsEmpty    (Stack x)    ->    BOOL;
   IsEmpty    [ ]          ->    TRUE;
   IsEmpty    s            ->    FALSE;
```

```
:: Push   x (Stack x)  ->   Stack x;
   Push   e s          ->   [ e | s ];

:: Pop  (Stack x)  ->   Stack x;
   Pop  [ e | s ]  ->   s;

:: Top  (Stack x)  ->   x;
   Top  [ e | s ]  ->   e;
```

Note that predefined types can be seen as special cases of abstract types.

8.2.3 Type specifications for functions

The type of a rewrite rule is either explicitly specified or it is inferred by the system. When it is explicitly specified the type specification must precede the corresponding rewrite rule. The type rule consists of one rule; free type variables may appear on the right-hand side.

> Using free type variables on the right-hand side of a type definition for a rewrite rule: F has as result type any list.

```
:: F   ->   [x];
   F   ->   [ ];
```

Typing partial functions

Some type errors cannot be detected at compile-time. A partial function can be called with an actual argument of the correct type (domain) for which no image exists, due to a failing pattern match. An error is generated at run-time if this leads to a wrong value.

> At run-time the application of F in the start rule will not match. So F 1 will not yield the required type: INT. Hence, at run-time a type error is generated:

```
:: F INT   ->   INT;
   F 0     ->   0;

:: Start   ->   INT;
   Start   ->   F 1;
```

However, a failing match does not always have to be wrong. A match may fail as long as no type conflicts are caused by this failure and safe rewrite rules are being used (see also Section 6.3.2). In FGRSs there is no special situation when a function application does not match any of the rewrite rules of the function: the result is a root head normal form. In Clean this is also the case as long as no type conflicts occur and functions are safely typed (see Section 6.3.2). So in Clean functions can appear on a 'constructor position'. In Miranda a non-matching function will always result in a run-time error: Miranda is a function constructor system.

Consider the following example:

```
TYPE
:: Num ->   Zero
       ->   Succ Num
       ->   Pred Num;

RULE
:: Succ Num        ->   Num;
   Succ (Pred n)   ->   n;

:: Pred Num        ->   Num;
   Pred (Succ n)   ->   n;

:: Start           ->   Num;
   Start           ->   Succ (Succ Zero);
```

The graph Succ (Succ Zero) in the start rule will not match any rule. But, the resulting graph is still correctly typed and has type Num. In Clean Succ and Pred have to be defined twice, once as function and once as constructor. Notice that the definitions of the functions Succ and Pred are safe according to the condition given in Section 6.3.2.

8.3 Strict annotations

By default Clean rules are reduced using the functional strategy. This strategy may be locally influenced by the use of *annotations* added to the Clean program. Annotations can be considered as parameters of the strategy function. They are very important if one wants to optimize the time and space behaviour of the reduction process.

In this section the **strict annotations** are discussed that can be added in Clean to the rewrite rules and to type rules with the effect that sometimes partially *eager* evaluation is used instead of *lazy* evaluation. Strict annotations are important because, in general, functions with annotated arguments can be implemented very efficiently (see Chapters 10 and 11). The largest gain in efficiency is obtained when arguments of the basic types are being annotated. Strict annotations are also convenient when Clean is used as an intermediate language for eager languages (such as HOPE (Burstall *et al.*, 1980) or FP (Backus, 1978)).

Strict annotations and the order of evaluation

Annotations let the reduction strategy deviate from the default functional evaluation order, making the evaluation order partially eager instead of lazy. Annotations can be placed in definitions of new types and in type specifications of rewrite rules (*global annotations*) as well as in the right-hand sides of the rewrite rules themselves (*local annotations*). If a strict annotation is specified, the evaluation of the indicated subgraph is forced. This forced evaluation will also follow the functional strategy, yielding a root normal form. After the forced evaluation has delivered the root normal form, the reduction process continues with the ordinary reduction order following the functional strategy.

Strict annotations can only be added safely when it is known that the termination behaviour of the original program is not changed.

A strict annotation might change the termination behaviour of a program: before the rewrite rule for F is applied, the reduction of the argument of F is forced due to the specified strict annotation. As a consequence, the normal form 1 of F W will not be reached any more.

```
:: Start   ->   INT;
   Start   ->   F !W;

:: W       ->   INT;
   W       ->   W;

:: F INT   ->   INT;
   F x     ->   1;
```

Strict annotations are in general used to force the evaluation of arguments of a function in the case that the function is known to be *strict* in these arguments (see Chapter 7). A strict argument can safely be evaluated in advance.

Ideally, a programmer should not be bothered at all with annotations to gain efficiency. As shown in Chapter 7, a good strictness analyser (such as incorporated in the Clean system) can detect many cases where strict annotations can be put safely. Therefore, user-defined strict annotations are generally only used when an ultimate gain in efficiency is demanded.

8.3.1 Global strict annotations in type rules

The strict annotations in a type specification are called **global** because they change the reduction order for *all* applications of a particular function. Annotations in a type specification of a function are allowed to be placed before the type specification of an argument on the left-hand side of the type rule.

Example of a global strict annotation in type rules:

```
:: Cond !BOOL  x     x    ->  x;
   Cond TRUE   then  else ->  then;
   Cond FALSE  then  else ->  else;
```

Note that the strict annotation will force the evaluation of the first argument before the Cond function is examined as a candidate for rewriting.

In reasoning about programs with global strict annotations it will always be true that the annotated argument is in root normal form when the corresponding rule is applied. In the pattern matching phase this knowledge can be used: one can start by comparing symbols.

Another example of a global strict annotation: the Nfib function calculates the number of times it is called. Nfib is frequently used to determine the number of function calls per second for a particular implementation.

```
:: Nfib !INT  ->  INT;
   Nfib n     ->  1,     IF < n 2
              ->  ++ (+ (Nfib (– n 1)) (Nfib (– n 2)));
```

Strict annotations can also be placed in type rules to indicate that the corresponding parts of an argument or a result will always be evaluated when the object as a whole is evaluated.

Example of global strict annotations in tuple types:

```
:: +C  !(!REAL, !REAL)  !(!REAL, !REAL)  ->  (!REAL, !REAL);
   +C  (r1, i1)         (r2, i2)         ->  (+R r1 r2, +R i1 i2);
```

Strict annotations may be used in the same manner in a type synonym definition. The meaning of these annotated synonym types can be explained with the aid of a simple program transformation with which all occurrences of these synonym types are replaced by their right-hand sides (annotations included).

Example of (partially) strict tuple types in a type synonym definition. The definition of +C is equivalent to the definition given above.

```
TYPE
:: Complex  ->  (!REAL, !REAL);

RULE
:: +C  !Complex  !Complex  ->  Complex;
   +C  (r1, i1)  (r2, i2)  ->  (+R r1 r2, +R i1 i2);
```

Allowing tuples to be strict makes it possible to define functions that deliver multiple results eagerly (i.e. all results already evaluated). This is in contrast with the general lazy case where the evaluation of the arguments of a tuple is not forced since the tuple constructor that 'glues' the results together induces a lazy context for these arguments. With a strict annotation it is possible to overrule this laziness. The use of (partially) strict data types can lead to very efficient code (Nöcker and Smetsers, 1993).

8.3.2 Local strict annotations in rewrite rules

Strict annotations in rewrite rules are called **local**. They change only the order of evaluation for a *specific* function application. Local strict annotations can be placed anywhere on the right-hand side of a rewrite rule, both on arguments as well as on nodes. If a local strict annotation is put on a node, this is equivalent to putting the annotation on each reference to that node. When a rewrite rule is applied, all strict annotated nodes of the right-hand side of the applied rewrite rule are evaluated before the evaluation continues.

Example of strict annotations on the right-hand side. For this particular occurrence of Cond (as defined in a previous example) it is indicated that a common part of the then and else part can be reduced safely.

```
F x y -> Cond x !y (++ !y);
```

Each *node* on the right-hand side is considered to be either **strict** (appearing in a **strict context**: it has to be evaluated to root normal form) or **lazy** (appearing in a **lazy context**: not yet to be evaluated to root normal form). The following rules specify whether or not a particular node is lazy or strict:

(1) the root node of the right-hand side is strict;
(2) the global annotated arguments of a strict node are strict;
(3) a local annotated node is strict;
(4) all the other nodes are lazy.

Before reducing the root node of the right-hand side all strict nodes other than the root node are evaluated to root normal form.

Example illustrating states of nodes:

```
:: F ![INT]   INT ->   [INT];
   F [ ]      n   ->   [ ];
   F [ a | b ] n  ->   [ n | F b (G a n) ];
```

```
G a b     ->     + a b;

Start w -> r: F a b,   a: F e c,   e: [ 1 ], c: ++ 5,   b: G 1 !d,   d: ++ 4;
```

In the Start rule, the nodes r, a, e and d are strict; the others are lazy.

8.3.3 Strictness analysis

A strictness analyser is incorporated in the Clean system. This analyser is based on *abstract reduction* (see Chapter 7). The analyser can often determine strictness and is quite fast. When a function is found to be strict in a certain argument, a global strict annotation is generated automatically. Certain strictness information is very difficult to detect. Finding information for tuple types is almost impossible since it would require an analysis of all the possible uses of the type.

Consider again the following example:

```
+C (r1, i1) (r2, i2)    ->    (+R r1 r2, +R i1 i2);
```

The only information that can be derived for the function +C is that it is strict in its arguments (because of the pattern matching). The result of the function is a tuple that is in root normal form. One generally cannot conclude that the tuple arguments are needed and hence they cannot be reduced in advance.

8.3.4 Strict annotations and gain in efficiency

The following example illustrates the gain in efficiency that is achieved when strict annotations are added to a Clean program. Consider the following Clean program that calculates the Ackermann function.

```
:: LazyAcker INT  INT  ->   INT;
   LazyAcker 0    j    ->   ++ j;
   LazyAcker i    0    ->   LazyAcker (-- i) 1;
   LazyAcker i    j    ->   LazyAcker (-- i) (LazyAcker i (-- j));

:: Start   ->   INT;
   Start   ->   LazyAcker 3 7;
```

Performing this computation on a MacIIx with a 4Mb heap takes 16.3 s + 0.2 s for garbage collection.

```
:: StrAcker   INT  INT  ->   INT;
   StrAcker   i    0    ->   StrAcker !(-- i) 1;
   StrAcker   i    j    ->   StrAcker !(-- i) !(StrAcker i (-- j));
```

The same computation (StrAcker 3 7), but now with local strict annotations added (as shown in the definition of StrAcker) will only cost 9.6 s + 0.1 s for garbage collection. The gain in efficiency is obtained because fewer nodes have to be made. In general, it is hard to predict how much gain will be achieved.

```
:: Acker  !INT   !INT  ->   INT;
   Acker  0      j     ->   ++ j;
   Acker  i      0     ->   Acker (-- i) 1;
   Acker  i      j     ->   Acker (-- i) (Acker i (-- j));
```

A significant gain in efficiency can be obtained when strict annotations are placed in global positions (see the (type) definition of Acker above). The same computation (Acker 3 7) will now only take 1.9 s + 0.0 s garbage collection. The gain is one order of magnitude compared with the previous definitions. It is now known that for *all* applications of the function the evaluation of the argument is needed, in particular for the recursive call itself. As will be explained in Chapter 11, no nodes are made at all (hence no garbage collection is needed) because both argument and result are of type INT. The calculation is performed on a stack and registers are used where possible. The speed is comparable with a recursive call in highly optimized C or with the speed obtainable when the function is programmed directly in assembler. The example already reveals the cost of lazy evaluation and pure graph reduction compared with eager evaluation using stacks and registers. Fortunately, with the help of strictness analysis, much strictness information can be found automatically (for instance in the case of the Ackermann function defined above).

8.4 Modules

For a practical useful language separate compilation is a must. A modular structure enables this with the facility to hide actual implementations of types and functions. This can also be used to specify abstract data types (see also Section 8.2). The Clean modular structure very much resembles the Modula2 approach (Wirth, 1982) with one major exception: Clean's implicit imports, which simplify the definition of modules that just collect and pass-through definitions of other modules.

A Clean program consists of *definition modules* and *implementation modules*. In general, each definition module has a corresponding implementation module. An implementation module and its corresponding definition module bear the same module name. Each module is stored in a separate file with the same name as the module, with an appropriate extension (e.g. name.icl, name.dcl).

8.4.1 Implementation modules

An *implementation module* consists of a sequence of type and rule definitions. The types and rules defined in such an implementation module have in principle only a *local scope*: they have meaning only in the implementation module in which they are defined.

Example of an implementation module:

```
IMPLEMENTATION MODULE ListOperations;
FROM deltaM IMPORT ABORT;
RULE
:: Hd   [x]      ->   x;
   Hd   [ x | y ] ->  x;
   Hd   x        ->   ABORT "head of empty list ?! ";

:: Tl [x]        ->   [x];
   Tl [ x | y ]  ->   y;
   Tl x          ->   ABORT "tail of empty list ?! ";

:: IsNil [x]     ->   BOOL;
   IsNil [ ]     ->   TRUE;
   IsNil x       ->   FALSE;
```

An executable Clean program should have an implementation module with a Start rule declared in it. This module is called the **start module**.

8.4.2 Definition modules

In a *definition module* one can specify which types and rules (defined in the corresponding implementation module) are **exported**, i.e. are made visible to the outside world. To export a type or a function from an implementation module one has to *repeat* its type definition in the corresponding definition module. All other definitions in the implementation module remain hidden.

Example of a definition module:

```
DEFINITION MODULE ListOperations;
RULE
:: Hd    [x]    ->   x;
:: Tl    [x]    ->   [x];
:: IsNil [x]    ->   BOOL;
```

An abstract type can be realized by exporting the name of an algebraic or synonym type, but not its concrete realization (see also Section 8.2.2). A definition module does not need to have a corresponding implementation module. This can be useful for defining types on a global level. Such a definition module can also serve as a 'pass-through' module (see Section 8.4.3).

System modules

System modules are special definition modules indicated by the keyword SYSTEM instead of DEFINITION. This indicates that the corresponding implementation module does not contain ordinary Clean rules, but abstract ABC machine code instead (the ABC machine is explained in Chapter 10). This facility makes it possible to program directly in ABC code. This can be used to increase execution speed of heavily used functions or complex data structures. On demand, the Clean compiler will substitute the ABC code of a function *in-line* at the place in which the corresponding function is called. In this way execution speed can be increased even more. An advantage of system modules is that a certain increase of efficiency can be obtained in a device-independent manner, since ABC code is device independent. It goes without saying that for ABC programming advanced knowledge is needed of the code generation schemes and the run-time behaviour of the ABC machine. Imprudent programming of system modules will generally lead to unpredictable errors. Typically, predefined δ-rules are implemented as system modules (see Appendix B).

8.4.3 Implicit and explicit importing

Via an *import* statement an exported definition can be used in another implementation or definition module. Imported types and rules can be regarded as being predefined. There are two kinds of import statement: *explicit* and *implicit* imports.

Explicit imports

Explicit imports are import statements in which every type or rule that has to be imported from a particular module is explicitly mentioned. In this way only these explicitly indicated types and rules are declared within the importing module.

Example of the use of explicit IMPORT statements: the sieve of Eratosthenes, which calculates prime numbers.

```
IMPLEMENTATION MODULE Eratosthenes;
FROM deltaI IMPORT ++, =, % ;
RULE
:: Start    ->    [INT];
   Start    ->    Sieve (Gen 2);
```

```
:: Sieve [INT]         ->    [INT];
   Sieve [ pr | str ]  ->    [ pr | Sieve (Filter pr str) ];

:: Filter INT [INT]      ->    [INT];
   Filter pr [ n | str ] ->    Filter pr str,         IF = (% n pr) 0
                         ->    [ pr | Filter pr str ];

:: Gen INT    ->    [INT];
   Gen n      ->    [ n | Gen (++ n) ];
```

Implicit imports

Implicit imports are import statements in which only the imported module name is mentioned. In this case *all* symbols that are **declared** (i.e. defined or imported) in the imported module are imported (and hence also declared in the module that contains the import statement). So not only are all symbols exported by the indicated module imported, but also all symbols which in their turn are imported in that definition module. In this aspect the Clean modular structure differs from the Modula2 approach. So with one simple IMPORT statement all related declarations are imported implicitly. Consequently, definition modules can serve as a kind of 'pass-through'.

> All delta-rules can be imported easily by importing the module delta via the implicit import statement: IMPORT delta; . This is due to the fact that *all* predefined definition modules for arithmetic are in their turn implicitly imported in the definition module delta.

```
DEFINITION MODULE delta;
IMPORT deltaB, deltaC, deltaI, deltaR, deltaS, deltaM;
```

8.5 Unique types and destructive updates

Section 2.6 describes the Miranda method of writing interactive programs. However, this approach has many disadvantages. To interact with the operating system the initial expression has to yield special constructors which have to be interpreted by the run-time system. To ensure referential transparency, certain restrictions are imposed on the kind of I/O that is permitted (e.g. a file cannot be rewritten). Furthermore, the solution is rather inefficient and the structure of highly interactive programs can become rather ugly. Generally, there is a direct relation between input and output which is not always clearly visible in the Miranda approach: input is converted into a list to read from, output has to be produced by an eager printing of the result yielded by the initial expression. Since the order in which functions are evaluated is hard to predict, a frequently occurring error consists of the specification of a program that demands input before a prompt for such is given. So the Miranda solution is not a satisfactory method for writing interactive programs.

On the other hand, it is not easy to find a good solution. The problem is that certain kinds of destructive updates, which occur for example in traditional file I/O, would be very nice to have. But one cannot have destructive updates in the functional framework without some drawbacks. So the questions that arise are:

- How is it possible to perform destructive updates efficiently without violating the functional properties of the program (referential transparency, Church–Rosser property)?
- Since the evaluation of a functional program is unpredictable, how can one control the order in which destructive updates are performed?

When are destructive updates safe?

What kind of problems are caused by functions that perform destructive updates? Such functions are, for example, functions that destructively update an array, instantaneously write to a file on disk or to a window on a screen.

Take, for example, file I/O. The most obvious and efficient way to perform file I/O is by implementing functions that directly read and write to a file, such as is common in imperative languages. However, a naïve implementation of such functions in a functional language would conflict with referential transparency. For instance, assume a function that upon evaluation directly writes a character to a given file. Assume that such a function is of type:

```
:: FWriteC CHAR FILE  ->    FILE;
```

This function takes a character and a file as an argument. However, the character cannot be written into the given file and returned as result because the original file can be shared and used in other function applications. Modification of the argument will therefore also affect the outcome of other computations that share the same argument. The result of a program will now depend on the evaluation order, and the Church–Rosser property is lost.

Example of an illegal destructive update:

```
:: F FILE ->    (FILE,FILE);
   F file  ->    (file1, file2),
                 file1: FWriteC 'a' file,
                 file2: FWriteC 'b' file;
```

> Assume that the function FWriteC would actually append the given character to the file it gets as an argument. Now, since the file is used twice in the function body of F the result will depend on the evaluation order. It will either be (file++'a', file++"ab") or (file++"ba", file++'b'). But, if FWriteC does not change the original file the result would be (file++'a', file++'b'), independent of the chosen evaluation order.

The destructive update is also in conflict with the standard graph rewriting semantics of FWriteC (see also Appendix B) that prescribes construction of a *new* file (contractum) in the function body with the contents of the given file and the given character. So each time a character is written such a data structure has to be constructed. This is of course very inefficient and it is not the intention either. One really wants to have the possibility of modifying an *existing* file *instantaneously*. The problem becomes even more obvious when one wants to write to a window on a screen: one would like to be able to draw in an *existing* window. In the standard semantics one would be obliged to construct a new window with each drawing command.

However, under certain conditions destructive updates *can* be allowed. If it can be guaranteed that an argument of a particular function application is not used by (shared with) other function applications, then the argument becomes garbage if it is not used in the corresponding function body. In principle one can destructively update such an argument to construct the function result. This would make it possible to construct a function FWriteC that can actually write the character to the given file, yielding the updated file. But, such a function can only restrictively be used. For example, the illegal example above would indeed not be allowed.

Controlling the evaluation order

Assume that we can define functions that perform destructive updates in such a way that the Church–Rosser property of the program is retained. One certainly would not want destructive updates such as interaction with the user to occur in arbitrary order. How can one ensure that destructive updates are performed in the intended order? A well-known method is environment passing. The state of the environment one wants to regard is then coded into an (abstract) object (e.g. a FILE in the case of file I/O). Each function that modifies the environment needs the current state of the environment as argument and yields the updated environment as result. In the case of file I/O this means that all functions that perform file I/O need a file as argument and return an updated file (see Section 8.5.2 and Appendix B). So such an object has to be passed from one function to another. When a function performs an update of an argument, it must be guaranteed that all previous updates of that argument by other functions have already taken place. So a function that updates an argument must be **hyper-strict** in this argument, i.e. it must be guaranteed that the argument is always in normal form before the function is applied. Passing around unique objects from just one function to another is called the **single-threaded** use of objects. For such use destructive updates are allowed and they take place in a fixed sequential order (innermost).

Solutions for incorporating destructive updates

Currently, there are two promising ways to incorporate destructive updates as described above in a pure functional language. The first method is by using **monads** (Peyton Jones and Wadler, 1993). Monads are abstract data structures on which functions are defined in such a way that a single threaded use of the monad is guaranteed. However, a disadvantage of the method is that one can only manipulate one monad at a time. So, for example, destructive file I/O and destructive array manipulation are hard to combine. In Clean a second method is introduced that does not have this disadvantage but it does require a special type system. One can assign a *unique type attribute* (Smetsers *et al.*, 1993) to an arbitrary object that can be used to guarantee that such an object can be destructively updated safely.

8.5.1 The unique type attribute

A node *n* of a graph *G* is **unique** with respect to a node *m* of *G* if *n* is only reachable from the root of *G* via *m* and there exists exactly one path from *m* to *n* (Figure 8.2).

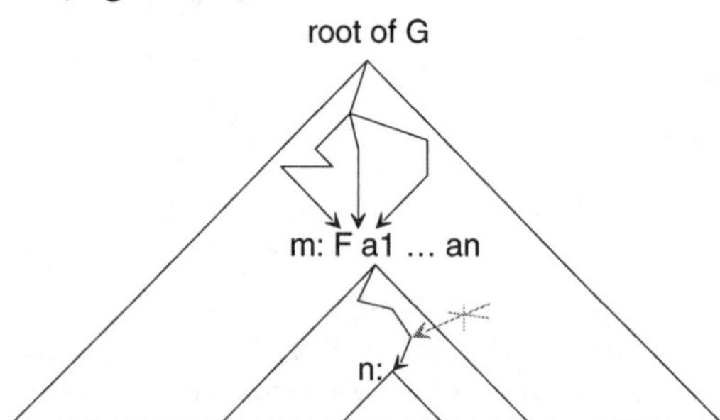

Figure 8.2 Unique node n with respect to the root m of the redex.

A property of a unique node is the fact that it has a reference count (in-grade) of one. A shared node which has a larger reference count than one clearly cannot be unique with respect to any node. A reference count of one is, however, not sufficient for uniqueness with respect to any other node: there can still be more paths leading to such a node. Assume that a node is passed as argument of a certain function application in such a way that the node is unique with respect to that function application: if such a node is accessed via a variable in a pattern of the corresponding rewrite rule and that variable is not used on the right-hand side of that rule, it can be considered as garbage and reused for building the contractum.

It would be nice if at compile-time the uniqueness of arguments and results of functions could be determined. Unfortunately, this is undecidable. In Clean a decidable approximation has been incorporated using **unique types**. Unique types (Smetsers *et al.*, 1993), defined on *graphs*, have many similarities with linear types, defined on *λ-terms* (Girard, 1987; Wadler, 1990). An important difference is that Clean's unique types give information about the way *a specific function* has to be *applied* (e.g. this function has to be called with an argument that is used in a linear way) while other linear type systems give information about the way expressions are being used in the function body (e.g. this argument of the function is used in a linear way in the function body).

Unique type specifications and functions

The type of a graph in a rewrite rule can have the **unique type attribute**, i.e. the graph can be of type UNQ T. *If a graph on a left-hand side or on the right-hand side of a rewrite rule is of type UNQ T, it is guaranteed that at run-time the root of the corresponding graph is unique with respect to the root of, respectively, the function application or contractum. When no contractum is specified, a result of type UNQ T means that a redirection is performed to an object that was unique with respect to the root of the function application.* When this cannot lead to confusion the phrase 'a unique graph' will be used instead of 'a graph which is unique with respect to the function application/contractum'.

The UNQ type attribute can be added by the programmer to any type to express the restricted use of an object of that type. To verify the correctness of the use of UNQ attributes the type system has been extended. This means that all applications on the right-hand side of a function are examined to check that when a parameter or a result of a UNQ type is demanded, a unique graph of the demanded type is offered. Here, demanded means that either the corresponding formal parameter of the applied function has a UNQ attribute or the result type of the defined function itself is attributed with UNQ. To get a well-typed program, the following general rules have to be obeyed:

- An applied occurrence of a node-id bound to a graph can have the UNQ type attribute only if there exists at most one path from the root of the right-hand side of a rule alternative to that applied occurrence.

Not well-typed example. The type specification of the function F defined below will be rejected since two paths are leading from the root of the contractum to the same node x. The unique argument of the function F is not unique any more in the resulting pair. So the following types for F would be accepted: ::F UNQ INT -> ([INT], [INT]) or ::F INT -> ([INT], [INT]).

```
:: F UNQ INT    ->    ( [UNQ INT], [UNQ INT] );
   F x          ->    ( y, y ),
                      y: [ x ];
```

Each function alternative is separately checked for consistency. Although in the definition of F below the unique node-id n is used twice this does not lead to a conflict: only one of the guarded expressions is chosen at run-time.

```
:: F  UNQ INT   INT   ->    UNQ INT;
   F  n         m     ->    n, IF = m 0
                      ->    F (G n) (-- m);

:: G  UNQ INT   ->    UNQ INT;
   ...
```

It is not always wrong to use a UNQ-typed graph more than once in one and the same function alternative. *A unique node-id may be shared between the guard and the guarded expression belonging to it.* The reason is that a guard is evaluated in advance to determine which of the function alternatives has to be chosen. A guard will yield a Boolean result that cannot contain references to UNQ nodes. To guarantee that no destructive updates occur when a guard is evaluated, a graph that is being used in both guard and guarded expression will lose its unique type attribute in the guard. This enables the non-destructive (observing) inspection of such a graph in a guard. This property for guards can be generalized to a more general property for uniqueness connected to the order of evaluation (see Smetsers *et al.*, 1993).

Example of sharing of a unique node-id in guard and right-hand side:

```
:: F  UNQ INT   ->    UNQ INT;
   F  n         ->    n, IF = n 0 || = n 1
                ->    F (G n);
```

Although the node-id n is shared between the guard and both guarded expressions this will not lead to an erroneous situation. After the evaluation of the guard still only one non-garbage reference to n exists. The type system will assign the type INT (and not UNQ INT) to both uses of n in the guard.

- Demanded UNQs have to be obeyed (with an exception for function types, see below): when a demanded type T and an offered type T' are unifiable (in the standard sense, ignoring the UNQ attributes) then for each position where in T the UNQ attribute occurs, there has to be a corresponding position in T' with the UNQ attribute.

Not well-typed example. F is recursively called with a graph of type INT, while in the type specification of F an argument of type UNQ INT is demanded. This will yield a type error.

```
:: F  UNQ INT   ->     INT;
   F  n         ->     F (G n);

:: G  INT       ->     INT;
   ...
```

For demanded *function types* with UNQ arguments the offered argument type need not be unique: a demanded type => UNQ T T' and an offered type => S S' are unifiable (when in the standard sense, ignoring the UNQ attributes, => T T' and => S S' are unifiable).

- When a UNQ type is offered but not demanded, this offered type is accepted (with an exception for function types, see below). This can be explained by the fact that a UNQ type imposes an additional restriction on the way the object is used. If this restriction is not demanded by the context this is of course fine. It does mean that *type conversions* have to take place. An offered object of type UNQ T is automatically converted to type T if this type is demanded from the context.

Take the previous example and consider the application of G n. G demands an argument of type INT while G is applied with a graph of type UNQ INT. The type system will automatically convert the UNQ INT to an INT and will then conclude that the type of the application G n is correct.

Offered *unique function types* are never converted: when a type UNQ => T T' is offered, the demanded type must be of type UNQ => S S' and unifiable in the standard sense.

```
:: F UNQ FILE CHAR       ->     UNQ FILE;
   F f c                 ->     FWriteC c f;

:: G (=> CHAR UNQ FILE)  ->     (UNQ FILE, UNQ FILE);
   G g                   ->     (g ‘a’, g ‘b’);
```

With the well-typed rules above the expression G (F StdErr) would be rejected. The type of F StdErr is UNQ (=> CHAR UNQ FILE) owing to the left to right UNQ propagation rule which is explained in the next subsection.

Furthermore, offered *function types* with UNQ arguments have to be obeyed: when a demanded type => T T' and an offered type => UNQ S S' are unifiable (in the standard sense, ignoring the UNQ attributes) then they are not unifiable taking UNQ into account. The demanded type must be => UNQ T T'.

```
:: UMap (=> UNQ x UNQ y)   [UNQ x]     ->   [UNQ y];
   UMap f                  [ ]         ->   [ ];
   UMap f                  [ x | xs ]  ->   [ f x | UMap f xs ];

:: WriteAll CHAR   [UNQ FILE]   ->   [UNQ FILE];
   WriteAll c      ufiles       ->   UMap (FWriteC 'a') ufiles;
```

This variant of Map is defined on functions that take a graph of type UNQ x and yield a graph of type UNQ y. UMap applies such a function to a unique list (see below) with elements of type UNQ x yielding a unique list with elements of type UNQ y. This function UMap is used in the function WriteAll to map a function FWriteC that writes a character into a unique file on a list of unique files. It has to be guaranteed that the offered function FWriteC is always applied to a unique file. From the type of the standard function Map one cannot deduce whether this condition is fulfilled. Therefore in this example the use of Map instead of UMap would have been rejected. Note that there is no distinction between the definition of the function Map and UMap: there is only a difference in the specified type.

When functions are allowed to be polymorphic in their UNQ attributes one can define a generic Map function that can be used both as the standard Map function and as the UMap function in the example above.

Defining types with UNQ attributes

A programmer can add unique type attributes to any type. List, tuples and function types, as well as their subtypes, can have the unique attribute. Furthermore, type attributes can be used in the definition of new types (algebraic, abstract and synonym types). In this section it is explained what the meaning of such a definition is.

An important aspect of a function application containing a unique graph is that it cannot be a part of a graph that is not unique with respect to that function application. In other words, when a graph with type T contains unique parts (which means that the type T has unique subtypes) the graph itself must be unique (this is called **the UNQ propagation rule**). Otherwise, there can be multiple paths leading to this graph which means that its components would not be unique any more. The propagation rule holds for all types, and also for function types. For non-function types UNQ attributes propagate from **inside-out**, for function types it propagates from **left to right**. In Clean, it is not necessary to give the full type specification; the propagation of the UNQ attributes is done automatically by the compiler.

Example of 'inside-out' propagation: consider the type (INT, UNQ CHAR). An instance of such a type is a pair containing an INT and a unique CHAR. Due to the propagation rule, the pair itself has to be unique as well, i.e. the full type specification is UNQ (INT, UNQ CHAR).
Example of 'left to right' propagation: take F typed as :: F UNQ INT INT -> INT; the type of the curried function F is => UNQ INT (=> INT INT). Now consider the curried application F 3. This application has taken a unique integer value. When there are multiple paths leading to F 3 there are also multiple paths leading to 3. So F 3 has to be unique as well. Hence, the full type specification for F is => UNQ INT UNQ (=> INT INT).

Synonym types

Synonym types can be used in the usual way.

```
TYPE
:: UTUPLE UNQ x -> (UNQ x, UNQ x);
```

Applying UNQ propagation to achieve the full type specification for this example gives UNQ UTUPLE UNQ x -> UNQ (UNQ x, UNQ x).

Algebraic types

The following rules guarantee that when unique substructures are being used, a consistent (recursive) algebraic data type is defined.

(1) All occurrences in both left- and right-hand sides of a certain type variable must have the same type attribute.

(2) All occurrences of a recursive algebraic type must be attributed uniformly.

(3) When the root of a right-hand side of a type alternative is attributed with UNQ, all other type alternatives will get the UNQ attribute on their root as well. Moreover, the algebraic type itself (and hence all occurrences of that type) will get the UNQ attribute.

A list with a unique spine but not necessarily with unique elements:

```
:: List x       ->   Cons x UNQ (List x)
                ->   Nil;
```

Due to the UNQ propagation rule the uniqueness of the spine will propagate over the Cons. As a consequence, Nil will get the UNQ attribute (being the root of the other type alternative) as well as all occurrences of List x (being the defined algebraic type). So the full definition deduced by the compiler is:

```
:: UNQ List x      ->   UNQ Cons x UNQ (List x)
                   ->   UNQ Nil;
```

For clarity, we advise specifying the left-hand side completely:

```
:: UNQ List x      ->   Cons x (List x)
                   ->   Nil;
```

A list with unique elements and hence with a unique spine:

```
:: List UNQ x      ->   Cons UNQ x (List UNQ x)
                   ->   Nil;
```

Owing to the UNQ propagation rule the uniqueness of list elements will propagate over the Cons. As in the case above, the root of both alternatives as well as the algebraic type itself become unique and therefore so does the whole spine. So the complete list has to be unique (lists elements as well as the spine). The full definition is:

```
:: UNQ List UNQ x     ->   UNQ Cons UNQ x UNQ (List UNQ x)
                      ->   UNQ Nil;
```

The advised definition is:

```
:: UNQ List UNQ x     ->   Cons UNQ x (List UNQ x)
                      ->   Nil;
```

Unique types can be used as instantiations of polymorphic types. The meaning of a type T parametrized with a unique type is rather obvious: the resulting type is deduced from the type obtained by substituting the parameters (including the UNQ attributes) in the definition of T.

Take for example the following common definition of a list:

```
:: List x    ->   Cons x (List x)
             ->   Nil;
```

Then for the type List UNQ INT the following full type definition is deduced:

```
:: UNQ List UNQ INT ->   UNQ Cons UNQ INT UNQ (List UNQ INT)
                    ->   UNQ Nil;
```

The substitution of a UNQ instantiation in a polymorphic type will not always yield a UNQ type as result.

Take for example the following definition:

```
:: T x          ->    C (=> x (=> INT INT));
```

Left to right propagation deduces for the type T UNQ INT the following:

```
:: T UNQ INT  ->    C (=> UNQ INT UNQ (=> INT INT));
```

Abstract types

Abstract types with UNQ attributes are specified by giving the *full* type specification of the left-hand side of the corresponding type definition in the implementation module.

The previous fully unique List type is turned into an abstract type as follows:

```
ABSTYPE
:: UNQ List UNQ x;
```

8.6 Input/output handling

Using the UNQ type attribute, single-threaded use of *file I/O* and *screen I/O* (in Clean called *event I/O*) can be assured. In this way incremental updates of persistent data are made possible (see Section 8.6.2). Specification of modern I/O that uses modules, windows, menus and the like can be done on a very high level of abstraction by making use of the predefined Clean library (Achten *et al.*, 1993) that heavily uses UNQ types. This library is part of Appendix B.

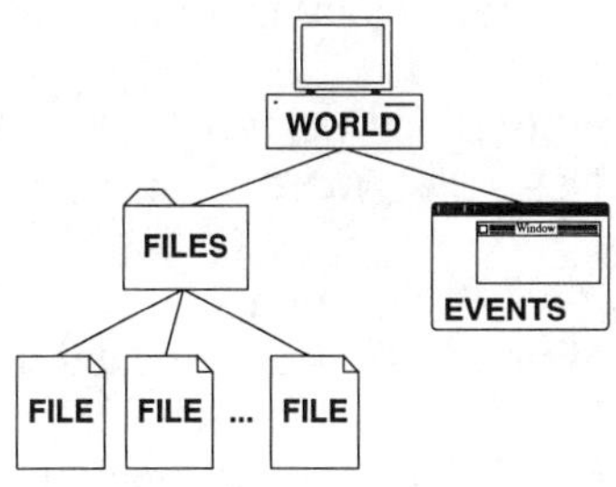

Figure 8.3 The I/O environment hierarchy of Clean.

The I/O constructs of Clean are referentially transparent and hence '100% functional'. An abstract object representing the outside world has been predefined with type UNQ WORLD. From this world the following disjoint abstract objects can be extracted (see Figure 8.3): an object of type UNQ EVENTS which is used to perform screen I/O and an object of type UNQ FILES (the file system) from which in its turn objects of type FILE (concrete files) can be extracted (opened) to perform file I/O. One can open unique files (if these files have to be modified) or non-unique ones (for read-only files).

8.6.1 The world

The world contains all the information about the concrete environment that is relevant to the program. There is no function to create a world. The world is an abstract object of predefined type UNQ WORLD optionally given to a Clean program as an argument of the Start rule:

```
RULE
:: Start UNQ WORLD -> ...     ==  any type
   Start w -> ...             ==  any computation yielding the indicated type;
```

Pure computations ignore the world and its subenvironments. Interactive programs need to access and change the world using functions which require a unique world. When the world becomes garbage it does not mean that the world has ceased to exist, but it means that the program no longer performs operations on the world. If the subenvironments have been retrieved earlier, then they can still be accessed in the program.

8.6.2 File I/O

FILES is the unique subenvironment of the world containing all the files that are visible to the program (the file system). The file system is retrieved from a unique world by the rule OpenFiles and can be put back again by the rule CloseFiles. Once the file system has been retrieved from the world, it cannot be retrieved again without closing it first.

```
:: OpenFiles UNQ WORLD -> (UNQ FILES, UNQ WORLD);
:: CloseFiles UNQ FILES UNQ WORLD -> UNQ WORLD;
```

A Clean file has type FILE. To open a file (to read or write) one needs the file system. Only writable files are opened as UNQ FILE; read-only files do not require the unique attribute. For example, the following functions have been predefined (there are many more: see Appendix B).

```
:: FOpen    STRING INT UNQ FILES -> (BOOL, UNQ FILE, UNQ FILES);
:: SFOpen   STRING INT UNQ FILES -> (BOOL, FILE, UNQ FILES);
:: FWriteC  CHAR UNQ FILE -> UNQ FILE;
:: SFReadC  FILE -> (BOOL, CHAR, FILE);
```

In the Clean library also an FSeek function is predefined with which the file pointer can be moved explicitly such that a file can be randomly accessed. Note that all functions return a (UNQ) FILE on which I/O functions can continue.

The following example illustrates the use of WORLD, FILES and FILEs:

```
RULE
:: Start UNQ WORLD -> UNQ FILE;
   Start w ->  CopyF sf df,
               (fs, w'):                OpenFiles w,
               (source_open, sf, fs' ): SFOpen "Source" FReadData  fs,
               (dest_open, df, fs''):   FOpen   "Dest"   FWriteData fs';

:: CopyF FILE UNQ FILE -> UNQ FILE;
   CopyF sf df   ->   df,                                  IF NOT read_ok
                 ->   CopyF sf' (FWriteC char df),
                      (read_ok, char, sf'):    SFReadC sf;
```

This program copies the contents of one file to another. First it retrieves the file system from the world. This file system is used to open the source and the destination file. The world and the file system are no further needed and become garbage. The source file is only being read (indicated by FReadData), so it does not have to be unique. The destination file is being written (FWriteData) and therefore this file must be unique. After completion of copying, the source file becomes garbage, and the program yields the written file. To do the actual copying on the open files CopyF is applied. When the source file is empty the destination file is yielded, otherwise CopyChars reads a character from the source file, writes it to the destination file and continues recursively.

It is possible that a UNQ FILE is used in such a way that it loses its UNQ attribute (e.g. when the file gets shared). Since all destructive operations on files require an object of type UNQ FILE, an ordinary (possibly shared) file of type FILE cannot be modified any more. But there are several non-destructive operations defined on an object of type FILE with which such a file can still be examined.

8.6.3 Event I/O

Event I/O is a different class of I/O than file I/O. In **event I/O** the objects that are being manipulated are graphical interface objects such as windows, menus and dialogs. Graphical interface systems are event driven: actions performed by the user generate events to the program. Clean's event I/O library (written in Clean) offers a way to define these graphical interface objects on a level that is very close to the way these objects actually appear on the screen. The library completely takes care of all the low-level event handling.

Devices

A **device** in Clean is an interface object such as a window or a menu. There are four devices predefined in the Clean library: the *menu device*, the *window device*, the *dialog device* and the *timer device*.

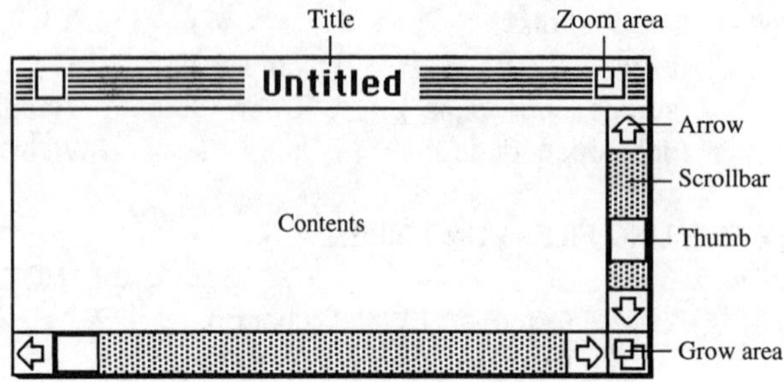

Figure 8.4 Example of a window.

A **window device** (see Figure 8.4) is an interactive device: it reacts on key presses and releases and mouse clicks and releases, coupled with mouse positions. Windows are the only way a program can visualize output. A window gives a view on a **picture** (again a UNQ abstract object) on which a set of drawing functions is defined.

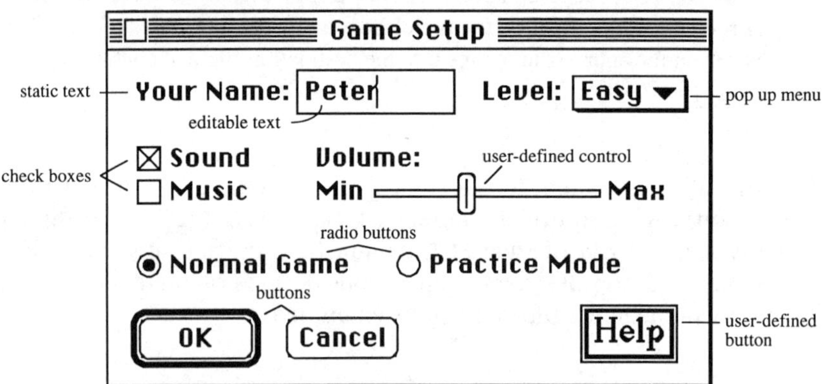

Figure 8.5 Example of a dialog.

The relationship between the visible part of the picture and the window is defined by the positions of the thumbs of the window's scroll bars. One can open several windows dynamically, at most one of them is active. Almost all window management is handled automatically by the library. The programmer just has to define the update management which is the redrawing that should be performed if an invisible part of the window becomes visible again. The programmer can also define what should be done when a window is closed.

The **menu device** (see Figure 8.7) conceptualizes choosing from a distinguished set of available commands. A menu device can contain pull-down menus each containing commands or submenus.

The **dialog device** (see Figure 8.5) conceptualizes structured communication between the program and the user via a form that has to be filled in. One can have modal and modeless dialogs, as well as notices. Modal and modeless dialogs can contain editable text fields, static text fields, pop-up menus, radio buttons, check boxes, buttons, final buttons and user-defined controls.

With the **timer device** a program can be synchronized (see Section 8.6.4): a function can be evaluated every time a certain time interval has passed. Several timers can be installed. When a time interval is set to zero, a timer event is generated whenever no other event is generated.

Interactions

The concept of events and devices can now be used to define **interactions**. An interaction is a *state transition system* in which I/O is performed. The state of an interaction is composed of two objects: the *program state* and the *I/O state*.

The **program state** is a program-defined data structure. The program state can be used by the programmer to maintain the current state of the program (which is dependent on the kind of program).

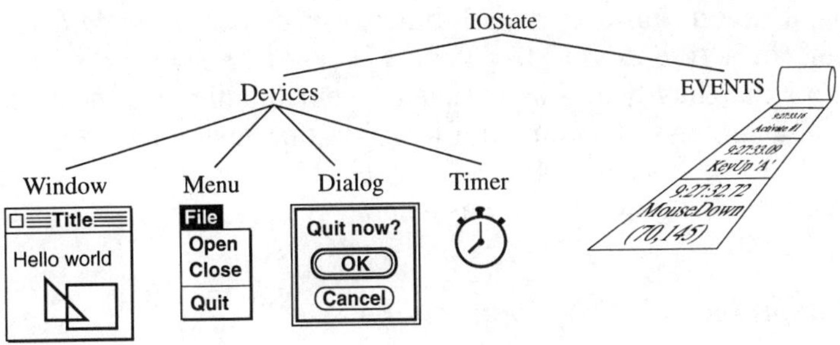

Figure 8.6 The contents of the IOState.

The **I/O state** is an abstract data type of type IOState that can be regarded as a *hidden* state used by the library to maintain the current state of the I/O interface. All interactions and I/O functions are defined on this type IOState, rather than on the EVENTS environment. In this way it is made explicit that all event handling is done by the library. The I/O state contains (see Figure 8.6):

- the event stream (modelled by the EVENTS);
- the definition of all the devices that participate in the interaction.

Transitions are triggered by the events in the event stream. Each event in the event stream is dispatched in the library to the proper device, which computes the next interaction state by calling the proper event handler.

The event stream

The event stream can be retrieved from and put back into the WORLD by means of the following predefined functions from the deltaEventIO module:

```
:: OpenEvents UNQ WORLD -> (UNQ EVENTS, UNQ WORLD);
:: CloseEvents UNQ EVENTS UNQ WORLD -> UNQ WORLD;
```

The definition of the devices

Devices are specified with the help of a predefined algebraic data type DeviceSystem. With this type actually a special kind of declarative language is introduced in which the programmer can specify the properties of the devices that are being used (see the example in Section 8.6.4). The programmer has to specify:

- *which* of the predefined I/O devices are being used;
- *how* these devices should be initialized;
- *which* **event handler** or **call-back routine** *has to be called* when a certain active device has been triggered (e.g. a particular menu item that has been chosen). An event handler is a user-defined higher order state transition function that takes the program state and I/O state as an argument to yield a pair with the new program state and the new I/O state as result.

Starting and terminating interactions

Starting and terminating interactions are handled by two special functions: StartIO and QuitIO. StartIO takes the specification of the set-up of the I/O system as described above, the initial program state s_0, a possibly empty list of functions that can be used to change the default settings of the system, and the event stream obtained from the world. StartIO takes the description of the devices, after which these devices are activated and drawn on the screen. Then, the device description and the event queue are stored in the I/O state. Finally, the default settings are set and an internal function DoIO is called with the initial program state

s_0 and the initial I/O state $IOState_0$. This function DoIO recursively calls itself. In each call an input event e_n is taken from the event stream. The input event is dispatched to the proper device which computes the next program state s_{n+1} and the next I/O state $IOState_{n+1}$ by applying the proper event handler. In this way a sequence of pairs of program state and IOState, starting from the program state s_0 and I/O state $IOState_0$, is computed. Below the simplified implementation of StartIO is given using internal library functions InitIO, DoIO, GetEvent, GetEvents and GetHandler.

```
StartIO device_defs program_state default_settings events
->      DoIO (program_state, io_state),
        io_state:   InitIO device_defs default_settings events;

DoIO (program_state, io_state: ClosedIO_State)
->      (program_state, GetEvents io_state);
DoIO (program_state, io_state)
->      DoIO (event_handler program_state io_state''),
        (event_handler, io_state''):  GetHandler event io_state',
        (event, io_state' ):          GetEvent io_state;
```

The order of evaluation guarantees that the transition triggered by event e_{n+1} is only reduced after the transition triggered by e_n has yielded a complete $IOState_{n+1}$. The interaction obtained in this way can only be terminated by having any of the device functions apply QuitIO to its IO-State argument. The function QuitIO produces a special I/O state, Closed-IO_State, in which all devices are closed. DoIO matches on this special state producing the final program state and the remaining event stream.

8.6.4 An example: the game of Life

In this section we present an example of a typical interactive Clean program that uses the Clean I/O library. The program describes the interface for a system playing the game of Life. This is a 'game' consisting of an infinite two-dimensional space (the universe). A cell is identified by a Cartesian position in the universe. A cell is either alive or dead. When an initial generation of living cells is given, each following generation is computed as follows:

- if a living cell has just two or three living neighbour cells, it survives to the next generation;
- if a dead cell has exactly three living neighbour cells, it becomes alive in the next generation.

In this example we concentrate on the specification of the interactive part of the program, so our prime interest is not, for instance, the function that calculates a new generation given the current generation.

Hence, we assume that the specifications of such functions are already given.

> The following functions are assumed to be given: LifeGame computes, given the current generation of cells, a triplet consisting of the next generation, and, to make drawing of cells easier, the collection of new-born cells and the cells that have passed away. RemoveCell deletes a cell from a generation; adding a cell to a generation is done by AddCell. They are used for the creation of the initial generation by the user.

```
:: LifeGame      Generation  ->  (Generation, Generation, Generation);
:: RemoveCell    LifeCell Generation   ->   Generation;
:: AddCell       LifeCell Generation   ->   Generation;
:: InitialGeneration   ->   Generation;
```

The initial generation of cells has to be specified by the player. The player can add or delete a cell at a certain position by clicking with a *mouse* in a *window*. Then the calculation of generations can be started. There are several options that can be chosen from a *menu* (Figure 8.7).

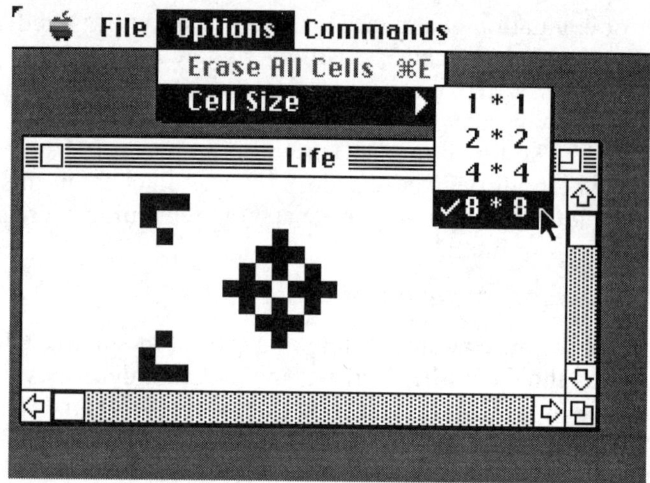

Figure 8.7 **Life** window, **Options** menu and **Cell Size** submenu.

The menu consists of:

- a pull-down menu named **File**, containing:
  - a **Quit** command to terminate the application.
- a pull-down menu named **Options**, containing:
  - an **Erase** command to clear the contents of the window and to create a fresh game with an empty generation;

- a submenu called **Cell Size** to change the size of the cells displayed in the window. Because at most one size is valid at a time, the items are organized as radio items (selection of an item causes the deselection of all others). The initial cell size will be set to **8 * 8** pixels.

- a pull-down menu named **Commands**, containing:
  - a **Play** command to start the continuous computation of next generations. **Play** disables itself such that the command cannot be chosen again. Furthermore, **Erase** will be disabled and **Halt** has to be enabled.
  - a **Halt** command to terminate the computation of generations and reverse all (dis)abling done by **Play**.

When **Play** is chosen from the menu, generations will be computed one after another. If nothing happens, this computation will go on forever. To stop it one has to choose **Halt** from the menu. To make this possible one has to ensure that the program inspects its event queue regularly to see if, for example, **Halt** has been chosen. This can be realized by using the *timer* device with the time interval set to zero. When no events are generated by the user, a timer event is generated automatically that is used to calculate the next generation. If there is a user event, it will get priority. In this way the calculation of generations can be interrupted.

```
MODULE LifeGame;
IMPORT delta;
IMPORT deltaEventIO, deltaMenu, deltaWindow, deltaTimer, deltaPicture;
IMPORT Life;
```

Constants to enhance comprehension and maintenance:

```
MACRO
   FileMenuId -> 1;        OptionsMenuId -> 2;       CommandsMenuId -> 3;
      QuitId -> 11;           EraseId -> 21;            PlayId -> 31;
                              CellSizeId -> 22;         HaltId -> 32;
                                 Size1Id  -> 221;
                                 Size2Id  -> 222;
                                 Size4Id  -> 223;
                                 Size8Id  -> 224;
   TimerID -> 1;              NullInterval    -> 0;
   LifeWindowId -> 1;         MinimumSizeOfWindow -> (50,    50);
   WindowPos    -> (0,0);     InitialSizeOfWindow -> (1000, 1000);
   PictureRange -> ((0,0), (1000,1000));
   ScrollBarH&V -> ScrollBar (Thumb 0) (Scroll 8);
```

The program state State consists of the current generation and the size of the cells displayed in the window. A synonym for the IOState is defined to prevent type rules from cluttering up.

```
TYPE
:: UNQ IO        ->    IOState State;
:: UNQ State     ->    (Generation, Size);
:: Size          ->    INT;
```

The execution of the program starts here. A window is created, to access a null device (which is not active yet) and a menu. The parameters have to obey the algebraic data type defined in the library. The symbols printed in *italic* are the user-defined event handlers. To each menu item a different label (an arbitrary constant number) is attached (an Id) such that one can refer to it later. Observe the close relation between the definitions of the window and menu device and their graphical appearance on the screen.

```
RULE
:: Start UNQ WORLD -> (State, UNQ EVENTS);
   Start world     ->
   StartIO [ menus, timer, window ] initial_program_state [ ] events,
   initial_program_state:  (InitialGeneration, 8),
   (events, world'):       OpenEvents world,
   menus:      MenuSystem [ file, options, cmnds ],
   file:       PullDownMenu FileMenuId "File" Able
                [ MenuItem QuitId "Quit" (Key 'Q') Able Quit     ],
   options:    PullDownMenu OptionsMenuId "Options" Able
               [  MenuItem EraseId "Erase All Cells" (Key 'E') Able Erase,
                  SubMenuItem CellSizeId "Cell Size" Able
               [  MenuRadioItems Size8Id
               [  MenuRadioItem Size1Id "1*1" NoKey Able (ChangeSize 1),
                  MenuRadioItem Size2Id "2*2" NoKey Able (ChangeSize 2),
                  MenuRadioItem Size4Id "4*4" NoKey Able (ChangeSize 4),
                  MenuRadioItem Size8Id "8*8" NoKey Able (ChangeSize 8)
               ]  ]  ],
   cmnds:      PullDownMenu CommandsMenuId "Commands" Able
               [  MenuItem PlayId "Play" (Key 'P') Able Play,
                  MenuItem HaltId "Halt" (Key 'H') Unable Halt
               ],
   timer:      TimerSystem
               [  Timer TimerID Unable NullInterval NextGeneration ],
   window:     WindowSystem
               [  ScrollWindow LifeWindowId WindowPos "Life"
                  ScrollBarH&V ScrollBarH&V PictureRange
                  MinimumSizeOfWindow InitialSizeOfWindow
                  UpdateWindow [ Mouse Able Track ]     ];
```

Next we define the user-defined event handlers. All handlers take two additional arguments of type State and IO and yield a pair of type (State, IO).

```
:: Quit State IO  -> (State, IO);
   Quit state iostate -> (state, QuitIO iostate);

:: Erase State IO -> (State, IO);
   Erase (g, s) io
   ->    (([ ], s), DrawInActiveWindow [ EraseRectangle PictureRange ] io);

:: ChangeSize INT State IO -> (State, IO);
   ChangeSize ns (g, s) io
   ->    ((g, ns), DrawInActiveWindow cells io),
         cells:    [ EraseRectangle PictureRange | Map (DrawCell ns) g ];

:: Play State IO  -> (State, IO);
   Play state io
   ->    (state, ChangeIOState [   DisableActiveMouse,
                                   DisableMenuItems [ PlayId, EraseId ],
                                   EnableMenuItems [ HaltId ],
                                   EnableTimer TimerID   ]   io);

:: Halt State IO  -> (State, IO);
   Halt state io
   ->    (state, ChangeIOState [   DisableTimer TimerID,
                                   DisableMenuItems [ HaltId ],
                                   EnableMenuItems [ PlayId, EraseId ],
                                   EnableActiveMouse     ]   io);
```

A timer event is generated when no other event is present and this is used to calculate a new generation of cells:

```
:: NextGeneration TimerState State IO -> (State, IO);
   NextGeneration tstate (g, s) io
   -> ((ng, s), ChangeIOState [    DrawInActiveWindow erasecells,
                                   DrawInActiveWindow newcells ]   io),
      erasecells:        Map (EraseCell s) died,
      newcells:          Map (DrawCell s) new,
      (ng, new, died):   LifeGame g;
```

UpdateWindow redraws all cells regardless of their visibility:

```
:: UpdateWindow UpdateArea State -> (State, [DrawFunction]);
   UpdateWindow update_area state:(g, s)
   ->    (state, [ EraseRectangle PictureRange | Map (DrawCell s) g ]);
```

Track evaluates all mouse activities in the window:

```
:: Track MouseState State IO -> (State, IO);
   Track (pos, ButtonUp, modifiers) state io   ->     (state, io);
   Track ((x,y), down, (shift,option,command,control)) (g, s) io
   ->     ((remove, s), DrawInActiveWindow erase io),          IF command
   ->     ((add, s), DrawInActiveWindow draw io),
          remove:    RemoveCell cell g,  erase:  [EraseCell s cell],
          add:       AddCell cell g,     draw:   [DrawCell s cell],
          cell:  (/ nx s, / ny s),       nx:   – x (% x s),   ny:   – y (% y s);
```

Auxiliary drawing functions have to be defined. DrawCell draws the cells that have been created and EraseCells draws the cells that have died.

```
:: DrawCell Size LifeCell -> DrawFunction;
   DrawCell s (x, y)     ->     FillRectangle ((px, py), (+ px s, + py s)),
                                px: * x s,    py: * y s;

:: EraseCell Size LifeCell -> DrawFunction;
   EraseCell s (x, y)    ->     EraseRectangle ((px, py), (+ px s, + py s)),
                                px: * x s,    py: * y s;
```

Note that the IOState (the parameter of type IO) is used single-threadedly everywhere in the program (otherwise this program would have been rejected by the compiler). In the example above this is generally done implicitly (using the predefined function ChangeIOState). It can also be done explicitly. Take for example the Play function as defined above. This function can also be defined as follows:

```
:: Play State IO ->    (State, IO);
   Play state io  ->    (state, play),
                        play :    EnableTimer TimerID
                                    ( EnableMenuItems [ HaltId ]
                                      ( DisableMenuItems [ PlayId, EraseId ]
                                        ( DisableActiveMouse io ) ) );
```

Or even more explicitly:

```
:: Play State IO ->    (State, IO);
   Play state io  ->    (state, io4),
                        io1:  DisableActiveMouse io,
                        io2:  DisableMenuItems [ PlayId, EraseId ] io1,
                        io3:  EnableMenuItems [ HaltId ] io2,
                        io4:  EnableTimer TimerID io3;
```

Summary

- Clean is a *lazy*, *higher order functional* programming language based on FGRSs.
- Clean can also be used as *intermediate language* in the compilation path from functional languages to concrete machine architectures.
- *Sharing of computation* can be expressed explicitly by the programmer in a general way, including the possibility of specifying cyclic structures.
- Clean is a *strongly typed* language (based on Milner–Mycroft typing extended for the use of patterns) including *polymorphic types*, *abstract types*, *algebraic types* and *synonym types*, as well as basic types; there are predefined type constructors for *lists*, *tuples* and (curried) *functions*. The type system enhances efficiency, modularity and understandability.
- A Clean program can be decorated with *annotations* that influence the evaluation order.
- With *strict annotations* the evaluation can be made (partially) *eager* instead of *lazy*. Strict annotations are only safe when they are used in such a way that the termination behaviour of the program is not changed. Generally, the annotations are placed on the strict arguments of a function.
- Annotations can be defined by the *programmer* but they can also be generated automatically by the built-in *strictness analyser* of the Clean system. An annotated program generally runs much faster and has a much better space behaviour than a program without annotations.
- Clean has a *modular structure* with *implementation modules* and *definition modules* including a facility to import definitions from other modules implicitly and explicitly; it includes predefined libraries for basic operations (δ-rules) on objects of basic types.
- A *unique type attribute* can be added to the type specification of any object. The type system ensures that such an object can only be used *single-threadedly*. When such an object is passed to a function it can in principle be reused for the construction of the function result. In this way functions can be constructed that perform destructive updates without loosing referential transparency.
- With the help of the unique type attribute and higher order functions a library has been written in Clean that enables a *high-level specification* of *interactive programs* that use *windows*, *dialogs*, *menus* and the like.

EXERCISES

8.1 Describe *all* reduction paths for the initial expression G (H 0) given the rules below if they are valid (a) Miranda, (b) Clean, (c) TRS, (d) GRS rules. Ignore small syntactic differences between the systems.

```
F (H 0)   x = x
F 1       x = x
H x = 1
G x = F x x
```

In the following exercises a task is given for which a Clean program has to be written. Specify the type of each rule. Invent appropriate (partially strict) data structures when necessary. Utilize sharing and cycles to prevent computations being carried out more than once.

8.2 Compute a list of all Fibonacci numbers.

8.3 Compute the powerset of a given set (represent a set as a list, multiple occurrences of an element in the list are not allowed).

8.4 Given a function f and a set of values X, compute the closure of f and X: $clos(f, X) = \{ f^n(x) \mid n \in Nat, x \in X \}$.

8.5 Compute Pascal's triangle (to a certain depth) in a neatly formatted way. This triangle consists of numbers such that each number is the sum of the numbers just to the right and just to the left of it, on the line above it. The sides of the triangle consist of 1s. Part of the triangle is given here:

```
         1
      1     1
   1     2     1
1     3     3     1
```

8.6 Read a file, named 'perm.in', containing some permutation of the numbers 1 to n. To determine n ask the user for input. After reading in this file find out which permutation cycles the permutation in the file consists of. Write these permutation cycles to a file named 'cycles.out'.

Suppose the file contains 2 4 3 1, which is a permutation of the numbers 1 to 4; then it consists of the permutation cycles (1 2 4) and (3).

8.7 Implement the functions LifeGame, RemoveCell, AddCell and InitialGeneration as applied in Section 8.6.4.

8.8* Refine the CopyF function of Section 8.6.2 such that it asks interactively the names of the files. Open StdIO to get a standard window to prompt the user for the file names. Open StdErr to display error messages. Allow StdIO as one of the file names. Make the program robust such that wrong file names cannot lead to abortion of the program. Make a more user-friendly version of the program by using file selector dialogs.

8.9* Program a simple pocket calculator that can be used by pressing buttons in a dialog definition.

8.10* Write the well-known Tetris game. Define suitable menus and dialogs. Add a help file and a high-score list.

8.11* Write a matrix multiplication program using a UNQ ARRAY INT and using an [[INT]]. Measure the time–space behaviour of both representations and explain the differences.

8.12* Write in C an imperatively written program (assignments allowed) that sorts a list using the quicksort algorithm. Write a quicksort function in Clean. Also write the quicksort algorithm defined on lists with a unique spine. Measure the differences in time–space behaviour and explain them.

8.13* Write a non-trivial program (e.g. the λ-reducer of Exercise 3.7) in Clean, an imperative language, an object oriented language and a logical language. Which style of programming did you like most? Why? Measure and compare the efficiency in both time and space. Also measure the effect of the strictness analyser.

Chapter 9
Translation into Clean

In this chapter the most important advanced language concepts offered by a lazy functional language such as Miranda are transformed into an FGRS-based language such as Clean (Figure 9.1). The transformation schemes take Miranda explicitly as the source language, but they can also serve as a guideline for the translation of other lazy functional languages.

As a 'side-effect', this chapter gives a better insight in the semantics of the treated language concepts, especially with respect to sharing.

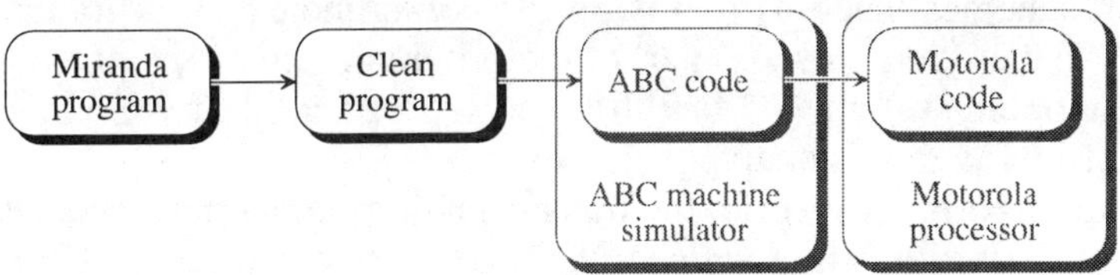

Figure 9.1 The first translation step: translating a Miranda script into an equivalent Clean program.

The goal of the transformation schemes is to obtain Clean code that is as efficient as possible. The transformation schemes presented in this chapter are based on the standard transformation techniques (Peyton Jones, 1987). However, some changes have been made to generate *better code* and to employ *sharing* as much as possible (Koopman and Nöcker, 1988) to avoid redundant computation.

During the transformation auxiliary functions are inevitably generated. The transformation schemes are designed in such a way that generation of new functions is reduced to a minimum.

A significant increase of execution speed can be obtained when a function is known to be strict in an argument of basic type (see Section 8.3). The corresponding analysis is not performed during the translation from Miranda to Clean but it is left to the strictness analyser of the Concurrent Clean System (see Chapter 7).

The transformation is performed in two phases. In the first phase a Miranda program is desugared by translating it into an equivalent program in a Miranda subset that is very Clean-like. This approach has the advantage that most transformations can be defined by using the semantics of Miranda itself (Section 9.1). As much as possible of Miranda is desugared in this way: list comprehensions (Section 9.3), local function definitions (Section 9.4) and various other small syntactical constructs (Section 9.2).

Phase two (Section 9.5) is relatively straightforward: an almost trivial syntactical transformation is needed to convert a program in the desugared language into an equivalent Clean program. Finally we discuss how sharing can be exploited in the transformation of Miranda to Clean (Section 9.6).

9.1 About the desugaring of the language

In the first phase Miranda programs are desugared by transforming them into a Miranda subset that is syntactically similar to Clean. These transformations can be split into relatively simple changes such as the transfer from infix into prefix notation and the more complex transformation schemes, such as removing list comprehensions. Miranda constructs that are more or less part of the programming environment, such as the module system, I/O facilities and predefined library modules, are not considered in this chapter.

An important aspect in the transformations concerns a special kind of local definition: the **local constant** definition, i.e. a local function definition with *zero* arguments or a local *tuple* definition. In the following a strict distinction will be made between local *constant* definitions and local *function* definitions (the other local definitions). Local constants can be defined in Clean as well as in Miranda and therefore they will *not* be moved to a global level (see Section 9.4). In the second phase (see also Section 9.5) the local constant definitions are translated directly into the equivalent node-id definitions in Clean. In Clean they will be *shared* automatically such that duplication of computation is avoided. In several transformation schemes local constant definitions are introduced to avoid duplication of work.

Most of the program transformations are easy, others are a bit more difficult. It is not always evident which transformation scheme will yield the most efficient code. In some cases several alternatives for a particular transformation are given. The following remarks hold for all transformations:

- The transformation schemes produce standard Miranda expressions (e.g. infix notation). This is merely done for readability. Actually, the expressions thus generated in their turn also have to be transformed into the wanted Miranda subset.
- Some transformations require the insertion of new local definitions. In Miranda local definitions are only allowed at particular places. The transformation schemes do not take this into account, simply because it would make the description unreadable.
- Often it does not matter very much in which order the transformations are being performed. But rule lifting, i.e. moving all local function definitions (including the ones inserted by the transformations) to a global level, should be done at the end.
- In some transformations (new) names are introduced. It is assumed that these names do not conflict with already existing names.

Trivial transformations are explained with the help of examples. In other cases the transformation schemes (called MirSMir) are more formally specified in the usual manner.

9.2 Simple transformations

Since pattern matching is available in Miranda as well as in Clean, pattern matching can generally be translated directly without any changes. However, some special patterns are allowed in Miranda and not in Clean. In particular, *irrefutable patterns*, *comparing rules*, *constructor definitions* and *omitted arguments in function definitions* have to be transformed into Clean-like definitions. Furthermore, Miranda allows *infix* notation and Clean generally allows only *prefix* notation.

Infix notation

In Miranda there are many predefined infix operators with various binding powers. User-defined infix operators are also possible. Furthermore, mathematical expressions like a < b < c can occur. In Clean, the prefix notation is generally used and all functions have the same binding power. Infix notations can be removed easily. The general transformation is (in which i_1, i_2 stand for infix symbols, and e_1, e_2 and e_3 stand for arbitrary expressions):

$$\text{MirSMir}\,[\![\, e_1\ i_1\ e_2\ i_2\ e_3 \,]\!] = (\&)\ ((i_1)\ e_1\ s)\ \text{MirSMir}\,[\![\, s\ i_2\ e_3 \,]\!]\ \text{where}\quad s = e_2$$
$$\text{MirSMir}\,[\![\, e_1\ i_1\ e_2 \,]\!] = (i_1)\ e_1\ e_2$$

For instance, a < b < c is translated as:

```
MirSMir ⟦ a < b < c ⟧  →  (&) ((<) a s) MirSMir ⟦ s < c ⟧   where  s = b
                       →  (&) ((<) a s) ((<) s c)            where  s = b
```

In the transformation new local constant definitions are generated to achieve sharing in Clean.

The match on syntactic constructs automatically takes care of the various binding powers, as illustrated in the example below:

```
MirSMir ⟦ 2 < 3 + 1 ⟧  →  (<) 2 MirSMir ⟦ 3 + 1 ⟧   →   (<) 2 ((+) 3 1)
```

Comparing rules

In Miranda a variable can occur multiple times on a left-hand side. Such a function alternative is called a **comparing rule**, which is only chosen if the values corresponding to this variable are equal.

The following rule will only be chosen if the two arguments are equal:

```
f x x  =  x
```

Comparing is not allowed in FGRSs and hence it is also prohibited in Clean. However, a δ-rule is defined that tests the equality of normal forms. The transformation is therefore the following:

Redefine the rule above by:

```
f x y  =  x,  if x = y
```

Since the guard is evaluated after the pattern is matched, in particular cases (e.g. when the left-hand side of the rule is f x x 2) one has to take care that the order in which the tests and matches are performed is not changed by the transformation. This can be realized by generating auxiliary function definitions.

Irrefutable patterns

In Miranda no evaluation is forced for an argument corresponding to a pattern if the type checker guarantees that the evaluated argument will always match the pattern. Such patterns are called **irrefutable patterns**.

Consider the following Miranda function definition:

```
f:: (*, **) -> num
f (x, y)   =  3
```

In this function a tuple is specified as pattern, but the tuple elements are not used in the function body. The type system guarantees that the function is always applied on a tuple. So pattern matching is in this case not necessary.

Clean would force evaluation for these kinds of pattern. This may lead to unintended non-termination if the function is not strict in its argument and the argument does not have a root normal form.

The problem is solved by eliminating the pattern match and including some way in which the components of the pattern can be accessed in a lazy manner. This is done by adding local constructor definitions (see below) or projection functions.

A correct translation of the example above is

```
f:: (*, **) -> num
f z    = 3  where (x, y)   = z
```

Constructor definitions

A **constructor definition** is a (possibly local) definition in which the defined symbol is not a function but a constructor. Such a definition is effectively used to define projection functions yielding the arguments of the constructor.

```
C 2 x y  = e
```

C is a Miranda constructor. In this way projection functions x and y are defined and a test on the value of the first argument of C is induced.

A possible translation involves the explicit definition of the corresponding objects using projection functions.

The example above is translated into:

```
x  =  f1 z
y  =  f2 z
z  =  e
f1 (C 2 a b)    =  a
f2 (C 2 a b)    =  b
```

If the definitions are local, then after the transformations of the second phase e will be shared in Clean.

A disadvantage of this method is the generation of new projection functions for each occurrence of a constructor definition. In practice the same projection functions can be used for many different occurrences.

Omitted arguments in function definitions

In Miranda it is not required to specify the same number of arguments in all alternatives of a function definition.

In the definition of f some of its arguments are omitted:

```
f 1    = fac
f a 2  = a * 3
f b    = (*) 5,     if b < 0
       = (–) 2,     if b > 5
f      = plus
```

In Clean function definitions have fixed arity so such definitions have to be transformed. The omitted arguments are added on the left-hand side as well as to corresponding expressions on the right-hand side.

The example above with added arguments becomes:

```
f 1 x  =  fac x
f a 2  =  a * 3
f b x  =  (*) 5 x,   if b < 0
       =  (–) 2 x,   if b > 5
f x y  =  plus x y
```

9.3 List comprehensions

In this section we shall formally specify how dotdot expressions and non-diagonalized *ZF*-expressions can be desugared into function definitions. Diagonalized *ZF*-expressions are not treated. For non-diagonalized *ZF*-expressions besides the standard transformation method (Peyton Jones, 1987) a method that generates more efficient code is described. This method makes use of patterns and compile-time continuations (Koopman and Nöcker, 1988).

9.3.1 Dotdot expressions

In Section 2.2 the semantics of dotdot expressions was explained with the help of two auxiliary functions, inbetween and from. The general translation of such dotdot expressions is as follows (in which a, b and c stand for arbitrary numeral expressions):

```
MirSMir ⟦ [a..b] ⟧     =  inbetween a b 1
MirSMir ⟦ [a..] ⟧      =  from a 1
MirSMir ⟦ [a, b..c] ⟧  =  inbetween s c (b – s)   where   s  =  a
MirSMir ⟦ [a, b..] ⟧   =  from s (b – s)          where   s  =  a
```

New local constant definitions are generated for the use of sharing.

9.3.2 *ZF*-expressions

The translation of non-diagonalized *ZF*-expressions is more difficult. Two methods are given. The first scheme is primarily given to make the semantics of non-diagonalized *ZF*-expressions clear, but it is not very efficient. At run-time a lot of time is wasted concatenating empty lists. The second scheme presented is more complex, but it also generates more efficient code.

Simple transformation of ZF-expressions

The following transformations are essentially the same as the basic transformation schemes given in Peyton Jones (1987). As with the transformation of the dotdot expressions, the original expression is not duplicated during the transformation. Instead new local definitions are generated in such a way that, after the transformations of the second phase, the original expression is shared in Clean.

ZF-expressions can be translated as follows (in which e stands for an arbitrary expression, b for a Boolean-valued filter, q for a list of qualifiers, p, p_1 and p_n for patterns, x, y and z for simple variables, and list and l_1 for a list-valued expression):

```
MirSMir ⟦ [e | b] ⟧               = cond b [e] [ ]
MirSMir ⟦ [e | b;q] ⟧             = cond b MirSMir ⟦ [e | q] ⟧ [ ]
MirSMir ⟦ [e | p <- list] ⟧       = flatmap f list
                                    where  f p   = [e]
                                           f x   = [ ]
MirSMir ⟦ [e | p <- list;q] ⟧     = flatmap f list
                                    where  f p   = MirSMir ⟦ [e | q] ⟧
                                           f x   = [ ]
MirSMir ⟦ [e | p1, ..., pn <- list] ⟧   = MirSMir ⟦ [e | p1 <- l1;...;pn <- l1] ⟧
                                    where  l1    = list
MirSMir ⟦ [e | p1, ..., pn <- list;q] ⟧ = MirSMir ⟦ [e | p1 <- l1;...;pn <- l1;q] ⟧
                                    where  l1    = list
```

The function cond is the conditional with boolean, 'then' part and 'else' part arguments. This function is used instead of guards, since guards cannot be nested easily. It is sensible to replace, at a later stage, the applications of cond as much as possible by guards.

The local constant definitions for l_1 are generated to create sharing in Clean. The local function definition for f is generated in order to achieve the proper projection from the pattern p to the expression e. The second alternative of f is only needed for the case where the pattern p is not just a simple variable.

The function flatmap is a variant of map (see Chapter 2). It is defined below:

```
flatmap:: (* -> [**]) -> [*] -> [**]
flatmap f [ ]        = [ ]
flatmap f (x : r)    = f x ++ flatmap f r
```

In spite of the introduced sharing the transformation scheme given above is not very efficient because at run-time many empty lists are concatenated.

Take the following Miranda expression computing all Pythagorean triangles with sides less than or equal to n and a<b<c:

```
pyth n   =  [ (a, b, c) | a, b, c <- [1..n]; a<b<c; a^2 + b^2 = c^2 ]
```

According to the simple transformation scheme given above, this *ZF*-expression will be translated into:

```
pyth n   =  flatmap f1 list
            where
            list  =  [1..n]
            f1 a  =  flatmap f2 list
                     where
                     f2 b  =  flatmap f3 list
                              where
                              f3 c  =  cond (a<b<c)
                                                 (cond (a^2+b^2=c^2) [(a, b, c)] [ ])
                                                 [ ]
```

The code yields the concatenation of almost n^3 empty lists.

More efficient transformation of ZF-expressions

There are several ways to improve the transformation schemes given above (see also Peyton Jones, 1987). We will treat here the scheme of Koopman and Nöcker (1988). It presents an alternative transformation by using patterns. Furthermore, an additional argument is used in the transformation scheme to remember where the generation of list elements has to be continued. The advantage of the scheme is that it does not generate empty lists nor append functions. The proposed scheme also contains a slight optimization in the sequence of filters.

```
MirSMir ⟦ [e | q] ⟧                  = MirSMir' ⟦ [e | q] ⟧ [ ]

MirSMir' ⟦ [e | b1;b2] ⟧ r           = MirSMir' ⟦ [e | b1&b2] ⟧ r
MirSMir' ⟦ [e | b1;b2;q] ⟧ r         = MirSMir' ⟦ [e | (b1&b2);q] ⟧ r
```

```
MirSMir' ⟦ [e | b] ⟧ r                 = cond b (e : r) r
MirSMir' ⟦ [e | b;q] ⟧ r               = cond b (MirSMir' ⟦ [e | q] ⟧ r) r
MirSMir' ⟦ [e | p <- list] ⟧ r         = f list
                                          where
                                          f [ ]     = r
                                          f (p : y) = e : f y
                                          f (x : y) = f y
MirSMir' ⟦ [e | p <- list;q] ⟧ r       = f list
                                          where
                                          f [ ]     = r
                                          f (p : y) = MirSMir' ⟦ [e | q] ⟧ (f y)
                                          f (x : y) = f y
MirSMir' ⟦ [e | p1, ..., pn <- list] ⟧ r   = MirSMir' ⟦ [e | p1 <- l1;...;pn <- l1] ⟧ r
                                              where  l1 = list
MirSMir' ⟦ [e | p1, ..., pn <- list;q] ⟧ r = MirSMir' ⟦ [e | p1 <- l1;...;pn <- l1;q] ⟧ r
                                              where  l1 = list
```

r is used to remember where the evaluation has to be continued if a generator has come to the end of the generated list. This is specified in the first alternative of the locally defined function f in the scheme. The last alternative of this function f is only needed when p is a pattern that is not just a simple variable.

An empty list is passed as an additional argument to the new transformation scheme. The previous transformation schemes are only slightly changed to pass the extra argument. Furthermore, two rules are inserted to obtain better code in the case that multiple filters are specified. Finally, the two rules for generators are replaced by two rules that employ the continuation passed in the extra argument.

With this new scheme the Pythagorean triangles will be translated into:

```
pyth n  = f1 list
          where
          list     = [1..n]
          f1 [ ]   = [ ]
          f1 (a:x) = f2 list
                     where
                     f2 [ ]   = f1 x
                     f2 (b:x) = f3 list
                                where
                                f3 [ ]   = f2 x
                                f3 (c:x) = cond (a<b<c & a^2+b^2=c^2)
                                                ((a, b, c) : f3 x)
                                                (f3 x)
```

ZF-expressions are very concise constructs. A disadvantage is that even with the most efficient transformation scheme they are transformed into many function definitions and applications. So a functional program with many *ZF*-expressions might be a beautiful specification, but it is in many cases an inefficient program.

Recurrent generators

The previous scheme for *ZF*-expressions is further extended such that it can also deal with recurrent generators. In Chapter 2 we explained that the meaning of a recurrent generator can be expressed with the help of the function iterate. So a recurrent generator can be translated by adding the following rules:

```
MirSMir' ⟦ [e | p <- e0, en..] ⟧ r      = MirSMir' ⟦ [e | p <- iterate g e0] ⟧ r
                                          where  g p  = en
MirSMir' ⟦ [e | p <- e0, en..;q] ⟧ r    = MirSMir' ⟦ [e | p <- iterate g e0;q] ⟧ r
                                          where  g p  = en
```

9.4 Local function definitions

A functional program containing local function definitions has to be transformed in such a way that all function definitions are on the global level, such as is the case in Clean. This transformation is called **rule lifting**. The general idea is to make the local functions self-contained by adding parameters for certain variables (*free* variables). The extra arguments have to be added in front of the original parameters, since for curried applications of functions generally not all original arguments are available (see also the example below).

Take the definition of a local function p in the following definition of filter:

```
filter a (b:x)   = p a,       if b mod a = 0
                 = g b p a,  otherwise
                   where p y  =  filter y x
g x y z          = x : y z
```

It will be first transformed into:

```
filter a (b:x)   = p x a,          if b mod a = 0
                 = g b (p x) a,    otherwise
                   where p x y   =  filter y x
g x y z          = x : y z
```

p is used in a curried way. Therefore it is necessary that the extra argument x is added in front of the original argument. This extra argument is added both to the definition of p as well as to the applications of p. Now the definition of p is self-contained and it can be lifted:

```
filter a (b:x)    = cond ((b mod a) = 0) (p x a) (g b (p x) a)
p x y             = filter y x
g x y z           = x : y z
```

A self-contained local definition can be moved freely to the global level. Of course, when moving a local definition to a global level, names have to be changed if the name of the function already occurred at that level. In this section rule lifting is discussed in general and an example is given of a rule lifter for Miranda.

λ-lifters are well-known lifting algorithms (Johnsson, 1985) that are defined for λ-calculus-based expressions. The lifting process defined in this section basically follows the same algorithm but there are some differences. In particular, *rule lifters* are able to handle patterns and multiple alternatives as well.

Rule lifting is not so easy. First of all, all rule alternatives of one function definition can be mutually dependent, and therefore they all have to be lifted together. In Miranda, even functions defined on different levels can depend on each other (see the example after the specification of the lifting algorithm). Therefore, all local functions of a global function have to be lifted simultaneously, taking the scope rules of Miranda into account. Furthermore, local *constant* definitions should *not* be lifted to the global level. However, local constant definitions can be nested (in contrast to node-id definitions in Clean) so they *do* have to be lifted to one and the same *local* level.

A rule lifter for Miranda

First of all, it is assumed that all names are (made) unique. Then, let f be a function, defined on the global level, and g_i be functions (not constants) defined locally at some level of that rule. Furthermore, where in the following definitions **right-hand side** is used, it stands for the expression on the right-hand side of a function definition *with* its local *constant* definitions but *without* the local *function* definitions. With these assumptions define:

$V(g_i)$: the set of *variables* on the right-hand sides of the rule-alternatives of g_i: i.e. all identifiers on the right-hand sides that are *neither defining names* of global definitions nor of local function definitions;

$LF(g_i)$: the set of names of *local functions* applied on a right-hand side of a rule-alternative of g_i;

$BV(g_i)$: the set of *bound variables* of the rule-alternatives of g_i; **bound variables** are the names that occur as (part of the) arguments on the left-hand side of a rule-alternative or as a defining name of a local constant definition that is contained within g_i;

FV(g_i): the complete set of **free variables** of a local function g_i. This set is defined by the following equation:

$$FV(g_i) = (V(g_i) \cup All\_FV(g_j)) - BV(g_i)$$

in which $All\_FV(g_j)$ is the union of all $FV(g_j)$, $g_j \in LF(g_i)$ and – denotes set difference.

Due to mutual dependencies in LF, the defining equation of FV can be recursive. So possibly a collection of recursive set equations has to be solved. This can be done by repeatedly substituting approximations in the equations until a fixed point is reached, i.e. all resulting sets of two subsequent approximations are the same. When empty sets are used as the initial approximation, the fixed point will be the least solution.

With these definitions the algorithm for lifting is the following:

(1) for each local function g_i determine the sets V, LF, BV and FV by solving the equations;
(2) add the elements of the set of free variables FV(g_i) as extra parameters (in front of the original parameters) to each occurrence of a function g_i and to its definition;
(3) move all local *function* definitions to the global level;
(4) lift all remaining local *constant* definitions to one local level in the rule in which they are defined.

The lifting algorithm is applied in the following function definition:

```
f x y z  =  g s s
            where
            s       =  r + k r
                       where
                       r       =  y + z
            g a b   =  h a a + k t
                       where
                       h 0 c   =  10 + t
                       h d e   =  g (b + e) (y + 1)
                       t       =  a + x
            k q     =  q + z
```

There are three local functions defined (g, h and k) and three local constants (s, r and t). All names are already unique.

Step 1. $V(g) = \{a, t, x\}$ $V(h) = \{b, y, e, t\}$ $V(k) = \{z, q\}$
$LF(g) = \{h, k\}$ $LF(h) = \{g\}$ $LF(k) = \{\}$
$BV(g) = \{a, b, t\}$ $BV(h) = \{c, d, e\}$ $BV(k) = \{q\}$

$$
\begin{aligned}
FV(g) &= (V(g) \cup FV(h) \cup FV(k)) - BV(g) \\
FV(h) &= (V(h) \cup FV(g)) - BV(h) \\
FV(k) &= V(k) - BV(k)
\end{aligned}
$$

So the following recursive set equations have to be solved:

$$
\begin{aligned}
FV(g) &= (\{a, t, x\} \cup FV(h) \cup FV(k)) - \{a, b, t\} \\
FV(h) &= (\{b, y, e, t\} \cup FV(g)) - \{c, d, e\} \\
FV(k) &= \{z, q\} - \{q\}
\end{aligned}
$$

Starting with the empty set as initial approximation for the recursive equation:

$$
\begin{aligned}
FV_1(g) &= (\{a, t, x\} \cup FV_0(h) \cup \{z\}) - \{a, b, t\} \\
&= (\{a, t, x\} \cup \{z\}) - \{a, b, t\} \\
&= \{x, z\} \\
FV_1(h) &= (\{b, y, e, t\} \cup FV_0(g)) - \{c, d, e\} \\
FV_1(h) &= (\{b, y, e, t\}) - \{c, d, e\} \\
&= \{b, y, t\} \\
FV(k) &= \{z\}
\end{aligned}
$$

The second subsequent approximation will be:

$$
\begin{aligned}
FV_2(g) &= (\{a, t, x\} \cup FV_1(h) \cup \{z\}) - \{a, b, t\} \\
&= (\{a, t, x\} \cup \{b, y, t\} \cup \{z\}) - \{a, b, t\} \\
&= \{x, y, z\} \\
FV_2(h) &= (\{b, y, e, t\} \cup FV_1(g)) - \{c, d, e\} \\
&= (\{b, y, e, t\} \cup \{x, z\}) - \{c, d, e\} \\
&= \{b, y, t, x, z\} \\
FV(k) &= \{z\}
\end{aligned}
$$

The result of the third subsequent approximation equals the second:

$$
\begin{aligned}
FV_3(g) &= (\{a, t, x\} \cup FV_2(h) \cup \{z\}) - \{a, b, t\} \\
&= (\{a, t, x\} \cup \{b, y, t, x, z\} \cup \{z\}) - \{a, b, t\} \\
&= \{x, y, z\} \\
&= FV_2(g) \\
FV_3(h) &= (\{b, y, e, t\} \cup FV_1(g)) - \{c, d, e\} \\
&= (\{b, y, e, t\} \cup \{x, y, z\}) - \{c, d, e\} \\
&= \{b, y, t, x, z\} \\
&= FV_2(h) \\
FV(k) &= \{z\}
\end{aligned}
$$

So the fixed point solution is:

```
FV (g)  = {x, y, z}
FV (h)  = {b, y, t, x, z}
FV (k)  = {z}
```

Step 2. To all occurrences of g, h and k the variables of the corresponding FV set are added as parameters in front of the original parameters:

```
f x y z  = g x y z s s
           where
           s          = r + k z r
                        where
                        r          = y + z
           g x y z a b = h b y t x z a a + k z t
                        where
                        h b y t x z 0 c = 10 + t
                        h b y t x z d e = g x y z (b + e) (y + 1)
                        t          = a + x
           k z q      = q + z
```

Step 3. All local function definitions are made global; the result will be:

```
f x y z          = g x y z s s
                   where  s  =  r + k z r
                                where  r  =  y + z
g x y z a b      = h b y t x z a a + k z t
                   where  t  =  a + x
h b y t x z 0 c = 10 + t
h b y t x z d e = g x y z (b + e) (y + 1)
k z q            = q + z
```

Step 4. Finally, all local constant definitions are lifted to the same local level:

```
f x y z          = g x y z s s
                   where  s  =  r + k z r
                          r  =  y + z
g x y z a b      = h b y t x z a a + k z t
                   where  t  =  a + x
h b y t x z 0 c = 10 + t
h b y t x z d e = g x y z (b + e) (y + 1)
k z q            = q + z
```

9.5 Translating the desugared language into Clean

The subset of Miranda resulting from the program transformations described in the previous sections is chosen in such a way that the translation of this subset into an equivalent Clean program is relatively straightforward: it is reduced to merely a syntax transformation. Expressions will be represented by graphs, and function definitions become rewrite rules. Variables in functions are represented by node identifiers. So in this way *sharing* of computation is actually introduced.

Furthermore, local constant definitions are syntactically transformed into node definitions, yielding again sharing of computation. For each kind of Miranda type there is an equivalent in Clean via a simple syntactic transformation that is not given here (see Chapter 8).

From function definitions to rewrite rules

The following syntax transformations are needed to change a function definition in the Miranda subset into a rewrite rule in Clean:

- Rename every function in such a way that it starts with an upper case character, to make it a proper Clean symbol (be careful to cause no name conflicts with constructors); also rename the standard basic functions to their Clean δ-rule equivalent.
- Add a ';' to the end of each function alternative.
- Replace the 'where' symbol by a ',', replace the '=' by a '->' where it separates left- and right-hand sides in a rule definition, but by a ':' where it is used to separate sides in a local constant definition;; in guards: replace 'if' by 'IF' and remove ',' and 'otherwise' where necessary; let introduced node definitions be preceded with a ','.
- Remove redundant brackets.

The example used in the section on rule lifting transformed into Clean:

```
F x y z           ->    G x y z s s,
                        s: + r (K z r),
                        r: + y z;
G x y z a b       ->    + (H b y t x z a a) (K z t),
                        t: + a x;
H b y t x z 0 c   ->    + 10 t;
H b y t x z d e   ->    G x y z (+ b e) (+ y 1);
K z q             ->    + q z;
```

Numerals

In Miranda, there is no upper bound to the numerals that can be used in arithmetic. In Clean however, the standard integer arithmetic available on the machine is used. So if the reach of this arithmetic is not sufficient one can either use Clean reals (floating-point numbers) or one has to define a suitable module that implements Miranda-like unbounded arithmetic on numbers.

9.6 The exploitation of sharing

The generation of sharing and of cycles is, in particular, very important, since it can greatly improve the efficiency of the program, effectively reducing the computational complexity of the specification. In the previous sections local constant definitions were introduced when possible such that expressions are not unnecessarily duplicated and become shared in Clean. In this section three important transformations are discussed that carry the exploitation of sharing even further: *sharing of common subexpressions*, *creating cycles* and *sharing results of partial applications*.

Find common subexpressions

For subexpressions that occur more than once on a right-hand side an extra constant definition can be inserted which induces sharing in Clean.

Sharing common subexpressions on the right-hand side:

```
f x    =  (x + 1) + (x + 1)
```

This can be transformed into:

```
f x    =  s + s     where   s  =  x + 1
```

This will lead to sharing the expression x + 1 in Clean.

It is also possible to make use of the occurrence of common subexpressions on the left- and right-hand sides. This is the case when a term is used as a pattern while this same term is also used in the function body. In Clean, rebuilding of the graph for such a term can be avoided by explicitly specifying a node-id for the term on the left-hand side and by using that node-id on the right-hand side instead of duplicating the term again.

Consider the Miranda definition:

```
f (Cons 1 (Cons a Nil))    x  =  Cons 1 (Cons a Nil)
f y                        x  =  x
```

In Clean, rebuilding the graph Cons 1 (Cons a Nil) can be avoided as follows:

```
F y : (Cons 1 (Cons a Nil))   x  ->   y ;
F y                           x  ->   x ;
```

Create cycles

The transformations described in the previous sections generate cycles in Clean if a local constant definition is recursive.

A recursive local constant definition generating a cycle in Clean:

```
f g   =  map g ones    where    ones = Cons 1 ones
```

Since the local constant definition is translated directly to a node-id definition this will create a cycle in Clean:

```
F g   =  Map g ones,
         ones: Cons 1 ones;
```

Generating cycles for global constant definitions can be achieved by generating extra local constant definitions.

A recursive global constant definition in Miranda:

```
ham  =  1 : merge (map (* 2) ham) (map (* 3) ham)
```

A cycle will be generated in Clean if this definition is transformed into

```
ham  =  x  where   x  =  1 : merge (map (* 2) x) (map (* 3) x)
```

Sharing results of partial applications

When in a lazy evaluation of a computation sharing is applied in such a way that even every partial application is evaluated at most once, this evaluation is called **fully lazy**. In general, computation in Clean is not fully lazy since the semantics of Clean does not require any special evaluation behaviour for partial applications.

Take the following Miranda program and its standard transformation to Clean:

```
g x y =  x * x + y
f x   =  x 3 + x 5
h x   =  f (g x)

G x y    ->     + (* x x) y;
```

```
F x     ->    + (x 3) (x 5);
H x     ->    F (G x);
```

Evaluating H 35 the partial application G 35 is constructed. But no special computation is involved for such a partial application. The two calls G 35 3 and G 35 5 are separately computed and * 35 35 will be computed twice. So in some sense the computation involved with the partial application G 35 is done twice. Hence, this evaluation is not fully lazy in Clean.

It is, however, possible to transform Miranda in such a way into Clean rules that effectively the Miranda computation is performed in a fully lazy manner. This can be achieved by generating *super-combinators* (Hughes, 1982). **Super-combinators** have the property that evaluation by standard graph rewriting is fully lazy.

In Clean, all classes of combinatory expressions can be expressed. Hence it is also possible to specify or generate super-combinators, which can be done as follows. First, the largest subexpressions that only depend on one argument of the function, the **maximal free expressions**, are determined. Then, for each maximal free expression a new function is defined of one argument, with as body the maximal free expression.

In the example above x * x is a maximal free expression in the function g. So a new function is defined: g' x = x * x.

Furthermore, a new function is defined with as body the body of the original function in which every maximal free expression is replaced by a fresh variable. In the parameter list of the new function such a fresh variable replaces the argument on which the corresponding maximal free expression depends. Finally, the original function body is adjusted, calling the newly created functions.

After defining the new function g'' and adjusting the definition of g the final set of function definitions becomes:

```
g' x     = x * x
g'' z y  = z + y
g a      = g'' (g' a)
f x      = x 3 + x 5
h x      = f (g x)
```

The main drawback of super-combinators is the huge number of combinator rules that are generated in this way. Besides that, they are only of use if there really are such partially applied shared functions. Even in that case it is doubtful whether the additional effort needed to maintain the sharing will be less than the resulting increase of execution speed. If the choice is made to transform a Miranda program into a super-combinator program this transformation has to be done before the rule lifting, and on local definitions the algorithm for generating super-combinators has to be slightly adapted. An example is given below.

Consider, for instance, the following definition:

```
f x    = g 3 + g 5   where  g y      = x * x + y
```

It can be translated into

```
f x    = g 3 + g 5   where  g'       = x * x
                            g'' z y  = z + y
                            g        = g'' g'
```

The definitions of g' and g are local constant definitions to increase sharing. The definition of g'' will be lifted to the global level afterwards.

Summary

- A Miranda program can be translated into an equivalent Clean program in the following way: first, a Miranda program is translated into an equivalent program in a Clean-like Miranda subset, then the program in this subset is transformed via simple syntactical rules into an equivalent Clean program.
- Most of these transformations are straightforward. The more difficult transformations are:
  - the translation of *ZF-expressions*;
  - the *lifting* of local definitions to one global level.
- The transformations give (as a side-effect) a better understanding of the precise meaning of many constructs in Miranda. One of the reasons for this is that by defining the transformation into a graph rewriting language one *automatically defines* the places where *sharing* is used in the computation.
- During the transformations *sharing* can be *introduced* in several ways: by introducing local constant definitions, by sharing common subexpressions, by creating cycles and by generating super-combinators. Sharing can greatly improve the efficiency of the computation.

EXERCISES

9.1 Use both of the given translation schemes for *ZF*-expressions to transform:

(a) `f = [ a | a,b <- [0..100]; a = b * b ]`
(b) `cartprod x y = [ (a,b) | a <- x; b <- y ]`

9.2 Apply the given rule lifting algorithm to:

```
f x    = h (a + a)
         where  a      = g x y
                         where  g   = h
                                y   = a * a
                h p q  = p + q + x
```

9.3* Translate the exercises of Chapter 2 to Clean. Explain which transformations have been used. Measure the time–space behaviour of the original programs and the Clean programs. Explain the differences.

Chapter 10
The abstract ABC machine

This chapter introduces the architecture and instruction set of an *abstract* machine: the *ABC machine* (Koopman *et al.*, 1990). The instruction set of the ABC machine is used as an intermediate language in the compilation path from functional language to concrete machine instructions (Figure 10.1). This intermediate language is on a much more concrete level of abstraction than Clean. With this abstract machine graph reduction can be described in terms of low-level, imperative machine instructions.

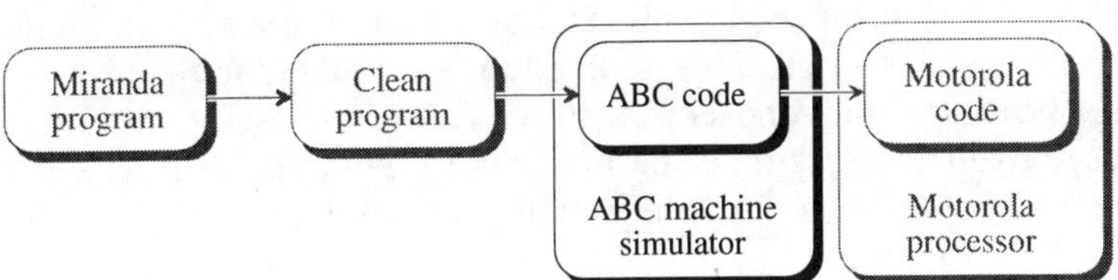

Figure 10.1 Graph rewriting on a more concrete level: the ABC machine and its instruction set.

First a motivation and global overview of the architecture of the ABC machine is given (Section 10.1). A, B and C stand for the three stacks of this abstract machine. The architecture of the ABC machine is a mixture between an idealized graph rewriting machine and a more traditional stack-based machine architecture.

The ABC machine is specified in a functional language, so in this chapter we also show that a very elegant specification of a highly imperative system can be given in a functional language. In this way a prototype implementation of the abstract machine is obtained, almost effortlessly, that can actually be used to execute ABC instructions. A complete specification of the ABC machine is found in Appendix C.

The ABC machine is composed of several kinds of *memory storage*. The contents of all these storages together define the *state* of the machine. Each storage is defined as an abstract data structure in the description. Access functions defined on these abstract data structures form the *micro-instructions* of the machine. The storage components of the ABC machine and the available micro-instructions are explained in Section 10.2. The actual *ABC machine instructions* are defined with the help of these micro-instructions in Section 10.3. The remaining parts of the machine (the *instruction fetch cycle* and a *bootstrapper*) are defined in Section 10.4. In order to allow the use of symbolic names one can add an assembler to convert ABC assembly statements into proper ABC instructions.

Chapter 11 discusses in detail how Clean programs can be compiled into ABC code. The translation of ABC code into concrete machine code is discussed in Chapter 12.

10.1 About the ABC machine

The additional intermediate level created with the abstract ABC machine is very important since it helps to get a more structured implementation. By specifying how an FGRS-based language like Clean can be implemented on an abstract machine, a general blueprint is available for actual implementations on a large class of concrete target architectures. When the abstraction is carefully chosen, irrelevant machine aspects can be left out. For instance, an unbounded amount of memory or an infinite number of processors can be assumed to be available in the abstract machine. Furthermore, one can abstract from addressing modes, word sizes, register use and other particularities. This makes it easier to understand how FGRSs can conceptually be implemented and what the trade-offs are.

Another advantage of the additional intermediate level is that a *compiler* structured in this way can be ported more easily: one only has to change the last part of such a compiler that translates ABC machine code into concrete machine code (see Chapter 12). The loss of efficiency introduced by this additional intermediate level is in most cases very small.

The definition of an abstract machine also makes it easy to achieve a machine-independent *interpreter* for functional languages, e.g. by implementing an ABC machine *simulator* in a portable high-level language. Such a simulator has to interpret ABC machine instructions.

Another well-known abstract machine for functional languages is the G machine (Johnsson, 1984). The objectives of this abstract machine are identical to those of the ABC machine: defining an imperative abstract graph rewriting machine as an intermediate level in the compilation of functional languages. Basically, the G machine and the ABC machine have much in common, although they differ in almost all details. The most important differences on the architecture level are caused by the different representation of nodes: ABC nodes have variable arity while the nodes in the G-machine are either leaf nodes or application nodes with two arguments. Furthermore, the ABC machine is designed to handle arbitrary constructors.

10.1.1 The basic architecture of the ABC machine

The architecture of the abstract ABC machine actually consists of a mixture of two abstract machines.

One part of the ABC machine consists of an idealized graph rewriting architecture with a graph storage designed to perform graph rewriting conveniently. However, it is not easy to map this part of the abstract machine efficiently on a traditional concrete machine. The present-day concrete machine architectures are not at all designed for graph rewriting. They do not have anything like a graph store. A graph on a concrete machine has to be represented by some data structure stored in a linear memory of the machine. The rewriting of the graph will lead to complex memory management problems at run-time, involving garbage collection.

When simple calculations are realized on a concrete machine by building graphs and performing redirections it must be clear that this will be terribly inefficient compared with the way computations are commonly performed on such a computer: registers and stacks are normally used where possible. This observation has triggered the introduction of the second part of the abstract ABC machine: an abstraction from a traditional stack-based architecture.

So the architecture of the ABC machine is a mixture between the idealized graph rewriting machine one would like to have in reality and an idealized concrete machine.

The most important optimization that results in an efficient implementation of functional languages is: use the instructions of the traditional part of the abstract machine where possible. These instructions have the property that they can relatively easily be mapped on a concrete architecture. Avoid the higher level graph rewriting instructions of the abstract machine because they are generally hard to implement efficiently on a concrete machine.

The **ABC machine** consists of the following memory components (Figure 10.2):

- a *graph store* containing the graph to be rewritten;
- a *program store* containing the instruction sequence to be executed;

- a *program counter* containing an identification of the instruction (instrid) to be executed;
- an *A(rgument)-stack* to reference nodes in the graph store;
- a *B(asic value)-stack* to deal with basic values efficiently;
- a *C(ontrol)-stack* to store and retrieve return addresses;
- a *descriptor store* containing information about the symbols used;
- an *I(nput)/O(utput) channel* to show the result of a function.

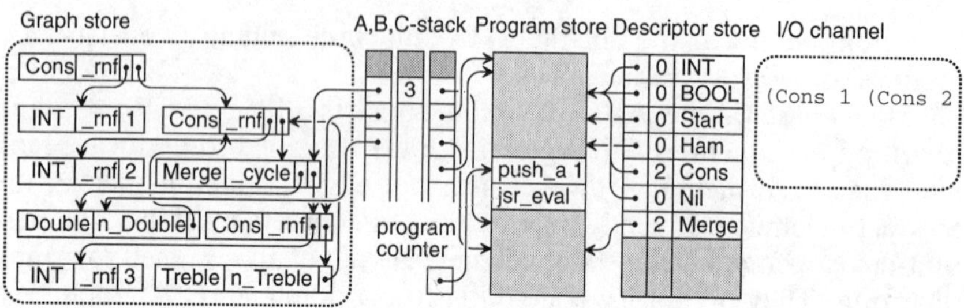

Figure 10.2 A snapshot of a possible state of the ABC machine (see Section 10.2). Not all pointers are drawn in order to keep the picture illustrative. The symbol names and labels in the nodes are actually pointers into the descriptor store and the program store.

The idealized and inefficient graph rewriting part of the ABC machine consists of the graph store, A-stack and descriptor store. The more traditional and efficient part of the abstract machine consists of the B-stack. The other, also conventional, components of the machine are shared by both parts: the program store, the program counter, the C-stack and the I/O channel.

10.1.2 The description method

The ABC machine is described in a functional language. Such a description has a number of advantages over conventional descriptions:

- Using the abstraction mechanisms of the language, like abstract data types, a hierarchical description can be given. A layered machine description enables a very clear description: details can be described without getting an overall view cluttered by too many details at the top level of the specification.
- The compiler can partially check the specification. This does not imply that the description is correct, but frequently occurring errors, like forgotten arguments, type conflicts and unbound identifiers, will be spotted by the compiler.

- The machine specification is its own prototype implementation, since it is a functional program. This implies that at an early stage the machine can be run to observe its dynamic behaviour.

A formal description of a representative subset (only Boolean and integer values are considered) of the ABC machine is given in Appendix C. The description method used below to define the ABC machine is also well suited for the description of arbitrary (concrete) machine architectures (Koopman *et al.*, 1993; Koopman, 1990).

Micro-instructions

The bottom layer of the description consists of the specification of the different kinds of memory storage that are visible to the programmer. Each memory component of the ABC machine, the A-stack (as), B-stack (bs), C-stack (cs), graph store (gs), descriptor store (ds), program counter (pc), program store (ps) and I/O channel (io), is described by an abstract data type with corresponding access operations. These access functions are called **micro-instructions** (see Section 10.2).

The state of the machine

The **state** of the machine is defined by the contents of all memory components. This state is described by a tuple:

```
state = = (astack,bstack,cstack,graphstore,descrstore,pc,programstore,io)
```

Machine instructions

Instructions change the state of the machine, e.g. they update one or more memory components. Hence, **ABC instructions** are functions that take the current machine state as argument and deliver a new state, changed by the instruction. So all instructions yield a function of the following type:

```
instruction = =   state -> state.
```

Memories can only be accessed using the micro-instructions of the machine. This means that ABC instructions are always described in terms of these micro-instructions. Each description of an ABC instruction shows how information flows between the different memory components when the instruction is executed (see Section 10.3).

Execution of the ABC machine

The specification of the ABC instructions and micro-instructions can be regarded as part of the interpretation circuit of the abstract machine. When a *bootstrapper* and a circuit to *fetch instructions* are added, a complete executable ABC machine is obtained (see Section 10.4).

10.2 Machine components and micro-instructions

In this section the rationale behind the different machine components with the available micro-instructions is given. The abstract data types for the memory storage of the ABC machine are assumed to be sufficiently defined by the specification of the abstract operations that can be applied to them. For further details the reader is referred to the concrete operational semantics of the micro-instructions given in Appendix C.

The following type synonyms are used to increase the clarity of the type definitions. The type nat stands for natural numbers including zero, and is represented by numbers (num).

```
arity    == nat     || the arity of a symbol
a_dst    == nat     || the index of the destination on the A-stack
a_src    == nat     || the index of the source on the A-stack
b_dst    == nat     || the index of the destination on the B-stack
b_src    == nat     || the index of the source on the B-stack
c_src    == nat     || the index of the source on the C-stack
nr_args  == nat     || the number of arguments involved
arg_nr   == nat     || the number of the argument involved
```

10.2.1 The program store

A Clean program is translated into a *sequence of ABC instructions*, the **ABC program**, which is stored in the **program store**. Each instruction has a unique identification. An instruction identification (an **instr-id**) is like an ordinary machine address. The instructions will rewrite the initial graph to its normal form according to the annotated functional strategy. Conceptually there are two algorithms involved, the *annotated functional reduction strategy* which indicates the next redex and the *rewriting* of that redex according to the Clean rules. These algorithms are merged in the ABC program to increase efficiency.

Each Clean rule alternative is translated into a sequence of ABC instructions. Such an instruction sequence controls the reduction order, checks whether the indicated subgraph matches the rule, and if so, builds a contractum in the graph store to which references to the root of the corresponding redex are redirected. If the rule alternative does not match the subgraph, the instruction sequence corresponding to the next rule alternative is executed. The execution of an instruction sequence corresponding to a Clean rule alternative does not always have to start with the same instruction. Depending on the circumstances under which a function is called (e.g. curried or not) a particular instruction **entry** (address of the first instruction of an instruction sequence) is chosen.

A program does not change during execution. It is loaded once in the machine (ps_init) when the machine is booted. Programs to be stored are denoted by a list of instructions (see Section 10.4). An instruction that has to be executed is fetched from the program store (ps_get).

```
ps_get  :: instrid -> programstore -> instruction
ps_init :: [instruction] -> programstore
```

10.2.2 The program counter

Since the ABC machine has an imperative nature it is essential to have a locus of control: the **program counter**. The program counter is an abstract data structure containing the *instr-id* of the next instruction to be executed. A micro-instruction (pc_init) is provided to initialize the program counter such that it points to the first instruction of the program. The program counter can be incremented: the next instruction in the sequence will be executed (pc_next), the counter can be set to indicate that the program is finished (pc_halt), or it can be checked whether the last instruction of the program is reached (pc_end). The instr-id can be fetched from (pc_get) and assigned to (pc_update) the program counter.

```
pc_init   :: pc
pc_next   :: pc -> pc
pc_halt   :: pc -> pc
pc_end    :: pc -> bool
pc_get    :: pc -> instrid
pc_update :: instrid -> pc -> pc
```

10.2.3 The graph store

The ABC machine has, of course, a piece of memory in which the graph to be rewritten is stored: the **graph store**. As in Chapter 5, each node in the graph has a unique identification, the **node-id**. There are micro-instructions to generate a new (empty) graph store (gs_init), to create a new (empty) node in the graph (gs_newnode) and to retrieve information stored in a node of the graph (gs_get). Finally, a node can be updated by a function passed as a parameter to the gs_update micro-instruction.

```
gs_get     :: nodeid -> graphstore -> node
gs_init    :: graphstore
gs_newnode :: graphstore -> (graphstore, nodeid)
gs_update  :: nodeid -> (node -> node) -> graphstore -> graphstore
```

The nodes in the graph store

A node in the graph store does not contain a *symbol*, but instead it contains a *descriptor identification* (**descr-id**) which is an **entry** (address where the information can be found) in the descriptor store (see Section 10.2.4). The advantage of this is that the (possibly long) symbol name need not be stored in a node. The actual name of a symbol is only needed when results have to be printed. During reduction it is only important that all symbols have a unique (short) representation such that the equality of symbols can be tested easily. This is accomplished by having a unique entry for each symbol in the descriptor table.

A node generally also contains a *sequence of node-ids* representing the arguments of the symbol. An exception is formed by arguments that are basic values, such as integers or booleans. For efficiency they are stored directly in the nodes themselves. This is in contrast with the way such graphs are structured in Chapter 5.

Each node furthermore contains a **code field** in which an instruction entry is stored. By convention, the execution of the corresponding sequence of ABC instructions will take care of the reduction of the node to root normal form. The contents of the code field can be *changed* at run-time, so it can be used as a kind of flag. Different kinds of code can be executed under different kinds of circumstances. For instance, it might be used at run-time to determine that a node is already under reduction. This means that there is a cycle of nodes each of which requires the evaluation of all the others in order to reach a root normal form: a **cycle-in-spine error**.

There are several micro-instructions to extract information stored in a node. The nodes themselves can be extracted from the graph store by the micro-instruction gs_get defined above.

```
n_arg      :: node -> arg_nr -> arity -> nodeid
n_args     :: node -> arity -> nodeid_seq
n_arity    :: node -> arity
n_B        :: node -> bool
n_descrid  :: node -> descrid
n_entry    :: node -> instrid
n_I        :: node -> int
n_nargs    :: node -> nr_args -> arity -> nodeid_seq
```

There are also micro-instructions to test whether a piece of a node has a certain value. They are important for pattern matching.

```
n_eq_arity     :: node -> arity -> bool
n_eq_B         :: node -> bool -> bool
n_eq_descrid   :: node -> descrid -> bool
n_eq_I         :: node -> int -> bool
n_eq_symbol    :: node -> node -> bool
```

The following micro-instructions to change the contents of a node are passed as argument to gs_update:

```
n_copy      :: node -> node -> node
n_fill      :: descrid -> instrid -> nodeid_seq -> node -> node
n_fillB     :: descrid -> instrid -> bool -> node -> node
n_fillI     :: descrid -> instrid -> int -> node -> node
n_setentry  :: instrid -> node -> node
```

In order to build a contractum new nodes have to be created in the graph store and redirections have to be performed. Redirections are conceptually elegant and explain the semantics of graph rewriting very well. However, it is very inefficient to examine the whole graph to substitute every reference to the root of a redex by a reference to the root of the contractum. Instead, it is actually much more efficient to *overwrite* the root node of the redex with the root of the contractum. The result is that all original references are automatically redirected to the contractum. The micro-instructions above show that the graph store can deal with variable sized nodes. So overwriting a node with another value is always possible. The update instruction is used both for overwriting old nodes as well as for the creation of new ones. New nodes are built as follows. First, a new empty node is created in the graph store (using gs_newnode). Then, the empty node is filled with the update instruction. To create an empty node first, which is filled later, is in particular convenient for the construction of cyclic structures (see Section 10.3).

10.2.4 The descriptor store

The ABC machine contains a piece of memory in which symbol descriptors are stored. This **descriptor store** contains information about the symbols used in the rewrite system. For each symbol and each basic type there is a unique entry in the descriptor store, labelled with the **descr-id**. Given a descriptor identification, a descriptor can be taken from the descriptor store (ds_get). This store can be initialized by passing a list of descriptors to the ds_init micro-instruction.

```
ds_get  :: descrid -> descrstore -> descr
ds_init :: [descr] -> descrstore
```

The descriptors

A **descriptor** contains information of the associated symbol: its *arity*, an instruction entry that is called for curried applications (see Section 11.2) and the *name of the symbol*. The symbol name is used only to print a representation of the graph in root normal form on the output channel. Information can be retrieved from a descriptor using the following micro-instructions:

```
d_ap_entry   :: descr -> instrid
d_arity      :: descr -> arity
d_name       :: descr -> string
```

10.2.5 The A-stack

The **A-stack** contains node-ids: references to nodes stored in the graph store. It is used to access the actual arguments and the result of the applied rewrite rule. As in imperative languages, instead of the data structure itself, a reference to it is passed to or returned from a function. The top of the stack has index 0 (as is the case for the other stacks). A new, empty, A-stack can be created by:

```
as_init      :: astack
```

An element at any depth, or a sequence of nr_args top elements, can be retrieved from the A-stack by:

```
as_get       :: a_src -> astack -> nodeid
as_topn      :: nr_args -> astack -> nodeid_seq
```

The type nodeid_seq represents a sequence of node-ids which can be taken from or pushed onto the A-stack, and it serves also as the argument sequence for a node. The A-stack can be updated by:

```
as_popn      :: nr_args -> astack -> astack
as_push      :: nodeid -> astack -> astack
as_pushn     :: nodeid_seq -> astack -> astack
as_update    :: a_dst -> nodeid -> astack -> astack
```

10.2.6 The B-stack

The ABC machine also has a stack to hold basic values (such as integers, reals and Boolean values). Basic values are stored and computed on this **B-stack** instead of in nodes in the graph store whenever this is possible. Temporary values are also held on this stack. All values are stored untagged on the stack. The initial, empty, B-stack is created by:

```
bs_init      :: bstack
```

Information can be obtained from the B-stack with:

```
bs_get       :: b_src -> bstack -> basic
```

```
bs_getB     :: b_src -> bstack -> bool
bs_getI     :: b_src -> bstack -> int
```

The B-stack can be changed with:

```
bs_copy     :: b_src -> bstack -> bstack
bs_popn     :: nr_args -> bstack -> bstack
bs_push     :: basic -> bstack -> bstack
bs_pushB    :: bool -> bstack -> bstack
bs_pushI    :: int -> bstack -> bstack
bs_update   :: b_dst -> basic -> bstack -> bstack
```

Besides these updating micro-instructions there are micro-instructions defined to perform computations with the basic values stored on the B-stack. Usually, the arguments are all on top of the B-stack and are replaced by the result of the operation. When arguments are not on the B-stack they are an argument of the micro-instruction. Some micro-instructions to handle integer values are:

```
bs_addI     :: bstack -> bstack
bs_eqI      :: bstack -> bstack
bs_eqIi     :: int -> b_src -> bstack -> bstack
bs_gtI      :: bstack -> bstack
```

A further optimization would be to include *registers* in the ABC machine to hold these basic values. However, the number of registers and the operations possible on them vary too much between different concrete machines. Register allocation is therefore left as a part of the implementation of the ABC machine (see Chapter 12).

10.2.7 The C-stack

The **C-stack** (control stack) is used to implement nested reductions in the abstract machine. It contains return addresses (instr-ids). The program counter can be stored and recovered from this stack.

```
cs_init     :: cstack
cs_get      :: c_src -> cstack -> instrid
cs_popn     :: nr_args -> cstack -> cstack
cs_push     :: instrid -> cstack -> cstack
```

10.2.8 The input/output channel

The abstract machine furthermore contains an **input/output channel**. In the description in this chapter only simple *output* is considered, such that the result of the reduction can be shown. A string is printed just by appending it to the output channel. This corresponds to classical character-based output.

```
io_init          :: io
io_print         :: string -> io -> io
io_print_symbol  :: node -> descr -> io -> io
```

With respect to more sophisticated input/output using modern facilities such as windows, menus and dialogs the available interface on the machine (e.g. Macintosh tool box or X Window System interface) is assumed to be called directly as a side-effect. This is possible due to the properties of UNQ types (see Chapter 8).

10.3 The machine instructions

The state of the ABC machine is completely determined by the contents of its eight stores: the A-stack, B-stack, C-stack, the graph store, descriptor store, program counter, program store and input/output channel. Each ABC instruction changes the state of the machine by changing the contents of one or more of these stores. The only way to change the contents or retrieve information from the stores is via the micro-instructions introduced in the previous section. So the *ABC instructions* are described in terms of *micro-instructions* and for each instruction we define how the information flows between these memories. In this way *imaginary data paths* are defined between the several stores. One can imagine that these data paths could actually be present in a concrete piece of hardware.

Not all ABC instructions are shown in this section. The specification in terms of micro-instructions is only given for the most important ones. For some other instructions, only the type and an informal explanation are given. The instructions shown here are classified according to their main purpose:

- graph manipulation
- retrieving information from a node
- manipulating the A-stack
- manipulating the B-stack
- changing the flow of control
- generating output.

10.3.1 Instructions for graph manipulation

There are several instructions to manipulate the graph store. With the instruction create a new empty node is created in the graph store. With other instructions the contents of an existing (possibly empty) node can be changed. Finally, there are also instructions that fetch information stored in the nodes of the graph. All instructions for graph manipulation (with the exception of the instruction create) have as operand an offset into the A-stack to find the node-id of the node to manipulate.

The instruction create creates a new empty node in the graph store, and the node-id of the new node is pushed on the A-stack. The create instruction is defined as:

```
create:: instruction
create (as,bs,cs,gs,ds,pc,ps,io)
   = (as',bs,cs,gs',ds,pc,ps,io)
     where  as'              = as_push nodeid as
            (gs', nodeid)    = gs_newnode gs
```

With the fill instruction one can update the contents of an existing node:

```
fill:: descrid -> nr_args -> instrid -> a_dst -> instruction
fill descr nr_args entry a_dst (as,bs,cs,gs,ds,pc,ps,io)
   = (as',bs,cs,gs',ds,pc,ps,io)
     where  as'     = as_popn nr_args as
            gs'     = gs_update nodeid (n_fill descr entry args) gs
            nodeid  = as_get a_dst as
            args    = as_topn nr_args as
```

As can be seen from this specification the arguments of the node are taken from the A-stack. The first argument is on top of the A-stack. Other instructions to change the contents of an existing node are:

```
fill_a     :: a_src -> a_dst -> instruction    || the copy node instruction
fillB      :: bool -> a_dst -> instruction     || fills the node with the given bool
fillB_b    :: b_src -> a_dst -> instruction    || fills with bool found on B-stack
fillI      :: int -> a_dst -> instruction      || fills the node with the integer
fillI_b    :: b_src -> a_dst -> instruction    || fills with integer found on B-stack
set_entry  :: instrid -> a_dst -> instruction  || changes code entry of node
```

Building a Clean node in the graph store involves at least two instructions: a create, which leaves a node-id on the A-stack, and one of the fill instructions.

To create the graph Cons 1 Nil, the following code fragment is written in the ABC assembly language introduced in Section 10.4.

```
[    Create                      ,   || node for Cons
     Create                      ,   || node for Nil; 2nd arg of Cons
     Fill "Nil" 0 "_rnf" 0       ,   || fill node just created
     Create                      ,   || node for 1; 1st arg of Cons
```

```
        Filll 1 0                              ,  || fill node just created
        Fill "Cons" 2 "_rnf" 2                 ]  || fill Cons node
```

It is assumed that calling the entry stored in the code field of a node will reduce the corresponding subgraph to root normal form. For subgraphs already in root normal form the instruction sequence can be one simple return instruction (rtn) assumed to be labelled by the entry _rnf. The descriptor-ids of Nil and Cons are indicated by "Nil" and "Cons".

Retrieving information from a node

The information retrieved from a node is generally stored on one of the stacks. The node-id of the node to fetch the information from is found at the indicated depth on the A-stack. There are also instructions to test whether the content of a node has a certain value.

```
push_args:: a_src -> arity -> nr_args -> instruction
push_args a_src arity nr_args (as,bs,cs,gs,ds,pc,ps,io)
   = (as',bs,cs,gs,ds,pc,ps,io)
     where  as'     = as_pushn args as
            args    = n_nargs (gs_get nodeid gs) nr_args arity
            nodeid  = as_get a_src as

pushI_a:: a_src -> instruction
pushI_a a_src (as,bs,cs,gs,ds,pc,ps,io)
   = (as,bs',cs,gs,ds,pc,ps,io)
     where  bs'     = bs_pushI int bs
            int     = n_I (gs_get nodeid gs)
            nodeid  = as_get a_src as

eqI_a:: int -> a_src -> instruction
eqI_a int a_src (as,bs,cs,gs,ds,pc,ps,io)
   = (as,bs',cs,gs,ds,pc,ps,io)
     where  bs'     = bs_pushB equal bs
            equal   = n_eq_I (gs_get nodeid gs) int
            nodeid  = as_get a_src as

eq_descr_arity:: descrid -> arity -> a_src -> instruction
eq_descr_arity descrid arity a_src (as,bs,cs,gs,ds,pc,ps,io)
   = (as,bs',cs,gs,ds,pc,ps,io)
     where  bs'     = bs_pushB equal bs
            equal   = n_eq_descrid node descrid & n_eq_arity node arity
            node    = gs_get nodeid gs
            nodeid  = as_get a_src as
```

Appendix C lists some more instructions for retrieving information from a node, such as extracting the arguments of a node or changing them.

10.3.2 Instructions to manipulate the A-stack

The A-stack is used to access the nodes involved in a rewriting. Via push instructions, new node-ids can be pushed on the stack. Furthermore, there are instructions provided to manipulate the A-stack:

```
pop_a:: nr_args -> instruction
pop_a n (as,bs,cs,gs,ds,pc,ps,io)
   = (as',bs,cs,gs,ds,pc,ps,io)
     where   as'       =  as_popn n as

push_a:: a_src -> instruction
push_a a_src (as,bs,cs,gs,ds,pc,ps,io)
   = (as',bs,cs,gs,ds,pc,ps,io)
     where   as'       =  as_push nodeid as
             nodeid    =  as_get a_src as

update_a:: a_src -> a_dst -> instruction
update_a a_src a_dst (as,bs,cs,gs,ds,pc,ps,io)
   = (as',bs,cs,gs,ds,pc,ps,io)
     where   as'       =  as_update a_dst nodeid as
             nodeid    =  as_get a_src as
```

The cyclic graph ones: Cons 1 ones is constructed as follows (here the advantages of separate create and fill instructions are seen).

```
[       Create                        ,  || node for Cons
        Push_a 0                      ,  || 2nd arg of Cons
        Create                        ,  || node for 1; 1st arg of Cons
        FillI 1 0                     ,  || fill node just created
        Fill "Cons" 2 "_rnf" 2        ]  || fill Cons node
```

10.3.3 Instructions to manipulate the B-stack

The B-stack has stack handling instructions similar to the A-stack:

```
pop_b      :: nr_args -> instruction
push_b     :: b_src -> instruction
pushI      :: int -> instruction
pushB      :: bool -> instruction
update_b   :: b_src -> b_dst -> instruction
```

There are many instructions to manipulate the basic values on this stack; they all follow the same scheme as the add instruction presented below.

```
addI:: instruction
addI (as,bs,cs,gs,ds,pc,ps,io)
```

```
    = (as,bs',cs,gs,ds,pc,ps,io)
      where  bs'      = bs_addl bs
```

10.3.4 Instructions to change the flow of control

The desired flow of control has to be realized by manipulating the program counter. Jumps can be unconditional but they can also be controlled by the Boolean value on top of the B-stack.

```
jmp:: instrid -> instruction
jmp address (as,bs,cs,gs,ds,pc,ps,io)
  = (as,bs,cs,gs,ds,pc',ps,io)
where  pc'      = pc_update address pc

jmp_false:: instrid -> instruction
jmp_false address (as,bs,cs,gs,ds,pc,ps,io)
  = (as,bs',cs,gs,ds,pc',ps,io)
    where  pc'      = pc, if bool
                    = pc_update address pc, otherwise
           bool     = bs_getB 0 bs
           bs'      = bs_popn 1 bs

jmp_true:: instrid -> instruction
jmp_true address (as,bs,cs,gs,ds,pc,ps,io)
  = (as,bs',cs,gs,ds,pc',ps,io)
    where  pc'      = pc_update address pc, if bool
                    = pc, otherwise
           bool     = bs_getB 0 bs
           bs'      = bs_popn 1 bs
```

When a jump to subroutine (jsr) instruction is executed, the current value of the program counter is stored on the C-stack. A return from subroutine instruction (rtn) will restore the program counter and pop the return address from the C-stack.

```
jsr:: instrid -> instruction
jsr address (as,bs,cs,gs,ds,pc,ps,io)
  = (as,bs,cs',gs,ds,pc',ps,io)
    where  pc'      = pc_update address pc
           cs'      = cs_push (pc_get pc) cs

rtn:: instruction
rtn (as,bs,cs,gs,ds,pc,ps,io)
  = (as,bs,cs',gs,ds,pc',ps,io)
    where  pc'      = pc_update (cs_get 0 cs) pc
           cs'      = cs_popn 1 cs
```

The jsr_eval instruction is a very important instruction since it starts the execution at the entry stored in the code field of the node on top of the A-stack. The return address is saved on the C-stack. In other words, the jsr_eval performs a jsr to the instr-id stored in the node. By convention, the execution of the instruction sequence will reduce the corresponding node to its root normal form.

```
jsr_eval:: instruction
jsr_eval (as,bs,cs,gs,ds,pc,ps,io)
    = (as,bs,cs',gs,ds,pc',ps,io)
      where  pc'     = pc_update (n_entry (gs_get nodeid gs)) pc
             nodeid  = as_get 0 as
             cs'     = cs_push (pc_get pc) cs
```

The program execution stops after the execution of a halt instruction. The instruction fetch_cycle will spot this instruction and the machine will stop (see Section 10.4).

```
halt:: instruction
halt (as,bs,cs,gs,ds,pc,ps,io)
    = (as,bs,cs,gs,ds,pc',ps,io)
      where  pc'     = pc_halt pc
```

10.3.5 Instructions to generate output

To show the result of the reduction there are print instructions. These instructions append strings to the output channel.

```
print:: string -> instruction
print string (as,bs,cs,gs,ds,pc,ps,io)
    = (as,bs,cs,gs,ds,pc,ps,io')
      where  io'     = io_print string io

print_symbol:: a_src -> instruction
print_symbol a_src (as,bs,cs,gs,ds,pc,ps,io)
    = (as,bs,cs,gs,ds,pc,ps,io')
      where  io'     = io_print_symbol node descr io
             nodeid  = as_get a_src as
             node    = gs_get nodeid gs
             descr   = ds_get (n_descrid node) ds
```

10.4 Program execution

As already explained in Section 10.1 the specification of the ABC instructions and micro-instructions can be seen as part of the interpretation circuit of the abstract machine. In order to obtain an executable specification of the ABC machine that can be used to execute ABC programs one needs an implementation of the abstract data structures which are discussed in Section 10.2. Such an implementation is given in Appendix C. Still there are some machine parts missing. An *instruction fetching* mechanism has to be defined and one needs a *bootstrapper* to initialize the machine. This bootstrapper needs an ABC program with corresponding descriptor values in a machine-readable format. For this purpose a small *assembler* is defined that can convert an *ABC assembly* program to the desired format. The ABC assembly language makes it possible to denote ABC instructions in a user-friendly notation.

10.4.1 The instruction fetch cycle

To run the ABC machine described here, the instructions must be applied to the state of the machine. In each machine cycle recursively the current instruction is fetched from the program store and is applied to the current state. The fetching (and hence the machine) stops when the program counter indicates that a halt instruction is executed.

```
fetch_cycle :: state -> state
fetch_cycle (as,bs,cs,gs,ds,pc,ps,io)
   = (as,bs,cs,gs,ds,pc,ps,io)                              , if pc_end pc
   = fetch_cycle (currinstr (as,bs,cs,gs,ds,pc',ps,io))   , otherwise
     where  pc'        = pc_next pc
            currinstr = ps_get (pc_get pc) ps
```

10.4.2 Booting the machine

Before it is possible to run the machine, the machine must be loaded (booted) with the initial state. The program and descriptors must be supplied as arguments to the boot function. All parts of the machine are initialized by the corresponding _init micro-instructions.

```
boot :: ([instruction],[descr]) -> state
boot (program,descriptors)
   = (as,bs,cs,gs,ds,pc,ps,io)
     where  pc   = pc_init
            as   = as_init
            bs   = bs_init
            cs   = cs_init
            gs   = gs_init
            ps   = ps_init program
            io   = io_init
            ds   = ds_init descriptors
```

10.4.3 ABC assembly language

For testing the machine specification with actual ABC programs it is convenient to have an ABC assembly language. For instance, in ABC instructions addresses (instr-ids) are actually required instead of symbolic labels. This is close to reality, but such abstract machine code is cumbersome to read and write for human beings. For this reason an assembly language is defined in which symbolic names are used instead of concrete machine addresses.

The ABC assembly language allows us to write, for example:

```
example1:: assembly
example1  = [            Label
             "Length1",  Jsr_eval                          ,
                         Eq_descr_arity "Cons" 0 0         ,
                         Jmp_false "Length2"               ,
                         Push_args 0 2 2                   ,
                         Create                            ,
                         Push_a 2                          ,
                         Fill "Length" 1 "n_Length" 1      ]
```

instead of the ABC instruction sequence that might correspond to it:

```
example2:: [instructions]
example2  = [            jsr_eval                          ,
                         eq_descr_arity 23 0 0             ,
                         jmp_false 62                      ,
                         push_args 0 2 2                   ,
                         create                            ,
                         push_a 2                          ,
                         fill 12 1 613 1                   ]
```

In this particular case, a program in ABC assembly language is represented by a Miranda data structure. Therefore, every ABC instruction is represented by a constructor with a similar name: the first character is changed to an upper case character to make it a constructor. Addresses are replaced by symbolic labels. Furthermore, there is a denotation for all objects involved. The use of a Miranda data structure has the advantage over the use of strings that it eliminates the generation and parsing of ABC assembly. It also enables easy printing and manipulating of ABC assembly statements (data structures) which is much harder for ABC machine instructions (functions).

An assembler translates an ABC assembly program into ABC instructions with the corresponding descriptors:

```
assembler:: assembly -> ([instruction], [descr])
```

10.4.4 Running a program

The ABC machine starts evaluating an assembly program as follows:

```
fetch_cycle (boot (assembler (assembly_program)))
```

Summary

- The ABC machine is an abstract machine in which two different kinds of architecture are combined:
  - one part of the abstract machine is an *idealized architecture* to perform *graph rewriting*;
  - the other part is an *abstraction* of a more or less *traditional stack-based machine architecture*.
- The ABC machine consists of the following components:
  - a *program store*, containing a sequence of instructions that controls the rewriting process;
  - a *program counter*;
  - a *graph store*, containing the graph to be rewritten;
  - an *argument stack*, containing node-ids;
  - a *basic value stack*, containing basic values;
  - a *control stack*, containing return addresses;
  - an *output channel*, to print the string representation of an obtained root normal form;
  - a *descriptor store*, containing the descriptors of function and constructor symbols.
- The instruction set of the machine offers another *machine-independent level of abstraction* for the implementation of functional languages.
- The imperative ABC machine can be specified elegantly in a functional language:
  - the *memory stores* are defined as abstract data types;
  - the machine has *micro-instructions*: operations defined on these abstract types to access the stores;
  - the *instructions* of the ABC machine are defined in terms of micro-instructions, thus defining the data flow between the several machine components;
  - an *assembly language* is defined that permits instruction labels and symbolic names to be used.
- The given specification of the ABC machine is executable. It can therefore be used as an interpreter of ABC instructions and, for

example with a Miranda to Clean compiler as an interpreter of Miranda scripts. In this way the behaviour of the ABC machine can be observed.

EXERCISES

10.1 Write small ABC assembly routines to accomplish the following tasks (the routines should remove their arguments and other created entries from the stacks with the exception of their result):

(a) A routine that takes two argument nodes containing integers on the A-stack, and leaves the sum of these integers on the B-stack.

(b) A routine that takes two integers on the B-stack and leaves only the greater of them on the B-stack (computes maximum).

(c) A routine that takes a boolean on the B-stack and builds a node containing the complement of this boolean (logical NOT).

10.2* Extend the machine with one register br that replaces the top of the B-stack. Define a suitable abstract data type for br. Give the definition and implementation of the following micro-instructions: br_getB, br_putB, br_getI, br_putI, br_init. Give the new definition of the ABC state. Give the new definition of pushB. Define new instructions that take advantage of the new micro-instructions.

10.3* Define the instruction set of a programmable pocket calculator using the description method introduced in this chapter. Define for such a machine: a program store and a stack. Define suitable micro-instructions on these machine components. Define the following instructions: addI, subI, mulI, divI, eqI, pop, push, label, jsr, rtn, jmp_false, start, stop. Define two instruction: one to clear the program store and one to add an instruction into the store. Program the machine to calculate the factorial function.

Chapter 11
Translating Clean into ABC code

This chapter discusses the transformation of Clean programs into ABC machine instructions (Figure 11.1). The relatively high-level functional language Clean is transformed into a low-level, imperative machine language. Hence, compared with the transformations described so far, the transformation from Clean into ABC code is the most complex one.

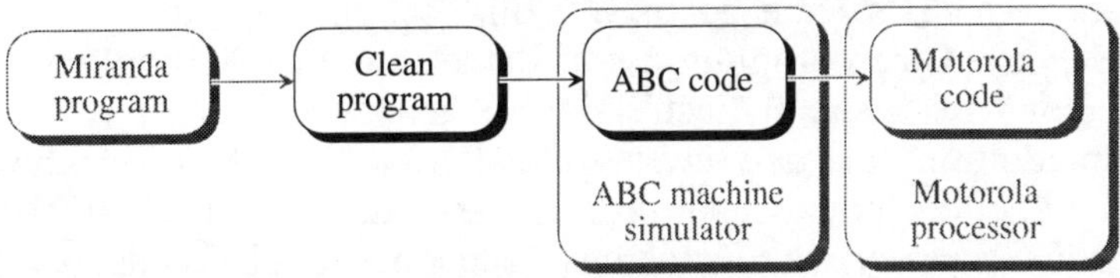

Figure 11.1 The second transformation step: Clean into ABC code.

The goal of the translation is, of course, to transform Clean programs into equivalent and efficient ABC programs. This ABC code is then further translated into instructions for the concrete target machine. The various target machines have quite different instruction sets, which makes it impossible to develop a compilation scheme to ABC code that is optimal for all possible concrete architectures. Nevertheless, several general optimizations can be used. These general optimizations consist of deviations from the standard operational semantics of Clean that are deliberately made to increase the performance of the generated code.

An important optimization is the following: although Clean graphs are mapped directly to graphs in the graph store of the ABC machine, this graph store is *not* updated after every rewrite step. During the rewriting the updating information is stored on the stacks and (implicitly) in the instruction sequence executed.

Another important optimization is induced by the fact that the performance of ABC programs heavily manipulating the graph store for simple computations will be low compared with ABC code that employs the B-stack whenever appropriate. So to achieve an efficient implementation of graph rewriting one should *avoid* the actual rewriting of the graph in the graph store where possible. For instance, in a straightforward scheme, subgraphs are constructed in the graph store to pass arguments from one function to another. But, when simple basic values are passed one does not need to construct these nodes at all: the values can be passed on the B-stack. The B-stack will be used in all cases where strict arguments of a basic type are passed to or returned by a function.

Section 11.1 informally describes graph rewriting on the ABC machine. Section 11.2 discusses the run-time system. Finally, Section 11.3 treats some high-level optimizations including the use of the B-stack.

11.1 Basic graph rewriting on the ABC machine

There are, in principle, many different ways to realize graph rewriting on the abstract ABC machine. This section discusses one straightforward method in an informal way. Only *pure* graph rewriting is considered. This means that only the graph rewriting part of the ABC machine is used. So the B-stack is not used in this section.

When a Clean program is translated into an ABC program, a sequence of ABC assembly instructions is generated for *each* rewrite rule and, in addition, for *each* rewrite rule alternative. In this code the functional reduction strategy and the graph rewriting operations are merged. For *each* Clean *rewrite rule* there is a sequence of ABC code to:

- construct a *stack frame* such that the arguments of the function can be accessed directly; furthermore, the arguments with global strict annotations are reduced to root normal form;
- handle the situation that none of the rule alternatives is applicable.

In addition, for *each* Clean *rule alternative* there is a sequence of ABC code to:

- determine whether the rule alternative matches the actual redex; if this is the case the corresponding rewrite is performed; if not, the next rule alternative is tried by executing its code.

Furthermore, there is a fixed piece of ABC code, called the **run-time system**, that

- initiates the reduction of a Start rule to *normal form*;

- *prints* the result of the computation on the input/output channel;
- *converts* curried applications into uncurried ones.

Entries (see Chapter 10) are important because they mark pieces of code that belong together. A sequence labelled with an entry can be executed by jumping to this entry (there are several jump instructions available). So entries can be called from outside. There are several kinds of entry generated in the ABC code. For each entry a certain **calling convention** is assumed: i.e. an interface between caller and callee. The different pieces of code, the entries and the calling conventions are described below.

11.1.1 Entries and calling conventions

One property of the functional strategy is that, once initiated, the reduction of a (sub)graph continues until it is in root normal form. This is realized as follows on the ABC machine. As was explained in the previous chapter, entries can be stored in the code field of a node. In general, the code field of a node will refer to a special entry, the **node entry**. When this node entry is called, the corresponding instructions will eventually reduce the subgraph rooted at that node to its root normal form (if it exists).

The reduction of a redex can be initiated by a jsr_eval instruction. This instruction calls the node entry stored in the code field of the root node of the redex and leaves a reference to this root on the top of the A-stack (see the definition of jsr_eval). When the node entry is entered, the root node is marked as being under reduction such that a cycle-in-spine can be detected. Since the ABC machine contains no tags, this marking is realized by overwriting the code field with a special entry (_cycle) that will produce an error message when it is called by a second attempt to reduce the same node.

Before the actual matching and rewriting can take place a stack frame is constructed on the A-stack. This **stack frame** contains:

- a reference to the root of the (sub)graph under reduction. This root is used as a **place-holder node** on the bottom of the stack frame. It will be updated with the root normal form when this is reached.
- the node-ids of all the arguments of the function that is called. The reference to the first argument is on top of the stack. The arguments that are marked as strict are in root normal form.

To construct the described stack frame, the arguments of the root node have to be pushed on the A-stack as well. Those arguments that are globally annotated as being strict are reduced to root normal form (again by using jsr_eval instructions). There is a special entry, called the

eval args entry (evaluate strict arguments), to reduce the corresponding arguments.

The actual matching and rewriting will take place depending on the actual rewrite rule alternatives (see Sections 11.1.2 and 11.1.3).

Consider the following rewrite rules:

```
:: F ![x]            ![x]       ->  INT;
   F [a | [b | c]]   [d | e]    ->  G f f , f: [b | e];

:: G [x] [x]    ->  INT;
   G a  b       ->  1;
```

Throughout this chapter, new parts in the pictures are printed bold. Graphs with unknown contents are drawn as grey boxes (Figure 11.2).

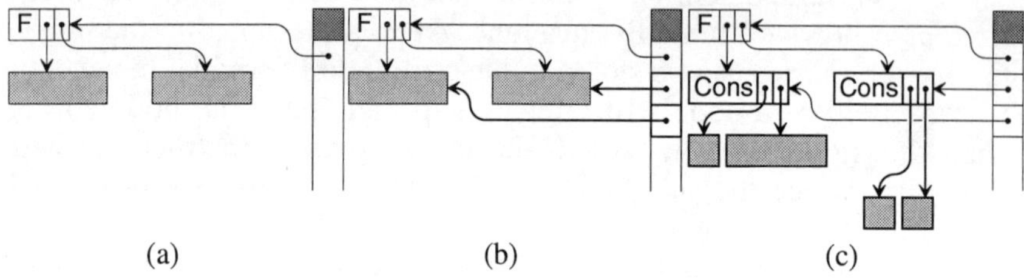

Figure 11.2 (a) The initial A-stack frame and graph just before entering the node entry. (b) The stack frame is extended with the node-ids of the arguments. (c) The stack frame as expected by the rule alternatives; both arguments are strict and hence both are reduced to root normal form.

For each rewrite rule alternative there is a separate **rule alternative entry**. Only the first rewrite alternative will be referenced outside the code for a particular rewrite rule. The code for each rule alternative entry consists of a *matching phase* which determines whether this alternative is applicable and a *rewriting phase* which performs the rewrite. When an alternative appears to be inapplicable, execution proceeds with the next one. Furthermore, for each rewrite rule, an **additional rule alternative entry** is generated that is executed when none of the rewrite rule alternatives is applicable. This means that a partial function has been called with a value on which it is not defined, which is generally considered as a run-time error (see Section 8.2.3). However, for well-typed partial functions it means the place-holder node can be updated with the root normal form reached.

A different situation arises when a *curried* function is used. As explained in Chapter 8, an automatic conversion has to convert a curried application into an uncurried one. For this purpose, a special internal

_AP-rule is defined in the run-time system (see Section 11.2). When sufficient arguments are supplied, the _AP-function will call the special **apply entry** of the rewrite rule. In this case, the node-id of the redex, the node-id of the last argument and a reference to the node containing the other arguments will be on the stack. To construct the same stack frame as described above, the last reference has to be replaced by the other arguments of the rewrite rule. Finally, the strict arguments have to be reduced to root normal form. So the eval args entry is called.

Summary of entries, calling conventions and their actions

Node entry

Called by: any function that needs the root normal form of the applied function.

Calling conventions:
- node-id of root of redex on top of A-stack.

Actions:
- mark root node redex for cycle-in-spine detection; this node now serves as place-holder node;
- push the node-ids of all the arguments of the redex on the A-stack; last argument on top of the stack;
- proceed with eval args entry.

Eval args entry

Called by: node entry as well as apply entry.

Calling conventions:
- node-id of place-holder node on the stack;
- node-ids of all arguments of the function called above it, node-id of first argument on top of A-stack.

Actions:
- reduce those arguments that are marked as strict to root normal form;
- proceed with first rule alternative entry.

Rule alternative entry

Called by: the first rule alternative can be called by any function; the other rule alternatives are called by the previous one when they do not match.

Calling conventions:
- the stack frame is complete: node-id of place-holder node on the stack, node-ids of arguments on top of it, strict arguments are in root normal form.

Actions:
- try to match this alternative;
- if no match, proceed with next rule alternative entry;
- if match, evaluate strict nodes of right-hand side and construct contractum;
- when a root normal form is reached, the place-holder node is overwritten with the contractum; return to caller;
- otherwise: build stack frame for root of right-hand side;

- proceed with the first rule alternative entry of the root of right-hand side.

Additional rule alternative entry

Called by: last rule alternative entry.

Calling conventions:
- a complete stack frame.

Actions:
- in general: generate an error message and halt the program;
- for well-typed partial functions: fill place-holder node with root normal form.

Apply entry

Called by: built-in _AP-function when a curried application has enough arguments.

Calling conventions:
- node-id of place-holder node on A-stack;
- node-id of node containing $n - 1$ arguments on top of it;
- node-id of last argument on top of A-stack.

Actions:
- pop the two node-ids on top and push the node-ids of all the arguments of the function called on the A-stack;
- proceed with eval args entry.

11.1.2 Matching

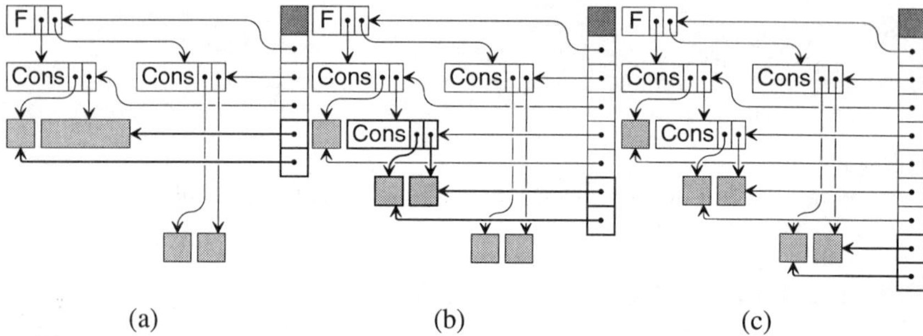

Figure 11.3 (a) The situation after matching the top level of the first argument and pushing its subarguments. (b) The second subargument of the first argument is reduced and matched. After the successful match the node-ids of the subarguments are pushed on the stack. (c) The second argument also matches. So this rule alternative is applicable.

In each rewrite rule alternative the arguments are matched from left to right. If the formal argument in the corresponding rewrite rule is a variable the argument trivially matches. Otherwise, when the actual argument is not known to be in root normal form already, it is brought in root normal form by calling its node entry. Now the symbol in the graph can be compared with the symbol specified in the redex pattern. When the symbols match (are equal), its subarguments are pushed on the A-stack as well (Figure 11.3). Subpatterns are matched in the same way. In this way all node-ids that appear on the left-hand side of the rewrite rule alternative are pushed on the A-stack. The advantage of this is that these node-ids and hence the corresponding nodes become directly accessible in the rewriting phase.

As soon as an argument is found that does not match the corresponding redex pattern, all subarguments are popped from the stack and execution proceeds with matching the next rule alternative. When the matching of all arguments succeeds the rewrite must be performed.

11.1.3 Rewriting

When the redex matches a rewrite rule alternative, the rewriting can take place. According to the semantics of GRSs, the contractum must be constructed (if present in the rule) and all references to the root of the redex must be redirected to the root of the contractum. During the matching phase all node-ids that appear on the left-hand side of the rewrite rule alternative have already been pushed on the A-stack such that they are directly accessible in the rewriting phase.

To increase the performance of the generated code some deviations of the standard GRS semantics are made.

As explained in Section 8.3.2, before reducing the root node of the right-hand side all strict nodes other than the root node are evaluated to root normal form. However, not the whole contractum is built before these strict nodes are evaluated. Only those parts of the contractum that are necessary for this evaluation (lazy subgraphs, sharing, cycles) are built before this evaluation is started.

Furthermore, as already mentioned in Section 10.2, it is very inefficient to examine the whole graph and replace every reference to the root of a redex by a reference to the contractum root. A more efficient implementation is achieved by *overwriting* the root of the redex with the root of the contractum. In this way all references to the redex are automatically redirected to the contractum.

Finally, the graph store is *not* updated after each rewrite step. It is only updated when a root normal form is reached. During the rewriting the information is stored on the stacks and (implicitly) in the instruction sequence executed. Three situations are distinguished: the contractum is *not known to be in root normal form*; the specified contractum is a *root normal form;* and *no contractum* is specified in this rule alternative.

Redirection to a reducible contractum

When the contractum is not known to be in root normal form, the rewrite rule associated with the symbol in this root must be applied. It makes no sense to fill the redex with the root of the contractum. The new rewrite rule would unpack this node immediately since the functional strategy will indicate this redex as the one to rewrite. So it is possible and more efficient to delay the update of the graph store until a root normal form is reached.

Hence, when the reduction of a new subgraph is demanded, the corresponding root of the redex is pushed once on the bottom of the stack frame. In the case that the reduction continues with the reduction of the contractum, a new stack frame is constructed for the first rule alternative of the corresponding rewrite rule. Rewriting proceeds immediately with that first alternative.

When the right-hand side root function is called, the current function does not need its own stack frame any more. So the space occupied by the old stack frame can be reused for building the new one. The original redex stays as place-holder on the bottom of the new stack frame such that it can be overwritten when the root normal form is reached. The node-ids of the old arguments are removed from the stack and the new ones are pushed instead. After that, a jump (and not a jsr_eval) is performed to the first rule alternative of the called function. In this way *tail recursion* is removed automatically.

Redirection to a contractum in root normal form

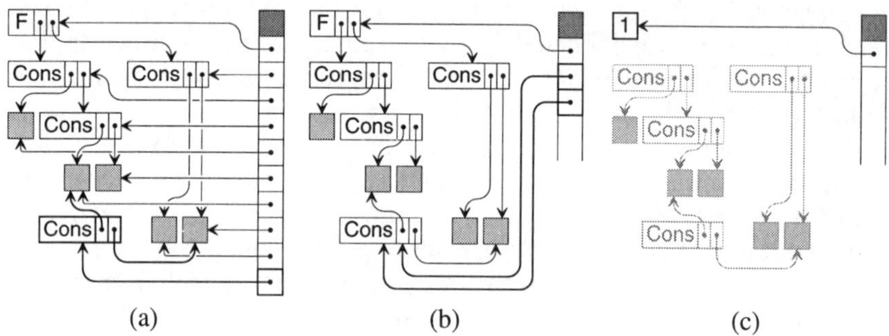

Figure 11.4 (a) The shared node, f, is constructed in the graph store. (b) The stack frame is ready for matching the first rule alternative of G. (c) The reduction according to rule G has been performed, a root normal form is reached; garbage nodes are drawn dotted.

The ABC machine has variable-sized nodes. This means that it is always possible to overwrite a node with arbitrary new contents, even if the new node is larger than the old one. So when the contractum is in root normal form, the place-holder node at the bottom of the stack frame is overwritten with the root of the contractum. In this way all references to the redex are automatically redirected to the contractum: a very cheap and commonly used implementation of redirection.

For a machine without variable-sized nodes the place-holder node is usually overwritten by an **indirection node**: a special node that fits in any node which points to the actual node. A drawback of indirection nodes is that they make an implementation a bit more complicated and inefficient because these indirection nodes can appear anywhere in a graph. So special attention has to be paid to deal with such nodes.

Redirection to an existing graph

When the right-hand side of a rewrite rule only consists of a redirection, there is a problem. The root of the redex has to be redirected to the root of an existing graph somewhere in the graph store. Introduction of indirection nodes may seem unavoidable.

However, the following approach is taken. After the redirection to some existing (sub)graph, the functional strategy will continue with the reduction of that (sub)graph to root normal form. The idea is now to postpone the redirection until after the reduction of the indicated subgraph (see Figure 11.5).

To illustrate these graph manipulations an example is shown .

```
:: Tl ![x]      ->   [x];
   Tl [ h | t ] ->   t;

:: F ->   [INT];
   F ->   [ 1 | F ];
```

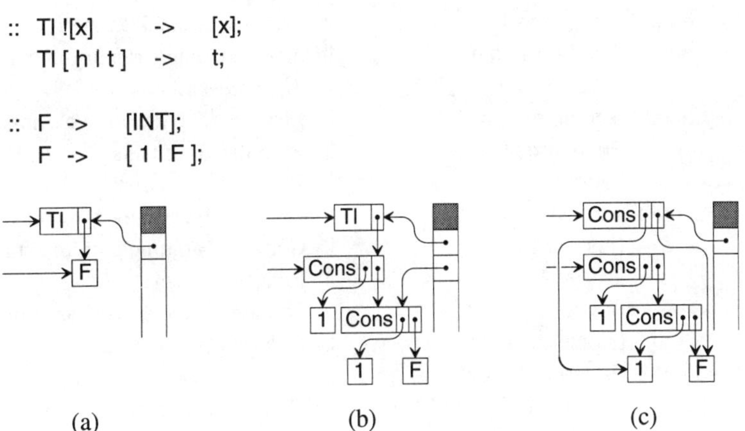

Figure 11.5 (a) Start of the reduction for the graph Tl F. State at the node entry. The arrows from outside indicate sharing. (b) After the reduction of the redex t, before the rewriting. (c) After copying the top node. Both nodes contain the proper root normal form.

This means that first the reduction to root normal form of the redex indicated by the redirection is started. When the root normal form is reached, the root node of this redex will be overwritten as usual. Next, the postponed redirection is performed. This is implemented by overwriting the place-holder node with a *copy* of the root node of the root normal form obtained.

This optimization results in a graph that is *different* from the one that should be obtained according to standard GRS semantics. The redirected arcs point to a copy of the root node instead of to the root node itself. Fortunately, both the graphs remain equal modulo unravelling (see also Chapter 14).

11.1.4 Example of the rewriting process

Consider the following Clean rewrite rule to compute the length of a list:

```
:: Length !INT   ![x]      ->  INT;
   Length n      [ a | b ] ->  Length (+ n 1) b;
   Length n      [ ]       ->  n;
```

The corresponding ABC code using the described calling conventions is:

```
[             Descriptor
"Length"      "a_Length" 2 "Length"     ,  || The generated descriptor
              Label                        || The apply entry
"a_Length",Repl_args 1 1                ,  || Prepare the stack frame
              Jmp "e_Length"            ,  || Start reducing strict arguments
              Label                        || The node entry
"n_Length",Set_entry "_cycle" 0         ,  || Mark node to detect cycle-in-spine
              Push_args 0 2 2           ,  || Push the arguments
              Label                        || The eval args entry
"e_Length",Jsr_eval                     ,  || Reduce first argument to rnf
              Push_a 1                  ,  || Copy 2nd argument on top stack
              Jsr_eval                  ,  || Reduce it to rnf
              Pop_a 1                   ,  || Pop duplicated second argument
              Label                        || Entry for first rule alternative
"Length1",  Eq_desc_arity "Cons" 2 1,      || Match second argument
              Jmp_false "Length2"       ,  || Goto next alternative if match fails
              Push_args 1 2 2           ,  || Push subarguments
              Push_a 1                  ,  || Rewrite according to alternative 1
              Jsr_eval                  ,  || Reduce b
              Create                    ,  || Node for result of + n 1
              Create                    ,  || Node for 1
              FillI 1 0                 ,  || Fill this node
              Push_a 5                  ,  || Push n; it is known to be a rnf
```

```
              Jsr "+1"                      , || Reduction of + n 1
              Update_a 1 5                  , || Adapt stack frame to call Length
              Update_a 0 4                  , ||
              Pop_a 4                       , || Remove old (sub)arguments
              Jmp "Length1"                 , || Goto alternative 1 of Length
              Label                           || Entry for second rule alternative
"Length2",    Eq_desc_arity "Nil" 0 1       , || Match argument
              Jmp_false "Length3"           , || Goto next alternative if match fails
              Fill_a 0 2                    , || Rewrite according to alternative 2
                                              || n known to be a rnf, so it is copied
              Pop_a 2                       , || Remove arguments from stack
              Rtn                           , || Rnf reached
              Label                           || Entry for additional alternative
"Length3",    Jmp "_mismatch"               ] || There is a mismatch
```

The machine state during reduction of this code for the graph Length 0 [1, 2] is shown in Figure 11.6:

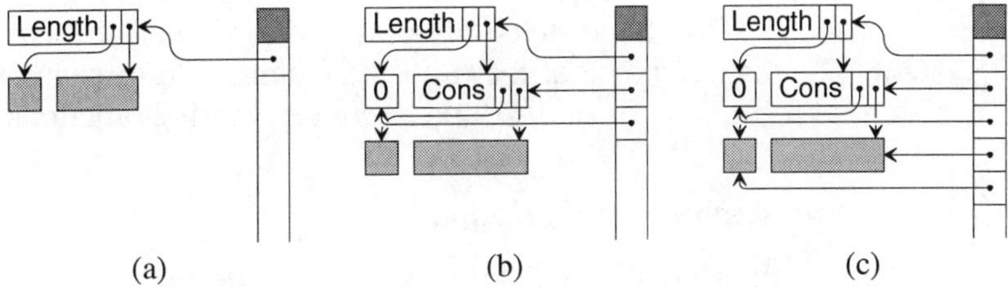

Figure 11.6 (a) Initial state at node entry. (b) Initial state at first alternative entry. (c) After successful match of first rule alternative.

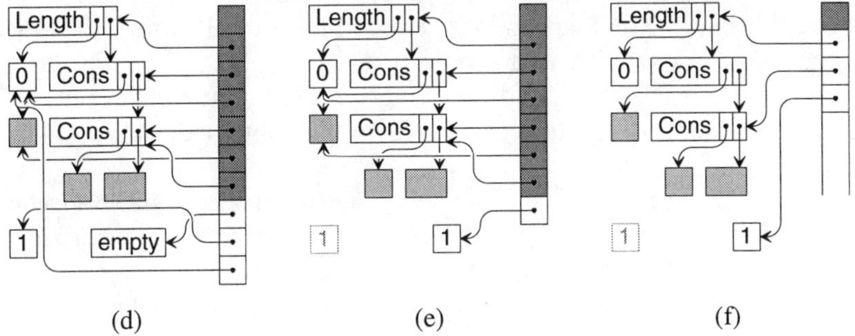

(d) Reduction according to the first rule alternative. First, the last strict argument is reduced. The state before calling + 1 to reduce the first strict argument is shown. (e) State returned by + 1. Garbage nodes are displayed dotted. (f) State before calling Length1 recursively. (*continued overleaf*)

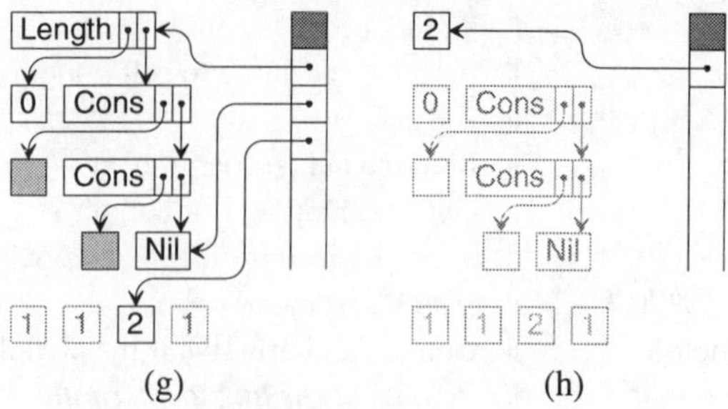

Figure 11.6 (*continued*) (g) State before last call of Length1. (h) State of ABC machine after reaching the rnf.

11.2 The run-time system

Each Clean rewrite rule is translated into a sequence of ABC instructions. To let the machine perform graph rewriting properly, some additional ABC instructions also have to be defined that are independent of a concrete program. This fixed piece of ABC code is called the **run-time system**. The main purpose of the run-time system is to force evaluation to normal form, to perform I/O, and to convert curried functions.

Reduction to normal form and printing

The compilation scheme explained above produces code such that a redex is reduced to root normal form. The run-time system contains the routine init_graph to build the initial redex, the Start node. Then, it initiates the reduction of this Start node to *normal form*. The reduction to normal form and the printing of subgraphs in normal form are done by the routine _driver. The Start node is reduced to normal form as follows: first the Start node is reduced to root normal form, the symbol in the resulting root node is printed and the driver process recursively continues with the arguments of the root normal form thus obtained.

```
[               Label                         || The initiator of graph reduction
"init_graph",   Create                    ,   || Create and fill the start node
                Fill "Start" 0 "n_Start" 0 ,
                Jsr "_driver"             ,   || Print the nf of start node
                Print "\n"                ,   || Print a newline
                Halt                      ,   || The program is finished
                Label                         || The global print driving routine
"_driver",      PushI 0                   ,   || Closing bracket count
                Label                         || Label for tail recursion
"_print",       Jsr_eval                  ,   || Reduce top node to rnf
                Get_node_arity 0          ,   || Get number of args in node
                Eql_b 0 0                 ,   || No arguments ?
```

```
                Jmp_false "_args"       ,
                Label                      || Print last argument
"_print_last",  Print_symbol 0          ,  || Do it
                Pop_a 1                 ,  || Remove node
                Pop_b 1                 ,  || Remove arity
                Label                      || Print the closing brackets
"_brackets",    Eql_b 0 0               ,  || Bracket count equal 0 ?
                Jmp_true "_exit"        ,  || Yes; finished
                Print ")"               ,  || No; print bracket
                Decl                    ,  || Decrement bracket count
                Jmp "_brackets"         ,  || Next bracket
                Label                      || Finished with this node
"_exit",        Pop_b 1                 ,  || Remove bracket count
                Rtn                     ,
                Label                      || Start the printing of arguments
"_args",        Print "("               ,  || An opening bracket
                Print_symbol 0          ,  || The symbol of the node
                Get_desc_arity 0        ,  || Arity corresponding to symbol
                Repl_args_b             ,  || Replace node by its arguments
                Pop_b 1                 ,  || Pop descriptor arity
                Label                      || Loop to print arguments
"_arg_loop",    Print " "               ,  || Space between elements
                Eql_b 1 0               ,  || Last argument ?
                Jmp_false "_next_arg"   ,
                Pop_b 1                 ,  || Remove arg counter
                Incl                    ,  || Increment bracket counter
                Jmp "_print"            ,  || Optimized tail recursion
                Label                      || Print an arg; not the last one
"_next_arg",    Jsr "_driver"           ,  || Recursion to print argument
                Decl                    ,  || Decr arg cnt; driver removes arg
                Jmp "_arg_loop"         ]  || Next argument
```

Miscellaneous definitions in the run-time system

The run-time system contains some special entries for general use and standard descriptors for elements of basic types. As in the previous chapter, only integer and Boolean values are considered here.

The _rnf entry is used as node entry for graphs in root normal form. The _cycle entry is stored upon entrance of a node entry when the reduction of the subgraph rooted with this node is started. In this way a cycle-in-spine error is detected when such a node is revisited. The _mismatch entry is used when none of the rule alternatives is applicable.

```
[               Descriptor
"INT"           "_rnf" 0 "integer"      ,  || Reserved first descriptor
                Descriptor
```

```
"BOOL"       "_rnf" 0 "boolean"          ,  || Reserved second descriptor
             Label                          || Node entry for graphs rnf
"_rnf",      Rtn                         ,  || Return immediately
             Label                          || Node entry to detect cycles
"_cycle",    Print "Cycle-in-spine: Reduction interrupted",
             Halt                        ,  || Stop the reduction
             Label                          || Exit when no alt. applicable!
"_mismatch", Print "Mismatch: Reduction interrupted",
             Halt                        ]  || Stop the reduction
```

Curried functions

To handle curried function applications, the run-time system contains a special predefined rule _AP. The generic _AP rule converts a curried symbol into its uncurried form as soon as all its arguments are available. To obtain this effect all occurrences of curried symbols in Clean are transformed into applications of the function _AP. If F is defined with arity n, say F a_1 a_2 ... a_n -> a_r, then _AP (... (_AP (_AP F a_1) a_2) ...) a_n reduces to F a_1 a_2 ... a_n (see Section 8.1.6).

So the call of a curried function is actually a call of the function _AP. This function is strict in its first argument: the function that has to be applied. Each _AP node provides one additional argument to the function. If there are too few arguments the expression is in root normal form. When all arguments are there the indicated function is called.

On the ABC machine the arguments of the curried function are collected one by one in the corresponding apply node. When the last argument is supplied and all other required arguments are already collected, a stack frame according to the apply entry is constructed and execution continues on that entry of the corresponding function. Otherwise, the next argument is collected in its turn and a root normal form is reached. The code for _AP is similar to the code for other functions.

```
[          Descriptor
"_AP"      "n_AP" 2 "_AP"
           Label                          || The node entry for _AP
"n_AP",    Set_entry "_cycle" 0        ,  || Mark node as being reduced
           Push_args 0 2 2             ,  || Push the function and its arg
           Jsr_eval                    ,  || Reduce curried function to rnf
           Label                          || Entry for rule alternative _AP
"_AP1",    Get_node_arity 0            ,  || Number of args in node
           Get_desc_arity 0            ,  || Number of args for symbol
           SubI                        ,  || Number of arguments needed
           EqI_b 1 0                   ,  || Last argument supplied?
           Jmp_false "yet_args_needed",   || No; update node and return
           Pop_b 1                     ,  || Yes; start reduction of function
           Push_ap_entry 0             ,  || Push apply entry on C-stack
```

```
                Rtn                              ,  || Jump to that entry
                Label                               || _AP doesn't supply last arg
"yet_args_needed"                                ,  || Update apply node and return
                Push_a 1                         ,  || Argument supplied here
                Add_args 1 1 3                   ,  || Update apply node
                Pop_a 2                          ,  || Clean up stacks
                Pop_b 1                          ,  ||
                Rtn                              ]  || Rnf reached
```

This is illustrated by the following example (Figure 11.7):

```
Start ->    Inc 2;
Inc   ->    Plus 1;
Plus  ->    +;
```

which is internally transformed into:

```
Start ->    _AP Inc 2;
Inc   ->    _AP Plus 1;
Plus  ->    +;
```

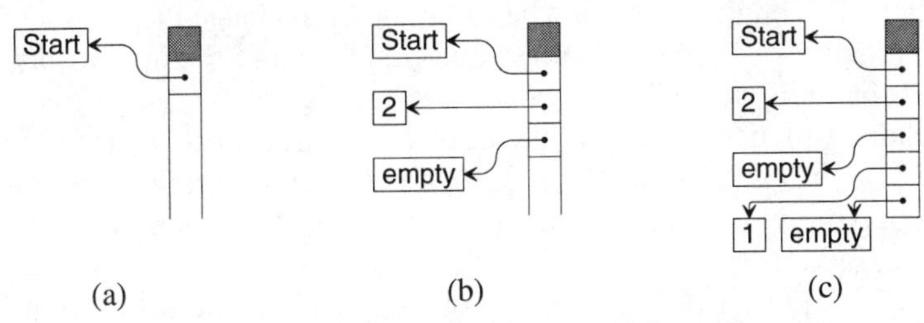

Figure 11.7 (a) Initial state. Reduction starts at the node entry of Start. (b) Creation of the arguments of _AP. Second argument is built. First argument is strict. (c) Reduction according to Inc. Second argument is created. First argument is strict.

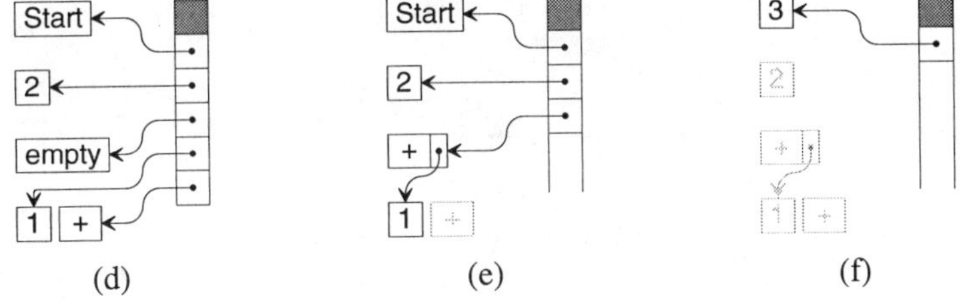

(d) Reduction according to Plus. The redex node is filled with an rnf. (e) + has not enough arguments to become a function. So the node is filled with the rnf. (f) After reduction according to + the top node is replaced by its rnf.

11.3 Optimizations

The code generated by the compilation scheme presented above can be improved at many places. The most important improvement is to use the B-stack instead of the nodes in the graph to pass basic values between functions. The use of the B-stack will be described informally and illustrated with an example. Afterwards some other high-level optimizations will be discussed.

11.3.1 The extended compilation scheme using the B-stack

Basic values are manipulated on the B-stack of the ABC machine. This implies that every computation involving basic values requires the transportation of the values to the B-stack and the shipment of the result back to a node in the graph store. When the result is used again as argument in another computation there is too much data transportation. To reduce the unnecessary movement of data, the compilation scheme must be changed such that basic values stay on the B-stack as much as possible. To achieve this, the stack frame expected by the rewrite alternatives is changed: strict arguments of *simple basic type* (integers, reals, characters, booleans, files) are passed on the B-stack and the result of a reduction is also left on the B-stack when it is of such a basic type.

The calling conventions for the node entry and the apply entry remain unchanged, but the code corresponding to the eval args entry has to be changed since it has to take care of the transport of basic values between the graph and the B-stack. After the reduction of a strict argument of a simple basic type, the value contained in the node in the graph store is copied to the B-stack. When the result of the function is also of a basic type the first rule alternative entry is called as a subroutine. The corresponding code will yield the root normal form on the B-stack. Returning from the subroutine call the result is stored in the place-holder node.

Summary of changed calling conventions and their actions

Eval args entry

Called by: node entry as well as apply entry.

Calling conventions:

- node-id of place-holder node on the stack;
- node-ids of all arguments of the function called above it, node-id of first argument on top of A-stack.

Actions:

- reduce those arguments that are marked as strict to root normal form;
- when the strict arguments are of a simple basic type, the values are pushed on the B-stack and the corresponding node-ids are popped;

- proceed with first rule alternative entry, but do this via a jsr when the result is of simple basic type in order to come back to copy this result from the B-stack back to the A-stack.

Rule alternative entry

Called by: the first rule alternative can be called by any function;
- the other rule alternatives are called by the previous one when they do not match.

Calling conventions:
- the stack frame is complete: node-id of place-holder node on the stack, node-ids of arguments on top of it, strict arguments are in root normal form, strict arguments of complex type on A-stack, the others on the B-stack.

Actions:
- try to match this alternative;
- if no match, proceed with next rule alternative entry;
- if match, evaluate strict nodes of right-hand side and construct contractum;
- when a root normal form is reached, the place-holder node is overwritten with the contractum; return to caller;
- otherwise: build stack frame for root of right-hand side;
- proceed with the first rule alternative entry of the root of right-hand side.

The complexity of the code generation is increased significantly by this new calling convention. Arguments and results must be moved to the desired place at every occurrence. This is not difficult, but it involves an elaborated case analysis.

An example of the use of the B-stack

To show the changes resulting from the new calling conventions the ABC code for the Length example of Section 11.1.4 is shown.

```
:: Length !INT  ![x]      ->   INT;
   Length n     [ a | b ] ->   Length (+ n 1) b;
   Length n     [ ]       ->   n;
```

Both arguments are strict. Note that the first argument is also a basic value, so it will be passed on the B-stack to the rule alternatives. They will also store the result on the B-stack. The integer addition used on the right-hand side also expects strict basic values as argument and it delivers a strict basic value as well. So no nodes have to be created when + is called, and all values are passed directly on the B-stack. The same holds for the first argument of Length when it calls itself recursively.

```
[           Descriptor
"Length"    "a_Length" 2 "Length"     ,   || The generated descriptor
            Label                         || The apply entry
"a_Length",Repl_args 1 1              ,   || Prepare the stack frame
```

```
            Jmp "e_Length"                   , || Start reducing strict arguments
            Label                              || The node entry
"n_Length",Set_entry "_cycle" 0              , || Mark node to detect cycle-in-spine
            Push_args 0 2 2                  , || Push the arguments
            Label                              || The eval args entry
"e_Length",Jsr_eval                          , || Reduce first argument to rnf
            PushI_a 0                        , || Copy first argument to the B-stack
            Pop_a 1                          , || Pop first argument from A-stack
            Jsr_eval                         , || Reduce second argument to rnf
            Pop_a 1                          , || Pop duplicated second argument
            Jsr "Length1"                    , || Initiate rewriting by alternatives
            FillI_b 0 0                      , || Fill node with result of reduction
            Pop_b 1                          , || Pop result of the reduction
            Rtn                              , || Done; node is in rnf
            Label                              || Entry for first rule alternative
"Length1", Eq_desc_arity "Cons" 2 0,           || Match argument
            Jmp_false "Length2"              , || Goto next alternative if match fails
            Push_args 0 2 2                  , || Push subarguments
            Push_a 1                         , || Rewrite according to alternative 1
            Jsr_eval                         , || Reduce b
            PushI 1                          , || Second argument for +
            Push_b 1                         , || First argument for +
            Jsr "+1"                         , || Reduction of + n 1
            Update_a 0 3                     , || Adapt A-stack frame to call Length
            Update_b 0 1                     , || Adapt B-stack frame to call Length
            Pop_a 3                          , || Remove old args from A-stack
            Pop_b 1                          , || Remove old args from B-stack
            Jmp "Length1"                    , || Goto alternative 1 of Length
            Label                              || Entry for second rule alternative
"Length2", Eq_desc_arity "Nil" 0 0           , || Match argument
            Jmp_false "Length3"              , || Goto alternative 3 if match fails
            Pop_a 1                          , || Remove arg
            Rtn                              , || Rnf reached
            Label                              || Entry for additional alternative
"Length3", Jmp "_mismatch"                   ] || There is a mismatch
```

In Figure 11.8 snapshots of the reduction process are shown (compare them with the pictures in Figure 11.6). The efficiency gained by this optimized compilation scheme depends on the rules to transform and the implementation of the ABC machine. The measured efficiency gain for the length rule given as an example using a reasonable implementation is about a factor of 2.5 when garbage collection is excluded (see Chapter 12 for more information on garbage collection). However, a lot of garbage collection is prevented as well. The efficiency gained by eliminating the garbage collection depends heavily upon the circumstances. Including the garbage collection the efficiency gain of the length function is typically about a factor of 6.5.

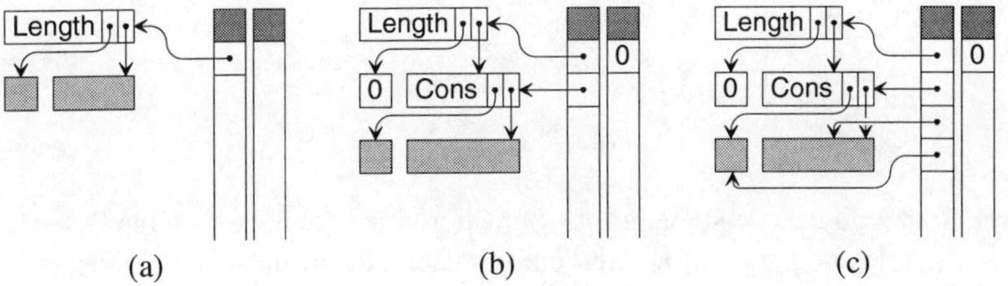

Figure 11.8 (a) Initial state at node entry. (b) State at first rewrite alternative entry. (c) After successful match of first rule alternative.

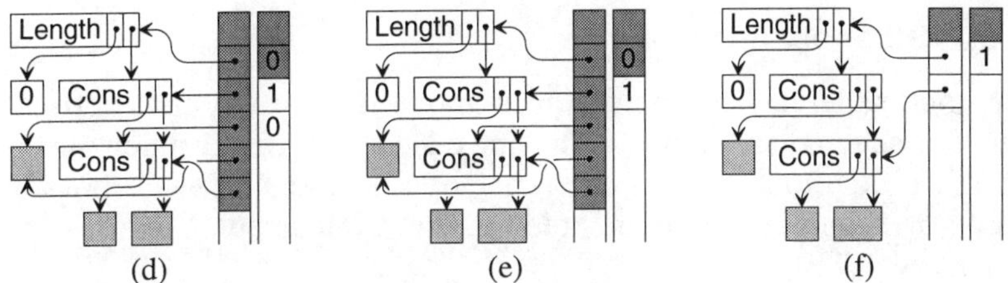

(d) Reduction according to the first rule alternative. State before calling +1. (e) State returned by +1. (f) State before calling Length1 recursively.

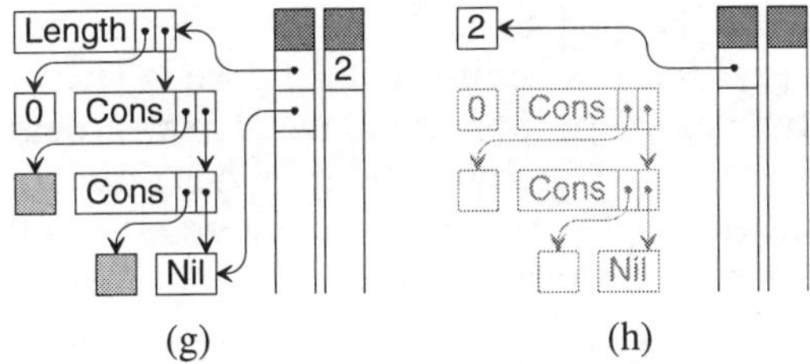

(g) State before last call of Length1. (h) State of ABC machine after the rnf is reached.

The example above shows the successful use of the B-stack. It included very little overhead involving the movement of data between the graph and B-stack. This is not always the case. It is possible to construct an example such that arguments just happen to be expected on the other stack. Projection functions, like the identity function, always work on the A-stack. This induces an overhead when they are called with arguments that live on the B-stack. A solution for this problem will be discussed in the next section.

Unnecessary overhead may occur when using the B-stack:

```
:: I !x    ->    x;
   I x     ->    x;

:: F !INT !INT   ->    INT;
   F a b         ->    + (I a) b;
```

Both arguments and the result of function F will be passed on the B-stack by the rule alternative entry. But, unfortunately, the identity function expects its polymorphic typed argument on the A-stack and also leaves its result there. So a has to be put back in a node to pass it to I and the result must again be extracted from a node to pass it to +.

11.3.2 Other optimizations

The code generated by the schemes above is generally more efficient than the scheme in Figure 11.6, but can be improved much further. Here, we mention some of the other optimizations that are possible. Many of them are implemented in the Concurrent Clean System (Smetsers, 1989).

- The elements of strict tuples can also be passed on the stacks instead of via a reference to a node in the graph. In addition, it is possible in Clean to put strict annotations in a tuple type appearing in a strict context (see Section 8.3). When these arguments are of a simple basic type they can also be passed on the B-stack instead of the A-stack. So in that case there is not much difference in terms of efficiency between a function with more than one argument and a function that carries its arguments in a strict tuple. When a function yields a tuple as result, the tuple arguments are returned via the stacks as well. Functions that return a tuple of which the basic typed arguments are marked as being strict can return the corresponding values via the B-stack.
- When a new stack frame is constructed over the old the references on the stack have to be rearranged in the right order. A simple solution uses temporary variables to construct the new frame before the old one is overwritten. A more clever algorithm will try to minimize the number of moves (updates) and additional amount of space needed for the construction of the new frame.
- As shown above, there are some cases where arguments are shipped from A-stack to B-stack and backwards frequently. The calling conventions for such functions can be changed such that they can handle items on both stacks. This requires, however, a number of entries that is exponential with respect to the number of

arguments since all cases have to be covered, so this will only be practical for functions with a very small number of arguments.

- For projection functions for which the right-hand side consists of a single node-id, the place-holder node of the function application can be used, so a new place-holder node need not be created. In this way one prevents a possible series of place-holder nodes to which results are copied.
- It is very important to use in-line code substitution for very short functions. Instead of performing a subroutine jump, the body of the routine is substituted in place. This makes it possible, for instance, to generate the AddI instruction instead of a Jsr +1.
- In the present compilation schemes the matching of each rule alternative starts from scratch. However, the use of information from the previous alternative and type information can speed up the matching process considerably. So it is better to use a finite state machine for the matching of the rule alternatives instead of starting all over again for each alternative.
- Constant graphs which occur on the right-hand side of rewrite rules need not be built each time the rule is used. These graphs can be created once. The node-ids of the root of these graphs can be used instead of building a new one at each occurrence.
- One can use scratch nodes for nodes which will be used once for a very short time. This occurs when a function delivers its result in the graph which is required on the B-stack; the result is stored in the node, moved to the B-stack and the node becomes garbage immediately.
- It is important that nodes are represented as compactly as possible. Special compact representations can be chosen for nodes containing basic values or nodes with few arguments.
- One can improve the performance of predefined functions (δ-rules) by hand-coding them in assembler.
- One can reuse UNQ-attributed function arguments (see Section 8.5) for the construction of the function result. This makes it, for example, possible to define a traditional sort function on a list with a unique spine. Sorting then can take place *in situ*: no new Cons nodes have to be constructed (Smetsers *et al.*, 1993).

Besides these optimizations in the area of code generation for the ABC machine there are also important optimizations possible on the level of the Clean language itself: Clean program transformations. Functions can be partially evaluated at compile-time. Clearly, this is possible for expressions that consist only of constants. One can create specialized function calls for certain function applications in which it is, for example, clear that one or more of the alternatives of the original function will never match, etc. Of course, the transformations must not change the termination behaviour of the program.

Another important optimization on the level of Clean itself concerns the analysis of *all* applications of a function. This can, for instance, greatly improve the strictness analysis of Chapter 7, in which only the function definition is taken into account.

11.3.3 Efficiency gain of the optimizations

To analyse the effect of a subset of the optimizations mentioned a measurement of the performance of the well known Nfib function is presented. The integer delivered by the Nfib function is the number of performed function calls. The Nfib-number is obtained by dividing this number by the execution time. So the **Nfib-number** is the number of function calls per second that is executed for the calculation of the result in this particular example. The Nfib 'benchmark' is often used as a measure for the basic efficiency of an implementation of a functional language. Although it gives some indication of the speed offered, it is not at all a representative benchmark. The Nfib-number is extremely sensitive to the optimizations discussed. It actually gives the maximum number of function calls per second under ideal circumstances.

```
:: Nfib !INT   ->   INT;
   Nfib 0      ->   1;
   Nfib 1      ->   1;
   Nfib n      ->   ++ (+ (Nfib (-- n)) (Nfib (- n 2)));
```

The table below gives an idea about the gain in efficiency obtained by the optimizations mentioned. Unless stated otherwise the measurements where done on a Sun 3/280 under SunOS 4.0.3 (using a straightforward code generation for the Sun). Measurements are accurate within 10%.

Nfib-number	*Conditions*
90 000	The basic translation scheme as given in Section 11.1.
280 000	The integers are passed on the B-stack.
415 000	In-line code substitution is also used for the δ-rules.
2 000	Same code interpreted by the PABC interpreter/simulator (Nöcker, 1989).
300 000	The Nfib function in C (Kernighan and Ritchie, 1978).
1 200	The Nfib function in Miranda, executed by the Miranda interpreter.
6	ABC machine as in Appendix C (Miranda interpreter).
220	ABC machine as in Appendix C, with Miranda converted to the Concurrent Clean System, executed by the Concurrent Clean System.

The code for the 415 000 Nfib in ABC assembly using the extended compilation scheme becomes:

```
[            Descriptor
 "Nfib"      "a_Nfib" 1 "Nfib"         , || The generated descriptor
             Label                       || The apply entry
"a_Nfib",    Pop_a 1                   , || Reference to node containing Nfib
             Jmp "e_Nfib"              , || Start reducing strict argument
             Label                       || The node entry
"n_Nfib",    Set-entry "_cycle" 0      , || Mark node to detect cycle-in-spine
             Push_args 0 1 1           , || Push argument on A-stack
             Label                       || The eval args entry
"e_Nfib",    Jsr_eval                  , || Reduce strict argument
             PushI_a 0                 , || Copy argument to B-stack
             Pop_a 1                   , || Remove argument from A-stack
             Jsr "Nfib1"               , || Initiate calculation on B-stack
             FillI_b 0 0               , || Copy result from B-stack to node
             Pop_b 1                   , || Remove result from B-stack
             Rtn                       , || Rnf reached
             Label
"Nfib1",     EqI_b 0 0                 , || Match rule 1; is argument 0?
             Jmp_false "Nfib2"         , || No; goto second rule alternative
             Pop_b 1                   , || Yes; remove argument
             PushI 1                   , || Store result
             Rtn                       , || Done
             Label
"Nfib2",     EqI_b 1 0                 , || Match rule 2; is argument equal 1
             Jmp_false "Nfib3"         , || No; goto rule alternative 3
             Pop_b 1                   , || Yes; remove argument
             PushI 1                   , || Push result
             Rtn                       , || Done
             Label                       || Rule alternative 3
"Nfib3",     PushI 2                   , || Compute – n 2
             Push_b 1                  , || Push n
             SubI                      , || In-line code substitution for –
             Jsr "Nfib1"               , || Compute Nfib (– n 2)
             Push_b 1                  , || Compute – – n; push argument
             DecI                      , || In-line code substitution for –
             Jsr "Nfib1"               , || Compute Nfib (– – n)
             AddI                      , || In-line code substitution for +
             Update_b 0 1              , || Replace argument by result
             Pop_b 1                   , || Remove copied result
             IncI                      , || In-line code substitution for ++
             Rtn                       ] || Done
```

With better code generation for the concrete machine the performance (including the Nfib-number) can be improved even further (see the next chapter).

Summary

- A Clean program can be translated into ABC code with the *basic translation scheme* in which Clean *graphs* are more or less directly *mapped onto graphs* in the graph store of the ABC machine.
- In this basic scheme the graph rewriting process is as follows: *redirection* is *implemented by overwriting* the root of the redex with the root of the contractum. Furthermore, *overwriting* of such a redex *is delayed* until the root normal form is reached.
- An important optimization is the use of the *B-stack* to pass arguments that are *both strict and of a basic type*. Results that are of a basic type are again returned on the B-stack. As a consequence, such basic calculations are actually not performed via graph rewriting at all but they *entirely* proceed on the B-stack.
- Many more optimizations are possible resulting in a code with an efficiency in *the same order of magnitude as classical imperative code*. Compiled code typically can be two orders of magnitude faster than when an interpreter is used.

EXERCISES

11.1* Consider the following Clean rule:

```
:: Filter INT [INT]    ->   [INT];
   Filter x  [ ]       ->   [ ];
   Filter x  [ e | es ] ->  r, IF = e x
                       ->   [ e | Filter e r ],
                            r: Filter x es ;
```

(a) Write the corresponding ABC code obeying the calling conventions.

(b) Add strictness annotations in the Clean rule where possible.

(c) Change the ABC code given above to obtain the most optimal code as explained in the textbook: use strictness annotations, in-line code substitution, B-stack parameter passing.

(d) Indicate explicitly which alterations, omissions or additions in the code are due to each optimization.

Chapter 12
Realizing the ABC machine

This chapter treats the last step in the implementation path of functional languages: the realization of the abstract ABC machine by translation of ABC machine code to executable code for a concrete machine (Figure 12.1).

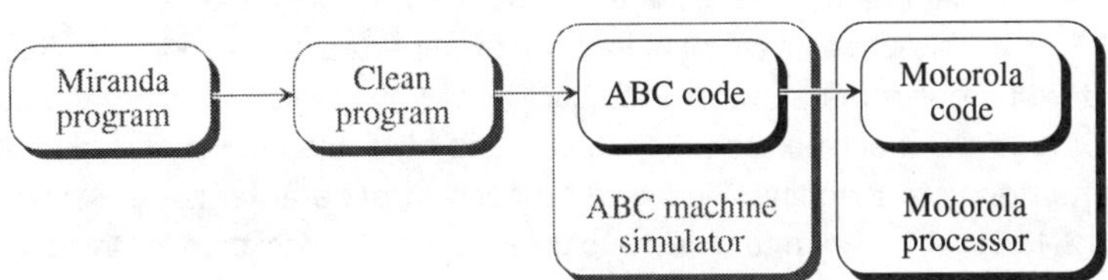

Figure 12.1 Realizing the ABC machine on a concrete machine.

In principle, an abstract machine such as the ABC machine can be realized either in hardware or by a software implementation running on standard hardware. With tailor-made hardware one should be able to obtain extremely good performance. However, the design of such a dedicated piece of hardware would take a lot of time and money. Furthermore, with present day compilation techniques it is possible to achieve efficient implementations on cheap standard hardware. So in practice there is no need for special purpose hardware reduction machines unless ultimate performance is demanded.

A software realization of the ABC machine can be achieved in two different ways. The first method is to write a program that interprets ABC machine code. Such an *interpreter* analyses and executes ABC code at run-time. In general, this is done instruction by instruction. Owing to the run-time analysis that has to be done, the most important disadvantage of an interpreter is that it is slow, independent of the language in which the interpreter is written. On the other hand, an interpreter has the advantage that it is easy to implement. Furthermore, it can be written in a portable language such as C (Kernighan and Ritchie, 1978) which makes an implementation available on many different kinds of machine. Tracing and debugging tools can also be encapsulated relatively easily into an interpreter. The formal definition of the ABC machine in Appendix C can be used as such an interpreter for ABC code.

The second method is to make a *code generator* that analyses sequences of ABC code at compile-time and generates executable code that does the actual work at run-time. In this way much time can be spent analysing the ABC code such that the code generated is as efficient as possible. Code generators are therefore generally much more complicated programs than interpreters. By making good use of the instructions and registers that are available on the concrete machine, code generators can produce efficient code that can do the work typically one order of magnitude faster than an interpreter running on the same machine. For ABC code sometimes an improvement of even two orders of magnitude has been measured (see Section 11.3). Concrete architectures differ much in detail (the instruction set, the memory management, number and kind of registers). Implementation tricks suited for one machine are usually not suited for others. So code generators that produce fast code are generally not very portable.

In this chapter we explain how to generate good code for standard hardware. First one has to decide how the logical memory stores of the ABC machine are mapped onto the available memory storage of the concrete machine. This is discussed in general terms in Section 12.1. Suitable concrete data structures have to be designed for this purpose. In general this will not cause many problems. The concrete data structures needed to implement the stores often directly follow the abstract definition in the ABC machine. An important difference between the ABC machine and a concrete machine is that the latter has a *limited* amount of memory. As a consequence, the memory management of the graph store becomes more complex. *Garbage collection* is needed to reclaim unused memory. Several techniques for garbage collection are discussed in Section 12.2.

Simple code generators (based on macro substitution of ABC instructions) are in principle not difficult to implement. But, when the context in which ABC instructions appear is taken into account, many optimizations can be performed. The ABC code generated is certainly not optimal in terms of efficiency. For example, many ABC instructions require their arguments on top of the stack whereas on a concrete machine the arguments of corresponding instructions can be accessed more directly using the addressing modes of the target machine. This implies that the copy actions specified by the ABC instructions are often not necessary. The ABC machine does not have registers. Registers have the property that their access time is much less than the access time of ordinary memory locations. Registers can be used for implementing the ABC stacks and heap, for storing temporary values, and for passing arguments and return values. To make optimal use of registers while avoiding unnecessary saving and restoring of information is a difficult task. Consequently, a good code generator for Clean is rather complex (Van Groningen, 1990). Some of the techniques that can be used are general techniques commonly used for the implementation of other types of languages (for example register allocation algorithms). Sometimes they have to be adapted because of the specific properties of both source language and target machine. Other optimizations are very specific for lazy functional languages, e.g. the implementation of higher order functions, efficient memory management and optimized graph reduction.

In the remaining sections of this chapter we describe how abstract ABC machine code can be translated to a specific target machine: the Motorola MC68020 processor. However, many of the ideas presented can be generally applied for other architectures as well. A brief summary of the Motorola architecture and instruction set is given in Section 12.3. A concrete representation of the ABC memory components chosen on the Motorola is presented in Section 12.4. How computations specified in ABC code can be optimized when generating concrete machine code is described in Section 12.5. A concrete example of the code generated is shown in Section 12.6. The measurements presented in Section 12.7 demonstrate that with all the optimizations discussed in this part of the book good code can indeed be generated.

12.1 Representing the ABC machine components

The first step in the realization of the ABC machine on concrete hardware is the design of the data structures that represent the several ABC machine memory components. This involves deciding how to map these data structures onto the concrete memory storages of the target machine. As already stated in the introduction, one of the main differences between the abstract machine and a concrete machine is that the latter has to deal with a limited amount of memory. So the data structures have to be chosen such that memory management of the components can be done efficiently. Furthermore, it is very important to achieve fast access on the elements of the several stores.

The actual design of the data structures and their mapping to the memory will be highly dependent on the architecture of the concrete machine. For some classes of architecture the mapping will be more difficult than others. One has to bear in mind that the ABC machine is a mixture between an idealized graph rewriting machine and a stack-based architecture. Therefore, it will be easier to find a suitable implementation for a Motorola-based architecture than for an IBM PC (poor support for a graph store due to its segmented memory) or transputer-based architecture (poor support for stacks due to limited number of registers and lack of suitable addressing modes). For some classes of architecture maybe a slightly different type of abstract machine would be more convenient. However, it is impossible to design an abstract machine that is equally easy to map to all existing kinds of concrete architectures. Concrete architectures for which the ABC machine is a suitable abstraction have:

- a reasonable amount of memory (a couple of megabytes);
- the possibility of reserving a large proportion of this memory to implement the graph store;
- support for the implementation of stacks (i.e. lots of registers with suitable addressing modes).

A concrete memory generally consists of a finite sequence of consecutive memory cells. Stacks and stores of the ABC machine are implemented on a consecutive partition of such a memory (see Section 12.4 for a possible partitioning). The registers of the concrete machine are generally used to store program counter and stack pointers and to store intermediate arithmetic results. Input and output have to be interfaced with the file system and the I/O facilities offered by the underlying operating system.

The program store

The program store contains concrete machine instructions:

- code produced by the code generator by translating rule-dependent ABC instructions;
- the run-time system including code for memory management like garbage collection.

The several entries (instr-ids) are represented by addresses in this store.

The program counter

The program counter of the ABC machine can of course be represented directly by the program counter of the concrete machine.

The A-stack, B-stack and C-stack

To make the mapping of ABC instructions to concrete instructions convenient it is necessary that a memory partition is allocated for each stack. For each stack a pointer pointing to the top element on the stack is needed. For reasons of efficiency these pointers are usually kept in registers.

Stacks on concrete machines cause the following memory management problems. First of all, concrete stacks have a finite size. So it is necessary to do a run-time *boundary check*. Some machines have hardware support for such a boundary check. Otherwise, additional code has to be generated to do a boundary check when something is pushed on a stack. This will slow down the performance (typically by 20–30 %). Another possibility, taken by many implementations of imperative languages, is simply to leave out the boundary check and take the risk that the system might crash. Other compilers generate boundary checks optionally. When a boundary check is implemented one can either stop the program when the limit is reached or try to dump part of the stack to secondary memory.

Another disadvantage of a stack is that at run-time it may occupy only a very small part of the partition that is reserved for it. In that case the other part of the partition is wasted. With three stacks three parts may be wasted. However, two stacks can be put in one partition in which they grow in opposite directions. In this way they share the free space. In Figure 12.10 this solution is chosen for the A- and B-stacks. Another solution is to allow the programmer, using a trial-and-error method, to specify the amount of memory that should be reserved for each stack. In this way the partitions for a specific application can be tuned by hand such that the stacks are big enough but the amount of wasted memory is minimal.

Another way to reduce the problems mentioned above is by reducing the number of stacks. It is not really necessary to implement every stack separately. It is also possible to merge two or even all three of them into one stack. The merging of the B- and C-stacks causes no problems and is certainly advisable when parallel code has to be generated (see Chapter 17). However, merging the A-stack has to be done in such a way that it is possible to recognize the elements belonging to the A-stack, since they are needed for garbage collection (see Section 12.2). This generally requires additional space for tagging stack elements and may cause a slightly more complex access or a more complex garbage collector. If one decides to merge stacks the code generation will get slightly more difficult, since the offsets of the ABC push and pop instructions will not correspond directly to offsets on the concrete stacks. To make code generation simple again one can incorporate the merging of stacks at the ABC level. One then obtains an A-B&C machine or an A&B&C machine. The translation from Clean to such a changed abstract machine with merged stacks is no more difficult than the code generation for the current ABC machine.

The graph store

The graph store is represented in a memory partition called the **heap**. A graph is composed of nodes. Node-ids are just addresses of memory cells. In principle there are many different choices possible for the representation of ABC nodes in memory. However, the ABC code that is generated by a Clean program (see Chapter 11) assumes that the node on the bottom of a stack frame can always be overwritten with another node. This can be implemented simply in a conventional memory when all nodes are equal in size. The problem is that Clean nodes have variable arity. To solve this problem without wasting memory one can split up an abstract node into two separate concrete nodes: a fixed-sized part and, optionally, a variable-sized part (see Figure 12.2).

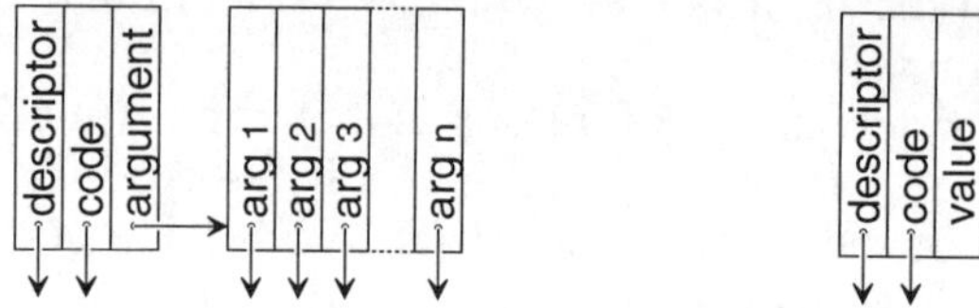

Figure 12.2 Two possible node structures.

The fixed-sized part generally contains:

- an entry in the descriptor store, the **descriptor pointer**, uniquely representing the corresponding Clean symbol (see below);
- a code field containing an address in the program store, called the **code pointer** (commonly pointing to the corresponding node entry);
- a field containing either the address of the variable-sized part or a basic value. The address is called the **argument pointer**.

The variable-sized part generally contains pointers. Each pointer refers to a node representing an argument of the symbol. It can also contain a basic value (string). In principle, no additional tags are needed in nodes. The split representation of nodes makes it always possible to overwrite the fixed-sized part with another fixed-sized part. This representation is essentially equivalent to (and developed independently from) the one chosen by Peyton Jones and Salkild in their spineless tagless G-machine paper (Peyton Jones and Salkild, 1989).

As is the case with stacks, the graph store in the ABC machine is unlimited. In a concrete machine that is not the case. When a new node has to be created in a full concrete graph store one can try to reuse parts of the heap filled with nodes that have become garbage because they are not connected to the data graph any more (see Chapter 5). This well-known technique is called **garbage collection**. A piece of code that takes care of this is called a **garbage collector**. Solutions for garbage collection are discussed in Section 12.2.

The descriptor store

Just as in the ABC machine an actual descriptor in the descriptor store should contain:

- the symbol name (as a string);
- the arity of the symbol;
- the address of the apply entry in the program store.

Furthermore, it is convenient for memory management reasons to store additional information on the kind of node, such as whether it contains a basic value and if so, of what type. The type and arity of a symbol can be used by a garbage collector to determine the structure of a node. The apply entry is used for curried functions.

The input/output channel

As soon as the reduct of the start rule has reached a root normal form the root symbol is written to the standard output channel of the concrete machine.

12.2 Garbage collection

In this section the implementation of garbage collection is discussed in the context of the realization of the ABC machine. In the literature many kinds of garbage collection algorithms can be found. It depends on the available hardware, on the demands of the user and on the properties of the programs which of these algorithms is suited best. Below several well-known algorithms are briefly discussed and their suitability for the collection of variable-sized Clean nodes stored in the heap is examined. First some terminology is introduced.

Terminology

In this section on garbage collection a **node** is defined as a number of contiguous computer cells that can be manipulated by the user program. For a garbage collector the representation of a Clean node as given in the previous section can actually consist of two nodes in memory: the fixed-sized part and the variable-sized part. If a node x contains a pointer to a node y, then x is called the **parent** of y, and y is called a **child** of x. Nodes that cannot be reached any more via pointers from the root(s) of the graph are called **garbage**.

The *storage allocator* and *garbage collector* together manage the memory. The **storage allocator** is a program that assigns storage (nodes) to the user program. For the storage allocator the memory consists of two parts: a part with unallocated nodes, the **free space**, and a part with allocated nodes. The storage allocator takes storage from the free space and makes it available to the user program in the form of nodes. The **garbage collector** retrieves allocated nodes that are not being used any more and reassigns them to the free space.

Garbage collection of nodes that are all of the same fixed size is generally easier than garbage collection of nodes that vary in size. In the proposed realization of the ABC machine the nodes in memory can have different sizes (due to the variable-sized parts). Therefore only garbage collectors are considered that can deal with variable-sized nodes.

Management of the free space

The free space generally consists either of a *linked list of unused nodes* or it consists of a *contiguous part of memory*.

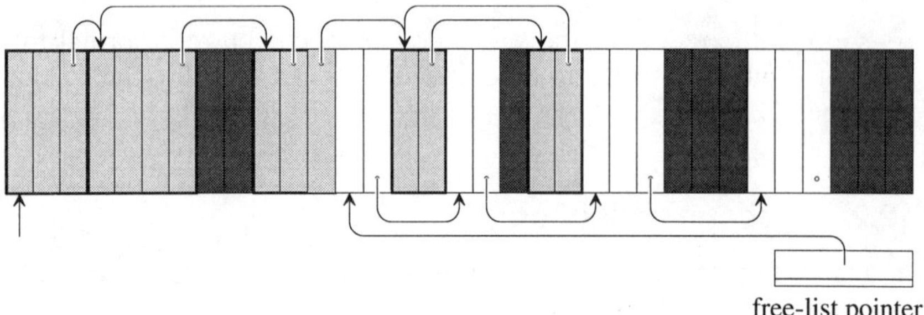

Figure 12.3 Free space management with a free-list. White cells are unused, light-grey cells are nodes in use, dark-grey cells are garbage.

When the free space is a *linked list*, a pointer to the head of the free-list is maintained, for instance in a register (see Figure 12.3). Such a linked list is called a **free-list**. The main disadvantage of a free-list is that storage allocation is more complex when one has to deal with variable-sized nodes. In general one has to walk through the linked list to find an unused node of a certain size. It can even happen that there are enough nodes available in the free-list, but none of them has the required size. So although there is space enough in the heap it cannot be used because of this **memory fragmentation.**

When there is no piece of contiguous memory of the right size available in the free-list one can move the available nodes in the memory such that they form a contiguous storage area. This process is called **compaction**. Compaction is a costly process since all nodes must be moved and pointers have to be adjusted such that the free-list fills a contiguous piece of memory. So it is important to avoid or postpone compaction as much as possible.

Morris (1978) introduces a compaction algorithm for variable-sized nodes. It does the compaction in linear time with respect to the number of non-garbage nodes and needs only one additional bit per pointer. The algorithm requires two scans. The first one only readjusts forward-pointing references. The second one updates references pointing backwards and does the compaction.

One way to postpone compaction is by keeping multiple free-lists (instead of one): i.e. besides the normal free-list with nodes of miscellaneous sizes a separate free-list is maintained for each node size commonly used in a program. An unused node is returned to the appropriate free-list. Requests for new nodes are handled according to their size. If the only node available is larger than needed, it is split into two nodes; the first is used to satisfy the request, the second is returned to one of the free-lists.

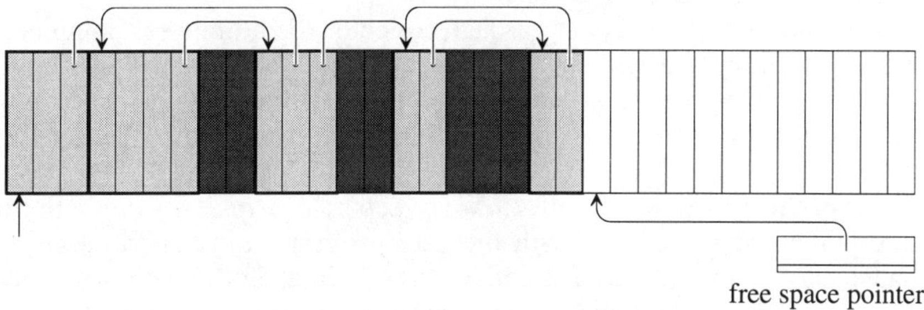

Figure 12.4 The free space contained in a contiguous part of memory.

When the free space is always a *contiguous part of memory*, the storage allocator is very simple: a pointer to the next free word is maintained (see Figure 12.4). If a request for a node with a size of n words is done, this pointer is simply moved n words further on. So having a free space that consists of a contiguous part of memory is ideal for storage allocation for variable-sized nodes. Another advantage of using a contiguous part of memory is that no compaction is needed.

The garbage collector

A garbage collector has the following tasks: the identification of the nodes that are garbage and the collection of these nodes into the free space. If the free space consists of a free-list it may be necessary to compact collected nodes such that they form a contiguous storage area (after or during the incorporation of the nodes into the free space).

One of the problems of garbage collection is that the garbage collector is invoked at the moment that there is no space available any more, perhaps not even for the garbage collector itself. So all the space that the garbage collector needs must be reserved in advance. A practical algorithm runs in a fixed and reasonable amount of space. Garbage collectors can be divided in two groups: *stop-and-collect* garbage collectors and *continuous* garbage collectors.

Mark–scan and *copying* garbage collectors belong to the stop-and-collect category. With **stop-and-collect** garbage collectors the execution of the regular user program is suspended when the user program asks for a new node and the free space contains not enough words to satisfy the request. The garbage collector is called to retrieve unused memory in the free space. Systems with a large (virtual) memory spend a fair amount of their time in garbage collection. The garbage collection time can be up to 30% of the CPU time.

For interactive systems stop-and-collect collectors may lead to intolerably long interruptions. This drawback can be attenuated by using **continuous** garbage collectors that continuously update the free space. Example of continuous collectors are *reference count* garbage collectors or *on-the-fly* garbage collectors.

With a reference count garbage collector the number of pointers to a node is administered in the node and updated when this number changes. In this way the collection is naturally distributed over time. A disadvantage of reference count garbage collectors is that they cannot reclaim cyclic graph structures.

On-the-fly garbage collectors are separate *processes* that can run interleaved or in parallel with the user program, thus distributing the pause caused by the garbage collector over time. Both *on-the-fly copying* as well as *on-the-fly mark–scan garbage* collection are possible.

12.2.1 Copying garbage collection

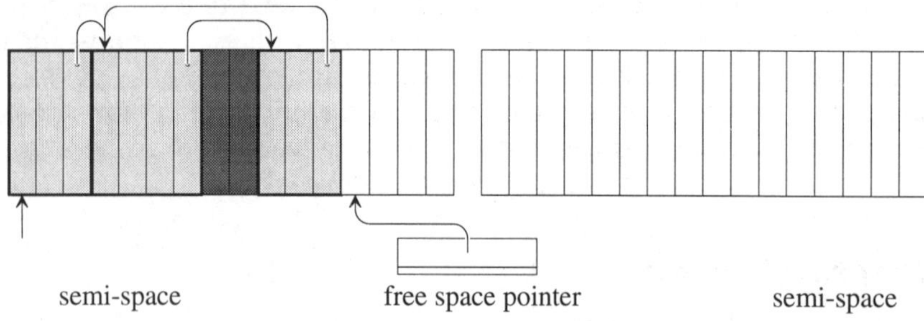

Figure 12.5 Semi-space organization for a copying garbage collector.

Copying garbage collectors generally split the heap into two areas called **semi-spaces**. At any given time, the storage allocator allocates nodes in only one of these semi-spaces. The free space consists of a contiguous part of memory in the active semi-space (see Figure 12.5).

When this free space gets exhausted, all non-garbage nodes are copied from one semi-space to the other unused one. From then on the allocator allocates nodes in the other semi-space until this gets exhausted, and so on. For the actual copying of the nodes there are many different algorithms that use or do not use a stack and/or markings in the nodes. Here only one copy algorithm is treated, which uses neither a stack nor marking bits. A more detailed description of the algorithm can be found in Minsky (1963).

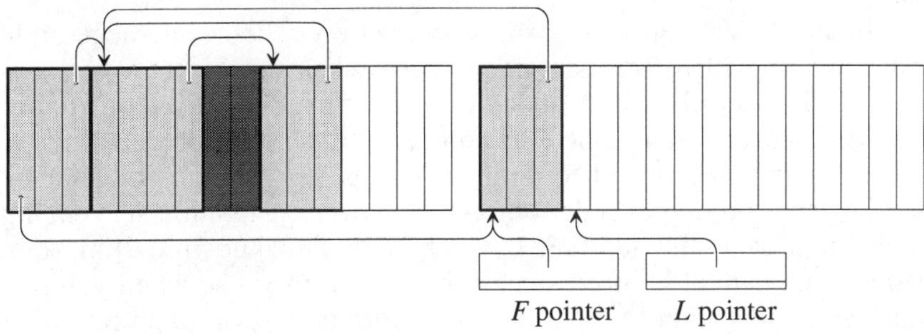

Figure 12.6 Snapshot: copying the used nodes in the unused semi-space.

The algorithm proceeds as follows when the old semi-space gets exhausted:

- First, all roots of the non-garbage graphs are copied to the new semi-space (Figure 12.6).
- Then, two pointers are positioned in the new semi-space, one at the beginning and one at the end of the roots. The pointers are used as follows: the first one, say *F*(irst), indicates the node of which the children are next to be copied to the new semi-space; the last one, say *L*(ast), indicates where copied nodes are to be put.
- All children of the node at *F* are now copied to the new semi-space *L*, and *F* is moved to the next node. This is repeated for the children of the next node, and so on. The copying algorithm terminates when *F* becomes equal to *L*. In this copying process, special precautions have to be taken to maintain sharing of nodes, and to guarantee termination if there are cycles in the graphs. Therefore, a node that resided in the old semi-space but which has been copied to the new semi-space, is overwritten with the address of its copy in the new semi-space. This address is called a **forwarding address** or **forwarding pointer**. Before a node is copied to the new semi-space, it is checked whether it contains a forwarding address.

If not, it is simply copied; if so, the pointer in its parent is changed to the new address.

In general, with a copying garbage collector twice as much storage is needed as the allocator has at its disposal. This is a very large amount, but it is fixed, so it can be reserved in advance. Furthermore, there is no other space needed nor any other stack allocation nor extra bits nor a free-list administration nor compaction, since in the new semi-space the non-garbage nodes are in a contiguous part of the memory. A copying garbage collector is very fast when there is a lot of garbage in the semi-space. But the performance drastically decreases if there is only a little garbage: the number of copy actions depends on the number of used nodes.

In the basic copying garbage collection scheme all accessible nodes are copied to the new semi-space when the old one gets exhausted. This implies that nodes that live very long are copied frequently from one semi-space to another. When such objects occupy much memory it is useful to optimize a copying garbage collector by avoiding the copying of older objects. However, generation scavenging (Liebermann and Hewitt, 1983), which is the best-known optimization of this kind, cannot be used since it is only of great use when younger nodes generally point to older nodes. Unfortunately, in graph rewriting systems older nodes generally point to younger ones.

12.2.2 Mark–scan garbage collection

A mark–scan garbage collector does not split up the heap, but uses a free-list. Hence, when variable-sized nodes are collected, fragmentation can occur (see above) and compaction is needed occasionally.

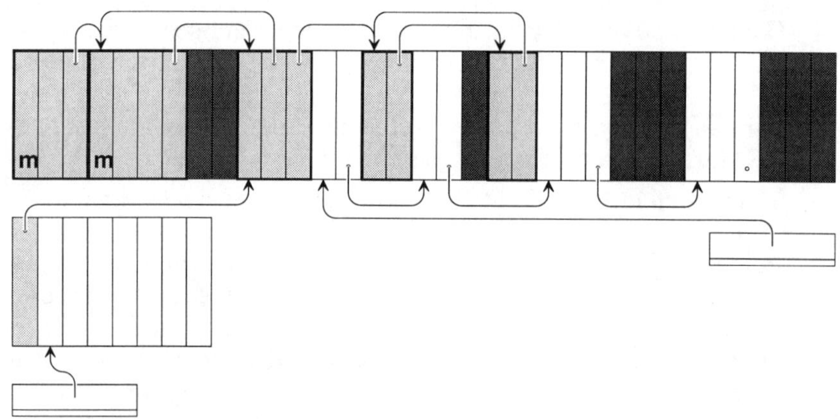

Figure 12.7 Mark–scan garbage collection: phase 1 using a recursive graph traversal stack.

The collector does its job in two phases. In the first phase, the **mark phase**, the accessible nodes are marked. Starting from all roots, the complete subgraphs reachable from these roots are traversed recursively and all encountered nodes are marked (see Figure 12.7). The reachable nodes can be marked by the following algorithm:

```
push all roots on a stack;
WHILE the stack is not empty
DO   mark the node indicated on top of the stack;
     replace it by all unmarked children
OD
```

In the second phase, the **scan phase**, the whole storage is scanned, node by node. Marked nodes are unmarked again, and unmarked nodes, which are garbage, are added to the free-list (see Figure 12.8).

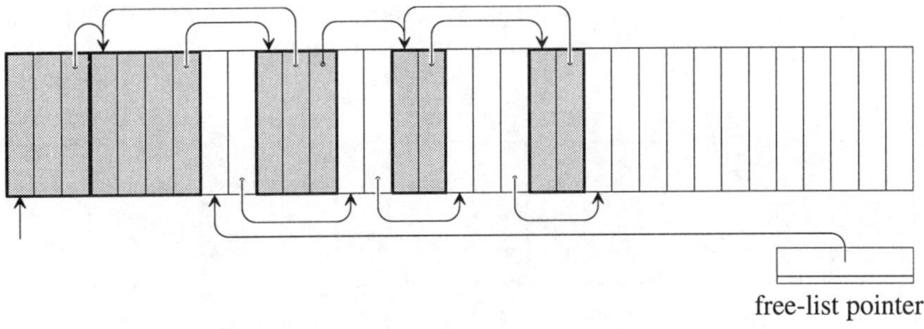

Figure 12.8 Mark–scan garbage collection: phase 2.

Mark–scan garbage collection is not as efficient as copying. In the worst case the complete heap has to be traversed twice: once for the mark and once for the collect phase. When the heap contains little garbage the performance decreases considerably. The mark phase has much more work to do and a large amount of additional space is needed for the recursion stack. In the worst case the size of the extra recursive graph traversal stack equals the total number of nodes available in the memory when there is no garbage and all nodes form a single linked list. However, there are several optimizations that use only a small, fixed-size stack or even no stack at all (by using pointer reversal). These algorithms and many others are discussed in Cohen (1981).

12.2.3 Reference count garbage collection

When garbage collection is done with reference counts, an additional field, a **reference count**, is reserved in each node. In this field the number of pointers to the node is administered. The reference count field must be large enough to hold the total number of nodes in the heap.

When nodes are generally small, this is a significant space overhead. Reference count garbage collectors use a free-list. So compaction may be needed once in a while.

All node creations and pointer manipulations are done by special procedures that not only perform the creation of the node and the pointer manipulation itself, but also maintain the correct reference count:

- new nodes are created with reference count 1;
- when a pointer to a node is copied, the reference count of the node is incremented by 1; when a pointer to a node is deleted, the reference count of the node is decremented by 1;
- when the reference count becomes zero, the node becomes garbage and can be added to the free-list. The reference count of all the children of the node can now also be decremented and they may become garbage too if they are not shared. A recursion stack is needed to adjust all children of a deleted node.

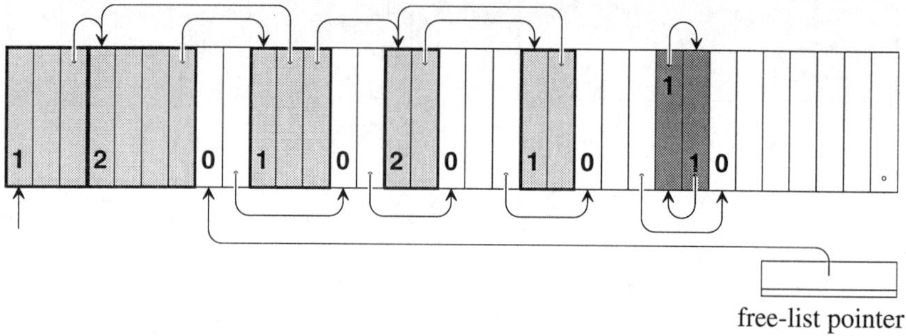

Figure 12.9 Reference count garbage collection. The dark grey cyclic structure cannot be collected.

The advantage of reference count garbage collection is that garbage can be collected immediately after it is created. The cost of reference counting garbage is independent of the proportion of the heap that is used. However, there are some severe drawbacks. For small nodes there is a significant space overhead in the form of the reference count. With each pointer manipulation an update of the counter has to be done. This means that, even if no garbage collection is needed, administrative work must still be done. Another important disadvantage of reference counting is that it is impossible to recover cyclic structures. In a cyclic structure all nodes have reference count greater than zero (see Figure 12.9). When such a cyclic structure becomes garbage it cannot be detected unless the whole memory is examined again.

An optimization that avoids the deletion recursion stack is called lazy garbage collection (Glaser and Thompson, 1985): when a node becomes garbage, it is added to the free-list. When the reference count field is large enough to hold a pointer, it can be used for the linking. Now, when a node is needed, it is taken from the free-list and its reference count is set to one. Next, the reference counts of the children of the node are decremented. The children that become garbage are put in the free-list in the same manner. In this way lazy garbage collection is obtained with the major advantage that the collection is only done when needed, while there is no need for a recursion stack.

A solution for the collection of cyclic structures is to combine the reference count technique with stop-and-collect garbage collection. The former would be used during most of the processing time. The latter would be used as a last resort when the storage area is fouled up with non-recyclable nodes. When reference count is combined with other methods, the reference count field does not have to be of maximum size. A smaller size can be used. When the smaller reference count field overflows, the nodes cannot be reclaimed by the reference count algorithm. Just like cycles, such nodes are reclaimed by the other method.

12.2.4 On-the-fly garbage collection

Another possible solution for continuous garbage collection is to have a separate garbage collection process (an **on-the-fly** garbage collector) that works concurrently (i.e. interleaved or in parallel) with the user program. Of course, for parallel garbage collection a second dedicated processor is required. The garbage collection is divided into two concurrent processes: the user program, in this context usually called the **mutator**, and the **collector**, which performs the marking/copying and the collection of the garbage. Being concurrent processes, some communication between mutator and collector is necessary.

The best-known on-the-fly garbage collection method, introduced by Dijkstra *et al.* (1978), is based on the *mark–scan* method. The mutator colours nodes to be examined by the collector. Therefore, three mark colours, white, grey and black, are introduced. White corresponds to no marking, and black to the marking done by the collector. The mutator only marks nodes grey to indicate to the collector that marking has to be done from this node on.

Copying garbage collection, which incorporates compaction via semi-spaces, can also be done on-the-fly (Baker, 1978). In this case the mutator must know that there are two semi-spaces in which nodes can reside. Allocation of new nodes is done in the semi-space to which the collector currently is copying all nodes.

On-the-fly garbage collectors are best suited for interactive programs. But, as with reference count garbage collection, they are also inefficient when they are executed in an interleaved manner. This is due to the communication and synchronization overhead between the mutator and the collector.

12.2.5 Comparison of the methods

When there is enough memory available and there are no strong requirements on the real-time behaviour of the program, copying garbage collection is generally the best method because it is a very simple and fast method (see Table 12.1).

Table 12.1 Summary of the different kinds of garbage collection methods: '+' means good, '–' means not so good, 'o' means 'neutral', '+/–' means good when there is a large amount of garbage and '–/+' means good when there is little garbage.

	Stop-and-collect		*Continuous collectors*		
	Copying	*Mark–scan*	*Reference count*	*On-the-fly copying*	*On-the-fly mark–scan*
Time efficiency	+/–	–/+	o	+/–	–/+
Space efficiency	–	+	–	–	+
Free-list not needed	yes	no	no	yes	no
No time overhead if space free	yes	yes	no	no	no
Collects cycles	yes	yes	no	yes	yes

If the amount of memory is too limited, mark–scan can be used instead of copying. A good solution is the following: implement both a copying as well as a mark–scan collector and automatically switch between them, depending on the actual memory consumption. If the real-time behaviour is very important one can use an on-the-fly variant of copying or mark–scan. A pure reference count collector is less desirable, because it cannot deal with cyclic structures.

When garbage collection has to be performed in a parallel environment, other problems can occur and the comparison between the algorithms will be different (see Chapter 17).

12.3 The Motorola MC68020 processor

There are two reasons for choosing the Motorola 680x0 family of processors (68010, 68020, 68030, 68040 ...) as target machine (Motorola, 1984–1985). First of all, they have been used in several widespread machines such as the Sun3, Apple Macintosh and Atari ST. Furthermore, the Motorola processors are very suitable as an actual target machine to illustrate how the ABC machine (and therefore functional languages in general) can be implemented efficiently. It should be no problem to use the ideas presented when generating actual target code for other register based processors (such as the Intel 80x86 family).

In this chapter the instruction set of the Motorola MC68020 processor is used as example. The MC68020 processor is a 32–bit machine which makes a large heap possible. Besides a *program counter* and a *status register* it contains two kinds of general purpose registers, namely *data registers* and *address registers*, eight of each kind. The status register contains the following condition codes: N (negative), Z (zero), V (overflow) and C (carry). The data registers, often denoted by d0–d7, are mainly used in arithmetical operations whilst the address registers (indicated by a0–a7) can be used to access data structures that are kept in memory. The address registers can be used in combination with many different addressing modes such as post-increment and pre-decrement. So stacks can be implemented very efficiently.

Summary of the addressing modes used in the examples:

(address)	take the contents of this address;
offset(address)	take the contents at address + offset;
(address)+	take the contents of this address and then increment the address in the register;
–(address)	first decrement the address in the register and then take the contents of this new address.

For the remaining parts of this chapter no further knowledge is assumed about the specific architecture of the MC68020 processor. Some general familiarity with assembly language will suffice to understand the examples of concrete code given in this section.

The following MC68020 machine instructions are used in the examples:

bra	branch; same as jmp in ABC machine, address must be nearby;
bcs	branch when the carry bit (C) is set in status register;
bmi	branch when negative bit (N) is set in status register;
beq	branch when equal bit (Z) is set in status register;
bne	branch when equal bit (Z) is not set in status register;
bsr	branch to subroutine; same as jsr, but address must be nearby;
jsr	equivalent to jsr in ABC machine;
rts	equivalent to rtn in ABC machine;
add.l	integer addition (32 bits);
addq.l	addition of small integer values (8 bits);
sub.l	integer subtraction;
subq.l	subtraction of small integer values;
muls.l	integer multiplication;

move.l	move a 32 bit long word from the source to the destination;
lea	load a 32 bit memory address in a register;
cmp.l	compare two 32 bit long words;
seq	set all bits in byte operand when Z is set; otherwise reset all bits;
extb.l	extend sign of byte to long word;
tst	test, compare with zero.

12.4 Representing ABC components on the MC68020

In this section we present a mapping of the basic ABC machine components onto a specific machine, the Motorola MC68020. The mapping of the different ABC memory storages onto the concrete memory is given in Figure 12.10.

The representation of the components of the ABC machine (i.e. ABC stacks, graph store (heap) and descriptors) on the MC68020 does not cause many difficulties. Stacks can be implemented simply using some of the address registers. Implementing the heap is somewhat more complicated. The structure of the descriptors mainly depends on how higher order functions are implemented.

The program store and program counter

The mapping of the program store and program counter is trivial: their concrete counterparts on the MC68020 can be used.

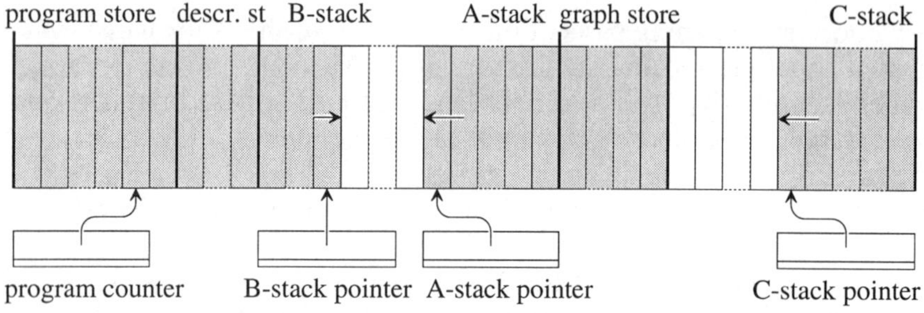

Figure 12.10 Mapping the ABC memory stores on a concrete linear store.

The A-stack, B-stack and C-stack

For the C-stack the system stack of the MC68020 is taken (i.e. the stack used by the processor itself when it performs a subroutine call). So the jmp and rtn instructions of the ABC machine can be mapped directly to those of the MC68020 (of course, for the jsr_eval instructions more things have to be done; see below). This implies that address register a7 (normally called sp (stack pointer)) is reserved as usual. The A- and B-stacks are allocated in one contiguous area of memory in such a way that they can grow in opposite directions. In this way a check on stack overflow of both the A- and B-stacks can be done with a few instructions (just compare the two stack pointers and check that their difference is not negative). The pointers to the tops of the stack are held in registers: for the A-stack register a3 is reserved, for the B-stack register a4 (from now on these registers will be called asp and bsp).

The graph store

For the graph store a *contiguous* area of memory is chosen and not a free-list. The pointer to the free area is stored in register a6 (called hp (heap)), whereas the number of free long words (i.e. 1 long word = 4 bytes) is stored in register d7 (fh from now on (free heap)). As explained in Section 12.2, with this representation the allocation of memory becomes cheap. Filling newly created nodes can be done very efficiently.

Suppose that a Cons node should be created that has two arguments. The references to both arguments are kept in the address registers a1 and a2. At the end a pointer to the new node is returned in register a0. First we have to check whether there is enough space in the heap. This is done by:

```
subq.l   #4, fh    ;  4 long words needed to store the new node
bcs      call_gc   ;  call the garbage collector if not enough free space
```

Now the heap pointer (held in register hp) refers to the first free long word in the heap. Filling the node by using hp is straightforward (for the actual representation of nodes see below):

```
return_from_gc:
move.l   hp, d0           ;  first the variable part is filled
                          ;  a pointer to it is temporarily stored in d0
move.l   a1, (hp)+        ;  store pointer to the first arg. in variable part
move.l   a2, (hp)+        ;  store pointer to the second arg. in variable part
                          ;  now the fixed part is treated
move.l   hp, a0           ;  store a pointer to it in a0
move.l   #Cons, (hp)+     ;  the descriptor field must point to entry of Cons
move.l   d0, (hp)+        ;  store argument pointer
```

Representation of nodes

As described earlier, a node in the ABC machine consists of fixed- and variable-sized parts. A drawback of the ABC node structure as suggested in Section 12.1 is that the size of the nodes is relatively large: the fixed part consists of 3 long words (12 bytes), one for the pointer to a descriptor, one for the code pointer and one for the pointer to the variable-sized part. It is important that nodes are as small as possible: creating, filling and copying of nodes can be done faster and because less memory is consumed the garbage collector will be called less often.

One can observe that if a node is in root normal form, its code pointer always points to the root normal form code. In that case only the pointer to the descriptor is of interest. On the other hand, if a node contains an (unevaluated) expression, only the code pointer is essential: the descriptor is not used. This observation makes it possible to combine the descriptor and code pointer into one field. This reduces the size of the fixed part of a node by one third. There remains one problem: the arity of a node, stored in the descriptor table, is needed for garbage collection. This information is not available when a code pointer is stored in the node. The problem can be solved by storing the arity in the program store, just before the node entry.

The space-saving new node structure is illustrated in Figure 12.11. The disadvantage is that a tag has to be inserted: the highest bit of the first word of the code/descriptor field (note that this field consists of two words) indicates whether it contains a descriptor or a code address. If this bit is set, the second word is an index in the descriptor table. Otherwise, the code/descriptor field contains a code pointer that is used to reduce the node to root normal form.

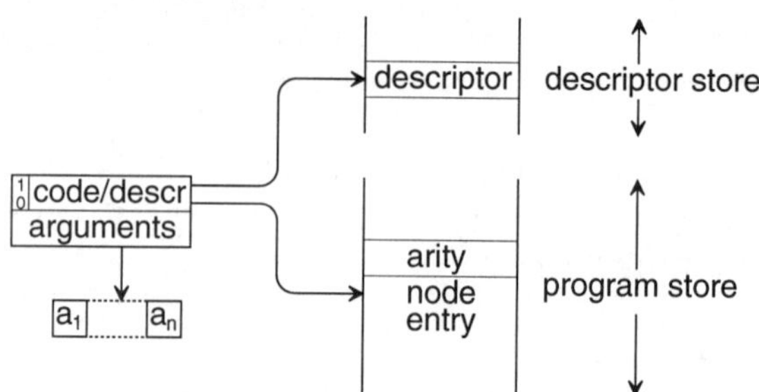

Figure 12.11 The structure of nodes and descriptors

In the ABC machine nodes can be evaluated to root normal form by means of the jsr_eval instruction. This instruction fetches the code address from the node on top of the A-stack and jumps to it. Owing to the combined code/descriptor we first have to check whether the node is already in root normal form before the jump to the evaluation code is made. The next piece of code shows how this can be achieved (assume that register a1 refers to the node to be reduced).

```
move.l  (a1), d6     ;  get the code/descriptor field
bmi     is_in_rnf    ;  check whether the highest bit is set
save all the registers in use
move.l  a1, a0       ;  ensure that a pointer to the node that
                     ;  is going to be evaluated is in reg. a0
move.l  d6, a1       ;  move the evaluation address in a1
```

```
jsr       (a1)       ; call the evaluation code
move.l  a0, a1       ; move the result of the evaluation back in a1
restore the previously saved registers
is_in_rnf:  ...
```

The loss of efficiency caused by the introduction of the tag is very limited while a lot of space (and hence time) is saved with this alternative representation.

When a node is not in root normal form, this alternative representation leads to slightly less efficient code (an extra move instruction and a conditional branch are needed). But when the node is already in root normal form the code becomes much faster. In that case the saving and restoring of the registers are not needed any more.

Garbage collection

Memory is recycled by a *copying garbage collector* that uses two semi-spaces (see Section 12.2). When one semi-space is filled up the garbage collector copies all the nodes still needed for the execution of the program to the other semi-space, leaving all the garbage behind.

The descriptor store

In Section 11.2 the ABC code for the apply function is given (_AP). The code shows that at run-time two arities are needed (the number of arguments collected in the node so far and the number of arguments needed). The apply entry of the curried function has to be called when all arguments are supplied. All this information has to be found via the descriptor that points to an entry of the descriptor table (Figure 12.12).

A straightforward translation of the ABC apply code will result in rather inefficient MC68020 code. To increase the efficiency a pointer is stored in the descriptor table that points to the code to be executed when the curried function is applied to an additional argument.

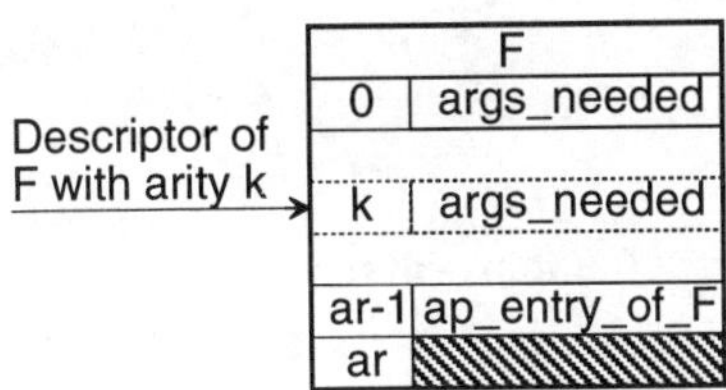

Figure 12.12 Lay-out of a descriptor in the descriptor table.

When F is a symbol defined with arity ar its descriptor contains a string representation of the name and ar+1 entries. The pointer stored in the descriptor field of a node is one of these entries. It indicates with which arity F is actually applied, which is used by the garbage collector. Furthermore, the entry contains a reference to the code to be reduced when a partial application of F is applied to an additional argument (with the (internal) apply function).

With the aid of the previous representation the translation of the apply code will result in the following ABC instructions (it is assumed that register a1 refers to the node containing the partial application and register a5 refers to the beginning of the descriptor table):

```
move    2(a1), a2  ; get the offset of the descriptor entry
add.l   a5 a2      ; add this offset to the beginning of the descriptor table
move.l  2(a2), a2  ; retrieve the reduction code
jsr     (a2)       ; call the reduction code
```

12.5 Generating MC68020 code

A straightforward way of generating concrete machine code is by means of *macro expansion*: each ABC instruction is considered to be a macro application that is substituted by a sequence of MC68020 instructions. The main disadvantage of this method is that the context in which the instruction appears is not taken into account.

An illustrating example is given by the next piece of ABC code together with macro expanded MC68020 code. Assume the following macro definitions:

```
#macro    push_b(n)       move.l  –((n+1)*4)(bsp), (bsp)+
#endmacro
#macro    addl            move.l  –(bsp), d0
                          add.l   d0, –4(bsp)
#endmacro
```

and the following ABC instructions:

```
push_b 0
push_b 2
addl
```

Applying the macro definitions will result in:

```
move.l  –4(bsp), (bsp)+
move.l  –12(bsp), (bsp)+
move.l  –(bsp), d0
add.l   d0, –4(bsp)
```

However, if the three ABC instructions were considered simultaneously, one could use the fact that the MC68020 add instruction does not require that the arguments are on top of the B-stack. By looking at the context in which instructions appear, the movement of data can be reduced. A more efficient code generator might compile the three ABC instructions into the following three MC68020 instructions, which are about 30% faster than the ones above:

```
move.l  –4(bsp), d0
add.l   –8(bsp), d0
move.l  d0, (bsp)+
```

So before generating code it is useful to group ABC instructions into blocks. These **basic blocks** can be considered as kinds of atomic action. They specify state transitions that convert the state of the ABC machine (which is determined by the contents of the stacks and the graph store) at the beginning of these blocks into the final state at the end of the basic blocks. Now the task of a code generator becomes to implement such actions as efficiently as possible.

The largest gain will be achieved when these basic blocks are as large as possible. In the current Clean code generator a basic block consists of the maximal sequence of ABC instructions that does not contain any label definitions or instructions that might change the flow of control (e.g. subroutine calls or conditional branches). Basic blocks can be made larger by replacing a subroutine call by its code. However, programs become larger in this way, and therefore code substitution is only advisable when the substituted code is relatively small.

12.5.1 Compile-time optimizations

With the aid of basic blocks the compile-time analysis of ABC programs is simplified. A few examples follow.

Flow of control

The original ABC instructions specify an evaluation order. Grouping these instructions into basic blocks allows us to deviate from this order as long as the new evaluation has no effect on the final result obtained at the end of the basic block (i.e. the new code sequence should specify the same state transition). Changing the evaluation order makes it possible to improve the generated code.

Suppose that d0+d1 and d0+d2 have to be computed in a register while d1 is used after these computations, but d0 and d2 not. First computing d0+d1 and then d0+d2 will give:

```
move.l    d0,  d3
add.l     d1,  d3
add.l     d2,  d0
```

It is better to compute d0+d2 first. It saves one instruction and one register.

```
add.l     d0,  d2
add.l     d0,  d1
```

In the ideal case the code generator will determine an evaluation order of instructions such that the execution costs of the generated code are as low as possible. The execution costs can be found by simply adding the execution times of all the individual instructions (one should note that the execution time of an instruction may depend on the preceding instructions). But the problem of finding an evaluation order in such a way that the total time is minimal is NP-complete, which makes an algorithm based on this strategy useless.

Optimize the use of the registers

A different approach is not to minimize the execution time but to minimize the number of registers needed to evaluate a basic block. This is a reasonable approach because, since the registers of a processor are relatively sparse, the quality of the generated code will strongly depend on how well they are utilized. Table 12.2 summarizes which of the 8+8 registers of the MC68020 have been reserved for special purposes.

Table 12.2 Summary of reserved registers

Mnemonic	*Register*	*Function*
fh	d7	number of free words in heap
asp	a3	pointer to the top of the A-stack
bsp	a4	pointer to the top of the B-stack
hp	a6	pointer to the first free node in the heap
sp	a7	pointer to the top of the C-stack

Parameters and results of functions are in principle passed via the A- and B-stacks. However, the efficiency can be increased a lot when registers are used instead. So arguments and results are kept in *registers* whenever possible. Only when there are not enough free registers are the values stored on the stacks.

In the ABC machine the conditional jump instructions base their decision whether or not to jump on the Boolean value that is on top of the B-stack. If this boolean is the result of some comparison (which is indeed often the case) then it is not necessary to calculate this value explicitly. Instead of that, the conditional jump can use the *condition codes* in the status register of the MC68020 that are set implicitly after performing the comparison.

Take for example the following ABC instructions:

```
eql_b +10 0
jmp_false label
```

The following code would have been generated if the boolean is calculated explicitly (assuming that the element on top of the B-stack is kept in register d0, register d1 is used to calculate the boolean and the value –1 and 0 represent respectively TRUE and FALSE):

```
cmpi.l   #10, d0
seq      d1
extb.l   d1
tst.l    d1
beq      label
```

Much better code is generated using the condition codes of the MC68020:

```
cmpi.l   #10, d0
bne      label
```

Heap allocation

A basic block may contain instructions that reserve space in the heap. Such an instruction has to check whether the heap contains enough free cells. If this is not the case the garbage collector has to be called. Since it is known at compile-time how many cells are actually needed in a certain basic block, all these checks can be done at once instead of performing separate checks for each instruction.

Stack use optimization

The generation of additional instructions for boundary checks of the stacks inside a basic block can be combined. For each block we can determine the maximal amount by which the stack will grow and perform the tests in one place. The same holds for the adjustment of the stack pointer (due to the various push and pop instructions).

Using alternative instructions

On the MC68020 there are several instructions that, when applied to certain arguments, can be replaced by other instructions having the same effect, but with the advantage that their execution time is less. This replacement can easily be performed during the last phase of the MC68020 code generation or even by the assembler.

12.5.2 The code generation process

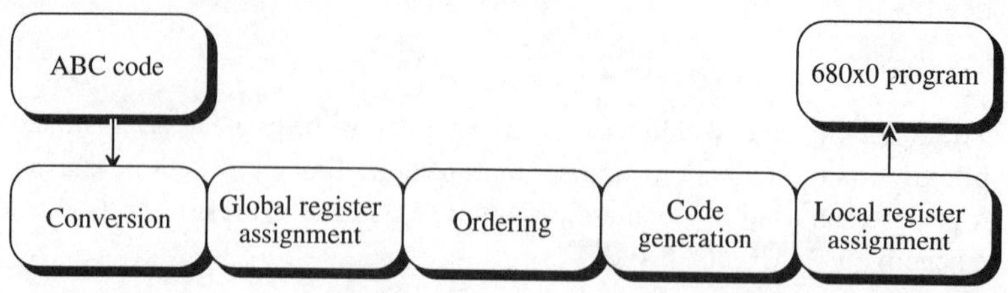

Figure 12.13 The code generation phases.

The actual code generation is divided into a number of phases (Figure 12.13). During the *conversion phase* the initial ABC program is divided into *basic blocks* and converted into an internal representation using graphs. The *global register assignment phase* determines which entries of the A- and B-stacks are kept in registers at the beginning and at the end of these basic blocks. The *ordering phase* determines the order in which all the subexpressions have to be evaluated. During the *code generation phase* (pseudo-) MC68020 code is generated according to the order specified by the previous phase. The only difference between real MC68020 code and the generated code is that in the latter an unlimited number of (virtual) registers are assumed. Finally, the *local register assignment phase* replaces virtual registers by real MC68020 registers.

The conversion phase

The correspondence between the initial stack frame S_b at the beginning of a basic block and the final stack frame F_b at the end is defined by the instructions of that basic block. A directed acyclic graph is a useful data structure for representing basic blocks such that automatic analysis of these blocks can be done more conveniently. Such a dag gives a picture of how the value computed by each statement in a basic block is used in subsequent statements in the block. The dag representation of a basic block that is used has the following properties:

- The leaves either represent constants or entries of S_b.
- All the other (interior) nodes represent applications of ABC instructions. The arguments of these nodes are the representations of the arguments of the corresponding instructions.

- If a node represents an instruction whose result appears in F_b, this node is labelled with an identification of the corresponding entry in F_b. All the other nodes are not labelled.

The next example illustrates the ABC to MC68020 translation process. Consider the following Clean rewrite rule for F:

```
:: F !INT !INT ->    INT;
   F a    b    ->    – (* a b) (+ a 3);
```

This rule is compiled into the following ABC instructions (only the code for the rule alternative entry is given):

```
F1:
pushI +3
push_b 1             || push a on top of the stack
addI                 || add b and 3
push_b 2             || push b on top of the stack
push_b  2            || push a on top of the stack
mulI                 || multiply a and b
update_b 1 3         || update the B-stack
update_b 0 2
pop_b 2
subI                 || subtract the topmost elements
rtn
```

The strict entry forms one basic block. The dag that is constructed is given in Figure 12.14. The meaning of the additional information stored in the dag is explained later.

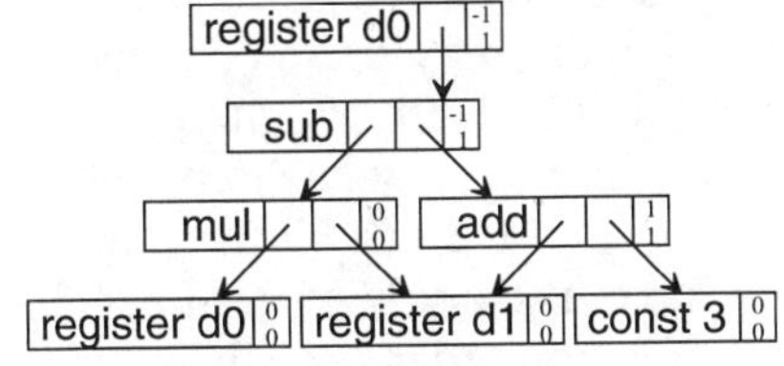

Figure 12.14 The dag of the strict entry.

The global register assignment phase

Global register assignment specifies which values of the initial and final stack frames of each basic block are kept in registers. The information that is used to determine this assignment is obtained from the original Clean program. The Clean compiler uses the type information of the Clean rules to insert special ABC directives in the corresponding ABC program. These directives specify the layouts of both the A- and B-stacks for both the beginning and the end of a basic block.

With the aid of the stack layout information the code generator reserves all the data and address registers that are needed for storing these elements at the beginning of a basic block if such a basic block starts with a label that corresponds to an entry point of a function. The directives describing the layout of the end of a basic block are used to ensure that, when a basic block is left at run-time, the results are kept in the right places (i.e. either in one of the registers or one of the final stack frames itself). The latter may require that the contents of certain registers in use have to be saved on the stack.

The result of the global register assignment of a basic block is administered in the corresponding dag with the aid of two kinds of special nodes, namely *register* and *store register* nodes. A **register node**, which refers to an entry of the initial stack frame S_b, indicates that the value of that entry is kept in a register when entering the basic block (note that register nodes are always leaves of the dag).

Consider Figure 12.14: owing to the global register assignment, a and b are kept in, respectively, data registers d1 and d0 and the final result should be stored in register d0. These register assignments are indicated with the aid of the register nodes.

A **store register node**, which refers to an entry of the final stack frame F_b, indicates that the value of that entry is held in a register when leaving the basic block. So store register nodes are always labelled.

The ordering phase

Under the assumption that none of the instructions in a basic block, except the very last instruction, may produce side-effects, the generation of code can be done independently of the original order of ABC instructions. The only requirement that has to be met is that when generating code for a certain node of the dag all the other nodes that are reachable from this node have already been treated. So we are allowed to change the original evaluation order as long as the previous requirement is fulfilled.

If a basic block does not contain any common subexpression (CSE) (so the corresponding dag is free of sharing), the problem of determining the reduction order such that the number of registers is minimal is simple. An algorithm (which makes some assumptions about the registers and instructions of the target machine) has been given in Aho *et al.* (1986). The problem with common subexpressions is that the results of these expressions have to be stored somewhere until they are used for the last time. This implies that after evaluating a certain subexpression, the number of registers in use does not always increase by exactly one (due to the additional register necessary to hold the value of that subexpression). It is possible that this increase is greater than one (if the cdag (connected dag; see below) contains CSEs that were not evaluated yet) or even smaller than one (if registers containing values of CSEs were used for the last time). Furthermore, the algorithm presented in Aho *et al.* (1986) cannot deal with values kept in registers at the beginning and at the end of a basic block. As with CSEs, such registers can be released as soon as their contents are not needed any more.

Before the modified algorithm (the algorithm and its proof can be found in van Groningen (1990) that determines the evaluation order is explained some notions have to be introduced. A **(rooted) connected dag** (abbreviated as **cdag**) is defined as a dag that has a node r (the **root of the cdag**) such that all the other nodes of this dag are reachable from r. Further, let n be the number of cdags that have to be evaluated and g_i denote the ith cdag ($1 \leq i \leq n$). The evaluation order can be expressed by means of a permutation π of $1..n$ such that the cdag g_i is evaluated before a cdag g_j if $\pi^{-1}(i) < \pi^{-1}(j)$. Define $I(\pi, i)$ and $U(\pi, i)$ as:

$I(\pi, i)$ = the increase of the number of used registers due to the evaluation of $g_{\pi(i)}$ after evaluating $g_{\pi(1)}, \ldots, g_{\pi(i-1)}$.
$U(\pi, i)$ = the (additional) number of registers required for the evaluation of $g_{\pi(i)}$ (also after evaluating $g_{\pi(1)}, \ldots, g_{\pi(i-1)}$).

Note that $I(\pi, i)$ can be negative but $U(\pi, i)$ cannot. Furthermore, note that $U(\pi, i) \geq I(\pi, i)$.

Given an evaluation order π, the maximum number of registers used during the evaluation of $g_{\pi(i)}$ is

$$R(\pi, i) = U(\pi, i) + \sum_{k=1}^{i-1} I(\pi, k)$$

The number of registers necessary to evaluate all the graphs in an order specified by π is

$$R_m(\pi) = Maximum\ \{R(\pi, i) \mid 1 \leq i \leq n\}$$

Hence, finding an optimal evaluation order is equivalent to determining a permutation π_{min} such that for all other permutations π of $1..n$ it holds that $R_m(\pi_{min}) \leq R_m(\pi)$.

A straightforward algorithm would generate all permutations π of $1..n$ and choose the one for which $R_m(\pi)$ is minimal. Unfortunately the complexity of such an algorithm is $O(n!)$ which is, of course, unacceptable.

The modified algorithm estimates the values of $I(\pi, i)$ and $U(\pi, i)$ beforehand (i.e. before determining the evaluation order) by respectively $I(i)$ and $U(i)$. It is required that the estimations are safe which implies that for all permutations π both $I(\pi, i) \leq I(i)$ and $U(\pi, i) \leq U(i)$ must be valid. After determining $I(i)$ and $U(i)$, the evaluation order of the cdags is given by the following two rules:

- first, evaluate all the cdags g_i with $I(i) \leq 0$ from low to high $U(i)$;
- then, evaluate all the other cdags from high to low $D(i)$, where $D(i)$ is defined as $U(i)–I(i)$.

It will be clear that the cdags g_i with $I(i) \leq 0$ have to be done first, for, after the evaluation of a graph with a non-positive I value, some registers may become free. To minimize the number of registers needed to evaluate the whole dag the cdags should be treated in ascending $U(i)$ order.

Why all the other cdags are ordered according to their D value is more difficult to see. This is illustrated with an example.

> Suppose there are three graphs g_1, g_2, and g_3 with $I(1)=1$, $U(1)=2$, $I(2)=1$, $U(2)=2$, $I(3)=1$ and $U(3)=5$. Starting with g_3 only five registers are needed. Starting with one of the other two graphs at least six registers are necessary.

The two types of register of the MC68020 processor are not generally exchangeable. Furthermore, not all registers are freely available. Both facts make it necessary to adapt the algorithm described above. This is done in two stages. First, for each node of the dag it is decided whether this node is computed in an address register or in a data register. After that, for each cdag g_i two values of $I(i)$ are calculated: one for each type of register. Now, the total increase $I_t(i)$ is defined as:

$$I_t(i) = a * I_d(i) + d * I_a(i)$$

where a, I_a, d, I_d are resp. the number of address registers, the increase of address registers, the number of data registers and the increase of data registers. In the same $U_t(i)$ is defined as:

$$U_t(i) = a * U_d(i) + d * U_a(i)$$

The evaluation order is obtained by applying the previous algorithm using the functions I_t and U_t instead of I and U.

> Consider again Figure 12.14: each node is supplied with two numbers, whereof the uppermost gives the I_d value of this node and the other number gives the U_d value. Since the I_a and U_a values do not matter they are omitted. The negative I values (of the sub and the uppermost register nodes) are a consequence of the fact that the contents of the register d1 are not needed any more after evaluating these nodes. The result of the mul node can be stored in

register d1 so, in contrast to the add node, no additional registers are needed to compute the result of this node.

The code generation phase

During the code generation phase, the dags of all the basic blocks are traversed. The order in which the cdags are treated is specified by the ordering phase. For each node of a cdag code is generated in a depth-first way: first, code is generated (recursively) for all of the arguments of a node (again in an order as specified by the ordering phase). Then the operation specified by the node is translated into one or more (pseudo-) MC68020 instructions assuming an unlimited number of (virtual) data and address registers.

The local register assignment phase

Finally, during the last phase of the translation real registers are assigned to the virtual registers allocated by the code generation phase. The algorithm that determines the evaluation order tries to minimize the number of data and address registers that are needed to evaluate a basic block. However, it may be the case that one of these numbers exceeds the number of registers that are actually available (i.e. the number of virtual registers exceeds the number of real registers). In that case it will be necessary to save the contents of one of the registers in memory in such a way that it can be used again. The problem is which register to choose. The strategy chosen takes the register of the required type whose contents will not be used for the longest time.

Consider Figure 12.14. During the last phase code is generated for this dag. The result is shown below:

```
F1:
muls.l   d1, d0
addq.l   #3, d1
sub.l    d1, d0
rts
```

12.6 Example of concrete code

In this section the quality of the code obtained by using the techniques described in this chapter is illustrated with the help of an example. For this purpose we take the Length example of Chapter 11.

```
:: Length !INT   ![x]      ->   INT;
   Length n      [ a | b ] ->   Length (+ n 1) b;
   Length n      [ ]       ->   n;
```

Consider the following Motorola code (some simplifications are made for reasons of clarity). When a function is called, the values on the bottom of a stack frame (see Chapter 11) are kept in registers. The registers a0–a1 are used for the bottom elements of the A-stack pointing to the root node to be overwritten and the first argument. The registers d0–d7 are used to transfer the bottom elements of the B-stack frame. Although the example above gives rise to many assembler instructions, the most important part of the resulting code that performs the recursive call of Length is a tight loop (between Length1 and Length2) that only takes a small number of instructions.

```
a_Length:                        ; The apply entry
                                 ; a0 points to (List x)
                                 ; a1 contains a pointer to (Length n)
    move.l  4(a1), a1            ; Fetch argument pointer
    move.l  (a1), a1             ; Fetch first argument n
    bsr     e_Length             ; Jsr to eval args entry
    subq.l  #2, fh               ; Reserve a node in the heap to store the result
    bcs     i_55                 ; Branch to the garbage collector
i_56:                            ; Returning from the garbage collector
    move.l  hp, a0               ; Store the pointer to the new node
    move.l  #INT–DT, (hp)+       ; Store offset integer descriptor in the node
    move.l  d0, (hp)+            ; Store the integer result in the node
    rts                          ; rtn
n_Length:                        ; The node entry
                                 ; a0 points to root (Length n (List x))
    lea     _cycle, a1           ; Store entry for cycle detection in a1
    move.l  a0, –(asp)           ; Save root pointer on A-stack
    move.l  a1, (a0)             ; Store cycle-in-spine entry in the root
    move.l  4(a0), a0            ; Fetch argument pointer of the root
    move.l  (a0)+, a1            ; Store first arg. (n) in a1
    move.l  (a0), a0             ; Store second arg. (List x) in a0
    bsr     e_Length             ; Jsr to eval args entry
    move.l  (asp)+, a0           ; Fetch root pointer from A-stack
    move.l  #INT–DT, (a0)        ; Store an integer descriptor in the node
    move.l  d0, 4(a0)            ; Store the integer result in the node
    rts                          ; rtn
e_Length:                        ; The eval args entry
                                 ; a0 points to (List x)
                                 ; a1 points to n
    move.l  (a0), d0             ; Fetch code/descriptor field second arg.
    bmi     e_0                  ; Test on root normal form
    move.l  a1, –(asp)           ; Not in rnf, store first arg. on A-stack
    move.l  a0, –(asp)           ; Store second arg. on A-stack
    move.l  d0, a1               ; Set code pointer in a1
    jsr     (a1)                 ; Evaluate second arg. to root normal form
```

```
    move.l  (asp)+, a0          ; Fetch second arg.
    move.l  (asp)+, a1          ; Fetch first arg.
e_0:                            ; Second arg. now in root normal form
    move.l  (a1), d0            ; Fetch code/descriptor field first arg.
    bmi     e_1                 ; Test on root normal form
    move.l  a0, -(asp)          ; Not in rnf, store second arg. on A-stack
    move.l  a1, a0              ; Root node always in a0
    move.l  d0, a1              ; Set code pointer in a1
    jsr     (a1)                ; Evaluate first arg. to root normal form
    move.l  a0, a1              ; Fetch first arg.
    move.l  (asp)+, a0          ; Fetch second arg.
e_1:                            ; First arg. now also in root normal form
    move.l  4(a1), d0           ; Store integer value n in d0
Length1:                        ; Entry for first rule alternative
                                ; a0 points to (List x)
                                ; d0 contains n
    cmp.w   #Cons+8-DT,2(a0)    ; Test whether list arg. is of type Cons a b
    bne     Length2             ; If not do second rule alternative
m_P1:                           ; First rule alternative is applicable
    move.l  a0, -(asp)          ; Save second arg. on A-stack
    move.l  4(a0), a0           ; Fetch argument pointer second arg.
    move.l  (a0)+, a1           ; Fetch pointer to a in a1
    move.l  (a0), a0            ; Fetch pointer to b in a0
    move.l  (a0), d1            ; Fetch code/descriptor field of b
    bmi     e_2                 ; Test on root normal form
    move.l  a1, -(asp)          ; Not in rnf, store pointer to a on A-stack
    move.l  a0, -(asp)          ; Store pointer to b on A-stack
    move.l  d0, (bsp)+          ; Store n on B-stack
    move.l  d1, a1              ; Set code pointer in a1
    jsr     (a1)                ; Evaluate to root normal form
    move.l  -(bsp), d0          ; Fetch n from B-stack
    move.l  (asp)+, a0          ; Fetch pointer to b in a0
    move.l  (asp)+, a1          ; Fetch pointer to a in a1
e_2:                            ; b in root normal form now
    addq.l  #1, d0              ; + n 1
    addq.l  #4, asp             ; Remove list argument
    bra     Length1             ; Recursion via a loop
Length2:                        ; Entry for second rule alternative
    cmp.w   #Nil+8-DT,2(a0)     ; Test whether list is a Nil
    bne     Length3             ; If not do additional rule alternative
m_P2:                           ; Second rule alternative is applicable
    rts                         ; Done, result in d0, rtn
Length3:                        ; Entry for additional alternative
    lea     l_1, a0             ; Load address of error message
    jsr     print               ; Print it out
    jmp     halt                ; Halted due to a mismatch
```

12.7 Performance

In this section the code generated using the optimization techniques presented in this chapter is compared with C (for a comparison of the execution speed offered by modern compilers for lazy functional languages we refer to Hartel and Langendoen (1993)). The gnu C compiler for the Sun3 is used, which generally gives faster code than the standard C compiler. It should be stated that, where possible, C has been used in an imperative way (i.e. using assignments and iteration instead of recursion where appropriate). The following test programs were used (see Smetsers *et al.*, 1991):

nfib — the well-known Nfib function with argument 30.

tak — the Takeuchi function, called with tak 24 16 8.

sieve — a program which generates the first 10 000 primes, using a quite optimal version of the sieve of Eratosthenes (outputs only the last one).

queens — counts all solutions for the (10) queens problem.

reverse — reverses a list of 3000 elements 3000 times.

twice — four times the twice function on the increment function.

rnfib — again the Nfib function, but now defined on reals, with argument 26.

fastfourier — the fast Fourier algorithm, on an array of 8K complex numbers. In the Concurrent Clean program a complex number is defined as a strict tuple of two reals.

Table 12.3 shows that recursive programs written in C appear to be slower than the ones written in Concurrent Clean. However, the iterative versions of the examples written in C are faster.

The test programs have the advantage that they are very small, such that a comparison can be made quickly. However, the question remains of how large 'real applications' written in a functional language behave compared to their imperative counterparts. Of course, it will depend highly on the kind of application. In general the functional program will run slower; not one or two orders of magnitude as was the case in the past, but some constant factor that depends on the kind of program. However, the loss of efficiency is already often quite acceptable. For example, a copy/paste editor written in Clean was, to our surprise, as fast as its imperative look-alike written in object-oriented C. It says something about both implementations. Anyhow, in comparison with the past, the difference in execution times between functional languages on the one hand and imperative languages on the other hand has significantly decreased.

Table 12.3 Performance measurements of the Concurrent Clean compiler version 0.7. The first three columns give the speed figures measured on different Macs using a 2Mb heap (with only 1Mb heap for the Mac+). All times are in seconds. The same programs are also tested on a SUN3/280, with a MC68020 processor running at 25 MHz, 2 Mb heap and compared with C. In Clean (!), strictness annotations are added by the programmer.

Program	*Clean* MacIIfx	*Clean* MacIIsi	*Clean* Mac+	*Clean* Sun3	*Clean (!)* Sun3	*C* Sun3
nfib	2.6	5.2	53	4.5	4.5	11
tak	2.6	5.3	53	4.9	4.9	11
sieve	4.4	9.4	260	8.1	6.8	4.5
queens	15	41	240	28	14	4.1
reverse	31	63	620	64	50	–
twice	0.86	1.8	Heap full	1.7	0.5	–
rnfib	6.1	13	2000	11	11	19
fastfourier	14	30	Heap full	34	19	9

The most worrying aspect is still the space consumption, which often is much too high for functional programs. Fortunately there are many more opportunities for efficiency improvement left: e.g. program transformations, sharing analysis, special code generation for UNQ-attributed objects, merging of B- and C-stacks etc. Also, the run-time system can be further improved. For instance, the current Clean system automatically switches between copying garbage collection (time-efficient) and mark–scan (space-efficient) to get the best of both worlds. All this will lead to much better efficiency in both time and space.

Summary

- The ABC machine can be realized in *hardware* or in *software*. A realization in hardware will be fast but such a machine will also be expensive. A software *interpreter* is easy to make, portable, but slow.
- A better performance can be obtained by a *code generator* that produces executable code from ABC instructions. To obtain a good performance one has to generate concrete target machine code. Such a code generator will probably be harder to port.
- Before code can be generated, *concrete data structures* have to be designed to represent the different memory components of the abstract ABC machine. Furthermore, one has to decide how to map these data structures onto the actual storages of the concrete architecture.

- In general the concrete data structures are quite similar to the abstract data structures. The main problem is caused by the fact that in the concrete case the available amount of memory is *limited*, so special actions are needed for memory management of the stacks (*boundary checks*) and the graph store (*garbage collection*).
- *Copying garbage collection* is very fast and a suitable method, but it needs a lot of memory. *Mark–scan garbage collection* can be used if there is not enough memory available for a copying collector. One can also implement both techniques and automatically switch between them. On-the-fly garbage collectors may be useful for real-time applications.
- Code generators try to use the available resources of the target machine as well as possible. Therefore one has to analyse whole sequences of ABC instructions (*basic blocks*). There are several optimization techniques possible to manipulate basic blocks: one can try to *change the flow of control* to minimize the unnecessary copying of information and to make an optimal use of the registers, one can try to *combine* boundary *checks* on stacks and on the heap, or replace any sequence of code by a more efficient one with the same effect.
- With the optimization techniques described in this part of the book it is possible to obtain efficient implementations of lazy functional languages on conventional architectures.

EXERCISES

12.1 Take the Concurrent Clean System and type in the Length function as defined in Section 12.6.

(a) Use the Clean System to generate ABC code. Compare this code with the code given in Section 11.3. What do you think is the purpose of the descriptors? How many stacks are there? What other kind of differences do you notice? Explain their purpose.

(b) Use the Clean System to generate assembly code. Compare the code with the code given in Section 12.6. Explain the differences.

12.2* Write the test programs of Section 12.7 in your favourite high-level functional language. Write the test programs in your favourite imperative language using an imperative programming style. Write the test programs in your favourite logical language. Measure the performance in both time and space of all programs. Compare the performance with the figures of Table 12.3. Explain the differences.

Part 5
Concurrency issues

Functions written in a functional program have the advantage that they can be evaluated in any order while the outcome of the computation remains the same. This property makes functional programs *conceptually* very suited for *concurrent* (i.e. *interleaved* or *parallel*) evaluation.

However, the exploitation of concurrency in functional programs is still in its infancy. Automatic creation of parallelism such that a significant speed-up is obtained is not easy to realize. It is also not clear yet what kind of primitives should be given to a programmer for a high-level specification of the required process structure and behaviour. So this part of the book is of a rather experimental nature, due to the many open research questions and the rapid developments in this interesting and promising area. Nevertheless, we hope that we can give a good impression of the conceptual and practical possibilities of the concurrent evaluation of functional programs.

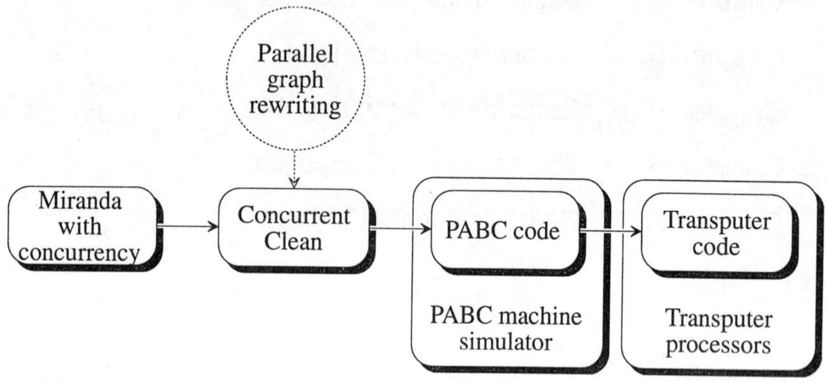

Figure P5.1 Implementing concurrent functional programming.

For simplicity we shall assume that concurrency is specified *explicitly* by the programmer via special *process annotations*. The presented annotations are especially designed to indicate the desired evaluation order for a multi-processor architecture where each processor is equipped with its own local memory. So functions (work) and constructors (data) have to be shipped from one local memory to another. Hence graphs have to be copied from one processor to another. This is modelled by the concept of *lazy copying* which extends the standard graph rewriting model. The implementation of concurrent functional programs on parallel architectures will be discussed via the same translation steps as were used for the sequential implementation (Figure P5.1).

Chapter 13
Basic language concepts

In a *concurrent* program the program is split up into parts (tasks) that are executed *concurrently*, i.e. *interleaved* or in *parallel* with each other. Each task is evaluated by a separate process. *Parallel* processes run on *different* processors. *Interleaved* processes run on the *same* processor. The result of a functional program is known to be independent of the chosen evaluation order (although one has to be a bit careful not to change the termination behaviour of a program). So functional programs seem to be very suited for concurrent evaluation. Conceptually it is indeed possible to evaluate functions interleaved or even in parallel with each other. By using mutual recursion arbitrary dependencies between these functions can be specified, thus creating a way to define *arbitrary networks of processes* (reducers). *Communication* and *synchronization* between the processes are realized *automatically* using the *lazy evaluation* principle. Communication takes place when a process demands a value that is being calculated by another process. No additional communication primitives are needed.

When concurrent evaluation is used to gain efficiency one actually would like to have an analyser that *automatically* marks expressions that can safely be executed in parallel. A strictness analyser can be used for this purpose. But one often also needs to know whether parallel evaluation of expressions is *worthwhile*. With the creation of each task a certain amount of *overhead* is involved, depending on the number of processes created and the amount of communication that takes place between them. One can only *gain* efficiency when a *sufficiently large amount of work* is assigned to a process which involves *limited inter-process communication* for the exchange of information. The amount of work performed by a process and the amount of inter-process communication that is needed to do the work is of course undecidable. The actual overhead will also depend on the concrete machine architecture the program is running on. How to split up work efficiently is therefore very problem- and machine-dependent and often difficult to solve, even for a human being. To make things easier, we assume from now on that the programmer has to define the concurrent behaviour of the functional program *explicitly*, either in order to achieve a certain desired concurrent structure or to achieve a faster program. Furthermore, we assume that concurrent functional programs at least have to run conveniently on a widely available class of parallel machine architectures: multiple instruction–multiple data machines with a distributed memory architecture. Such a machine can consist of hundreds or even thousands of more or less conventional processors that are connected via a communication network.

In spite of the conceptual possibilities, *concurrent functional programming* is still in its infancy. At the moment, none of the commercially available functional languages supports concurrent programming. However, in several experimental languages concurrency primitives have been proposed in the form of annotations or special functions (Kluge, 1983; Goguen *et al.*, 1986; Hudak and Smith, 1986; Burton, 1987; Glauert *et al.*, 1987; Vree and Hartel, 1988; Van Eekelen *et al.*, 1991; Darlington *et al.*, 1991). With these primitives the default evaluation order of an ordinary functional program can be changed such that a concurrent functional program is obtained. However, there is not yet a common view on which kinds of primitives are handy or definitely needed for concurrent functional programming.

This chapter therefore does not reflect *the* way to achieve concurrency, but it presents *one* of the methods to define concurrency. In the presented method the concurrent behaviour of a program is defined by means of special high-level concurrency *annotations* with an associated *type system*. By combining the use of higher order functions with the type system it is possible to specify a very large class of process structures in an elegant manner.

This chapter first gives a brief introduction on concurrency in general and concurrency in the context of functional languages (Section 13.1). Then the annotations and the type system are introduced in a Miranda-like syntax (Section 13.2). Section 13.3 shows some more elaborate examples of concurrent functional programs. Section 13.4 discusses the advantages and the disadvantages of the functional concurrency primitives that are used in this chapter.

13.1 Concurrency and functional programming

A **concurrent program** is a program in which parts of the program (called **processes**) are running **concurrently**, i.e. *interleaved* or in *parallel* with each other. An algorithm that is to be executed is called a **task**. Each task involves a certain amount of work. In a concurrent program the task to be performed is split up into *subtasks*. Each subtask is assigned to a process. **Parallel processes** are processes that perform their task at the *same* time. **Interleaved processes** perform their task *merged* in some unknown *sequential* order on a time-sharing basis.

13.1.1 Why concurrent programming?

Concurrent programming is mainly used for the following reasons:

(1) To *obtain efficiency*: concurrent programs are used to decrease the time needed to accomplish the complete program task by assigning subtasks to *parallel* executing processes. Of course, one needs a multi-processor machine architecture for the execution of these processes to actually gain efficiency.

(2) To *structure software*: some programs are logically composed of components that perform subtasks concurrently (take for instance the components of an operating system). These subtasks can run interleaved on a single processor machine or in parallel on a multi-processor machine.

(3) To *program parallel hardware* such as a system that consists of autonomous components that interact with each other, e.g. a multi-processor architecture or a system configuration consisting of a processor, a printer and a tape unit.

The design and implementation of concurrent programs are a difficult job for a human being. One not only has to decide *which* subtasks are to be assigned to processes, but one also has to decide *how* and *when* the corresponding processes have to communicate with each other. The interaction between the processes must be programmed in such a way that at any moment any communication with another process is handled in the intended manner. In general, special language facilities or system calls are available that define the creation of processes with their tasks. Also, primitives are needed to enable the control over communication and synchronization between the processes.

When concurrent programming is used to *structure software* or to *program parallel hardware* the design of the concurrent program is substantially determined by the subtasks that need to be performed by the separate components in the system. Such a program can become complex when there are many tasks created that heavily depend on each other. For a human being it is very difficult to think of all the possibilities that can arise in such a complex concurrent environment.

Gaining speed with concurrent programming

When concurrent programming is used to obtain a more *efficient* program the subtasks performed by a program must be assigned to parallel executing processes in such a way that they indeed increase the efficiency. But with each process created and each communication that takes place some overhead is involved. An increase in efficiency can actually only be obtained when the subtask that has been assigned to a parallel process represents a sufficiently large amount of work. The additional overhead needed for process creation and inter-process communication should be low. The problem is now how to tune the number of processes and the kind and size of the tasks such that an optimal gain in efficiency is obtained on a certain concrete architecture.

Fine-grain versus coarse-grain parallelism

One can split up a program into *tiny* subtasks in which a relatively small amount of work is performed. In general, a lot of this **fine-grain parallelism** can be found in a program. It is even often possible to find many of these fine grains automatically. For example, the strict arguments of a function can safely be evaluated in parallel. Efficiency gain can only be achieved with tiny tasks if there is almost no overhead penalty for the creation of these tasks on the underlying architecture. However, in reality it may well be the case that the additional overhead needed to create these tiny subtasks becomes larger than the speed gained by evaluating them in parallel. The reason for this is that the overhead costs are generally dependent on the *number of tasks* and the *amount of communication* between them, but not on the amount of work performed by a task.

An efficiency gain can be obtained when it is possible to split up a program into subtasks that consist of a relatively large amount of work with only limited communication between the tasks. But, in general, only a *limited* amount of this **coarse-grain parallelism** can be found. Besides the knowledge that it is safe to fork off a task one also has to take the complexity of a task and the amount of communication between tasks into account. These last two entities are in general undecidable. Furthermore, it is even for a human being often rather difficult to find a suitable coarse-grain partitioning of a program. It generally means that one has to redesign the algorithm. When not enough coarse-grain parallelism can be found or created the capacity of a parallel machine cannot be used in an optimal manner.

Importance of the underlying concrete parallel architecture

The optimal tuning of a program will not only depend on the problem one has to solve but will also depend heavily on the concrete architecture of the parallel machine that is actually being used. There are single instruction–multiple data (SIMD) machines and multiple instruction–multiple data (MIMD) machines. In an **SIMD** machine a very large number (say, thousands) of tiny processors all execute the *same* instruction at the *same time*, albeit on *different data*. They are especially suited to performing the same type of calculation on a large data structure (array or vector processing). In an **MIMD** machine there are fewer (say, hundreds) 'ordinary' processors working independently. These architectures are generally more suited for executing concurrent functional programs. There are MIMD architectures with *shared memory* and with *distributed memory*.

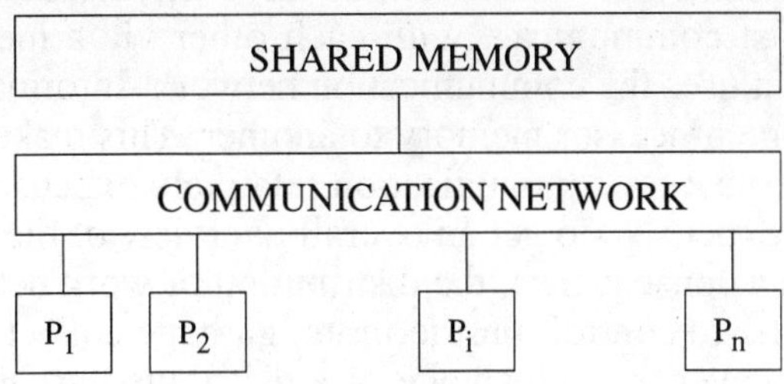

Figure 13.1 Parallel architecture with shared memory.

In a **shared memory architecture** (Figure 13.1) all processes share the same memory via a communication device such as a bus or a special network switch. Shared memory architectures have the advantage that all processes can communicate with each other via global data. This makes creation of processes and inter-process communication cheap. The status of each processor can also be inspected relatively easily by the operating system of the machine. As a consequence, the distribution of work between the processors can also be controlled relatively easily. A shared memory architecture is therefore best suited for automatic creation of parallelism. A disadvantage of such an architecture is that there are two bottlenecks, one formed by the communication network and one formed by the shared memory: generally only one memory access is possible at the same time. So only a certain limited number of processors (say, tens of processors with current technology) can effectively contribute in a shared memory configuration.

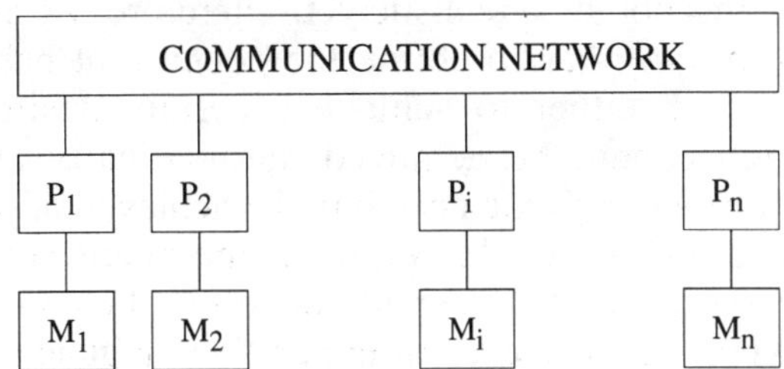

Figure 13.2 Parallel architecture with distributed memory.

In a **distributed memory architecture** (Figure 13.2) each processor has its own local memory. Processors are (sparsely) connected via some special communication network. In a distributed architecture generally not all processors are directly connected to each other. A fully connected network would be too complex and too expensive. An important property of distributed architectures is that for each processor it is more efficient to access objects located in its own local memory than to use the communication medium to access remote objects.

Distributed memory architectures have the disadvantage that all processors must communicate with each other via a message-passing mechanism that uses the communication network. Information has to be copied from one processor memory to another. This makes process creation and inter-process communication relatively expensive. Generally, it is also very expensive to get an overall overview of the status of such a machine. As a consequence, the distribution of work between the processors is harder to control. Furthermore, garbage collection is difficult to realize. However, the advantage of a distributed architecture is that the network is only used for global memory access but not for local memory access. So the bottleneck formed by the communication network is not so serious when local memory access happens frequently compared with global memory access. With a suitable network topology generally hundreds of processors can be connected to each other in such a way that they effectively work with each other.

Assumptions

When concurrency is used to speed up execution the actual speed-up one can obtain is highly dependent on the algorithm being used, the number and the kind of subtasks that are created and the actual multiprocessor architecture the program is running on. How to split up work efficiently is an undecidable problem. It is often even difficult for a human being to find an acceptable solution. Even when concurrency is used to structure software it is often very hard for a human being to come up with a good design and specification for the desired structure.

So an automatic partitioning of a program in concurrently executable parts seems not to be realistic yet. Therefore, we assume that the programmer *explicitly* has to define the concurrent behaviour of the functional program, either to achieve a certain desired concurrent structure (which cannot be achieved automatically anyway) or to achieve a faster program (which can only be achieved automatically under certain conditions). For this purpose one needs special language constructs for expressing the desired concurrent behaviour. One basic approach to express concurrence in imperative languages can be found in Hoare (1978). Furthermore, we assume that concurrent functional programs at least have to run conveniently on MIMD machines with a distributed memory architecture. They are widely available and generally contain more processors than shared memory architectures.

13.1.2 Why concurrent *functional* programming?

Imperative programming languages have the disadvantage that one cannot always assign an *arbitrary* subtask (such as a procedure call) to a process. A procedure call can have side-effects via access to global variables (see Chapter 1). When such a procedure is executed concurrently, the correctness of the program is no longer guaranteed. Furthermore, inter-process communication has to be defined *explicitly*. All possible communication situations have to be handled. Programs tend to become very complex.

Advantages of concurrent functional programming

In a concurrent functional program a task assigned to a process consists of the evaluation of a function. *Any* function (redex) can be assigned to a process. Since there are no side-effects, the outcome of the computation, the normal form, is independent of the chosen evaluation order. Interleaved as well as parallel evaluation of redexes is allowed. Communication between the processes takes place *implicitly*, simply when one process (function) needs the result calculated by another. No additional primitives for process communication are needed. Reasoning about the concurrent algorithm is for most properties similar to reasoning about any other functional program.

The fact that the evaluation order cannot influence the outcome of a computation also gives additional *flexibility* and *reliability* for the evaluation of functional programs on parallel architectures. When a processor becomes defective or when it is overloaded with work it is in principle possible to change the evaluation order and the number of tasks created in optimal response to the actual run-time situation.

Besides the advantages mentioned above, the programmer of concurrent functional programs has the full power of a functional language at his or her disposal. This means that the general advantages of functional programming are also applicable in a concurrent context.

Disadvantages of concurrent functional programming

Concurrent functional programming means that the programmer explicitly defines how the concurrent evaluation of the program must take place. As a consequence, a program in a functional language can no longer be regarded as an executable specification. How expressions are being evaluated is now of importance.

Actually, already for ordinary lazy functional programs there are situations in which a programmer cannot be totally unaware of the evaluation order of his or her program. For instance, patterns specified on a left-hand side of a function definition force evaluation. Whether or not a function can be called with an argument representing an infinite computation will depend on how the function is defined. Furthermore, most functional languages have facilities to influence the default evaluation order: LML (Augustsson, 1984), Miranda (Turner, 1985), Haskell (Hudak *et al.*, 1992) and Clean (Brus *et al.*, 1987). When these facilities are used one also has to be aware of how and when certain expressions are evaluated. So although functional languages focus on a declarative style of programming there are some points where this goal is not totally met.

In concurrent functional programming the programmer has to be even more aware of the evaluation order. This actually means that the evaluation order becomes part of the specification. However, when a functional program is compiled many transformations are needed to map the high-level specification efficiently onto the low-level instruction set of the machine. As a consequence, it is very hard to predict in which order arbitrary expressions are being evaluated. So the tools given to a programmer should make it possible to specify the reduction order in such a way that the desired concurrent behaviour becomes clear without detailed knowledge of a particular implementation.

13.2 Annotations for concurrency

13.2.1 Creating parallel processes

Suppose that one would like to increase the execution speed of the following function by introducing parallelism into the computation.

```
fib:: num -> num
fib 1  =  1
fib 2  =  1
fib n  =  fib (n – 1) + fib (n – 2),      if n > 2
```

Since both arguments of the addition have to be calculated before the addition can take place one could try to optimize the performance by calculating the two recursive calls of fib in parallel, each on a different processor. This is a typical example of **divide-and-conquer** parallelism. We assume that one can create a parallel process for the reduction of a function application by prefixing the application with a special annotation: {Par}. A process created with a **{Par}** has as task to evaluate the annotated function in *parallel* to *normal form*. With this annotation the desired parallel divide-and-conquer variant of fib is specified as follows:

```
fib:: num -> num
fib 1  =  1
fib 2  =  1
fib n  =  {Par} fib (n – 1) + {Par} fib (n – 2),      if n > 2
```

The use of {Par} in such a recursive function definition creates a new process for each annotated function application in each call of the function. In this way a tree of processes is created. The bottom of the tree consists of processes that execute the non-recursive alternative of the function definition (Figure 13.3).

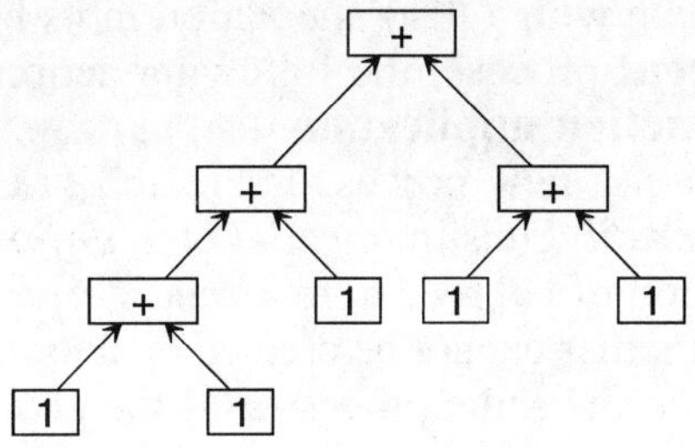

Figure 13.3 Snapshot of a tree of processes computing fib 5; the arrows indicate the direction of the flow of information between the processes.

It will often not be worthwhile to evaluate fib n in parallel in such a way. To turn the *fine-grain* parallelism into *coarse-grain* parallelism, a threshold is introduced that ensures that the processes at the bottom of the tree have a substantial amount of work to do (Figure 15.4).

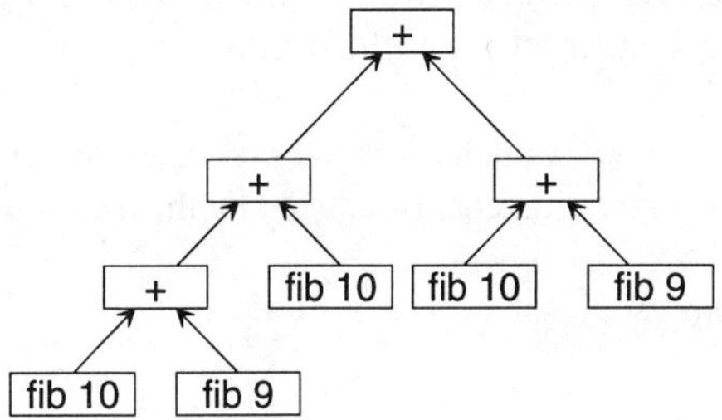

Figure 13.4 Tree of processes with threshold computing fib 13.

Divide-and-conquer Fibonacci with threshold:

```
fib:: num -> num
fib 1  =  1
fib 2  =  1
fib n  =  {Par} fib (n – 1) + {Par} fib (n – 2),     if n > threshold
       =  fib (n – 1) + fib (n – 2),                 if n > 2

threshold:: num
threshold  =  10
```

The {Par} annotation can be used in the body (the right-hand side) of any function definition. In order to keep the semantic description of the {Par} annotation as simple as possible, {Par} is only defined for an argument that is a function application of the form f a_1 a_2 ... a_n. The {Par} annotation is not defined on *ZF*-expressions and the like. This is of course not a fundamental restriction.

When a function with a {Par} annotation in its body is evaluated by a process (the **parent** process) the following action is taken. For each **Par-annotated function application** {Par} f a_1 a_2 ... a_n specified in the body of the function a new process is created (a **child** process). This child process *preferably* runs in *parallel* on a *different* processor, with as task the evaluation of f a_1 a_2 ... a_n to *normal form*. If the child process for one reason or another cannot be created on another processor it is allowed to create it on the same processor as the parent process. Parallel processes are usually created to perform a substantial task. Therefore, a task performs the reduction of the indicated expression to *normal form* and not just to *head normal form*. When the child processes have been created the parent process continues as usual with the regular evaluation of the function body. Consequently, the creation of parallel processes will not influence the termination behaviour of a program.

13.2.2 Creating interleaved processes

In the solutions presented so far processes have not been used in an optimal way. The parent process did not do much useful work because it had to wait for the results of its child processes.

Consider again the fib example. A better processor utilization may be achieved when one of the two arguments is reduced by the parent process.

```
fib:: num -> num
fib 1  =  1
fib 2  =  1
fib n  =  fib (n – 1) + {Par} fib (n – 2),      if n > threshold
       =  fib (n – 1) + fib (n – 2),            if n > 2
```

The intention in the fib example above is that the first argument is reduced on the parent processor in parallel with the evaluation of the second argument. As specified, the first argument *will* be calculated by the parent process and the second one by another parallel process. However, the solution assumes that the parent process directly continues with the evaluation of the first argument. In reality, this may not be the case. If the parent process happens to start with the calculation of the second argument first, it waits until the child process has communicated the result, after which the parent process can evaluate the first argument. So although the specification is fulfilled, the desired parallel effect may not be obtained.

The problem illustrated in the example arose because the programmer had made some (possibly wrong) assumptions on the precise evaluation order of the program (in the case above this concerned in particular the order of evaluation of the strict arguments of δ-rules). It is generally very dangerous to make any assumptions on the evaluation order. Therefore, we have chosen to be very *explicit* about the evaluation order when processes are created. A new annotation is introduced that creates an *interleaved* executing child process on the same processor as the parent process: the *{Self} annotation* (Figure 13.5).

Divide-and-conquer Fibonacci with parent processor (not the parent process) participating in the work:

```
fib:: num -> num
fib 1  =  1
fib 2  =  1
fib n  =  {Self} fib (n – 1) + {Par} fib (n – 2),     if n > threshold
       =  fib (n – 1) + fib (n – 2),                   if n > 2
```

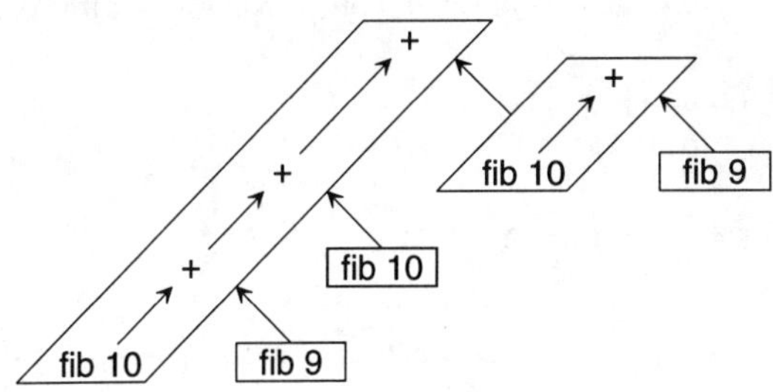

Figure 13.5 Tree of processes for fib; the left branch is computed on the same processor by different interleaved running processes.

The {Self} annotation can be used like a {Par}: in the body (the right-hand side) of any function definition. When a function with {Self} annotations in its body is evaluated by the parent process the following action is performed. For each **self-annotated function application** {Self} f a_1 a_2 ... a_n a new *child* process is created as a subprocess. This child process runs *interleaved* on the *same* processor as the parent process with as task the evaluation of f a_1 a_2 ... a_n to *normal form.*

In many cases a better utilization of the machine capacity can be achieved when a subprocess is created on the same processor as the parent process. Furthermore, the {Self} annotation is in particular handy to create **channel processes**. When several processes demand information from a particular process, it is useful to create a (channel) subprocess for each demanding process to serve the communication demands.

13.2.3 Communication and lazy evaluation

In the sequential case, when a value is needed, it is evaluated by the process itself. In the concurrent case such a value can be evaluated by another process, possibly on another processor. Clearly, the only sensible thing to do for a demanding process is to *wait* until the needed value becomes available. However, for efficiency it is important that a demanding process can continue as soon as possible. Such a process should not wait until the *whole* normal form has been calculated. As soon as part of it is known it can be communicated. This prompt communication of information can be compared with the way the result of an ordinary program is printed. So communication can take place as soon as a head normal form is reached. That part of the result which is still under evaluation will be communicated later when it becomes needed as well. So *communication* is defined *implicitly* by making use of the lazy evaluation order. This way of communication can be used to create *information streams* between processes.

A communication stream between processes (Figure 13.6). The function generator is also used later on in several other examples in this chapter.

```
generator:: num -> [num]
generator n = [n..100]

map (* 2) ({Par} generator 3)
```

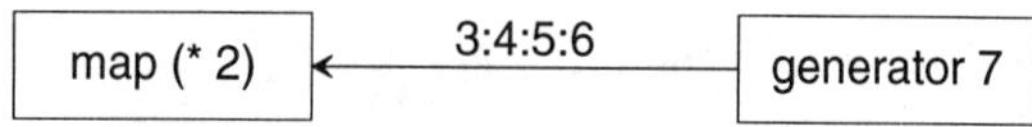

Figure 13.6 Simple pipeline between the processes map and generator; in the snapshot the values 3:4:5:6 are being communicated.

When the parent process needs a value of the child process and the child process has produced a head normal form, the requested information is communicated to the parent process. That part which is still under evaluation will be communicated later when there is a demand for it. In this way the generator and the map process are effectively operating in a (very small) pipeline.

13.2.4 Expressive power of concurrent functional programs

An advantage of functional languages is that it is relatively easy to define general tools for the creation of parallelism by using annotations like {Par} in combination with the ordinary expressive power of higher order functions in these languages.

Divide-and-conquer parallelism can be expressed in a general way using higher order functions:

```
divconq:: (* -> **) -> * -> (* -> bool) -> (** -> ** -> **) -> (* -> (*,*)) -> **
divconq f arg threshold conquer divide
        = f arg,                                                        if threshold arg
        = conquer ({Self} divconq f left threshold conquer divide)
                  ({Par} divconq f right threshold conquer divide),otherwise
          where  (left, right) = divide arg


pfib:: num -> num
pfib n  = divconq fib n threshold (+) divide
          where  threshold n    = n <= 10
                 divide n       = (n – 1, n – 2)
```

Function composition can be used to create pipelines of processes.

Static pipeline of processes (Figure 13.7):

```
stat_pipe:: * -> (* -> **) -> (** -> ***) -> (*** -> ****) -> ****
stat_pipe i f1 f2 f3 = f3 ({Par} f2 ({Par} f1 ({Par} i)))

stat_pipe (generator 3) (map fib) (map fac) (map (* 2))
```

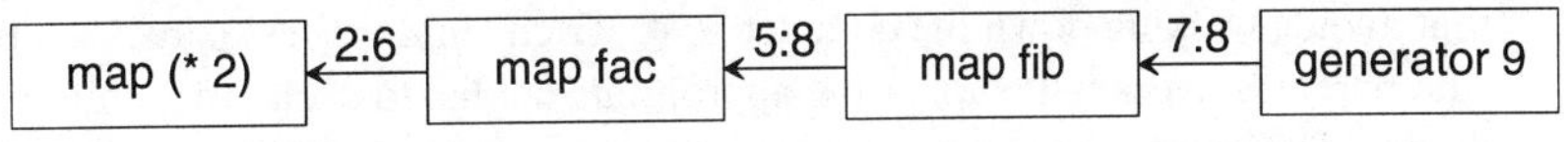

Figure 13.7 Snapshot of a static pipeline of four processes.

With higher order functions general skeletons can be defined to create frequently occurring process structures (this is essentially different from the process skeletons in Darlington *et al.* (1991), which are inherently predefined). Often parallel variants of the basic building blocks given in Chapter 2 can be used.

A general pipeline defined with the {Self} annotation:

```
parfoldr:: (* -> ** -> **) -> ** -> [*] -> **
parfoldr f i [ ]        = i
parfoldr f i (x : xs)   = {Par} f x in     where   in = {Self} parfoldr f i xs


parfoldr map (generator 3) [(* 2), fac, fib]
```

A parallel version of map implementing vector-like processing: it creates a parallel process for each element in a given list.

```
parmap:: (* -> **) -> [*] -> [**]
parmap f (x : xs) =  {Par} f x : {Self} parmap f xs
parmap f [ ]      =  [ ]
```

then

```
parmap (twice fac) [0, 1, 2, 3]
→ {Par} twice fac 0 : {Self} parmap (twice fac) [1,2,3]
→ {Par} twice fac 0 : {Par} twice fac 1 : {Self} parmap (twice fac) [2,3]
...    →     [1, 1, 2, 720]
```

A process can create one or more subprocesses with the {Self} construct. These subprocesses (running interleaved on the same processor) can be used to serve communication channels with other processes. Each communication link of a process has to be served by a separate subprocess that reduces the demanded information to normal form. A process with its subprocesses in a functional language acts more or less like a process with its channels in a message-passing language like CSP (Hoare, 1978). Serving subprocesses is like sending information over a channel to any process requesting that information.

In the following parallel version of the quicksort algorithm (see also Chapter 2) two child processes are created when the list to be sorted contains more than threshold elements (this is checked by the predicate too_few_elements that avoids walking down the complete list). Each child process sorts a sublist. The parent process will supply the appropriate sublist to each of its child processes. The parent process can perform both these tasks 'simultaneously' with the help of two subprocesses running interleaved with each other.

```
sorter:: [num] -> [num]
sorter list  =  quick_sort list,       if too_few_elements list threshold
             =  par_quick_sort list,   otherwise

threshold:: num
threshold  =  7

quick_sort:: [num] -> [num]
quick_sort [ ]        =  [ ]
quick_sort (x : xs)   =  quick_sort [b I b <- xs ; b <= x]
                         ++ [x] ++ quick_sort [b I b <- xs ; b > x]

par_quick_sort:: [num] -> [num]
par_quick_sort (x : xs)    =  {Par} sorter ({Self} smalleq x xs)
                              ++ [x] ++ {Par} sorter ({Self} larger x xs)
                              where   smalleq x xs   =  [b I b <- xs ; b <= x]
                                      larger x xs    =  [b I b <- xs ; b > x]
```

```
too_few_elements:: [num] -> num -> bool
too_few_elements [ ]          n  =  True
too_few_elements xs           0  =  False
too_few_elements (x : xs)     n  =  too_few_elements xs (n – 1)

sorter [6,3,1,4,2,7,3,12,5,1,4,97,3,2,17,6,93,114]
```

13.2.5 Specifying process types

In the examples shown so far, processes only *locally* appeared in the function body. Complex process topologies can be specified more elegantly if processes can be passed as arguments to functions or returned as function results. The consistent use of processes can be checked by the compiler. Furthermore, for code generation it can be important to know that an expression will be (or has been) evaluated by a process. So a special type attribute {proc} is introduced. This type attribute indicates that an expression is known to be in process normal form.

When an expression is in **process normal form (PNF)** it will, *when its evaluation is demanded*, either be *in* normal form or it will be *reduced to* normal form by one or more *processes*. The PNF property is in general undecidable. However, it is possible to introduce a type system to achieve a decidable approximation of the PNF property (*known to be* in PNF). Clearly, an expression annotated with a {Par} annotation or a {Self} annotation is known to be in PNF since a process is created to reduce it to normal form. There are more cases in which expressions are known to be in PNF. A complete survey of these cases is given below. In the following we shall use *in PNF* instead of *known to be in PNF* when there can be no confusion.

An expression has type **{proc} T** when it is of type T and in PNF. This type can be used in the type definition of a function. An expression is said to have a **process type** when its type has the type attribute {proc}.

A tool to create a dynamic pipeline of processes of arbitrary length:

```
pipeline:: * -> [* -> *] -> {proc} *
pipeline gen filters  =  npipe ({Par} gen) filters

npipe:: {proc} * -> [* -> *] -> {proc} *
npipe in [ ]          =  in
npipe in (x : xs)     =  npipe ({Par} x in) xs

pipeline (generator 3) [map fib, map fac, map (* 2)]
```

In the function npipe the newly created parallel process will be evaluating a function x applied on an argument evaluated by another process. Due to the recursive call a pipeline of processes is created.

A type inferencer can derive that an argument of a function has a process type. However, in many cases the programmer wants to be more restrictive, indicating process types *explicitly*. A type *checker* can then check the consistency of the type attributes and assign process types to subexpressions of function definitions accordingly. For reasons of simplicity it is assumed that these actions are performed after the normal type inferencing/checking.

The following expressions are known to be in PNF and therefore a process type can be assigned to them:

- expressions of the form {Par} f e_1 ... e_n or {Self} f e_1 ... e_n for $n \geq 0$;
- an argument of a function if on the corresponding position in the type definition a process type is specified and a result of a function if on the corresponding position in the type definition a process type is specified;
- expressions of the form C a_1 a_2 ... a_n, where C is a constructor of which all the arguments a_i have a process type (*composition*);
- arguments a_i of an expression that has a process type and that is of the form C a_1 a_2 ... a_n, where C is a constructor (*decomposition*);
- expressions statically known to be in normal form, e.g. expressions not containing any function applications.

The decomposition case reflects the property that when a process returns a complex value the information that a process is evaluating this value should not be lost when an object contained in this complex value is selected. This property is called the **decomposition property**.

Assume that g is of type [num]; then using the decomposition property x is of type {proc} num in (for more practical examples see the next section):

```
x where (x : xs) = {Par} g
```

With similar reasoning the following type specification is accepted:

```
phd:: {proc} [num] -> {proc} num
phd (x : xs)    = x
```

With the assigned process types the standard type substitutions and unifications are performed, with the following two exceptions:

- Where a process type is specified but a process type cannot be assigned, a process type error will occur.

This definition of pipeline will be rejected since on the right-hand side in the application of npipe for gen no process type is assigned, while in the type definition of npipe a process type is specified:

```
pipeline:: * -> [* -> *] -> {proc} *
pipeline gen filters  =  npipe gen filters

npipe:: {proc} * -> [* -> *] -> {proc} *
```

- Where a non-process type is specified but a process type is assigned no error will occur. In that case the specified type is used in substitutions and for unification (**deprocessing**). This deprocessing, however, does not exclude the possibility that process types are substituted for type variables.

With the following definition:

```
f:: [num] -> num
f (x : xs)     =  x
```

f ({Par} generator 3) has type num due to deprocessing. But, with the more general polymorphic definition:

```
f:: [*] -> *
f (x : xs)     =  x
```

f ({Par} generator 3) has type {proc} num by decomposition and substitution.

The type system is such that in well-typed programs it is guaranteed that expressions that have a process type are in PNF.

13.3 Examples of concurrent functional programs

In this section two more elaborate examples of concurrent functional programs are given: the sieve of Eratosthenes computing prime numbers and Warshall's algorithm solving the shortest path problem. The purpose of the examples is to show that more complex process topologies can be expressed elegantly with help of the presented annotations and type attributes. It is not the intention to show how ultimate speed-ups can be achieved for the problems in question.

13.3.1 Sieve of Eratosthenes

The sieve of Eratosthenes (see also the sequential Clean version in Chapter 8) is a classical example generating all prime numbers. In the parallel version a pipeline of processes is created. There is a process for each sieve. Those sieves hold the prime numbers in ascending order, one in each sieve. Each sieve accepts a stream of numbers as its input. Those numbers are not divisible by any of the foregoing primes in the pipeline. If an incoming number is not divisible by the local prime as well, it is sent to the next sieve in the pipeline. A newly created sieve process accepts the first incoming number as its own prime and returns this prime as result such that it can be printed. After that it starts sieving. A generator process is used to feed the first sieve in the pipeline with a stream (list) of increasing numbers greater than one (see Figure 13.8).

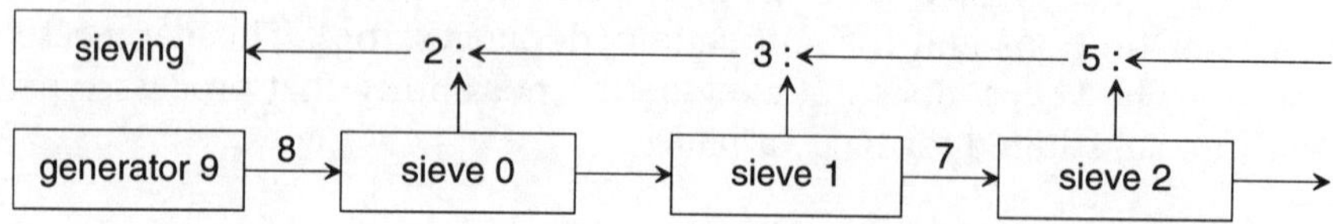

Figure 13.8 Snapshot of the process structure of the sieve processes.

In the programs below two concurrent solutions for the sieve of Eratosthenes are given. In the first toy example only a fixed number (four) of sieve processes is created. No more prime numbers can be found than the number of sieves created. So only four prime numbers will be found. The program shows very clearly that each sieve process is returning two results in a tuple: the prime number and a stream of numbers that is communicated to the next sieving process.

Sieve of Eratosthenes with a fixed number of sieve processes in the pipeline:

```
static_sieving:: [{proc} num]
static_sieving   = [p1, p2, p3, p4]  where  s0       = {Par} generator 2
                                            (p1, s1) = {Par} sieve s0
                                            (p2, s2) = {Par} sieve s1
                                            (p3, s3) = {Par} sieve s2
                                            (p4, s4) = {Par} sieve s3

sieve:: [num] -> (num, [num])
sieve (prime : stream) =  (prime, filter prime stream)

generator:: num -> [num]
generator n    =  [n..100]

filter:: num -> [num] -> [num]
filter n [ ]        =  [ ]
filter n (x : xs)   =  x : filter n xs,   if (x mod n) ~= 0
                    =  filter n xs,       otherwise
```

The local selector function (p_i, s_i) in static_sieving selects objects being evaluated by a (parallel) process. So the argument s_i of a sieve is already under calculation by the previous sieving process. As explained in Section 13.2.5, a process type can be assigned to the sieve arguments. In this way the required communication stream between the sieving processes is accomplished.

In the second more general solution as many sieves are created as necessary. Each time a new prime number is produced at the end of the pipeline a fresh sieve is created and the pipeline is extended. Each individual sieve works as described above.

Sieve with as many sieve processes as necessary in the pipeline (with the functions sieve and generator as defined above).

```
dynamic_sieving:: [{proc} num]
dynamic_sieving    = dynpipe ({Par} generator 2)

dynpipe:: {proc} [num] -> [{proc} num]
dynpipe [ ] = [ ]
dynpipe in = p : {Self} dynpipe s    where  (p, s)   = {Par} sieve in
```

13.3.2 Warshall's algorithm

The following algorithm is a parallel version of Warshall's solution for the *shortest path problem*:

Given a graph G consisting of N nodes and directed edges with a distance associated with each edge, the graph can be represented by an $N * N$ matrix in which the element at the ith row and jth column is equal to the distance from node i to node j. Warshall's shortest path algorithm is able to find the shortest path within this graph between any two nodes.

Warshall's shortest path algorithm:

A path from node j to node k is said to contain a node i if it can be split in two paths, one from node j to node i and one from node i to node k ($i \neq j$ and $i \neq k$). Let $SP(j,k,i)$ denote the length of the shortest path from node j to node k that contains only nodes less than or equal to i ($0 \leq i$ and $1 \leq j,k$ and $i,j,k \leq N$).

So

$$
\begin{aligned}
SP(j,k,0) &= 0 && \text{if } j=k \\
&= d && \text{if there is an edge from } j \text{ to } k \text{ with distance } d \\
&= \infty && \text{otherwise} \\
SP(j,k,i) &= \mathit{minimum}\,(SP(j,k,i-1),\ SP(j,i,i-1) + SP(i,k,i-1))
\end{aligned}
$$

Define a matrix M as follows: $M[j,k] = SP(j,k,i)$ for some i. The final shortest path matrix can be computed iteratively by varying i from 0 to N using the equations as described above. In the ith iteration it is considered for each pair of nodes whether a shorter path exists via node i.

The Warshall algorithm is an interesting algorithm to test the expressiveness of parallel languages (Augusteijn, 1985) since it requires a special process structure containing a cycle (Figure 13.9).

To illustrate the algorithm it is applied to the graph on the right with the corresponding matrixes given below:

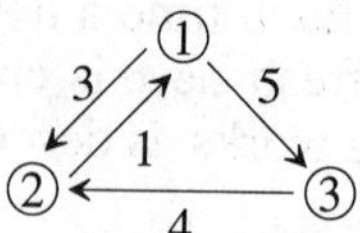

$M[j,k]_0$

0	3	5
1	0	∞
∞	4	0

$M[j,k]_1$

0	3	5
1	0	6
∞	4	0

$SP(2,3,1) = min\ (SP(2,3,0), SP(2,1,0)+SP(1,3,0)) = min\ (\infty, 1+5)$

$M[j,k]_2$

0	3	5
1	0	6
5	4	0

$SP(3,1,2) = min\ (SP(3,1,1), SP(3,2,1)+SP(2,1,1)) = min\ (\infty, 4+1)$

$M[j,k]_3$

0	3	5
1	0	6
5	4	0

Observing the algorithm it can be concluded that during the ith iteration all updating can be performed in parallel. It seems a good decision to create N parallel processes: one for each row that updates its row during each iteration step. In the ith iteration all the parallel processes need to have access to row i as well as to their own row. This can be achieved by letting parallel process i distribute its own row as soon as the ith iteration starts. At the end of the distributed computation the rows of the solution have to be collected.

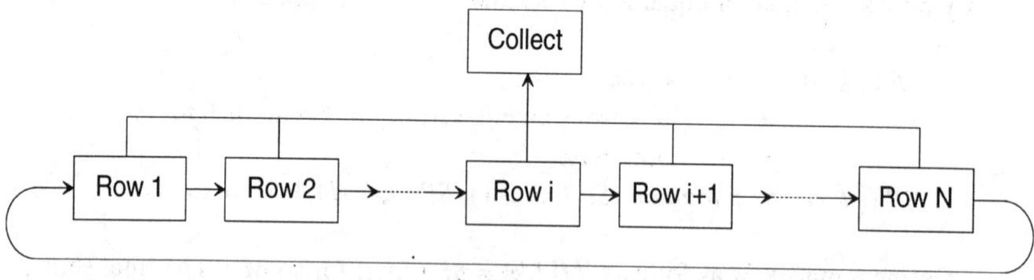

Figure 13.9 Snapshot of the process structure of Warshall's algorithm.

Initially, a parallel process $rowproc_i$ is created for each row of the matrix. Before $rowproc_i$ performs its *i*th iteration it distributes its own row to the other rowprocs. This is done in a cyclic pipeline, i.e. $rowproc_i$ sends its own row to $rowproc_j$ via $rowproc_{i+1}$, ... , $rowproc_{j-1}$ and $rowproc_j$ (counting modulo *N* from *i* to *j*).

It is rather difficult to express this distributing, updating and iterating in a parallel functional language. The cyclic process structure is created via a recursive local definition of a pair with as first element the final solution and as second element the output that will be produced by the *N*th process after it is created.

```
matrix * ==   [ [*] ]

warshall:: matrix num -> matrix num
warshall mat
   = solution
     where (solution, output_rp_N) = create_procs (#mat) 1 mat output_rp_N

create_procs:: num -> num -> matrix num -> {proc}[[num]]
                                     -> ([{proc}[num]], {proc}[[num]])
create_procs size k [row_N] input_left_rp
   = ([row_N_solution], output_rp_N)
     where   (row_N_solution, output_rp_N)
                     = {Self} iterate size k 1 row_N input_left_rp
create_procs size k (row_k : restmat) input_left_rp
   = (row_k_solution : rest_solutions, output_rp_N)
     where   (row_k_solution, output_rp_k)
                     = {Self} iterate size k 1 row_k input_left_rp
             (rest_solutions, output_rp_N)
                     = {Par} create_procs size (k+1) restmat output_rp_k

iterate:: num -> num -> num -> [num] -> [[num]] -> ([num],[[num]])
iterate size k i row_k rows
   = (row_k, [ ]),                     if iterations_finished
   = (solution, row_k : rest_output),  if start_sending_this_row
   = (solution, row_i : rest_output),  otherwise
     where   iterations_finished       = i > size
             start_sending_this_row    = i = k
             row_i : xs                = rows
             (solution, rest_output)   = iterate size k (i+1) next_row_k xs
             next_row_k    = row_k,                              if i = k
                           = updaterow row_k row_i dist_k_i,     otherwise
             dist_k_i      = row_k ! (i – 1)

updaterow::[num] -> [num] -> num -> [num]
updaterow [ ]                   row_i                 dist_j_i  =  [ ]
```

```
updaterow (dist_j_k : restrow_j)   (dist_i_k : restrow_i)   dist_j_i
   = min dist_j_k (dist_j_i + dist_i_k) : updaterow restrow_j restrow_i dist_j_i
     where  min m n   = m,   if m < n
                      = n,   otherwise

warshall [ [   0, 100, 100,  13, 100, 100 ],
           [ 100,   0, 100, 100,   4,   9 ],
           [  11, 100,   0, 100, 100, 100 ],
           [ 100,   3, 100,   0, 100,   7 ],
           [  15,   5, 100,   1,   0, 100 ],
           [  11, 100, 100,  14, 100,   0 ] ]
```

13.4 Discussion

Writing concurrent programs is in general a much more difficult task than writing ordinary sequential programs. Writing concurrent programs in a functional language instead of in an imperative language has certain advantages and disadvantages.

With only *two* annotations, one for the creation of parallel processes and one for the creation of interleaved processes, already very complicated concurrent programs can be specified in an elegant and readable way using the associated type system. Processes can be created dynamically. For the communication between processes no additional primitives are needed. Communication is demand driven: whenever a process needs information from another process the information is communicated as soon as it is available. Flexible and powerful tools for the construction of frequently occurring process topologies can be defined using the expressive power of functional languages. Concurrent functional programs can be executed on any processor configuration, in parallel or just sequentially. In principle, the programmer can start with writing an ordinary sequential program. When this program is finished he or she can turn this program into a parallel version by creating processes for some of the function applications in the program.

Of course, many problems remain that are connected with concurrent programming in general. Sometimes it is very difficult to tell which function application really is worthwhile to be evaluated in parallel. In the worst case, the program has to be fully rewritten simply because the chosen algorithm is not suited for parallel evaluation at all. So one cannot expect a real speed-up when the chosen algorithm is not suited for parallel evaluation.

It is possible to write complicated concurrent functional programs with the proposed language extensions, but there are still many things to be desired. With explicit use of sharing, e.g. in graph rewriting systems, it would be not only possible to specify cyclic structures explicitly, but it would also be possible to specify process topologies directly. Besides, for some applications one would like to have the possibility of creating processes that reduce to head normal form or to spine normal form instead of to normal form. Furthermore, it should be possible to assign a particular process to a specific concrete processor. With such a facility a concurrent program can be optimally tuned to the available parallel architecture. For certain applications one would also like to have better control of the kind of information that is passed from one process(or) to another. One would like to ship not only data but also work (redexes). The control of the amount of information that is communicated and the moment at which this happens (synchronous, asynchronous, blocked) can be important as well.

To tackle the problems and desires mentioned above it is necessary to extend the graph rewriting model (see Chapter 14).

Summary

- A functional program can be turned into a *concurrent* functional program with help of a {Par} annotation (for the creation of *parallel* processes) and a {Self} annotation (for the creation of *interleaved* subprocesses).
- For the *communication* between processes *no special primitives are needed* since due to the lazy evaluation scheme process communication is also lazy.
- A process can *communicate* with *several other processes* at the same time using subprocesses that run interleaved *serving* demanding processes.
- In the *type specifications* of the function definitions the programmer can explicitly indicate that certain subexpressions of the program will be evaluated by a process. In this way complex process topologies can be specified in a clear way.
- With the proposed primitives and the use of higher order functions and function composition complex concurrent programs can be expressed elegantly. Divide-and-conquer parallelism can be specified, but also more complicated process topologies such as a *pipeline* of processes or a *cyclic* process structure.
- Concurrent functional programming is still in its infancy. Many other language constructs for special forms of concurrency are possible.
- For a better understanding of the possibilities, limits and properties of concurrent functional programming the underlying computational model of graph rewriting has to be extended to a parallel context.

EXERCISES

13.1 Give a sequential definition of fib n that has a linear complexity with respect to n. Discuss the differences in efficiency compared with the parallel version of Figure 13.5.

13.2* Write a Miranda function that computes the determinant of a matrix. Use this function to compute the inverse of a matrix using the method of Cramer. Use {Par} and {Self} to construct a parallel program. Let the main process compute the determinant of the matrix. Each element of the inverse matrix is computed by a parallel process.

13.3 Write a function that computes the *n* queens problem (see Exercise 2.5) in parallel using a divide-and-conquer approach. The function should take the board size and a threshold as an argument.

Chapter 14
Parallel graph rewriting

This chapter will show that processes and inter-process communication can be modelled by extending the GRS model presented in Chapter 5. For reasons of simplicity this extension will be restricted to TGRSs. The extensions made to the TGRS model are inspired both by the concurrency primitives that we would like to have on the language level as well as by the target architectures we are aiming for (see Chapter 13).

Owing to the absence of global memory on loosely coupled parallel architectures it is no longer realistic to share graphs across processor boundaries. In a concrete implementation graphs have to be copied from one local processor memory to another. This copying is so important and complex that we do not want to regard it as a minor implementation issue. So we want to obtain this behaviour as a basic aspect in the underlying model of computation. In order to be able to copy graphs in a flexible way TGRSs are extended with the concept of *lazy copying*.

Furthermore, we want to be able to specify *dynamic process creation* explicitly in a TGRS. For this purpose the strict annotations as introduced in Clean (Chapter 8) are generalized to *strategy annotations* that influence a single incarnation of a reduction strategy and *process annotations* that create new incarnations of a reduction strategy. However, it has to be sound to consider a graph rewrite step as an indivisible step in order to make reasoning about rewriting systems possible. This implies that with process annotations only *interleaved* processes can be created. Still, of course, one would like to be able to create reducers of which the rewrite steps can actually be performed in *parallel* instead of *interleaved*. A special combination of process annotations and lazy copying does allow such a parallel evaluation.

Section 14.1 introduces *strategy annotations* and *process annotations* to control the sequential and the concurrent evaluation order. With process annotations *interleaved*, executing reducers can be created. In

Section 14.2 *copying* and *lazy copying* are introduced. Section 14.3 shows that lazy copying and process annotations can be seen as basic primitives with which higher level annotations such as {Par} and {Self} (as introduced in Chapter 13) can be created. Similar annotations, {P} and {I}, are introduced to create processes that reduce to *root normal form*. These annotations are more primitive, but they allow finer control over the distribution of data and work (see also Chapter 15).

14.1 Annotations to control the reduction order

This section introduces *strategy annotations* and *process annotations* in TGRSs as generalizations of the strict annotations used in Section 8.3.

The semantics of strategy and process annotations on a *right-hand side* are effected after a rewrite of the corresponding rule alternative but before the function at the root of the right-hand side is considered for evaluation. In the case that in a single right-hand side more than one annotation is used, the order in which these annotations are dealt with takes the graph structure into account. The annotations are in principle effected depth-first. In order to obtain a higher degree of flexibility the annotations in this section are parametrized with a strategy σ.

14.1.1 Strategy annotations in TGRSs

In TGRSs strategy annotations, denoted by $\{!_\sigma\}$, can be placed at arguments on the right-hand side of a rewrite rule.

The semantics of a **strategy annotation in a TGRS** is as follows. When the current strategy considers as a candidate for reduction a function application that has an argument which is annotated in the rewrite rule with a strategy annotation σ, then the current strategy is *temporarily* interrupted: instead the strategy σ is applied on the subgraph corresponding to the argument. The interrupted strategy will continue again (e.g. with another annotated argument or with the application of the function itself) when no redexes are indicated by σ, i.e. when the subgraph is in **σ normal form**.

Looking at the overall strategy function one can observe that it is composed of several strategy functions that invoke each other. Each of them is invoked on the indicated subgraph where an annotation occurs in the contractum pattern. However, at each moment only *one* strategy σ is actively applied; all the others are interrupted.

We distinguish three kinds of *strategy annotation*:

- The **rnf annotation** {!} invokes the *functional strategy to strong root normal form* (used, for example, in Section 8.3).
- The **nf annotation** {!!} invokes the *functional strategy to normal form* (used for the evaluation of the Start node (see Section 11.2)).

- The **step annotation** {*} is used to invoke a *zero or one step reduction* strategy function that performs one rewrite on the annotated function application if it is a redex (used, for example, to force copying of graphs in Sections 14.3 and 14.4).

14.1.2 Graph rewriting with interleaved semantics

When a *parallel* reduction strategy is used, *several* redexes are indicated as candidates for reduction (see Section 5.7). However, in principle it is not allowed to rewrite all these redexes simultaneously. Unpredictable graphs may be constructed if matching, contractum construction, redirection and garbage collection of several rewrites were to take place in parallel. Therefore, without additional restrictions it is *a priori not* sound to rewrite in *parallel*, even when a so-called *parallel reduction strategy* is being used. In order to be able to reason about the result of reductions indicated by a parallel strategy, it is assumed that 'parallel' rewriting has interleaved semantics, i.e. parallelism is *simulated* by *interleaving* ordinary, *sequential* rewrite steps. The rewrite step itself is considered to be *indivisible*. So when a parallel reduction strategy is used, only one of the indicated redexes is chosen in an arbitrary way and rewritten as usual. Then the parallel reduction strategy will determine the next candidates. It will always be assumed that the parallel strategy will at least offer the not-chosen candidates for the next round. To obtain a proper simulation of parallel reduction it is assumed that the rewriting will be **fair**, i.e. a redex repeatedly indicated by the parallel strategy will *eventually* be rewritten by the reducer.

Section 14.3 will discuss cases for which the *interleaved* semantics is not required, allowing a more realistic *truly parallel* evaluation.

14.1.3 Process annotations in TGRSs

By using **process annotations** in the rewrite rules one can indicate on which part of the graph strategy σ has to be applied in an *interleaved* way. As with strategy annotations, several sequential strategy functions are invoked at several places (subgraphs) in the graph. The difference with strategy annotations is that for a process annotation a *new* incarnation of a sequential reduction strategy is created such that *multiple strategy incarnations* now *remain* active. These strategies together form a **parallel strategy**: each of them delivers one candidate for rewriting. The parallel strategy thus constructed is completely determined by the sequential strategies that are activated and by the set of root nodes of the several subgraphs on which they are applied.

A reducer is a process that repeatedly chooses and rewrites one of the redexes indicated by the (parallel) reduction strategy. In the case of a parallel strategy specified by using process annotations one can equally well assume that there are several **interleaved reducers**, where each reducer is attached to one of the sequential strategies that the parallel strategy is composed of. So TGRSs are extended in the following way. For each sequential strategy σ on a right-hand side of a rewrite rule process annotations {p_σ} can be specified.

Example of {p_σ} annotation on a right-hand side:

```
Fib 0   →   1
Fib 1   →   1
Fib n   →   + ({pσ} Fib (– n 1)) ({pσ} Fib (– n 2))
```

A process annotation changes the default sequential strategy into a parallel one by applying the sequential strategy σ on the indicated subgraph as well. As a result a new sequential reducer is created with the following properties:

- the new reducer reduces the corresponding subgraph with strategy σ and dies when no more redexes are indicated;
- the new reducer proceeds *interleaved* with the parent reducer;
- all rewrites are *indivisible* actions.

Locking of reducers

A process created with a process annotation may hit on a shared redex which is already under reduction by another process. We have already argued in Chapter 13 that in such a situation it would be best for efficiency reasons to wait until the first process is finished, i.e. has delivered its σ normal form. Therefore we assume that a process that needs information which is already being calculated by another process is **suspended (locked)** until the result becomes available.

Such a locking has to be realized by the overall strategy function. Each of the incarnations of a sequential strategy delivers a candidate for rewriting. But when the same redex is indicated by more than one incarnation, only one of them is allowed to reduce the redex until the intended σ normal form is reached. The others are not chosen and locked in that way. *From now on we only consider process annotations that invoke such locking strategies.*

In this chapter two special (locking) *process* annotations are used to model higher level process behaviour like, for example, the behaviour induced by the {Par} and {Self} annotations of Chapter 13.

- The **p-rnf process annotation {p!}** invokes a *process* with the *functional strategy* to *strong root normal form.*
- The **p-nf process annotation {p!!}** invokes a *process* with the *functional strategy* to *normal form.*

14.1.4 Deadlock

When processes need information from each other in order to continue a **deadlock** situation may be created (i.e. none of the processes involved can make any progress). This is easily avoided by the programmer through the following important property. When all process annotations occur on positions that are needed for the sequential evaluation, the following holds: if, due to the process annotations, a deadlock situation occurs, ignoring the process annotations would have led to a sequential cycle-in-spine error.

Correspondence between deadlocks of processes and cycle-in-spine errors:

```
Start   →   x: {p!} F y,
            y: {p!} G x

F 0     →   1
G 0     →   1
```

The processes created will be in deadlock because they need each other's result. When the annotations are ignored a cycle-in-spine error occurs.

14.2 GRSs with lazy copying

TGRSs have the advantage over TRSs that by sharing it is possible to avoid duplication of work. But in order to model the inter-processor communication on a distributed machine architecture a facility to express graph *copying* has to be added to TGRSs. One might expect that it is already possible to express copying in (T)GRSs. However, this is not true: only a very limited kind of graph copying can be expressed.

Clearly, the following function does not copy its argument since it creates two pointers to the argument instead of duplicating the argument itself.

```
Duplicate x   →   Pair x x
```

```
@1: Duplicate @2,
@2: Pair @3 @2,
@3: 1
```

This graph reduces to

```
@4: Pair @2 @2,
@2: Pair @3 @2,
@3: 1
```

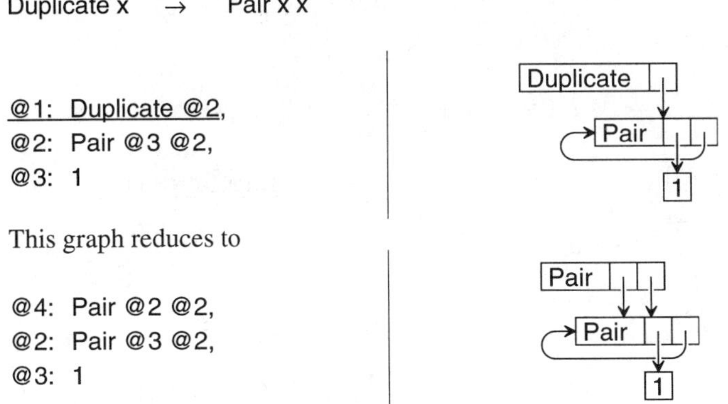

In order to copy a node in a GRS one has to define a rewrite rule in which the pattern is used to determine the node symbol such that a new copy of this node containing the same symbol can be created on the right-hand side. Such a copying rewrite rule is needed for each kind of node that has to be copied. Since it is not possible to match on an arbitrary symbol one cannot define a rewrite rule that can copy an *arbitrary* unknown graph structure. In a special case, i.e. when all the possible symbols of the nodes to copy are known, rules can be defined that can copy a graph structure composed of these nodes. But even in that case, copying remains difficult when shared graph structures are involved. The different sharing structures have to be distinguished. This is only possible in comparing systems. For this purpose the theory of comparing systems would have to be further developed (see Section 5.6.1).

So for reasons of expressiveness and of efficiency of communication it is necessary somehow to include the possibility of copying arbitrary graph structures in the standard semantics of GRSs. This requires in some way finding a construct with semantics in between the semantics of TRSs (in which multiple occurrences of variables on the right-hand side always indicate that duplicates are made) and the semantics of GRSs (in which multiple occurrences of variables on the right-hand side always indicate that a structure with sharing has to be made).

14.2.1 Eager copying

Such a construct is created by extending graph rewriting systems with a function Copy which produces as its result a *full* copy of its argument graph. This function is defined by extending the semantics of graph rewriting. The moment at which this function is executed is, of course, indicated by the reduction strategy. A node containing an application of the Copy function is also called a **copy node**.

The way of copying defined in this section is called **eager copying**, in contrast to *lazy copying*, which will be defined in the next section.

With the following Duplicate rule an arbitrary graph structure can be copied:

```
Duplicate x    →    Pair x (Copy x)
```

The cyclic graph @2: Pair @3 @2, @3: 1 can be copied as follows:

```
@1:    Duplicate @2,
@2:    Pair @3 @2,
@3:    1
```

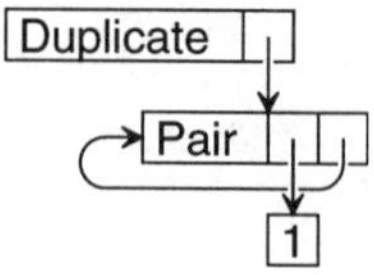

which reduces first to:

```
@4:    Pair @2 @5,
@2:    Pair @3 @2,
@3:    1,
@5:    Copy @2
```

and then to:

```
@4:    Pair @2 @12,
@3:    1,
@2:    Pair @3 @2,
@12:   Pair @13 @12,
@13:   1
```

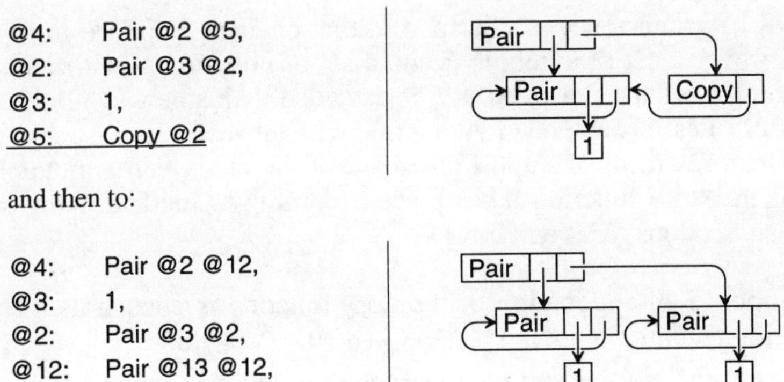

Copy nodes are not treated specially during graph rewriting. Consequently, when the argument of a copy node is a cyclic graph containing again the very same copy node, this node is copied with the rest of the cyclic graph. The copy node will occur again in the result of the copy.

Take the following cyclic graph:

```
@1:    Pair @2 @3,
@2:    1,
@3:    Copy @1
```

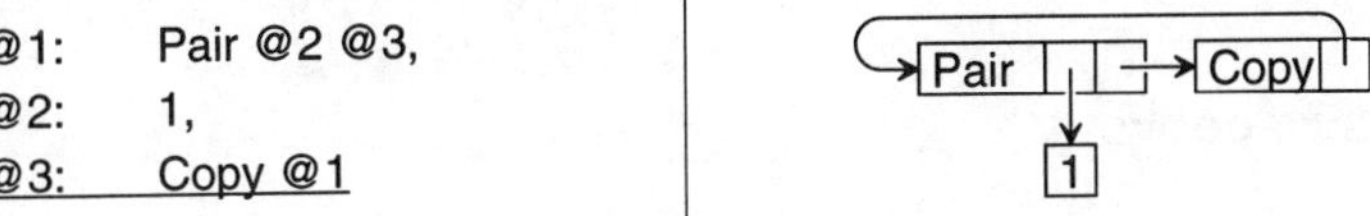

The result after executing the Copy function:

```
@1:    Pair @2 @11,
@2:    1,
@11:   Pair @12 @13,
@12:   1,
@13:   Copy @11
```

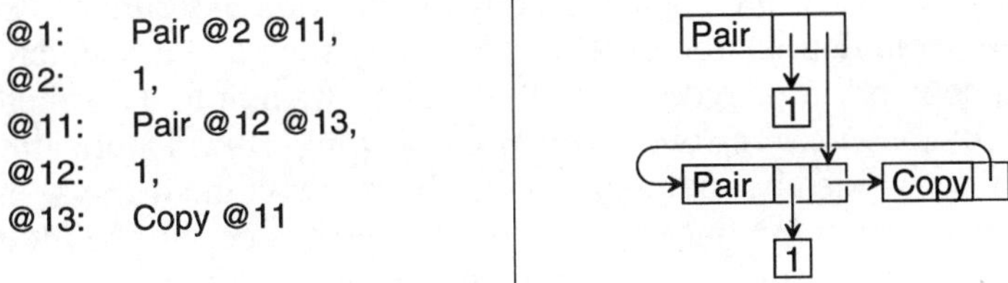

Semantics of eager copying

The Copy function uses the internal structure of its argument to create the result. The copy it makes is a full isomorphic copy of its argument graph. We saw that possible occurrences of the Copy function itself do not play a special role: they will also be copied. An application of the Copy function is treated just as any other function. Also, with respect to the evaluation order no special treatment is necessary. Evaluating an application of the Copy function simply yields a copy of its argument with which evaluation can continue.

Using the terminology of Chapter 5 the operational semantics of eager copying is defined as follows as an extension of the standard semantics of graph rewriting defined in that chapter. Suppose there is a graph γ over a set of symbols F and a set of node-ids N with contents function C_γ and a set of rules ρ. F is extended with a new symbol: Copy, the set of rules ρ is extended with a rule with left-hand side r: Copy x.

Then, rewriting a graph in the case of the redex being an application of the Copy function takes place according to the following steps (see also Sections 5.3.3 and 5.6.1):

(1) Suppose an application of the Copy function is chosen as a redex with matching mapping μ, i.e. $C_\gamma(\mu(\mathrm{r})) = \mathrm{Copy}\ \mu(\mathrm{x})$

(2) Then, the contractum is constructed as follows: using new node-ids, i.e. node-ids not present in γ, a graph γ' is constructed which is equivalent to the subgraph of $\mu(\mathrm{x})$ in γ.
(Owing to the equivalence and the use of new node-ids γ' is in fact the required copy of the subgraph of $\mu(\mathrm{x})$ in γ.)

(3), (4) and (5) In the standard way, the graph γ' is united with γ, $\mu(\mathrm{r})$, redirected to the root of γ' and garbage collection takes place.

So the function Copy produces as its result a graph copy of its argument.

14.2.2 Lazy copying

Copying *redexes* corresponds to copying *work*. Copying *normal forms* (or certain parts of the graph that will not be reduced anymore) corresponds to copying *data* (in many cases the result of work that has been performed). However, using eager copying the choice is either to share a graph to avoid duplication of work or to copy such a graph which will include a copy of *all* its redexes. In this section we aim to do something in between: *copying of graphs without duplicating work*. Duplication of work can be avoided by maintaining the sharing with the original graph as long as the subgraph to copy has not been evaluated. So the intuitive idea is to *defer* the copying action as long as the work is not finished. After the work is done the copy can be made.

Copying with the choice of breaking up the sharing or maintaining the sharing by deferring the copying is called **lazy copying** (Van Eekelen,1988; Van Eekelen *et al.*,1991). For this reason a node in the graph is extended with the ability to have a **defer attribute**. A node which has this defer attribute is accordingly called a **deferred node**.

The defer attribute is generally assigned to and removed from a node by the reduction strategy. A natural way to do this is to create nodes with the deferred attribute, if this is indicated, on a right-hand side of a rule. When such a deferred node is rewritten it seems reasonable to make the result of the rewrite inherit the deferred attribute, since the 'work' is still going on. Furthermore, it seems sensible to remove the deferred attribute when a node is in σ normal form, since then the 'work' is done. *From now on we shall always assume that every reduction strategy deals with deferred nodes in this way.*

For lazy copying, in the same way as in the previous section, a new primitive can be defined: a function LCopy, which produces as its result a partial copy of its argument graph in which the copying is deferred for those nodes that have the defer attribute. A node containing an application of the LCopy function is also called a **lazy copy node**.

So when the function LCopy hits a deferred node the **copying is deferred**, i.e. stopped *temporarily* until this node loses its defer attribute. This is done as follows: instead of making a copy of the deferred node, a node is created with an application of the function LCopy with the deferred node as its argument. The semantics of the LCopy function deals with deferring the copy in that case simply by the fact that an application of the LCopy function with, as its argument, a deferred node is not considered to be a redex. After creating such a node, the original LCopy function continues as if the deferred node (with its descendants) was copied.

Semantics of lazy copying

Like the Copy function, the LCopy function uses the internal structure of its argument to create the result. Again, possible occurrences of the LCopy function itself do not play a special role: they will also be copied.

Using the terminology of Chapter 5 the operational semantics of lazy copying is defined as follows as an extension of the standard semantics of graph rewriting defined in that chapter. Suppose there is a graph γ over a set of symbols F and a set of node-ids N with contents function C_γ and a set of rules ρ. F is extended with a new symbol: LCopy, the set of rules ρ is extended with a rule with left-hand side r: LCopy x. Furthermore, a predicate P will be defined as a function from N to {*True, False*} indicating for each node whether the node has the deferred attribute or not. The actual concrete definition of P is determined by the reduction strategy. For this purpose, syntactically on a right-hand side nodes can be attributed with a subscript d indicating to the reduction strategy that the corresponding created node has to be deferred. The **non-deferred subgraph of a node-id** n in a graph g is defined as the connected subgraph of g which is rooted at n and contains the node definitions of all non-deferred nodes in g that are reachable from n via non-deferred nodes only.

Then, rewriting a graph in the case of the redex being an application of the LCopy function takes place according to the following steps (see also the previous section and Sections 5.3.3 and 5.6.1):

(1) An application of the LCopy function can only be chosen as a redex *if the corresponding argument does not have the deferred attribute.*

Now suppose this is the case: there is a matching mapping μ, i.e. $C_\gamma(\mu(\text{r}))$ = LCopy μ(x) and μ(x) does not have the deferred attribute.

(2) Then the contractum is constructed as follows: using for the node definitions new node-ids, i.e. node-ids not present in γ, a graph γ' is constructed which is equivalent to the non-deferred subgraph of μ(x) in γ.

Since γ' is equivalent to the non-deferred subgraph of μ(x) in γ and new node-ids are used for the node definitions only, γ' can contain nodes n that have arguments that are deferred nodes in γ. Let δ be the (not connected) graph containing the node definitions of all such nodes n of γ' (δ contains precisely those nodes that have deferred arguments for which copying has to be deferred).

Now, for all nodes n in δ, each deferred argument x of n is redirected in γ' to a node with a new node-id y and the following definition: y: LCopy x. In this case new node-ids are node-ids not present in γ nor in γ' (it is easy to check that the order in which this is done does not influence the result).

This results in a new graph γ''.

(3), (4) and (5) In the standard way, the graph γ'' is united with γ, μ(r) is redirected to the root of γ'' and garbage collection takes place.

So the function LCopy produces as its result a (possibly partially deferred) graph copy of its argument.

A lazy copying example reduced with the functional strategy.

```
Start          →   Duplicate (Facd 6)

Duplicate x    →   Pair (LCopy x) x

Fac 0          →   1
Fac n          →   * n (Fac (-- n))
```

The following rewrites occur (see also Figure 14.1):

```
@1: Start
→   @2: Duplicate @3,   @3: Facd 6
→   @4: Pair @3 @5,     @5: LCopy @3,   @3:    Facd 6
→*  @4: Pair @6 @5,     @5: LCopy @6,   @6:    720d
=   @4: Pair @6 @5,     @5: LCopy @6,   @6:    720
→   @4: Pair @6 @16,    @6: 720,        @16:   720
```

Note that the d attribute was inherited when the node @3 was redirected to @6 which corresponded with the reduction of the node. The deferred attribute of the node @6 is removed when the root normal form is reached.

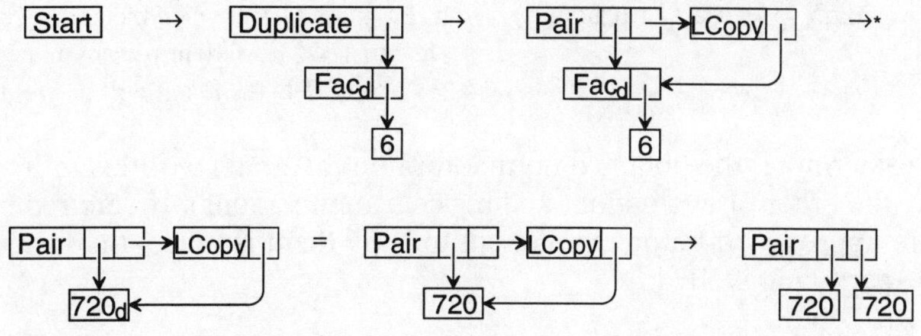

Figure 14.1 Example of lazy copying.

14.2.3 Properties of TGRSs extended with lazy copying

The semantics of graph rewriting with lazy copying is in some sense in between the semantics of term rewriting and the semantics of graph rewriting. The choice can be made either to *share* or to *copy*. When no copying is used a GRS is obtained, when all arguments are copied a TRS is obtained. But the choice can be made in a very flexible way since the copying can be demanded and deferred at any node.

An interesting aspect of lazy copying is that normal forms do not contain defer attributes nor LCopy nodes. In a normal form every subgraph is trivially in σ normal form. Evaluation of nodes to σ normal form eliminates the defer attributes such that all strict applications of the LCopy rule can be reduced.

The following rules:	result in the following normal forms:
Start → x: Pair 1 x	@1: Pair 1 @1
Start → x: Pair$_d$ 1 x	@1: Pair 1 @1

Evidently, (lazy) copying influences the normal forms in the graph world in a trivial way, since copies are made which mean that the resulting graphs are not graph equivalent anymore. However, the normal forms in the graph world can also be influenced in a more subtle way, since sharing can be broken up when a cycle is copied which contains LCopy nodes or deferred nodes. The result will be partly unravelled with respect to a full copy (a similar property holds for eager copying).

Partial unravelling (and in both cases an infinite normal form) due to copying:

```
Start → x: Pair 1 (LCopy x)    @1:  Pair 1 @11,   || a cycle with a copy in it
                               @11: Pair 1 @21,   || yields a partly unrav-
                               @21: LCopy @11     || elled cyclic structure.
```

Start → x: Pair_d 1 (LCopy x)   @1: Pair 1 @11, || when the node is not
                                                        @11: Pair 1 @21, || deferred anymore the
                                                        @21: LCopy @11 || result will be yielded.

Furthermore, the obtained normal form in the graph world is influenced by the order of evaluation (and hence by annotations). If deferred nodes are not reduced before an attempt to copy them is made, the result will be partly unravelled.

Normal forms of TGRSs with lazy copying are influenced by the reduction order. Consider the following rules:

Start →   r: LCopy (A x z),
              x: I_d z,
              z: B
I x   →   x

After the Start rule has been applied there are two possible reduction orders that can be taken by a reduction strategy: First one can do the lazy copy.

@1:   LCopy @2,
@2:   A @3 @4,
@3: I_d @4,
@4:   B

The identity function cannot be copied because it is deferred. This is remembered by the new LCopy node. Now the identity rule is applied. Then, the deferred property can be removed since the result is in σ normal form. Finally the deferred copying can be completed.

@12:	A @13 @14,	@12:	A @13 @14,
@13:	LCopy @3,	@13:	LCopy @4,
@14:	B,	@14:	B,
@3:	I_d @4,	@4:	B_d
@4:	B		

@12:	A @13 @14,	@12:	A @24 @14,
@13:	LCopy @4,	@24:	B,
@14:	B,	@4:	B
@4:	B		

The alternative is to do first the identity rule and then the lazy copy. This leads to another graph normal form (shown below). So depending on the reduction order chosen by the strategy, we have two different graph normal forms. The unravellings of the two normal forms are equivalent.

```
@1: LCopy @2,                    @1: LCopy @2,
@2: A @3 @4,                     @2: A @4 @4,
@3: Id @4,                       @4: Bd
@4: B

@1: LCopy @2,                    @12:  A @14 @14,
@2: A @4 @4,                     @14:  B
@4: B
```

The unravelling of the normal forms of a rule system with lazy copying will *always* be the same as the unravelling of the normal forms of the same rule system without lazy copying (Barendsen and Smetsers, 1992; Smetsers, 1993). In other words, unravelling is *invariant* with respect to lazy copying. This is a very important property for term graph rewriting and for the implementation of functional languages.

An important property for implementations based on lazy copying has to do with copying LCopy nodes. It can happen that the evaluation of the LCopy itself hits on an LCopy node that refers to a deferred node. Then according to the semantics for that deferred node a new LCopy node is created as usual. This, however, may lead to chains of LCopy nodes. An optimized implementation can do the following: if the LCopy action hits an LCopy node referring to a deferred node, only one new LCopy node is created referring directly to the deferred node. It can be proven that this leads to semantically equivalent results.

14.3 Modelling parallel graph rewriting

This section considers FGRSs only. Parallel instead of interleaved reduction is possible when it is guaranteed that the parallel rewrite steps cannot interfere with each other. It will be shown that one can describe the divide-and-conquer type of parallel graph reduction on distributed architectures by using a special combination of lazy graph copying and p-nf process annotations. This idea is extended to a more general method that can be used to model the {Par} and {Self} annotations introduced in the previous chapter. A variant of this method using p-rnf process annotations is shown to have even greater flexibility for modelling all kinds of process behaviour. Due to the use of lazy copying one can control when graphs are copied from one processor to another while it is possible to ship either work (redexes) or data (root normal forms).

14.3.1 Divide-and-conquer parallelism

With the help of strategy annotations, process annotations and lazy copying we are going to model divide-and-conquer parallelism suited for parallel evaluation on a distributed architecture. For divide-and-conquer evaluation, work (a redex) has to be copied to another processor.

When the work is finished the result (a normal form) has to be shipped back to the original processor. So lazy copying has to be performed *twice*: one lazy copy is directly made when a parallel process is created and one lazy copy is made later when the result is demanded by the parent process. The redex gets the defer attribute to ensure that it is not copied back before the normal form is reached.

When the result is demanded by the parent process it has to wait until this result has been calculated. This locking can be realized easily: just create a process on the redex. A demanding process now automatically will have to wait until this process has delivered its normal form while it is guaranteed that the work is indeed being evaluated.

A subgraph is **self-contained** when the root of the subgraph is the only connection between the subgraph and the other parts of the graph. The rewriting of such a self-contained subgraph cannot be interfered with by rewriting actions performed elsewhere on other parts. Therefore it is safe to evaluate the redex *in parallel* with the other rewriting steps.

A divide-and-conquer example in FGRSs (Figure 14.2):

```
Fib 0    →    1
Fib 1    →    1
Fib n    →    + (LCopy left) (LCopy right),
              left:     {p!!} Fibd (– ({*} LCopy n) 1),
              right:    {p!!} Fibd (– ({*} LCopy n) 2)
```

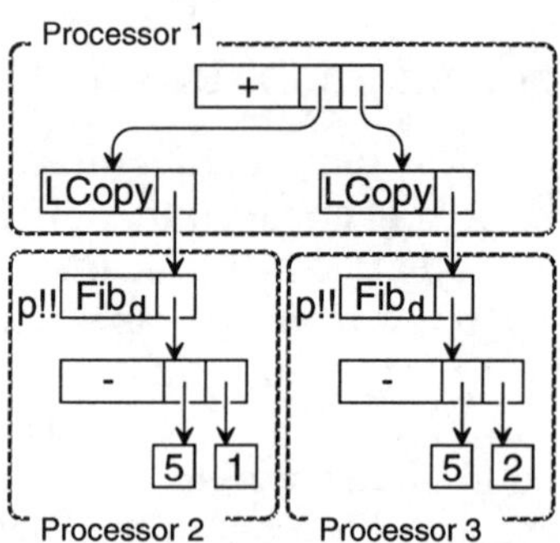

Figure 14.2 The process structure after one reduction of Fib 5. Each process may be executed in parallel on a different processor.

This particular combination of {p!!} annotations with the LCopy functions and defer indications makes it possible to evaluate both calls of Fib on another processor after which the result is copied back to the original demanding processor. The two process annotations indicate the reduction of the arguments with the functional strategy to normal form. The subgraph on which each process runs is made *self-contained* by actively taking copies (say n' and n") of the shared argument n. This lazy copy is made via the one step reduction {*}. So on one processor the graph Fib$_d$ (– n' 1) is created, on the other Fib$_d$ (– n" 2). Furthermore, the parent process demands a lazy copy of the results to perform the addition, but the shipped redex is deferred and a process is created on it. So the parent process will wait until the shipped redex has been reduced to normal form, after which the lazy copy can be made.

14.3.2 Modelling loosely coupled evaluation

A method which makes it possible to model process behaviours that are more general than divide-and-conquer must provide a way to define *arbitrary* connections between processes and processors.

A lazy copy of a subgraph is generally *not* self-contained since it may contain lazy copy nodes that point to those parts in the graph that have to be copied later when they are in σ normal form and needed for the evaluation. So the lazy copy nodes form the border of the copy. Lazy copy nodes are natural candidates for serving as interconnections between parallel executing processes because they induce further copying when they are accessed. Hence, communication between parallel processes can be realized via lazy copy nodes. In this context lazy copy nodes are also called **communication channels**, or just **channels**, because these nodes will provide the communication between processors. The semantics of lazy copy nodes implies that the flow of data through a channel is the reverse of the direction of the node-id in the graph. Since channels are ordinary nodes, they can be passed as parameters or be copied as well.

A subgraph is **loosely connected** if channels (lazy copy nodes) are the only connections between the subgraph and the rest of the graph. So a self-contained subgraph is loosely connected if its root is a channel. Also, a loosely connected subgraph has the property that its nodes can be reduced *in parallel* when they are prohibited from being accessed by reducers running on other processes. Hence, a problem arises when a reducer demands information from a channel that points to a subgraph located on another processor. The root node of such a subgraph is called a **global node**. There are two possibilities:

- The demanded subgraph is in σ normal form. The information can be lazy copied to the demanding process, yielding again a loosely connected subgraph of which the copied parts can be reduced in parallel.
- The demanded subgraph is *not* in σ normal form. The demanding processor is not able to reduce the demanded subgraph when it is located on another processor. Therefore, the demanding process *has to be suspended* (*locked*) until the demanded information has been reduced to σ normal form by another process (on the corresponding processor). When the σ normal form is reached the sus-

pended process can be awoken and it can continue as explained in the previous case.

So processes running on different loosely connected subgraphs can run *in parallel* with each other *provided that these processes are locked when they demand information from a channel pointing to a subgraph which is not in σ normal form.* To make safe parallel evaluation possible this locking condition has to be fulfilled. This can be accomplished quite easily: always create a process on those subgraphs which channels of a loosely connected subgraph refer to. So processes are created on every deferred global node.

14.3.3 Translating {Par} and {Self}

In this subsection it is shown how annotations like {Par} and {Self} can be expressed in FGRSs using process annotations {p!!} and lazy copying.

To realize the parallel evaluation of the indicated function, with lazy copying a loosely connected subgraph is built. On this subgraph a parallel reducer {p!!} is created which reduces the spawned-off redex to normal form. The result has to be copied back lazily as well, so the root of the subgraph has to be created with the deferred attribute such that the result is not copied before the normal form is reached.

Each occurrence of:	will be substituted by:
n : {Par} Sym a_1 ... a_m	n : LCopy x, x : {p!!} I_d ({*} LCopy y), y : Sym a_1 ... a_m
n : {Self} Sym a_1 ... a_m	n : {p!!} Sym_d a_1 ... a_m

I is the identity function: I x → x. The lazy copy created for the parallel process is loosely connected.

The semantics of {Self} just demands an interleaved executing process yielding a normal form for which the {p!!} annotation can be used. To prevent a subgraph being reduced by an interleaved reducer from being (lazy) copied while it is not yet in normal form, the subgraph is marked deferred as well. So indeed, all created processes (parallel as well as interleaved) are created on deferred subgraphs. In this way no lazy copies can be made of a subgraph under reduction. So {Par} and {Self} *processes act as copy-stoppers*. In fact, when this scheme is followed the only way to defer copying of a subgraph is by creating such a process on it. Hence, channels *always* refer to deferred subgraphs on which processes are created. The lazy copied subgraph on which a parallel process is created can have references to other parts somewhere in the original graph (see Figure 14.3). The copying of these parts is postponed because they were under reduction by another process at the time the lazy copy was made. Such a part will be lazy copied later to the created parallel process in the usual way when it is needed for evaluation and in normal form. Consequently, the process topologies that can be created with these annotations can become very complex.

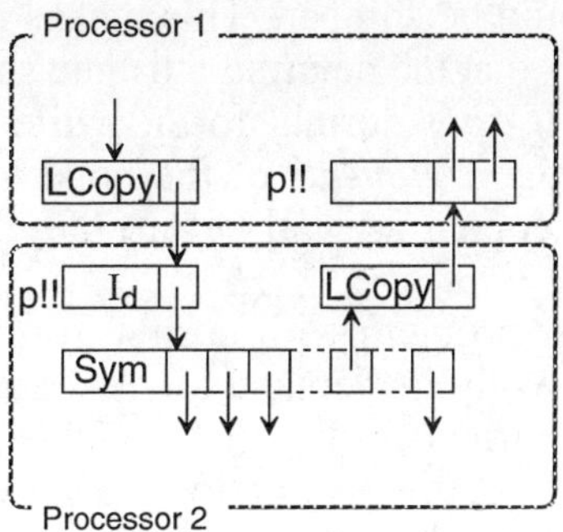

Figure 14.3 {Par} in terms of process annotations and lazy copying.

For instance, consider the following example using {Par} and {Self}:

Fib 0 → 1
Fib 1 → 1
Fib n → + left right,
left: {Par} Fib (– n 1),
right: {Self} Fib (– n 2)

This can be translated to:

Fib 0 → 1
Fib 1 → 1
Fib n → + (LCopy left) right,
left: {$p_{!!}$} I_d ({*} LCopy y),
y: Fib (– n 1),
right: {$p_{!!}$} Fib_d (– n 2)

The translation can be further optimized to:

Fib 0 → 1
Fib 1 → 1
Fib n → + (LCopy left) right,
left: {$p_{!!}$} Fib_d (– {*} (LCopy n) 1),
right: {$p_{!!}$} Fib_d (– n 2)

With the scheme above the semantics of {Par} and {Self} are *almost* completely expressed in terms of the primitives introduced in this chapter. There is one aspect which is different. In the scheme above a demanding reducer has to wait until the result is in normal form. We argued in Chapter 13 that to achieve optimal performance reducers should deliver their results as soon as possible. So one should not wait until the whole result is in normal form. Instead, that part of the graph that is already being calculated should be shipped. This means in the parallel case for normal form reducers that the deferred attribute should be taken away as soon as the root is in root normal form, while the deferred attribute should be added to the *arguments* of the node in root normal form to prevent them being copied as well before they have been reduced to root normal form.

There is another problem with normal form processes in general which also has to do with the demand to yield a result as soon as possible. Suppose that a normal form process yields an n-tuple. The functional strategy will force the evaluation of the elements of this tuple from left to right. But, in a parallel environment there may be a process demanding the result of the first element while another process may demand the result of the last element. It would be nice if this last process did not have to wait until all other tuple elements have been calculated. To make this possible one should create an (interleaved executing) process on any tuple element there is a demand for. One can also see that this is conceptually sound due to the decomposition property (see Chapter 13). If a tuple is known to be in PNF, so are the tuple elements (which means that it is sound to create a process on each of the tuple elements as well).

Concluding, {Par} and {Self} can be modelled as described above. However, an efficient implementation of normal form processes is rather complicated (see also Chapters 16 and 17).

14.3.4 Basic primitives for modelling process behaviour

The {Par} and {Self} annotations are high-level process annotations yielding a specific process behaviour suited for high-level functional programming. Their semantics is based on a strategy that reduces to normal form. However, in inter-process communication root normal forms play an essential role. So when process behaviours in general are investigated, it seems to be more natural to consider semantics based on processes that reduce to root normal form.

For that purpose in this section two new annotations are introduced: **{P}** for parallel processes and **{I}** for interleaved processes. The only difference with the {Par} and {Self} annotations is that root normal form processes {p!} are being used instead of normal form processes. The {P} and {I} annotations have the advantage that they create processes that deliver a result as soon as a root normal form is reached. Furthermore, these annotations have the advantage (and disadvantage) that one explicitly can (has to) specify what has to happen with this root normal form. Without special actions the whole subgraph in root normal form (possibly containing redexes) is lazily copied back to the demanding process. If the intention is only to ship the root in normal form one should explicitly start new processes (using either {P} or {I} annotations) on the arguments of this root node.

Each occurrence of:	will be substituted by:
n : {P} Sym a_1 ... a_m	n : LCopy x, x : $\{p_!\}$ I_d ({*} LCopy y), y : Sym a_1 ... a_m
n : {I} Sym a_1 ... a_m	n : $\{p_!\}$ Sym_d a_1 ... a_m

So in this scheme one has very fine control over what is shipped (work or data) and when (by creating a root normal form or not). This is handy when such fine tuning is needed. Take, for example, a function application that delivers a large structure after relatively few reduction steps. If a graph containing such a function application is submitted to another processor then it is preferable for the communication cost not to reduce this application before the submission. The fine control gets very annoying when one actually wants to ship a normal form. In that case the evaluation to normal form has to be programmed in the rewrite rules using root normal form processes.

The {P} and {I} annotations are interesting to study the behaviour of concurrent processes in functional languages due to the fine process tuning they offer (see Chapter 15). Furthermore, they have the advantage that they are relatively easy to implement (see Chapters 16 and 17).

Summary

- *Strategy annotations* are introduced in TGRSs. They make it possible to influence a single incarnation of a reduction strategy: the current strategy function is interrupted and the specified strategy function is applied on the indicated subgraph. When finally a σ normal form is reached, the interrupted strategy continues.
- *Process annotations* are introduced in TGRSs. They make it possible to change the reduction strategy into a parallel strategy with multiple incarnations of a reduction strategy: both the current strategy function and the new strategy function deliver candidates for rewriting. A reducer can be attached to each strategy function. So reducers are created dynamically and they die when a σ normal

form is reached. Parallel reduction is allowed under certain conditions only. In general, processes have to be *interleaved.*

- With *eager copying* a complete subgraph can be duplicated. Eager copying implies duplication of work.
- With *lazy copying*, one can copy a graph without duplicating work. This is realized by deferring the copy action until the graph that has to be copied is in σ normal form.
- With the lazy copy, primitive graph rewriting systems can be specified for which *the semantics are* in some sense *in between the semantics of term rewriting and of graph rewriting*. Subexpressions can be shared as well as copied. For certain redexes copying can be deferred until these redexes are in σ normal form.
- The use of lazy copying influences the resulting graph normal forms. The resulting graph normal form can even depend on the reduction order. But *the unravellings of the normal forms will always be equivalent*, which is required for term graph rewriting.
- A subgraph is *loosely connected* when lazy copy nodes (*channels*) are the only connections between the subgraph and the rest of the graph. Reduction on different loosely connected subgraphs can be done in *parallel.* Communication between loosely connected subgraphs can be modelled via *lazy copying.*
- The annotations {Par} and {Self} of the previous chapter can be modelled by using the proper combination of lazy copying with process and strategy annotations.
- More basic primitives are the introduced {P} and {I} annotations with semantics based on root normal form reduction. They can be used to specify various process behaviours (see the next chapter).

EXERCISES

14.1 Parallel reduction always has to be fair, but it may in practice be wise to reschedule certain reducers with a very low priority. Why?

14.2 Why is a deadlock in practice much more difficult to detect than a cycle-in-spine error?

14.3 A graph that has to be lazy copied to another machine will in practice probably be copied twice. Why?

14.4 Is the following type: `LCopy:: * -> UNQ *` correct? Would the `LCopy` function be useful as a primitive function for a Clean programmer? How about the `Copy` function? Which one do you prefer and why?

Chapter 15
Concurrent Clean

This chapter extends the language Clean (see Chapter 8) with the possibility to create parallel and interleaved executing processes. The resulting language *Concurrent* Clean offers the {P} and {I} annotations as introduced in Chapter 14. A refined version of the {P} annotation is introduced as well. It can be used to give a more precise description of the processor on which a parallel process has to be allocated.

The Concurrent Clean annotations are explained in Section 15.1. How they can be used for the creation of various process topologies is explained in Section 15.2. The chapter is concluded with a discussion on how the {Par} and {Self} annotations of Chapter 13 can be translated into Clean's {P} and {I} annotations.

15.1 Extending Clean to Concurrent Clean

Concurrent Clean (Nöcker *et al.*, 1991b) incorporates a single extension with respect to Clean as defined in Chapter 8: *process annotations*. The **process annotations** of Concurrent Clean are precisely the {P} and {I} annotations presented in Chapter 14. There is an additional option to control the **process allocation**, i.e. one can specify with more or less precision on which concrete processor a new process has to be created.

The process annotations are *local* annotations (see Section 8.3) that can be specified on the right-hand side of a rewrite rule. They can be put on a node (before the symbol) or on a node-id. Just as with local strict annotations, it holds that if a local process annotation is put on a node, this is equivalent to putting the annotation on each reference to that node. Process annotations can have the form {P}, {I} or {P AT location} (see Appendix B). The semantics of {P} and {I} in Concurrent Clean fully conform with the definitions of {P} and {I} for parallel graph rewriting in Chapter 14. The effect of the annotations is summarized below. Furthermore, some explicit choices related to the order in which local and global annotations are effected in Clean are explained. The semantics of {P AT location} will be a small extension of the semantics of {P}.

15.1.1 Creation of processes on processors

When, in Concurrent Clean, a process annotation occurs in a contractum pattern, during a rewrite with the corresponding rule a new reducer will be created with as task the evaluation of the corresponding subgraph.

With the {I} annotation a new **interleaved reducer** is created on the *same* processor that reduces to root normal form (following the functional strategy). Such an interleaved reducer dies when the root normal form is reached. However, during the evaluation of this result other reducers may have been created.

With the {P} annotation a new **parallel reducer** is created. This reducer is *preferably* located on a *different* processor working on a lazy copy of the corresponding subgraph, but, when this is somehow not possible, it may be created on the *same* processor. Reducers that are located on different processors can be executed in parallel with each other. Reducers that run on the same processor run interleaved.

15.1.2 Locking

As explained before, an interleaved or parallel reducer will be *locked* if it wants to reduce a redex that is already being reduced by some other reducer. A locked reducer can continue when the redex has been reduced to root normal form. A reducer can demand the evaluation of a subgraph located on another processor. Such a demand always takes place via a *communication channel* (a lazy copy node). If the channel is referring to a subgraph in root normal form, a lazy copy of this subgraph is made on the processor such that it can be further evaluated by the demanding reducer. If the subgraph is not yet in root normal form, the demanding process is locked. In that case, on the other processor a reducer will always exist that reduces the subgraph to its root normal form. So all communication channels are always being *served* by processes to ensure that demanding processes are not locked unnecessarily.

15.1.3 Annotations and evaluation order

When there are several local annotations specified in a contractum, the *order* in which they have to be effected is, as is defined in the previous chapter, in principle depth-first with respect to the subgraph structure. The underlying philosophy here is that in many cases it makes sense to deal with the arguments before a function is called. In fact, the definitions of {P} and {I} in Chapter 14 also rely on this philosophy.

Local and global annotations

An extra complication with respect to the semantics of annotations in Concurrent Clean is the fact that Clean (and hence Concurrent Clean) also allows strict annotations to appear in the type specification of a function, the *global* strict annotations (see Section 8.3.2). Consequently, it has to be defined in what order local and global annotations are effected. The general idea here is that local annotations are used by a programmer to control explicitly the order of evaluation of the right-hand side of a rewrite rule. Global annotations should not influence this explicit control. So the choice has been made to give priority to local annotations over global annotations. Of course, it still holds that when a chosen function is actually evaluated, first its globally annotated arguments will be reduced.

Maximizing actual parallelism

When there is not a clear hierarchy between annotations, it would be nice if the degree of parallelism would be maximized in choosing between the various possibilities.

So for these cases the choice has been made first to effect {P}s, then {I}s, and finally {!}s. These priorities also hold for the cyclic case and for the case in which several annotations are put on the same node. At first sight it may not seem to make much sense even to allow the latter case because only one reducer will be able to reduce the indicated subgraph. All others will be locked until the reduction is finished. However, a user may want to specify such a behaviour in which, for example, first a parallel reducer is started on a node (with a {P}) and immediately the parent process will wait for the result (due to a {!}).

However, parallelism can be even further maximized, as is clarified by the following situation: suppose that a local process annotation and a global strict annotation are both valid for the same node. Then, as defined above, the priority lies with creating the child process first in order to maximize the parallelism. It can, however, be the case that the parent process has again the choice between waiting for the child process to produce its result and, for instance, evaluating another argument of the corresponding function call. Then the parallel behaviour of the program is improved when the other argument is chosen first. Otherwise, the parent process would just be waiting in parallel.

So when arguments are equal in priority (e.g. they are either both globally strict annotated or both locally strict annotated) the choice is made to effect first those strict annotations for which it is known that (owing to an analysis of the right-hand side of the corresponding rule) yet another process is not already evaluating the corresponding subgraph. In this way unintended waiting is avoided.

Example of maximizing parallelism:

```
:: Fib INT    ->    INT;
   Fib n      ->    + ({P} Fib (– n 1)) (Fib (– n 2));
```

+ is globally strict in both arguments. A child process reduces a lazy copy of the first argument in parallel. The parent continues with the second argument.

```
   Fib n      ->    + (Fib (– n 1)) ({P} Fib (– n 2));
```

But if a child were to be created on the second argument instead, the parent process would evaluate the first argument. In this way a nice symmetric behaviour is obtained, with the maximum amount of actual parallelism.

15.1.4 Controlling process allocation

Processors in a distributed architecture are generally sparsely connected. When two parallel processes communicate heavily with each other it is efficient to locate them on processors that are directly connected via a hardware link. If one is aiming for optimal performance the actual location of a process should be definable. For this reason there is a possibility in Concurrent Clean to specify the processor on which a parallel process should be created. The use of this possibility might make the efficiency of the program fully dependent on the actual machine the program is running on. So the user is advised to refrain from the use of this feature as much as possible.

The {P} annotation can be extended with a **location directive** {P AT location}, where location is an expression of predefined type PROCID indicating the processor on which the parallel process has to be created. In the library deltaP (see Appendix B) functions are given that yield an object of this type. Some of the primitives can be used without detailed knowledge of the actual processor topology. For instance, with the function NeighbourP one can create a process *n* links (hops) away from another processor (e.g. the current processor CurrentP). With the primitive ITOP one can specify exactly which processor is intended. The primitive converts an integer value to a value of type PROCID. It is assumed that each processor of a concrete architecture can be uniquely identified by an integer value. How this mapping is defined is implementation-dependent. So the programmer must know this mapping and the actual processor topology to make optimal use of it.

In any case, it holds that whatever the use of process locations is, the *result of the program cannot be influenced*. The process locations influence only the actual process allocation on the machine.

15.2 Specifying process structures

The fact that Concurrent Clean is a graph rewriting language is clearly an advantage for the specification of process topologies. The graph structure can be used to define explicitly the demanded process topology. This makes, for instance, the creation of cyclic process structures much better to understand. To illustrate the use of graph rewriting in specifying process topologies, several Concurrent Clean examples are given below.

15.2.1 A hierarchical process topology

Divide-and-conquer parallelism is expressed with hierarchical process topologies. They have a straightforward process behaviour. This can be expressed very easily in Concurrent Clean.

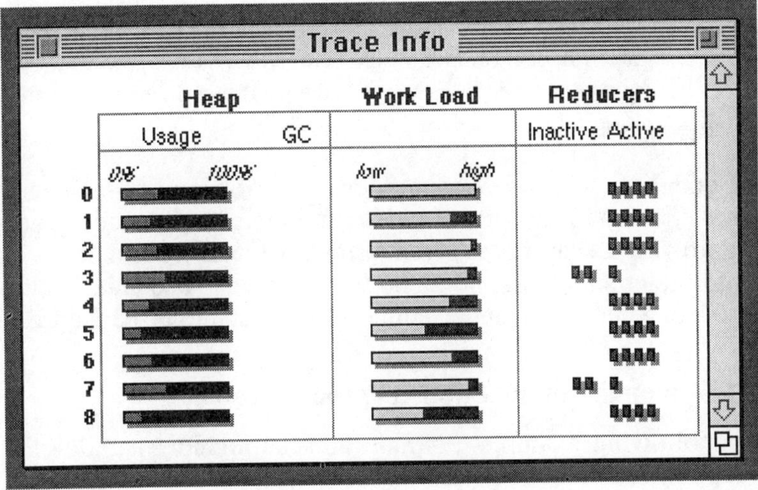

Figure 15.1 Trace information shown by the Concurrent Clean simulator. For each simulated processor the heap usage is displayed, along with the workload relative to the other processors as well as the number of inactive (locked) and active reducers.

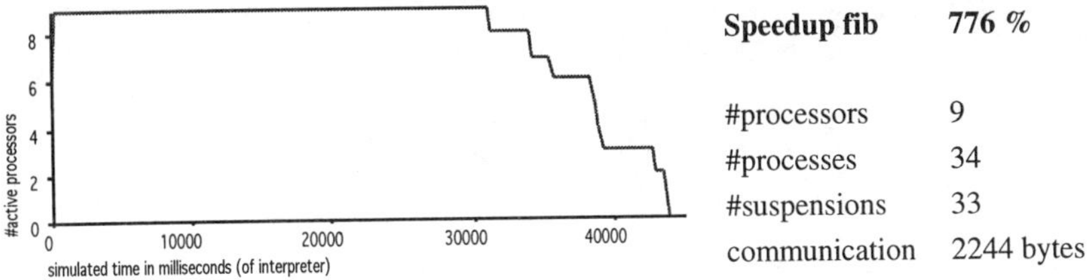

Figure 15.2 During simulation all kinds of statistical information can be written to a file and examined afterwards.

A hierarchical process topology in Concurrent Clean.

```
:: Fib INT ->   INT;
   Fib 0   ->   1;
   Fib 1   ->   1;
   Fib n   ->   + {P} left {P} right,      IF > n Threshold
           ->   + left right,              IF > n 2
           ->   ABORT "Fib called with negative value",
                left:    Fib ! (– n 1),
                right:   Fib ! (– n 2);
```

Both calls of Fib can be evaluated in parallel on another processor. First (– n 1) and (– n 2) are evaluated, forced by the local strict annotations because these annotations are put on subgraphs of the graphs on which the process annotations are put. Next, two parallel processes are created on lazy copies of right and left respectively. The parent process continues with the addition, but it has to wait until the arguments are evaluated and have been lazy copied back. A more efficient solution would be to create a child process for just one of the arguments. The parent process then will automatically calculate the other. This version has been used in Figures 15.1 and 15.2.

The Concurrent Clean system provides tools to simulate the behaviour of parallel programs, using either the interpreter or the code generator. In Figure 15.1 a snapshot is given of the trace information displayed by the interpreter simulating Fib 22 on 9 processors. Also statistical information can be produced and examined after execution (see Figure 15.2).

15.2.2 A simple non-hierarchical process topology

In the following example a simple non-hierarchical parallel reducer topology is demonstrated. It serves the purpose of explaining how more complicated parallel reducer topologies can be expressed.

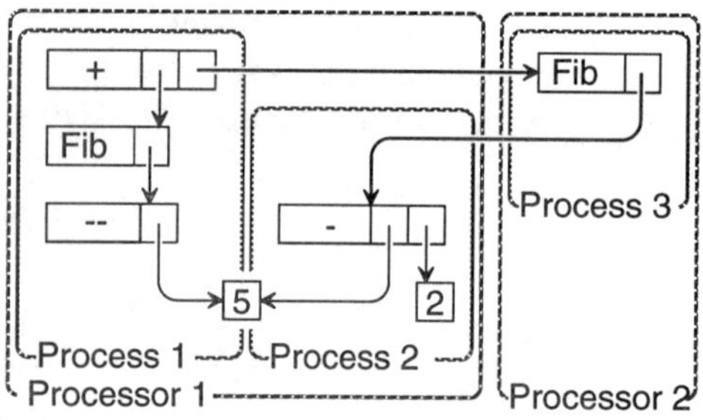

Figure 15.3 Intended distribution of the processes across the processors. A snapshot of the program execution of Fib 5 is given.

A non-hierarchical parallel reducer structure: the second argument of Fib will be executed by another parallel reducer, but the argument of that call is reduced interleaved on the original processor (see Figure 15.3).

```
:: Fib INT ->    INT;
   Fib 0   ->    1;
   Fib 1   ->    1;
   Fib n   ->    + (Fib (-- n)) m,
                 m:    {P} Fib o,
                 o:    {I} – n 2;
```

15.2.3 Asynchronous process communication with streams

The small examples above are very similar to the examples using {Par} and {Self} since only simple basic values are communicated. For graphs yielding basic values the root normal form is also the normal form.

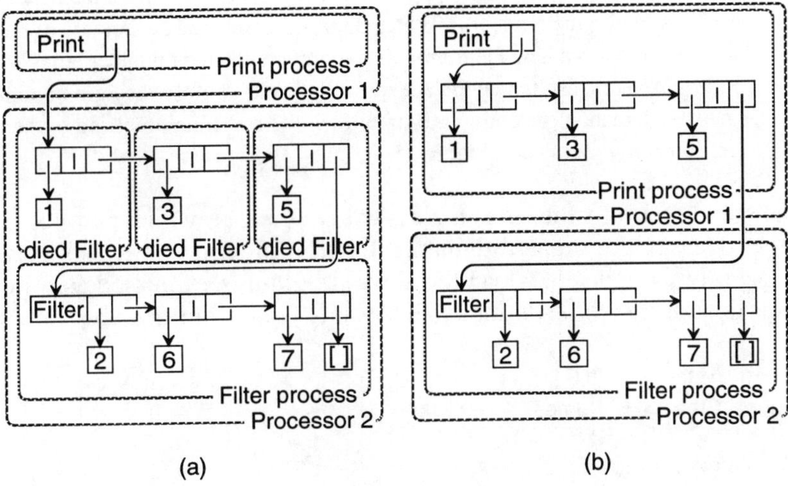

Figure 15.4 (a) Snapshot of the filtering process working on a list containing the natural numbers from 1 to 7. (b) The root normal forms yielded by successive interleaved Filter processes have been shipped with one lazy copy action. The active interleaved Filter process acts as a copy-stopper and a new channel has been created to this process. If more results are demanded, the lazy copy action will be continued as soon as new results become available.

To express a general asynchronous communication stream a sequence of interleaved reducers has to be created. Each interleaved reducer computes a partial result that can be sent across a channel. Just before the reducer delivers its root normal form (and dies) it creates a new interleaved reducer that delivers the next result in the same way. When partial results are delivered more frequently than is demanded, all partial results (a **burst**) are sent at the same time. The lazy copy will copy all partial results at once, but it stops at those nodes that are under reduction by a reducer. In this way a parallel reducer can have several streams and all kinds of (cyclic) graphs can be sent to another processor.

Example of an asynchronous communication behaviour with streams:

```
:: PrintList [INT]          ->    [CHAR];
   PrintList list           ->    Print ({P} Filter 2 list);

:: Filter   INT  [INT]      ->    [INT];
   Filter   p    [ ]        ->    [ ];
   Filter   p    [ f | r ]  ->    Filter p r,           IF = (% f p) 0
                            ->    [ f | {I} Filter p r ];
```

The process reducing PrintList creates a new parallel reducer: Filter. This process removes from its second argument, which is a list, all the elements that are divisible by the number 2. When Filter has computed an element of the result list it creates a new Filter process to compute the next number, after which it dies. Several results may be added to the stream before they are communicated on demand. The end of the stream will be a channel referring to the current filtering process (see Figure 15.4).

The sieve of Eratosthenes is a classical example in which parallel sieving processes are created dynamically in a pipeline (see also Section 13.3.1). In Concurrent Clean the sieve program is expressed as follows (Limit is assumed to be defined in a MACRO, Filter is defined above):

```
:: Start ->    [INT];
   Start ->    Primes;

:: Primes ->    [INT];
   Primes ->    Sieve ({P} Gen 2);

:: Gen INT    ->    [INT];
   Gen Limit  ->    [ ];
   Gen n      ->    [ n | {I} Gen (++ n) ];

:: Sieve [INT]      ->    [INT];
   Sieve [ ]        ->    [ ];
   Sieve [ p | s ]  ->    [ p | {P} Sieve ({I} Filter p s) ];
```

15.2.4 Communicating work or data

When a reducer yields a root normal form it dies and the yielded subgraph in root normal form can be lazy copied to a demanding process.

The copying process will postpone copying on those parts of the graph that are under reduction by another process. This makes it possible to decide which part of the graph is lazy copied back. The subgraph in root normal form will generally contain several redexes (work). When such a redex is returned in the lazy copy, work is shipped from one processor to another. One can choose whether or not work should be locally calculated before it is shipped. In that case an interleaved process should be created on the corresponding redex before the root normal form is delivered. So for each redex one can choose how it should be handled.

Choosing between data or work:

```
:: F (=> INT INT) BOOL  ->  [ INT ];
   F g            h     ->  Map g ({P} BigList h);

:: BigList BOOL  ->  [ INT ];
   BigList h     ->  [ 0 | Gen 2 ],  IF h
                 ->  [ 1 | {I} CompList ];
```

The function F maps a function g over a list that is computed by a parallel process BigList (Map is defined in Section 8.1.6). Depending on the evaluation of h, either a simple big list is returned or a big list that takes some computing power. In the first case, work is copied back: the list itself is not returned but an expression is returned that computes this list when it is evaluated. In the second case data is copied, computed by an interleaved process CompList that is created to compute the list before it is shipped.

15.2.5 Cyclic process topologies with location directives

The following example creates a cyclic parallel process structure, i.e. a number of parallel reducers that are mutually dependent. In a similar way cyclic process structures can be explicitly specified in more elaborate examples, such as the Warshall example of Chapter 13.

```
:: Start ->     [INT];
   Start ->     last: CreateProcs NrOfProcs last;

:: NrOfProcs ->     INT;
   NrOfProcs ->     5;

:: CreateProcs INT [INT]   ->   [INT];
   CreateProcs 1   left    ->   Process 1 left;
   CreateProcs pid left    ->   CreateProcs (-- pid)
                                     ({P} Process pid left);

:: Process INT  [INT]   ->   [INT];
   Process n    left    ->   [ n | {I} Process (+ n (Hd left)) (Tl left) ];
```

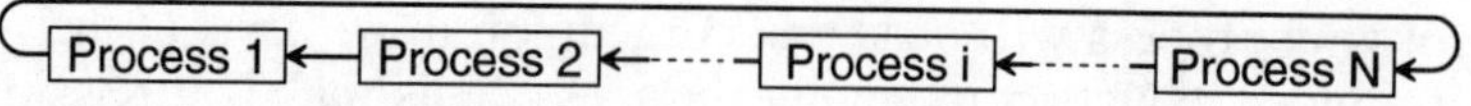

Figure 15.5 A cyclic process structure.

CreateProcs is initially called with a reference to itself, thus forming a cyclic process structure of length one. CreateProcs recursively creates new processes Process. Each Process has a process number. CreateProcs will finally form the first Process in the cycle with process number 1. Each Process is connected to the next one, i.e. the one with the next pid number, by means of a channel (see Figure 15.5). During the creation of the processes this channel is passed as a parameter: left. Hd and Tl take, in a lazy way, respectively the head and the tail of the channel. Note that the type of left has to be the same as the result type of CreateProcs and Process. The function Process will in general produce a lazy stream of values (in the example integer values) that can be used as input by another Process. Owing to the use of {I} annotations recursively a part of the stream can be produced as a result. In the example an infinite list of rapidly increasing numbers is generated ([1, 3, 8, 20, 48, …]).

As explained in Chapter 14, one has to be careful not to introduce deadlock when cyclic process topologies are specified using recursive functions. A subtle deadlock example is given by a variant of the function definition Process of the cyclic process topology example above.

```
:: Process INT  [INT]         ->   [INT];
   Process n    [ hd | tl ]   ->   [ n | {I} Process (+ n hd) tl ];
```

A deadlock occurs since each process, due to the pattern match, wants the result of the previous process before it creates a result itself.

Location directives

In the cyclic example given above every process is communicating heavily with both its neighbours. So it is probably more efficient to create a new process on a processor to which a direct link exists. This can be done by replacing the {P} annotations above by the location directive {P AT NeighbourP 1 CurrentP}. However, this only guarantees that the new process will be located on a direct neighbour: it can happen that effectively only two processors are used. This can be avoided by making use of knowledge about the actual machine topology, e.g. using the location function ITOP (see also Appendix B).

A cycle of processes assuming that a neighbouring processor has an identification one lower than the previous one.

```
CreateProcs p l -> CreateProcs (-- p) ({P AT ITOP p} Process p l);
```

15.3 Translation into Concurrent Clean

In many cases it is possible to translate {Par} and {Self} annotations to a collection of {P}, {I} and {!} annotations. When root normal forms are equivalent to normal forms (e.g. for simple basic values) the translation is trivial. When this is not the case, a sequence of annotations is needed to achieve the evaluation to normal form. A process reducing to normal form can be realized by creation of a new interleaved process just before the current one delivers its root normal form. Compare for instance the sieve example in this chapter with the sieve example in Chapter 13. The creation of additional interleaved processes has to be explicitly specified in the rewrite rules. Consequently, it is not possible to use this translation scheme to force normal form evaluation of an arbitrary function passed as an argument to a function.

Limitation of simulating normal form processes via a sequence of root normal form processes:

```
:: ParMap (=> x y) [x] -> [y];
   ParMap f [ ]          ->    [ ];
   ParMap f [ x | xs ]   ->    [ {P} f x | {I} ParMap f xs ];
```

The parallel process that is created in the ParMap example only evaluates the unknown function application f x to *root* normal form. It is not possible to force the evaluation of such an unknown function to normal form.

So the ability to create processes that reduce arbitrary unknown functions to normal form gives more expressive power to the language. As already stated in Chapter 13, normal form processes are often useful, but also hard to implement efficiently. Process types (see Chapter 13.2.5) can help to set up efficient communication streams between normal form processes.

The {P} and {I} annotations have the advantage that they allow a more precise control over the interaction between processes. So they are also very useful primitives. They are less suited when evaluation to normal form is demanded.

In future versions of Concurrent Clean normal form processes with process types will be added in addition to the current annotations. But it remains to be seen what kind of annotations in the long term are both suitable from a programming point of view as well as efficiently implementable on a wide range of architectures. A different approach can be found in Darlington *et al*. (1991), who propose a wide range of special purpose annotations (called skeletons) for all kinds of architectures (varying from MIMD to SIMD machines).

Summary

- Concurrent Clean extends Clean with *process annotations* {P}, {I} and {P AT location}. Their semantics *conforms* fully to *the semantics of parallel graph rewriting* as given in Chapter 14.
- With the {I} annotation a new *interleaved reducer* is created on the *same* processor reducing to root normal form following the functional strategy. With the {P} annotation a *parallel reducer* is created *preferably* running on a *different* processor. Communication takes place via lazy copying, as explained in the previous chapter.
- A *location directive* can be added to indicate on which processor a process should be created. Location directives cannot influence the result of the program.
- It is not always possible to translate {Par} and {Self} annotations to a collection of {P}, {I} and {!} annotations. Both kinds of annotation are useful. {P} and {I} give precise control over the distribution of work or data and are efficiently implementable because they fit very well in the default evaluation order (which is root normal form evaluation). {Par} and {Self} are much more difficult to implement efficiently but they are user friendly because processes are in practice often created to yield a normal form.

EXERCISES

15.1 What other kind of location directives can you imagine as being useful? Explain why.

15.2 Rewrite Exercises 13.2 and 13.3 in Concurrent Clean. Simulate parallelism using the simulator on 1, 2, 4, 8 and 16 processors. Measure the speed-ups. Explain the results.

15.3 Answer the questions of Exercise 15.2 for the sieve example given in Section 15.2.3.

15.4 Would it not be better for parallel evaluation to have an eager language instead of a lazy one?

15.5 Can branch-and-bound parallelism be expressed in a pure functional language?

Chapter 16
The Parallel ABC machine

This chapter presents the PABC machine, a parallel version of the abstract ABC machine (see Chapter 10). This PABC machine serves as an abstraction of the class of concrete parallel machines we focus on: MIMD machines with distributed memories. These concrete machine architectures are much more complex than their sequential counterparts. There are many difficult implementation problems that have to be solved before parallel programs can be executed efficiently on them. For example, one has to control the distribution of work such that each processor has enough work to do, one has to take care of the routing of messages over the communication network, garbage has to be collected that can be spread across several processors, and so on. Many of these problems are inherent to these MIMD architectures. They have to be solved for *any* parallel program, regardless of the language.

The PABC machine level abstracts from most of these implementation issues. The abstract machine would otherwise become much too complex. We will focus on the essential aspects of parallel graph rewriting only, such as *process creation*, *lazy copying* and the *communication* between arbitrary processes and processors.

For the description of the PABC machine the specification of the ABC machine presented in Chapter 10 is taken and extended. In this way again an executable specification is obtained. It is remarkable that the concurrency aspects of the machine can still be described understandably in a sequential functional language.

First, Section 16.1 discusses some basic ideas behind the architectural design of the PABC machine. Then, it will be described in detail how {P} and {I} annotations are handled. The design of the PABC machine architecture is such that the machine is also capable of dealing with more sophisticated annotations, such as {Par} and {Self}. In

Section 16.2 *interleaved* reduction is described, while *parallel* reduction is treated in Section 16.3. How the execution of the different (parallel) machine components is handled is explained in Section 16.4. Section 16.5 contains a small example showing how Concurrent Clean's process annotations are straightforwardly translated into PABC code.

16.1 About the PABC machine

In Section 13.1 we have assumed that concurrent functional programs at least have to run conveniently on MIMD machines with a distributed memory architecture. The main goal of the PABC design (Nöcker *et al.*, 1991a) is to introduce an abstract machine which can be efficiently implemented on those kinds of architecture. The PABC machine is defined as an extension of the ABC machine such that the sequential optimizations can still be applied in the parallel case.

The machine components of the PABC machine are more complex than those of the ABC machine. Instead of having one reducer, there are now *several reducers* possible on one single processor, while there are *several processors* as well. All processes and processors can communicate with each other. Processes are created *dynamically*, have to be scheduled and can be active or suspended (locked). In order to let this whole machinery work, it is no longer possible to have only *passive* machine components. As in real life an *operating system* is required as one of the processes on a processor. Furthermore, a *communication process* is provided on each processor to take care of the communication with the other processors.

16.1.1 The basic architecture of the PABC machine

The PABC machine consists of a number of *processors*. On each processor several processes are running interleaved with each other: zero or more *reducers*, an *operating system* and a *communication process*.

In principle, each reducer requires a private ABC machine (as introduced in Chapter 10). However, some of the ABC machine components can be *shared* by reducers executing on the *same* processor. The contents of the *program store* and *descriptor store* do not change during execution and are identical for each reducer. They can therefore be shared without problems. Interleaved reducers all have direct access to the graph, so the graph store has to be shared as well. The contents of this store can be changed by the reducers running on the processor. So one has to be careful and make sure that the graph store always remains in a consistent state. It will be clear that the *A-*, *B-* and *C-stacks*, as well as the *program counter*, cannot be shared between the reducers. Each reducer gets a private local version of these storages (see Figure 16.1).

Compared with the sequential ABC machine, there are also some differences. Input/output handling, as well as all interaction with the other processors, will now be handled by the *operating system* in collaboration with the *communication process*. Hence, *input/output channels* are no longer needed. There are also two new components needed for each reducer. One new machine component, the *N-queue*, is used by a reducer to store the node-ids of subgraphs that have to be reduced by it (the *N*odes to be reduced). This is convenient for the creation of reducers that reduce to normal form or that use some other reduction strategy. Another new component, the *waiting list register*, is a register used by a reducer to temporarily store the list of locked reducers that have to be awakened when the root normal form is reached. Finally, there is a small *administration* store located on each processor that, among other things, is used to identify the current reducer running on it.

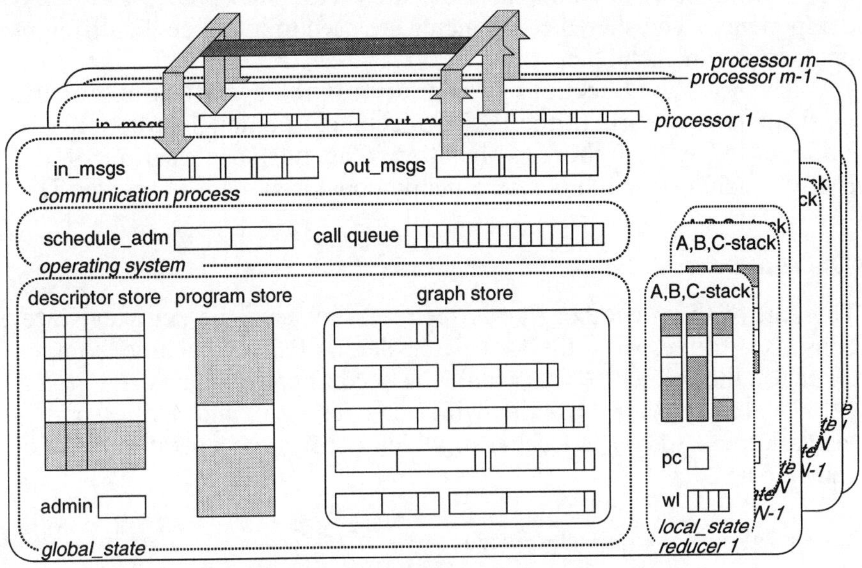

Figure 16.1 The basic architecture of the parallel ABC machine.

The *operating system* deals with the scheduling of the interleaved reducers and the communication requests coming from the reducers or the communication process. All processes can ask assistance from the operating system by putting a request in a queue (the *call queue*) of the operating system. The operating system process handles these requests. It can ask assistance from the *communication process* to handle *communication* between parallel reducers executing on different processors.

16.1.2 The description method

For the description of the PABC machine the specification of the ABC machine presented in Chapter 10 is taken and extended in the same spirit. But there are some differences. As explained above, there are several *kinds* of process on each processor: reducers, an operating system, and a communication process. Each such process performs different kinds of state transitions, and therefore different kinds of instructions are needed. Of course, it would have been possible to define instructions that work on the machine as a whole. But such a design would have led to a very ugly specification. So in the PABC machine specification **active components** are added: processes like the operating system and the communication process that have their own instruction set. Hence, besides ordinary *PABC instructions* (for reducers), there are *operating system instructions* (stored in the call queue) and *communication process instructions* (a fixed program). Each process uses some of the components of the machine for its own purpose (*local* components) while other components are shared with other processes (*global* components). The shared components are used to interface the different processes with each other.

The following sections briefly discuss the specifications of the most interesting parts of the PABC machine. The new instructions are summarized with a short explanation. The full specification of the PABC machine (including micro-instructions) is given in Appendix D.

The reducers

The part of the processor that is seen by a reducer, the **reducer state**, consists of three parts: the first part contains PABC machine storages *local* for the reducer (local_state), the second part contains the *global* storages (global_state) it shares with other reducers, and the last part is the call queue (opsys_callqueue) in which calls to the operating system can be put.

```
instruction    ==  state -> state
state          ==  (local_state, global_state, opsys_callqueue)
local_state    ==  (astack, bstack, cstack, nqueue, pc, wlist)
global_state   ==  (admin, graphstore, descrstore, programstore)
```

The PABC machine in principle incorporates all sequential ABC machine instructions. However, owing to the new state structure the description of each of these ABC instructions has to be slightly adapted.

The PABC specification of the pop_a instruction (see also Section 10.3.2):

```
pop_a:: nr_args -> instruction
pop_a nr_args ((as,bs,cs,nq,pc,wl),glob,cq)
    = ((as',bs,cs,nq,pc,wl),glob,cq)
      where  as'   = as_popn nr_args as
```

This actually shows a weakness of a specification in which state transition functions are being used. Even a small change in the state has as a consequence that all functions acting on that state have to be changed as well. A **record**-like data structure with named fields (as is present in ML and in many imperative programming languages) solves this problem. Record structures will be incorporated in a future version of Clean.

Some of the ABC machine instructions have to be changed somewhat further to incorporate context switches (see Section 16.2.2).

There are of course also several new machine instructions added for the control of process creation and communication. These new instructions are listed below (see also Sections 16.2 and 16.3).

```
new_ext_reducer   :: instrid -> a_src -> instruction   || create a {P} reducer
new_int_reducer   :: instrid -> a_src -> instruction   || create a {I} reducer
stop_reducer      :: instruction                       || stop current reducer

newP            :: instruction            || get processor-id for new process
randomP         :: instruction            || get a random processor-id
currentP        :: instruction            || get current processor-id
neighbourP      :: instruction            || get processor-id of a neighbour
channelP        :: a_src -> instruction   || get processor-id stored in channel

create_channel  :: instruction                      || create new channel
send_graph      :: a_src -> a_src -> instruction    || lazy copy graph
send_request    :: a_src -> instruction             || request for lazy copy

is_empty_n      :: instruction            || are there node-ids in the N-queue?
get_node        :: instruction            || fetch node to reduce from N-queue
set_continue    :: a_src -> instruction   || store node to be reduced in N-queue

set_wait        :: a_src -> instruction   || administer reducer waiting for rnf
suspend         :: instruction            || lock current reducer
getWL           :: a_src -> instruction   || store locked reducers in register wl
release         :: instruction            || unlock reducers stored in wl
```

The operating system

The new parallel reducer instructions generally end with a request via the call queue (opsys_callqueue) to the operating system to do the actual work. Such an **operating system call** is an *instruction* that can be executed by the operating system (opsys_instruction). If the operating system gets control, it executes these calls, removing them from the queue.

As in real life, the operating system can be seen as the software extension of the machine. So the complete state of the processor is determined by the state of the operating system itself (opsys_state). The operating system has complete control over all processes on the processor. It therefore manages its own administration (schedule_adm) that gives the possibility to control (schedule) all the reducers living on the machine. To control communication the operating system also has access to the shared global components of the reducers. To communicate with the communication process it furthermore has access to the input and output list of messages (in_msgs, out_msgs).

```
processor        ==  opsys_state
opsys_state      ==  (schedule_adm,
                        in_msgs, out_msgs, global_state, opsys_callqueue)
schedule_adm     ==  ([ active ], [ passive ])
active           ==  reducer
passive          ==  reducer
reducer          ==  (redid, local_state)
```

A full list of the *operating system instructions* is given below.

```
opsys_instruction   ==   opsys_state -> opsys_state

os_suspend_reducer :: opsys_instruction
os_schedule        :: opsys_instruction
os_reducerprio     :: opsys_instruction

os_send_newreducer :: instrid   -> nodeid   -> opsys_instruction
os_new_reducer     :: instrid   -> nodeid   -> opsys_instruction
os_stop_reducer    :: opsys_instruction
os_halt            :: opsys_instruction

os_send_newchannel :: procid    -> nodeid   -> opsys_instruction
os_send_graph      :: nodeid    -> nodeid   -> opsys_instruction
os_send_request    :: nodeid    -> opsys_instruction
os_setwait         :: nodeid    -> opsys_instruction
os_release         :: wlist     -> opsys_instruction

os_print           :: string    -> opsys_instruction
```

The communication process

The communication process handles all interaction with other processors. The communication process is a simple process which repeatedly performs the *same* single instruction (cp_accept_msg). This instruction will see to it that a message is delivered to the intended processor.

```
comproc_instruction   ==   comproc_state -> comproc_state
cp_accept_msg::    msg_contents -> comproc_instruction
```

The communication process has access to the global structures of the processor such that it can read from and write to the graph store to ship lazy copies. A request for an outgoing message is done by the operating system. It puts a message into the output message list (out_msgs) of the communication processor. The incoming messages are fully dealt with by the communication process (in_msgs). For this purpose, the communication process can call the operating system if necessary via the call queue.

```
comproc_state   ==  (in_msgs, out_msgs, global_state, opsys_callqueue)
in_msgs         ==  [ msg_contents ]
out_msgs        ==  [ message ]
message         ==  (proc_src, proc_dst, msg_contents)
```

The communication network

An outgoing message sent away by a communication process has to be sent across a *communication network* such that it can be received as an incoming message by the communication process of the indicated processor. A simple communication network is chosen: all processors are connected with each other. Another option would have been to model a sparsely connected network topology as well as the routing of messages across such a network. This is assumed to be out of the scope of our abstract specification. Of course, if one is interested in modelling these aspects, they can be specified in any detail.

```
network          ==   [network_element]
network_element  ::=  P processor
```

16.2 Interleaved reduction

16.2.1 Creation and abortion of interleaved reducers

The PABC instruction new_int_reducer creates a new interleaved executing process reducing a graph of which the root is assumed to be on the A-stack (a_depth). The current reducer executing this instruction asks the operating system to perform the creation (os_new_reducer is put in the call queue with the micro-instruction os_call). The operating system will administer the new reducer as *active* and initialize the local storages such as the A-, B- and C-stacks, as usual.

Reducers created by an {I}-annotation reduce the graph to root normal form. To support other kinds of reducers, new_int_reducer is parametrized with an entry (instrid) to the code that drives the execution of the reducer to (root) normal form.

```
new_int_reducer:: instrid -> a_src -> instruction
new_int_reducer code a_depth ((as,bs,cs,nq,pc,wl),glob,cq)
   = ((as,bs,cs,nq,pc,wl),glob,cq')
     where  nid   = as_get a_depth as
            cq'   = os_call cq [ os_new_reducer code nid ]

os_new_reducer code nid (rs,in,out,(ad,gs,ds,ps),instrs)
   = (rs',in,out,(ad',gs,ds,ps),instrs)
     where  rs'                     = (act_reds ++ [ new_red ], pass_reds)
            (act_reds, pass_reds) = rs
            (ad', new_redid) = ad_new_redid ad
            new_red            = (new_redid,(as,bs,cs,nq,pc,wl))
                                 where  as    = as_init
                                        bs    = bs_init
                                        cs    = cs_init
                                        nq    = nq_new nid
                                        pc    = pc_update code pc_init
                                        wl    = wl_init
```

A reducer can quit with the instruction stop_reducer. This means that the reducer is stopped and all its stacks frames are released. This is effectively achieved by the operating system instruction os_stop_reducer.

16.2.2 Scheduling

Several reducers can exist on one processor. But only one of them can be executing: this is called the **current reducer**. All others have to wait until it is their turn for execution. At a certain point in time a **context switch** takes place: the execution of the current reducer is interrupted and the execution can proceed with one of the other reducers, which then becomes the new current reducer. Some kind of **scheduling** mechanism is needed: a mechanism that decides, when a context switch occurs, *which* of the active reducers on a processor is chosen for execution. Such a scheduling mechanism has to fulfil several requirements.

- Some kind of *fairness* should be assured (see Section 14.1). A fair distribution of the execution power avoids unnecessary locking of reducers and is furthermore needed because one can create reducers that do not contribute to the computation of the final result. So one should switch between interleaved processes *regularly*.
- The semantics prescribes that a context switch is only allowed after a rewrite step. And indeed, context switches cannot be allowed at arbitrary moments. When a process is manipulating globally accessible information (such as the graph store) it is possible that this information is temporarily in an inconsistent state. A context switch at such a moment is prohibited. Since graph rewriting on the

(P)ABC machine is optimized, there are some places in the code where it can be shown that a context switch cannot do any harm (for instance, a node is only rewritten when a root normal form is reached (see Chapter 11)).

- The sequential parts of the parallel ABC code should be amenable to the *same* optimizations as the sequential ABC code. In a basic block various kinds of optimization are performed (see Chapter 12). These optimizations would no longer be applicable if context switches within a basic block were allowed.
- A context switch is an *expensive* operation on a concrete machine (although the costs may vary from machine to machine). It should therefore be *avoided* as much as possible. Furthermore, on some machines context switches are only possible at *specific points* (e.g. transputers generate switches on jump instructions only).

Therefore, in the PABC machine the current reducer will never get interrupted by another reducer unless it executes an instruction in which *explicitly* a scheduling request is made to the operating system (using the instruction os_schedule). This happens in all instructions that end a sequential basic block (jmp, jsr, print, print_symbol) and furthermore in a few new instructions added for parallel processing (explained later on).

```
jsr address ((as,bs,cs,nq,pc,wl),glob,cq)
    = ((as,bs,cs',nq,pc',wl),glob,cq')
      where   pc'   = pc_update address pc
              cs'   = cs_push (pc_get pc) cs
              cq'   = os_call cq [os_schedule]

print string (loc,glob,cq)
    = (loc,glob,cq')
      where   cq'   = os_call cq [ os_print string, os_schedule ]
```

Given the generated code it can be shown that, when these instructions are being used and a context switch is requested, all the globally accessible stores on a processor will be in a consistent state.

The abstract operating system uses a very simple scheduling algorithm. The reducers living on a processor are divided into **active reducers** (wanting a time slice) and **inactive reducers** (that are **locked** or **suspended** because they are waiting for information). A context switch means that the current reducer is put at the end of a queue of active reducers and the next active reducer is fetched from the start of the queue. This **round robin** scheduling algorithm is just one method of dividing processor time fairly between active reducers. Any other algorithm can also be used as long as it obeys the fairness condition discussed above.

```
os_schedule ((act_reds,pass_reds),in,out,glob,instrs)
   = ((act_reds,pass_reds),in,out,glob,instrs),   if act_reds = [ ]
   = (rs',in,out,glob,instrs).                    otherwise
     where  rs'                  = (new_act_reds, pass_reds)
            new_act_reds         = rest_act_reds ++ [ red ]
            red : rest_act_reds  = act_reds
```

16.2.3 Locking of reducers

If a reducer wants to reduce a node that is already under reduction, it has to be *locked* until the reduction of that node is finished (see Section 14.3). The first reducer that takes a node under reduction will *reserve* it before doing anything else. Of course, such a reservation can be done by a mark in the node, but it is more elegant and efficient to use the code field in the root node. In that case no flags nor tests are necessary. For this purpose, the node entry of the reduction code of each function has to be changed (see Section 11.1).

```
[       Label
"n_entry"                          ,  || The node entry
        Set_entry "_reserve" arity ,  || Reserve this node
        Push_args 0 arity arity    ,  || Proceed as usual with the node entry
        ...
```

As a result, another reducer accessing a node with _reserve as code field (such a **node** is said to be **reserved** or **locked**) will enter the _reserve code instead of entering its node entry. The reserve code takes care of the suspension (or locking) of other reducers executing this code.

```
[       Label
"_reserve"           ,  || Code for locked nodes
        Set_wait 0   ,  || Put this reducer in the waiting list of this node
        Suspend      ,  || Lock this reducer
        Rtn          ]  || Return when awake again
```

By executing the set_wait instruction of the reserve code the current reducer is administered as being waiting for the result of the redex under reduction, after which the reducer locks itself with the suspend instruction. The operating system will put the reducer in the list of inactive reducers and perform a context switch to one of the active ones.

Reducers that hit a locked node are collected in a waiting list. A pointer to this list is stored in the node on which they are waiting. When such a node is overwritten with its root normal form, the locked reducers have to be released and made active. This has to be done *after* the update because otherwise the node is not in a consistent state yet. However, when the update takes place, the pointer to the waiting list is lost.

Therefore, the pointer is temporarily stored (using the getWL instruction) in a special register (the **waiting list register** wl) *before* the update takes place. *After* the update the reducers stored in this register are released by the release instruction.

```
getWL:: a_src -> instruction
getWL a_depth ((as,bs,cs,nq,pc,wl),(ad,gs,ds,ps),cq)
    = ((as,bs,cs,nq,pc,wl'),(ad,gs,ds,ps),cq)
      where  wl'   = n_wl_get (gs_get nid gs)
             nid   = as_get a_depth as

release:: instruction
release ((as,bs,cs,nq,pc,wl),glob,cq)
    = ((as,bs,cs,nq,pc,wl),glob,cq')
      where  cq'   = os_call cq [ os_release wl ],  if ~ wl_empty wl
                   = cq,                            otherwise
```

An example of the use of these instructions for an integer node:

```
      GetWL a_depth          , || Get waiting list from node in wl
      FillI 3 a_depth        , || Update the node with integer value 3
      Release                , || Release locked reducers
      ...
```

16.2.4 *N*-queue

The ***N*-queue** is a special store in the PABC machine containing the node-ids of the root nodes of subgraphs that have to be reduced to root normal form by the corresponding reducer. A reducer stops if its queue is empty. For a root normal form reducer ({P} and {I} annotations) one node is stored in the *N*-queue when the reducer is created.

```
[          Label
"_rnf_reducer"               , || Code for a root normal form reducer
           Get_node          , || Get the node from the N-queue
           Jsr_eval          , || Reduce that node
           Pop_a 1           , || Clean up stack
           Stop_reducer      ] || Rnf reached: stop
```

The *N*-queue store is added to the PABC machine to make the implementation of other kinds of reducer (such as normal form reducers) possible. The code for a normal form reducer very much resembles a driver in the sequential case (see Section 11.2) recursively invoking root normal form reducers. Each node that has to be reduced to normal form is stored in the queue. When the root normal form is reached the corresponding node is removed from the queue, while its arguments are stored. In their turn they will be evaluated in the same way until a normal form is obtained. The parallel context offers the opportunity to reduce the nodes in the N-queue in any order, even interleaved. This makes it possible to increase the effective parallelism. For instance, when a normal form reducer is locked it can still continue with any of the other nodes in the N-queue. Also, when a request from another reducer comes in, a normal form reducer can choose to create a new internal reducer to reduce the corresponding node in the N-queue such that the request can be answered swiftly. This requires a special code generation scheme for normal form processes. For optimal performance it might be better to create more special PABC machine instructions to deal with such situations. Accessing the N-queue requires two new instructions: get_node, which moves the first node in the N-queue to the A-stack (and pushes a boolean on the B-stack that indicates this was possible), and set_continue which appends a node to the N-queue.

```
get_node:: instruction
get_node ((as,bs,cs,nq,pc,wl),glob,cq)
   = ((as',bs,cs,nq',pc,wl),glob,cq)
     where  as'  =  as_push n as
            n    =  nq_first nq
            nq'  =  nq_remove nq

set_continue :: a_src -> instruction
set_continue depth ((as,bs,cs,nq,pc,wl),glob,cq)
   = ((as,bs,cs,nq',pc,wl),glob,cq)
     where  n    =  as_get depth as
            nq'  =  nq_add n nq
```

16.2.5 Representing deferred nodes

The semantics of the {P} and {I} annotation prescribes that all processes are created on a deferred node. In the PABC machine a node with a deferred attribute is represented by a special indirection node. So all pointers to a node with a deferred attribute will actually point to such a **deferred indirection node**. The advantage of this representation is that such a deferred indirection node can easily be treated specially by using a special descriptor (important for lazy copying). When the indirection node is overwritten the deferred attribute is automatically removed. Processes that are trying to evaluate a deferred node which is already under reduction have to be locked, as is explained in Section 16.2.3.

```
[ Label
"_defer_code"                  ,  || Code for evaluating a
                               ,  || deferred indirection node
         Set_entry "_reserve" 1  ,  || Reserve this node
         Push_args 0 1 1         ,  || Get graph to evaluate
```

```
Jsr_eval                              ,  || Evaluate graph
GetWL 1                               ,  || Save locked reducers in wl
Fill_a 0 1                            ,  || Update node with result
Release                               ,  || Release locked reducers
Pop_a 1                               ,  || Clean up stack
Rtn                                   ]  || End of defer code
```

16.3 Parallel reduction

16.3.1 Creation of parallel reducers

The creation of a parallel reducer is split into several *phases* to keep the machine as flexible as possible:

(1) *build the graph* that has to be reduced in parallel;
(2) *find a processor* on which the reducer can be created;
(3) *create a channel* to that processor;
(4) make a *lazy copy of the graph to be reduced*;
(5) start *a new parallel reducer* on the remote graph.

A typical PABC instruction sequence resulting from a {P} annotation:

```
...                                        ,  || Code for building the graph
NewP                                       ,  || Destination proc-id on B-stack
Create_channel                             ,  || Create channel to that processor
Send_graph 1 0                             ,  || Send lazy copy graph to reduce
New_ext_reducer "_rnf_reducer" 0,             || Create external reducer process
```

Build the graph

When a redex is lazy copied to another processor the corresponding subgraph has to exist on the shipping processor. Due to the optimizations this might not always be the case. Then, additional code has to be generated that constructs a proper subgraph on the local processor before it is lazy copied to the destination processor. No new instructions are needed for this graph construction.

Find a processor

In Concurrent Clean processes can be created with a location directive (see Chapter 15). In the PABC machine each processor has a unique identification, the **processor-id**. Special instructions are provided (newP, randomP, currentP, neighbourP and channelP) that push a processor-id on top of the B-stack to support these location directives.

Create a channel

References to nodes on another processor are represented by **channel nodes** (a lazy copy node). On the PABC machine level, a special indirection node is used with an argument field containing an identification of the process on the remote processor. The instruction create_channel assumes the remote processor-id for the channel to be on top of the B-stack. To inform the remote processor that a channel has to be created, a message is sent to it. The remote processor will create a new empty global node. Its node-id will be returned over the communication network. With the processor-id it is stored in the new channel node.

```
create_channel:: instruction
create_channel ((as,bs,cs,nq,pc,wl),(ad,gs,ds,ps),cq)
   = ((as',bs',cs,nq,pc,wl),(ad,gs',ds,ps),cq')
     where bs'        = bs_popn 1 bs
           pid        = bs_getP 0 bs
           (gs',nid)  = gs_newchannel pid gs
           as'        = as_push nid as
           cq'        = os_call cq [ os_send_newchannel pid nid,
                                     os_setwait nid,
                                     os_suspend_reducer ]
```

Make a lazy copy of the graph

send_graph sends the graph that has to be reduced in parallel to its destination. The destination address is fetched from the channel node.

```
send_graph:: a_src -> a_src -> instruction
send_graph graph_depth chan_depth ((as,bs,cs,nq,pc,wl),glob,cq)
   = ((as,bs,cs,nq,pc,wl),glob,cq')
     where chanid  = as_get chan_depth as
           graphid = as_get graph_depth as
           cq'     = os_call cq [ os_send_graph graphid chanid ]
```

The lazy copying algorithm is given in Appendix D. Copying has to preserve the structure of the graph. The algorithm requires two scans of the graph: one scan to build the copy and one scan to remove all the forwarding references and markers that have been created to preserve the shared structure in the copy.

Start a new parallel reducer

Finally, the new reducer will be started on the remote processor (remembered in the channel node) using the instruction new_ext_reducer. A message is sent to the remote processor for creating the new reducer. The reducer is created with a label code indicating the kind of reduction code that has to be executed (e.g. to root normal form or to normal form). The remote processor will create and initialize a new reducer and put the root node of the remote graph in the N-queue as usual.

```
new_ext_reducer:: instrid -> a_src -> instruction
new_ext_reducer code chan_depth ((as,bs,cs,nq,pc,wl),glob,cq)
   = ((as,bs,cs,nq,pc,wl),glob,cq')
     where  chanid  =  as_get chan_depth as
            cq'     =  os_call cq [ os_send_newreducer code chanid ]
```

16.3.2 Demanding a lazy copy across a channel

The result of a parallel process is communicated to a demanding reducer when it is needed, i.e. when a corresponding channel node is evaluated. A channel node is evaluated as any other node: by executing its code.

```
[       Label
"_channel_code"              ,  || The code associated with a channel node
        Set_entry "_reserve" 0,  || Reserve the channel node
        Send_request 0       ,  || Send a demand for the result
        Set_wait 0           ,  || Put reducer in waiting list of this node
        Suspend              ,  || Lock the current reducer
        Rtn                  ]  || Return when awake again
```

First, the channel node will be reserved as for any other node: other reducers that need the result just have to wait. Then, the instruction send_request asks the remote processor for the result of the reduction of the graph belonging to the channel node.

```
send_request:: a_src -> instruction
send_request chan_depth ((as,bs,cs,nq,pc,wl),glob,cq)
   = ((as,bs,cs,nq,pc,wl),glob,cq')
     where  cq'     =  os_call cq [ os_send_request chanid, os_reducerprio ]
            chanid  =  as_get chan_depth as
```

After sending the request the demanding reducer is suspended to wait for the result (with the instructions set_wait and suspend). The instruction os_reducerprio guarantees that administration and suspension are done with highest priority, i.e. before the result is already communicated.

The request is answered as soon as the requested node is in root normal form (regardless of whether the reducer reduces to root normal form or to normal form). The result can be returned immediately as a lazy copy if it is available. Otherwise, the request is stored in the waiting list of the remote node under reduction. In that case the request will be answered when a release instruction is executed for this node. On the demanding processor the actual update with the lazy copy of the result will be performed automatically by the communication process.

16.4 Program execution

In order to obtain an executable specification of the PABC machine one needs an implementation of the abstract data structures and micro-instructions, as in Section 10.4. For the PABC machine this includes a specification of the rather powerful operating system instructions and the instructions of the communication process. Furthermore, one needs to define how communication (and lazy copying) takes place.

This section only treats the PABC *bootstrapper* and *instruction fetch* mechanisms (for the other aspects we refer to Appendix D). A special solution is necessary since real parallelism and non-deterministic interleaving are *not* directly expressible in a functional language. The concurrent behaviour has to be *simulated* in some way.

16.4.1 The instruction fetch cycle

To run the PABC machine one not only has to specify the execution behaviour of a single processor (which involves fair interleaving of operating system, communication process and reducers), but also the behaviour of the network of parallel processors (which involves simulation of parallelism and distribution of messages across the network). Altogether the specification of the behaviour of the machine implies *several* instruction fetch cycles that call each other.

The PABC machine cycle

The PABC machine consists of a number of processors connected via a very simple communication network. In a PABC machine cycle all messages on outgoing lines from the processors are collected, removed and distributed to the incoming lines. Outgoing messages that are the output of the overall reduction process are added to the final output of the PABC machine. The parallelism is simulated by giving each processor a time slice by calling the processor cycle for it.

```
output      ==  [ msg_contents ]

machine_cycle:: network -> output
machine_cycle nw
   = output                                        , if op_halt output
   = op_append output (machine_cycle nw')          , otherwise
     where  output  =  nw_output nw
            nw'     =  nw_exec proc_cycle (nw_distribute_msgs nw)
```

The processor cycle

Each processor has to guarantee a fair distribution of CPU time between the processes running on it. The choice has been made to give the communication process and the current reducer each a time slice in each processor cycle. In order to handle operating system calls as soon as possible, the operating system gets a time slice both after the reducer cycle and after the communication process cycle.

```
proc_cycle:: processor -> processor
proc_cycle =  opsys_cycle . red_cycle . opsys_cycle . comproc_cycle
```

The communication process cycle

The communication process handles all incoming messages in one cycle. However, it can happen that the current reducer has requested priority over the communication process (see Section 16.3). In that case communication will not be handled in the current processor cycle.

```
comproc_cycle:: processor -> processor
comproc_cycle (rs, in, out, (ad,gs,ds,ps), cq)
   = (rs, in, out, (ad',gs,ds,ps), cq),   if ad_prio ad = Prio_Reducer
     where   ad'   = ad_new_prio No_Prio ad
comproc_cycle (rs, [ ], out, glob, cq)
   = (rs, [ ], out, glob, cq)
comproc_cycle (rs, (msg : msgs), out, glob, cq)
   = comproc_cycle (rs, in', out', glob', cq')
     where   (in', out', glob', cq')  =  cp_accept_msg msg (msgs,out,glob,cq)
```

The operating system cycle

The operating system performs all pending calls in one cycle.

```
opsys_cycle:: processor -> processor
opsys_cycle (rs, in, out, glob, cq)
   = (rs, in, out, glob, cq),                                   if os_cq_empty cq
   = opsys_cycle (os_first_call cq (rs,in,out,glob, os_rest_calls cq)),otherwise
```

The reducer cycle

The cycle of the current reducer calls fetch_cycle to execute the current reducer. The execution of a reducer is driven by a slightly modified version of the instruction fetch cycle of Section 10.4.1. fetch_cycle terminates when the current reducer calls the operating system.

```
red_cycle:: processor -> processor
red_cycle ((act_reds, pass_reds), in, out, glob, cq)
```

```
    = ((act_reds, pass_reds), in, out, glob, cq),   if act_reds = [ ]
    = (rs', in, out, glob', cq'),                   otherwise
      where rs'                = ((rid, loc') : reds, pass_reds)
            (rid, loc) : reds  = act_reds
            (loc', glob', cq') = fetch_cycle (loc, glob, cq)

fetch cycle:: state -> state
fetch_cycle ((as,bs,cs,nq,pc,wl), (ad,gs,ds,ps), cq)
    = ((as,bs,cs,nq,pc,wl), (ad,gs,ds,ps), cq),             if ~ os_cq_empty cq
    = fetch_cycle (currinstr ((as,bs,cs,nq,pc',wl) ,(ad,gs,ds,ps), cq)), otherwise
      where pc'        = pc_next pc
            currinstr  = ps_get (pc_get pc) ps
```

16.4.2 Booting the machine

To boot the PABC machine not only do program and descriptors have to be supplied, but also the number of processors.

```
boot:: nat -> ([ instruction ], [ descr ]) -> network
boot nr_proc (program, descriptors)
    = nw_init nr_proc (program, descriptors)
```

16.4.3 Running a program

So the PABC machine starts evaluating a program as follows.

machine_cycle (boot *nr_of_processors* (assembler (*program*)))

16.5 Translating Concurrent Clean into PABC code

The PABC instructions are on a high level, very close to the process annotations available in Concurrent Clean. So the translation is straightforward. The important aspects are already covered in the previous sections. In this section an example is given of code generated accordingly.

Take the second rule alternative of Sieve in an example of Section 15.2.3:

```
Sieve [ p | s ]  ->     [ p | {P} Sieve ({I} Filter p s) ] ;
```

The generated code for the right-hand side of this alternative (extra instructions needed for the interleaved and parallel evaluation are emphasized):

```
[  Label
"Sieve2"                         ,  || Entry for the second alternative
   Push_args 0 2 2               ,  || Push the arguments
   Create                        ,  || Node for defer attribute
```

```
Create                                     ,  || Node for result of Filter
Push_a 2                                   ,  || Push second argument of Filter
Push_a 4                                   ,  || Push first argument of Filter
Fill "Filter" 2 "n_Filter" 2               ,  || Fill node for Filter
Fill "_Defer" 1 "_defer_code" 1            ,  || Fill deferred indirection node
Create                                     ,  || Node for result of Sieve
Push_a 1                                   ,  || Push argument of Sieve
Fill "Sieve" 1 "n_Sieve" 1                 ,  || Fill node for Sieve
NewP                                       ,  || Destination proc-id on B-stack
Create_channel                             ,  || Create channel to that processor
Send_graph 1 0                             ,  || Send lazy copy graph to reduce
Update_a 0 1                               ,  || Update Sieve node with channel
Pop_a 1                                    ,  || Remove channel from A-stack
New_int_reducer "_rnf_reducer" 1,             || Create internal reducer process
New_ext_reducer "_rnf_reducer" 0,             || Create external reducer process
Push_a 0                                   ,  || Push second argument of Cons
Push_a 3                                   ,  || Push first argument of Cons
GetWL 7                                    ,  || Save locked reducers in wl
Fill _Cons 2 "_rnf" 7                      ,  || Update root node of process
Release                                    ,  || Release the locked reducers
Pop_a 5                                    ,  || Clean up stack
Rtn                                        ]  || End of alternative
```

Summary

- The PABC machine is an abstract distributed machine which is an extension of the sequential ABC machine such that the sequential optimizations can still be applied.
- The PABC machine consists of the following components:
  - a *network* of *processors* that communicate messages;
  - a *communication process* on each processor that deals with outgoing and incoming messages;
  - an *operating system* on each processor which can be called via a queue of pending operating system instructions. The operating system deals with lazy copying, scheduling, creation and locking of reducers etc.;
  - a number of *reducers* on each processor. A single reducer performs sequential reduction like the sequential ABC machine.
- The instruction set of the PABC machine extends the sequential ABC machine for communication and synchronization with a relatively small number of instructions based on lazy copying and parallel graph rewriting.
- The PABC machine can be specified elegantly in a functional language in very much the same way as the sequential ABC machine.

- A Concurrent Clean program can be translated to PABC code quite straightforwardly. Code has to be generated for locking and releasing of reducers. Furthermore, each process annotation gives rise to a sequence of specific PABC machine instructions.

EXERCISES

16.1 Compile the parallel programs written in the previous exercises to PABC code. Study the generated code. Some PABC instructions are different. Which ones? Can you explain what the advantages of these changes are?

16.2 Refine the PABC machine specification such that processors are connected via a sparsely connected communication network instead of a fully connected network. Define the simulated topology in a table such that it can be changed easily. Also define in a table how messages have to be routed to the intended destination. Change the communication processor such that it can take care of the routing of messages. Then, define the instructions newP, randomP, currentP, neighbourP and channelP properly within the PABC specification.

16.3* Suppose that you had to design an *S*ABC machine to model a *shared* memory architecture instead of a *distributed* memory architecture.

(a) Is lazy copying still necessary? Is it necessary to make a distinction between {P} and {I} processes? Which PABC components would you still need? Which ones can be shared? Which of the PABC instructions are not needed any more? Are there any new instructions needed?

(b) The SABC machine has a different architecture from the PABC machine. This means that all PABC machine instructions have to be adapted such that they can be applied on the new state. Are there also non-trivial changes in instructions necessary? Hint: remember that parallel evaluation is only allowed when the rewritings cannot interfere with each other.

(c) Give a picture similar to Figure 16.1 depicting the SABC architecture.

16.4* Specify the SABC machine.

Chapter 17
Realizing the PABC machine

This chapter discusses the concrete realization of the PABC machine. For this purpose one at least needs a good *sequential* code generator. Such a code generator can be developed using the techniques described in Part 4. First, Section 17.1 treats in general terms the many additional problems one has to solve when 'going parallel'. Suitable representations of the different new PABC machine components are given. In particular, attention is given to the rather long list of run-time support that has to be offered on the concrete target machine in either hardware or software. Garbage collection on a distributed machine architecture is discussed separately (Section 17.2).

The remaining part of this chapter treats the realization of the PABC machine on a specific machine, a 32 node transputer architecture. The transputer processor is explained in Section 17.3. A concrete representation of each of the PABC components on this processor is given (Section 17.4). Finally, the most important concrete aspects of actual code generation are treated, including a discussion of the obtained performance (Section 17.5).

17.1 Representing the PABC machine components

The PABC machine has been specifically designed to be realized on a concrete MIMD architecture in which each processor has its private memory and processors are (sparsely) connected via some special communication network. This section briefly explains how each of the PABC machine components can be realized on concrete architectures.

The most complex component of the PABC machine is clearly the abstract operating system. The PABC machine abstracts from a lot of problems for which a solution has to be found on a concrete architecture. So one not only has to provide facilities like lazy copying and communication between arbitrary processes and processors: one also has to take care of the collection of garbage that can now be distributed over the different processors and of the memory management for the allocation of the dynamically created stacks. Furthermore, the distribution of tasks has to be dealt with such that all processors are utilized in the best possible way. All these activities have to be performed by the run-time system of the application in combination with the support offered by the concrete operating system of the machine. The complexity of the concrete run-time system therefore depends heavily on the facilities offered by the processor and the concrete operating system.

17.1.1 Representing the reducer components

The program store and the program counter

Each processor in a distributed memory machine will need its own copy of the program in its private memory. The easiest way to accomplish this is by copying the complete program to a particular location in the store of each of the processors *before* the execution starts (**static loading**). Most concrete machines have instructions to support this. Another strategy is to load precisely that part of the program into each memory that is actually being used by the corresponding reducer (**dynamic loading**). This saves memory occupation but it may become an inefficient strategy if process creation occurs very frequently and different pieces of code have to be (re)loaded often. Also the addressing may become more complex, especially when the architecture has no facility to support dynamic loading.

The program counter of an abstract PABC reducer can, of course, be directly represented by the program counter of the concrete processor the reducer is running on.

The A-stack, B-stack and C-stack

Because several reducers may run on one processor, *several* stacks have to be allocated in memory instead of just *three* stacks as in the sequential case. Furthermore, stacks are created dynamically when a new reducer is created. Consequently, the stack (frame) management is much more complicated than in the sequential case. In general, it is not known in advance how large a stack a reducer needs. If (too) small stack frames are allocated initially, problems arise when the stacks become too large. If too big stacks are allocated initially, heap space is wasted. One solution is to use linked stacks, but then stack addressing becomes more complicated. Another solution is to allocate small stacks initially and to *reallocate* these when necessary. In that case a new and larger stack frame is allocated in a contiguous piece of memory to which the contents of the old one are copied. This copying seems to be a quite inefficient solution, but it often works satisfactorily in practice. Normally, reducers only use small stacks and reallocations are not often needed.

When a reducer dies, its stacks become garbage. They have to be collected such that the space they occupy can be reused. An obvious solution for this problem is to handle stacks as normal heap objects, such that their space can be reclaimed by an ordinary garbage collector. When stacks are incorporated into the heap one has the additional advantage that no distinction has to be made between the amount of memory available for stacks and the amount of memory available for graphs. This division can automatically be tuned at run-time. If stacks are allocated randomly in the heap (just as ordinary nodes) they will always be copied during a garbage collection when a copying or compacting garbage collector is activated. To avoid this problem it is better to reserve a special part of the heap to accommodate stack frames (which makes the heap management a bit more complicated).

As discussed in Chapter 12, one can combine the stacks of a reducer in an actual implementation. Merging the B- and C-stacks is certainly advisable for parallel environments. It makes the management of stack frames easier and reduces the amount of boundary checks. For garbage collection it is convenient to keep a separate A-stack such that pointers to nodes can easily be distinguished from other data.

The N-queue and the waiting list register

The implementation of an *N*-queue can be realized in the same way as the implementation of stacks, e.g. as a special relocatable object in the heap space. For the waiting list register any free machine register or memory location can be used.

The graph store

A new aspect of the graph store is that one now has to deal with waiting lists and with defer attributes. Defer attributes can either be represented by a special indirection node (as suggested in the PABC machine) or by a tag in the node itself.

Waiting lists are more problematic. The easiest way to represent them is by inserting an additional field in the fixed part of a node containing a pointer to the actual waiting lists. The waiting list itself can be represented in the heap. Adding an additional field has the disadvantage that all nodes become larger. This gives rise to increased memory consumption. However, in practice it is possible to (mis)use one of the existing fields that is not being used when the waiting list has to be constructed. For instance, it is possible to use one of the argument fields of a node because a node with a waiting list is certainly being reduced and for a node being reduced the original arguments have already been saved on the stack.

Another solution is not to use waiting lists at all. Instead, waiting reducers can execute a polling loop in which they examine whether the node they are waiting for is updated or not. With clever scheduling scheme polling can be cheaper than a waiting list administration with explicit reactivation of locked reducers (Van Groningen *et al.*, 1992).

The descriptor store

The descriptor store can be treated in the same way as the program store: a copy of (a part of) the store has to be loaded either statically or dynamically into each of the processor stores.

17.1.2 Operating system and communication process

The abstract parallel reducer instructions are effectively all handled by the operating system located on the corresponding abstract processor. The operating systems communicate with each other via the communication processes. In practice, the tasks performed by these abstract components are realized by the *run-time system* of the program with the help of the concrete operating system running on top of the concrete machine. Furthermore, many other tasks which we have abstracted in the PABC machine have to be performed by these systems.

Process creation, scheduling and context switching

Not all kinds of processor have direct hardware support for process creation, scheduling and context switching. In most cases additional software support is needed. The PABC machine instructions specify when a context switch between processes is allowed. The scheduling has to be fair. This means that the generated code must be such that context switches indeed take place regularly and that all reducers eventually will get a time slice. Some concrete processors (like, for example, the transputer) support an automatic context switch (consisting of a move of merely two pointers) on certain instructions (e.g. after each jump instruction). This makes switching reasonably efficient. Other systems offer a possibility to raise interrupts at a specified time interval. When the interrupt occurs it can be used by the interrupt handler to schedule another process. In that case one has to ensure that context switches only take place when the stores are in a consistent state and no critical actions are being undertaken (e.g. garbage collection). A context switch can then also be done rather efficiently, but special code is needed to prevent switching at unwanted moments. If the individual processors are of a more conventional type (like Motorola's) special code has to be inserted at certain places that forces a switch on a regular basis. Context switches are probably a bit more expensive in this way. Anyhow, every context switch will cause a certain amount of overhead for saving the old context and restoring a previous one. So on the one hand one should switch regularly for fairness reasons and on the other hand one should not switch unnecessarily to avoid wasting of CPU time.

Communication between processors

The PABC instructions require that any two processes located on arbitrary processors can directly communicate with each other. In practice, the processors in a distributed memory architecture are only sparsely connected in some network topology. Some systems provide the possibility for any two processors to communicate with each other even if there is no direct hardware link between them. Other systems only provide communication between processors that have a direct link. In that case additional communication software (a **router**) is needed to provide reliable and fast communications between arbitrary processors.

Load balancing

Parallel reducers can be created on arbitrary processors. The operating system is free to use any information to select such a processor. In order to obtain ultimate performance the system should distribute the work evenly over the available processors. This distribution of work is called **load balancing.** In an *optimal* balanced system all processors have an equal amount of work to do: they all have enough free memory while the communication overhead is minimal due to the fact that processes which communicate heavily with each other are ideally located.

Load balancing is an important task of the operating system. However, in general it is undecidable to determine an optimally balanced distribution of tasks. To find a good approximation, ideally all processors should always be kept completely informed about the status of the whole machine. This is hard to realize on a distributed memory architecture without introducing an unacceptable amount of communication overhead. Therefore, in practice a suitable processor has to be chosen based on only *partial* knowledge about the workload of other processors. Neighbouring processors or processors with which communication is already taking place are good candidates to obtain the above information without facing too much communication overhead.

Process migration

It is a waste of machine capacity if the load is not well distributed and some processors have too little work or even nothing to do at all. Things become problematic when processors have so much work to do that they are running short of memory space (even after garbage collection has been performed). In that case one either has to stop the whole machine or one has to try to get the system in balance by transferring work from overloaded processors to other processors. Moving work effectively means moving a reducer by making a lazy copy of its graph. This is a delicate task since there is probably not much heap space on the overloaded processors to prepare the lazy copy.

Channels and global nodes

A channel node refers to a global node located on a remote processor. Such a reference cannot simply be the address of that node on the remote machine. Global nodes are, like ordinary nodes, sometimes moved by the garbage collector. An *indirection table* on the remote machine can be used to obtain a fixed address location. A channel node then refers to a fixed location in the table in which the varying address of the global node is stored. The table can also be used to store a reference count (representing the number of channels pointing to the graph) used for global garbage collection (see next section).

When a processor has to answer a request it must know to which processor it has to send the graph such that the channel node on the requesting reducer can be overwritten with the result. Clearly, channel nodes can be moved around by the garbage collector as well. Therefore, the address of a requested channel node has to be stored in an indirection table as well.

Lazy copying

A lazy copy of a graph must preserve the graph structure. One cannot simply apply an algorithm like those often used by copying garbage collectors: forwarding pointers (see Section 12.2) violate the original graph. Furthermore, garbage collection cannot be allowed during a lazy copy action: the garbage collector should not find the heap in an inconsistent state. There are several possible solutions, each with their own space-time behaviour. An important aspect to keep in mind is that graphs to be copied are expected to be relatively small, since otherwise the communication overhead would probably be too large.

One solution uses pointer reversal to traverse the original graph in advance to compute the size of the graph before copying starts. Next, the garbage collector is called (if necessary), directly followed by the (indivisible) copy action itself using forwarding addresses. Finally the original graph is restored, again using pointer reversal to traverse it. An advantage of this algorithm is that it does not require more memory than needed to store the lazy copy itself. A disadvantage is that it requires three scans of the graph to be copied.

Another solution uses the end of the heap temporarily as a stack to keep track of the original nodes. Whenever a node is encountered for the first time during copying its address is pushed on this stack. After copying has taken place the stack is traversed and all nodes encountered are restored. Finally, the stack is removed. If the garbage collector has to be called during copying the original graph must be restored in advance (again using the stack at the end of the heap). The copy that has been built so far has to be considered lost. After the garbage collection has been performed the copying must start all over again, increasing the cost of a copy action considerably (in the worst case it takes twice as long). But this situation is not likely to happen very often.

Sending of graphs

Sending a graph to another processor is usually realized as follows. Locally a lazy copy of the graph is made, as explained above. This copy is provided with relocation information. The copy cannot be sent away immediately. On the destination processor enough heap space must be available as well. This implies that first enough heap space on the remote processor has to be reserved. Further sending has to be suspended until an acknowledgement has been received that the amount of memory indeed could be reserved. Hereafter the graph can be sent away and, finally, when the graph arrives at the destination, all pointers in the graph have to be adjusted using the relocation information.

Deadlock detection

It is possible to write functional programs that contain deadlock (see Chapter 14). It would be nice if deadlock could be detected by the system. This is certainly important in a multi-user environment where a deadlock blocks (a whole) part of the machine. Deadlock that involves reducers located on one processor is not difficult to detect: one has to check whether locked reducers are mutually waiting on each other. Of course, deadlock will be much harder to detect without considerable communication overhead when the reducers involved are located on different processors.

Input/output

The treatment of I/O highly depends on the kind of I/O (file I/O, screen I/O) and the architecture of the concrete machine. In most concrete architectures only a few of the available processors will have a direct connection to secondary memory (disk) or to a video processor. Most of the time only one processor offers such facilities, sometimes indirectly via a connection with a host machine. This means that all I/O actions have to be realized by sending messages across the communication network to this particular processor. I/O is therefore typically a facility offered by the operating system of the concrete machine.

17.2 Garbage collection on a distributed machine

It is difficult to accomplish efficient garbage collection on a distributed machine. The possibly cyclic graph is now distributed across the different processors. To determine whether or not a node has become garbage references to that node from other processors have to be taken into account. One certainly would not like to stop the whole machine because one of its processors needs a garbage collection. Therefore, generally the collection process is first split into a local part and a global part (Kingdon *et al.*, 1991). The **global garbage collection** tries to determine which of the *global nodes* are garbage. The **local garbage collection** basically removes garbage locally, knowing which of its global nodes are garbage or not. Often for local and global garbage collection different techniques are combined. To recover all cyclic structures, information has to be passed from the local to the global collector and vice versa. There still does not exist a completely satisfactory solution to recover *all* distributed garbage efficiently.

Local garbage collection

In principle, local garbage collection can be done by using a standard copying garbage collector/mark–scan technique (see Chapter 12). Each of the non-garbage global nodes must now be regarded as a root of a subgraph that cannot be collected. The global nodes themselves are collected differently (see below).

In a sequential implementation the garbage collector is only invoked when a processor runs out of heap memory. In a parallel implementation garbage collection needs to occur more regularly (for instance with the help of a timer) even when there is enough local memory available. Suppose a processor p_1 holds a node n_1 that contains a reference to a node n_2 on another processor p_2 and suppose that n_2 is the root of a large graph. At some point in time n_1 may become garbage but p_1 will not discover this until it performs a local garbage collection. Consequently n_2 will not be removed before this time either.

In a parallel implementation it is very important that collection takes place as soon as possible. When a processor cannot reclaim its heap space because it is unaware of the status of its global nodes, none of its reducers can continue either and eventually the whole parallel machine will get blocked. Furthermore, if a process has been created on a node that has become garbage (a **garbage reducer**), it has to be stopped quickly because such a process is actively creating garbage, wasting the resources of the computer.

Global garbage collection

For garbage collection of global nodes a reference count garbage collector has certain advantages over copying/mark–scan. With a reference count collector a global node (and the possibly large subgraph with this node as root) can be collected locally as soon as its reference count becomes zero. When a channel node containing a reference to a global node is collected by its local garbage collector, a message is sent to the corresponding processor to decrement the reference count of the global node. When a channel node is copied or requested, a message is sent to increase the global reference count. A disadvantage of reference counting is that it cannot reclaim cyclic structures (see Chapter 12).

The straightforward implementation of global reference counting may cause severe problems. When a decremental message arrives before an incremental one it can result in removal of a global node that is not garbage at all. This problem can be solved by a **weighted reference count** algorithm (Bevan, 1987; Watson and Watson, 1987). The advantage of this algorithm is that *only* decremental messages are needed. Initially, a huge power of two is stored as reference count in both the channel node and the corresponding global node. When a channel node is copied its reference count is divided by two. This new reference count is stored in the original channel node as well as in its copy. When the reference count drops down to one (which is not very likely to happen often in practice) a new indirection node to the channel is created, again containing a huge power of two. When a channel node is deleted its reference count is sent to the processor it is referring to, such that the reference count of the global node can be decremented by that number. When this reference count drops down to zero the global node has become garbage and it can be collected.

Removal of cyclic structures

Cyclic structures that are distributed over multiple processors cannot be collected when a reference count collector is being used. An option is to use a mark–scan collector (for the whole network, for all local and global nodes) as a *secondary* collector, solely to remove cyclic structures when memory gets scarce in spite of local and global collecting attempts. For this purpose either a stop-and-collect or an on-the-fly collector can be used.

Removal of garbage reducers

To check whether a reducer is a garbage reducer it is sufficient to check whether all the nodes the reducer has reserved have become garbage.

17.3 The transputer processor

A transputer is a processor with hardware support for concurrent processing. It has instructions to start and stop processes at two priorities. *Low-priority processes* are automatically time-sliced in a round robin fashion by means of a hardware scheduler. *High-priority processes* are not time-sliced. Each transputer has four hardware links with which it can be connected to four other transputers (Figure 17.1). Instructions exist that enable a process to communicate with another process over such a link or with another process on the same transputer. Each transputer has some on-chip memory (static RAM) and a memory interface to connect it to at most 4 Gbyte of external memory. The access time of the static RAM is 3 to 5 times smaller than the access time of the external memory.

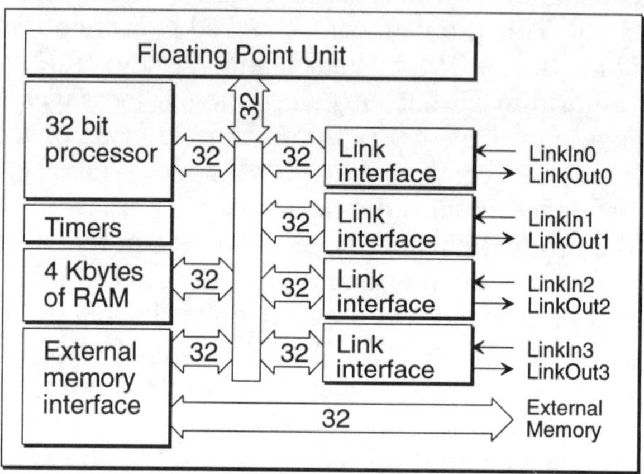

Figure 17.1 Architecture of the transputer processor.

Several types of transputer exist (T212, T414, T800 and T9000). The main differences between these processors can be found in speed, word size, instruction set and size of on-chip memory. The instruction set of newer processors is basically a superset of the older ones.

The transputer has only six registers. None of them is a general purpose register like the ones available in more traditional processors. The *workspace pointer* (wsp) is a register containing a pointer to some piece of memory which is called the workspace of a process. Addressing takes place relative to this workspace pointer. The *instruction pointer* (iptr) indicates the next instruction to be executed. The *operand register* (Operand) is used to construct large operands. Finally, there are three registers (called Areg, Breg and Creg) that form a tiny evaluation stack. These registers are the sources and destinations for most arithmetic and logical operations. Loading a value into this stack pushes B into C and A into B before the value is loaded into A. The contents of C are lost. Storing the value of A into memory pops B into A and C into B.

The value of *C* is left undefined when this happens. The contents of these registers are not saved when a context switch occurs. Only a few instructions exist at which a context switch is possible.

> Some important transputer instructions: in the listed instructions '(expression)' stands for the *contents* of the address indicated by this expression. wordlength is the word length of the machine. Only the j instruction can cause a context switch.

```
ldl offset       ; load (wsp + offset * wordlength) into Areg
stl offset       ; store Areg into (wsp + offset * wordlength)
ldnl offset      ; replace Areg by (Areg + offset * wordlength)
stnl offset      ; store Breg into (Areg + offset * wordlength)
ldnlp offset     ; add offset * wordlength to Areg
ldpi             ; add iptr to Areg
dup              ; Creg := Breg, Breg := Areg
rev              ; swap Areg and Breg
mint             ; load –2^(wordlength–1) into Areg
ldc constant     ; load constant into Areg
adc constant     ; add constant to Areg
add              ; Areg := Breg + Areg,  Breg := Creg
sub              ; Areg := Breg – Areg,  Breg := Creg
mul              ; Areg := Breg * Areg,  Breg := Creg
and              ; Areg := Breg & Areg,  Breg := Creg
gt               ; Areg := Breg > Areg,  Breg := Creg
cj label         ; jump to label if Areg == 0
j label          ; jump to label, context switch possible
gcall            ; jump to Areg, Areg := return address
runp             ; start process of which Areg contains the wsp
stopp            ; stop current process
```

17.4 Representing PABC components on transputers

This section discusses a concrete realization of the PABC machine on a ParSyTec transputer architecture (Kesseler, 1991; 1992). The concrete network being used consisted of 32 T800s, each running at 25 MHz and having 4 Kbyte of static RAM and 4 Mbyte of external memory. The discussed implementation describes one of the many ways in which a concrete implementation can be obtained. A different transputer implementation of the PABC machine based on the ZAPP design (Burton and Sleep, 1981) can be found in Goldsmith *et al.* (1993).

17.4.1 Representing the reducer components

A PABC machine can conveniently be implemented on a concrete machine that has a reasonable number of general purpose registers.

Clearly, the transputer is not such a machine. To overcome this problem, the on-chip static RAM is regarded as a large collection of registers. Each reducer is implemented as a single low-priority transputer process with a private 'register' set, a fixed amount of memory of the on-chip static RAM: the **workspace frame**. The elements of this set are called the **locals** of a reducer. The workspace pointer of each reducer points to the start of these locals and can be used to identify each reducer uniquely (Figure 17.2). There can be locals to cache top values of the A- and B-/C-stacks, to remember the number of cached values (information used by the garbage collector) and to store stack pointers. Furthermore, two locals can be used to refer respectively to data that is different for each reducer and to data that is shared by all reducers.

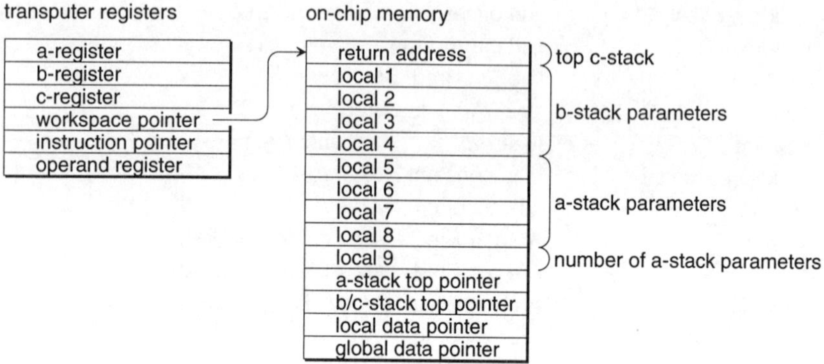

Figure 17.2 Layout of a workspace frame.

The program store and the program counter

The external memory and instruction pointer register are respectively used to represent the program store and the program counter. Into each external memory of the transputer a complete copy of the program is statically loaded when execution is initialized.

The A-stack, B-stack and C-stack

Two of the locals are used as a stack pointer for the A-stack, and the combined B-/C-stack. So each stack access requires an indirection, which is not very efficient. However, the locals provide enough spare registers for each reducer, such that in many cases stack access can be avoided (see Chapter 12). In practice, this solution gives good results.

All stacks are allocated in the heap and occupy one contiguous area of memory. The B- and the C-stacks are merged. A- and B-stacks grow in opposite direction such that their sizes can be checked at the same time by comparing the two stack pointers.

Each reducer gets small stacks initially. When necessary, a larger one (typically 1/8 larger) is allocated and the contents of the old stack are copied to the new one. The old stack then becomes garbage. Boundary checks cause a noticeable but not too serious overhead (worst case about 10%).

The N-queue and the waiting list register

The *N*-queue is stored in the heap. The waiting list register is a local.

The graph store

To store the graph each processor has a heap consisting of a contiguous piece of its external memory. The free space is a contiguous area within the heap: each reducer can reserve memory by taking the shared pointer to the first free word and advancing it the required number of words.

Representation of nodes

The node representation is basically the same as for sequential implementations, albeit that the waiting list has to be taken into account. For this purpose an extra field is added into the fixed part of the node in which a reference to a waiting list can be stored (see Figure 17.3).

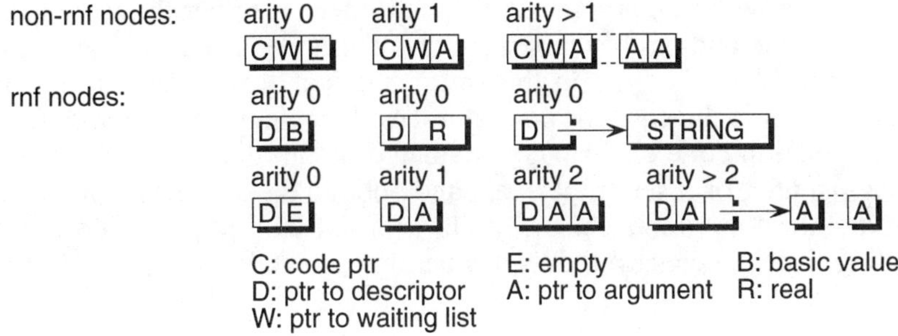

Figure 17.3 Chosen rnf and non-rnf node representations.

A positive field value D indicates that the node is in root normal form and a pointer to the descriptor can be computed by taking –D. A negative value C means the node is not in root normal form and C is a pointer to the code of the node (on the transputer the lowest address starts at $-2^{\text{wordlength}-1}$). Note that this only works as long as the transputer has no more than 2 Gbyte of memory. A pointer to a waiting list (Figure 17.4) is stored in a dedicated field of each non-root normal form node. As a consequence of this node representation a reducer has to check whether a node is in root normal form each time it tries to evaluate it.

Code for PABCs Jsr_eval (local 5 is assumed to refer to the node to reduce):

```
        ldl 5                 ; get pointer to node
        ldnl code             ; get code/descriptor of node
        mint                  ; load hex 80000000
        and                   ; 0 if descriptor
        cj .is_in_rnf         ; jump if descriptor
        check_stacks          ; macro call, check if enough space on stacks
        save_                 ; macro call, save all locals in use on stacks
        ldl 5                 ; get pointer to node
        ldnl  code            ; get evaluation code of node
        gcall                 ; evaluate the node
        restore_              ; macro call, restore previously saved locals
.is_in_rnf
```

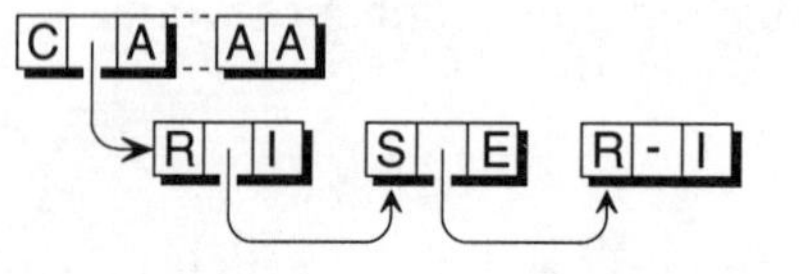

C: code ptr
A: ptr to argument
E: external address (of channel)
I: internal address (of reducer)
R: release code ptr (of internal reducer)
S: send code ptr (to external address)

Figure 17.4 Representation of a waiting list.

Each element in the waiting list is implemented as an ordinary graph node with one argument. This argument is either the workspace pointer or the address of the remote channel node. The next element of the waiting list is stored in the waiting list field of each waiting list node, just as is the case for normal nodes. Depending on the argument, the evaluation code either puts a reducer back in the scheduling list of the transputer, or it sends the evaluated node to the requesting processor and updates the remote channel node with it. So all requests stored in a waiting list can be answered by evaluating each node in it.

The descriptor store

Each processor gets a copy of the representation of the descriptor store when program execution is initialized. The representation is conceptually the same as for sequential implementations.

17.4.2 The run-time system

A transputer has primitives for process creation, abortion and context switching. It has a hardware round robin scheduling mechanism. Reducers are automatically time-sliced by the transputer hardware when jump and loop end instructions are executed. However, this feature sometimes gets in the way at those places where context switches are not allowed. On the transputer there are basically two ways to prevent context switches. A process can run at high priority (high-priority processes are not time-sliced at all) or the use of those instructions that cause a context switch is totally avoided. One can replace those instructions by conditional jump instructions. In this way one can prevent other low-priority processes from getting a time slice. Interrupts from high-priority processes are still possible. Since it is relatively expensive to change the priority of a process the second solution is used where possible. In order to obtain a fair scheduling transputer jump instructions are used sometimes between adjacent basic blocks to jump across data.

Locally, an ordinary copying garbage collector is used. Globally, a weighted reference count algorithm is implemented. So cyclic structures across process boundaries are currently not removed. The program is aborted when a processor, in spite of garbage collection, runs out of memory space.

Indirection tables are used to store channel node addresses, global node addresses and a reference count. A stack is used for graph copying, since pointer reversal is relatively expensive. Currently, no load balancing information is taken into account to find a suitable processor for an arbitrary created parallel process. A simple pseudo-random generator is used. Running tasks or processes are not migrated to other processors.

17.4.3 Communication between processors

Each of the four transputer links provides two uni-directional links, one in each direction. So a fully connected network of transputers cannot be constructed with more than five transputers. However, the transputer hardware does not support the communication between transputers that have no direct link. So for the implementation of the parallel instructions of the PABC machine a complete communication system has to be provided including support for file I/O. None of the available standard communication software facilities could be used because they were not implemented reliably, efficiently or flexibly enough. Therefore, a dedicated communication system (a router) has been implemented directly on top of the low-level communication primitives of the transputer. The lowest level of the router is a communication layer that provides deadlock-free *routing* of packets to arbitrary destinations. These packets are not allowed to be larger than a certain maximum size. Messages larger than the maximum packet size are broken into a number of packets, which are sent separately. Each packet gets a number that indicates its position in the original message. The order in which packets arrive at the destination is not necessarily the same as the order in which they are sent. Packets cannot get lost.

The router employs a modified algorithm based upon the algorithm presented in Annot and Van Twist, (1987). It uses a fixed amount of buffers and a class-climbing algorithm to prevent *deadlock* under the assumption that each packet that reaches its destination is consumed within a finite amount of time. *Starvation* is avoided by a mechanism that locks out links from accessing buffers of a certain class if they recently used such a buffer and others are trying to access it as well. The algorithm does not use a fixed path to route packets, so *hot spots* in the network are avoided to some extent.

17.5 Generating transputer code and performance

Efficient sequential code generated for a single processor is the basis of an efficient parallel implementation. Despite the fact that the transputer architecture is quite different from the M680x0, the code generator presented in Chapter 12 can successfully be retargeted to transputer code. There are some small differences because the transputer has only six registers (but it has an on-chip memory) and a small evaluation stack. Also some adaptations are needed for dynamic stack allocations. However, with a reasonable amount of locals assigned to each process most of the optimizations discussed in Chapter 12 remain applicable.

Example of generated code. Consider again (see also Section 12.5.2):

```
:: F !INT !INT   ->   INT;
   F a b         ->   - (* a b) (+ a 3);
```

The generated Motorola code for this rule alternative:

```
muls.l  d1, d0      ; multiply a and b
addq.l  #3, d1      ; add a and 3
sub.l d1, d0        ; subtract both results
rts                 ; return to caller
```

The corresponding transputer code:

```
ldl 1               ; push b on evaluation stack
ldl 2               ; push a on evaluation stack
mul                 ; multiply a and b
ldl 2               ; push a on evaluation stack
adc 3               ; add a and 3
sub                 ; subtract both results
stl 1               ; store result on top of B-stack
ldl 0               ; get return address
gcall               ; return to caller
```

This may seem a bit long, but the code actually occupies only 10 bytes of memory. The top of the B-stack is cached in local 2, the second entry resides in local 1. The caller expects the result to be returned in local 1. On entry to this function the return address is stored in local 0. No stack checks are needed since only locals are used.

Performance

Table 17.1 shows some performance results (see also Table 12.3).

nfib 30	each task computes nfib 30.
sieve	10 000 primes, one task for every 20 prime numbers.
queens	counts all solutions for the (10) queens problem.
rnfib 30	each task computes nfib 30.
fastfourier	on an array of 8000 complex numbers.
mandelbrot	calculates Mandelbrot fractals, resolution 530 x 320, depth 128.

Table 17.1 Performance in seconds on respectively 1, 2, 4, 8, 16 and 32 T800 processors of some well-known benchmarks on 32 processors connected in a grid topology.

Program	*Number of processors*					
	1	*2*	*4*	*8*	*16*	*32*
nfib	12.2	6.5	3.5	2.2	1.4	1.1
sieve	19.4	31.2	32.1	23.6	16.9	14.5
queens	47.9	28.5	15.1	9.0	6.2	4.7
rnfib	23.7	12.2	7.1	3.9	2.2	1.6
fastfourier	13.8	11.2	8.7	6.3	5.6	5.6
mandelbrot	147.0	91.0	54.3	34.3	18.2	10.6

The main difference from the sequential implementation discussed in Chapter 12 is that stacks are handled less efficiently in the transputer version. In the Motorola implementation, stack frames are allocated once outside the heap. In the transputer implementation programs are started with an initial stack size of 0 bytes in the heap. The stacks are automatically reallocated and resized, implying that boundary checks have to be performed. So the Motorola programs actually use more memory than their transputer counterpart because their A-, B- and C-stacks are allocated outside the heap. A disadvantage of a T800 is that the processor needs quite some time to fetch instructions and data from off-chip memory. If a program is placed in the 4K on-chip memory (only the code, while keeping the data in the same place) it runs about 1.6 times faster. But, of course, most useful programs are larger than 4K. A T800 produces good results for computations with reals due to the speed of the on-chip floating-point processor.

The parallel results are obtained with medium-sized randomly distributed tasks. A small task size degrades performance by introducing a relatively large communication and process management overhead. Large tasks limit the total number of tasks, thereby increasing the chance that a bad load distribution will occur.

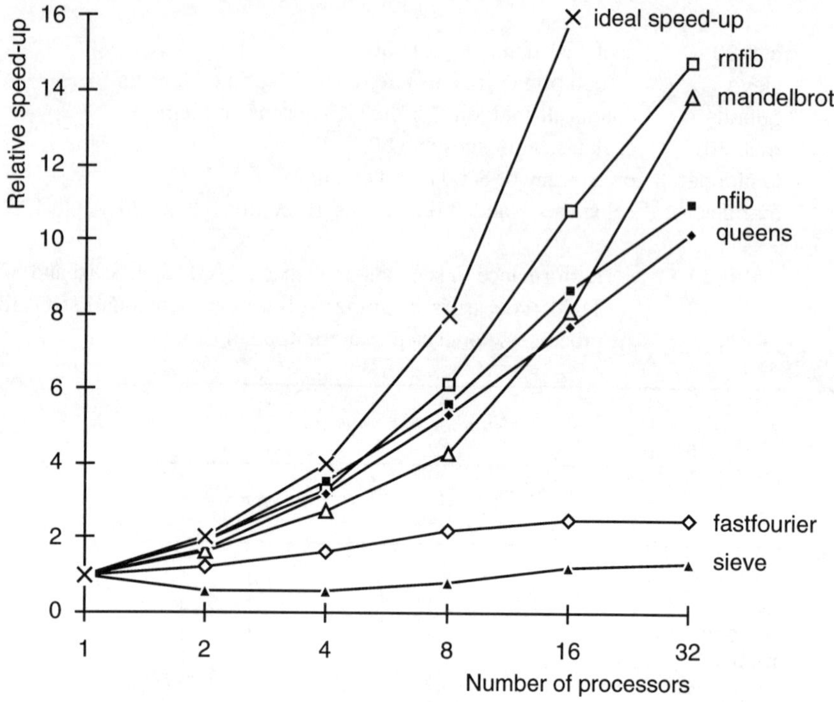

Figure 17.5 A graphical representation of the speed-up obtained for the different test programs.

Figure 17.5 shows that some examples (like sieve and fastfourier) do not have a lot of inherent parallelism, although a lot of processes are generated. The communication overhead is inherently too large for these examples. They serve as an exercise in expressing certain process topologies, but not as examples of good speed-ups. The other examples show a reasonable performance considering that a random process distribution was used.

Further code optimizations

The code as tested (see Table 17.1) can be improved in several ways. Many small improvements for the sequential code (see Chapter 12) are not yet implemented. Besides these standard optimizations for sequential code there are also many possible improvements related to the parallel parts of the machine. Certain PABC instructions that involve communication between processors often appear in a certain order. It is sometimes possible to combine PABC instructions to reduce the amount of communication between these processors. Furthermore, the initialization of a new process can be done more cheaply by reusing the stacks of a previously stopped process. Processes are created randomly. No heuristic for workload balancing is being used. A lazy copy sent across a network can be represented more compactly (Van Groningen, 1992). Process communication and synchronization as well as scheduling can be automatically tuned to optimize the communication between a producing process and a consuming process. All these optimizations are subjects of future research.

Summary

- The sequential implementation technique presented in this book can also successfully be applied on a transputer processor, even though its architecture is quite different from the more traditional architectures such as those offered by a Motorola processor.
- The PABC machine abstracts from many implementation problems. Therefore, the realization of the PABC machine is considerably more work than the realization of the ABC machine. The actual effort will depend heavily on the facilities offered by the concrete MIMD machine hardware and software. Typical features that have to be solved in one way or another include *stack checking*, *stack reallocation*, *local* and *global garbage collection*, *removal of garbage reducers*, *context switching*, deadlock and starvation-free efficient *routing of messages* between arbitrary processors, *load balancing*, *deadlock detection*, *process migration* and *I/O support.*
- Most of the items on the previous list also have to be addressed when other kinds of programming languages (imperative, logical, object oriented) are to be implemented on an MIMD architecture.
- The PABC machine has been realized on a 32 node ParSyTec transputer system. Although a transputer does not have a large set of general purpose registers, the actual implementation on one transputer performs reasonably well.
- MIMD architectures are generally quite expensive. An implementation of Concurrent Clean (and the PABC machine) is also available for a, generally less expensive, heterogeneous network (AppleTalk/Ethernet) of Macintosh and Sun workstations. This will offer the opportunity to use concurrent functional programming not only for gaining speed but also for writing *distributed interactive multi-user applications* (e.g. spreadsheets, databases) combining Clean's event I/O with process annotations.

EXERCISES

17.1 Use the code generator to generate parallel code for the programs of Exercises 15.2 and 15.3. Generate parallel code for one machine. Measure the differences between parallel code and pure sequential code. If it is possible on your system, measure the speed-ups on as many distributed processors as are available. Also measure the communication costs. Compare the actual results with the results predicted by the simulator. Explain the differences.

17.2 Measure the nfib example using different allocation strategies and topologies. Does the chosen topology make much difference? Does the chosen allocation strategy make much difference? Explain the results.

17.3* Assume that you would have used {Par} and {Self} annotations instead of {P} and {I}. Would the programs of Exercise 17.1 perform better, worse or the same?

17.4 Assume that you would have used a shared memory architecture instead of a distributed memory architecture. What would be the expected performance compared with distributed implementations?

Appendices

Appendix A
Syntax of the example programs

The example functional programs in this textbook are generally written in a Miranda-based notation. These examples obey the BNF-style context-free syntax rules given in this appendix.

Conventions used in the syntax specification below

[non-term] means that the presence of non-term is optional
[non-term]+ means that non-term occurs at least once
{non-term} means that non-term can occur zero or more times
terminals are enclosed by single quotes
symbols are printed in *italic*

Script

script = {declaration} ;
declaration = function_decl | type_decl ;

Definition

function_decl = def_lhs def_rhs ;
def_lhs = pattern | function_form ;
pattern = formal | *constructor* [formal]+
| '(' pattern ')' [formal]+
| pattern '$' *constructor* pattern ;
formal = *variable* | *constructor* | *literal*
| '(' pattern ')' | tuple_formal | list_formal ;
tuple_formal = '(' ')' | '(' pattern [',' pattern]+ ')' ;
list_formal = '[' ']' | '(' pattern ':' pattern ')'
| '[' pattern {',' pattern} ']' ;
function_form = *variable* [formal]+
| pattern '$' *variable* pattern
| '(' function_form ')' {formal} ;
def_rhs = {def_case} def_lastcase [where_def] *terminator* ;
def_case = '=' expression ',' guard *terminator* ;
expression = prefix_operator [expression]
| infix_operator
| [simple_expr]+
| expression infix_operator expression
| expression '$' *variable* expression
| expression '$' *constructor* expression ;
simple_expr = *variable* | *constructor* | *literal*
| '(' expression ')'
| '(' infix_operator expression ')'
| '(' expression infix_operator ')' | tuple | list ;

```
tuple           = '(' ')'          | '(' expression [',' expression]+')' ;
list            = '[' ']'          | '[' expression {',' expression} ']'
                | dotdot_expr      | zf_expr ;
dotdot_expr     = '[' expression [',' expression] '..' [expression] ']' ;
zf_expr         = '[' expression '|' qualifier {';' qualifier} ']'
                | '[' expression '//' qualifier {';' qualifier} ']' ;
qualifier       = expression   | generator ;
generator       = pattern {',' pattern} '<-' expression
                | pattern '<-' expression ',' expression '..' ;
prefix_operator = '~'  | '-'  | '#' ;
infix_operator  = '++' | ':'  | '\/' | '&'  | '>'  | '>=' | '~='
                | '<=' | '<'  | '='  | '+'  | '*'  | '/'  | 'div'
                | '^'  | '.'  | '!'  | '-'  | '--' | 'mod' ;
guard           = [ 'if' ] expression ;
def_lastcase    = '=' expression ',' guard        | '=' expression ',' 'otherwise'
                | '=' expression ;
where_def       = 'where' [function_decl]+ ;
```

Type declaration and specification

```
type_decl       = abstype_def | typesyn_def | type_def    | type_spec ;
abstype_def     = 'abstype' type_form {',' type_form} 'with' signature terminator ;
type_form       = type_name {type_variable}
                | type_variable '$'type_variable type_variable ;
signature       = [type_spec]+ ;
type_spec       = type_variable {',' type_variable} '::' type terminator
                | type_form {',' type_form} '::' 'type' terminator ;
type            = simple_type   | type_name [simple_type]+
                | type '->' type | type '$'type_variable type ;
simple_type     = type_name     | type_variable | '(' type ')'
                | tuple_type    | list_type ;
tuple_type      = '(' ')'       | '(' type [',' type ]+')' ;
list_type       = '[' type ']' ;
typesyn_def     = type_form '==' type terminator ;
type_def        = type_form '::=' type_construct {',' type_construct} terminator ;
type_construct  = '(' type_construct ')' {simple_type}
                | constructor {simple_type}     | type '$'constructor type ;
```

Symbols

```
variable        = IDENT ;
type_name       = IDENT ;
type_variable   = TYPEVAR ;
constructor     = CONS ;
literal         = NUMERAL       | CHAR        | STRING ;
terminator      = ';'           | OFFSIDE ;
```

Lexical classes used in the syntax specification above

IDENT	identifiers starting with a lower case letter, e.g. f, f', longer_name
CONS	identifiers starting with an upper case letter, e.g. Cons, Tree
TYPEVAR	one or more asterisk, e.g. *, **, ***
NUMERAL	numeral denotation, e.g. 1.0, 2, 3.3e7
CHAR	character denotation, e.g. 'c', '\n'
STRING	string denotation, e.g. "hello world\n"
OFFSIDE	not a proper terminal: represents an application of the offside rule

Appendix B
Concurrent Clean syntax and library

This appendix uses the same conventions as Appendix A.

B.1 Concurrent Clean syntax

Clean program

```
CleanProgram    = {Module} ;
Module          = DefModule          | ImplModule ;
DefModule       = 'DEFINITION' 'MODULE' ModuleId ';' {Def}
                | 'SYSTEM' 'MODULE' ModuleId ';' {Def} ;
ImplModule      = ['IMPLEMENTATION'] 'MODULE' ModuleId ';' {Impl} ;
Def             = Import             | Type-Block    | AbsType-Block
                | DefRule-Block      | Macro-Block ;
Impl            = Import             | Type-Block    | ImplRule-Block
                | Macro-Block ;
Import          = 'IMPORT' ModuleId {',' ModuleId} ';'
                | 'FROM' ModuleId 'IMPORT' Symbol {',' Symbol} ';' ;
Type-Block      = 'TYPE' [TypeRule]+ ;
AbsType-Block   = 'ABSTYPE' [AbsTypeRule]+ ;
DefRule-Block   = 'RULE' [TypeRule]+ ;
ImplRule-Block  = 'RULE' [StrategyDef] [[TypeRule] Rule]+ ;
Macro-Block     = 'MACRO' [Rule]+ ;
StrategyDef     = 'STRATEGY' Strategy ';' ;
Strategy        = 'FUNCTIONAL' ;
```

Type definitions

```
TypeRule        = '::' TypeAlt {'|' TypeGraph} ';'
                | '::' TypeAlt {'->' TypeGraph} ';' ;
AbsTypeRule     = '::' TypeGraph ';' ;
TypeAlt         = TypeGraph '->' TypeGraph ;
TypeGraph       = Graph ;
```

Rule definitions

```
Rule           = [RuleAlt]+ ;
RuleAlt        = Graph '->' GuardedRhss {',' NodeDef} ';' ;
GuardedRhss    = GuardedRhs ['->' GuardedRhss]  |  Rhs ;
GuardedRhs     = Rhs [','] 'IF' Guards ;
Rhs            = NodeId                    |  [NodeId ':'] Node ;
Guards         = Guards {'&&' Guards}      |  Guards {'||' Guards}
               | '(' Guards ')'            |  Rhs ;
Graph          = [NodeId ':'] Node {',' NodeDef} ;
NodeDef        = NodeId ':' Node           |  NodeIds ':' ListNode
               | NodeIds ':' ApplyNode     |  NodeIds ':' SimpleNode
               | NodeIds ':' [Annot] NodeId ;
NodeIds        = '(' NodeId [',' NodeId]+ ')' ;
Node           = TupleNode   |  ListNode  |  ApplyNode   |  SimpleNode ;
TupleNode      = [AnnOrAttr] '(' UnBrackArg [',' UnBrackArg ]+ ')';
ListNode       = [AnnOrAttr] '[ ]'
               | [AnnOrAttr] '[' UnBrackArg {',' UnBrackArg } ['|' UnBrackArg ] ']' ;
ApplyNode      = [AnnOrAttr] NodeId [Arg]+ ;
SimpleNode     = [AnnOrAttr] Symbol {Arg} ;
Arg            = [AnnOrAttr] NodeId    |  [AnnOrAttr] [NodeId ':'] ArgNode ;
ArgNode        = Symbol  |  '(' Node ')'  |  TupleNode    |  ListNode ;
UnBrackArg     = [AnnOrAttr] NodeId    |  [AnnOrAttr] [NodeId ':'] Node ;
```

Annotations and attributes

```
AnnOrAttr       = Annotation Attribute     |  Annotation     |  Attribute ;
Annotation      = '{' StrictAnnot '}'  |  '{' ProcessAnnot '}'  |  StrictShorthand ;
StrictAnnot     = '!' ;
ProcessAnnot    = 'I'                  |    'P' ['AT' Graph] ;
StrictShorthand = '!' ;
Attribute       = UniqueAttribute ;
UniqueAttribute = 'UNQ' ;
```

Symbol and node identifiers

```
Symbol          = SymbolId   |  BasicType  |  BasicValue    |  PredefinedType ;
BasicType       = 'INT'      |  REAL'      |  'CHAR'        |  'BOOL'
                | 'STRING'   |  'FILE'     |  'PROCID' ;
BasicValue      = IntDenot   |  RealDenot  |  CharDenot     |  BoolDenot
                | StringDenot ;
PredefinedType  = '=>' ;
```

Identifiers and denotations

A dot (.) is used for concatenation of characters. Reserved words are not allowed as identifiers.

```
ModuleId       = LowerCaseChar.{RestChar}   |  UpperCaseChar.{RestChar}
               | Class1Char.{RestChar} ;
NodeId         = LowerCaseChar.{RestChar} ;
SymbolId       = UpperCaseChar.{RestChar}   |  Class1Char.{RestChar} ;
LowerCaseChar  = 'a' | 'b' | ... | 'z' ;
UpperCaseChar  = 'A' | 'B' | ... | 'Z' ;
Digit          = '0' | '1' | ... | '9' ;
OctDigit       = '0' | '1' | ... | '7' ;
RestChar       = LowerCaseChar |  Class1Char   |  Digit
               | UpperCaseChar |  CharDel      |  StringDel ;
CharDel        = ''' ;
```

```
StringDel      = '"' ;
IntDenot       = [Sign].[Digit]+ ;
RealDenot      = [Sign].[Digit]+.'.'.[Digit]+.[Exponent] ;
Exponent       = 'E'.[Sign].[Digit]+ ;
CharDenot      = CharDel.Char.CharDel ;
Char           = LowerCaseChar | Class1Char | Digit
               | UpperCaseChar | Class2Char | Special ;
BoolDenot      = 'TRUE'        | 'FALSE' ;
StringDenot    = StringDel.{Char}.StringDel ;
Sign           = '+' | '-' ;
Class1Char     = '@' | '#' | '$' | '%' | '^' | '&'
               | '?' | '*' | '-' | '+' | '/' | '='
               | '<' | '>' | '_' | '.' | '`' | '"' ;
Class2Char     = '|' | '!' | '(' | ')' | '{' | '}'
               | '[' | ']' | ':' | ';' | '~' | ',' ;
Special        = '\n' | '\r' | '\f' | '\b' | '\t' | '\\'
               | '\'.CharDel | '\'.StringDel | '\'.OctDigit.OctDigit.OctDigit ;
```

Reserved words

```
'AT'            'FROM'            'PROCID'      'UNQ'
'ABSTYPE'       'FUNCTIONAL'      'REAL'        '->'
'BOOL'          'IF'              'RULE'        '=>'
'CHAR'          'IMPLEMENTATION'  'STRATEGY'    '&&'
'CODE'          'IMPORT'          'STRING'      '||'
'DEFINITION'    'INT'             'SYSTEM'      '<<'
'FALSE'         'MACRO'           'TRUE'        '>>'
'FILE'          'MODULE'          'TYPE'        '=='
```

B.2 δ-rules

General library entrance (delta)

```
DEFINITION MODULE delta;
IMPORT   deltaB, deltaC, deltaI,  deltaR, deltaS, deltaM;
```

Imports all library operations excluding deltaP and the I/O library.

Operations on booleans (deltaB)

```
SYSTEM MODULE deltaB;
RULE
:: NOT !BOOL        ->  BOOL;     == Boolean negation
:: AND !BOOL !BOOL  ->  BOOL;     == Boolean AND
:: OR  !BOOL !BOOL  ->  BOOL;     == Boolean OR
:: =B  !BOOL !BOOL  ->  BOOL;     == Boolean equal
:: <>B !BOOL !BOOL  ->  BOOL;     == Boolean not equal
:: BTOS      !BOOL  ->  STRING;   == BOOL to STRING conversion
```

Operations on characters (deltaC)

```
SYSTEM MODULE deltaC;
RULE
:: =C  !CHAR !CHAR ->  BOOL;      == character equal
:: <>C !CHAR !CHAR ->  BOOL;      == character not equal
:: <C  !CHAR !CHAR ->  BOOL;      == character less than
```

```
:: >C  !CHAR !CHAR ->  BOOL;      == character greater than
:: <=C !CHAR !CHAR ->  BOOL;      == character less than or equal
:: >=C !CHAR !CHAR ->  BOOL;      == character greater than or equal
:: CTOI      !CHAR ->  INT;       == CHAR to ASCII conversion
:: CTOS      !CHAR ->  STRING;    == CHAR to STRING conversion
```

Operations on integers (deltaI)

```
SYSTEM MODULE deltaI;
RULE
:: +       !INT !INT ->  INT;     == integer addition
:: -       !INT !INT ->  INT;     == integer subtraction
:: *       !INT !INT ->  INT;     == integer multiplication
:: /       !INT !INT ->  INT;     == integer division
:: %       !INT !INT ->  INT;     == integer modulus
:: ++      !INT      ->  INT;     == integer increment
:: --      !INT      ->  INT;     == integer decrement
:: =       !INT !INT ->  BOOL;    == integer equal
:: <>      !INT !INT ->  BOOL;    == integer not equal
:: <       !INT !INT ->  BOOL;    == integer less than
:: >       !INT !INT ->  BOOL;    == integer greater than
:: <=      !INT !INT ->  BOOL;    == integer less than or equal
:: >=      !INT !INT ->  BOOL;    == integer greater than or equal
:: AND%    !INT !INT ->  INT;     == integer bitwise AND
:: OR%     !INT !INT ->  INT;     == integer bitwise OR
:: NOT%    !INT      ->  INT;     == integer bitwise NOT
:: XOR%    !INT !INT ->  INT;     == integer exclusive OR
:: SHIFTL% !INT !INT ->  INT;     == integer shift left
:: SHIFTR% !INT !INT ->  INT;     == integer shift right
:: ITOC    !INT      ->  CHAR;    == INT to CHAR conversion
:: ITOR    !INT      ->  REAL;    == INT to REAL conversion
:: ITOS    !INT      ->  STRING;  == INT to STRING conversion
```

Operations on reals (deltaR)

```
SYSTEM MODULE deltaR;
RULE
:: +R     !REAL !REAL ->  REAL;   == real addition
:: -R     !REAL !REAL ->  REAL;   == real subtraction
:: *R     !REAL !REAL ->  REAL;   == real multiplication
:: /R     !REAL !REAL ->  REAL;   == real division
:: =R     !REAL !REAL ->  BOOL;   == real equal
:: <>R    !REAL !REAL ->  BOOL;   == real not equal
:: <R     !REAL !REAL ->  BOOL;   == real less than
:: >R     !REAL !REAL ->  BOOL;   == real greater than
:: <=R    !REAL !REAL ->  BOOL;   == real less than or equal
:: >=R    !REAL !REAL ->  BOOL;   == real greater than or equal
:: SIN    !REAL       ->  REAL;   == sine
:: COS    !REAL       ->  REAL;   == cosine
:: TAN    !REAL       ->  REAL;   == tangent
:: ASIN   !REAL       ->  REAL;   == arc sine
:: ACOS   !REAL       ->  REAL;   == arc cosine
:: ATAN   !REAL       ->  REAL;   == arc tangent
:: LN     !REAL       ->  REAL;   == logarithm base e
:: LOG10  !REAL       ->  REAL;   == logarithm base 10
:: EXP    !REAL       ->  REAL;   == raise e to power
:: POW    !REAL !REAL ->  REAL;   == raise to power
```

```
:: SQRT     !REAL          ->  REAL;     == square root
:: ENTIER   !REAL          ->  INT;      == entier
:: RTOI     !REAL          ->  INT;      == round REAL to INT
:: RTOS     !REAL          ->  STRING;   == REAL to STRING conversion
```

Operations on strings (deltaS)

```
SYSTEM MODULE deltaS;
RULE
:: +S     !STRING   !STRING     ->  STRING;   == concatenate arg2 to arg1
:: =S     !STRING   !STRING     ->  BOOL;     == string equal
:: <>S    !STRING   !STRING     ->  BOOL;     == string not equal
:: <S     !STRING   !STRING     ->  BOOL;     == string less than
:: >S     !STRING   !STRING     ->  BOOL;     == string greater than
:: <=S    !STRING   !STRING     ->  BOOL;     == string less than or equal
:: >=S    !STRING   !STRING     ->  BOOL;     == string greater than or equal
:: INDEX  !STRING !INT          ->  CHAR;     == get the arg2nd char from arg1
:: SLICE  !STRING !INT !INT     ->  STRING;   == get substring arg2 .. arg3
                                              == from arg1
:: UPDATE !STRING !CHAR !INT -> STRING;       == replace arg3rd char in arg1
                                              == with arg2
:: LENGTH  !STRING              ->  INT;      == string length
```

String comparison is based on lexical order. String indices range from 0. Note that as a consequence LENGTH gives the number of characters in the string and not the index of the last character.

Miscellaneous operations (deltaM)

```
SYSTEM MODULE deltaM;
RULE
:: ABORT     !STRING   ->   x ;           == stop reduction, print arg1
```

Processor location operations (deltaP)

```
SYSTEM MODULE deltaP;
RULE
:: CurrentP                    ->  PROCID;  == proc-id of the current processor
:: ITOP !INT                   ->  PROCID;  == convert an integer to a proc-id
:: RandomP                     ->  PROCID;  == generate a random proc-id
:: NeighbourP !INT !PROCID     ->  PROCID;  == proc-id of nth neighbour
:: ChannelP x                  ->  PROCID;  == returns the proc-id of arg1
```

B.3 I/O library

Operations on files (deltaFile)

```
SYSTEM MODULE deltaFile;
ABSTYPE
:: UNQ FILES;

MACRO            ==   File modes
   FReadText     ->   0;                  == read from a text file
   FWriteText    ->   1;                  == write to a text file
```

```
    FAppendText   ->   2;              == append to an existing text file
    FReadData     ->   3;              == read from a data file
    FWriteData    ->   4;              == write to a data file
    FAppendData   ->   5;              == append to an existing data file
                                       == seek modes:
    FSeekSet      ->   0;              == new position is the seek offset
    FSeekCur      ->   1;              == relative to current position
    FSeekEnd      ->   2;              == relative to end of file

RULE
:: OpenFiles !UNQ WORLD   ->   (!FILES, !UNQ WORLD);
```
Opens the file system (FILES) containing all accessible files. The file system is used as argument for the functions that open and close files (deltaFile.dcl). Attempts to open a file system that is already open will result in a run-time error.

```
:: CloseFiles !FILES !UNQ WORLD   ->   UNQ WORLD;
```
Closes the file system.

```
:: FOpen    !STRING !INT !FILES   ->   (!BOOL, !UNQ FILE, !FILES);
```
Opens a file in a certain mode (read, write or append, text or data). The Boolean output parameter reports success or failure. An attempt to open a file that is already open will result in a run-time error.

```
:: FReOpen  !UNQ FILE !INT        ->   (!BOOL, !UNQ FILE);
```
Re-opens an open file in a possibly different mode. The boolean indicates whether the file was successfully closed before reopening.

```
:: FClose   !UNQ FILE !FILES      ->   (!BOOL, !FILES);
```
Closes a file such that it can be opened again with FOpen. The boolean indicates whether the file was successfully closed.

```
:: FReadC   !UNQ FILE             ->   (!BOOL, !CHAR, !UNQ FILE);
```
Reads a character from a text file or a byte from a data file. The Boolean parameter reports success or failure of the operation.

```
:: FReadI   !UNQ FILE             ->   (!BOOL, !INT, !UNQ FILE);
```
Reads an integer from a text file by skipping spaces, tabs and newlines and then reading digits, which may be preceded by a plus or minus sign. From a data file FReadI will just read four bytes (a Clean INT).

```
:: FReadR   !UNQ FILE             ->   (!BOOL, !REAL, !UNQ FILE);
```
Reads a real from a text file by skipping spaces, tabs and newlines and then reading a character representation of a real number. From a data file FReadR will just read eight bytes (a Clean REAL).

```
:: FReadS   !UNQ FILE !INT        ->   (!STRING, !UNQ FILE);
```
Reads *n* characters from a text or data file, which are returned as a STRING. If the file does not contain *n* characters the file will be read to the end of the file. An empty string is returned if no characters can be read.

```
:: FReadLine !UNQ FILE            ->   (!STRING, !UNQ FILE);
```
Reads a line from a text file (including a newline character, except for the last line). FReadLine cannot be used on data files.

```
:: FWriteC  !CHAR !UNQ FILE       ->   UNQ FILE;
```
Writes a character to a text file. To a data file, FWriteC writes one byte (a Clean CHAR).

```
:: FWriteI  !INT !UNQ FILE        ->   UNQ FILE;
```
Writes an integer (its textual representation) to a text file. To a data file, FWriteI

writes four bytes (a Clean INT).

```
:: FWriteR    !REAL !UNQ FILE          ->     UNQ FILE;
```
Writes a real (its textual representation) to a text file. To a data file, FWriteR writes eight bytes (a Clean REAL).

```
:: FWriteS    !STRING !UNQ FILE        ->     UNQ FILE;
```
Writes a string to a text or data file.

```
:: FEnd     !UNQ FILE                  ->     (!BOOL, !UNQ FILE);
```
Tests for end-of-file.

```
:: FError   !UNQ FILE                  ->     (!BOOL, !UNQ FILE);
```
Has an error occurred during previous file I/O operations?

```
:: FPosition !UNQ FILE                 ->     (!INT, !UNQ FILE);
```
Returns the current position of the file pointer as an integer. This position can be used later on for the FSeek function.

```
:: FSeek    !UNQ FILE !INT !INT        ->     (!BOOL, !UNQ FILE);
```
Move to a different position in the file, first integer argument is the offset, second argument is a seek mode (see above). True is returned if successful.

```
:: StdIO    !FILES                     ->     (!UNQ FILE, !FILES);
```
Open the 'Console' for reading and writing.

```
:: StdErr                              ->     !UNQ FILE;
```
The StdErr file is a write-only file (the 'Errors' file) that need not be opened or closed.

```
:: SFOpen       !STRING !INT !FILES ->    (!BOOL, !FILE, !FILES);
:: SFReadC      !FILE               ->    (!BOOL, !CHAR, !FILE);
:: SFReadI      !FILE               ->    (!BOOL, !INT, !FILE);
:: SFReadR      !FILE               ->    (!BOOL, !REAL, !FILE);
:: SFReadS      !FILE !INT          ->    (!STRING, !FILE);
:: SFReadLine   !FILE               ->    (!STRING, !FILE);
:: SFSeek       !FILE !INT !INT     ->    (!BOOL, !FILE);
```
With SFOpen a file can be opened for reading more than once without closing it first. On a file opened by SFOpen only the operations beginning with SF can be used. The SF... operations work just like the corresponding F... operations.

```
:: FShare       !UNQ FILE !FILES    ->    (!FILE, !FILES);
```
Change a file so that from now on it can only be used with SF... operations.

```
:: SFEnd        !FILE               ->    BOOL;
:: SFPosition   !FILE               ->    INT;
```
The functions SFEnd and SFPosition work like FEnd and FPosition, but do not return a new file on which other operations can continue. They can be used for files opened with SFOpen or after FShare, and in guards for files opened with FOpen or FReOpen.

General operations on the IOState (deltaEventIO)

```
DEFINITION MODULE deltaEventIO;
IMPORT deltaIOSystem;
ABSTYPE
:: UNQ EVENTS;
= = The event stream.
:: UNQ IOState UNQ s;
= = The environment on which all event I/O functions operate.
```

```
TYPE
:: InitialIO s  ->     [=> s (=> (IOState s) (s, IOStates))]
```
= = The I/O functions that will be evaluated before starting the interaction.

```
RULE
:: OpenEvents  !UNQ WORLD  ->   (!EVENTS, !UNQ WORLD);
```
Retrieves the event stream from the world. Attempts to retrieve the event stream from the world more than once without putting it back result in a run-time error.

```
:: CloseEvents  !EVENTS  !UNQ WORLD  ->   UNQ WORLD;
```
Puts the event stream back into the world.

```
:: StartIO  !(IOSystem s (IOState s))   !s !(InitialIO s)  !EVENTS
                                                  ->    (!s, !EVENTS);
```
Starts a new interaction. The initial state of this interaction is composed of the program state (s) and the initial I/O state, which consists of the devices participating in the interaction (defined in the IOSystem argument) and the event stream (EVENTS). Of each device in the initial IOSystem only the first occurrence is taken into account. The program state must be unique. Before starting the interaction the InitialIO functions are evaluated. At the end of the interaction StartIO returns the final program state and the resulting event stream, from which the events that have been handled during the interaction have been removed.

```
:: NestIO  !(IOSystem s (IOState s))   !s !(InitialIO s)  !(IOState t)
                                                  ->    (!s, !IOState t);
```
Starts a nested interaction. It replaces the current interaction (as specified by the IOState argument) with a completely new one (as specified by the IOSystem argument). It hides the devices of the current interaction (if any) and fills a new IOState with the devices that are specified in the IOSystem and with the event stream of the old IOState. The program state argument (s) serves as initial program state of the new interaction. Before starting the nested interaction the InitialIO functions are evaluated. NestIO returns the final program state of the new interaction and the original IOState, such that the original interaction reappears.

```
:: QuitIO  !(IOState s)   ->    IOState s;
```
Closes all devices that are held in the IOState argument. The resulting IOState will cause StartIO or NestIO to terminate.

```
:: ChangeIOState  ![=> (IOState s) (IOState s)] !(IOState s)   ->    IOState s;
```
Applies all functions in its first argument in consecutive order to the second (IOState) argument.

Definition of the I/O system (deltaIOSystem)

```
DEFINITION MODULE deltaIOSystem;
FROM deltaPicture IMPORT Picture, Rectangle, DrawFunction;
ABSTYPE
:: UNQ DialogState UNQ s UNQ io;
:: DialogInfo;

TYPE
:: IOSystem UNQ s UNQ io      ->   [DeviceSystem s io];
:: DeviceSystem UNQ s UNQ io  ->   TimerSystem    [TimerDef  s io]
                              ->   MenuSystem     [MenuDef  s io]
                              ->   WindowSystem   [WindowDef  s io]
                              ->   DialogSystem   [DialogDef s io];
```

The timer device responds only to timer events. A timer event occurs as soon as a certain TimerInterval has expired since the last time it was ‘sampled’. A TimerInterval is defined as a number of ticks. A macro TicksPerSecond is defined in delta-

Timer.dcl. The timer event causes one of the programmer-defined TimerFunctions to be evaluated. The TimerState argument of a TimerFunction indicates how many times the TimerInterval has passed since the last timer event for that timer. When the TimerInterval of one of the timers is smaller than 1 the corresponding TimerFunction is called as often as possible.

```
:: TimerDef UNQ s UNQ io
     ->    Timer TimerId SelectState TimerInterval (TimerFunction s io);
:: TimerId                          ->    INT;
:: TimerInterval                    ->    INT;
:: TimerFunction UNQ s UNQ io       ->    => TimerState (=> s (=> io (s, io)));
:: TimerState                       ->    INT;
```

The menu device consists of several PullDownMenus. PullDownMenus are logically grouped into a menu bar, in the same order as they are specified. They are selected by pressing the mouse on their MenuTitle in the menu bar. Menus contain MenuElements. The corresponding MenuFunctions are executed when these elements are selected.

```
:: MenuDef UNQ s UNQ io
     ->    PullDownMenu MenuId MenuTitle SelectState [MenuElement s io];
:: MenuElement UNQ s UNQ io
     ->    MenuItem MenuItemId ItemTitle KeyShortcut SelectState
                                                    (MenuFunction s io)
     ->    CheckMenuItem MenuItemId ItemTitle KeyShortcut SelectState MarkState
                                                    (MenuFunction s io)
     ->    SubMenuItem MenuId ItemTitle SelectState [MenuElement s io]
     ->    MenuItemGroup MenuItemGroupId [MenuElement s io]
     ->    MenuRadioItems MenuItemId [RadioElement s io]
     ->    MenuSeparator;
:: RadioElement UNQ s UNQ io
     ->    MenuRadioItem MenuItemId ItemTitle KeyShortcut SelectState
                                                    (MenuFunction s io);

:: MenuFunction UNQ s UNQ io     ->    => s (=> io (s, io));
:: MenuId                        ->    INT;
:: MenuTitle                     ->    STRING;
:: MenuItemId                    ->    INT;
:: MenuItemGroupId               ->    INT;
:: KeyShortcut                   ->    Key KeyCode | NoKey;
```

The window device consists of several ScrollWindows or FixedWindows. A ScrollWindow is defined by the following arguments:

- WindowId: the number by which the programmer refers to the window.
- WindowPos: the position of the upper-left corner of the window.
- WindowTitle: the title of the window.
- ScrollBarDefs: the horizontal and vertical scroll bars (in that order).
- PictureDomain: the range of the drawing operations in the window.
- MinimumWindowSize: the smallest dimensions of the window.
- InitialWindowSize: the initial dimensions of the window.
- UpdateFunction: the function to redraw parts (UpdateArea) of the window.
- An attribute list that may contain the following window attributes:
  - Activate: the way to respond to activation of the window.
  - Deactivate: the way to respond to de-activation of the window.
  - GoAway: the way to respond when the window is closed.
  - Keyboard: the way the window responds to keyboard input.
  - Mouse: the way the window responds to mouse events.
  - Cursor: the shape of the cursor (mouse pointer) inside the window.
  - StandByWindow: when this attribute is present the window will be a so-called stand-by window.

A FixedWindow has a fixed size, which is defined by its PictureDomain. Therefore it has no scroll bars and no size parameters. When the PictureDomain of a Fixed-Window is or becomes greater than one of the screen's dimensions it becomes a ScrollWindow.

```
:: WindowDef UNQ s UNQ io
   -> ScrollWindow     WindowId WindowPos WindowTitle
                       ScrollBarDef ScrollBarDef PictureDomain
                       MinimumWindowSize InitialWindowSize
                       (UpdateFunction s) [WindowAttribute s io]
   -> FixedWindow      WindowId WindowPos WindowTitle PictureDomain
                       (UpdateFunction s) [WindowAttribute s io];

:: WindowId                 ->   INT;
:: WindowPos                ->   (!INT, !INT);
:: WindowTitle              ->   STRING;
:: ScrollBarDef             ->   ScrollBar ThumbValue ScrollValue;
:: ThumbValue               ->   Thumb INT;
:: ScrollValue              ->   Scroll INT;
:: MinimumWindowSize        ->   (!INT, !INT);
:: InitialWindowSize        ->   (!INT, !INT);
:: UpdateFunction UNQ s     ->   => UpdateArea (=> s (s, [DrawFunction]));
:: UpdateArea               ->   [Rectangle];

:: WindowAttribute UNQ s UNQ io
   ->   Activate      (WindowFunction s io)
   ->   Deactivate    (WindowFunction s io)
   ->   GoAway        (WindowFunction s io)
   ->   Mouse         SelectState (MouseFunction s io)
   ->   Keyboard      SelectState (KeyboardFunction s io)
   ->   Cursor        CursorShape
   ->   StandByWindow;

:: WindowFunction     UNQ s UNQ io ->   => s (=> io (s, io));
:: MouseFunction      UNQ s UNQ io ->   => MouseState (=> s (=> io (s, io)));
:: KeyboardFunction   UNQ s UNQ io ->   => KeyboardState (=> s (=> io (s, io)));

:: CursorShape ->     StandardCursor |  BusyCursor       |  IBeamCursor |
                      CrossCursor    |  FatCrossCursor   |  ArrowCursor |
                      HiddenCursor;
```

The dialog device: dialogs given in the initial I/O system will be opened as modeless dialogs. Use the Open(Modal)Dialog function (deltaDialog.icl) to open dialogs during the interaction. PropertyDialogs are special dialogs that can only be modeless. They are used to change certain properties (default values, preferences etc.) of a program. They have two predefined buttons: the Set and the Reset buttons. A CommandDialog can be any kind of dialog. A PropertyDialog is defined by the following attributes:

- DialogId: a number by which the programmer can refer to the dialog.
- DialogTitle: the title of the dialog.
- A list of attributes that may contain the following dialog attributes:
  - DialogPos: the position of the dialog on the screen.
  - DialogSize: the size of the dialog.
  - DialogMargin: the horizontal and vertical margins between the borders of the dialog and the items.
  - ItemSpace: the horizontal and vertical space between the items of the dialog.
  - StandByDialog: when this attribute is present the dialog will be a so-called stand-by dialog.

  When none of these attributes is specified the dialog is centred on the screen, a size is chosen such that all items fit in the dialog and save default margins, and item spaces are chosen.
- SetFunction/ResetFunction: the button function for the set/reset button.

- A list of DialogItems: other items such as CheckBoxes, Controls etc.

A CommandDialog also has an id, a title, a position, a size and a list of DialogItems. Furthermore it has the following attribute:

- DialogItemId: the item id of the default button.

In the AboutDialog, information about the application (version, authors etc.) can be presented. It may also contain a button that should provide a help facility. The first AboutDialog that is encountered in the initial dialog device becomes the AboutDialog of the application. Attempts to open AboutDialogs with Open(Modal)Dialog are ignored. The AboutDialog will be accessible by the user during the interaction in a system-dependent way.

```
:: DialogDef UNQ s UNQ io
   -> PropertyDialog     DialogId DialogTitle [DialogAttribute] (SetFunction s io)
                         (ResetFunction s io) [DialogItem s io]
   -> CommandDialog      DialogId DialogTitle [DialogAttribute] DialogItemId
                         [DialogItem s io]
   -> AboutDialog        ApplicationName PictureDomain [DrawFunction]
                         (AboutHelpDef s io);

:: DialogId           ->  INT;
:: DialogTitle        ->  STRING;
:: DialogAttribute    ->  DialogPos     Measure Measure
                      ->  DialogSize    Measure Measure
                      ->  DialogMargin  Measure Measure
                      ->  ItemSpace     Measure Measure
                      ->  StandByDialog;
:: Measure            ->  MM REAL | Inch REAL | Pixel INT;
:: ApplicationName    ->  STRING;
:: AboutHelpDef UNQ s UNQ io
   -> AboutHelp ItemTitle (AboutHelpFunction s io)
   -> NoHelp;
:: AboutHelpFunction UNQ s UNQ io   ->    => s (=> io (s, io));
```

A DialogItem can be a final button (DialogButton), a final button with a user-defined look (DialogIconButton), an unchangeable piece of text (StaticText), a changeable piece of text (DynamicText), an editable text field (EditText), a pop-up menu (DialogPopUp), a group of RadioButtons, a group of CheckBoxes, or a user-defined Control. The ItemPos specifies the position of the item relative to the other items. When the ItemPos is Left, Center or Right the item is placed left-aligned, centred or right-aligned, respectively, beneath all other items.

```
:: DialogItem UNQ s UNQ io
   -> DialogButton DialogItemId ItemPos ItemTitle SelectState
                         (ButtonFunction s io)
   -> DialogIconButton DialogItemId ItemPos PictureDomain IconLook
                         SelectState (ButtonFunction s io)
   -> StaticText DialogItemId ItemPos STRING
   -> DynamicText DialogItemId ItemPos TextWidth STRING
   -> EditText DialogItemId ItemPos TextWidth NrEditLines STRING
   -> DialogPopUp DialogItemId ItemPos SelectState DialogItemId
                         [RadioItemDef s io]
   -> RadioButtons DialogItemId ItemPos RowsOrColumns DialogItemId
                         [RadioItemDef s io]
   -> CheckBoxes DialogItemId ItemPos RowsOrColumns [CheckBoxDef s io]
   -> Control DialogItemId ItemPos PictureDomain SelectState ControlState
                         ControlLook ControlFeel (DialogFunction s io);

:: DialogItemId  ->   INT;
:: ItemPos       ->   Left | Center | Right | RightTo DialogItemId |
                      Below DialogItemId | XOffset DialogItemId Measure |
                      YOffset DialogItemId Measure | XY Measure Measure |
                      ItemBox INT INT INT INT;
```

```
:: IconLook       ->   => SelectState [DrawFunction];
:: TextWidth      ->   Measure;
:: NrEditLines    ->   INT;
:: RowsOrColumns   ->     Rows INT | Columns INT;

:: RadioItemDef UNQ s UNQ io
   -> RadioItem  DialogItemId ItemTitle SelectState (DialogFunction s io);
:: CheckBoxDef UNQ s UNQ io
   -> CheckBox  DialogItemId ItemTitle SelectState MarkState
                (DialogFunction s io);
```

Attributes of a user-defined Control: the ControlState can be a boolean, an integer, a real or a string. The look of the control is defined by the DrawFunctions (see deltaPicture.dcl) returned by the ControlLook function. The ControlFeel defines the way to respond to mouse clicks inside the control's picture domain.

```
:: ControlState ->    BoolCS BOOL          | IntCS INT            |
                      RealCS REAL          | StringCS STRING      |
                      ListCS [ControlState] | PairCS ControlState ControlState;
:: ControlLook  ->    => SelectState (=> ControlState [DrawFunction]);
:: ControlFeel  ->    => MouseState (=> ControlState
                                    (ControlState,[DrawFunction]));
```

Types of the several dialog item functions:

```
:: SetFunction      UNQ s UNQ io   ->    ButtonFunction s io;
:: ResetFunction    UNQ s UNQ io   ->    ButtonFunction s io;
:: DialogFunction   UNQ s UNQ io
     -> => DialogInfo (=> (DialogState s io) (DialogState s io));
:: ButtonFunction   UNQ s UNQ io
     -> => DialogInfo (=> s (=> io (s, io)));
```

A notice is a simple, modal dialog containing only text and final buttons. It can be used to inform the user about unusual or dangerous situations. A notice is defined by the following attributes:

- A list of STRINGs: each string is a line of the message of the notice.
- A NoticeButtonDef: the default button of the notice.
- A list of NoticeButtonDefs: the other buttons of the notice.

```
:: NoticeDef          -> Notice [STRING] NoticeButtonDef [NoticeButtonDef];
:: NoticeButtonDef    -> NoticeButton NoticeButtonId ItemTitle;
:: NoticeButtonId     -> INT;
```

Keyboard input: a window may respond to keyboard events. Each such event causes the KeyboardFunction to be evaluated. For certain special keys constants of type KeyCode are provided in deltaSystem.dcl.

```
:: KeyboardState   ->    (!KeyCode, !KeyState, !Modifiers);
:: KeyCode         ->    CHAR;
:: KeyState        ->    KeyUp | KeyDown | KeyStillDown;
```

Mouse input: windows and controls may respond to mouse events. Each such event causes the MouseFunction to be evaluated.

```
:: MouseState      ->    (!MousePosition, !ButtonState, !Modifiers);
:: MousePosition   ->    (!INT, !INT);
:: ButtonState     ->    ButtonUp | ButtonDown | ButtonDoubleDown    |
                         ButtonTripleDown | ButtonStillDown;
```

For each modifier or meta-key (Shift, Option (Alternate), Command, Control) a boolean in Modifiers indicates whether it was pressed (TRUE) or not (FALSE). On keyboards that have no Command key both the third and the fourth boolean in Modifiers become TRUE when Control is pressed.

```
:: Modifiers        ->     (!BOOL, !BOOL, !BOOL, !BOOL);
```

Other common types:

```
:: ItemTitle         ->    STRING;
:: SelectState       ->    Able | Unable;
:: MarkState         ->    Mark | NoMark;
:: PictureDomain     ->    Rectangle;
```

Operations on the timer device (deltaTimer)

```
DEFINITION MODULE deltaTimer;
IMPORT deltaIOSystem, deltaEventIO;
MACRO
   TicksPerSecond    ->    ... ;   == system dependent

TYPE
:: CurrentTime -> (!INT, !INT, !INT);
   (hours (0–23), minutes (0–59), seconds (0–59))
:: CurrentDate -> (!INT, !INT, !INT, !INT);
   (year, month (1–12), day (1–31), day of week (1–7, Sunday=1, Saturday=7))

RULE
:: OpenTimer    !(TimerDef s io)  !(IOState s)   ->   IOState s;
:: CloseTimer   !TimerId          !(IOState s)   ->   IOState s;
   Open (install) a new timer, close (remove) an existing timer.

:: EnableTimer  !TimerId     !(IOState s)   ->    IOState s;
:: DisableTimer !TimerId     !(IOState s)   ->    IOState s;
:: ChangeTimerFunction       !TimerId    !(TimerFunction s (IOState s))
                                                  !(IOState s)   ->    IOState s;
:: SetTimerInterval    !TimerId     !TimerInterval    !(IOState s)   ->    IOState s;
:: GetTimerBlinkInterval !(IOState s)    ->    (!TimerInterval, !IOState s);
   Enable, disable, change the TimerFunction and TimerInterval of a Timer. Get-
   TimerBlinkInterval returns the number of ticks that should pass between a blink of
   the cursor (also called caret time).

:: Wait     !TimerInterval    x        -> x;
:: UWait    !TimerInterval    UNQ x    -> UNQ x;
   Delay the evaluation of the second argument for a certain TimerInterval.

:: GetCurrentTime !(IOState s)    ->    (!CurrentTime,    !IOState s);
:: GetCurrentDate !(IOState s)    ->    (!CurrentDate,    !IOState s);
   GetCurrentTime / GetCurrentDate return the current time and date.
```

Operations on menus (deltaMenu)

```
DEFINITION MODULE deltaMenu;
IMPORT deltaIOSystem, deltaEventIO;
```

Menu operations on unknown MenuIds/MenuItemIds are ignored.

```
RULE
:: EnableMenuSystem     !(IOState s)    ->    IOState s;
:: DisableMenuSystem    !(IOState s)    ->    IOState s;
   Enable and disable the complete menu system. Enabling the menu system will
   make the previously enabled menus and menu items selectable again. Operations
```

on a disabled menu system take effect when the menu system is re-enabled.

```
:: EnableMenus    ![MenuId] !(IOState s) ->    IOState s;
:: DisableMenus   ![MenuId] !(IOState s) ->    IOState s;
```

Enable, disable menus. Disabling a menu causes its contents to be unselectable. Enabling a disabled menu with partially selectable contents causes the previously selectable items to become selectable again.

```
:: InsertMenuItems     !MenuItemGroupId !INT ![MenuElement s (IOState s)]
                                               !(IOState s)    ->    IOState s;
:: AppendMenuItems  !MenuItemGroupId !INT ![MenuElement s (IOState s)]
                                               !(IOState s)    ->    IOState s;
:: RemoveMenuItems            ![MenuItemId] !(IOState s)       ->    IOState s;
:: RemoveMenuGroupItems   !MenuItemGroupId ![INT]
                                               !(IOState s)    ->    IOState s;
```

Addition, removal of MenuItems in MenuItemGroups. InsertMenuItems inserts menu items before the item with the specified index, AppendMenuItems inserts them after that item. Items are numbered starting from one. Indices smaller than one or greater than the number of elements cause the elements to be inserted, respectively, before the first and after the last item in the group. Only (Check)MenuItems and MenuSeparators are added to MenuItemGroups. RemoveMenuItems only works on items that are in a MenuItemGroup. RemoveMenuGroupItems removes the items with the specified indices (counting from one) from the specified MenuItemGroup.

```
:: SelectMenuRadioItem     !MenuItemId !(IOState s)     ->     IOState s;
```

Select a MenuRadioItem: the mark will move from the currently selected item in the group to the item with the specified id.

```
:: EnableMenuItems   ![MenuItemId] !(IOState s)    ->    IOState s;
:: DisableMenuItems  ![MenuItemId] !(IOState s)    ->    IOState s;
:: MarkMenuItems     ![MenuItemId] !(IOState s)    ->    IOState s;
:: UnmarkMenuItems   ![MenuItemId] !(IOState s)    ->    IOState s;
:: ChangeMenuItemTitles ![(MenuItemId, STRING)] !(IOState s)   ->    IOState s;
:: ChangeMenuItemFunctions     ![(MenuItemId, MenuFunction s (IOState s))]
                                              !(IOState s)    ->    IOState s;
```

Enable, disable, mark, unmark, change titles and functions of MenuElements.

Operations on windows (deltaWindow)

```
DEFINITION MODULE deltaWindow;
IMPORT deltaIOSystem, deltaEventIO, deltaPicture;
```

Functions applied on non-existing windows or unknown WindowIds are ignored. Functions that operate on the active (or frontmost) window have the same effect as those operating on a (list of) WindowId(s) but are (slightly) faster.

```
RULE
:: OpenWindows          ![WindowDef s (IOState s)] !(IOState s)  ->     IOState s;
```

The windows are opened in the same order as specified in the list of WindowDefinitions. If one of these windows has the same WindowId as a window that is already open, then this window is not opened. Each new window is always the active window and is placed in front of all existing windows.

```
:: CloseWindows          ![WindowId] !(IOState s)  ->     IOState s;
```

The windows are closed in the same order as specified in the list.

```
:: CloseActiveWindow    !(IOState s)    ->     IOState s;
```

The active window is closed.

```
:: GetActiveWindow        !(IOState s)    ->     (!BOOL, !WindowId, !IOState s);
```
Returns the id of the active window. If there is no active window the boolean will be FALSE.

```
:: ActivateWindow         !WindowId !(IOState s)    ->     IOState s;
```
Activates the indicated window. No effect, if the window is already active.

```
:: ChangeUpdateFunction !WindowId !(UpdateFunction s) !(IOState s)-> IOState s;
:: ChangeActiveUpdateFunction !(UpdateFunction s) !(IOState s) -> IOState s;
```
Change the update function of the indicated window.

```
:: ChangeWindowTitle    !WindowId !WindowTitle !(IOState s) ->    IOState s;
:: ChangeActiveWindowTitle   !WindowTitle !(IOState s)      ->    IOState s;
```
Change the window title of the indicated window.

```
:: ChangeWindowCursor !WindowId !CursorShape !(IOState s)   ->    IOState s;
:: ChangeActiveWindowCursor   !CursorShape !(IOState s)     ->    IOState s;
```
Change the local cursor shape of a window. When the mouse pointer moves over the content region of the window the cursor will take the indicated shape.

```
TYPE
:: ScrollBarChange
   ->    ChangeThumbs INT INT   == set new horizontal and vertical thumb values
   |     ChangeScrolls INT INT  == set new horizontal and vertical scroll values
   |     ChangeHThumb INT       == set new horizontal thumb value
   |     ChangeVThumb INT       == set new vertical thumb value
   |     ChangeHScroll INT      == set new horizontal scroll value
   |     ChangeVScroll INT      == set new vertical scroll value
   |     ChangeHBar INT INT     == set new horizontal thumb and scroll values
   |     ChangeVBar INT INT;    == set new vertical thumb and scroll values
```

```
RULE
:: ChangeScrollBar !WindowId !ScrollBarChange !s !(IOState s) -> (!s, !IOState s);
:: ChangeActiveScrollBar !ScrollBarChange !s !(IOState s) ->    (!s, !IOState s);
```
Change the scroll bar(s) of a window according to the ScrollBarChange.

```
:: ChangePictureDomain !WindowId !PictureDomain !s !(IOState s)
                                                   -> (!s, !IOState s);
:: ChangeActivePictureDomain !PictureDomain !s !(IOState s) -> (!s, !IOState s);
```
Change the PictureDomain of the indicated window. The settings of the scroll bars are automatically adjusted. Windows will be resized in cases where the size of the new PictureDomain is smaller than the current size of the window.

```
:: DrawInWindow !WindowId   ![DrawFunction] !(IOState s)    ->    IOState s;
:: DrawInActiveWindow       ![DrawFunction] !(IOState s)    ->    IOState s;
```
Apply the list of DrawFunctions (see deltaPicture.dcl) to the Picture of the window in the given order.

```
:: DrawInWindowFrame !WindowId !(UpdateFunction s) !s !(IOState s)
                                                   -> (!s, !IOState s);
:: DrawInActiveWindowFrame !(UpdateFunction s) !s !(IOState s)-> (!s,!IOState s);
```
The UpdateFunction has a list of visible rectangles as parameter. Using this list it is possible to return a list of drawing functions that only draw in the visible part of the window.

```
:: WindowGetFrame !WindowId !(IOState s)  ->    (!PictureDomain, !IOState s);
:: ActiveWindowGetFrame  !(IOState s)     ->    (!PictureDomain, !IOState s);
```
Return the visible part of the Picture of the indicated window in terms of the PictureDomain. Returns ((0, 0), (0, 0)), if the indicated window does not exist.

```
:: EnableKeyboard          !WindowId !(IOState s)    ->    IOState s;
:: DisableKeyboard         !WindowId !(IOState s)    ->    IOState s;
:: EnableActiveKeyboard    !(IOState s)              ->    IOState s;
:: DisableActiveKeyboard   !(IOState s)              ->    IOState s;
:: ChangeKeyboardFunction   !WindowId !(KeyboardFunction s (IOState s))
                                         !(IOState s)    ->    IOState s;
:: ChangeActiveKeyboardFunction !(KeyboardFunction s (IOState s))
                                         !(IOState s)    ->    IOState s;
```

Enable, disable, change KeyboardFunction of a window.

```
:: EnableMouse        !WindowId !(IOState s)    ->    IOState s;
:: DisableMouse       !WindowId !(IOState s)    ->    IOState s;
:: EnableActiveMouse  !(IOState s)              ->    IOState s;
:: DisableActiveMouse !(IOState s)              ->    IOState s;
:: ChangeMouseFunction !WindowId !(MouseFunction s (IOState s)) !(IOState s)
                                                  -> IOState s;
:: ChangeActiveMouseFunction !(MouseFunction s (IOState s)) !(IOState s)
                                                  -> IOState s;
```

Enable, disable, change MouseFunction of a window.

Operations on dialogs (deltaDialog)

DEFINITION MODULE **deltaDialog**;
IMPORT deltaIOSystem, deltaEventIO;

Functions applied on non-existent dialogs or unknown ids are ignored.

```
TYPE
:: DialogChange s -> => (DialogState s (IOState s)) (DialogState s (IOState s));
```

RULE

OpenDialog opens a PropertyDialog or CommandDialog as a modeless dialog.

```
:: OpenDialog !(DialogDef s (IOState s)) !(IOState s) -> IOState s;
```

OpenModalDialog opens a CommandDialog as a modal dialog. The function terminates when the dialog is closed (by means of Close(Active)Dialog). Attempts to open property dialogs with this function are ignored.

```
:: OpenModalDialog !(DialogDef s (IOState s)) !s !(IOState s) -> (!s, !IOState s);
```

Close(Active)Dialog closes the indicated dialog.

```
:: CloseDialog !DialogId !(IOState s) -> IOState s;
:: CloseActiveDialog !(IOState s) -> IOState s;
```

OpenNotice opens a notice and returns the id of the selected notice button.

```
:: OpenNotice !NoticeDef !(IOState s) -> (!NoticeButtonId, !IOState s);
```

A Beep is the simplest kind of notice.

```
:: Beep !(IOState s) -> IOState s;
```

With the following functions the state of dialog items can be changed. They have no effect when an id is specified for an item for which the state change is invalid.

```
:: EnableDialogItems       ![DialogItemId] !(DialogState s (IOState s))
                            ->    DialogState s (IOState s);
:: DisableDialogItems      ![DialogItemId] !(DialogState s (IOState s))
                            ->    DialogState s (IOState s);
```

```
:: MarkCheckBoxes          ![DialogItemId] !(DialogState s (IOState s))
                           ->    DialogState s (IOState s);
:: UnmarkCheckBoxes        ![DialogItemId] !(DialogState s (IOState s))
                           ->    DialogState s (IOState s);
:: SelectDialogRadioItem   !DialogItemId !(DialogState s (IOState s))
                           ->    DialogState s (IOState s);
:: ChangeEditText          !DialogItemId !STRING !(DialogState s (IOState s))
                           ->    DialogState s (IOState s);
:: ChangeDynamicText       !DialogItemId !STRING !(DialogState s (IOState s))
                           ->    DialogState s (IOState s);
:: ChangeIconLook          !DialogItemId !IconLook !(DialogState s (IOState s))
                           ->    DialogState s (IOState s);
```

Functions to change state, look and feel (behaviour) of Controls. When the id is not the id of a Control the functions have no effect.

```
:: ChangeControlState   !DialogItemId !ControlState !(DialogState s (IOState s))
                        ->    DialogState s (IOState s);
:: ChangeControlLook    !DialogItemId !ControlLook !(DialogState s (IOState s))
                        ->    DialogState s (IOState s);
:: ChangeControlFeel    !DialogItemId !ControlFeel !(DialogState s (IOState s))
                        ->    DialogState s (IOState s);
```

Functions to change the functions related to dialog items.

```
:: ChangeDialogFunction    !DialogItemId !(DialogFunction s (IOState s))
                        !(DialogState s (IOState s)) -> DialogState s (IOState s);
:: ChangeButtonFunction    !DialogItemId !(ButtonFunction s (IOState s))
                        !(DialogState s (IOState s)) -> DialogState s (IOState s);
:: ChangeSetFunction       !(SetFunction s (IOState s))
                        !(DialogState s (IOState s)) -> DialogState s (IOState s);
:: ChangeResetFunction     !(ResetFunction s (IOState s))
                        !(DialogState s (IOState s)) -> DialogState s (IOState s);
```

Get(Active)DialogInfo returns the current settings (DialogInfo) of the indicated dialog. The boolean indicates whether the indicated dialog is open. When it is FALSE a dummy DialogInfo is returned.

```
:: GetDialogInfo !DialogId   !(IOState s)   ->   (!BOOL, !DialogInfo, !IOState s);
:: GetActiveDialogInfo       !(IOState s)   ->   (!BOOL, !DialogInfo, !IOState s);
```

DialogStateGetDialogInfo returns the DialogInfo corresponding to a DialogState.

```
:: DialogStateGetDialogInfo     !(DialogState s (IOState s))
   ->    (!DialogInfo, !DialogState s (IOState s));
```

The following functions return the current settings of certain dialog items (those that can be changed by the user). When the corresponding item does not exist a run-time error occurs. The id passed to GetSelectedRadioItemId must be the id of a DialogPopUp or a group of RadioButtons. The function CheckBoxesMarked returns the settings of a group of CheckBoxes. The id passed to it must be the id of such a group.

```
:: GetEditText              !DialogItemId !DialogInfo  ->  STRING;
:: GetSelectedRadioItemId   !DialogItemId !DialogInfo  ->  DialogItemId;
:: CheckBoxesMarked         !DialogItemId !DialogInfo  ->  [(DialogItemId, BOOL)];
:: CheckBoxMarked           !DialogItemId !DialogInfo  ->  BOOL;
:: GetControlState          !DialogItemId !DialogInfo  ->  ControlState;
```

ChangeDialog can be used to modify open dialogs.

```
:: ChangeDialog   !DialogId   ![DialogChange s]   !(IOState s)   ->   IOState s;
```

The file selector dialogs (deltaFileSelect)

DEFINITION MODULE **deltaFileSelect**;
IMPORT deltaFile, deltaEventIO;

With the functions defined in this module, standard file selector dialogs can be opened, which provide a user-friendly way to select input or output files. The layout of these dialogs depends on the operating system.

RULE

```
:: SelectInputFile !FILES !(IOState s)    -> (!BOOL, !STRING, !FILES, !IOState s);
```

Opens a dialog in which the user can traverse the file system to indicate an existing file. The Boolean result indicates whether the user has pressed the Open button (TRUE) or the Cancel button (FALSE). The STRING result is the complete path name of the selected file. If the Cancel button has been pressed, an empty string will be returned.

```
:: SelectOutputFile !STRING !STRING !FILES !(IOState s)
   ->    (!BOOL, !STRING, !FILES, !IOState s);
```

Opens a dialog in which the user can specify the name of a file that should be created in a certain directory. The first parameter is the prompt of the dialog (default: "Save As:"). The second parameter is the default file name. The Boolean result indicates whether the user has pressed the Save button (TRUE) or the Cancel button (FALSE). The STRING result is the complete path name of the selected file. If the Cancel button has been pressed, an empty string will be returned. When a file with the indicated name already exists in the indicated directory a confirm dialog will be opened after pressing Save.

Predefined Controls (deltaControls)

DEFINITION MODULE **deltaControls**;
IMPORT deltaIOSystem, deltaEventIO;

General scrolling list and slider bar definition. These predefined dialog items are implemented entirely in Concurrent Clean as a user-defined Control.

TYPE

```
:: NrVisible        -> INT;
:: SliderDirection  -> Horizontal | Vertical;
:: SliderPos        -> INT;
:: SliderMax        -> INT;
```

RULE

A ScrollingList is defined by the following attributes:

- Id, ItemPos and SelectState (like other dialog items).
- The minimum width of the scrolling list (Measure).
  This attribute is important only when ChangeScrollingList is used. Use a minimum width of zero when the scrolling list is not changed.
- The number of items that is visible in the list (NrVisible).
- The item that is initially selected (ItemTitle).
- The list of items ([ItemTitle]).
- A DialogFunction that is called whenever a new item is selected.

The function ScrollingList returns a DialogItem (a Control) that can be used in any dialog definition.

```
:: ScrollingList !DialogItemId !ItemPos !Measure !SelectState !NrVisible !ItemTitle
      ![ItemTitle] !(DialogFunction s (IOState s))  ->     DialogItem s (IOState s);
```

With ChangeScrollingList the items in the scrolling list can be changed. Its arguments are the id of the scrolling list, the newly selected item and the new list of items. When the id is not the id of a ScrollingList a run-time error is generated.

```
:: ChangeScrollingList !DialogItemId !ItemTitle ![ItemTitle]
      !(DialogState s (IOState s))  ->    DialogState s (IOState s);
```

GetScrollingListItem returns the currently selected item in the scrolling list with the indicated id from the DialogInfo parameter. When the id is not the id of a ScrollingList a run-time error is generated.

```
:: GetScrollingListItem    !DialogItemId !DialogInfo    ->    ItemTitle;
```

A SliderBar is defined by the following attributes:

- Id, ItemPos and SelectState, like other DialogItems.
- SliderDirection: Horizontal or Vertical.
- SliderPos: the initial position of the slider. This position is always adjusted between 0 and SliderMax.
- SliderMax: the slider can take on positions between 0 and SliderMax.
- A DialogFunction that is called whenever the slider moves.

```
:: SliderBar !DialogItemId !ItemPos !SelectState !SliderDirection !SliderPos
      !SliderMax !(DialogFunction s (IOState s))  ->    DialogItem s (IOState s);
```

ChangeSliderBar moves the slider of the indicated slider bar to the new position. The position is always adjusted between 0 and SliderMax.

```
:: ChangeSliderBar !DialogItemId !SliderPos !(DialogState s (IOState s))
   ->    DialogState s (IOState s);
```

GetSliderPosition returns the current slider position of the slider bar with the indicated id from the DialogInfo parameter. When the id is not the id of a SliderBar a run-time error is generated.

```
:: GetSliderPosition    !DialogItemId !DialogInfo    ->    SliderPos;
```

Miscellaneous operations (deltaIOState)

DEFINITION MODULE **deltaIOState**;
IMPORT deltaIOSystem, deltaEventIO;
RULE

```
:: SetGlobalCursor    !CursorShape    !(IOState s)    ->    IOState s;
```

Sets the shape of the cursor (mouse pointer) globally. This shape overrules the local cursor shapes of windows. Attempts to set the global cursor to HiddenCursor are ignored.

```
:: ResetCursor  !(IOState s)    ->    IOState s;
```

Undoes the effect of SetGlobalCursor. It resets the cursor to the standard shape outside windows with a local cursor shape and to the local shape inside such windows.

```
:: ObscureCursor  !(IOState s)    ->    IOState s;
```

Hides the cursor until the next time that the mouse is moved.

```
:: SetDoubleDownDistance    !INT  !(IOState s)    ->    IOState s;
```

Set the maximum distance (in pixels) between two mouse clicks such that they will be treated as a ButtonDoubleDown or ButtonTripleDown.

Operations on pictures (deltaPicture)

```
DEFINITION MODULE deltaPicture;
IMPORT deltaFont;
ABSTYPE
:: UNQ Picture;

TYPE
:: DrawFunction    ->     => Picture Picture;
```

The predefined figures that can be drawn:

```
:: Point              ->    (!INT, !INT);
:: Line               ->    (!Point, !Point);
:: Curve              ->    (!Oval, !INT, !INT);
:: Rectangle          ->    (!Point, !Point);
:: RoundRectangle     ->    (!Rectangle, !INT, !INT);
:: Oval               ->    Rectangle;
:: Circle             ->    (!Point, !INT);
:: Wedge              ->    (!Oval, !INT, !INT);
:: Polygon            ->    (!Point, !PolygonShape);
:: PolygonShape       ->    [Vector];
:: Vector             ->    (!INT, !INT);
```

The pen attributes influence the way figures are drawn. The PenMode also influences the way text is drawn. The Not... modes do not work when text is drawn. When the PenMode is a Not... mode text is drawn in OrMode.

```
:: PenSize      ->  (!INT, !INT);
:: PenMode      ->  CopyMode       | OrMode          | XorMode        |
                    ClearMode      | NotCopyMode     | NotOrMode      |
                    NotXorMode     | NotClearMode    | HiliteMode;
:: PenPattern   ->  BlackPattern   | DkGreyPattern   | GreyPattern    |
                    LtGreyPattern  | WhitePattern;
```

The predefined colours:

```
:: Colour ->  RGB REAL REAL REAL         |
              BlackColour | WhiteColour | BlueColour   | CyanColour |
              RedColour   | GreenColour | YellowColour | MagentaColour;

MACRO
   MinRGB  ->   0.0;
   MaxRGB  ->   1.0;

RULE
```

Rules setting the attributes of a Picture:

SetPenSize (w, h) sets the PenSize to w pixels wide and h pixels high.
SetPenMode sets the drawing mode of the pen.
SetPenPattern sets the pattern of the pen.
SetPenNormal sets the PenSize to (1,1), the PenMode to CopyMode and the PenPattern to BlackPattern.

```
:: SetPenSize     !PenSize     !Picture ->   Picture;
:: SetPenMode     !PenMode     !Picture ->   Picture;
:: SetPenPattern  !PenPattern  !Picture ->   Picture;
:: SetPenNormal                !Picture ->   Picture;
```

Colour: there are two types of Colour: RGB colours and basic colours. An RGB colour defines the amount of red (r), green (g) and blue (b) in a certain colour by the tuple (r,g,b). These are REAL values and each of them must be between MinRGB and MaxRGB (0.0 and 1.0). The colour black is defined by (MinRGB, MinRGB, MinRGB) and white by (MaxRGB, MaxRGB, MaxRGB). Given an RGB colour, all amounts are adjusted between MinRGB and MaxRGB.

SetPenColour sets the colour of the pen.
SetBackColour sets the background colour.

```
:: SetPenColour    !Colour !Picture  ->    Picture;
:: SetBackColour   !Colour !Picture  ->    Picture;
```

Fonts: the initial font of a Picture is the default font (see deltaFont.dcl).

SetFont sets a new complete Font in the Picture.
SetFontName sets a new font without changing the style or size.
SetFontStyle sets a new style without changing font or size.
SetFontSize sets a new size without changing font or style. The size is always adjusted between MinFontSize and MaxFontSize (see deltaFont.dcl).

```
:: SetFont          !Font          !Picture ->    Picture;
:: SetFontName      !FontName      !Picture ->    Picture;
:: SetFontStyle     ![FontStyle]   !Picture ->    Picture;
:: SetFontSize      !FontSize      !Picture ->    Picture;
```

PictureCharWidth (PictureStringWidth) yield the width of the given CHAR (STRING) given the current font of the Picture. PictureFontMetrics yields the FontInfo of the current font.

```
:: PictureCharWidth    !CHAR     !Picture ->    (!INT,       !Picture);
:: PictureStringWidth  !STRING   !Picture ->    (!INT,       !Picture);
:: PictureFontMetrics            !Picture ->    (!FontInfo,  !Picture);
```

Absolute and relative pen move operations without drawing.

```
:: MovePenTo   !Point   !Picture ->    Picture;
:: MovePen     !Vector  !Picture ->    Picture;
```

Absolute and relative pen move operations with drawing.

```
:: LinePenTo   !Point   !Picture ->    Picture;
:: LinePen     !Vector  !Picture ->    Picture;
```

DrawChar (DrawString) draws a character (string) in the current font. The baseline of the characters is the *y*-coordinate of the pen. The new position of the pen is directly after the (last) character (of the string).

```
:: DrawChar     !CHAR     !Picture ->    Picture;
:: DrawString   !STRING   !Picture ->    Picture;
```

All following rules do not change the position of the pen after drawing.

Draw(C)Point draws the pixel (in the given colour) in the Picture.
Draw(C)Line draws the line (in the given colour) in the Picture.
Draw(C)Curve draws the curve (in the given colour) in the Picture. A Curve is a part of an Oval o starting from angle a up to angle b (both in degrees modulo 360): (o, a, b). Angles are always taken anticlockwise, starting from 3 o'clock.

```
:: DrawPoint    !Point   !Picture ->    Picture;
:: DrawLine     !Line    !Picture ->    Picture;
:: DrawCurve    !Curve   !Picture ->    Picture;
:: DrawCPoint   !Point   !Colour  !Picture ->    Picture;
:: DrawCLine    !Line    !Colour  !Picture ->    Picture;
```

```
:: DrawCCurve !Curve !Colour !Picture -> Picture;
```

A Rectangle is defined by two diagonal corner points.
DrawRectangle draws the edges of the rectangle.
FillRectangle draws the edges and interior of the rectangle.
EraseRectangle erases the edges and interior of the rectangle.
InvertRectangle inverts the edges and interior of the rectangle.
MoveRectangleTo moves the contents of the rectangle to a new top-left corner.
MoveRectangle moves the contents of the rectangle over the given vector.
CopyRectangleTo copies the contents of the rectangle to a new top-left corner.
CopyRectangle moves the contents of the rectangle over the given vector, but leaves the original untouched.

```
:: DrawRectangle   !Rectangle  !Picture ->  Picture;
:: FillRectangle   !Rectangle  !Picture ->  Picture;
:: EraseRectangle  !Rectangle  !Picture ->  Picture;
:: InvertRectangle !Rectangle  !Picture ->  Picture;

:: MoveRectangleTo  !Rectangle !Point  !Picture ->  Picture;
:: MoveRectangle    !Rectangle !Vector !Picture ->  Picture;
:: CopyRectangleTo  !Rectangle !Point  !Picture ->  Picture;
:: CopyRectangle    !Rectangle !Vector !Picture ->  Picture;
```

Rounded corner rectangles: a RoundRectangle with enclosing Rectangle r and corner curvatures x and y is defined by the tuple (r, x, y). x and y define the horizontal and vertical diameter of the corner curves. They are always adjusted between 0 and the width (height) of r.

```
:: DrawRoundRectangle    !RoundRectangle  !Picture ->  Picture;
:: FillRoundRectangle    !RoundRectangle  !Picture ->  Picture;
:: EraseRoundRectangle   !RoundRectangle  !Picture ->  Picture;
:: InvertRoundRectangle  !RoundRectangle  !Picture ->  Picture;
```

An Oval is defined by its enclosing Rectangle.

```
:: DrawOval   !Oval  !Picture ->  Picture;
:: FillOval   !Oval  !Picture ->  Picture;
:: EraseOval  !Oval  !Picture ->  Picture;
:: InvertOval !Oval  !Picture ->  Picture;
```

A Circle with centre c (a Point) and radius r (an INT) is defined by the tuple (c, r).

```
:: DrawCircle    !Circle  !Picture ->  Picture;
:: FillCircle    !Circle  !Picture ->  Picture;
:: EraseCircle   !Circle  !Picture ->  Picture;
:: InvertCircle  !Circle  !Picture ->  Picture;
```

A Wedge is a part of an Oval o starting from angle a up to angle b (both in degrees modulo 360): (o, a, b). Angles are taken anticlockwise, starting from 3 o'-clock.

```
:: DrawWedge   !Wedge  !Picture ->  Picture;
:: FillWedge   !Wedge  !Picture ->  Picture;
:: EraseWedge  !Wedge  !Picture ->  Picture;
:: InvertWedge !Wedge  !Picture ->  Picture;
```

A Polygon is a figure drawn by a number of lines without taking the pen off the Picture, starting from and ending at some Point p. The PolygonShape is a list of Vectors ($[v_1,...,v_n]$) that defines how the Polygon is drawn: (p, $[v_1,...,v_n]$).

ScalePolygon scales the polygon. Non-positive scale factors are allowed.
MovePolygonTo changes the starting point into the given Point and

MovePolygon moves the starting point by the given Vector.

```
:: ScalePolygon     !INT    !Polygon  ->   Polygon;
:: MovePolygonTo    !Point  !Polygon  ->   Polygon;
:: MovePolygon      !Vector !Polygon  ->   Polygon;

:: DrawPolygon      !Polygon  !Picture ->  Picture;
:: FillPolygon      !Polygon  !Picture ->  Picture;
:: ErasePolygon     !Polygon  !Picture ->  Picture;
:: InvertPolygon    !Polygon  !Picture ->  Picture;
```

Operations on fonts (deltaFont)

```
DEFINITION MODULE deltaFont;
ABSTYPE
:: Font;

TYPE
:: FontName ->    STRING;
:: FontStyle  ->  STRING;
:: FontSize   ->  INT;
:: FontInfo   ->  (!INT, !INT, !INT, !INT);

MACRO
   MinFontSize ->   ... ;      == system dependent
   MaxFontSize ->   ... ;      == system dependent

RULE
```

SelectFont creates the font as specified by the name, the stylistic variations and size. The size is always adjusted between MinFontSize and MaxFontSize. The Boolean result is TRUE if the font is available and need not be scaled. In cases where the font is not available, the default font is chosen in the specified style and size.

```
:: SelectFont    !FontName ![FontStyle] !FontSize ->    (!BOOL, !Font);
```

DefaultFont returns the default font, specified by name, style and size.

```
:: DefaultFont  ->    (!FontName, ![FontStyle], !FontSize);
```

FontNames returns the FontNames of all available fonts.
FontStyles returns the available FontStyles for a certain font.
FontSizes returns all FontSizes of a font that are available without scaling.
In cases where the font is not available, the styles or sizes of the default font are returned.

```
:: FontNames                     ->   [FontName];
:: FontStyles     !FontName      ->   [FontStyle];
:: FontSizes      !FontName      ->   [FontSize];
```

FontCharWidth(s) and FontStringWidth(s) return the width(s) in terms of pixels of given character(s) or string(s) in a certain Font.

```
:: FontCharWidth       !CHAR      !Font    ->    INT;
:: FontCharWidths      ![CHAR]    !Font    ->    [INT];
:: FontStringWidth     !STRING    !Font    ->    INT;
:: FontStringWidths    ![STRING]  !Font    ->    [INT];
```

FontMetrics yields the FontInfo in terms of pixels of a given Font. The FontInfo is a 4-tuple (ascent, descent, maxwidth, leading), which defines the font metrics:

- ascent is the maximum height of a character measured from the base line.

- descent is the maximum depth of a character measured from the base line.
- maxwidth is the width of the widest character.
- leading is the vertical distance between two lines of the same font.

The full height of a line is the sum of the ascent, descent and leading.

```
:: FontMetrics   !Font   ->   FontInfo;
```

System-dependent constants and functions (deltaSystem)

DEFINITION MODULE **deltaSystem**;
MACRO
Keyboard constants (of type KeyCode):

```
UpKey        -> ...;          BackSpKey   -> ...;
DownKey      -> ...;          DelKey      -> ...;
LeftKey      -> ...;          TabKey      -> ...;
RightKey     -> ...;          ReturnKey   -> ...;
PgUpKey      -> ...;          EnterKey    -> ...;
PgDownKey    -> ...;          EscapeKey   -> ...;
BeginKey     -> ...;          HelpKey     -> ...;
EndKey       -> ...;
```

Separator between directory and filenames in a pathname (of type CHAR):

```
DirSeparator    -> ...;
```

Constants to check which of the meta-keys (modifiers) is down (of type Modifiers):

```
ShiftOnly       -> (TRUE,FALSE,FALSE,FALSE);
OptionOnly      -> (FALSE,TRUE,FALSE,FALSE);
CommandOnly     -> ...;   == depends on whether the keyboard of the system
ControlOnly     -> ...;   == has a Command key.
```

The minimum and maximum sizes of a picture domain (of type INT):

```
MinPictureDomain -> ...;          MaxPictureDomain -> ...;
```

RULE
The function HomePath prefixes the pathname given to it with the full pathname of the home directory of the user (on single-user systems this is the current working directory). ApplicationPath prefixes the pathname given to it with the full pathname of the directory in which the application resides.

```
:: HomePath           !STRING  -> STRING;
:: ApplicationPath    !STRING  -> STRING;
```

Functions to retrieve the horizontal and vertical screen resolution.

```
:: MMToHorPixels     !REAL  ->   INT;
:: MMToVerPixels     !REAL  ->   INT;
:: InchToHorPixels   !REAL  ->   INT;
:: InchToVerPixels   !REAL  ->   INT;
```

The maximum width and height for the indicated type of window such that the window will fit on the screen. For FixedWindows this is the maximum size of the PictureDomain such that the window does not become a ScrollWindow.

```
:: MaxScrollWindowSize   ->   (!INT, !INT);
:: MaxFixedWindowSize    ->   (!INT, !INT);
```

Appendix C
ABC machine specification

This appendix summarizes the machine instructions of the ABC machine. The most representative instructions (marked with •) are formally specified together with the used micro-instructions. The actual ABC machine (Koopman *et al.*,1990) has some facilities (such as directives and calling external functions) that are not included here.

C.1 The ABC instruction set

```
state = = (astack,bstack,cstack,graphstore,descrstore,pc,programstore,io)
instruction     = =   state -> state

a_dst       = =   nat
a_src       = =   nat
ap_entry    = =   instrid
arg_nr      = =   nat
arity       = =   nat
b_dst       = =   nat
b_src       = =   nat
c_src       = =   nat
descrid     = =   num
graph       = =   [node]

int         = =   num
instrid     = =   num
name        = =   [char]
nat         = =   num
nodeid      = =   nat
nodeid_seq  = =   [nodeid]
nr_args     = =   nat
real        = =   num
string      = =   [char]
```

Instruction set

```
•  add_args          ::  a_src -> nr_args -> a_dst -> instruction
•  create            ::  instruction
•  del_args          ::  a_src -> nr_args -> a_dst -> instruction
•  eq_descr          ::  descrid -> a_src -> instruction
•  eq_descr_arity    ::  descrid -> arity -> a_src -> instruction
•  eq_symbol         ::  a_src -> a_src -> instruction
•  eqB               ::  instruction
•  eqB_a             ::  bool -> a_src -> instruction
•  eqB_b             ::  bool -> b_src -> instruction
   eqC_a             ::  char -> a_src -> instruction
   eqC_b             ::  char -> b_src -> instruction
```

```
• eqI               :: instruction
• eqI_a             :: int -> a_src -> instruction
• eqI_b             :: int -> b_src -> instruction
  eqR_a             :: real -> a_src -> instruction
  eqR_b             :: real -> b_src -> instruction
  eqS_a             :: string -> a_src -> instruction
• fill              :: descrid -> nr_args -> instrid -> a_dst -> instruction
• fill_a            :: a_src -> a_dst -> instruction
• fillB             :: bool -> a_dst -> instruction
• fillB_b           :: b_src -> a_dst -> instruction
  fillC             :: char -> a_dst -> instruction
  fillC_b           :: b_src -> a_dst -> instruction
• fillI             :: int -> a_dst -> instruction
• fillI_b           :: b_src -> a_dst -> instruction
  fillR             :: real -> a_dst -> instruction
  fillR_b           :: b_src -> a_dst -> instruction
  fillS             :: string -> a_dst -> instruction
  fillS_symbol      :: a_src -> a_dst -> instruction
• get_descr_arity   :: a_src -> instruction
• get_node_arity    :: a_src -> instruction
• halt              :: instruction
• jmp               :: instrid -> instruction
• jmp_eval          :: instruction
• jmp_false         :: instrid -> instruction
• jmp_true          :: instrid -> instruction
• jsr               :: instrid -> instruction
• jsr_eval          :: instruction
• no_op             :: instruction
• pop_a             :: nr_args -> instruction
• pop_b             :: nr_args -> instruction
• print             :: string -> instruction
• print_symbol      :: a_src -> instruction
• push_a            :: a_src -> instruction
• push_ap_entry     :: a_src -> instruction
• push_arg          :: a_src -> arity -> arg_nr -> instruction
• push_arg_b        :: a_src -> instruction
• push_args         :: a_src -> arity -> nr_args -> instruction
• push_args_b       :: a_src -> instruction
• push_b            :: b_src -> instruction
• pushB             :: bool -> instruction
• pushB_a           :: a_src -> instruction
  pushC             :: char -> instruction
  pushC_a           :: a_src -> instruction
• pushI             :: int -> instruction
• pushI_a           :: a_src -> instruction
  pushF_a           :: a_src -> instruction
  pushR             :: real -> instruction
  pushR_a           :: a_src -> instruction
• repl_args         :: arity -> nr_args -> instruction
• repl_args_b       :: instruction
• rtn               :: instruction
• set_entry         :: instrid -> a_dst -> instruction
• update_a          :: a_src -> a_dst -> instruction
• update_b          :: b_src -> b_dst -> instruction

• addI              :: instruction
• decI              :: instruction
  divI              :: instruction
• gtI               :: instruction
• incI              :: instruction
• ltI               :: instruction
• mulI              :: instruction
  modI              :: instruction
```

```
• subI          :: instruction

  acosR         :: instruction
  addR          :: instruction
  asinR         :: instruction
  atabR         :: instruction
  cosR          :: instruction
  decR          :: instruction
  divR          :: instruction
  entierR       :: instruction
  expR          :: instruction
  incR          :: instruction
  gtR           :: instruction
  lnR           :: instruction
  log10R        :: instruction
  ltR           :: instruction
  mulR          :: instruction
  powR          :: instruction
  remR          :: instruction
  sinR          :: instruction
  sqrtR         :: instruction
  subR          :: instruction
  tanR          :: instruction

  catS          :: instruction
  cmpS          :: instruction
  indexS        :: instruction
  lenS          :: instruction
  sliceS        :: instruction
  updateS       :: instruction

  andBit        :: instruction
  notBit        :: instruction
  orBit         :: instruction
  xorBit        :: instruction
  shiftlBit     :: instruction
  shiftrBit     :: instruction

  andB          :: instruction
  notB          :: instruction
  orB           :: instruction

  gtC           :: instruction
  ltC           :: instruction

  convertCtoI   :: instruction
  convertItoC   :: instruction
  convertItoR   :: instruction
  convertRtoI   :: instruction

  endF     :: instruction
  getFC    :: instruction
  getFS    :: a_dst -> instruction
  openF    :: a_src->a_src->instruction
  putFC    :: instruction
  putFS    :: a_src -> instruction
  reopenF:: instruction
```

Specification of representative instructions

```
int_descr      = 0
bool_descr     = 1
rnf_entry      = 1

add_args a_src nr_args a_dst (as,bs,cs,gs,ds,pc,ps,io)
  = (as',bs,cs,gs',ds,pc,ps,io)
    where as'        = as_popn nr_args as
          gs'        = gs_update dstid (n_fill descrid entry newargs) gs
          dstid      = as_get a_dst as
          srcid      = as_get a_src as
          node       = gs_get srcid gs
          descrid    = n_descrid node
          entry      = n_entry node
          newargs    = n_args node arity ++ as_topn nr_args as
          arity      = n_arity node

create (as,bs,cs,gs,ds,pc,ps,io)
  = (as',bs,cs,gs',ds,pc,ps,io)
    where as'            = as_push nodeid as
          (gs',nodeid)   = gs_newnode gs

del_args a_src nr_args a_dst (as,bs,cs,gs,ds,pc,ps,io)
  = (as,bs,cs,gs',ds,pc,ps,io)
    where gs'        = gs_update dstid (n_fill descrid entry newargs) gs
          dstid      = as_get a_dst as
          srcid      = as_get a_src as
          node       = gs_get srcid gs
          descrid    = n_descrid node
          entry      = n_entry node
```

```
                newargs    = n_nargs node (arity – nr_args) arity
                arity      = n_arity node

eq_descr descrid a_src (as,bs,cs,gs,ds,pc,ps,io)
   = (as,bs',cs,gs,ds,pc,ps,io)
     where  bs'        = bs_pushB equal bs
            equal      = n_eq_descrid node descrid
            node       = gs_get nodeid gs
            nodeid     = as_get a_src as

eq_descr_arity descrid arity a_src (as,bs,cs,gs,ds,pc,ps,io)
   = (as,bs',cs,gs,ds,pc,ps,io)
     where  bs'        = bs_pushB equal bs
            equal      = n_eq_descrid node descrid & n_eq_arity node arity
            node       = gs_get nodeid gs
            nodeid     = as_get a_src as

eq_symbol a_src1 a_src2 (as,bs,cs,gs,ds,pc,ps,io)
   = (as,bs',cs,gs,ds,pc,ps,io)
     where  bs'        = bs_pushB equal bs
            equal      = n_eq_symbol node1 node2
            node1      = gs_get nodeid1 gs
            node2      = gs_get nodeid2 gs
            nodeid1    = as_get a_src1 as
            nodeid2    = as_get a_src2 as

eqB (as,bs,cs,gs,ds,pc,ps,io)
   = (as,bs',cs,gs,ds,pc,ps,io)
     where  bs'        = bs_eqB bs

eqB_a bool a_src (as,bs,cs,gs,ds,pc,ps,io)
   = (as,bs',cs,gs,ds,pc,ps,io)
     where  bs'        = bs_pushB equal bs
            equal      = n_eq_B (gs_get nodeid gs) bool
            nodeid     = as_get a_src as

eqB_b bool b_src (as,bs,cs,gs,ds,pc,ps,io)
   = (as,bs',cs,gs,ds,pc,ps,io)
     where  bs'        = bs_eqBi bool b_src bs

eqI (as,bs,cs,gs,ds,pc,ps,io)
   = (as,bs',cs,gs,ds,pc,ps,io)
     where  bs'        = bs_eqI bs

eqI_a int a_src (as,bs,cs,gs,ds,pc,ps,io)
   = (as,bs',cs,gs,ds,pc,ps,io)
     where  bs'        = bs_pushB equal bs
            equal      = n_eq_I (gs_get nodeid gs) int
            nodeid     = as_get a_src as

eqI_b int b_src (as,bs,cs,gs,ds,pc,ps,io)
   = (as,bs',cs,gs,ds,pc,ps,io)
     where  bs'        = bs_eqIi int b_src bs

fill descr nr_args entry a_dst (as,bs,cs,gs,ds,pc,ps,io)
   = (as',bs,cs,gs',ds,pc,ps,io)
     where  as'        = as_popn nr_args as
            gs'        = gs_update nodeid (n_fill descr entry args) gs
            nodeid     = as_get a_dst as
            args       = as_topn nr_args as

fill_a a_src a_dst (as,bs,cs,gs,ds,pc,ps,io)
   = (as,bs,cs,gs',ds,pc,ps,io)
```

```
        where  gs'          = gs_update nodeid_dst (n_copy node_src) gs
               node_src     = gs_get nodeid_src gs
               nodeid_dst   = as_get a_dst as
               nodeid_src   = as_get a_src as

fillB bool a_dst (as,bs,cs,gs,ds,pc,ps,io)
   = (as,bs,cs,gs',ds,pc,ps,io)
     where  gs'     = gs_update nodeid (n_fillB bool_descr rnf_entry bool) gs
            nodeid  = as_get a_dst as

fillB_b b_src a_dst (as,bs,cs,gs,ds,pc,ps,io)
   = (as,bs,cs,gs',ds,pc,ps,io)
     where  gs'     = gs_update nodeid (n_fillB bool_descr rnf_entry bool) gs
            bool    = bs_getB b_src bs
            nodeid  = as_get a_dst as

fillI int a_dst (as,bs,cs,gs,ds,pc,ps,io)
   = (as,bs,cs,gs',ds,pc,ps,io)
     where  gs'     = gs_update nodeid (n_fillI int_descr rnf_entry int) gs
            nodeid  = as_get a_dst as

fillI_b b_src a_dst (as,bs,cs,gs,ds,pc,ps,io)
   = (as,bs,cs,gs',ds,pc,ps,io)
     where  gs'     = gs_update nodeid (n_fillI int_descr rnf_entry int) gs
            int     = bs_getI b_src bs
            nodeid  = as_get a_dst as

get_descr_arity a_src (as,bs,cs,gs,ds,pc,ps,io)
   = (as,bs',cs,gs,ds,pc,ps,io)
     where  bs'     = bs_pushI arity bs
            arity   = d_arity (ds_get descrid ds)
            descrid = n_descrid (gs_get nodeid gs)
            nodeid  = as_get a_src as

get_node_arity a_src (as,bs,cs,gs,ds,pc,ps,io)
   = (as,bs',cs,gs,ds,pc,ps,io)
     where  bs'     = bs_pushI arity bs
            arity   = n_arity (gs_get nodeid gs)
            nodeid  = as_get a_src as

halt (as,bs,cs,gs,ds,pc,ps,io)
   = (as,bs,cs,gs,ds,pc',ps,io)
     where  pc'     = pc_halt pc

jmp address (as,bs,cs,gs,ds,pc,ps,io)
   = (as,bs,cs,gs,ds,pc',ps,io)
     where  pc'     = pc_update address pc

jmp_eval (as,bs,cs,gs,ds,pc,ps,io)
   = (as,bs,cs,gs,ds,pc',ps,io)
     where  pc'     = pc_update (n_entry (gs_get nodeid gs)) pc
            nodeid  = as_get 0 as

jmp_false address (as,bs,cs,gs,ds,pc,ps,io)
   = (as,bs',cs,gs,ds,pc',ps,io)
     where  pc'     = pc, if bool
                    = pc_update address pc, otherwise
            bool    = bs_getB 0 bs
            bs'     = bs_popn 1 bs

jmp_true address (as,bs,cs,gs,ds,pc,ps,io)
   = (as,bs',cs,gs,ds,pc',ps,io)
     where  pc'     = pc_update address pc, if bool
```

```
                        = pc, otherwise
              bool      = bs_getB 0 bs
              bs'       = bs_popn 1 bs

jsr address (as,bs,cs,gs,ds,pc,ps,io)
    = (as,bs,cs',gs,ds,pc',ps,io)
      where   pc'       = pc_update address pc
              cs'       = cs_push (pc_get pc) cs

jsr_eval (as,bs,cs,gs,ds,pc,ps,io)
    = (as,bs,cs',gs,ds,pc',ps,io)
      where   pc'       = pc_update (n_entry (gs_get nodeid gs)) pc
              nodeid    = as_get 0 as
              cs'       = cs_push (pc_get pc) cs

no_op state     = state

pop_a n (as,bs,cs,gs,ds,pc,ps,io)
    = (as',bs,cs,gs,ds,pc,ps,io)
      where   as'       = as_popn n as

pop_b n (as,bs,cs,gs,ds,pc,ps,io)
    = (as,bs',cs,gs,ds,pc,ps,io)
      where   bs'       = bs_popn n bs

print string (as,bs,cs,gs,ds,pc,ps,io)
    = (as,bs,cs,gs,ds,pc,ps,io')
      where   io'       = io_print string io

print_symbol a_src (as,bs,cs,gs,ds,pc,ps,io)
    = (as,bs,cs,gs,ds,pc,ps,io')
      where   io'       = io_print_symbol node descr io
              nodeid    = as_get a_src as
              node      = gs_get nodeid gs
              descr     = ds_get (n_descrid node) ds

push_a a_src (as,bs,cs,gs,ds,pc,ps,io)
    = (as',bs,cs,gs,ds,pc,ps,io)
      where   as'       = as_push nodeid as
              nodeid    = as_get a_src as

push_ap_entry a_src (as,bs,cs,gs,ds,pc,ps,io)
    = (as,bs,cs',gs,ds,pc,ps,io)
      where   cs'       = cs_push (d_ap_entry (ds_get descrid ds)) cs
              descrid   = n_descrid (gs_get nodeid gs)
              nodeid    = as_get a_src as

push_arg a_src arity arg_nr (as,bs,cs,gs,ds,pc,ps,io)
    = (as',bs,cs,gs,ds,pc,ps,io)
      where   as'       = as_push arg as
              arg       = n_arg (gs_get nodeid gs) arg_nr arity
              nodeid    = as_get a_src as

push_arg_b a_src (as,bs,cs,gs,ds,pc,ps,io)
    = (as',bs,cs,gs,ds,pc,ps,io)
      where   as'       = as_push arg as
              arg       = n_arg (gs_get nodeid gs) arg_nr arity
              nodeid    = as_get a_src as
              arg_nr    = bs_getI 0 bs
              arity     = bs_getI 1 bs

push_args a_src arity nr_args (as,bs,cs,gs,ds,pc,ps,io)
    = (as',bs,cs,gs,ds,pc,ps,io)
```

```
        where  as'     =  as_pushn args as
               args    =  n_nargs (gs_get nodeid gs) nr_args arity
               nodeid  =  as_get a_src as

push_args_b a_src (as,bs,cs,gs,ds,pc,ps,io)
    =  (as',bs,cs,gs,ds,pc,ps,io)
        where  as'     =  as_pushn args as
               args    =  n_nargs (gs_get nodeid gs) nargs arity
               nargs   =  bs_getI 0 bs
               nodeid  =  as_get a_src as
               arity   =  bs_getI 1 bs

push_b b_src (as,bs,cs,gs,ds,pc,ps,io)
    =  (as,bs',cs,gs,ds,pc,ps,io)
        where  bs'     =  bs_push basic bs
               basic   =  bs_get b_src bs

pushB bool (as,bs,cs,gs,ds,pc,ps,io)
    =  (as,bs',cs,gs,ds,pc,ps,io)
        where  bs'     =  bs_pushB bool bs

pushB_a a_src (as,bs,cs,gs,ds,pc,ps,io)
    =  (as,bs',cs,gs,ds,pc,ps,io)
        where  bs'     =  bs_pushB bool bs
               bool    =  n_B (gs_get nodeid gs)
               nodeid  =  as_get a_src as

pushI int (as,bs,cs,gs,ds,pc,ps,io)
    =  (as,bs',cs,gs,ds,pc,ps,io)
        where  bs'     =  bs_pushI int bs

pushI_a a_src (as,bs,cs,gs,ds,pc,ps,io)
    =  (as,bs',cs,gs,ds,pc,ps,io)
        where  bs'     =  bs_pushI int bs
               int     =  n_I (gs_get nodeid gs)
               nodeid  =  as_get a_src as

repl_args arity nr_args (as,bs,cs,gs,ds,pc,ps,io)
    =  (as',bs,cs,gs,ds,pc,ps,io)
        where  as'     =  as_pushn args (as_popn 1 as)
               args    =  n_nargs (gs_get nodeid gs) nr_args arity
               nodeid  =  as_get 0 as

repl_args_b (as,bs,cs,gs,ds,pc,ps,io)
    =  (as',bs,cs,gs,ds,pc,ps,io)
        where  as'     =  as_pushn args (as_popn 1 as)
               args    =  n_nargs (gs_get nodeid gs) nr_args arity
               nodeid  =  as_get 0 as
               arity   =  bs_getI 0 bs
               nr_args =  bs_getI 1 bs

rtn (as,bs,cs,gs,ds,pc,ps,io)
    =  (as,bs,cs',gs,ds,pc',ps,io)
        where  pc'     =  pc_update (cs_get 0 cs) pc
               cs'     =  cs_popn 1 cs

set_entry entry a_dst (as,bs,cs,gs,ds,pc,ps,io)
    =  (as,bs,cs,gs',ds,pc,ps,io)
        where  gs'     =  gs_update nodeid (n_setentry entry) gs
               nodeid  =  as_get a_dst as

update_a a_src a_dst (as,bs,cs,gs,ds,pc,ps,io)
    =  (as',bs,cs,gs,ds,pc,ps,io)
```

```
        where  as'     = as_update a_dst nodeid as
               nodeid  = as_get a_src as

update_b b_src b_dst (as,bs,cs,gs,ds,pc,ps,io)
    = (as,bs',cs,gs,ds,pc,ps,io)
        where  bs'     = bs_update b_dst basic bs
               basic   = bs_get b_src bs

addl (as,bs,cs,gs,ds,pc,ps,io) = (as,bs',cs,gs,ds,pc,ps,io) where bs' = bs_addl bs
decl (as,bs,cs,gs,ds,pc,ps,io) = (as,bs',cs,gs,ds,pc,ps,io) where bs' = bs_decl bs
gtl  (as,bs,cs,gs,ds,pc,ps,io) = (as,bs',cs,gs,ds,pc,ps,io) where bs' = bs_gtl bs
incl (as,bs,cs,gs,ds,pc,ps,io) = (as,bs',cs,gs,ds,pc,ps,io) where bs' = bs_incl bs
ltl  (as,bs,cs,gs,ds,pc,ps,io) = (as,bs',cs,gs,ds,pc,ps,io) where bs' = bs_ltl bs
mull (as,bs,cs,gs,ds,pc,ps,io) = (as,bs',cs,gs,ds,pc,ps,io) where bs' = bs_mull bs
subl (as,bs,cs,gs,ds,pc,ps,io) = (as,bs',cs,gs,ds,pc,ps,io) where bs' = bs_subl bs
```

C.2 Running ABC programs

Booting and instruction fetching

```
boot:: ([instruction],[descr]) -> state
boot (program,descriptors)
    = (as,bs,cs,gs,ds,pc,ps,io)
        where  pc   = pc_init
               as   = as_init
               bs   = bs_init
               cs   = cs_init
               gs   = gs_init
               ps   = ps_init program
               io   = io_init
               ds   = ds_init descriptors

fetch_cycle:: state -> state
fetch_cycle (as,bs,cs,gs,ds,pc,ps,io)
    = (as,bs,cs,gs,ds,pc,ps,io)                        , if pc_end pc
    = fetch_cycle (currinstr (as,bs,cs,gs,ds,pc',ps,io)) , otherwise
        where  pc'        = pc_next pc
               currinstr  = ps_get (pc_get pc) ps
```

ABC assembly language

```
assembler:: assembly -> ([instruction], [descr])
assembler asm_prog
    = (translate asm_prog loc_count sym_table, descr_table asm_prog sym_table)
        where  loc_count    = 0
               descr_count  = 0
               sym_table    = collect asm_prog loc_count descr_count
```

The specification of translate, descr_table and collect that translate the ABC assembly program and produce its ABC instructions with its description table would require many (rather trivial) lines. For the full specification the reader is referred to Koopman *et al.* (1990).

The ABC assembly language is defined by the algebraic data structure given below. Most assembly statements are equal to their ABC instruction counterpart, but their names begin with an upper case character. The statements in *italic* are slightly different because symbolic names are used instead of addresses. In addition, the assembler allows the definition of labels and descriptors. Furthermore, Branch instructions are added to allow the specification of relative jumps. The assembler will convert them to jump instructions. These extra assembly statements are also shown in *italic*.

```
assembly        ==  [statement]
red_label       ==  label
descr_label     ==  label
label           ==  [char]
nr_instr        ==  int

statement
::= Label            label                       | No_op                         |
    Descriptor descr_label red_label arity name  | Pop_a          nr_args        |
    Br               nr_instr                    | Pop_b          nr_args        |
    Br_false         nr_instr                    | Print          string         |
    Br_true          nr_instr                    | Print_symbol   a_src          |
    Add_args         a_src nr_args a_dst         | Push_a         a_src          |
    Create                                       | Push_ap_entry  a_src          |
    Del_args         a_src nr_args a_dst         | Push_arg   a_src arity arg_nr |
    Eq_descr         descr_label a_src           | Push_arg_b     a_src          |
    Eq_descr_arity descr_label arity a_src       | Push_args  a_src arity arg_nr |
    EqB                                          | Push_args_b    a_src          |
    EqB_a            bool a_src                  | Push_b         b_src          |
    EqB_b            bool b_src                  | PushB          bool           |
    EqI                                          | PushB_a        a_src          |
    EqI_a            int a_src                   | PushI          int            |
    EqI_b            int b_src                   | PushI_a        a_src          |
    Fill      descr_label nr_args label a_dst    | Repl_args      arity nr_args  |
    Fill_a           a_src a_dst                 | Repl_args_b                   |
    FillB            bool a_dst                  | Rtn                           |
    FillB_b          b_src a_dst                 | Set_entry      label a_dst    |
    FillI            int a_dst                   | Update_a       a_src a_dst    |
    FillI_b          b_src a_dst                 | Update_b       b_src b_dst    |
    Get_descr_arity  a_src                       |
    Get_node_arity   a_src                       |
    Halt                                         | AddI                          |
    Jmp              label                       | DecI                          |
    Jmp_eval                                     | GtI                           |
    Jmp_false        label                       | IncI                          |
    Jmp_true         label                       | LtI                           |
    Jsr              label                       | MulI                          |
    Jsr_eval                                     | SubI
```

C.3 The ABC micro-instructions

```
abstype    astack, bstack, cstack, graphstore, descrstore, pc, programstore, io
  with

  ps_get         :: instrid -> programstore -> instruction
  ps_init        :: [instruction] -> programstore

  pc_end         :: pc -> bool
  pc_get         :: pc -> instrid
  pc_halt        :: pc -> pc
  pc_init        :: pc
  pc_next        :: pc -> pc
  pc_update      :: instrid -> pc -> pc
```

```
gs_get          :: nodeid -> graphstore -> node
gs_init         :: graphstore
gs_newnode      :: graphstore -> (graphstore,nodeid)
gs_update       :: nodeid -> (node -> node) -> graphstore -> graphstore

n_arg           :: node -> arg_nr -> arity -> nodeid
n_args          :: node -> arity -> nodeid_seq
n_arity         :: node -> arity
n_B             :: node -> bool
n_copy          :: node -> node -> node
n_descrid       :: node -> descrid
n_entry         :: node -> instrid
n_eq_arity      :: node -> arity -> bool
n_eq_B          :: node -> bool -> bool
n_eq_descrid    :: node -> descrid -> bool
n_eq_I          :: node -> int -> bool
n_eq_symbol     :: node -> node -> bool
n_fill          :: descrid -> instrid -> nodeid_seq -> node -> node
n_fillB         :: descrid -> instrid -> bool -> node -> node
n_fillI         :: descrid -> instrid -> int -> node -> node
n_I             :: node -> int
n_nargs         :: node -> nr_args -> arity -> nodeid_seq
n_setentry      :: instrid -> node -> node

ds_get          :: descrid -> descrstore -> descr
ds_init         :: [descr] -> descrstore

d_ap_entry      :: descr -> instrid
d_arity         :: descr -> arity
d_name          :: descr -> string

as_get          :: a_src -> astack -> nodeid
as_init         :: astack
as_popn         :: nr_args -> astack -> astack
as_push         :: nodeid -> astack -> astack
as_pushn        :: nodeid_seq -> astack -> astack
as_topn         :: nr_args -> astack -> nodeid_seq
as_update       :: a_dst -> nodeid -> astack -> astack

bs_get          :: b_src -> bstack -> basic
bs_getB         :: b_src -> bstack -> bool
bs_getI         :: b_src -> bstack -> int
bs_init         :: bstack
bs_popn         :: nr_args -> bstack -> bstack
bs_push         :: basic -> bstack -> bstack
bs_pushB        :: bool -> bstack -> bstack
bs_pushI        :: int -> bstack -> bstack
bs_update       :: b_dst -> basic -> bstack -> bstack

bs_addI         :: bstack -> bstack
bs_decI         :: bstack -> bstack
bs_eqB          :: bstack -> bstack
bs_eqI          :: bstack -> bstack
bs_eqBi         :: bool -> b_src -> bstack -> bstack
bs_eqIi         :: int -> b_src -> bstack -> bstack
bs_gtI          :: bstack -> bstack
bs_incI         :: bstack -> bstack
bs_ltI          :: bstack -> bstack
bs_mulI         :: bstack -> bstack
bs_subI         :: bstack -> bstack

cs_init         :: cstack
cs_get          :: c_src -> cstack -> instrid
```

```
cs_popn          :: nr_args -> cstack -> cstack
cs_push          :: instrid -> cstack -> cstack

io_init          :: io
io_print         :: string -> io -> io
io_print_symbol  :: node -> descr -> io -> io
```

Program store

```
programstore ==  [location]
location     ::= I instruction

ps_get target ps               = instr      where   I instr   = ps ! target

ps_init (instruction : rest)   = I instruction : ps_init rest
ps_init [ ]                    = [ ]
```

Program counter

```
pc       ==   instrid

pc_end instrid           = instrid < 0
pc_get instrid           = instrid
pc_halt instrid          = –1
pc_init                  = 0
pc_next instrid          = instrid + 1
pc_update instrid pc     = instrid
```

Graph store

```
graphstore     ==   (graph, nat)

gs_get nodeid (nds,free)  =  nds ! (nodeid – free – 1)
gs_init                   =  ([ ], store_size)

store_size:: nat
store_size  =  100            || some natural number indicating the size

gs_newnode (nds,0)        =  error "graph-store is full"
gs_newnode (nds,free)     =  ((Empty : nds, free – 1), free)

gs_update nid f (nodes,free) =  (upd (nid – free –1) nodes f, free)
                                where   upd 0 (nd : nds) f = f nd : nds
                                        upd n (nd : nds) f = nd : upd (n – 1) nds f
```

Nodes

```
node ::=    Node descrid instrid nodeid_seq I Basic descrid instrid basic I Empty
basic ::=   Int int     I    Bool bool

n_arg node n arity    =  args ! (n – 1)   where    args  =  n_args node arity
n_args (Node descrid entry args) arity = args ||   arity can be used for optimizations

n_arity (Basic descrid entry basic)     =  0
n_arity (Node descrid entry args)       =  # args

n_B (Basic descrid entry (Bool b))      =  b
n_copy new old                          =  new
```

```
n_descrid (Node descrid entry args)      = descrid
n_descrid (Basic descrid entry basic)    = descrid

n_entry (Node descrid entry args)        = entry
n_entry (Basic descrid entry basic)      = entry

n_eq_arity  node n                       = n_arity node = n
n_eq_B      node b                       = n_B node = b
n_eq_descrid node descrid                = n_descrid node = descrid
n_eq_I      node i                       = n_I node = i
n_eq_symbol (Node descrid1 entry1 args1) (Node descrid2 entry2 args2)
                                         = descrid1 = descrid2
n_eq_symbol (Basic descrid1 entry1 basic1) (Basic descrid2 entry2 basic2)
                                         = descrid1 = descrid2 & basic1 = basic2
n_eq_symbol node1 node2                  = False
n_fill descr entry args node             = Node descr entry args
n_fillB descr entry b node               = Basic descr entry (Bool b)
n_fillI descr entry i node               = Basic descr entry (Int i)
n_I (Basic descrid entry (Int i))        = i
n_nargs node arg_count arity             = take arg_count (n_args node arity)

n_setentry newentry (Node  descrid entry args) = Node descrid newentry args
n_setentry newentry (Basic descrid entry basic) = Basic descrid newentry basic
```

Descriptor store

```
descrstore      ==   [descr]

ds_get target ds     = ds ! target
ds_init descriptors  = descriptors
```

Descriptors

```
descr    ::=   Descr ap_entry arity name

d_ap_entry   (Descr ap_entry arity name)   = ap_entry
d_arity      (Descr ap_entry arity name)   = arity
d_name       (Descr ap_entry arity name)   = name
```

A-stack

```
astack   ==   [nodeid]

as_get target as         = as ! target
as_init                  = [ ]
as_popn n as             = drop n as
as_push nodeid as        = nodeid : as
as_pushn nodeids as      = nodeids ++ as
as_topn n as             = take n as

as_update 0 nodeid (a : x)   = nodeid : x
as_update n nodeid (a : x)   = a : as_update (n – 1) nodeid x
```

B-stack

```
bstack   ==   [basic]

bs_get target bs     = bs ! target
bs_getB n bs         = b      where   Bool b  =  bs_get n bs
```

```
bs_getI n bs           = i       where  Int i      = bs_get n bs
bs_init                = [ ]
bs_popn n bs           = drop n bs
bs_push basic bs       = basic : bs
bs_pushB b bs          = Bool b : bs
bs_pushI i bs          = Int i : bs

bs_update 0 basic (b : x)  =  basic : x
bs_update n basic (b : x)  =  b : bs_update (n – 1) basic x

bs_addI    (Int i1 : Int i2 : r)      =  Int (i1 + i2) : r
bs_decI    (Int i : r)                =  Int (i – 1) : r
bs_eqB     (Bool b1 : Bool b2 : r)    =  Bool (b1 = b2) : r
bs_eqBi    b          n         bs    =  bs_push (Bool (b = bs_getB n bs)) bs
bs_eqI     (Int i1 : Int i2 : r)      =  Bool (i1 = i2) : r
bs_eqIi    i          n         bs    =  bs_push (Bool (i = bs_getI n bs)) bs
bs_gtI     (Int i1 : Int i2 : r)      =  Bool (i1 > i2) : r
bs_incI    (Int i : r)                =  Int (i + 1) : r
bs_ltI     (Int i1 : Int i2 : r)      =  Bool (i1 < i2) : r
bs_mulI    (Int i1 : Int i2 : r)      =  Int (i1 * i2) : r
bs_subI    (Int i1 : Int i2 : r)      =  Int (i1 – i2) : r
```

C-stack

```
cstack   = =    [instrid]

cs_init               =  [ ]
cs_get target cs      =  cs ! target
cs_popn n cs          =  drop n cs
cs_push c cs          =  c : cs
```

I/O channel

```
io  = =    [char]

io_init                      =  [ ]
io_print string output       =  output ++ string

io_print_symbol (Basic descrid ap_entry (Int i)) descr output     =  output ++ show i
io_print_symbol (Basic descrid ap_entry (Bool b)) descr output    =  output ++ show b
io_print_symbol (Node descrid entry args) (Descr ap_entry arity name) output
                                                                   =  output ++ name
```

Appendix D
PABC machine specification

The PABC machine is a parallel extension of the ABC machine. This extension has some consequences for the sequential ABC instructions presented in Appendix C. For most instructions only the machine state has to be extended. Together with the extension of the assembly language for the new instructions this is left to the reader.

For some sequential instructions a call to the operating system has to be included. This is fully specified together with the parallel instructions that are marked ("•") in the summary below. The instructions newP, randomP, currentP, neighbourP and channelP require some extensions of the specification (see Exercise 16.2).

D.1 The PABC instruction set

Sequential and parallel reducer instructions

```
instruction   ==  state -> state
state         ==  (local_state,global_state,opsys_callqueue)
local_state   ==  (astack,bstack,cstack,nqueue,pc,wlist)
global_state  ==  (admin,graphstore,descrstore,programstore)

•  halt              :: instruction
•  jmp               :: instrid -> instruction
•  jsr               :: instrid -> instruction
•  print             :: string -> instruction
•  print_symbol      :: a_src -> instruction

   channelP          :: a_src -> instruction
•  create_channel    :: instruction
   currentP          :: instruction
•  get_node          :: instruction
•  getWL             :: a_src -> instruction
•  is_empty_n        :: instruction
   neighbourP        :: instruction
```

```
• new_ext_reducer      :: instrid -> a_src -> instruction
• new_int_reducer      :: instrid -> a_src -> instruction
• newP                 :: instruction
  randomP              :: instruction
• release              :: instruction
• send_graph           :: a_src -> a_src -> instruction
• send_request         :: a_src -> instruction
• set_continue         :: a_src -> instruction
• set_wait             :: a_src -> instruction
• stop_reducer         :: instruction
• suspend              :: instruction
```

Operating system instructions

```
opsys_instruction   ==  opsys_state -> opsys_state
opsys_state == (schedule_adm,in_msgs,out_msgs,global_state,opsys_callqueue)

• os_halt              :: opsys_instruction
• os_new_reducer       :: instrid -> nodeid -> opsys_instruction
• os_print             :: string -> opsys_instruction
• os_reducerprio       :: opsys_instruction
• os_release           :: wlist -> opsys_instruction
• os_schedule          :: opsys_instruction
• os_send_graph        :: nodeid -> nodeid -> opsys_instruction
• os_send_newchannel   :: procid -> nodeid -> opsys_instruction
• os_send_newreducer   :: instrid -> nodeid -> opsys_instruction
• os_send_request      :: nodeid -> opsys_instruction
• os_setwait           :: nodeid -> opsys_instruction
• os_stop_reducer      :: opsys_instruction
• os_suspend_reducer   :: opsys_instruction
```

Communication process instructions

```
comproc_instruction  ==  comproc_state -> comproc_state
comproc_state        ==  (in_msgs,out_msgs,global_state,opsys_callqueue)

• cp_accept_msg    :: msg_contents -> comproc_instruction
```

Specification of sequential reducer instructions

```
halt ((as,bs,cs,nq,pc,wl),glob,cq)
   =  ((as,bs,cs,nq,pc,wl),glob,cq')
      where  cq'  =  os_call cq [os_stop_reducer, os_halt]

jmp address ((as,bs,cs,nq,pc,wl),glob,cq)
   =  ((as,bs,cs,nq,pc',wl),glob,cq')
      where  pc'  =  pc_update address pc
             cq'  =  os_call cq [os_schedule]

jsr address ((as,bs,cs,nq,pc,wl),glob,cq)
   =  ((as,bs,cs',nq,pc',wl),glob,cq')
      where  pc'  =  pc_update address pc
             cs'  =  cs_push (pc_get pc) cs
             cq'  =  os_call cq [os_schedule]

print string (loc,glob,cq)
   =  (loc,glob,cq')
      where  cq'  =  os_call cq [os_print string, os_schedule]

print_symbol a_src ((as,bs,cs,nq,pc,wl),(ad,gs,ds,ps),cq)
```

```
  = ((as,bs,cs,nq,pc,wl),(ad,gs,ds,ps),cq')
    where  cq'      = os_call cq [os_print string, os_schedule]
           nodeid   = as_get a_src as
           node     = gs_get nodeid gs
           string   = ds_get_repr node ds
```

Specification of parallel reducer instructions

```
create_channel ((as,bs,cs,nq,pc,wl),(ad,gs,ds,ps),cq)
  = ((as',bs',cs,nq,pc,wl),(ad,gs',ds,ps),cq')
    where  bs'        = bs_popn 1 bs
           pid        = bs_getP 0 bs
           (gs',nid)  = gs_newchannel pid gs
           as'        = as_push nid as
           cq'        = os_call cq [os_send_newchannel pid nid,
                                    os_setwait nid, os_suspend_reducer]

get_node ((as,bs,cs,nq,pc,wl),glob,cq)
  = ((as',bs,cs,nq',pc,wl),glob,cq)
    where  as'  = as_push n as
           n    = nq_first nq
           nq'  = nq_remove nq

getWL a_depth ((as,bs,cs,nq,pc,wl),(ad,gs,ds,ps),cq)
  = ((as,bs,cs,nq,pc,wl'),(ad,gs,ds,ps),cq)
    where  wl'  = n_wl_get (gs_get nid gs)
           nid  = as_get a_depth as

is_empty_n ((as,bs,cs,nq,pc,wl),glob,cq)
  = ((as,bs',cs,nq,pc,wl),glob,cq)
    where  bs'  = bs_pushB (nq_empty nq) bs

new_ext_reducer code chan_depth ((as,bs,cs,nq,pc,wl),glob,cq)
  = ((as,bs,cs,nq,pc,wl),glob,cq')
    where  chanid  = as_get chan_depth as
           cq'     = os_call cq [os_send_newreducer code chanid]

new_int_reducer code a_depth ((as,bs,cs,nq,pc,wl),glob,cq)
  = ((as,bs,cs,nq,pc,wl),glob,cq')
    where  nid  = as_get a_depth as
           cq'  = os_call cq [os_new_reducer code nid]

newP ((as,bs,cs,nq,pc,wl),(ad,gs,ds,ps),cq)
  = ((as,bs',cs,nq,pc,wl),(ad',gs,ds,ps),cq)
    where  bs'        = bs_pushP pid bs
           (ad',pid)  = ad_new_procid ad

release ((as,bs,cs,nq,pc,wl),glob,cq)
  = ((as,bs,cs,nq,pc,wl),glob,cq')
    where  cq'  = os_call cq [os_release wl]    , if ~ wl_empty wl
                = cq                            , otherwise

send_graph graph_depth chan_depth ((as,bs,cs,nq,pc,wl),glob,cq)
  = ((as,bs,cs,nq,pc,wl),glob,cq')
    where  chanid   = as_get chan_depth as
           graphid  = as_get graph_depth as
           cq'      = os_call cq [os_send_graph graphid chanid]

send_request chan_depth ((as,bs,cs,nq,pc,wl),glob,cq)
  = ((as,bs,cs,nq,pc,wl),glob,cq')
    where  cq'     = os_call cq [os_send_request chanid,os_reducerprio]
           chanid  = as_get chan_depth as
```

```
set_continue depth ((as,bs,cs,nq,pc,wl),glob,cq)
  = ((as,bs,cs,nq',pc,wl),glob,cq)
    where   n     = as_get depth as
            nq'   = nq_add n nq

set_wait a_depth ((as,bs,cs,nq,pc,wl),glob,cq)
  = ((as,bs,cs,nq,pc,wl),glob,cq')
    where   nid   = as_get a_depth as
            cq'   = os_call cq [os_setwait nid,os_reducerprio]

stop_reducer ((as,bs,cs,nq,pc,wl),glob,cq)
  = ((as,bs,cs,nq,pc,wl),glob,cq')
    where   cq'   = os_call cq [os_stop_reducer]

suspend ((as,bs,cs,nq,pc,wl),glob,cq)
  = ((as,bs,cs,nq,pc,wl),glob,cq')
    where   cq'   = os_call cq [os_suspend_reducer]
```

Specification of operating system instructions

```
schedule_adm    ==   ([active], [passive])
active          ==   reducer
passive         ==   reducer
reducer         ==   (redid, local_state)

os_halt (rs,in,out,(ad,gs,ds,ps),instrs)
  = (rs,in,out',(ad,gs,ds,ps),instrs)
    where   out'     = out ++ [(my_pid, 0, Msg_Halt)]
            my_pid   = ad_pid ad

os_new_reducer code nid (rs,in,out,(ad,gs,ds,ps),instrs)
  = (rs',in,out,(ad',gs,ds,ps),instrs)
    where   rs'                     = (act_reds ++ [new_red], pass_reds)
            (act_reds, pass_reds)   = rs
            new_red                 = (new_redid,(as,bs,cs,nq,pc,wl))
                                      where  as   = as_init
                                             bs   = bs_init
                                             cs   = cs_init
                                             nq   = nq_new nid
                                             pc   = pc_update code pc_init
                                             wl   = wl_init
            (ad', new_redid)        = ad_new_redid ad

os_print string (rs,in,out,(ad,gs,ds,ps),instrs)
  = (rs,in,out',(ad,gs,ds,ps),instrs)
    where   out'     = out ++ [(my_pid, 0, Msg_Print string)]
            my_pid   = ad_pid ad

os_reducerprio (rs,in,out,(ad,gs,ds,ps),instrs)
  = (rs,in,out,(ad',gs,ds,ps),instrs)
    where   ad'      = ad_new_prio Prio_Reducer ad

os_release wl (rs,in,out,(ad,gs,ds,ps),instrs)
  = (rs',in,out',(ad,gs,ds,ps),instrs)
    where   (reds,reqs,nid)         = (wl_reds wl, wl_reqs wl, wl_nid wl)
            (old_acts, old_pass)    = rs
            graph         = gs_copy nid my_pid ds gs
            rs'           = (new_acts, new_pass)
            new_acts      = old_acts ++ rel_reds
            new_pass      = old_pass -- rel_reds
            rel_reds      = [(rid,loc) | (rid,loc) <- old_pass; rid' <- reds; rid' = rid]
```

```
          out'          = out ++ [(my_pid, n_pid_of_global dst,
                                   Msg_Graph graph dst) | dst <- reqs]
          my_pid        = ad_pid ad

os_schedule ((act_reds,pass_reds),in,out,glob,instrs)
  = ((act_reds,pass_reds),in,out,glob,instrs)    , if act_reds = [ ]
  = (rs',in,out,glob,instrs)                      , otherwise
    where rs'                  = (new_act_reds, pass_reds)
          new_act_reds         = rest_act_reds ++ [red]
          red : rest_act_reds  = act_reds

os_send_graph graphid chanid (rs,in,out,(ad,gs,ds,ps),instrs)
  = (rs,in,out',(ad,gs,ds,ps),instrs)
    where out'    = out ++ [(my_pid, pid, Msg_Graph graph' dstid)]
          graph   = gs_copy graphid my_pid ds gs
          graph'  = gs_root_update (n_setdescr defer_descr) graph
          pid     = n_pid_of_global dstid
          dstid   = n_dest (gs_get chanid gs)
          my_pid  = ad_pid ad

os_send_newchannel pid chanid (rs,in,out,(ad,gs,ds,ps),instrs)
  = (rs,in,out',(ad,gs,ds,ps),instrs)
    where out'      = out ++ [(my_pid, pid, Msg_CreateChannel chan_eid)]
          chan_eid  = n_global my_pid chanid
          my_pid    = ad_pid ad

os_send_newreducer code chanid (rs,in,out,(ad,gs,ds,ps),instrs)
  = (rs,in,out',(ad,gs,ds,ps),instrs)
    where chan    = n_dest (gs_get chanid gs)
          out'    = out ++ [(my_pid, pid, Msg_NewReducer chan code)]
          pid     = n_pid_of_global chan
          my_pid  = ad_pid ad

os_send_request chanid (rs,in,out,(ad,gs,ds,ps),instrs)
  = (rs,in,out',(ad,gs,ds,ps),instrs)
    where out'    = out ++ [(my_pid, pid, Msg_Request srcid dstid)]
          srcid   = n_global my_pid chanid
          pid     = n_pid_of_global dstid
          dstid   = n_dest (gs_get chanid gs)
          my_pid  = ad_pid ad

os_setwait nid (rs,in,out,(ad,gs,ds,ps),instrs)
  = (rs,in,out,(ad,gs',ds,ps),instrs)
    where gs'                    = gs_update nid (n_wl_add_red rid) gs
          (rid, loc)             = red
          (red : reds, pass_reds) = rs

os_stop_reducer (rs,in,out,glob,instrs)
  = (rs',in,out,glob,instrs)
    where rs'                        = (act_reds, pass_reds)
          (red : act_reds, pass_reds) = rs

os_suspend_reducer (rs,in,out,glob,instrs)
  = (rs',in,out,glob,instrs)
    where rs'                        = (act_reds, red : pass_reds)
          (red : act_reds, pass_reds) = rs
```

Specification of communication process instructions

```
in_msgs      ==  [msg_contents]
out_msgs     ==  [message]
message      ==  (proc_src, proc_dst, msg_contents)
```

```
msg_contents
 ::= Msg_CreateChannel ext_nid          | Msg_Channel ext_nid ext_nid
   | Msg_Request ext_nid ext_nid        | Msg_Graph graph ext_nid
   | Msg_NewReducer ext_nid instrid     | Msg_Print string          | Msg_Halt
proc_src        == procid
proc_dst        == procid
ext_nid         == (procid, nodeid)

cp_accept_msg (Msg_CreateChannel src_eid) (in,out,(ad,gs,ds,ps),instrs)
   = (in,out',(ad,gs',ds,ps),instrs)
     where (gs', rqid) = gs_newnode gs
           out'        = out ++ [(my_pid, pid, Msg_Channel rq_eid src_eid)]
           rq_eid      = n_global my_pid rqid
           pid         = n_pid_of_global src_eid
           my_pid      = ad_pid ad
cp_accept_msg (Msg_Channel rq_eid dst_eid) (in,out,(ad,gs,ds,ps),instrs)
   = (in,out,(ad,gs',ds,ps),instrs')
     where nid     = n_local dst_eid
           gs'     = gs_update nid (n_putchannel rq_eid) gs
           wl      = n_wl_get (gs_get nid gs)
           instrs' = os_call instrs [os_release wl]
cp_accept_msg (Msg_NewReducer rq_eid code) (in,out,(ad,gs,ds,ps),instrs)
   = (in,out,(ad,gs,ds,ps),instrs')
     where instrs' = os_call instrs [os_new_reducer code (n_local rq_eid)]
cp_accept_msg (Msg_Request chan_eid rq_eid) (in,out,(ad,gs,ds,ps),instrs)
   = (in,out',(ad,gs',ds,ps),instrs)
     where rqid = n_local rq_eid
           rnf  = n_entry (gs_get rqid gs) = rnf_entry
           out' = out ++ [(my_pid, pid, Msg_Graph graph chan_eid)]  , if rnf
                = out                                               , otherwise
                  where pid    = n_pid_of_global chan_eid
                        graph  = gs_copy rqid my_pid ds gs
                        my_pid = ad_pid ad
           gs'  = gs_update rqid (n_wl_add_req chan_eid) gs   , if ~ rnf
                = gs                                          , otherwise
cp_accept_msg (Msg_Graph gr dst_eid) (in,out,(ad,gs,ds,ps),instrs)
   = (in,out,(ad,gs',ds,ps),instrs')
     where gs'     = gs_store nid gr gs
           wl      = n_wl_get (gs_get nid gs)
           nid     = n_local dst_eid
           instrs' = os_call instrs [os_release wl]
```

D.2 Running PABC programs

Booting and instruction fetching

```
boot:: nat -> ([instruction],[descr]) -> network
boot nr_proc (program,descriptors)  =  nw_init nr_proc (program,descriptors)

machine_cycle:: network -> output
machine_cycle nw
          = output                                    , if op_halt output
          = op_append output (machine_cycle nw')      , otherwise
            where output = nw_output nw
                  nw'    = nw_exec proc_cycle (nw_distribute_msgs nw)

proc_cycle:: processor -> processor
proc_cycle   = opsys_cycle . red_cycle . opsys_cycle . comproc_cycle

comproc_cycle:: processor -> processor
```

```
comproc_cycle (rs,in,out,(ad,gs,ds,ps),cq)
   =  (rs,in,out,(ad',gs,ds,ps),cq)        , if ad_prio ad = Prio_Reducer
      where   ad'   =  ad_new_prio No_Prio ad
comproc_cycle (rs,[ ],out,glob,cq)
   =  (rs,[ ],out,glob,cq)
comproc_cycle (rs,(msg:msgs),out,glob,cq)
   =  comproc_cycle (rs,in',out',glob',cq')
      where   (in',out',glob',cq')    =  cp_accept_msg msg (msgs,out,glob,cq)

opsys_cycle:: processor -> processor
opsys_cycle (rs,in,out,glob,cq)
   =  (rs,in,out,glob,cq)                                    , if os_cq_empty cq
   =  opsys_cycle (os_first_call cq (rs,in,out,glob,os_rest_calls cq)), otherwise

red_cycle:: processor -> processor
red_cycle ((act_reds,pass_reds),in,out,glob,cq)
   =  ((act_reds,pass_reds),in,out,glob,cq)                  , if act_reds = [ ]
   =  (rs',in,out,glob',cq')                                 , otherwise
      where   rs'              =  ((rid,loc') : reds, pass_reds)
              (rid,loc) : reds =  act_reds
              (loc',glob',cq') =  fetch_cycle (loc,glob,cq)

fetch_cycle:: state -> state
fetch_cycle ((as,bs,cs,nq,pc,wl),(ad,gs,ds,ps),cq)
   =  ((as,bs,cs,nq,pc,wl),(ad,gs,ds,ps),cq)                , if ~ os_cq_empty cq
   =  fetch_cycle (currinstr ((as,bs,cs,nq,pc',wl),(ad,gs,ds,ps),cq)), otherwise
      where   pc'         =  pc_next pc
              currinstr   =  ps_get (pc_get pc) ps
```

D.3 The new micro-instructions

```
abstype    astack, bstack, cstack, nqueue, pc , wlist,
           admin, graphstore, descrstore, programstore,
           opsys_callqueue, network, output
   with    ...
   gs_copy            ::  nodeid -> procid -> descrstore -> graphstore -> graph
   gs_newchannel      ::  procid -> graphstore -> (graphstore,nodeid)
   gs_root_update     ::  (node -> node) -> graph -> graph
   gs_store           ::  nodeid -> graph -> graphstore -> graphstore

   n_dest             ::  node -> dest
   n_global           ::  procid -> nodeid -> ext_nid
   n_local            ::  ext_nid -> nodeid
   n_pid_of_global    ::  ext_nid -> procid
   n_putchannel       ::  ext_nid -> node -> node
   n_setdescr         ::  descrid -> node -> node
   n_wl_add_red       ::  redid -> node -> node
   n_wl_add_req       ::  request -> node -> node
   n_wl_clear             ::  node -> node
   n_wl_get           ::  node -> wlist
   n_wl_put           ::  wlist -> node -> node

   ds_get_repr        ::  node -> descrstore -> string

   bs_getP            ::  b_src -> bstack -> procid
   bs_pushP           ::  procid -> bstack -> bstack

   nq_add             ::  nodeid -> nqueue -> nqueue
   nq_first           ::  nqueue -> nodeid
   nq_init            ::  nqueue
   nq_empty           ::  nqueue -> bool
```

```
nq_new                 :: nodeid -> nqueue
nq_remove              :: nqueue -> nqueue

wl_clear               :: wlist -> wlist
wl_empty               :: wlist -> bool
wl_init                :: wlist
wl_new                 :: nodeid -> wlist
wl_nid                 :: wlist -> nodeid
wl_reds                :: wlist -> [redid]
wl_reqs                :: wlist -> [request]

ad_init                :: procid -> procid -> admin
ad_new_redid           :: admin -> (admin,redid)
ad_new_procid          :: admin -> (admin,procid)
ad_new_prio            :: schedule_priority -> admin -> admin
ad_nr_pids             :: admin -> procid
ad_pid                 :: admin -> procid
ad_prio                :: admin -> schedule_priority

os_call            :: opsys_callqueue -> [opsys_instruction] -> opsys_callqueue
os_clear           :: opsys_callqueue
os_first_call      :: opsys_callqueue -> opsys_instruction
os_init            :: procid -> procid -> [instruction] -> [descr] -> opsys_state
os_cq_empty        :: opsys_callqueue -> bool
os_rest_calls      :: opsys_callqueue -> opsys_callqueue

nw_distribute_msgs     :: network -> network
nw_exec                :: (processor -> processor) -> network -> network
nw_init                :: procid -> ([instruction],[descr]) -> network
nw_output              :: network -> output

op_append              :: output -> output -> output
op_halt                :: output -> bool
```

Graph store

```
gs_copy top pid ds gs
   =  copy
      where   (copy,bindings)  =  copy_nodes [top] pid ds gs 0 empty_bindings

gs_newchannel pid (nds,0)
   =  error "cannot create new channel; graph-store is full"
gs_newchannel pid (nds,free)
   =  ((nds++[new_channel],free-1),nid)
      where   nid             =  store_size-free
              new_channel     =  Channel (wl_new nid) new_channel_entry (pid,(-1))

gs_root_update f (n : r)    =  f n : r

gs_store nodeid graph (old_graph,free)
   =  error "cannot store graph; graph-store is full"   , if size_graph > free
   =  (new_graph,free-size_graph+1)                     , otherwise
      where   size_graph       =  # graph
              size_old_graph   =  # old_graph
              offset           =  size_old_graph – 1
              (top:rest)       =  graph
              new_graph        =  upd nodeid old_graph (n_copy' top) ++
                                              [adjust_nids node | node<-rest]
              n_copy' (Node descrid wl entry args) old
                        =  Node descrid (n_wl_get old) entry [arg+offset|arg<-args]
              n_copy' (Basic descrid wl entry basic) old
                        =  Basic descrid (n_wl_get old) entry basic
```

```
n_copy' (Channel wl instrid dest) old
          = Channel (n_wl_get old) instrid dest
upd 0 (nd : nds) f    =  f nd : nds
upd n (nd : nds) f    =  nd : upd (n - 1) nds f
adjust_nids (Node descrid (rd,rq,nid) entry args)
   = Node descrid (wl_new (nid+offset)) entry [arg+offset|arg<-args]
adjust_nids (Basic descrid (rd,rq,nid) entry basic)
   = Basic descrid (wl_new (nid+offset)) entry basic
adjust_nids (Channel (rd,rq,nid) instrid dest)
   = Channel (wl_new (nid+offset)) instrid dest
```

The lazy copying algorithm

```
bindings = =   nodeid -> nodeid

copy_nodes:: [nodeid] -> procid -> descrstore -> graphstore -> nodeid -> bindings
                                                              -> (graph, bindings)
copy_nodes [ ] pid ds gs n bindings
   =  ([ ],bindings)
copy_nodes (nid : rest) pid ds gs n bindings
   =  copy_nodes rest pid ds gs n bindings     , if ~ bindings_is_empty bindings nid
   =  (nodes,bindings")                        , otherwise
      where  node                =  gs_get nid gs
             nodes               =  new_node : nodes'
             (new_node,args)     =  copy_node pid ds n node bindings"
             bindings'           =  bind nid n bindings
             (nodes',bindings")
                           =  copy_nodes (args++rest) pid ds gs (n+1) bindings'

copy_node:: procid -> descrstore -> nodeid -> node -> bindings -> (node, args)
copy_node pid ds nid (Node descrid wl entry args) bindings
   =  ((Channel (wl_new nid) new_channel_entry rq_eid),[ ])
                              , if descrid = defer_descr \/ entry = reserved_entry
   =  ((Node descrid (wl_new nid) new_entry new_args),args)           , otherwise
      where  new_entry        =  d_node_entry (ds_get descrid ds)
             new_args         =  map bindings args
             rq_eid           =  (pid,wl_nid wl)
copy_node pid ds nid (Basic descrid wl entry basic) bindings
   =  ((Basic descrid (wl_new nid) entry basic),[ ])
copy_node pid ds nid (Channel wl entry dest) bindings
   =  ((Channel (wl_new nid) entry dest),[ ])

bind:: nodeid -> nodeid -> bindings -> bindings
bind src dst bindings n      =  dst          , if n  =  src
                             =  bindings n   , otherwise

empty_bindings:: bindings
empty_bindings nodeid     =  –1

bindings_is_empty::bindings -> nodeid -> bool
bindings_is_empty b n     =  b n = –1
```

Nodes

```
node      :: =   Node descrid wlist entry nodeid_seq |   Channel wlist entry dest  |
                 Basic descrid wlist entry basic     |   Empty
basic     :: =   Int int          |  Bool bool       |   Pid procid
entry     = =    instrid
dest      = =    (procid,nodeid)

reserved_entry      =  3
```

```
new_channel_entry =  4
defer_descr       =  3

n_dest (Channel wl instrid dest)    =  dest
n_global pid nid                    =  (pid, nid)
n_local (pid, nid)                  =  nid
n_pid_of_global (pid, nid)          =  pid
n_putchannel ext_nid (Channel wl entry dest) = Channel (wl_clear wl) entry ext_nid
n_setdescr new_descr (Node descr wl entry args) = Node new_descr wl entry args

n_wl_add_red rid (Node descr (rids,reqs,nid) entry args )
                                        =  Node descr (rid:rids,reqs,nid) entry args
n_wl_add_red rid (Basic descr (rids,reqs,nid) entry basic )
                                        =  Basic descr (rid:rids,reqs,nid) entry basic
n_wl_add_red rid (Channel (rids,reqs,nid) entry dest)
                                        =  Channel (rid:rids,reqs,nid) entry dest

n_wl_add_req req (Node descr (rids,reqs,nid) entry args )
                                        =  Node descr (rids,req:reqs,nid) entry args
n_wl_add_req req (Basic descr (rids,reqs,nid) entry basic )
                                        =  Basic descr (rids,req:reqs,nid) entry basic
n_wl_add_req req (Channel (rids,reqs,nid) entry dest)
                                        =  Channel (rids,req:reqs,nid) entry dest

n_wl_clear (Node descr wl entry args )  =  Node descr (wl_clear wl) entry args
n_wl_clear (Basic descr wl entry basic) =  Basic descr (wl_clear wl) entry basic
n_wl_clear (Channel wl entry dest)      =  Channel (wl_clear wl) entry dest

n_wl_get (Node descr wl entry args)     =  wl
n_wl_get (Basic descr wl entry basic)   =  wl
n_wl_get (Channel wl entry dest)        =  wl

n_wl_put (reds,reqs,nid) (Node descr (reds',reqs',nid') entry args )
                                        =  (Node descr (reds,reqs,nid') entry args )
n_wl_put (reds,reqs,nid) (Basic descr (reds',reqs',nid') entry basic )
                                        =  (Basic descr (reds,reqs,nid') entry basic )
n_wl_put (reds,reqs,nid) (Channel (reds',reqs',nid') entry dest)
                                        =  (Channel (reds,reqs,nid') entry dest)
```

Descriptor store

```
descr       ::=  Descr ap_entry node_entry arity name
node_entry  ==   instrid

d_node_entry (Descr ap_entry node_entry arity name)    =  node_entry
ds_get_repr (Basic descrid wl entry (Int i)) ds        =  show i
ds_get_repr (Basic descrid wl entry (Bool b)) ds       =  show b
ds_get_repr (Node descrid wl entry args) ds            =  d_name (ds_get descrid ds)
```

B-stack

```
bs_getP n bs    =  p where Pid p = bs_get n bs
bs_pushP p bs   =  (Pid p):bs
```

N-queue

```
nqueue  ==   [nodeid]

nq_add     n nq       =  nq ++ [ n ]
nq_first   (n : nq)   =  n
```

```
nq_init                  = [ ]
nq_empty  (n : q)        = False
nq_empty  [ ]            = True
nq_new     n             = [ n ]
nq_remove    (n : nq)  = nq
```

Waiting lists

```
wlist     = =   ([redid], [request],nodeid)
request = =   ext_nid

wl_clear (reds,reqs,nid)   =  ([ ],[ ],nid)
wl_empty ([ ],[ ],nid)     =  True
wl_empty wl                =  False
wl_init                    =  ([ ],[ ], -1)
wl_new nid                 =  ([ ],[ ],nid)
wl_nid (reds,reqs,nid)     =  nid
wl_reds (reds,reqs,nid)    =  reds
wl_reqs (reds,reqs,nid)    =  reqs
```

Global administration

```
admin   = =   (nr_procids,new_procid,this_procid,redid,schedule_priority)
nr_procids           = =   procid
new_procid           = =   procid
this_procid          = =   procid
procid               = =   num
redid                = =   num
schedule_priority    :: =  No_Prio | Prio_Reducer

ad_init nr_pids pid  =  (nr_pids, 0, pid, 0, No_Prio)
ad_new_redid (nr_pids,new_pid,pid,rid,prio)
                     =  ((nr_pids,new_pid,pid, rid',prio), rid')
                        where    rid'   =  rid + 1
ad_new_procid (nr_pids,new_pid,pid, rid,prio)
                     =  ((nr_pids,new_pid',pid, rid,prio),new_pid')
                        where    new_pid'   =  1 + (new_pid mod nr_pids)
ad_new_prio new_prio (nr_pids,new_pid,pid, rid,prio)
                     =  (nr_pids,new_pid,pid, rid,new_prio)
ad_nr_pids    (nr_pids,new_pid,pid, rid,prio)  =  nr_pids
ad_pid        (nr_pids,new_pid,pid, rid,prio)  =  pid
ad_prio       (nr_pids,new_pid,pid, rid,prio)  =  prio
```

Operating system interface

```
opsys_callqueue    = =   os_cq
os_cq              :: =  OS_cq [opsys_instruction]

os_call (OS_cq instr) new             =  OS_cq (instr ++ new)
os_clear                              =  OS_cq [ ]
os_first_call (OS_cq (first : rest))  =  first
os_cq_empty (OS_cq (first : rest))    =  False
os_cq_empty (OS_cq [ ])               =  True
os_rest_calls (OS_cq (first : rest))  =  OS_cq rest

os_init nr_pids procid program descriptors
   =  (rs,in,out,glob,instrs)
      where   rs      =  ([(rid_main, (as,bs,cs,nq,pc,wl))], [ ])     , if procid = 1
                      =  ([ ], [ ])                                   , otherwise
                         where    as     =  as_init
```

```
                          bs     = bs_init
                          cs     = cs_init
                          nq     = nq_init
                          wl     = wl_init
                          pc     = pc_init
        (ad_main,rid_main)       = ad_new_redid (ad_init nr_pids 1)
        glob      = (ad,gs,ds,ps)
                    where ad     = ad_main                  , if procid = 1
                                 = ad_init nr_pids procid   , otherwise
                          gs     = gs_init
                          ps     = ps_init program
                          ds     = ds_init descriptors
        in        = [ ]
        out       = [ ]
        instrs    = os_clear
```

The communication network

```
network            ==   [network_element]
network_element    ::=  P processor
processor          ==   opsys_state
output             ==   [msg_contents]

nw_distribute_msgs processors
   = [ P (rs,in ++ select_msgs (ad_pid ad) msgs,out,(ad,gs,ds,ps),instrs) |
                                   P (rs,in,out,(ad,gs,ds,ps),instrs) <- new_procs]
     where  msgs = [msg |
                       P (rs,in,proc_out,glob,instrs)<-processors;msg<-proc_out]
            new_procs = [ P (rs,in,[ ],glob,instrs) |
                                     P (rs,in,proc_out,glob,instrs) <- processors]
            select_msgs pid msgs = [cts | (src,dst,cts) <- msgs; dst = pid]

nw_exec proc_cycle processors
   = [ P (proc_cycle processor) | P processor<-processors]

nw_init nr_procids (program,descriptors)
   = [ P (os_init nr_procids procid program descriptors) | procid<-[1..nr_procids]]

nw_output processors
   = [ cts | P (rs,in,proc_out,glob,instrs)<-processors;(src,dst,cts)<-proc_out;dst=0]

op_append o1 o2     =  o1 ++ o2
op_halt msgs        =  foldr (\/) False (map (= Msg_Halt) msgs)
```

Bibliography

Abramsky S. (1990). The lazy lambda calculus. In *Research Topics in Functional Programming, Austin Year of Programming Series* (Turner D., ed.), Austin TX, pp. 65–117. Reading MA: Addison-Wesley.

Achten P.M., van Groningen J.H.G. and Plasmeijer M.J. (1993). High-level specification of I/O in functional languages. In *Proc. 1992 International Workshop on Functional Languages,* Glasgow. Workshop Notes in Computer Science. Berlin: Springer-Verlag., in press.

Aho A.V., Sethi R. and Ullman J.D. (1986). *Compilers – Principles, Techniques and Tools*. Reading MA: Addison-Wesley.

Annot J.K. and Twist R.A.H. van (1987). A novel deadlock free and starvation free packet switching communication processor. In *Proc. Parallel Architectures and Languages Europe (PARLE '87),* Eindhoven (Bakker J.W. de, Nijman A.J. and Treleaven P.C., eds.), *LNCS*, **258**, pp. 68–85. Berlin: Springer-Verlag.

Augusteijn L. (1985). *The Warshall shortest path algorithm in POOL–T.* Internal Report Esprit Project 415 A, Doc. 0105. Eindhoven: Philips Research Laboratories.

Augustsson L.A. (1984). A compiler for lazy ML. In *Proc. ACM Symposium on LISP and Functional Programming,* Austin TX, pp. 218–227. ACM Press.

Backus J. (1978). Can programming be liberated from the Von Neumann style? A functional style and its algebra of programs. *Comm ACM,* **21**, pp. 613–641.

Baeten J.C.M., Bergstra J.A. and Klop J.W. (1987). Term rewriting systems with priorities. In *Proc. Conference on Rewriting Techniques and Applications,* Bordeaux (Lescanne P., ed.), *LNCS*, **256**, pp. 83–94. Berlin: Springer-Verlag.

Bakel S.J. van, Brock S. and Smetsers J.E.W. (1992). Partial type assignment in left-linear term rewriting systems. In *Proc. 17th Colloquium on Trees in Algebra and Programming (CAAP '92),* Rennes (Raoult J.C., ed.), *LNCS*, **581**, pp. 300–321. Berlin: Springer-Verlag.

Baker H.G. (1978). List processing in real time on a serial computer. *Comm ACM,* **4**, (21), pp. 280–294.

Barendregt H.P. (1984). *The Lambda-Calculus, its Syntax and Semantics*. Amsterdam: North-Holland.

Barendregt H.P., Eekelen M.C.J.D. van, Glauert J.R.W., Kennaway J.R., Plasmeijer M.J. and Sleep M.R. (1987a). Term graph rewriting. In *Proc. Parallel Architectures and Languages Europe (PARLE '87),* Eindhoven (Bakker J.W. de, Nijman A.J. and Treleaven P.C., eds.), *LNCS*, **259**, II, pp. 141–158. Berlin: Springer-Verlag.

Barendregt H.P., Eekelen M.C.J.D. van, Glauert J.R.W., Kennaway J.R., Plasmeijer M.J. and Sleep M.R. (1987b). Towards an intermediate language based on graph rewriting. In *Proc. Parallel Architectures and Languages Europe (PARLE '87),* Eindhoven (Bakker J.W. de, Nijman A.J. and Treleaven P.C., eds.), *LNCS*, **259**, II, pp. 159–175. Berlin: Springer-Verlag.

Barendregt H.P., Eekelen M.C.J.D. van, Glauert J.R.W., Kennaway J.R., Plasmeijer M.J. and Sleep M.R. (1988). LEAN: An intermediate language based on graph rewriting. *Parallel Computing,* **9**, pp. 163–177.

Barendsen E. and Smetsers J.E.W. (1992). *Graph rewriting and copying*. Technical Report 92-20, University of Nijmegen.

Berkling K.J. and Fehr E. (1982). A consistent extension of λ-calculus as a base for functional programming languages. *Information and control,* **55**, (1–3), pp. 89–101.

Bevan D.I. (1987). Distributed garbage collection using reference counting. In *Proc. Parallel Architectures and Languages Europe (PARLE '87),* Eindhoven (Bakker J.W. de, Nijman A.J. and Treleaven P.C., eds.), *LNCS*, **259**, pp. 176–187. Berlin: Springer-Verlag.

Bird R.S. and Wadler P. (1988). *Introduction to Functional Programming*. Englewood Cliffs NY: Prentice-Hall.

Bruijn N.G. de (1972). Lambda calculus notation with nameless dummies, a tool for automatic formula manipulation. *Indagationes Mathematicae,* **34**, (2), pp. 381–39.

Brus T., Eekelen M.C.J.D. van, Leer M. van, Plasmeijer M.J. and Barendregt H.P. (1987). Clean – a language for functional graph rewriting. In *Proc. Conference on Functional Programming Languages and Computer Architecture (FPCA '87),* Portland OR (Kahn G., ed.), *LNCS*, **274**, pp. 364–384. Berlin: Springer-Verlag.

Burks A.W., Goldstine H.H. and Neumann J. von (1946). Preliminary discussion of the logical design of an electronic computing instrument. In *John von Neumann, Collected Works*, **5**, pp. 35–79.

Burn G.L., Hankin C.L. and Abramsky S. (1985). The theory of strictness analysis for higher order functions. In *Proc. Workshop on Programs as Data Objects,* Copenhagen (Ganzinger H. and Jones N.D., eds.), *LNCS*, **217**, pp. 42–62. Berlin: Springer-Verlag.

Burstall R.M., MacQueen D.B. and Sanella D.T. (1980). Hope: an experimental applicative language. In *Proc. ACM Symposium on LISP and Functional Programming,* Stanford CA, pp. 136–143. University of Stanford.

Burton F.W. (1987). Functional programming for concurrent and distributed computing. *Computer J,* **30**, (5), pp. 437–450.

Burton F.W. and Sleep M.R. (1982). Executing functional programs on a virtual tree of processors. In *Proc. Conf. Functional Programming Languages and Computer Architecture (FPCA '82),* Portsmouth, New Hampshire, pp. 187–194.

Church A. (1932). A set of postulates for the foundation of logic. *Annals of Mathematics,* **2**, (33), pp. 346–366.

Church A. (1933). A set of postulates for the foundation of logic. *Annals of Mathematics,* **2**, (34), pp. 839–864.

Church A. (1936). An unsolvable problem of elementary number theory. *American J Mathematics,* **58**, pp. 354–363.

Church A. and Rosser J.B. (1936). Some properties of conversion. *Trans American Mathematical Society,* **39**, pp. 472–482.

Cohen J. (1981). Garbage collection of linked data structures. *Computing Surveys,* **13**, (3), pp. 341–367.

Curien P.-L. (1986). *Categorical Combinators, Sequential Algorithms and Functional Programming*. New York: Pitman/Wiley.

Curry H. B. (1930). Grundlagen der Kombinatorischen Logik. *American J of Mathematics,* **52**, pp. 509–536, 789–834.

Curry H.B. and Feys R. (1958). *Combinatory Logic*. **1**. Amsterdam: North-Holland.

Darlington J., Field A.J., Harrison P.G., Harpe D., Jouret G.K., Kelly P.L., Sephton K.M. and Sharp D.W. (1991). Structured parallel functional programming. In *Proc. 3rd International Workshop on the Implementation of Functional Languages on Parallel Architectures,* Southampton (Glaser H. and Hartel P., eds.). Technical Report 91-07, pp. 31–51, University of Southampton.

Dershowitz N. and Jouannaud J.P. (1990). Rewrite systems. In *Handbook of Theoretical Computer Science* (van Leeuwen J., ed.), pp. 52–66. Amsterdam: North-Holland.

Dijkstra E.W. (1968). GOTO statement considered harmful. *Comm ACM,* **11**, pp. 341–346.

Dijkstra E. W., Lamport L., Martin A.J., Scholten C.S. and Steffens E.F.M. (1978). On-the-fly garbage collection: an exercise in cooperation. *Comm ACM,* **21**, (11), pp. 966–975.

Eekelen M.C.J.D. van (1988). *Parallel graph rewriting, some contributions to its theory, its implementation and its application*. Ph.D. Thesis, University of Nijmegen.

Eekelen M.C.J.D. van, Plasmeijer M.J. and Smetsers J.E.W. (1991). Parallel graph rewriting on loosely coupled machine architectures. In *Proc. Conditional and Typed Rewriting Systems (CTRS '90),* Montreal (Kaplan S. and Okada M., eds.), *LNCS*, **516**, pp. 354–

369. Berlin: Springer-Verlag.

Eekelen M.C.J.D. van, Huitema H., Nöcker E.G.J.M.H., Plasmeijer M.J. and Smetsers J.E.W. (1992). *Concurrent Clean, Language Manual – Version 0.8*. Technical Report 92-18, University of Nijmegen.

Ehrig H., Pfender M. and Schneider H.J. (1973). Graph-grammars: an algebraic approach. In *Proc. IEEE Conf. on Automata and Switching Theory*, pp. 167–180.

Field A.J. and Harrison P.G. (1988). *Functional Programming*. Reading MA: Addison-Wesley.

Fraenkel A.A. (1922). Zu den Grundlagen der Cantor-Zermeloschen Mengenlehre. *Mathematische Annalen,* **86**, pp. 230–237.

Girard J.-Y. (1987). Linear logic. *Theoretical Computer Science,* **50**, pp. 1–102.

Glaser H.W. and Thompson P. (1985). Lazy garbage collection. *Software Practice & Experience,* **17**, (1), pp. 1–4.

Glauert J.R.W., Kennaway J.R. and Sleep M.R. (1987). DACTL: a computational model and compiler target language based on graph reduction. *ICL Technical J,* **5**, pp. 509–537.

Goguen J., Kirchner C. and Meseguer J. (1986). Concurrent term rewriting as a model of computation. In *Proc. Workshop on Graph Reduction,* Santa Fe NM (Fasel J.H. and Keller R.M., eds.), LNCS, **279**, pp. 53–94. Berlin: Springer-Verlag.

Goldsmith R., McBurney D.L. and Sleep M.R. (1993). Parallel execution of Concurrent Clean on ZAPP. In *Term Graph Rewriting* (Sleep M.R., Plasmeijer M.J. and Eekelen M.C.J.D. van, eds.). New York: John Wiley.

Groningen J.H.G. van (1990). *Implementing the ABC-machine on M680x0 based architectures*. Master Thesis, University of Nijmegen.

Groningen J.H.G. van, Nöcker E.G.J.M.H. and Smetsers J.E.W. (1992). Some implementation aspects of Concurrent Clean on distributed memory architectures. In *Proc. 4th International Workshop on the Implementation of Functional Languages on Parallel Architectures,* Aachen (Kuchen H. and Loogen R., eds.). Aachen: RWTH.

Groot D. de and Lindstrom G (1986). *Logic Programming: Functions, Relations, Equations*. Englewood Cliff NY: Prentice-Hall.

Harper R., MacQueen D. and Milner R. (1986). *Standard ML.* Internal Report ECS-LFCS-86-2, Edinburgh University.

Hartel P.H. and Langendoen K.G. (1993). Benchmarking implementations of lazy functional languages. In *Proc. Functional Programming and Computer Architectures (FPCA '93),* Copenhagen. ACM Press, in press.

Hindley J.R. (1969). The principal type scheme of an object in combinatory logic. *Trans American Mathematical Society,* **146**, pp. 29–60.

Hoare C.A.R. (1978). Communicating sequential processes. *Comm ACM,* **21**, (8), pp. 666–677.

Hudak P. and Smith L. (1986). Para-functional programming: a paradigm for programming multiprocessor systems. In *Proc. 12th ACM Symp. on Principles of Programming Languages*, pp. 243–254.

Hudak P., Peyton Jones S., Wadler Ph., Boutel B., Fairbairn J., Fasel J., Hammond K., Hughes J., Johnsson Th., Kieburtz D., Nikhil R., Partain W. and Peterson J. (1992). Report on the programming language Haskell. *ACM SigPlan Notices,* **27**, (5), pp. 1–164.

Huet G. and Lévy J.-J. (1979). *Call-by-need computations in non-ambiguous linear term rewriting systems.* Internal Report 359, INRIA.

Huet G. and Oppen D.C. (1980). Equations and rewrite rules: a survey. In *Formal Languages: Perspectives and Open Problems* (Book R. V., ed.). London: Academic Press.

Hughes R.J.M. (1982). Super-combinators: a new implementation method for applicative languages. In *Proc. ACM Symposium on Lisp and Functional Programming,* Pittsburgh, pp. 1–10.

Johnsson Th. (1984). Efficient compilation of lazy evaluation. In *Proc. ACM SIGPLAN '84, Symposium on Compiler Construction,* Montreal, pp. 58–69.

Johnsson Th. (1985). Lambda lifting: transforming programs to recursive equations. In *Proc. Conference on Functional Programming Languages and Computer Architecture,* Nancy (Jouannaud J.P., ed.), *LNCS*, **201**, pp. 190–203. Berlin: Springer-Verlag.

Kennaway J.R. (1988). The correctness of an implementation of functional Dactl by parallel rewriting. In *Proc. UK IT 88 ("Alvey") Conference (I.E.E.)*, pp. 254–257. British Computer Society.

Kennaway J.R. (1990). Graph rewriting in a category of partial morphisms. In *Proc. 4th International Workshop on Graph Grammars and their Applications,* Bremen (Ehrig H., Kreowski H.J. and Rozenberg G., eds.), *LNCS*, **532**, pp. 490–504. Berlin: Springer-Verlag.

Kennaway J.R., Klop J.W., Sleep M.R. and de Vries F.J. (1993a). An infinitary Church–Rosser property for non-collapsing orthogonal term rewriting systems. In *Term Graph Rewriting* (Sleep M.R., Plasmeijer M.J. and Eekelen M.C.J.D. van, eds.). New York: John Wiley.

Kennaway J.R., Klop J.W., Sleep M.R. and de Vries F.J. (1993b). The adequacy of term graph rewriting for simulating term rewriting. In *Term Graph Rewriting* (Sleep M.R., Plasmeijer M.J. and Eekelen M.C.J.D. van, eds.). New York: John Wiley.

Kernighan B., Ritchie W. and Dennis M. (1978). *The C Programming Language*. Englewood Cliff NY: Prentice-Hall.

Kesseler M.H.G. (1991). Implementing the ABC machine on transputers. In *Proc. 3rd International Workshop on Implementation of Functional Languages on Parallel Architectures,* Southampton

(Glaser H. and Hartel P., eds.). Technical Report 91-07, pp. 147–192, University of Southampton.

Kesseler M.H.G. (1992). Communication issues regarding parallel functional graph rewriting. In *Proc. 4th International Workshop on the Implementation of Functional Languages on Parallel Architectures,* Aachen (Kuchen H. and Loogen R., eds.). Aachen: RWTH.

Kingdon H., Lester D. and Burn G.L. (1991). The HDG-machine: a highly distributed graph-reducer for a transputer network. *The Computer J,* **34**, (4).

Klop J.W. (1992). Term rewriting systems. In *Handbook of Logic in Computer Science* (Abramsky S., Gabbay D. and Maibaum T., eds.), **2**, pp. 2–108. Oxford: Oxford University Press.

Kluge W.E. (1983). Cooperating reduction machines. *IEEE. Transactions on Computers,* **C-32**, (11), pp. 1002–1012.

Koopman P.W.M. (1987). Interactive programs in a functional language: a functional implementation of an editor. *Software Practice & Experience,* **17**, (9), pp. 609–622.

Koopman P.W.M. (1990). *Functional programs as executable specifications*. Ph.D. Thesis, University of Nijmegen.

Koopman P.W.M. and Nöcker E.G.J.M.H. (1988). *Compiling functional languages to term graph rewriting systems*. Technical Report 88-1, University of Nijmegen.

Koopman P.W.M., Eekelen M.C.J.D. van, Nöcker E.G.J.M.H., Plasmeijer M.J. and Smetsers J.E.W. (1990). *The ABC-machine: a sequential stack-based abstract machine for graph rewriting*. Technical Report 90-22, University of Nijmegen.

Koopman P.W.M., Eekelen M.C.J.D van and Plasmeijer M.J. (1993). Operational machine specification in a functional programming language. *Software Practice & Experience,* in press.

Lamping J. (1990). An algorithm for optimal lambda calculus reduction. In *Proc. 17th ACM Symp. of Principles of Programming Languages,* San Francisco, pp. 16–30.

Landin P.J. (1964). The mechanical evaluation of expressions. *Computer J,* **6**, pp. 308–20.

Landin P.J. (1966). The next 700 programming languages. *Comm ACM,* **9**, (3), pp. 157–164.

Lévy J.J. (1980). Optimal reductions in the lambda-calculus. In *To H.B. Curry: Essays on Combinatory Logic, Lambda-Calculus and Formalism* (Seldin J.P. and Hindley J.R., eds.), pp. 159–191. New York: Academic Press.

Liebermann H. and Hewitt C. (1983). A real-time garbage collector based on the lifetime of objects. *Comm ACM,* **26**, pp. 419–429.

Markovsky G. (1976). Chain-complete p.o.-sets and directed sets with applications. *Algebra Universalis,* **6**, pp. 53–68.

McCarthy J. (1960). Recursive functions of symbolic expressions and their computation by machine. *Comm ACM,* **4**, pp. 184–195.

Meinke K. and Tucker J.V. (1992). Universal algebra. In *Handbook of Logic in Computer Science* (Abramsky S., Gabbay D. and Maibaum T., eds.), **1**, pp. 189–398. Oxford: Oxford University Press.

Milner R.A. (1978). Theory of type polymorphism in programming. *J of Computer and System Sciences,* **17**, (3), pp. 348–375.

Minsky M.L. (1963). *A Lisp garbage collection algorithm using serial secondary storage.* Project MAC Memo 58 (rev.), Massachusetts Institute of Technology.

Morris F.L. (1978). A time- and space-efficient garbage compaction algorithm. *Comm ACM,* **21**, (8), pp. 662–665.

Motorola (1984–1985). *MC68020 32-Bit Microprocessor User's Manual.* Englewood Cliff NY: Prentice-Hall.

Mycroft A. (1981). *Abstract interpretation and optimising transformations for applicative programs.* Ph.D. Thesis, University of Edinburgh.

Mycroft A. (1984). Polymorphic type schemes and recursive definitions. In *Proc. International Conference on Programming,* Toulouse (Paul M. and Robinet B., eds.), LNCS, **167**, pp. 217–239. Berlin: Springer-Verlag.

Nöcker E.G.J.M.H. (1988). Strictness analysis based on abstract reduction of term graph rewrite systems. In *Proc. Workshop on Implementation of Lazy Functional Languages,* University of Göteborg (Johnsson Th., Peyton Jones S. and Karlsson K., eds.). Report 53, pp. 451–462, Chalmers University of Technology, Programming Methodology Group.

Nöcker E.G.J.M.H. (1989). *The PABC Simulator, v0.5. Implementation Manual.* Technical Report 89-19, University of Nijmegen.

Nöcker E.G.J.M.H. (1990). *Strictness analysis using abstract reduction.* Technical report 90-14, University of Nijmegen.

Nöcker E.G.J.M.H. (1993). Strictness analysis using abstract reduction. In *Proc. Conference on Functional Programming Languages and Computer Architectures (FPCA '93),* Copenhagen. ACM Press, in press.

Nöcker E.G.J.M.H. and Smetsers J.E.W. (1993). Partially strict non-recursive data types. *J of Functional Programming*, in press.

Nöcker E.G.J.M.H., Plasmeijer M.J. and Smetsers J.E.W. (1991a). The parallel ABC machine. In *Proc. 3rd International Workshop on Implementation of Functional Languages on Parallel Architectures,* Southampton (Glaser H. and Hartel P., eds.), Technical Report 91-07, pp. 383–407, University of Southampton.

Nöcker E.G.J.M.H., Smetsers J.E.W., Eekelen M.C.J.D. van and Plasmeijer M.J. (1991b). Concurrent Clean. In *Proc. Parallel Architectures and Languages Europe (PARLE '91),* Eindhoven (Aarts E.H.L., Leeuwen J. and Rem M., eds.), *LNCS*, **506**, pp. 202–219. Berlin: Springer-Verlag.

O'Donnell M.J. (1985). *Equational Logic as a Programming Language.* Foundations of Computing Series. Massachusetts: MIT Press.

Ong C.-H. L. (1988). *Lazy lambda calculus: an investigation into the foundations of functional programming.* Ph.D. Thesis, Imperial College, London.

Peyton Jones S.L. (1987). *The Implementation of Functional Programming Languages.* Englewood Cliffs NY: Prentice-Hall.

Peyton Jones S.L. and J. Salkild (1989). The spineless tagless G-machine. In *Proc. Conference on Functional Programming Languages and Computer Architectures (FPCA '89)*, pp. 184–201. Reading MA: Addison-Wesley.

Peyton Jones S.L. and Wadler P. (1993). Imperative functional programming. In *Proc. POPL '93*, in press.

Plasmeijer M.J., Eekelen M.C.J.D. van, Nöcker E.G.J.M.H. and Smetsers J.E.W. (1991). The Concurrent Clean System, functional programming on the Macintosh. In *Proc. 7th Internernational Conference of the Apple European University Consortium,* Paris, pp. 19–24. Apple Consortium.

Raoult J.C. (1984). On graph rewritings. *Theoretical Computer Science,* **32**, pp. 1–24.

Renardel de Lavalette G.R. (1988). *Strictness analysis for POLYREC, a language with polymorphic and recursive types.* Technical Report, University of Utrecht.

Robinson J.A. (1965). A machine-oriented logic based on the resolution principle. *J of the ACM,* **12**, (1), pp. 23–41.

Schönfinkel M. (1924). Über die Bausteine der mathematischen Logik. *Mathematische Annalen,* **92**, pp. 305–316.

Smetsers J.E.W. (1989). *Compiling Clean to abstract ABC-machine code.* Technical Report 89-20, University of Nijmegen.

Smetsers J.E.W. (1993). *Graph rewriting and functional languages.* Ph. D. Thesis, University of Nijmegen.

Smetsers J.E.W., Barendsen E., Eekelen M.C.J.D. van and Plasmeijer M.J. (1993). *Guaranteeing safe destructive updates through a type system with uniqueness information for graphs.* Technical report 93-4, University of Nijmegen.

Smetsers J.E.W., Nöcker E.G.J.M.H., Groningen J.H.G. van and Plasmeijer M.J. (1991). Generating efficient code for lazy functional languages. In *Proc. Conference on Functional Programming Languages and Computer Architecture (FPCA '91),* Cambridge MA (Hughes J., ed.), *LNCS*, **523**, pp. 592–617. Berlin: Springer-Verlag.

Staples J. (1980). Computation on graph-like expressions. *Theoretical Computer Science,* **10**, pp. 171–185.

Stoy J.E. (1977). *Denotational Semantics: The Scott–Strachey Approach to Programming Language Theory.* Massachusetts: MIT Press.

Toyama Y., Smetsers J.E.W., Eekelen M.C.J.D. van and Plasmeijer

M.J. (1993). The functional strategy and transitive term rewriting systems. In *Term Graph Rewriting* (Sleep M.R., Plasmeijer M.J. and Eekelen M.C.J.D. van, eds.). New York: John Wiley.

Turing A.M. (1937). Computability and λ-definability. *J of Symbolic Logic*, **2**, pp. 153–163.

Turner D.A. (1979a). A new implementation technique for applicative languages. *Software Practice & Experience*, **9**, (1), pp. 31–49.

Turner D.A. (1979b). *SASL Language Manual*. St. Andrews: University of St Andrews.

Turner D.A. (1985). Miranda: a non-strict functional language with polymorphic types. In *Proc. Conference on Functional Programming Languages and Computer Architecture*, Nancy, France (Jouannaud J.P., ed.), *LNCS*, **201**, pp. 1–16. Berlin: Springer-Verlag.

Vree W.G. and Hartel P.H. (1988). *Parallel graph reduction for divide-and-conquer applications; Part I – program transformations*. PRM Project Internal Report D-15, University of Amsterdam.

Wadler P. (1987). Strictness analysis on non-flat domains (by abstract interpretation over finite domains). In *Abstract Interpretation of Declarative Languages* (Abramsky S. and Hankin C., eds.). Chichester: Ellis Horwood.

Wadler P. (1990). Linear types can change the world! In *Programming Concepts and Methods* (Broy M. and Jones C.B., eds.). Amsterdam: North-Holland.

Wadsworth C.P. (1971). *Semantics and pragmatics of the lambda-calculus*. Ph.D. Thesis, University of Oxford.

Watson P. and Watson I. (1987). An efficient garbage collection scheme for parallel computer architectures. In *Proc. Parallel Architectures and Languages Europe (PARLE '87)*, Eindhoven (Bakker J.W. de, Nijman A.J. and Treleaven P.C., eds.), *LNCS*, **259**, pp. 432–443. Berlin: Springer-Verlag.

Wirth N. (1982). *Programming in Modula-2*. Berlin: Springer-Verlag.

Zermelo E. (1908). Untersuchungen über die Grundlagen der Mengelehre. *International Bibliography, Information and Documentation*, **65**, pp. 261–281.

Index

Emboldened terms indicate where a term has been defined in the text.

Q

R